In 2004, librarian and dancer Cherie sold her belongings, cashed in her pension and moved to Buenos Aires forever, with only her sheet music, a metronome and an over-anxious cat for company. This memoir offers a fascinating insight into her experience—as both dancer and teacher—of the Buenos Aires tango subculture: its complicated codes and etiquette, its charming practitioners, the lonely foreigners looking for love. Magnus also offers us a poignant account of how seductive, and potentially dangerous, it can be to abandon everything in pursuit of a dream.

—Miranda France, author of *Bad Times in Buenos Aires*

INTOXICATING TANGO:
MY YEARS IN BUENOS AIRES

INTOXICATING TANGO: MY YEARS IN BUENOS AIRES

A Death Dance Destiny Book

CHERIE MAGNUS

INTOXICATING TANGO is my personal story. Every word is true, but I have changed some names. I am not a sociologist, anthropologist, or psychologist, but this is my truth of living in Argentina, my story as it happened to me.

ISBN 978-0-578-55256-9 (print)
ISBN 978-0-578-55257-6 (ebook)

Cover art of La Confitéria L'Ideal by Andy Bridge

Printed in the United States of America

Mirasol Press
cheriemagnus.com

Other music exists to heal wounds; but the tango when sung and played is for the purpose of opening them...to tear them until they bleed.

—Ramon Gomez de la Serna,
1888 (Madrid)–1963 (Buenos Aires)

I come from a sad country.

—Jorge Luis Borges

PROLOGUE

June 2014

I should have left when he hit me. Just packed up my piano music and my cat and left Buenos Aires behind me.

Who was I to think at middle age I could start a new life alone in a new country, a machista country, and to find love and happiness?

I first went to Buenos Aires on a tango tour in 1998, with no expectations, only that I would be learning from the masters, whomever they might be, and dancing the tango for ten days. I knew nothing about the codigós, or La Confitería L'Ideal (not yet the Belle Époque setting of all the tango movies), or Comme Il Faut, the Manolo Blahnik's of tango shoes (which didn't yet exist), or even what or who was a milonguero. Or what being a woman in a macho culture would mean to me. I just hoped for a fun dance vacation in an exotic locale.

I didn't know then that I would become addicted to the tango, that I would soon do anything for a fix. Nor could I have imagined how the machismo I found so beguiling at first would completely transform my life.

TEN YEARS EARLIER

CHAPTER 1

To the TourisTango Woman: ...they find the warm embrace, sweet promises of eternal love, an arm that surrounds their back and is laid at their waist, a warm hand that 'talks' to theirs, the invitation to have the usual coffee after the dance, at first they feel invaded, and I say at first, because after a while, that attitude becomes a need...the woman's soul is universal and I do not know any who does not like being wanted.

—Victor Raik, milonguero

March 2004

It was just before dawn, and our small group of Argentines and Americans were tired and filled with reverie after a night of Tango. We were drooped over *cafés con leche* on an old wooden table in a run-down nineteenth-century coffee shop. The large party over by the dark windows also looked like they had been up all night having a good time. The men were wearing jackets, the women their décolletage, all somewhat portly and of "a certain age."

Suddenly one of the men stood up and began to sing, loudly, proudly, passionately. Heads nodded with approval. A woman in gold beads joined in. Several others, our table included, brightened with the music and began to clap along.

I didn't understand all of the words, but I knew it was the tango—love, life, disappointment, desire, joy and sadness.

Luis couldn't resist the siren call of the emotional song, even after dancing all night. He was Argentine. He looked at me purposefully, and we danced a tango on the cracked black and white marble floor around the men having breakfast with their newspapers on their way to work.

It was a normal morning in Buenos Aires.

I am a tango addict, you might even say a "tango bum," traveling wherever I must to get my tango fix. There are people all over the world who feel the same way—intoxicated by the tango. Maybe it's the embrace, at least the special close embrace of the *milongueros* of Buenos Aires, that made us crave more, want more, need more. No matter how we felt when we arrived at the tango hall—sick or depressed or tired—we left renewed by hours of moving to haunting music while clasped tightly to the chest of another. And we knew we had to have it again, soon, now. After a fix of a night of dancing, we were relaxed, sated. But within hours the need would build, and anxiety and hunger would drive us back to the *milonga* (tango dance hall) for more.

I had always danced, beginning with ballet at age three. I had majored in dance at UCLA, marrying before my delayed graduation, but children turned me toward something more practical—getting my master's in information science. Still, I had danced while working my day job at the Los Angeles Public Library. Dancing had saved me after my beloved husband died too young. And it was then the tango found me.

I was alone and lonely after Jack died. So to be able to communicate in a spiritual, soulful way with another person with no other commitment besides mutual enjoyment for ten minutes was a blessing. I was a dancer, now at an age when a classical *pas de deux* was impossible, but a *tanda* of tango–a dance set of three or four songs–to music that echoed my feelings of loss and regret, helped me be at peace for the first time after relentless suffering. In the arms of strangers I was myself again.

We humans need connection, but relationships are among the most difficult of life's challenges. We need touch, but in English-based cultures it can be difficult to fulfill that need unless we have equally affectionate people surrounding us. (Some people find it easier to have a pet.) Hugs can be healing, but often complicated. The tango embrace, however, is uncomplicated. When it's right you feel connected, whole, a part of the perfect universe, complete in the yin/yang circle of life—the complementary, interconnected, interrelated dualism that exists in the natural world. And once you felt this, you have to have it again. You become addicted to the tango and the resulting endorphins, dopamine, and serotonin that give you a chemical high. If tango is a "feeling that is danced" as the milongueros, the men who grew up dancing tango in the milongas, say, you are driven to feel it again and again.

Now after moving from San Miguel de Allende where I had lived for almost three years, I had rearranged my life so every morning was a Buenos Aires morning! I arrived in Argentina with my cat, Phoebe, from Mexico City and went straight to my two-bedroom furnished apartment on *Calle Mejico* (Mexico Street—certainly a good omen) in Congreso, the heart of the capital city. My five suitcases had gone to Rio according to AeroMexico.

The loss of my bags was a repeat of my arrival in Mexico in 2001 when everything but Phoebe was left behind at the airport on Christmas Eve. Phoebe "the Expat Cat" was still most important to me, and she was ready to start her new life in Argentina along with me.

But how I missed my sons. I was now so very far away. My two adult boys, Adam and Jason, were my only family for I had no siblings, aunts, or cousins. I seldom got to see Adam or my grandson, Dominic, because they lived in the mountains outside Sacramento in a "Fellowship," and travelled down to L.A. only occasionally. Jason lived in Hollywood but he was a busy young man trying to reconstruct his life after giving up his successful classical ballet career at the time of Jack's death. (He had toured for six weeks throughout Central and, ironically, South America where he had danced lead roles in the famous Teatro Colon of Buenos Aires.) Because I rarely saw my sons—and had no other family—I had been more motivated to leave L.A. If it were impossible geographically to get together with my boys, maybe I wouldn't feel so redundant. And the abundant tango hugs and little-kiss greetings of daily life would soothe my feelings of disconnection as I got my fix of tango.

After five days my luggage arrived and I spread my Mexican rugs on the floor, hung my "shoes in a suitcase" painting, filled the little closet with my clothes. I had already checked out the kitchen equipment—the toaster was one of those old fashioned things with clamps you hold over the fire—bought some cat food and cat litter, and so I was settled, more or less.

The every-two-weeks maid, Fernanda, came with the apartment. Her function was more that of spying for the landlord than cleaning. She examined everything I owned and paid too much attention to what I was doing. Stringy and small, toasty brown in color, she always brought with her the smell of cigarettes, which lingered long after she left.

As soon as I could, I anxiously got ready to go dancing as Fernanda was finishing up. She called out, "Hasta luego, Señora" and slammed the front door while I was in the bathroom scrunching my short red hair and putting on mascara. I usually didn't wear much makeup, but now that I was middle-aged, I needed to compete for the best tango partners with the local women who spared no effort in looking good in the milongas. Plus I was tall, which often worked against me, as the milongueros who were the best dancers, were old and usually short. Some didn't mind dancing with a tall woman—in fact they often enjoyed being at her chest level, especially if she were wearing décolleté. But others didn't. And my four-inch tango heels didn't help.

Sporting sneakers, I grabbed my tango shoe bag and a sweater as I was going on foot to the matinee at Lo de Celia. I liked that I could dance early and come home early, although sometimes I might then go to another milonga if I met up with a new friend. There were milongas from three in the afternoon to six in the morning every night. It was a feast of riches for the visiting dancers in this mecca of tango who were accustomed to only one or two milongas a week in their home towns, and now a nightly dream come true for me.

I'd been a tango tourist in Buenos Aires many times since my first visit six years ago. Finally I had made the big leap of moving to the tango capital, and now I guessed I could be called a *porteña*, a resident of Buenos Aires. After a decade of trying to find a permanent home in France and then Mexico, at last I felt I had found it on a new continent, in a different hemisphere, where I hoped I could live out my life on the limited means I had, but rich with lots of wonderful tango.

I had taken an early retirement from the Los Angeles Public Library due to the heavy breast cancer treatment I'd received back in 1994 and then again in 2002. But my pension simply didn't provide enough to live on in one of the most expensive cities in the U.S., Los Angeles. I felt then that this was my chance, my reason and excuse, to live in an entirely different culture, to learn a new language, to enjoy and experience as much as I could, and so I had moved to Mexico. Trying my best to survive had brought me now at last to Buenos Aires, the birthplace of the tango, where I could dance whenever I wanted.

After checking my lipstick in the entryway mirror, I grabbed the door handle to leave the apartment. It didn't budge. There were three locks on the door plus a chain and I only had two keys, which I tried over and over in all the locks. Evidently Fernanda had a third key that I didn't have and she had locked all three when she left. In Buenos Aires locks had to be locked and unlocked on both sides with keys. I was trapped.

I banged on the door just in case someone would hear me at the end of the long hall. Perhaps the porter would be around. I stood at the window looking down three stories, concentrating on the proprietor of the hardware store directly across the street. When I had gone there the day before to buy a voltage regulator, he had been so nice, finishing the sale with the *cualquier cosa* that I hadn't yet learned was ubiquitous in BA

(Buenos Aires), not meaning really that he'd help with anything I needed, only a polite way to end a transaction. This moment of panic was quite a "cosa" or thing I needed help with.

He was standing directly below me, in front of my building, leaning against the bright red wall of his shop, smoking a cigarette. I willed him to look up, to see me in panic three floors up, and rescue me like Rapunzel in the fairy tale. But soon a customer arrived, and they both vanished inside. There were pedestrians below and finally I yelled to them. "Help me, *Ayudame*!" I felt like an idiot. But it didn't matter as no one heard me or paid any attention anyway. First my lost luggage, then this.

I started to go a little crazy with being locked in, a prisoner. I opened the window completely—"Help! *Ayudame! Mira arriba! Look up!*" Frantically I yelled out in alarm to no one and everyone.

I had no cell phone but the apartment came with a landline. I didn't have the *portero*'s contact information yet, or any other number besides that of Cristina, the tango house maven I had stayed with many times during my vacation visits. After several calls to her, thank goodness she answered at last. She sent her ex-husband over to ring the portero's bell and both men came upstairs to release me from being imprisoned in my own apartment. Evidently the maid had locked the dead bolt when she left that afternoon, and it needed to be unlocked with a key even from the inside. Like the main door to the building, key in, key out was the BA security system. If a crook got in he couldn't get out with all your valuables in hand without a key. Hugo, the portero gave me a copy of the deadbolt key and I now had four keys on my new key ring.

At last I could go to the milonga. I had been a captive for almost three hours and I was ready to dance!

CHAPTER 2

Before touching your lips, I want to touch your heart, and before conquering your body, I want to conquer your love.

—piropo (compliment)

March 2004

I walked the few blocks over broken sidewalk tiles and past derelict buildings to Lo de Celia on the corner of Entre Rios and Humberto Primo, so happy to be out of the apartment, free, and to be going somewhere where almost everyone knew me. I climbed the stairs with a beating heart and bought my two-peso *entrada* ticket, and then went through the red draperies to be greeted by Celia, the organizer. She led me to a small table on the women's side of the room facing the men across the square dance floor. I felt immediately at home. Dany the DJ waved at me, and Jony the tuxedoed waiter quickly came over to welcome me with a *besito* on the cheek and a glass of champagne.

I slipped into the ladies' room to change my shoes, and checked out all of the cheap and fancy dancing clothes hanging everywhere, on the doors, the mirrors, the light fixtures–filling up the small space. It was possible to go into the bathroom in one outfit, and come out dressed in a completely new one. It was a way for the attendant to make a little more money than just tips and it added to the fun of the milonga.

That afternoon my dance partners all asked me when I had arrived in Buenos Aires and how long I would be staying this trip, as they asked all the visiting foreign ladies. They seemed taken aback when I replied, "I've moved here, I'm staying forever, *hasta siempre, hasta el final!*" They didn't know what to say to that, so they just opened their arms to take me in an embrace and then we stepped forward to join the line of dance, the *ronda,* on the floor. I think the milongueros liked the foreign women to come and then to leave. But now all of a sudden my status had changed. I would be around to see and be seen, to watch, to know, and to expect, and suddenly everything was more complicated.

The traditional milongas like Celia's were worth the long flights the many tango tourists took to get there. I loved the *codigós,* the unspoken rules of the tango salon. I felt so empowered (an unusual feeling for a woman in that *machista* culture). Because of the *cabeceo,* the traditional way of inviting and accepting dance invitations with nods of the head, nobody knew if I refused someone, there was no walk of shame for a rejected man returning to his table. I gave no mercy dances. I danced with whom I wanted, to the music I liked. I felt in control; no man could approach my table without permission from my eyes. There was none of the uninvited sitting down and monopolizing a woman that often occurs in the U.S.

I didn't like the popular milongas for young people with no codigos, where I felt vulnerable and with less control. *Prácticas* and milongas like La Viruta in the Armenian Club in Palermo across town, for example, were informal and anyone could grab anyone else for a dance. I felt invaded when that happened. I loved having my space at a table that no one could properly enter without permission. I felt safe.

Traditional tango, with its code of behavior and etiquette rules, is all about role-playing: the man leads, the woman follows. The man decides where and how the woman steps. The man protects the woman, turning and receiving the brunt of a collision that might otherwise hurt her. A woman needs to feel safe in the man's embrace so she can give up control, close her eyes, and go to the blissful state of tango heaven. And when that happens, the man is proud because he feels responsible for her pleasure. He also takes great delight in showing her off, letting her shine, because he knows that makes him look good.

The codigos also require the man to walk the woman back to her table after the tanda, to protect her until she is out of his care. For the woman the tanda is like a ten-minute vacation when she can give up control, be taken care of, and she doesn't have to worry about anything. For many women, these temporary roles are a brief and welcome respite from the real world of choices, decisions, and the anxiety of responsibility. You know what you have to do, you do it, and you get pleasure from it. You submit to the codigos of the tango and are rewarded with enjoyment and gratification.

The whole tango scene is very sexist, but as long as you understand that you are merely playing a role, it works for the length of the "play." While dancing, the men are rugged and aggressive, the women soft and yielding. For 150 years the tango has been danced this way–with all the codigos and the machismo of the dance salons. That is why so many tango tourists, including me, flock to Buenos Aires.

These male/female roles came out of the macho lifestyle of a Latin culture. That and the pervasive sadness and nostalgia of Buenos Aires is the reason the tango is Argentino and not gringo. And while Argentine women are resilient and outspoken, the residual machismo is still a strong societal norm: different pay scales, distinct retirement ages, various prices at milongas, men letting women board the bus first (although then it was a free-for-all for available seats), waiters and taxi drivers not acknowledging women when they were with a man, and the codigos of tango.

A woman might be a CEO, or "wear the pants" in her family, or even is *La Presidenta de la Republica*. But when she dances the tango, she wants to be feminine and follow the lead of a man. She wants to submit to machismo. And now that I lived in Tango Land, that's what I wanted too, as often as I could get it on the dance floor.

However when the cumbia tanda began, a set of *tropical* (a variety of other dance music, including merengue and even rock 'n roll), I visited the ladies' room. I preferred to save my energy for the tango. An Australian woman I knew was sitting weeping on one of the chairs where the ladies changed their shoes. A beautiful, tall, surgery-enhanced older woman, she was hunched over and crying, shoulders shaking with her silent sobs, her hands twisting the tissues in her lap.

"Loretta, you're back in BA. I just arrived too. But what's wrong? Can I help?"

"Remember Carlos? The man I liked last year? The tall one with the mustache?"

"Yes, what about him? What happened?" I pulled over another chair and sat down.

Carlos was a man much younger than Loretta who frequented the milongas where tourists went. Several visiting women were enamored of him, although I couldn't understand why. Carlos seemed slimy to me, a bottom-feeder, the epitome of a "Latin Lover. When she originally asked me about him last year, I had counseled her at the time to have fun with him, just enjoy him. Not to fall in love with him. But she had let him seduce her, and had become emotionally involved.

When we didn't understand the language and all the nuances, nor the culture, it was so easy to misread someone, to imagine that what would be true in our countries, wasn't necessarily true in a different one. We wanted to believe the smiles, the direct gazes, the touching and little kisses, the charm and chivalry. And the men were delighted when we did.

"We kept corresponding after I returned to Perth," she said, wiping her eyes, not careful of her mascara, "and he begged me to come back and rent a nice apartment for a longer stay, and we would live together for a little while. So I arrived two weeks ago.

"Oh, Cherie," she said, "the first few days were bliss! But then he kept returning later and later to the apartment, and when I questioned him about it, we ended up fighting. I don't know why he wanted me to come back here."

"Oh I'm sorry, Loretta." I put my arm around her shoulders, giving her a soft hug.

"And then he hit me!" With this revelation, she broke down completely, sobbing and gulping air. The other women in the bathroom and the attendant tried not to pay attention. After all, it was nothing they hadn't all heard a hundred times before.

When she recovered enough to talk, she said, "I made him get out and I haven't seen him since except in the milongas. I paid a lot for the long-term apartment, and I don't like being there alone, but maybe he will come back."

I wondered why she would want someone who hit her to return, yet I completely understood the tango trance that was worth almost anything to many dancers. There's a saying that the men dance with the women so that they will go to bed with them, and the women go to bed with the men so that they will dance with them. To the addicted, the dance is everything.

"Now he won't even look at me in the milongas," she said as the tears flowed down her cheeks. "At least he should dance with me!"

CHAPTER 3

Bank accounts frozen and the Argentine peso reduced to rubble...In just one day, dozens were killed as riots consumed Buenos Aires...By the time it was all over, fifty percent of Argentines were poor and the economy had cratered more than 20% in just a few years. Of course, the already rampant inflation rates got far, far worse as the value of the Argentine peso, no longer able to rest on its US dollar peg, collapsed.

— NomadCapitalist.com, Andrew Henderson, 2001

The previous December I had travelled from Mexico over the holidays to look for a place in BA so Phoebe and I could immediately settle in upon our arrival three months later in March. Mexico had become too expensive for me, and with the economic crash two years previously in Argentina, the dollars of my pension could go farther. However the poor Argentines had lost everything in *el corralito,* the economic measures taken at the end of 2001 by Minister of Economy Domingo Cavallo in order to stop a bank run.

It was devastating. A milonguero told me he had purchased his apartment for $50,000usd when the peso was one to one. But after the crash, the peso was devalued and suddenly his mortgage payments were three times as much. He lost his property. And many folks lost their jobs as well. With five presidents within two weeks, the country had been in chaos. Overnight women had stopped wearing makeup and nice clothes on the street in order not to draw attention to themselves and attract thieves. They carried their pretty things in bags and dressed up when they arrived at their destination. They even stopped wearing costume jewelry in public.

But now things had settled down, and I felt I could build my future in Argentina. I still had some funds from the sale of my house in Los Angeles, but my travellers' cheques were getting fewer. In San Miguel de Allende I had lived beyond my pension every month. In BA I hoped I could live within my means.

So last December I had left Phoebe with a friend in Mexico while I apartment hunted in BA. I had landed sick with what I would later call the Buenos Aires Crud that everyone got upon arrival: lung congestion, sore throat, a cough. For me it then would develop into asthma, which I had never had before. In December it was hot and humid, the air was heavy with moisture and pollution. I was feverish and in a kind of hell in the stifling, tiny, uncomfortable apartment I had rented sight unseen from a friend in Palermo for two weeks.

I had a few friends in BA who I had met over the years on my many short visits to the city to dance. Corrie, my hostess was one, and Brian, an expat from England, was another. I also counted Cristina, and another expat, Janet, as friends I could depend on. I tried to call Corrie with the number she left but there was never any answer, so I called Brian. "Brian, I can't stay here. And I'm too sick to figure anything out. Please help me."

He came over in a taxi, took one look around the hell hole I was in, grabbed the bag I had hastily packed, and bundled me downstairs to the waiting cab. I left a note for Corrie with the full amount of the rent we had agreed upon on the table, as well as the items she had asked me to bring her from the States. Brian saw that and was upset. "She is gouging you. She thinks because you're American you're rich. She could never, ever, rent this awful place to an Argentine for that much. I know a good hotel that's safe and not expensive close to several milongas in Congreso. Let's go there."

"Oh Brian, you're wonderful. Thank you so much. Yes, a hotel. Oh yes."

Right away I felt better in the Hotel Lyon. There was air conditioning, and a TV where I could watch the 24-hour tango channel. With my room service breakfast of *café con leche, media lunas* and sweet orange juice, I watched videos of tango lessons and performances and began to feel better.

It wasn't long before I recovered and was ready to meet up with my tango-house friend Cristina and her group of foreign dancers at one milonga after another. The men at hotel reception and the night guard were helpful, friendly, and solicitous and I felt quite safe returning alone late after a milonga. The *taxista* always waited, watching me, until I was securely inside the hotel before driving away.

Normally there were no milongas or transportation in BA on the nights of December 24 or 31, but Cristina knew about a private New Year's Eve tango party at the antique Hotel Dandi in San Telmo. She picked me up in her car packed with guests from her tango house, and we brought in 2004 with champagne and tango.

During my two weeks of reconnaissance, I asked everyone I met if they knew of a furnished apartment for rent come March. At first I had this romantic idea of living in a building with the old French-style architecture for which BA was famous. The city was called "The Paris of South America," for all of the art nouveau and architectural copying that had filled the city in the boom of the teens and 1920s. The buildings were of varying heights, not the six floors that made Paris so symmetrical, and possessed their own Argentine flamboyance. And now many of them, outside of the fancy barrios, had fallen into disrepair.

I quickly changed my mind about living in one when I looked at a few—too dark, too many cockroaches. I had a strong need to see the sky when I was inside, and those *casas de chorizo* had all rooms facing inside, perhaps for coolness during the sweltering summer months. But I needed to look up and out, to the infinite blue. Seeing the sky was critical to my mood and well-being.

An Argentine tanguero who also lived in New York had a furnished two-bedroom apartment for rent, in a rather modern building from the '50s or '60s. On the street, it had a "French balcony," meaning the glass window went to the floor and opened inward, but you couldn't step out or put plants there. Only a few blocks from the milongas of Nino Bien, Gricel, and Lo de Celia, it was $350usd / mo, including all utilities and a maid. My apartment in San Miguel de Allende was a studio for $600usd with nothing included. If I took this apartment, I could finally relax about money, my constant, nagging worry, and the big reason I had left Los Angeles and then Mexico.

After New Year's, I returned to San Miguel and began packing, selling and giving away possessions—oh so familiar–and looking forward, albeit with a lot of fear as well as excitement, to my big move to a new continent and a new life. San Miguel de Allende had become even more expensive with all of the wealthy Texans and Canadians building million-dollar houses, and besides, there was no tango there. Every so often, when the urge to dance became too strong I took a four-hour bus trip to Mexico City and stayed overnight in a hotel by myself, just to attend a milonga in an Argentine restaurant.

CHAPTER 4

No doubt the Argentines are indeed "sexy"; however, experience has revealed that this trait it is not in a pleasingly seductive or sensual way, but instead, in a disgustingly carnal manner.

—Enna Morgan, Quora.com

March 2004

Now as a resident of Buenos Aires, a *porteña,* I began doing what I always did—get into a routine. I planned to attend meetings of BAIN—Buenos Aires International Newcomers—where I hoped to make friends and connections. I also tried to find a cancer support group, either in Spanish or English, but with no luck. I had gone faithfully to cancer meetings in Mexico, not only to help myself, but I felt my presence was encouraging to the other members. They seemed to appreciate having a two-time survivor among the attendees since nearly every month someone in the group passed away.

I spent my days getting to know my barrio of Congreso, or more specifically Balvanera. The portero's wife, Susana, was outgoing and occasionally invited me into their miniscule apartment for coffee. The couple and their teenaged son shared one small room at the back of the ground floor, with sheets as dividers for sleeping spaces.

Susana was lonely and bored at home and quite curious about me. We communicated well despite my Mexican Spanish and she taught me new words in *castellano*, the Argentine Spanish. She walked me around the neighborhood and showed me things I never would have found on my own. We hiked down to the Ecological Reserve at Puerto Madero, and just a block away, she pointed out a nondescript building that had been used for detaining and torturing political prisoners during the Dirty War of the military junta.

The portero, Hugo, was too friendly I thought, especially when I was going out to dance all dressed up and met him in the hall. He would compliment me with a gleam in his eye. "Señora, que pinta!" he always said. "Wow!"

I went to milongas almost every night, where I saw my favorite milongueros and the women friends I had made over so many visits. I felt I had friends in BA, or at least people who knew me, which was more than I had had when I moved to Mexico in 2001 from L. A. During that group tango tour six years ago I became bewitched by the tango life I experienced in BA–the historical salons where the milongas were held, the emotional close embrace of the old milongueros, the excitement of a culture in which the tango was everything. Nothing mattered–not your job, car, social status, age–only how you danced. So thrilling and different from dancing tango anywhere else.

Despite the embraces on the dance floor and the seductive ways of the porteño men in the milongas, I didn't plan on falling in love or having any kind of relationship in my new country that was any more than "fun." My husband Jack and I had been so compatible, and our relationship so loving and supportive, that after his death when I was only forty-six, I hadn't thought it would be all that hard to have a loving partner once again, even if he were nothing like Jack. It had been easy with Jack. Now I was just trying my best to build a new life and be happy. I knew Jack would want that.

I had met Olivier in Paris a year after Jack's death. He was a beautiful man who owned a large, gorgeous art nouveau apartment in Paris' 3eme arrondissement, and my lifetime desire to live in France seemed about to come true. I couldn't believe that Olivier loved me, wanted to marry me, and live with him in Paris. It was like a fairy tale. But then just as I was about to leave Los Angeles for Paris, I was diagnosed with breast cancer and I learned the truth about him. Although he came to L.A. and took care of me after my surgery, drove me daily to radiation, was solicitous of my well-being when I visited Paris and had a chemo treatment in the Hôpital Saint Louis, once I began to recover, he changed. When we flew to Paris together from L.A. on Christmas Eve with all my belongings, and me with no hair, he suddenly realized the fantasy was over and reality had begun. I could tell he was scared.

Though Olivier was well-educated and from a good and respected family, somehow it had turned out that I paid for everything including his paranoia. Because of the French divorce laws, he was petrified that his wife, who had lived and worked in Katmandu for years, would discover I was living with him in his apartment, meaning that she might have a claim on it, even though it had been a gift from his father long before his marriage. So I paid for the blinds he installed on all of the apartment windows to hide my being there from the neighbors. He also insisted we leave and arrive to the apartment separately in case his wife had spies watching him. And we had to sleep separately in case the police arrived before dawn to check the warmth of the bed linens!

I understood at last that because of his status as the only

boy in a family of five children, his good looks and intelligence, that he had been raised to expect things would be given to him. He didn't really know what struggle meant. He was a narcissist, but that didn't seem to matter at first. It was easy for me to love and give, and love and give I did.

So after Olivier, and my year of convalescence in France, when I realized the relationship could never work out, I returned home to L.A. to work again at the library. And then I just tried to enjoy myself with whatever interesting man came my way. After two bouts with cancer and watching Jack die too young, I believed in living in the present.

Now in Argentina I wasn't going to search for a partner but do my best to build a life, to dance, and just be happy. And if that occasionally included a man (or two), so much the better.

I had lived in BA for two weeks, and it was my birthday. As always wherever I was, I planned a party to celebrate. This year marked the beginning of not only a new life in South America but I was turning sixty and a new decade—a testament to having followed my bliss—was beginning. But who to invite? I didn't want to ask people from the milonga who I didn't really know to come to my apartment. Cristina had always told me never to tell the milongueros where I lived or that I lived alone. I agreed, having learned my lesson last birthday in Mexico when I invited strangers to my party, and even though it was on the roof, I ended up getting robbed. There was Corrie but, after the fiasco of renting her awful place last December, we no longer were close. I invited Brian, and Cristina of course, who asked if she could bring the Australian dancers staying at her tango house. Perfect! A ready-made party. (I invited Janet too, but she was having a spat with Cristina so she declined.)

Among the Australian guests was a musician who brought his violin and improvised. The living room was small but everyone danced. I got out my finger cymbals and belly dancing veil and improvised as well.

I had ordered a birthday cake at a local deli, and specified writing a *Feliz Cumple a Cherie* on top. The clerk looked at me strangely when I described the *pastel* I wanted, but accepted the order and payment. But when I went to pick it up—it was a meatloaf! Sure enough my name was written on top in ketchup. Pastel was a cake in Mexico, but a meat or potato savory loaf in Argentina. As I stuck a candle in it, everyone laughed and sang Happy Birthday in English and Spanish.

It was a relief to speak English with my party guests. I had managed in Mexico after studying Spanish full time at the Academia Hispanico, but here the accent, grammar and vocabulary were so different—like "pastel." Few people I came in contact with on a daily basis spoke English in Buenos Aires. So I was determined to improve my castellano, which was Spanish but with a lot of Italian and slang (*lunfardo*) mixed in, as well as another kind of "pig latin" slang, *vesre*—pronouncing words backwards. Cristina recommended a teacher who gave private classes not far away.

Carolina lived in Congreso, in one of the old-style French buildings I had long admired. A young, petite, pleasant girl with intelligent laughing blue eyes and short curly black hair, answered the big carved front door of the building and we went up together in the ornate two-passenger cage elevator to the third floor and her apartment at the front. We entered a small vestibule and she ushered me into the living room that was no bigger than a closet. Books and CDs surrounded a very small sofa and a chair, and a huge white tomcat slept on the windowsill. The first lesson went well and so we scheduled two private lessons per week, conversation only. I explained it was useless to give me homework; I was motivated to learn but I needed as much time as possible for dancing, and I would be practicing castellano at the milongas.

I also wanted to continue my classes of flamenco that I began in Mexico, where I studied for two years and had even performed with my teacher's troupe in a Spanish restaurant. Brian knew a flamenco teacher he danced tango with at milongas, so I called her and signed up for two classes a week and one private in her studio in Almagro.

I was learning to get around on public transportation, which made me feel more like a local. You could get anywhere on the buses and subways of BA, but it took a little practice. Kioscos sold bus directories, but how to get from here to there wasn't simple to figure out. (Tourists joked that you needed a degree in astrophysics.) Because almost all of the streets were one way, it wasn't easy to know where to wait and where to get off, as the stops weren't well marked or obvious. This was especially true for me who, except for in Paris, had never taken public transportation. In Los Angeles, like most Angelenos, I'd always had a car.

Everyone lined up at the bus stops, but when the bus arrived, the men stepped aside and let the women get on first. I had never seen this level of courtesy toward women. Ironically however, once inside the bus, everyone fought over the seats. Maybe because I was noticeably a foreigner, no one ever offered me his seat when I was standing, and I was glad. I was just as capable of holding a strap as any man. There were laws posted about saving the front seats for pregnant women,

women carrying children, and the handicapped—rules that weren't always obeyed.

My flamenco teacher, Graciela, was a decade younger than I was, and had danced contemporary professionally as well as flamenco. Very pretty, with long black curly hair, and a dancer's slim and graceful shape, she had turned her living room into a dance studio by knocking out a wall and installing mirrors. Sheets of plywood protected the hardwood floor from the nails of the dancers' shoes as they stomped and clicked through the various rhythms of *solea, bulerias, alegrias.*

I had loved my fun flamenco classes in Mexico. But Graciela's classes were work. She was extremely serious and pushed me and the other three much younger students hard. *"Braceo! Codos arribas! Taco, planta, punta, planta! Venga!"* she commanded over and over, with vigorous handclaps. *"Otra vez!"* Again!

CHAPTER 5

**Shipwrecked survivors of the world who have lost their heart*

—"Fog of the Riachuelo" tango

May 2004

I was learning a lot about my new chosen country. Obviously it was one thing to be there on vacation and quite another to move there for the rest of my life. It meant everything to me that I had Phoebe at my side in Argentina, as she had been in Mexico and in Los Angeles. She was my constant, with all of her goofy ways, and she made wherever I was, a home. Home was where my cat was.

For an older woman like me, and the many tango tourists from around the world, the machista culture of Argentina was a surprisingly pleasant change from a background of large personal space. Here it was normal to touch strangers and give kisses as greetings to everyone. Whereas mature women were invisible at home, suddenly in Buenos Aires we were admired, complimented, flirted with, and often even propositioned.

This behavior was so ingrained in the culture and the men did it so charmingly, having learned their smooth ways from their fathers, uncles, and grandfathers, that a woman could almost believe it was true–that every man she met found her sexy and wanted to bed her. Consequently the local women knew that the power they had was sexual and they did their best to prolong it as long as possible, with plastic surgery, keeping their figures, lots of makeup, and sexy clothes.

Men theoretically gave up their seats on the bus to women just because they were women and "delicate." Men ordered for women in restaurants (not too long ago women didn't even get menus). Men made the decisions. Men met their friends for dinner, went out alone to dance, felt free to have affairs—it was their right as men.

Women in Argentina couldn't vote until 1947 and, as a predominantly Catholic country, abortion was still not legal today under any circumstances. Women could retire younger than men, and they often could pay less for entrance fees. I didn't know about salaries, but I was sure it wasn't equal pay for equal work. The whole culture defined women as less than men in every way. The gratuitous courtesy didn't fool me for a minute; well, to be honest, maybe for one minute I did believe that I was still desirable and sexy as an older woman, and that was a nice minute!

I was actually going out on "dates" with some of the men I danced with in the milongas. In Lo de Celia's, I danced with big and tall Hector, a dancer with a great embrace, who was very sensuous, complimentary, flirtatious as they all were.

One afternoon I agreed to go to coffee with him before a milonga. I thought before was safer than after. Hector picked me up in his fancy black SUV. A handsome and sexy man, he was beautifully dressed, lavishly cologned. He was such a gentleman, opening the car door, buckling my seat belt, putting the sugar into my coffee for me and stirring it with the accompanying tiny spoon.

I was tired from closing three milongas the previous night and dancing for ten hours, but Hector wanted to go to Salon Canning after coffee. I enjoyed dancing with him, so I wanted to make the most of the opportunity to have several tandas together during our date. We discussed sitting together or separately, because where you sit and with whom carried meaning according to the codigos.

I entered the milonga by myself and bought my own ticket, and later Hector came in, sitting several tables away with the men. We danced two different romantic tandas, but during the second one I could tell something was wrong.

"Que pasa?" I asked him during the pause between tangos on the dance floor, the only time historically men and women could talk alone and privately. In the past women were always accompanied to milongas by a chaperone—their mother, sister, or aunt—so *entre tango y tango* was the traditional time for flirtation and getting to know each other, and the opportunity for the *chamuyero* to charm his partner with compliments.

Hector said he was dismayed, but the ex-novia was there, even though they had worked out their milonga schedules previously so that no one would feel uncomfortable. He went to this one, she went to that one, all organized so they wouldn't run into each other.

"Do you want to leave?" I asked him.

"No, no, esta bien," he said.

We finished the tanda and returned to our respective tables. But then I saw him talking to her and when he sat down he looked sick.

The DJ began a romantic Pugliese tanda, a favorite of foreigners, sensuous dancers, and lovers. (The Osvaldo Pugliese Orchestra, the last in the pantheon of the Golden Age orchestras of the 30s, 40s, and 50s, played complex musical arrangements with slow parts, then fast sections, some jazzy moments, all with a passionate and theatrical bravado. It was beloved by beginners who couldn't hear the variations in tempo and theme and felt they could dance anything they liked. Pugliese, along with music of Astor Piazzola, was always played in tango stage shows and performances.)

I stared at Hector for a cabeceo, the silent invitation to dance, but he didn't look at me. Finally I accepted a cabeceo and danced with someone else, and over the shoulder of my partner while dancing, I saw Hector put on his coat and leave. Without me!

After the tanda, I left too, thinking perhaps he was waiting for me outside or in his car, but there I was on the dark street alone in my spiked-heeled tango shoes in the glacial cold. There was no sign of Hector or his SUV. I was embarrassed to return to the salon so when a lone taxi cruised by, I threw up my arm. Once home, I called him. He sounded horrible when he answered, like he was choking.

"Why did you leave me there?" I said. "I have never been abandoned by the man I came with. You could at least have left me a note or a message with the waiter! *Grosero,* so rude!"

"*Perdon,* I'm sorry, but I'm sick."

"So," I said, "you're still in love with your ex?"

"No," he said.

"But then why were you so thoughtless?" I asked. "It alarmed me, and made me uncomfortable. What if I hadn't had any money for a taxi?"

"I am sorry," he said again.

Frustrated, I just said, "Ciao!" and hung up. Treating me like a fairy doll and then leaving me high and dry? That seemed crazy to me. Was this normal in the culture I now found myself living in? Men just do whatever they want?

I learned that BAIN, the Buenos Aires International Newcomers club, had Friday afternoon meetings at the expensive Hotel Emperador in Recoleta, the Beverly Hills of BA. I got dressed up in a black pantsuit I hadn't worn since Los Angeles. Feeling a little like a bat, I grabbed a taxi in the street. I laughed to myself when the taxista addressed me respectfully as "Doctora," as I got out of the cab. Passing by the many suited security guards decorating the front and in the lobby of the modern hotel, I found my way downstairs to the meeting room and filled out a nametag.

There were about twenty-five attendees, mostly women and no one I recognized from the milongas. I grabbed a coffee and a little ham and cheese *miga* sandwich from the buffet and found a seat. When the meeting began I had to introduce myself as a first timer. After a presentation by an East Indian woman about her recent trip to India, there were announcements and socializing. People were from many different English-speaking countries, most wives of diplomats and businessmen. They definitely seemed affluent. I was glad I had worn my nice librarian suit.

BAIN held a luncheon every month at a different restaurant and I planned to go. It felt good to add dates to my calendar, to be organized in a sense, as that was what I had always been. And also it would be fun to discover restaurants I would never have found on my own.

At the restaurant excursion a few weeks later in Palermo, the expat barrio where the most interesting eateries were, I met handsome Mexican-American Mike (he didn't like to be called Miguel), who was in BA on business. His company provided him with a gorgeous three-bedroom apartment in Recoleta in a very tony building. He didn't speak Spanish even though he had been raised in a Mexican barrio of L.A. He was pleasant and easy on the eyes, but quite strange—secretive, suspicious, fearful and, I thought, probably emotionally unavailable. He was about 50, never married, no kids, not close with his family. His company had paid to ship his belongings to BA, but even though he had been there two years, his framed pictures were still on the floor facing the wall, along with boxes of belongings still unopened.

He was a member of International Toastmasters and invited me to go to a meeting, held in the sophisticated Club Militar not far from his place in Recoleta. All my life I had wanted to conquer my huge fear of public speaking, so this seemed like a good opportunity to try. After all it was rather now or never, wasn't it?

Entering the old world private club reminded me of my life with Jack and the many times we went to the elegant Jonathan Club in downtown L.A. When I inquired, "Toastmasters?" the Club Militar doorman sent me up the ornate wood-paneled stairs to the first floor, a splendid place, full of carved wood and colorful stained glass. Although most members were Argentine with the odd foreigner like myself, the meeting was conducted in English, and Mike had prepared me that I would have to stand up and introduce myself. Already my legs were shaking, my stomach churning. But I did it, although I was too shy to try speaking on a "Table Topic" that first night. Afterwards Mike invited me and his friend Silvina for dinner in the Club's restaurant. As it was a lovely autumn evening we dined in the back garden full of flowers, grass and a burbling fountain.

From then on I added Toastmasters on Thursday evenings to my schedule. I usually went dressed to dance and taxied to the Club Español afterwards.

Club Español was an iconic building on Bernardo Yrigoyen, close to the famous Obelisco. An amazing cupola of bronze crowned by a sculpture of Aladdin's Genie, that once upon a time held a light that was lit on special holidays, distinguished the stunning structure from far away. Buenos Aires' private clubs were often in the best condition as they had European money to maintain them. There were many Spanish and Italian clubs in BA, but this one was breathtakingly gorgeous, full of marble sculptures, gilt, wood carvings and in the basement, tiled walls worthy of the Alhambra.

The milonga was on the second floor (third to Americans), and dancers went up in a large gilded cage elevator with a red velvet bench for resting between stops. Because the salon was so elegant, dancers tended to dress up more than for other milongas, and the *pista* seemed to sparkle and gleam from the shine of the ladies dresses, the men's polished shoes, the gilt on the walls and ceiling, and the mirrors that reflected it all.

I met a blind dancer there who asked me to spend the day with him in the Delta of Tigre. I had never been but I had heard for years how lovely it was. I was nervous because my castellano still wasn't very good and Jorge spoke no English. He gave me detailed instructions on how to take the Tren de la Costa and where to meet him. I managed to find him at the station but from then on I was in panic mode. He asked me about directions and signs which I couldn't read or understand, and my only thought was to keep him from falling in the water as we got in and out of the water taxi and then walked around an island on a narrow dirt footpath next to a canal, he holding onto my elbow and tapping with his cane.

It was late fall and bitter cold in the delta, gray with a slight mist. I was grateful for my old Lands' End green parka. Somehow we found a cozy restaurant for lunch. Jorge paid for everything. He also confessed he was married and lived with his wife because "being blind he couldn't live alone." He may not have been a milonguero—he was a terrible dancer, and contrary to my preconceived ideas about blind people, he didn't listen to the music at all—but he obviously played around just the same. When I got home I was exhausted. I vowed to go back to Tigre in the summer and with someone more appropriate.

CHAPTER 6

The amount of our furniture we bring with us represents how much of a past we're willing to give up on, share, or ignore.

—Robert Kaplan, psychologist

June 2004

My New York-based landlord had figured out he could get more money renting the Congreso apartment short-term to tourists because each time someone left, he could raise the rent, so he wanted me to leave by August.

I was searching anyway for a new unfurnished place, a permanent home, but taking my time. Now knowing I had to leave soon made me nervous and anxious. This "kicking the widow into the street" seemed to be a pattern since Jack had passed away. I had been cheated out of my lovely old family home in Los Angeles by the realtor who still lived in it years later, and unbelievably, also out of my apartment in Evian-les-Bains, France, where Jack was buried. After his death, when my half of the apartment was paid off by mortgage insurance, my partners, the couple we had purchased it with, had pulled a fast one on me via an expensive California lawyer, and I lost that too. And at Chateau Rodney in Hollywood where I'd lived so happily for the six years after the end of my relationship with Olivier, all of the tenants were forced to leave when the building was sold.

But no one in BA wanted to rent long term to a foreigner. Owners were afraid the foreigner would skip back to where they came from without paying what they owed. Therefore the precaution the landlords took so that wouldn't happen, was not to rent to foreigners.

I worried and complained in castellano during my language classes with Carolina and one day she said she had some good news. Her father, a doctor, had just finished renovating a nice apartment in Caballito that he had inherited from his parents and now he was ready to rent it.

But in order to rent it, and with no guarantee by a cosigner who owned property in BA, I had to pay the whole two years (the usual length of a lease) in advance! In cash! But I did have American Express traveller's cheques and I found out at BAIN that I could cash them with no service charge in Retiro at the American Express office there.

However I was afraid to walk around afterwards looking for a taxi with thousands of pesos in my pocket. Even though the lovely park San Martin, with the grand Torre de los Ingleses in the center, was surrounded by elegant official buildings and palaces, it was close to the Retiro train station with a huge *villa miseria*, or shantytown slum, behind. Many tourists I knew had been robbed there. So I hired Cristina's ex-husband Ricardo to drive me and be my bodyguard.

I paid the twenty-four months plus the last month's rent and security deposit, signed a lease, and I had a place to live for at least two years. I could imagine living there forever. I was so excited to have a new home at last.

Moving day I just took what I arrived with in BA in a taxi over to my new place. It was completely empty except for an old cook stove in the long narrow mustard yellow kitchen on the other side of the dark burgundy hallway. (I wondered about Carolina's grandparents and their color choices.) I felt I was in Argentina for the long haul, forever, to the end, so buying furniture was an investment in my future. Even if I moved again after my two years in Caballito, I'd still need furniture and household items.

Originally I had planned to ship down the furniture I had put in storage from my big house in L.A. I had checked with many transportation companies about procedures and prices. Shipping furniture with a tourist visa was a way to go both crazy and broke. I heard stories at BAIN meetings about containers of household goods arriving at the port and being stored for months, held hostage for lack of papers at a great price. I hadn't thought about needing legal residency in order to bring a piano. There were probably a million things I had never thought of that were involved in my big move. Luckily I woke up and had smelled the coffee and had sent my Knabe parlor grand piano, large Persian rugs, and other beloved items to auction instead and just brought my sheet music and metronome in my suitcase.

I had always imagined having my things would help me to feel more at home, although many expats I met said they were glad to rid themselves of material objects to begin a new life. Perhaps those expats had fled from sad lives with bad memories of divorce and who knew what, unlike me who had only happy memories of the life I led before Jack died.

Of course there were many things I wished I still had besides my piano. I also missed sleeping on my Ralph Lauren sheets (the BA thin polyester sheets were rubbing my skin off), eating off of my grandmother's collection of Fiestaware from the '30s, and sitting on a comfortable chair to read. But you couldn't have everything, and I still had Phoebe.

Caballito was a nice family neighborhood with trees and cobblestone streets. Attractive restaurants and shops as well as a large park catered to the more middle-class residents than in my old working-class barrio of Balvanera. My new home was in a low-rise building about seventy years old, not the French style that I had hoped to find, but more or less art deco, which I also liked. The first-floor (second floor in the U.S.) apartment had a long balcony on the street that Phoebe learned to love, plus everything else I wanted—high ceilings, wood floors, lots of storage—and more, such as a maid's room and another half-bath, called the *dependencias*. The apartment had been designed so that the maid could enter, go through the kitchen to the dependencias, and not intrude on the family.

I taxied up Rivadavia to a huge antique warehouse with dusty items of every kind stacked and piled all over, my kind of place. I had my list. The salesman followed me around, writing things down on his notepad. Between answering questions about the furniture, he asked me about my "husband," where he was, why I was alone, and wouldn't I like some company?

When I was ready to buy, I asked for a package price, his best price, including delivery. When he named a figure, implying it would be less if I went out with him, I negotiated down and we finally agreed, although not before he said I could get a better discount if he took me for coffee.

My three months allotted stay in Argentina as a tourist was

almost up and it was time to exit the country to get my passport stamped. Most of the expats I knew took the ferry across the wide Rio de la Plata to Uruguay for the day. I had been to Montevideo on one of my tango trips to BA, so I chose instead to go to Colonia del Sacramento, a UNESCO World Heritage Site—closer to BA than Uruguay's capital city. I booked a tour that included the boat, lunch, and a city excursion. There was not a whole lot to see, especially as I had lived in a historical colonial town in Mexico, but every three months I'd have to do this to get a new tourist visa. Budgeting for it was important.

After a windy and rough crossing, the ferry brought me back to Retiro about nine p.m. I was wobbly disembarking and looking for a taxi in the dark, but at least I had no luggage. It was a cold winter night, and my apartment even colder. I found Phoebe curled up on the Yorkshire wool afghan on my bed looking lonely and giving me accusatory stares. When I tried to light with a match the old unventilated gas heater in the long dark hall, flames shot up with a smell of gas. I was frightened of it, so I called the landlord the next day. He said, "It was just fine for my father, and heated the apartment for the fifty years he lived there, so you can manage too."

I was so cold one night that, when Mike called, I complained and he sent over by taxi an electric portable heater, a white fleece jogging suit, and a warm blanket. I was afraid to use the jogging suit though as he was so particular that I didn't want to return it to him with any kind of a mark. I didn't know if it was a loan or a gift. But I was very happy using the blanket and heater.

I went to an appliance store in Boedo and bought a new wall heater, as well as a fridge, a microwave, and a tube TV. Then, because I had brought from Mexico the big box of VHS cassette tapes I had taken there from L.A., I bought a VHS player.

However what I had not taken into account was that the apartment could not support all of these new appliances electrically. There had never been an electricity upgrade; it was all the original wiring. Carolina's grandparents may not have had any electrical appliances, but now I sure did. I called Dr. Landlord: same answer—it was good enough for his father so it was my problem.

I hired an electrician, Fernando, to rewire everything. In Mexico it was commonplace for renters to fix up, improve, and even remodel apartments at their own expense. But not so much in Argentina. Still I had to make the apartment usable and comfortable for me. I hoped to live there a long time so I just went ahead and paid Fernando, who worked for three weeks to bring it up to code, if there even was a code. I made sure he wrote receipts and I saved them to show to the Doctor.

Fernando was extremely handsome in the tall, dark, Argentine way, and part of his service I gathered was seducing the lady of the house, despite the fact that he was married. I said no, but he didn't believe me and kept trying. He reminded me of Maximiliano el Magnifico, the famous dancer I had hosted for only four days out of the agreed upon ten in Los Angeles before I told him to leave.

It was awkward to be in the apartment alone with Fernando, yet I didn't want to leave him by himself with everything I owned. And I was uneasy repeatedly rejecting his advances. Argentine men seemed to think that any woman alone wanted a man, any man, and they were always ready to accommodate. Men thought when a woman said "no," she meant "maybe" and they just had to keep trying.

Electricity upgraded, next was a piano. I put an ad on the

BA Newcomers internet list and right away had a response from a piano teacher in Martinez—an upscale barrio north of town. She had a small upright that she wanted to keep but didn't need, as she had two grand pianos. She gave me detailed instructions on getting to her house, and that weekend I took two buses, a train, and a taxi to get to her lovely ranch-style home on a tree-shaded street. She was Asian, married to a British lawyer who worked in BA for a London firm.

After tea and cookies, I couldn't wait to try the piano, and was thrilled with it. It had great tone, a wonderful touch, and was perfectly in tune. We made a rental agreement for two years on condition that I would have it tuned when it arrived and would pay both ways for the transportation by special piano movers.

I was in heaven having the beautiful little piano in my living room. I got out my big pile of music and began to play. With no furniture but my bookcase and dining table, and no carpet or draperies in the room, the acoustics were superb. I played the blues, the French songs of Charles Aznavour, the tangos I had been collecting, and Chopin. I felt so at home.

At the age of five, I had learned to read music before I could read words. At that time my parents and I lived in a rented room off Pico Blvd. in L.A. My grandma, my mother's mother, gave us the small Crown upright piano she had purchased in the Depression with wages she had earned as a practical nurse.

That piano was my best friend, moving along with me to the tens of places I lived in before I got my Knabe grand in the late '70s. I loved that old piano as much as anyone can love an object. It was with me through thick and thin, through the yearly moves to different tract houses in the Valley, including my playing it in the back of a pickup truck going down

Sepulveda Blvd., to my student apartment in Westwood, to the apartments in Hollywood where I lived as a young wife and mother, and finally to the large family home in Los Feliz. When I finally sold it in 1978, the young pianist paid $200, the same price my grandma had paid for it in the '30s.

Along with the piano was the stack of precious sheet music that I took with me wherever I went—the two months of University of Hawaii summer school where I studied hula, the tiny practice rooms at UCLA during a free period, Paris where I played the piano that Maurice Ravel played when he visited Olivier's parents, Mexico where I rented playing privileges of the concert grand Bosendorfer at the Hotel Real de Minas and carried its key on my key ring, and now, finally here in BA.

I wasn't a great pianist despite my many years of playing, but music was a part of me. I was an "amateur" pianist—a lover of playing music. Playing music completed me, allowed me to express myself much as dancing did. Music was always in my home growing up, and especially later when my sons were playing, practicing, and performing. There were constant brass quintets, trios, solos around the Knabe grand in our living room, and once even a Chamber Music in Historic Sites recital.

I was sick a lot that winter. For the first time in my life I had asthma, thanks to the pollution and the humidity of BA. But my main concern was getting my cancer checkups on time. I found a gynecologist just a few blocks away who ordered my lab tests and mammogram. While the mammogram was ok, she found something worrisome in the pelvic exam, and so put me on watch. After surviving two cancers, I could never really relax about possible recurrences.

The three months went by fast and it was time to get my passport stamped again. The weather was still polar, I didn't want to do that boat trip across the very wide, rough river, but I had to, so I did.

CHAPTER 7

For me no matter how 'nice' the comment is on the street, when a man catcalls it is a painful reminder I'm treated as less than human.

—Zerlina Maxwell, on Twitter

September 2004

Late September in Buenos Aires, the sun shone at last, flowers were for sale on every corner, and even people you didn't know on the street wished you, *Feliz Primavera!*, Happy Spring! Those of us who lived in a country as far south as possible had survived a winter with no festivities to break up the dull dark days and spring was a waited for miracle of sunshine and flowers. Starting in August even the TV news had a daily Countdown to Spring.

Unfortunately spring down south for me turned out to mean terrible, awful, suffering allergies. I even had to go to the hospital one morning for a shot of cortisone. Next September, especially if I didn't have my residency papers yet, I wanted to leave the country for the whole month. Even though I had been sick during various tango visits, I never imagined I would get asthma and such bad allergies living in BA. Because my father had been a chain smoker, I was constantly sick as a child with one "cold" after another. No one knew back then the harmful effects of secondary smoke. My colds were always upper respiratory, I never had problems with my lungs until I moved to BA with the damp, pollution-choked streets, pulsing with black smoke from buses and cars using unleaded gasoline and without smog control laws. And it seemed like everyone was a smoker.

Everything felt topsy-turvy in this down-under land where Christmas was in summer, Easter was in the fall, and the water ran down the drain backwards (so it was said). I was still not used to the different stars in the sky and that the north wind was hot.

But in the milongas, nothing changed. Tourists came and went, and the porteños sat at the same tables where they'd sat for years. The same music was played that was played in the thirties, forties, and fifties, and no one was ever tired of it. For a change of pace from tango, sometimes the disk jockey played a set of Argentine folkdances, cumbia, or American Dixieland (everyone called it jazz) and dancers let loose on the floor.

At the same time, folks north of the Equator were easing into autumn with the thought of winter not far away. In the Northern Hemisphere there were the holidays to look forward to during winter, with all the warmth implied in those Hallmark card commercials and of course there was the Super Bowl. Up north in September the malls were dusting off their Thanksgiving decorations that go up in October. But in Argentina it was spring at last.

Some milongas had a Queen of Spring contest, and many businesses gave women carnations on the first day of spring, September 21st. It was a very big deal. I knew it was a compliment to be asked to participate in the pageant of women parading around the salon to be voted on in a kind of beauty contest, but I found it degrading and declined the honor when I was asked to take part. I hoped I didn't offend anyone, but it just seemed to me to be another example of women as dolls and sex objects. I was already sick to death of seeing nudie-cutie girlie magazines on full display everywhere, in supermarkets and kioscos on the street, with naked women on the covers, bare bosoms at eye level of all and sundry.

Once September was over and the pollen let up, I felt better physically except my feet and ankles hurt, and the flamenco didn't help. My recent checkups were all good except for "watching" whatever was happening in my pelvis. I danced tango four or five days a week (sometimes six), and flamenco two, although because I was preparing to be in Graciella's flamenco recital in December, there were additional rehearsals, often with live musical accompaniment.

My castellano lessons twice a week were slow going as I read and wrote too much in English to make a lot of progress. Many of my travel articles were being published in newspapers and magazines in paper and online, and I continued to work on my memoir of cancer and loss, love and disillusion in four countries, *The Church of Tango*.

Pedro, a milonguero I had known ever since I first visited BA, had a weekly *práctica*. When I entered the Salon de Fiestas on Avenida Independencia, there were six milongueros in suits and ties sitting around a table, smoking and talking. It looked like an audition for the Godfather. I was the only woman. Pedro had dragged in several of his friends to dance with the foreign ladies at the práctica with the bonus of free *vino tinto*. All the visiting *tangueras* wanted to dance with milongueros, the old men who never had a dance lesson in their lives yet danced like a dream, the way the tango should be danced.

After kissing them all hello, I sat down to listen. They were talking about tango, the old days, the orchestras, the music, the legendary golden age, when each night one could choose which famous live orchestra to dance to. They argued about steps, and one grabbed me and led something complicated. "No, no, that's not the way it was!" another one insisted and took me in his arms and said, "This is the way to do it." Pretty soon the two old men were dancing with each other, working out the step. It was like a movie.

Over the best vino tinto they discussed the tango and how it used to be. But eventually, being men, even if very old, they all turned their attention to me for compliments, *piropos*, questions, and teasing. When a couple of women and some foreign dancers finally arrived, the práctica began in earnest. But for me, the best part was over. I had witnessed something rare and special—which one day soon would be extinguished with these men—the living history of the authentic tango.

Afterwards, two of the milongueros and an Australian and I went to Lo de Celia's and took a corner table in the back. I alternated dancing with the two milongueros who plied me with piropos. "You are a fantastic dancer, but as beautiful as you dance, it's not as beautiful as you are."

The Australian didn't dance but ordered another bottle of vino tinto for all of us, hoping to keep the men talking. You could tell he also was a tango addict, thrilled and awed to be a quiet part of the old world of tango for a few moments, and he just breathlessly soaked it in, thankful to be there. As was I.

I saw Mike occasionally, sometimes at BAIN meetings, sometimes at Toastmasters, and sometimes dinner at his place or in a restaurant, always with champagne. I met his housekeeper who did his cooking and asked her if she could work a few hours for me every two weeks, and she agreed. I thought if "Mr. Wary and Suspicious Mike" trusted her, I certainly could. Whenever he visited me the first thing he did was to look out all the windows and then close the draperies. Poor Phoebe usually barfed after he left. She was a very nervous cat and had been on kitty Prozac for years.

Mike asked me to go to church with him one Sunday way out in Olivos, another upscale barrio north of town. I liked going to church, most any religious event, so I agreed. He picked me up at 8:30am in order to attend the Bible study class before the service.

I sat through the Bible class, and then during the service I was surprised when the pastor declared from the pulpit that no woman would ever stand there, would never deliver a sermon, or certainly not ever be a pastor. And he went on in a very misogynistic way, about how women would never be equal in the church and they were there to help the men do God's work. I couldn't believe my ears. I looked around the small hall filled with worshippers who didn't seem to be upset or surprised by these comments. I especially studied the faces of the women for expressions of discontent, but all were calm and accepting. Most of these attendees were foreigners, the service was in English, yet the sexism had spread even to them. I looked around the room at other women, nodding, silently agreeing with the pastor.

When the service ended and people filed out, some shaking hands and chatting softly, Mike and I stayed in our folding chairs. Mike was an Elder or Deacon of the church and now there was a business meeting he had to attend. I was uncomfortable and restless, and one of only a couple of women left in the hall. I was cold, thirsty, and my back hurt from the metal chair. I tuned out the discussion, anxious to leave.

Once in the car driving back to town Mike asked, "Did you enjoy the service? It's a nice church, isn't it? Friendly."

I was truthful. "Mike, the four hours were really a long time to sit on folding chairs, and with no refreshment. And what's up with the pastor declaring that women are second-class citizens? For a pastor to preach with such machismo isn't very Christian in my view."

Mike suddenly began to shout at me. "Cherie, it's Bible-based! There's a reason for that point of view. It's God's law that women are to serve. Go read 1 Timothy 2:11-12! 'Let the women learn in silence with all subjection.' A woman must be quiet! And in I Corinthians: 'For the man is not of the woman; but the woman of the man. Neither was the man created for the woman; but the woman for the man."

"What? That's insane! This is the 21st Century."

Mike pounded the steering wheel. "It's in the Bible!" His handsome face was turning red. "Full submission!"

His quick escalation to rage scared me. He had never mentioned his faith or religion before in any of our conversations. I was shaken by his sudden violent reaction and misogynistic attitude. He was American, but also of Mexican heritage, and just as macho as any Argentine. Full submission?

"Stop now! I want out!" We were somewhere in the middle of nowhere on Avenida Santa Fe. I didn't care, I just wanted to get away from him. He frightened me, the quick change from nice, pleasant, polite guy to fury. I never saw it coming. I grabbed the door handle as we sped along.

"No, you went with me and I'll see you home. My mother taught me to be a gentleman."

"A gentleman who insists women wait on him and to be at his service? A gentleman who believes women are less than men? That's crap! Once we arrive at your house I'll take a taxi home, thank you."

Obviously his mother never taught him that women and men were equal. What did being a gentleman mean to him, following fake etiquette rules without the accompanying respect? We continued in silence to Recoleta, where as he pulled into the garage I jumped out and hailed a passing cab.

I never saw him again. I asked Mari the maid about him, and she said he moved away, perhaps to Brazil, she didn't know. One day he and all of his stuff were in the apartment, and the next, he was gone. How bizarre. I secretly thought he might be CIA or some undercover government organization, but his strangeness was scary. Mari even suggested that maybe he had plastic surgery not to make him younger or more handsome, but to disguise his looks.

Despite the macho moves of some of the men I met, I felt blessed. I had a lovely apartment that I could afford in a nice neighborhood, I had organized a wonderful piano, I was learning castellano and flamenco, and making new friends as well as seeing tango dancers I knew from Los Angeles and all over the U.S. as well as Europe. The tango world was really small and everyone eventually showed up in Buenos Aires.

I felt like I was putting down some roots at last, unlike the feelings I had had in Mexico. Maybe it was the lack of good tango, or the rising prices of everything, or that I had to make all new friends, but as much as I loved San Miguel de Allende, I never felt "permanent," even after almost three years. I did miss Mexico—the colors, the food, the history and spirituality, the friends I had made there. I thought Mexican Spanish was the best Spanish to learn, but it was difficult in San Miguel because everyone spoke English. Now I had to unlearn all my Mexicano in order to speak castellano, and it was not easy. I didn't know why anyone would come to Argentina to learn Spanish with all of the complicated slang unless they were planning on staying, like me.

CHAPTER 8

For women, street harassment is not a compliment; it's a constant reminder and reinforcement of the fact that our bodies are perceived by many to be public property.

—Emily Jensen

December 2004

December was hot, and people wore shorts in the street, girls showed even more of their toned stomachs above low-cut jeans, and the clothes in the shop windows were in pastel colors. I would never get used to the mannequins in bikinis with Christmas tinsel around their necks.

The many ice cream parlors had long lines under the blooming purple jacaranda trees. Summer fruit was for sale in the *verdulerias*. An Argentine mockingbird began his mating mantra in the tree outside my window. The stores of cheap Chinese imports on every block were full of plastic Christmas trees and ornaments. At Las Violetas, a restored Belle Époque *confitéria*, they were putting up their huge artificial tree covered with plastic snow while running the air conditioner at full blast. On the other side of the stained glass windows, moist smoky heat filled the street at midnight as customers in shorts and sandals came and went, buying the traditional *pan dulce* gorgeously wrapped for Christmas giving.

At a nursery I bought a small blue cedar tree for my balcony. I brought it inside and decorated it on December 8,' *El Dia de la Virgin*, as was the tradition. Most people just took their little plastic trees out of the closet and set them up on that day, and that was it.

The annual recital of Graciela's students was a flamenco show held in her studio. She asked me if I'd like to also perform a tango, and of course I did want to, so I asked Luis to be my partner for two songs. Cristina recommended him as he gave lessons at her tango house, and I had danced with him at milongas. I didn't enjoy dancing with him as he always seemed slightly off the beat of the music, and liked to do fancy show steps, but it would be fine at a flamenco show. It was an incredibly hot and humid day, and more so with all of us dancers sweating and stomping, and the large audience packed in the back of her studio creating even more heat. The refreshments served outside on her patio were a relief.

With the flamenco show out of the way, I planned a Christmas tango party in December, on Jack's birthday–but only I knew I was celebrating him. It was also sort of a housewarming since I wanted to show off my lovely apartment in Caballito. I went to Salon Canning to dance on party night, but before the milonga I crossed the street to a Lebanese restaurant and ordered lots of food to take out, and then simply picked it up afterwards to carry home in the taxi. I had eaten there before in the garden after a milonga and the food was delicious.

My American, English and Mexican guests enjoyed it, but my porteño friends looked at all the food laid out on my new antique dining table covered with a hand-loomed cloth from Oaxaca with suspicion. Many asked if the food was spicy or garlicky, and what the ingredients were. I don't think they even tried anything, and stayed with the vino tinto and potato chips—and the Christmas sweet bread that was everywhere in summer.

Of course we danced, the salvation and reason for being for many of us. Lots of tango, and Graciela and I danced the Sevillanas to enthusiastic clapping. Many Argentines came from Spanish backgrounds so it was like folk dance to them. But the most fun for me was when we danced the Argentine folk dance, *la chacarera*.

I had bought white and red wine as well as 7-Up, and many guests had also brought wine, and I could not believe how many empty bottles I threw away afterward. Everyone seemed to have a good time and stayed until early morning. One of the last to leave was a tall milonguero I had danced with for years in the milongas. As I walked him downstairs to let him out of the main door with my key, instead of a besito on the cheek as was the custom, he grabbed me and stuck his tongue in my mouth. I pushed him out the door and onto the sidewalk with disgust, my warm feelings from the party dissipated.

During the holidays Buenos Aires became a ghost town. Everyone either was with family and/or went to the beach in Mar del Plata to get out of the heat. All BA was pretty much closed over the two holiday weeks.

I invited people for dinner, but nobody could come. Even all the movie theaters were closed. I thought about going away, just escaping Christmas in BA, but all the spas and resorts were also closed over the holidays. It was a family time and everyone planned to be with their families.

After Jack's death, during the holidays in Los Angeles, I tried to plan something nice for myself every year. Once I even went to Amsterdam on Christmas Eve for a tango festival and the tango marathon at El Corte in Nijmegen.

I remembered all of the fabulous Christmases we had when Jack was alive. Every year we had a big open house on Christmas Eve in our beautiful old Spanish home in Los Feliz, complete with mariachis, omelet chefs, and festive decorations. I always cooked a Christmas goose the following day and served it on my grandma's Bavarian china. Jason would be performing in the Nutcracker somewhere and Adam would be busy playing his horn in Christmas church concerts around the city. Such happy years! As I had often thought before, it was actually easier to be so far away that there was no prospect of spending special days with my sons, no disappointment or hope of family time.

However this year, my son Jason's friend Connie and her friend Ceci were visiting BA for the holidays, and I was overjoyed. Even though Connie and I didn't know each other well, I was ecstatic to see someone from home and to have a companion to do things with.

Pilar, who also had a tango house for foreign dancers like Cristina's, luckily had a party on Christmas Eve to entertain her guests who otherwise wouldn't have anything to do. Ceci, Connie, and I went, taking a cake for the buffet table and a bottle of Lopez vino tinto. We all danced—even Ceci and Connie who had never danced tango in their lives.

When the party was over Ceci grabbed a ride from someone going to Recoleta where their hotel was, and Connie and I went out looking for a taxi. I had forgotten that on the 24th and the 31st of December there was no transportation in BA—no taxis, no subway or buses, nothing. We waited on the corner of empty Avenida Rivadavia for what seemed like hours in the warm night. Whenever a rare taxi came by, there was a huge altercation on each of the four corners who was going to get it. Unbeknownst to me, we could have walked to my place, but I was still uncertain about distances and the map. Maps of BA were every which way; north wasn't always, or rarely, north, or at the top of the map. You had to figure where you were differently with each map, usually by the proximity to the river. In L.A. it was easy to know where you were, because the landscape told you: the mountains were to the north and the sea was to the west. At night in Hollywood I used to look for the illuminated Griffith Park Observatory hovering on the mountain above Los Feliz and my home.

Eventually we got back to my apartment and Connie slept on my new loveseat sofabed, and found a taxi the next morning to return to Recoleta, Ceci, and her hotel.

A week later Ceci made plans excluding Connie for the 30th, so I invited Connie to come over to my apartment. We planned to have dinner at a nice little restaurant around the corner that had become my go-to friendly place; dinner was always very late in Buenos Aires. But first I wanted to attend a milonga at Gricel, and Connie volunteered to meet me there. I admired her courage to get to the milonga (not in a great part of town), negotiate buying a ticket, passing through the velvet curtain and finding me in the smoky gloom, all without knowing Spanish. I was quite glad to see her. None of my other foreign dancer friends were in town any more as they all had gone home for the holidays.

Connie, a lovely young woman of Greek descent, had big eyes, beautiful long dark brown hair, and a slender figure. I warned her not to look at any of the men lined up at tables on the opposite side of the dance floor, as they would try to cabeceo her—unless she wanted to try out dancing in a milonga in BA for her diary.

When we got back to my apartment after dinner and turned on the TV news, we learned of a horrible fire in a nightclub not far away—the *Republica Cromagon* in Balvanera. The capacity was 1500 attendees but there had been more than 3000 people packed into the two-story club. The owner had chained and padlocked all of the exit doors to prevent teens from sneaking in, and during a fire caused by fireworks being let off on stage, many youngsters had died from being trampled and of smoke inhalation. Some teenaged parents had even brought their babies to the club and the upstairs bathroom had been turned into a nursery. Two hundred people died, and about 1500 were injured.

Connie and I sat glued to the awful TV broadcasts. The next night was Friday and New Year's Eve, and now it was a national day of mourning and disbelief. Everything was closed. There was no transportation. I had nothing to eat in my refrigerator but there was a bottle of champagne. We sat on the balcony, waving away the mosquitos, and passed the hot sad night with tumblers of champagne, TV news checks, and deep conversation.

Despite the tragic reports, it felt so good to talk to someone from my old life, someone who knew my native city, who shared a little of my history. Connie was Jason's age, but she was a wise soul. We confided intimate thoughts, personal stories of our own past tragedies, and became fast friends as summer insects buzzed around us and through the trees that canopied the balcony. A male mockingbird sang his seasonal refrain claiming his territory.

That night came to be known in Buenos Aires as "the night the tango died." There was to be no tango that night, or the next night *in memoriam,* but soon a moratorium on all dance clubs and concerts was passed by President Néstor Kirchner. The idea was to get safety issues checked out, exits inspected by the fire department, and so on, but that quickly became a whole other story of bribes and payoffs.

New Year's Day Ceci had the idea of having brunch at the Alvear Palace—a five star French-style deluxe hotel in Recoleta. I met them at their hotel and we walked to the Alvear, where Ceci marched to the front of the line and insisted to the hostess that we had reservations and we needed to be seated immediately! And soon we had a lovely table in the garden room close to the fabulous buffet that reminded me of my old life in L.A. and the fancy brunches at the Jonathan Club. All kinds of dishes were there for the taking, items that were considered exotic and that I had never seen on regular BA menus. I was delighted after a year of beef and potatoes and plates of plain beige food to have smoked salmon, baby lamb chops, asparagus, crepes suzettes, raspberries, and goat cheese. With flutes of champagne we toasted the New Year and Connie and Ceci's return to the States, and I hoped, a return to BA in the near future.

After the *Cromanon* tragedy, one of the few milongas that was allowed to stay open in BA was Club Español. Dany Borelli, the DJ, used the tango jazz music of Piazzola as the *cortinas,* or the breaks between sets of dance music, because all other music was banned. Or rather, for fear of being closed as were most of the milongas, only *"musica nacional"* was played. Now there were no tandas of tropical or rock 'n roll, because salsa clubs, rock clubs, and all other dance venues were shuttered. Frantic dancers, starved of tango, came to Club Español every Thursday afternoon and waited in the lobby to be allowed to enter. The energy was palpable.

Club Español escaped by virtue of being a private club, and as it was the only milonga available in town, everyone tried to get in. Dancers crammed into the anteroom waiting for someone to leave so they could enter. The fire laws and fire inspectors had suddenly become strict. People were desperate to dance, and folks who never normally attended this milonga panted to get in. After all, it was the only game in town, a feeding frenzy for all the tango-aholics who were used to dancing every night, or whenever they wanted to.

Other nights they were able to go far outside of the city limits where the closures were not in effect: La Glorieta (inside the city limits but allowed dancing because it was an outdoor venue), Banco Provincia, Circulo Trovador. Tango house parties became the norm for those who had space in their apartments for dancing. You could bet I went to them all. I spent a lot on taxis.

Being summertime in Argentina and winter in other parts of the world, there were lots of planned tango trips to BA from other countries but now were canceled. Buenos Aires suffered from tango withdrawal as well as the loss of tourist funds, not to mention the psychic pain of the tragedy even for those not personally involved. Some tango venues such as Lo de Celia were closed for six months or more. Many never fully recovered their cachet.

This time when my visa was up and I had to leave the country, instead of going to Uruguay for my mandatory passport stamps, I planned to go to Cuba. I had friends in Havana and wanted to watch the amazing Cuban Ballet, listen and dance to salsa (*son*), and relax on the beach. This would be my sixth trip to Havana and going from Argentina was so much easier than from the U.S.

To make myself Cuba-ready, I went to a salon on Avenida Entre Rios to get my hair colored, and I left with five different hues layered throughout: magenta red, warm red, blond, brown, and black.

CHAPTER 9

The love I have for you
I cannot deny…
I just can't help myself.

—"Chan Chan" by Compay Segundo

February 2005

Havana felt like home. I loved the friendliness of the people, their grace and beauty, the ubiquitous music, and the mojitos. (There never was much food to speak of.) I was anxious to see my friends again and to have some fun—a much better plan than going to Uruguay.

But after my midnight arrival at the Jose Marti airport, I went into shock when unexpectedly I had to exchange my dollars into *pesos convertibles* in order to take a taxi into dark and otherworldly Havana. A new ten-percent government commission on dollars meant that right away I lost a significant amount of cash. I had no idea that, unlike my previous five trips to Cuba, dollars were no longer accepted as legal tender. As an American there was no way to get more money if I ran out. I was panicked that my funds wouldn't last the nine days of my trip, and there was no fall-back position of credit cards or checks for Americans.

Dear Miriam and her tall twenty-three year-old son Fernan

were waiting for me at the little apartment I had always rented on San Miguel. But now someone else had my usual room despite my reservation via Miriam. It was clear that you have to be flexible in Cuba, a trait that was hard for me. So, no matter, we all trooped around the corner to another "friend's" apartment. All Cubans knew someone who had a room for rent.

Then I invited Miriam and Fernando to go to the *Hotel Telegrafo* for mojitos. We toasted to us having all of the fun together that we always had during my nine days in Havana and to my new life in Argentina.

But in the light of the next day I noticed the apartment was grim. So I went walking the streets in search of better lodgings. I didn't want to bother Miriam, or wait for her to help me as she always had in the past. She was working a lot and just seemed so tired, unusual for her.

I looked at several rooms in the Vedado neighborhood, feeling proud of myself to be handling the search and the Cuban Spanish on my own. Then I found a restored elegant old palacio with a terraza and many bedrooms, full of marble and stained glass and 40 foot ceilings. The location was perfect. So I took a room there and moved my stuff over on a bicitaxi.

On Sunday Miriam and I walked to the *Callejon Hamel* for the *rumba,* an Afro-Cuban music and dance fest with religious roots. We were late and most of the excitement was over. The drummers were packing up and spectators wandered away, some into the studio of the internationally well-known painter Salvador Gonzalez Escalona. We dropped in to visit Miriam's friend Carina who lived right in the center of the callejon.

As we drank rum and lemon soda and took in the action from the veranda, I saw a man sitting across the way watching us, a very handsome black man with shiny aviator sunglasses. We looked at each other across the alley for a while, and then Miriam went over and invited Rey to join us at Carina's. We liked one another and made a plan to meet later. Miriam and I agreed that he was a *tremendo mangon*—a hot and sexy man.

I was an American woman—a tall, pale-skinned redhead; there was no way I could blend in. It was impossible to walk down any street in Havana day or night without every man on it calling out or hissing in a particularly Cuban-construction-worker way. It was just part of their macho roles but a female tourist all alone felt vulnerable wherever she went, despite the policeman on nearly every Havana street corner, day and night, as well as CCTV. Even Miriam didn't like to be out alone without her son or a male friend at night.

I was lucky to have Miriam who had become close to me over the years. When I was with her I was just another dancer on the Prado in the middle of Cuban friends passing around a bottle of rum. Because of Miriam I went to a Senior Citizens Sunday afternoon soiree in the club on top of the Teatro Nacional and danced old-fashioned Cuban Danzon with a dapper old man in a white suit and white fedora. Because of her I danced at a fiesta in a private palacio, and with friends and family in Miriam's small home.

I realized I had made a mistake to come to Havana for so little time. It was too expensive and too far not to stay longer. I also needed time to get used to things. This whole week I felt people making demands of me. I never realized until Rey told me, that everyone was on the take. If someone could get you to rent a room from his friend, or buy a Che Guevara T-shirt in a back alley, or hire a car, or go to a nightclub, he got a commission. That was how they lived. Everything was illegal in Cuba, but they managed to survive this way. I was so used to being independent and alone, that it was difficult for me to adjust to all the desperation and attention. I felt like they were drowning, their arms reaching for me from everywhere, while I was on land, helpless to help them. But sometimes I was drowning too.

Now I realized a lot more about my past visits to Havana—the hangers-on, the people one collected in the streets. Sure, the Cubans were extremely outgoing and friendly and your visit to their country was all they could know of the outside world, but still, if they could get you to spend money while you were with them, they could make a few dollars to buy meat and eggs and soap. They were only able to buy the most basic and meager of supplies with their ration books and pesos.

My farewell dinner was supposed to be at Miriam's. She had always cooked for me the night before my departure. But she had been working so hard all week that I thought I could give her a special treat of a festive dinner at a famous *paladar* that had been featured in the movie, *Strawberries and Chocolate.*

Rey and I went early in the afternoon to look at the menu and check the prices, so I knew exactly how much it was going to be when I invited the three of them. I had just enough left for the dinner and to pay the $20 departure tax at the airport the next day.

The restaurant, *La Guarida,* was on the top floor of an incredible 200-year-old mansion that had mostly fallen down. Still, people were living in this once-fabulous grandeur. Marble staircases and sculptures, broken stained glass windows, two-story lobby, ruined walls, laundry flying from the ceiling—indeed it looked like a movie set.

Upstairs we rang the doorbell of the restaurant, and when we entered, I thought we were in New York or a dream. There were three dining rooms and a foyer, with photos of kings and queens and movie stars who had dined there covering the walls. The food was artistically presented and tasty, but not abundant. We ate every grain of rice and each bean. I felt like I had enough, but for hungry people, it wasn't sufficient, and the Cubans were always hungry, especially for meat.

When the bill arrived, I noticed there was coffee on it, and we hadn't had coffee. Rey took the bill out of my hand and checked it, and mentioned that it was $84. Miriam and Fernan almost fainted. I hadn't wanted them to know how much it cost. She said very quietly that she had to work for three months for that much money, and Fernan said there hadn't been enough to eat on the plates. They were appalled. I realized then that this was my (American) kind of place, and I should have taken them to a lively Cuban restaurant with music and piles of food where they would have felt more comfortable. This dinner only underlined the great economic disparity between us, so instead of bringing us closer, it threw up a kind of wall between Miriam and myself. We had always pretended we were the same, that we were sisters of different colors, but in reality we were not.

Usually Miriam and Fernando went to the airport to see me off, but this time we said our farewells after dinner downstairs in the street and I felt oh so sad. She was too tired and discouraged to be afraid of speaking against Fidel and the government in public on the street corner, where she knew cameras and microphones were recording her words and photographing her face.

"I can't take it. It's too much. Cuba is a hell. Fidel is its demon. We work so hard and we have nothing! Not even hope." she cried.

Fernan hugged her and said, "Hush, mami!"

And Miriam answered, "I don't care anymore, I just don't care."

I watched them, frustrated and sad and helpless. Tears rolled down my cheeks. This wasn't what I had wanted, what I had planned for on my trip.

Miriam had had no working refrigerator for over three years, no TV after her Soviet black-and-white died, no electricity in the living room, where two posts propped up the ceiling to keep the upstairs apartment upstairs. There was no water in the bathroom, only cold water in the kitchen, no access to toilet paper, no toilet seat. The many hurricanes that smashed into Havana regularly had just made it all the worse for the residents.

It was difficult and awful to see how elegant and educated folk had to live in squalor like this. Many Cubans were able to live better because they found something to sell: a waiter could "get" you cheap bottles of liquor, a cigar factory worker sold cigars out of his apartment; even at the ballet, the only available seats were from scalpers. But Miriam was a journalist; what did she have to sell?

I clearly saw for the first time, despite the many suitcases of useful things I always brought to give away, and paying for a bit of good food and fun once I was there, that trying to help my Cuban friends was like emptying the ocean with a teaspoon.

Once in Rey's friend Luis' '50s Caddy Sunday morning at 5am, me in the front with Luis, and Rey in the back hanging over the front seat, I felt better. We didn't meet another car on the entire drive to the airport.

I paid the $20 exit fee, the last of my pesos convertibles. Rey started to cry, his handsome face crimson with blushes and crumpled with emotion, when we kissed goodbye at the security line. "Chan Chan" played on the loudspeakers, and I was crying too.

I just can't help myself.

CHAPTER 10

only something in me understands
the voice of your eyes is deeper than all roses

—e.e. cummings

March 2005

By the end of March most of the milongas in the city of BA had reopened, with more fire extinguishers, or, as in the case of Viejo Correo, a knocked-out wall for a fire exit. Tango life was getting back to normal and I danced as much as I could—almost every night. After the forced diet, I was a happy glutton.

In several milongas I noticed a striking dancer who was very musical, who danced like I wanted to dance. But he never asked me to dance. The codigos demanded that the woman from across the room looked, stared in fact in a *mirada*, at the man she wished to dance with, and if he wanted to invite her, he nodded his head in a cabeceo. If she accepted this invitation, she nodded back with a smile, and he crossed the floor to her table and they began to dance.

I stared at this man, Ramon, for two months at different milongas with no result. I became obsessed with dancing with him. I even smiled at him when he was dancing with other women in front of my table. But still there was no cabeceo and I was disappointed.

The cabeceo was magical for many reasons, but it was hard for foreign women to get used to it. In other cultures it was too aggressive to look fixedly at someone. But in tango it not only was the way of asking and accepting dances, the cabeceo prevented the embarrassment of invitations being turned down. Gazing into someone's eyes was incredibly powerful. It could lead to a feeling of melding oneself with another, of sharing a special moment, a spiritual feeling of touching souls—exactly what a great tango was. After that strong visual connection, women felt safer, relying on their partner to dance them well and to protect them on the dance floor. And those feelings of trust often left the salon with the dancers and out into normal life and a relationship.

I celebrated my birthday in 2005 at my favorite milonga, where they honored popular dancers with a special "gang dance" or *agasajo,* when the honoree dances with several partners for a few seconds each. I was disappointed not to see Ramon in the salon as he was always there on Saturdays. The organizer Enrique presented me to the crowd, wished me a *Feliz Cumpleaños* and started the music (a tango vals). Ramon shot out from behind the bar as if from a cannon and took me in his arms. We had our first dance together for thirty seconds. We fit together like two puzzle pieces, like we were magnets, like old lovers. It was almost painful when we had to separate so I could dance a few seconds each with the men who had formed a line at the edge of the *pista.* From then on, he cabeceoed me several times during the two or three milongas per week we both attended. And it became my mission at a milonga to dance with Ramon.

I had been a dancer all of my life. I was a professional belly dancer with my own cabaret dance company, The Perfumes of Araby. I also was a soloist in Avaz, an international folk dance company in L.A. I had performed all over California and in Las Vegas. When I was learning to survive after Jack's premature death, I danced every night at a country and western club. I studied flamenco and had performed in Mexico. I choreographed Broadway shows for amateur productions and dinner theater. And now it was the tango. But it took two, and when Ramon danced with me, I felt like myself. It was a high, I supposed like cocaine, and certainly it was addictive. To many tangueros, and certainly to me, the tango was a drug. And dancing with Ramon was my cocaine.

You couldn't always tell by looking how much you would enjoy dancing with someone. A connection, the feel of the embrace, the lead and follow, the sensuality and musicality were secrets between the couple, first promised with the eyes. Many times I had been disappointed after actually dancing with someone I had admired from a distance. It wasn't as good every time as it looked. But dancing with Ramon was even better than I had anticipated. I closed my eyes and let him take me to tango heaven. I entrusted my body to him, to keep me safe, to dance me well, and he did.

He invited me for coffee at the historic Café Tortoni. ("Coffee" in Buenos Aires could mean much more than coffee and sometimes there was no coffee included at all.) I had coffee, he had nothing—because he had no money. We sat at a round marble-topped table next to a fat maroon pillar for two hours talking, as the tourists and businessmen came and went. He knew little English but we communicated very well. He was an expert at reading people, at body language.

"Why didn't you ask me to dance in all this time?" I asked him in Spanish. "You knew I wanted to dance with you by the way I stared."

"Si, tu mirada. Pero remember at Lo de Celia cuando you danced with mi amigo Jaime, with the eyeglasses?" He held his hands up in front of his eyes, making little circles. "I was sitting with him. And after the tanda, when he returned to our table, Jaime said you were going to be his *novia,* his girlfriend."

"I remember dancing that one tanda with Jaime, but he never again danced with me. Anyway, I wanted to dance with you."

This comment by his friend in effect had put dibs on me, which the men all honored. Jaime had put me in lay-away for two months. Until he decided not to use his reserve, his friends had to respect his claim of rights. There was an undeniably stronger code of honor among men than between men and women. In a way it was like war, with the men figuratively on one side and the women on the other, like the seating at a traditional milonga. But the sides weren't evenly matched. One side—the machos—played the role of being strong, powerful, able, and in control, and the other side—the feminine—were seen as delicate, helpless, fragile, dainty and had sex as their only weapon. It made perfect sense to me that the nostalgia and sadness of Buenos Aires, the machista capital of the world, was the home of the tango.

When we couldn't occupy the table any longer under the gaze of the line of tourists waiting to sit down, I uncomfortably paid the handsome silver-haired waiter for my coffee. In a world where the men had the control, it was embarrassing for a woman to take charge, to pay, even for herself when she was with a man.

I could tell Ramon wanted me to invite him home, but instead he walked me to the subway across the street and we said good night. I understood we both felt the connection but I wasn't going to make it easy for him.

A few nights later we met in the lobby of another milonga. "Please, to come to my *oficina*," he said as he gestured toward the salon's balcony. I knew he wanted to kiss me but no way was that going to happen in public at a milonga—my reputation would be ruined.

If he wanted me, he needed to expend a little effort. I was not going to invite him home to my apartment.

Then I shocked myself. "Well, when will you take me to a *telo*?" I boldly asked him. Why put off something pleasurable that you knew was going to happen? Life was short.

"I do not have the cost today, but we can go on Thursday after Club Español *si queres*, if you like." His dark brown eyes sparkled.

We went back into the salon, he to the men's side and me to the women's, both of us with little smiles.

Telos were the love hotels everywhere in BA and were clean and respectable. In crowded living conditions, it was difficult for couples to find privacy and these hotels that could be rented by the hour or for the night, were a popular option. There was nothing sleazy about them; they were just practical and safe solutions. (Once, some years previously, I had been to one with the milonguero I called The Beauty.) As a teenager in Los Angeles, everyone had a car to be private in, especially at favorite parking places like Mulholland Drive or the beach. My boyfriend Paul and I had spent hours steaming up the windows when I was a student at UCLA. But lovers had other options in BA.

Everyone seemed to know on Thursday that it was a special night for Ramon and me. A friend took our picture and we appeared happy and excited. Although both of us were dressed in black, we looked like newlyweds.

We walked to the Hotel Waikiki after the milonga. He was a good lover that night, as a matter of fact the best he ever was with me. But I was nervous, I didn't know why. I think I was afraid for some reason. I kept wanting to go home. I told him I needed to go home. But he said he had paid for the whole night, and it included breakfast in the morning. He seemed excited about the breakfast. So I stayed for breakfast. And then he walked me home to Caballito.

CHAPTER 11

I was warned about some of these milongueros. I felt a lot of them were married but did not want to let you know.

—Anonymous, Milonguero online survey response.

May 2005

My favorite place to dance was Saturday afternoons at the club Centro Región Leonesa, Milonga de los Consagrados. On Thursday midnight it was the setting for the famous milonga, Nino Bien, but I didn't enjoy Nino Bien that much these days. It was less about great dancing and more about see-and-be-seen. Región Leonesa was another Spanish club, not so gilded and luxurious as Club Español, but still gorgeous with an old-world grandeur—red velvet draperies, mirrors, a large skylight, a stage, and the most beautiful big wooden dance floor in Buenos Aires.

All of my favorite partners went there, and most specifically, Ramon. I always danced with several men, including a French man named Laurence, who attended Saturdays and sometimes on Thursdays at Club Español. He was tall with close-cropped graying hair and blue eyes behind rimless glasses. He had a great embrace, and deeply felt the music. He especially liked to dance the Pugliese tandas with me.

One afternoon Laurence said goodbye to me in the lobby

as he was leaving to return to France. He gave me his card and asked me to keep in touch. I didn't think much about it, and just tossed it on my desk, but several weeks later I found myself writing him a polite email, wishing him a nice summer. He wrote back to invite me to accompany him on his sailboat on a week of sailing around the islands in the Mediterranean off the coast of France.

He had never showed any special interest in me other than liking to dance with me. He had never asked me for coffee or anything else in BA, and now this. I needed to exit Argentina as usual every three months, so why not France instead of Uruguay? And then I could also go to Evian and see my friends there, and visit Jack's grave. So via email we made a plan: three nights in Paris, TGV, the high speed train, to Evian, and then TGV to Marseille where he would meet me and we'd go to his boat. I didn't tell him I got seasick and couldn't swim. I'd work it out somehow.

My friends and family in L.A. were aghast when I told them I was going sailing for a week in a small boat with a man I didn't know. "He could be an ax murderer!" they said. "Something could happen to you and you'd get thrown overboard and no one would ever know." I didn't care. I had seen death up close, I had been near to death myself—this time was gravy, what did I have to lose?

I found a cheap hotel near Les Halles in the heart of Paris for the weekend. It was completely charmless, with cardboard walls and rickety stairs. It was so strange that I understood everything I heard in France, but when I opened my mouth only castellano came out. At the hotel they called me La Argentine!

I had made plans via email to meet my ex-fiancé Olivier who agreed to come in from Lyon where he was now living.

After our horrible breakup in Los Angeles, we hadn't communicated, but I thought ten years later maybe we could be friends. I never forgot how he cared for me after my cancer surgery, during chemotherapy and radiation, and no matter how it had turned out, I was still grateful to him.

During luncheon under the trees in Paris, he filled in the blanks of the last decade. He never worked again, living very comfortably in Lyon off the proceeds of the sale of his apartment and art nouveau furniture. His father had died and left him something too. The book Olivier had written on the student upraising in Paris in May 1968 had been reissued and was now the standard text on the subject. He got fat and grew his curly greying hair long because he admitted he was too lazy to cut it, and now wore it in a ponytail. He never again had another girlfriend.

I offered him the box of *alfajores* I had brought from Buenos Aires, the much-coveted gourmet cookie of Argentina. He waved his hand in the air with a flourish, "Oh, I'm gluten-free now, so no thanks."

"Well please give them to your mother then," I countered.

"She watches her weight you know," he said with a French shrug.

This luncheon was a mistake. More narcissistic and angry than ever, he accused me of turning him misogynistic. What had I been thinking when I contacted him about being in Paris? I guessed that maybe ten years had changed him, or perhaps I had forgotten the truth. I had really loved him—or at least the man I used to think he was.

The next morning I boarded the high-speed train at the Gare de Lyon to Evian-les-Bains, where Edith was waiting for me in the station. Edith had been my next-door neighbor to the penthouse apartment that Jack and I had bought with another couple when we knew he was dying. He had hoped to leave me something so wonderful, a gift that would make me happy, for when he was gone.

Friendly Edith and her family had burst into our lives like a breath of fresh French air. They gave me love and support to the end and after. She had also fed and watched over me when I was recovering from my cancer treatment after leaving Paris and Olivier. All I did in those convalescent winter months on the shore of Lac Léman was build fires in the fireplace, watch the changing moods of the lake, visit Jack's grave in the village, and go next door to Edith's to eat.

As Edith drove through Evian and on to the village of Lugrin, approaching the lakeshore, it was hard to look at that amazing apartment that now belonged to someone else. I know Jack had hoped, as had I, that one day I could live there. And that was why I had chosen the little cemetery behind the village church as his last resting place. What a horrible shock it was when the other couple, our partners who we had thought were our friends, cheated me out of it.

Edith's life had changed too. She and Michel had divorced and sold their apartment next to mine, and she lived in a lovely apartment built by her son in a tiny village near her grandchildren. Mémé, the grandmother, had bone cancer and was suffering terribly. I loved her with all my heart as if she were my own grandmother, an incredible woman with extraordinary stories of survival in the war, her husband losing his life in the Resistance, leaving her alone with a baby—Michel.

It was so beautiful there in Haute Savoie, more beautiful than Provence, the Cote D'Azur, or anywhere else on the planet in my opinion. Why had I waited eight years to return?

I visited Jack's grave in the sweet village cemetery of Lugrin, which had grown residents by leaps and bounds. I felt so bad to have made the choice of burying him there, but at the time I thought I'd be living one day in my apartment on the lakeshore.

Too soon I hopped the bullet train to Marseille, to Laurence and his sailboat. He greeted me with a "French kiss" but I didn't feel like it, after all I didn't know him at all. I knew though that I'd have to come through somehow during the week on the boat. I didn't understand why he'd invited me for a week's cruise when he had never invited me for coffee in Buenos Aires. When I asked him why, he said that it seemed like a good idea. Well, I guessed it had seemed like a good idea to me, too!

I had never been to Marseille, and wished there was time to explore as we walked from the train station down to the marina and his little sailboat. He had sent me a photo of himself at the wheel of a friend's large sailboat but I wasn't disappointed that his was small. It didn't matter to me as long as he didn't expect me to know how to sail.

How could I describe the boat? It was cute with a minuscule galley, tiny head with a pump toilet, and a large bed built under the bow. There was a closet of sorts below the stern where I stashed my suitcase, with my "yacht clothes."

I just let him do everything, as I was ignorant of how to work a boat. I told him that if he needed help, to just let me know, but I never lifted a finger the whole week. He had stocked the galley with provisions, mostly cans of things, and I happily ate whatever he threw together. He wasn't a marvelous cook like Olivier had been, I was a bit disappointed about that, but he was a perfect gentleman. And patient at night when I got cramps in my feet, and when I had to wear the Mae West life vest to go swimming. It was my first time sailing and I loved it. When we got to Saint Tropez, though, I invited him to a restaurant dinner in town, which he seemed happy enough about, and I was delighted.

That first night was awkward as there was no choice but to sleep together on the only bed, but I told him I wasn't yet comfortable to do more than sleep, and he was fine with that.

During the day we swam, me with a life vest on, and took the skiff to shore where I checked my email. I took a Bonine tablet every day and so didn't suffer any seasickness. He asked me if I minded if he took off his shorts to sunbathe nude and of course I didn't. I was hoping to get to know him better during all the hours we were alone together, but he didn't talk much, so I just made the most of the quiet time myself. I gleaned very little about him: he had been married, had daughters whom he never saw, worked in some technical field and had taken an early retirement, and was atheist. That was it.

Despite the lack of deep conversation, it was like a fantasy to be sailing the Mediterranean in a small boat with a sexy Frenchman. Even though I couldn't swim, I wasn't afraid of the water and in fact I adored the sea. I was completely happy,

By then my brain had made the switch and I could speak the French that had lain dormant in my head all those years. It had taken two weeks. (And, ironically, when I arrived back in Argentina, only French came out of my mouth.)

Laurence would be returning to Argentina in the autumn (spring there) to study tango and castellano. He was on his boat until September. I didn't know how I felt about him or his upcoming return visit to BA. I liked him well enough, but even after the physical intimacy of the boat, I didn't know him at all.

It was a long way home to Buenos Aires, what with the train back to Paris and the flight, but it was all worth it.

Thanks to Edith, I had brought bits of food in my suitcase like some *Tomme de Chévre*—my favorite cheese from *Le Temple du Fromage*—some canned fancy entrees, dried herbs, amazingly chunky sea salt, dried cèpes, and flavored oil. Edith had always seen to it that she fed me well. What pleasure it had been to pick fresh lettuce, green beans, and white raspberries from Mémé's garden.

France at the end of June is quite expensive and it hadn't cost me more than my train tickets and three nights in a cheap Paris hotel. I was very lucky to have been invited. I had gone from bleak winter in Argentina to full summer in France. I was in Evian with my friends and eating straight out of their garden. And I was also in a small sailboat out of Saint Tropez eating out of cans, but still…it was France!

I returned to bitter winter—one degree Celsius (33.8 F) in the morning! After I picked her up from Brian's, poor Phoebe stayed huddled by the electric radiator, refusing to look at me.

CHAPTER 12

Tango is my mistress—only she has my heart.

—Gavito

June 2005

La Confitería Ideal was the iconic tango salon of Buenos Aires. When tourists and dancers alike passed through the double doors on Suipacha near Corrientes, they felt in their gut they were entering the historic soul of tango. In fact, La Ideal had spent most of its life since it was first built in 1912, as a pastry shop and salon de té, a confitería. The original owners were pastry chefs and entrepreneurs from Spain, who required that the building be constructed of expensive materials imported from all over Europe. It wasn't until the 1990s that tango dancing became its *raison d'être.*

The French *Fleur de Lys* became the enigmatic emblem because at that time all of the expensive buildings in Buenos Aires were influenced by the French architectural design of *La Belle Époque* of a few decades past. It was partly for that reason that the premises seemed much older than a scant century. Plus, it was now shabby and rundown. The gorgeous cage elevator hadn't worked in decades, and the iconic stained glass *quiosco glorieta* for the presentation of fancy pastries now sat empty but for the occasional tango shoe display.

I would never forget walking up its marble staircase for the first time seven years ago, smelling the mustiness, the cat piss, the burning incense lit to hide the odors of a building past its prime. I was a beginning tanguera in a culture that had seen very few tango tourists up until then. The milonga habitués looked upon our tour group from America as exotic creatures from another world, as I supposed in a way we were. That's how we too viewed the salon and the dancers of La Ideal, adding to its faded glamour and mystique.

It had been used as a location for all of the tango movies, so first-time visitors felt a sense of *déjà-vu*, or of having dreamed this place. Several years before, the gigantic central chandelier below the skylight on the second floor, worthy of the Phantom of the Opera, crashed to the floor, never to be seen again. A tanguero was dancing below on the marble floor and was injured by the huge fixture. He was taken to the hospital, where his wife was called. She was furious because she never even knew he danced the tango. Many scenes in my previous memoir, *The Church of Tango*, take place in La Ideal.

Lots of rumors surrounded La Ideal, and no one seemed to actually know who owned it—some said the government—but the truth was that it was owned by a private organization that received no government help to maintain this historic structure. Unfortunately, it was falling apart before our eyes, even though it was now proclaimed an official *Bar Notable*. I got used to the many blackened and spotted mirrors in the ladies' room, that only one of the three toilets worked, and that frequently there was no water in the marble wash basins. I wouldn't be surprised if one day a foreign investor stepped in to save it—in the manner of Versailles in France. Sometimes those who don't live in a place value its heritage more than the locals.

On my original visit to La Ideal, the site of my first tango classes in BA, there had been only one milonga there, the Friday afternoon matinée of Diego y Zoraida. A few years later there were more than twelve milongas every week in the same space, with classes from different teachers every day, and sometimes performances at night.

When I returned from France, I met Ramon at La Ideal on a date to celebrate. It was the first time Ramon and I sat together at a milonga—I was still speaking SpanFrench, and he kept repeating, "*No entiendo,* I can't understand a word you're saying!"

He was in mourning for his parents, and I felt bad that I hadn't been in BA when he lost them. When I got my email on one of the French islands, I learned that both his parents died within one week of each other. I hadn't told him about sailing with Laurence, only that I was visiting Edith in Evian and checking on Jack's grave that was only leased, unlike plot ownership in the U.S.

That was the same week that I found out Gavito had passed away, too.

Carlos Gavito was a world famous tango superstar. He appeared in most of the tango movies, on international TV, and on Broadway. Older than most professional stage dancers, tall, gray-haired and elegant, his passionate, sensuous dancing style was my favorite, his workshops always the best. I had first met him in San Francisco at Norah's Tango Week in the late 90s. I loved his group classes, which incorporated tango stories as well as technique and new ways to do old things. So over the years I took private and group lessons from him whenever he was in town with the touring show, "Forever Tango." I couldn't imagine how disappointed he must have been, when he was in L.A., sponsored by Yolanda

Rossi, that very few students showed up for his classes. I was also saddened in that I'd hoped he would be teaching lots of local dancers to dance better, more like him. He had advised me then not to go dancing in L.A., just to save up to visit BA as often as I could.

He was always with the youngest and most beautiful women, and everyone knew he was married, or had been married a few times, and that he had a lover in each city he visited on his world tours. He hid nothing, put on no acts offstage. He had tremendous charisma, both onstage and off. When he danced, he made even a beginner look—and feel—like a queen.

Over the years I had taken many of his classes in my around-the-world tango bum odyssey and was smitten with his style. He taught with humor, wisdom, personality, and a charming humility. He had the ability to convey how to dance, not just do steps. I loved it that he only spoke French to me.

Once in BA he had cabeceoed me in Gricel, and I received so many dirty looks, I thought the other women at my table were going to kill me. But another year during Norah's Tango Week in San Francisco, the year that he and El Indio did a fantastic *zapateo* dance-off, he had tried to cabeceo me from across the room and I was frightened and so I didn't look at him. I was afraid of becoming too fond of him, and then, naturally, getting hurt.

One night in Los Angeles when he needed a ride, I volunteered to pick him up at his hotel in Beverly Hills. At the milonga we sat together at his table of friends and well-known fellow performers, and he was considerate, gracious, and generous to me. I was the first person he asked to dance. Of course I knew what everyone was thinking, but I was proud anyway.

He always wore the same exquisite Italian cologne, and even the aroma of his French cigarettes didn't detract. I was happy to go along with the program.

On the way back from the dance, he invited me to dinner at an all-night restaurant on Melrose, a favorite of visiting professional Argentinian dancers. Just the two of us at one in the morning (usually impossible in L.A.), we sat in the patio warmed by heat lamps and plants and flowers, and he ordered Chateau Lafitte Rothschild and the best imported steaks. I knew what was coming.

He spoke several languages, and was the most sophisticated man I'd ever had dinner with. Certainly, his stories and conversation were all about him, but they were fascinating stories and interesting conversation. He told me about his childhood, how tango seduced him, how he began his career as a teenager and had been dancing and traveling around the world ever since. I enjoyed every minute of listening. I had little to say to him, but everything to hear.

As expected, he asked me in when we got to his hotel. I went, more curious than anything. Later I rather wished I hadn't seen him naked, with his skinny brown legs and small potbelly. The sex was quick, boring and perfunctory, almost obligatory. Many great tango dancers expressed all of their passion and emotion on the dance floor and there was very little left for the bedroom. Perhaps the public show of taking care of a woman didn't translate to what happened privately in bed.

There is no question that I preferred dancing with Gavito to making love with him. I would rather dance with him than anyone else in the world, and now that was ruined by having gone to bed with him. I felt uncomfortable when I saw him, even though he always treated me special in public, calling me *Corazón* and other endearments, as he did with all of his women. To be fair, it was me who "rejected" him afterwards. He never did the Latino conquistador move of bedding and then casting me aside. I never gave him the chance. He was always a gentleman. But I lost my fantasy that night, and it left a small hole in my life.

A couple of years later on one of my tango trips to BA, I saw him by accident at La Catédral, a huge old wooden warehouse turned into a funky tango salon, with brilliant colored paintings all over the walls, candelabras with melting wax candles, beat-up couches and easy chairs, and a horrible pitted and uneven wooden floor. Gavito asked me to hold his drink while he took a hit of cocaine in the men's room, and couldn't seem to understand why I didn't want to go back to his hotel. When I refused, he looked at me for a long time, seemingly unable to process the information through the alcohol and drugs. His professional partner had just left town to visit her family in the north, and I guessed he didn't like to be without a woman. Any woman, even me.

After that I avoided him and so lost my favorite teacher and favorite dance partner, as well as my flight of the imagination that always took me to Tango Heaven.

I saw him once more before his death from cancer. It was late at La Viruta and he was sitting with friends near the dance floor. He couldn't dance anymore but the milonga was his home. Watching the dancers and listening to the music with a cigarette and whiskey, perhaps allowed him to forget. He saw me across the floor and smiled, so I went over and kissed him. He was too weak to stand, but he hugged me and said in French, *Cherie, tu me manques.* I miss you. I tried to hide my tears, kissed him again on the cheek and went back to my table, bereft.

CHAPTER 13

I loved the embrace. And I even embraced the come-ons. I was over 55 when I first went to BA and the flirtations were an affirmation of my femininity.

—Anonymous response
to online Milonguero survey

July 2005

Ramon was sort of my novio, my boyfriend now. The night in the telo in the autumn had been a one-off until I returned from France. But now I was more interested in being with him and seeing how long a real relationship could work rather than my being fancy-free. When Laurence came back to BA around the holidays in the summer, he would probably expect me to see him but I wouldn't risk the still-tenuous bond with Ramon. In the macho world it was perfectly fine for a man to have relationships with many women, in fact it was encouraged. The men urged each other to do so, and congratulated the ones who did. And most of them did. But women didn't have that privilege.

Our dating life was quite limited. We couldn't even go to a movie or out for coffee. We either danced at a milonga (sitting separately) or hung out in my apartment. He lived with his son and grandchildren outside of town in a house he had built with his own hands decades ago and only came in to the city a couple of times a week to dance, which was enough for me. He seemed simple and humble, and I was a sucker for a pretty face, and above all for a great dancer. I had always believed that a man could be either handsome, a good person, or an excellent dancer—not all three. I joked to my friends about picking two out of the three qualities when dating. But now I wondered if perhaps Ramon were all three. He seemed to have everything, except a job and money. Somehow that didn't seem to matter.

It was watching him dance that got me hooked. When I first saw him at Club Español, I knew I simply had to dance with him. And then when I did, I loved the connection and his style of dancing—he was so natural, so graceful and creative, so musical and athletic on the floor—and there was instant chemistry. I no longer cared about dancing with anyone else, except occasionally with friends.

I watched him not only when he was dancing, but also helping behind the bar, or sometimes when he was just sitting, gazing at the floor, listening to the music, looking sad in that Argentine way.

We came from different cultures, spoke different languages, had different backgrounds socially, educationally, economically. We had nothing in common. Nothing but the tango. But I enjoyed being with him. I relaxed and took it easy. He didn't seem like the other milongueros; Ramon never offered piropos or compliments, never lied about only being separated and not divorced, never seemed to crave attention, and in fact seemed rather shy and self-effacing. He did enjoy women and seemed to light-up when speaking or dancing with an attractive one, especially if she spoke a latin language—his own, or Italian, or French, or Portuguese. And I couldn't help but notice that the women lit up too. He was very flirtatious, but I accepted that as his way. My son Jason, also a dancer, was the same. It was fun, I understood that. And after all, Ramon was good-looking, danced like a dream, had a great personality—I didn't blame him. But he wasn't at all the Latin Lover type, or a Lounge Lizard, and I saw plenty of those kinds of men in the milongas.

I thought he was not a typical Argentino, in that there was no poetry, no bullshit; he was just unassuming and honest. He was responsible, always called when he said he would, always did what he promised, always showed up on time. I hadn't expected a milonguero to be like that.

At the beginning I had smelled cigarette smoke on him, but when I told him how allergic I was, that even the secondary odor of smoke on his clothes, hair and breath caused me respiratory problems, he uncomplainingly gave it up. I never saw him smoke a cigarette.

He had a great voice, and when he sang to my piano playing, I was delighted. He also seemed to understand what I meant even if my castellano was imperfect. One night when he came over I asked him to dance with me to a Piazzola tango. I didn't know then that milongueros didn't dance those tangos that were mixed with jazz, or the newer electronic ones like Gotan Project from France that so many younger dancers were crazy about, or even to recordings of Carlos Gardel. So he was surprised but agreed, and away we went to "Libertango" in my living room. He only enjoyed the music of the Golden Age, those great old legendary orchestras, that was played in the traditional milongas, but he could dance to anything. He had even been a rock n' roll champion when he was young.

He didn't seem to dance to seduce women, but because

he loved to dance. However his dancing and the twinkle in his eye were very seductive. Women embarrassed themselves trying to get his attention. But, despite all of his other good qualities, he was still very macho, too macho, and we later had problems stemming from the machismo.

The biggest problem we had, of course, was that he didn't have steady work and had no money. He didn't ask me for any and I didn't offer any. But it was very difficult to go out and do things without a peso. He only attended the milongas where he didn't pay admission—Club Español, Los Consagrados, Lo de Celia, El Beso. He had worked for a television station for twenty years as a chauffeur / driver, and had driven all around Argentina for work. He had loved it. He used to dance all night, sleep in his car for a few hours, and then go to work a happy man. But he had lost his employment in 2001 during the "crisis," and after that he sold his van, did odd jobs, and repaired cars in order to survive. His son lived with him, as well as three of his grandchildren, and he tried to provide for them as best he could, as his son didn't manage to work much either. Ramon also taught tango in his barrio just outside of the city.

Because Ramon had only a couple of shirts, I wanted to buy him a new one, but I agonized over the propriety of doing so. I even wrote to a psychiatrist girlfriend in the States to ask if I would be setting a bad precedent, or sending the wrong message. She replied that it all depended on the message I sent with it.

So I wandered the streets of Caballito looking in the windows of all the men's clothing stores. Finally I got an idea of what I wanted—a long-sleeved black shirt with tiny colored pinstripes. I considered several and settled on one, fairly sure I could get the size right. I bought it and gave it to him, it fit perfectly, and he wore it to a milonga, where it seemed everyone instantly knew where the sharp new shirt came from. I didn't care if they talked. It was nobody's business but mine, and he looked handsome and elegant when I caught a glimpse of us dancing reflected in the sparkling mirrors surrounding the dance floor. I supposed the message that went with the new shirt was that I cared for him, and that he would look handsome in a new shirt. I didn't know what message he received.

I had always said I never wanted to dance with just one man, even if he were Gavito, because one challenge for a woman in the tango was to be able to dance well with any man, to follow the improvisation of whatever partner she danced with. Ramon's dancing was so fabulous and creative that I really didn't care about dancing with anyone else. Ramon was constantly inventive, always had a surprise for me, was never boring—and was at all times one with the music and rhythm. Sometimes he danced to the bandoneon, other times to the violin, other times to the piano or the singer. Ramon had a lot of wonderful qualities, but first was his natural sense of rhythm and love of the music. He never danced the same tango / vals / milonga twice.

I think if Ramon and I had met before I was getting bored with my various partners in the milongas and how they tended to dance the same way every time with me (Jorge for the Tanturi tanda, Alberto for the vals, Juan Carlos for the milonga, Osvaldo for Pugliese, etc.), maybe I wouldn't have been so quick to fall for him. It was absolutely true that timing was everything. I had been dancing with everyone for many years, both in the States and on my many visits to BA, and now I could be happy dancing less and with the best. Less was more, and Gavito was gone.

Although I had continued to attend the several milongas

where I was a regular, I had begun to feel that it was all too predictable. I enjoyed seeing my friends at Canning and El Arranque, but I found myself wishing for Ramon. I kept one eye trained on the door in case he walked in. I was getting tired of "dancing around," of looking for that elusive tango experience that satisfied me on all levels, when I could always count on it dancing with Ramon.

I was already more or less persona non grata with the other men and didn't get invited the way I used to, but I didn't care at that point. The men's macho code meant they always stuck together. The other milongueros weren't going to dance with Ramon's woman.

We didn't sit together but everybody knew it all anyway, just by looking. Everyone saw everything at the milonga. We all watched and knew things we shouldn't.

There was no future for Ramon and me, how could there be when we were so completely different in every way? So I was just going to enjoy what I could while I could, and that meant the best dancing of my tango life. Still we continued this sham of sitting separately. I was scared to just capitulate and to be joined at the hip with him because who knew how long this would go on? If we broke up then I'd have to start over in the milongas. And how many milongas would I have to go to by myself before I would be "available" to dance again in the milongueros' eyes?

But eventually, after many months of sitting apart, Ramon on one side of the dance floor with the men, and me on the other side with the women, I gave in. I wanted to sit with Ramon because he was so much fun. We laughed, drank champagne together, and I only wanted to dance with him anyway. He said it would be fine to sit together, he didn't mind. Easy for him for no matter where he sat, he could dance with anyone he wanted. But when we shared the same table, everyone knew I was "taken" and the other men would have to ask Ramon's permission to dance with me, and that wouldn't happen. Now we were known as a couple.

I wasn't following my own advice to visitors. I had been dishing out wisdom to *extranjeras* (non-Argentine women) for a long time, but somehow never thought it applied to me: "Have fun with them, but never fall in love with them."

Soon Tango Tourist Season would be in full bloom in Buenos Aires. In spring and autumn the milongas were swamped with people who had come halfway around the world to dance, preferably with the locals, the porteños and porteñas.

Middle-aged women flocked to Buenos Aires to dance, maybe because in their own countries they were overlooked as sexual beings and ignored in life as well as in the milongas of their hometowns. Here they (we) were welcomed and made to feel like queens, and it could be addictive. *Was* addictive, along with the tango itself. And many women came here twice a year, spring and fall, every year, because in Buenos Aires they felt desirable once again. In their home countries they were invisible. Past the time of the construction workers' whistles, past being the new girl in town at their local milongas, where there were always younger newbies ready to make a man feel like Pablo Verón, the sexy star of *The Tango Lesson* movie.

In Buenos Aires the female tango tourists were desirable women to be courted by the locals because:

- They would leave soon (very sexy);

- They were better dancers than the Argentinas (sometimes);
- They might be up for paying for private lessons or restaurant dinners (often);
- They might invite a milonguero to their home countries (did happen);
- They might be hot to trot so far from home and didn't have the time to waste on slow seduction;
- And, just perhaps, they were sexy, sensuous women unappreciated at home.

CHAPTER 14

Is your name Google? Because you are the answer to all of my questions.

—piropo

September 2005

The weather in BA is not so bad in winter, it's just that the porteños can't take the cold. Not that I could either, never having really lived in cold weather, but the coldest it got was about 2 or 3 degrees Celsius, 35-36 Fahrenheit. I wished I could wear my beautiful warm mink coat that Jack had bought me in the Las Vegas Neiman Marcus, but there was no way I could parade around the bus stops in that, attracting attention. So I bundled up with a wool coat and a shawl.

Ever since my move to Argentina, I had been sick more than usual. Springtime was the worst. On my vacation visits to BA I used to get sore throats and one time a very bad ear infection, but I just put that down to flying and recirculating air. But now I had asthma. Something I never had in my life. The doctor had said it was the BA humidity and the pollution.

That September I had been coughing and asthmatic off and on for some time like last spring, but after a few weeks I developed other symptoms: skin rash, sore throat, earache, sinus infection, eye oozing, and a temperature. I was really a mess.

Ramon went to the pharmacy and bought flu medicine and paracetemol and ibuprofen. I didn't remember ever being so sick, aside from the effects of my chemo and cancer therapy.

Some years before, when I was visiting BA and staying at Cristina's tango house, I had had an ear infection caused, I was sure, by flying with a stuffed up nose. I knew I needed antibiotics. Cristina had called a doctor to make a house call and all he did was instruct me to inhale eucalyptus vapor from boiling the dried leaves. I did it, but I knew I needed antibiotics. I suffered such pain no matter how many aspirins I took, which only got worse until finally I went to see an ear, nose and throat specialist who gave me a shot of penicillin and I was better in a few hours.

Now I called my Spanish teacher to ask her for a recommendation of a good GP. Her father was a pediatrician but in no case did I want to consult him, my landlord. She knew a doctor who was semi-retired, was of the highest caliber, and lived and worked close by in Caballito. I was too ill to figure it out, but Ramon took me. Dr. Alvarez had a *consultorio* in his big beautiful house. His wife answered the door and showed us past the piano in the hall, into his large front office. He was very old, a bit stocky, with thin white hair, a pink complexion, and a deep voice. I liked and trusted him immediately. He saw how sick I was at first glance. He asked me to step behind a screen and disrobe where there was a pressed white linen gown, and then he examined me on the corner table covered with elegant embroidered linen and trimmed with lace like an altar cloth.

"Si Señora, you have many things going on in your body. Indeed you are ill."

It didn't take a $300usd doctor bill and an armload of prescriptions to tell me that, but at least I felt better knowing

I was on the way to recovery. I gave Ramon money for the drugs and had hope for the first time in many days that I would feel better. Ramon made chicken soup and bought the sugared liquid that passed for juice in the supermarkets. When I went back to Dr. Alvarez, he smiled at me. *Ay, eso es la dama!* Now here is the lady!"

I was teaching tango now—and in fact a DVD had just come out in the States with me teaching with my old milonguero friend, Pedro. I was happy to assist him in teaching his classes in various salons, but I thought it was only because I was bilingual and any tanguera who spoke English and Spanish would have done. Unfortunately, the end result of so much dancing along with the percussion of flamenco, was that I got a minor fracture along with tendinitis and shin splints, and didn't dance anything for over two months.

But thanks to the Chinese-Argentine acupuncturist I found through the BANewcomers online mailing list, my dancing feet improved greatly except for the cramps I got whenever I lay down, so I kept going to him so that I could dance again pain free. He put bundles of herbs on the ends of the needles and lit them. The smoke smelled just like pot so maybe that's why I felt better when I left his office, which was usually so crowded with patients waiting that there were not enough chairs.

For so very long I had had to sleep with ice ankle wraps after dancing, but the acupuncturist had helped me. He was now trying to fix my imbalance of yin (too much) and yang (not enough.) He said my soul was "sick." He also said I needed to work on my yang, and he could help with that, but

I had to really want it. I wasn't quite sure how much I wanted to work on increasing my yang, though I understood that my energy was low and I had a faint pulse—symptoms of too little yang. What I really wanted was to be pain and cramp free and to dance as much as I liked. Every night in France I had been plagued with terrible cramps in both ankles, forcing me to get up and walk around two to three times a night (not easy on the boat). But I had no pain dancing or walking. Back in BA I resumed my regular twice a week acupuncture appointments. And through it all, I was still dancing the tango in stiletto heels! It's possible my soul was ailing, but without my regular tango fix, I was sure it would be sicker.

CHAPTER 15

I gave Viviana a goodbye kiss and headed downstairs to find a taxi. The sidewalk was busy with children coming home from soccer and ballet, and friends parting ways after work. An unoccupied taxi was just coming into view as the silhouette of a man came up the street. I saw only dark hair, a brown coat. But then his eyes pierced mine and with the practiced flourish of a piropeador, he gestured at my luggage and asked, 'Oh sweetness, must you leave so soon?' ...and he disappeared into the hazy pink evening.

—Kaitlin Quistgaard, The Argentine Art of Flirting, Salon, May 7, 1999

October 2005

I guessed I was in love. With somebody with no job or money and who lived with his family. He wasn't great in bed because it was all about him. But he had such soft, smooth, satin skin and a wonderful muscular back and shoulders that I enjoyed touching him and embracing him, and it was enough. I had had a lot of great sex in my life, so I thought I could live without it now, since Ramon gave me other delightful things. No relationship was perfect, I knew that. However he wanted to do things in bed that I didn't like. I also didn't like saying no to him. I explained that to him. I thought once should be enough. But he continued to ask me. Finally I told him to leave me, to go "out there" and find another woman to do those things with, of course practicing safe sex, and then come back to me when he'd had enough. I really meant it. It would have been fine with me. But he said, no, he didn't want another woman, he wanted me to do those things.

I couldn´t even have fun cheating on him. Well, I thought I probably could have with Laurence if we'd been back on the boat, far away from BA. But I felt committed to Ramon now.

Laurence wrote to say he couldn't wait to "take me to coffee" when he arrived soon for his summer in BA. I didn´t know what to do. I wanted my cake and to eat it too. I didn't want to forsake all chances I had of a future with somebody, I was tired of "dating" and remembered what a wonderful happy relationship I'd had with Jack. Ramon was in BA, and Laurence was still in France. But I was in Argentina. So many years of loneliness… You just never knew. And anyway, there was no guarantee with anybody. Jack and I both knew we would love each other forever, and look what happened. He left me because he had no alternative: he died.

But people made choices. Like I chose not to be with Gavito, because I wanted a real, long-term relationship and I knew that could never happen with him. But could it happen with Ramon? Did I want it to?

I had learned the Argentine folkdance, la chacarera, and leaped up to dance it whenever it was played as a break from all the tango at the milongas. Some years before I had seen a performance at a milonga of a folk dance group who danced la zamba (which is in fact the National Dance of Argentina, rather than the tango). I never forgot how emotional the music and movements of the dancers and their swirling handkerchiefs were. The DJs never played the zamba at milongas because few tangueros knew how to dance it. The chacarera was easy, but the zamba had 85 steps.

I knew a woman from the milongas who taught folklore, so I asked Victoria to come to my apartment and teach la zamba to Ramon and me. I enjoyed learning it, but we only had two private lessons before Ramon told me he couldn't take a lesson from a woman, that a woman couldn't tell him what to do. I had never heard anything so machista and ridiculous before. I was stunned. I could have continued on my own of course, but then who would I dance it with? I made an excuse to Victoria and that was that.

I once heard an American man say he didn't like the male posturing and role-playing of the chacarera folk dance. He preferred dances when everyone danced the same thing, and he enjoyed an interchange of lead and follow in tango, which was fine in my opinion for those who wanted to eliminate the "man" and the "woman" roles in tango, and just dance. (But for me, that would miss the whole point of the tango.) In most folk dances that men and women dance together, the simple moves act out the basic roles in society: the men stomp their feet and the women twirl their skirts. Or the men and women dance separately.

In la zamba, the man and woman danced the same steps around each other, never touching, swirling handkerchiefs while maintaining a lot of eye contact. Yet the goal in the zamba was to seduce the other person, and at times was more sensuous than the tango.

In other couple dances like salsa, rock 'n roll, ballroom, or square dancing, the couple also did the same steps, but the male / female connection was not important—two girls could often have just as much fun dancing together. The macho part of swing was the acrobatic lifts and spins. Some couple dances can even be done alone: salsa, disco, cha cha cha, mambo, samba, Charleston. But the tango takes two, who dance with one body.

I found the Anglican Cathedral, San Juan de Bautista, online and Sunday morning made my way by subte down to El Central. Constructed in 1831 in the neo-classical style, it was the oldest non-Catholic church building in South America. Only three blocks from the Casa Rosada, the seat of Argentine government, the financial area bustled during the week, but was creepily vacant on Sunday. Not many folks were in attendance at the bilingual church service, but the familiar ritual and hymns accompanied by the organ made me feel comfortable and at home. Everyone was friendly and welcoming.

During coffee hour in the fellowship hall, I met some sociable church members and the English priest, and I ended up volunteering to come to the weekly sewing circle to teach the women how to dance. I had always enjoyed volunteering at church—in San Miguel I was the Crucifer at St. Paul's, and in L.A. I had volunteered every week in the office of Hollywood Lutheran Church.

On the following Wednesday I hauled my boombox downtown to the church on the crowded subte. I walked across the windy Plaza de Mayo dotted with hawkers of Argentine flags and souvenir mate cups, and over the white painted silhouettes of head kerchiefs on the red brick ground of the plaza.

The kerchief graffiti symbolize the Mothers of the Plaza de Mayo who have demonstrated there every Thursday since 1977, wearing white kerchiefs in memory of their children who disappeared during the Dirty War. There are also graffiti drawings of the bodies of the lost. I tried to avoid stepping on any of the white outlines as I sadly remembered what they symbolized.

In the fellowship hall of the church, the street women were crocheting items to sell in the Afternoon Tea Fête fundraisers held twice a year. I was shy about my castellano, but I just plugged in the music and plowed ahead.

Hola damas. Encanto de conocerlas. Me gustaria compartir con ustedes un poco del tango, si quieren. "Hello ladies. It is a pleasure to meet you. I would like to share with you a little of the tango, if you would like. But first let's warm up and have some fun." I put on the "Hokey Pokey" and showed them how to "shake it all about." And then we did the "Bunny Hop." From there we went into the basic walk of the tango. They loved it, and were smiling and laughing. After learning the walk forward and backward, I paired them up to practice walking in unison, and we moved on to walking together in the line of dance. After a few weeks we progressed to the *ochos*, the second basic step of the tango, the first being the walk. I felt such pleasure at the thought of me teaching Argentinas how to dance the tango.

We did this every Wednesday afternoon. I wished I had a solution to not having to carry the awkward boombox as I returned home at rush hour, and the subte was jammed. I felt vulnerable holding the machine, my bag, and trying to hang onto the pole all while being squashed by the other riders.

Soon I got acquainted with several church members who helped out at the knitting circle. Many of the volunteers and the priest were English, or rather of British descent. I became especially close to Judy, an elderly woman whose family, originally from Scotland, had come to Argentina in the huge English migration to build the railroads in the 19th Century. She had grown up on a big estancia out of town, and now widowed, had a very British apartment in Recoleta. She ran the *Roparia,* a boutique of used men's clothing where street people and the homeless could shop for free every Saturday morning upstairs in the fellowship hall. A beautiful lady still, but fragile because of her age and recent knee surgery, I couldn't see how she could manage by herself, lugging the bags of donated men's clothing around and up the stairs. So I volunteered to help.

Working with the homeless men and Judy became a blessing in my life. My castellano improved—I learned words never heard in Mexico, like *chomba* (a sweatshirt), *remera* (tee shirt), and *campera* (jacket). The men would enter the small room one at a time and select an entire outfit from shoes to tie from the donated clothes on the racks. There was a small changing area and a mirror so they could feel like they were shopping in a store. We included small bags of hotel soap, shampoo, and a razor if we had some when we wrapped their items. They were always polite and we treated them with the utmost respect, something that they perhaps never got outside of the church.

Judy was smart and funny and she taught me a lot about my new country. We became fast friends.

CHAPTER 16

Did it hurt when you fell down from heaven?

—piropo

October 2005

After one of my flamenco lessons, Graciela and I sipped green tea in her lovely dining room filled with antique oak furniture, Spanish shawls, and fresh flowers. The double doors were wide open to the leafy patio and a cool spring breeze wafted in and refreshed my hot, damp face.

"Have you ever been to Machu Picchu?" she asked me all of a sudden as she replaced her cup onto the saucer. Obviously she had been thinking about it.

"No, but I've always wanted to."

"Let's you and me go, then," she said. "I think we would travel well together."

"Why not? Let's do it! It's not that far away!" I suddenly realized.

What a great opportunity to visit Peru. And because Graciela didn't speak English, I would have a week of intense Spanish practice. It would be fun to travel with a local—I wouldn't feel so lost, although she had never been there either. But at least she was a native speaker.

I wanted to compare tours online, but she insisted we take

several buses to a travel agent in the north, in Olivos. The trip took a whole day combined with the transportation and the long wait at the agency while the agent made calls and figured out dates and numbers. It was cheaper because the agent was Graciela's friend, and I wasn't charged the Yanqui Tax. So we were booked. How exciting! I had loved visiting the ancient ruins of Mexico.

Graciela was vivacious, lively and passionate about flamenco and I thought she was right that we would make good travel partners. She had been alone for many years since her divorce, and had her ways about her, but then so did I.

Ramon teased me about the possibility of falling in love with an Inca, and while I really loved strong noses, Peruvians in general were a bit too short for me.

Surprisingly enough, Lima was a lot like L.A.—the cliffs of the Palisades, the palm trees, the climate where it never rained, and everyone spoke Spanish, although a different Spanish. When Graciela and I spoke castellano, the Peruvians looked at us like we were from Mars. We went to the Mercado de Artesanias and by my second day, my one little suitcase was already stuffed. I even bought a carved folding wooden table/stool as well as an embroidered shirt for Ramon.

I had been worried that I was too tired to make this trip, having only recently recovered from the devastating flu. But Graciela wanted to sleep more than I did. So I took advantage of my free time in the hotel lobby and wrote emails while sucking alternately on coca tea for the altitude and on Pisco Sours. Graciela didn't drink and was a vegetarian and surprisingly for a porteña, went to bed very early at night. I had also bought a cute flask and filled it with Absolut Citron for the trip.

We went to the Ollantaytambo ruins and many others

along the way, climbing around and over them like alpacas. In Machu Picchu we both managed to hike all around the ruins with our guide who was hired by the tour company just for the two of us. Graciela, a real New-Ager, was feeling the energy, chanting to the sun, hugging the ancient stones, while I was listening hard to the guide as she pointed out the interesting features of the site. Later Graciela asked me what she said.

To celebrate my homecoming, Ramon wanted to make empanadas Tucumánas, his specialty. He said he loved to cook and was happily comfortable in the kitchen. I had seen Cristina's friend Gustavo make empanadas at her house, but he used the prepared rounds of dough available at the supermarket. Ramon did everything from scratch: he made the pastry, using a water bottle to roll out the dough because I had no rolling pin and cutting up the cooked meat in precise little cubes—no ground meat for him. They were delicious: light, flakey, tasty, and non-greasy. He talked about other dishes he wanted to cook for me, things he had learned from watching his mother in the kitchen when he was growing up in Tucumán. He said the secret ingredient in all of his cooking was love.

I knew that most Argentines drank *yerba mate,* and sipped on it all day long. Wanting to surprise Ramon, I made sure I had a mate gourd and bought some yerba, a special loose-leaf tea, at the market, just randomly picking one brand from the myriad on display. Ramon was delighted when I offered him some, and, after making sure the gourd was cured properly, he went to the kitchen to prepare it in the exact way necessary. He explained that the tradition came from the Guarani, the indigenous people of Argentina, who had been drinking it for centuries, and it was the favorite drink of the gauchos. There was a ritual, spiritual and social, somewhat like the tea ceremony of Japan. One didn't drink mate alone—it was a social event, with the gourd first drained by someone through the *bombilla* or metal straw, hot water refilled from a thermos, and then passed to another. It was all about sharing and connecting. But I was very disappointed that I didn't like the taste! Ramon put a lot of sugar into it, so it was very sweet, and also so acidic that it hurt my stomach. So rather than drink it alone, he just had coffee or tea with me instead and I think he was disappointed too.

One day Ramon took me in his old clunker (it was worse than anyone could ever imagine here in the States) on an excursion to Lujan, about an hour out of town and a tourist site because of its huge and beautiful basilica. Right next to the church were rusty roller coasters and octopus rides and many booths of cheap religious kitschy souvenirs made in China. I bought a book and Ramon a plastic rosary (for his car) and we had them blessed by the priest, along with his car keys. We stuffed ourselves on barbecued meat and rode horses along the river for a few minutes (2 pesos each), and relaxed on a patch of grass on the car floor mats he removed for us to lie on. Then he changed the flat tire that happened while we were having lunch and we spent some time in the tire repair shop fixing the old one, and then joined the hordes on the autoroute back to BA. That afternoon probably cost me around $30 US. It wasn't that much, but with the food and wine of other days we spent together, it all added up. I wished I could stop fretting about money and I wished Ramon could contribute something.

I didn't believe Ramon would ever have any money. When he would reach 65, he would get a minute amount of "social security" but he was only just 52. And he needed everything he had just to survive. But he especially needed medical treatment for his various ailments, and it broke my heart.

CHAPTER 17

The milongueros were very charming except for one who tried to rub his penis against me.

—Anonymous online Milonguero Survey response

November 2005

We were invited to the wedding of friends, a milonguero and an American woman. They reserved an entire restaurant for the dinner and then there was dancing in the basement. It was lovely, except for the cigarette smoke, but Ramon and I had a fight. I got very angry, I think it had to do with the money situation, but also he had eyes on a young pretty woman during the dancing, and he was drinking too much. With that and the choking smoke, I told him to just go for her and I ran out like a bat out of hell and into a taxi to go home.

I told him later it was mostly because of my preoccupation with money and the fact that he didn't have any, and I felt better after talking to him about it. It wasn't that he could do anything about no money, and whatever he did earn went to his family. He had sixteen grandchildren and three great-grandchildren.

However, his flirting and drinking didn't help matters and really annoyed me. But I usually rationalized, as many women do, that it was a wedding, a chance to have fun and relax, and that was his macho culture, which I didn't really understand. He was sweet and good and loving most of the time. I went crazy swerving back and forth between his good and bad attributes.

I only went to dance tango about three times a week now. There were so many places I just didn't enjoy. I went to Maipu 444 on Saturday for the first time, and I had to rush out of there after only an hour—so little fresh air, so much smoke. I couldn't breathe, it was crowded and I couldn't even see across the room. Lots of my favorite dancers were there, but the hall was impossible. So I went to Nino Bien, or Los Consagrados, which was in such a lovely salon. I saw Hector, the tall bear of a man who had left me alone at Canning. He seemed to be every place now that he was "single" again. But I didn't dance with him anymore.

Cristina had a party at her tango house and invited Ramon and me. We brought bottles of wine and Ramon's empanadas to share. Cristina and her boyfriend had made a lentil stew and charged us for it, even though we brought food and drink. Evidently foreigners were charged (as in many places) and locals were not. However Ramon was definitely a porteño and I was too now, wasn't I? Plus Cristina was my friend, wasn't she?

There was a little dancing but mostly it was a chatting get-together. One of Cristina's guests was an interesting Swede, and he and I stood in the dining room talking about mutual tango friends, the milongas, and what he thought of BA. It was normal party talk. But when I rejoined Ramon, he was furious.

"How dare you ignore me in public to talk so long to another man! *No me das bola*!"

"Don't be ridiculous! It's a party. Everyone talks with every-"

"You humiliated me!"

"Sorry. But that was not my intention. Guests are supposed to circulate at a party. Why didn't you chat with-"

"Nobody interesting speak Spanish," he said, talking over me. "*De todos modos* you are my partner and I *verguenza,* (embarrassed). *Falta de respecto,*" he pointed at his chest.

The party was over for me then and I just wanted to go home. I felt bad that we were somewhere where we could have some fun, and Ramon had to ruin it. I didn't think he wanted me to have a life, or be an interesting person, or to exist without him. Maybe that's the expected role of women in Argentina. But that wasn't me at all. And yet I was living in BA to dance, wasn't I? (And also because it worked for me economically). And there was no better tango for me than in Ramon's arms. So I shut up and put up—but ran away when it was too uncomfortable, like I had done at the wedding.

Ramon unfortunately was the kind of man who took out his frustrations on those nearest. So after Cristina's party, the Thursday night milonga wasn't that much fun with him (except for the dancing part), and the following Saturday he was really in a snit by the time I showed up at Los Consagrados. We usually met there instead of going together, as I enjoyed the drama of entering alone and getting a rush seeing him at our table. But tonight I just grabbed my bag and left while he was dancing. When I got home I gathered the things he had at my apartment and threw them over the balcony into the street. I was done. There was no reason for me to put up with his difficult behavior. I wouldn't let him take his frustrations and disappointments out on me.

He had to be right all the time, he never had to explain himself, he could never say he was sorry—all of that machismo crap that was so prevalent everywhere in Argentina. He called later but I didn't answer the phone. He called for several days but I didn't answer. That night he did pick up his clothes from the sidewalk though. I heard his old batata approach, idle a moment, and then roar off over the cobblestones.

I was willing to tolerate certain things, of course nobody's perfect, but there was a limit. I missed him a lot that week and felt bad, but not enough to call. I went to El Beso and Canning where he never went, but truthfully, I really only wanted to dance with Ramon. He was the best. I was going through tango withdrawal even though I danced with others. And so after several days, I did answer the phone and we made up and went dancing. Ramon and I somehow had gotten back together again. And it had only taken one tango.

CHAPTER 18

I learned that women needed to be protected, controlled, and left at home. I learned that men led, women followed…that women are there to be kissed… In movies, male domination sometimes includes punishment that's framed as playful…One of John Wayne's screenwriters once said, 'All you gotta have in a John Wayne picture is a hoity-toity dame with big tits that Duke can throw over his knee and spank.'

—Manohla Dargis, "What the Movies Taught Me About Being a Woman," New York Times

December 2005

In Argentina, everyone used nicknames. Unlike in the U.S., nicknames based on your appearance were terms of endearment. No one was offended if they were called Fatty, Skinny, Blackie, China, Kid, Baldy, or whatever they looked like. Jewish people were called *Ruso*; Italians, *Tano*; Spaniards, *Gallego*–(Gallego was somewhat disparaging due to envy, I thought, because the Spanish tended to be wealthy.)

Ramon was called *El Negrito* because of his dark complexion, or *El Tuco* because of the northern province where he was born—Tucumán. In Tucumán also there were many people of Arabic descent. Whether their ancestors were from Egypt,

Lebanon, Iraq or Turkey, it was all the same in Argentina—*El Turco.*

Ramon was born in a tiny village in Tucumán, where he had lived with his parents and two sisters in a little stone cottage without running water. He had to quit school in the fourth grade to work in the fields cutting sugarcane to help his family. Finally his father took the two older children to Buenos Aires to look for a better job and left Ramon with his mother in Santa Ana.

The cinema became Ramon's refuge as a young man. He haunted the theater, catching every new film that played there. He was a huge fan, especially of the great old Hollywood stars. John Wayne was his favorite. He had seen all of the classics and as many other American movies as he could. All he knew of the United States was through the movies and rock 'n roll. Like most South Americans, American movies, music, and TV were the source of knowledge about American culture and history. And often what was depicted was macho men having their way with women. In Hollywood, fathers always knew best, as did husbands. And love often began with a man physically overcoming a woman's protests, not taking no for an answer, from "Gone With the Wind" to "A Streetcar Named Desire" to "A Quiet Man" and many more. Hollywood reinforced the machismo that already existed around the world.

When Ramon was fourteen, he and his mother joined his father and sisters in BA, where he would hang out at the tango halls and watch his father dance.

Graciela had her flamenco recital again, but this year she

wanted me to do a "surprise" belly dance solo, which I was only too happy to agree to, as there was a definite connection between the two art forms. I had brought two costumes with me—somehow I just hadn't been able to let them go—and now I was glad I had them. I had also performed in a theater in Mexico with a flamenco troupe as a "surprise guest artist." And Ramon agreed to demonstrate a tango with me.

It was December and therefore stifling and sultry in her studio, so that it was difficult peeling the three different costumes on and off, but it was still fun. And once again the venue was packed. However, because my knees and ankles hurt so much after dancing flamenco, this recital would be my flamenco swan song. I had to save myself for the tango.

Since I had a novio now, I had hoped that maybe I wouldn't be alone during the holidays. But he always had to be with his family, Ramon told me, in any case until after midnight on the 24th and the 31st. These weren't the first holidays I had spent alone since Jack died, so it was no big problem for me. Phoebe and I would hide from the fireworks and be happy with just each other. With this horrible summer heat, I was thinking of going to Mexico maybe in January for my visa stamp, but it was expensive and not easy to get to San Miguel. I would so love to go to the beach—I never went to a Mexican beach in the two and a half years I lived there. But in January I made the usual turnaround trip to Uruguay instead.

Carnival in Argentina was something I really wanted to experience. When I read that BANewcomers had organized a turnaround trip to *Carnaval en Guayleguaychu*, I booked the two of us. We went to the downtown pickup spot at noon on Saturday, and rode with ten others in a van the three and a half hours to Guayleguaychu in the province of Entre Rios, northeast of BA, arriving in time to relax in the park by the river and to have dinner in a restaurant. Then we attended the amazing five-hour parade with dancers, floats, orchestras, and then found our way back to the van for the all-night return trip—a nightmare journey as a drunken woman was vomiting and Ramon had a horrible gall bladder attack. He turned completely yellow. Upon arrival in BA, we went straight to the hospital.

Ramon was incredibly ill. He had told me he had gall bladder trouble, but this time he was jaundiced from the whites of his eyes to his skin. A friend had recommended a gall bladder cleanse of olive oil and lemon juice, but all it did was make him vomit. He had had problems with his gall bladder for quite some time, he admitted, but had done nothing about it.

I found a specialist online and made Ramon go to see him. The doctor confirmed my fear, that he needed immediate surgery at a cost of several thousand dollars. Ramon refused as there was no money; his attack subsided, and I tried to forget about it. But I was more motivated than ever to get both of us some kind of health insurance.

I too needed health insurance, but I couldn't get it once I admitted on the applications my pre-existing condition—two occurrences of breast cancer. I applied and was turned down everywhere. I was very discouraged. Ramon wanted to inquire if his old TeLeFe union—TV Salud—would take me. We went and filled out all the forms truthfully. And they accepted me as a member. Ramon knew a woman in the membership office. I asked how much a policy for Ramon would cost, and it was much less than mine because he was younger, male and had no medical history, unlike me. So I signed us both up for a health plan and immediately began to breathe easier, despite the added pressure of another monthly bill.

We had medical insurance together, we sometimes gave tango classes in my living room, we sat together at the milongas—I guessed now I was committed to this relationship. When we had classes or milongas, he stayed with me, but then he would go home to his house in Banfield—primarily to smoke, I thought, but he also worried about his grandchildren. It was a comfortable arrangement. Like I told everyone, I was always happy to see him arrive and then glad to see him leave.

CHAPTER 19

...men could be whatever they liked; it was only unforgiveable for a woman to age or grow fat.

—Miranda France, *Bad Times in Buenos Aires*

March 2006

For my birthday in 2006, I had the best, most thrilling celebration of my life. Since all my tango friends went to Club Español on Thursday nights and my birthday fell on Thursday, what better place to celebrate than in the most beautiful venue in Buenos Aires? Somehow the plans grew—with Ramon speaking to Julio the organizer behind the scenes, and Pato the waitress, and Dany the DJ—and we were going to do a demonstration! In front of everyone for Club Español was always packed, especially ever since the closures caused by the Cromagnon tragedy. A good tanguero friend, Oscar Casas, volunteered to professionally video the festivities. And when I watched the video later on YouTube, I noticed Laurence, who was still in BA, taking pictures of us as we performed, and somehow that touched me.

Laurence was more infatuated with me than before, and I think it was from watching me dance with Ramon. Everybody watched us dance. People stopped me on the street to comment about how amazing it was to see us on the floor.

Perhaps because of the birthday celebration and our performance, and because so many people asked us, we considered entering the big Buenos Aires Tango Championships, first organized by the government in 2003.

The qualifying rounds for the *Campeonato Metropolitano de Tango* began early in May at most of the milongas in BA. Over a period of three weeks, more than 500 couples entered the contest. At least one member of the couple had to prove he lived in the city of Buenos Aires, because the winning couple in August would represent the city in the World Championships.

These preliminary rounds were entertaining, with friends cheering the dancers on in a relaxed atmosphere. Ramon and I qualified at Club Español. At this level there were three judges. There were some irregularities as you might expect —for example, one judge danced afterward with the sexy young foreigner he had selected. One young girl was obviously wearing no underwear. One couple were students of one of the judges, and so on.

Osvaldo and Coca Cartery, winners in 2004, sat with a friend of ours at a table watching us qualify. When we did, Osvaldo commented to our friend that he thought "foreigners could never dance the tango well." And he said this despite the fact that he made a living teaching foreigners. Our friend Alberto was surprised at this comment, as was I when he relayed it, but Ramon wasn't the least surprised. "That man is a *pelotudo*, an asshole," he said.

Ramon and I went to a few milongas we normally didn't attend in order to watch the other qualifying rounds to check out our competition. One night we were in Flores at El Pial, eating pizza and enjoying ourselves with some friends, when there was an announcement by the organizer: "And now El

Flaco Dany will perform a milonga with Cherie!" El Flaco Dany was a well-known dancer famous for his milonga dancing (a happy kind of tango rhythm in 4/4 time), whom I had never danced with before. I wasn't worried about performing with him because I could always follow a good leader, but I was stunned that he hadn't asked me first. I felt flattered, but still, it seemed so rude to surprise me like that. After all I was there with my partner and friends and in the middle of a pizza. What if I hadn't wanted to do it? What then?

Dany and I performed the milonga, and I sat down again at the table. Ramon was furious that Dany hadn't asked his permission—never mind mine. I felt proud that the famous dancer had wanted to demonstrate with me, and that we had performed so well together but also I felt like a sack of potatoes, a body that could dance, a non-person. Maybe Ramon was proud of me, but he sulked. And certainly didn't give me a pat on the back.

Ramon and I progressed to the Semifinals in July in Salon Argentina. This time there were five judges, Maria Nieves, superstar of "Tango Argentino" and other stage shows, and the ex-wife of Juan Carlos Copes, the man who made stage tango an international sensation, among them. It was less fun, because we came on time and had to wait several hours in the freezing green room before we got to dance in the two rounds of five or six couples each. It was long and arduous. Several couples were fighting over how to do a step and why they weren't selected and because they were cold and hungry. But eventually the eliminations were made and we could go home after being there for over five hours. At least Ramon and I went home as *Finalistas*. Even in the Semifinals, I was the only foreigner in the Tango Salon division, a fact of which I was very proud, and also that Maria Nieves had given us an almost perfect score.

Ramon and I didn't practice for the Finals that were being held in August. Our dance was completely improvised; we didn't do choreography. But several couples worked hard to prepare: taking classes, practicing, and going to milongas every night.

I did find a dressmaker who advertised in the tango magazines. I went to his studio on Avenida Rivadavia and we discussed what I wanted as he took measurements and showed me some of his other work for tango shows. I returned after a week to see the fabric samples he had chosen from the garment district, He had found the color I wanted—teal—in lace for the bodice and silk organza for the layered full skirt.

While working with Judy at the church's Roparia, I told her about the championships and my dress, and thought maybe there would be a suit there that Ramon could wear. The following week Judy brought in a gorgeous Saville Row wool suit that had belonged to her late brother, and it fit Ramon perfectly.

Even though I was backstage at the Finals, I had no idea that the fabulous music we heard while waiting to dance was played live by Emilio Balcarce's Orchestra. Ramon and I had seen and loved the film of his Escuela de Tango Orchestra, *Si Sos Brujo*. The event at the large venue of La Rural in Palermo was well organized, but they told us, the dancers, nothing at all about what was happening during the program, just when and where to line up.

After dancing a ronda to three orchestras in different styles (we had Di Sarli, D'Arienzo, and "Patético" by Pugliese), I was gratified that Ramon and I made the final cut, one of 16 couples out of the 32 finalist pairs. When I considered that more than 500 couples entered the contest in May, we were honored to be in the final 16 group, especially as 13 of the couples were youngsters. The other three couples who finished in the finals of the Finals were over fifty, including Ramon and myself. And like in the Semifinals, I was the only foreigner in the Tango de Salon competition. Judy was in the front row with one of her daughters, clapping furiously when we placed.

As in any arts contest, there was a lot of subjectivity. How could you choose between the five best movies, or five best actors, or books, or paintings, or dancers? It was not a science, and many people griped about the politics of the Campeonato, saying you had to know the judges or have taken lessons from them or whatever, but we didn't "know" anybody and we still made it almost to the end.

Of course in the Championships there were issues like the fact that Ramon and I followed completely the written contest rules—feet on floor, no pauses, no choreographed figures, total improvisation, no breaking of the embrace, etc.—and yet the youngsters' legs were flying all over the place in high kicks and the judges went for that. The rules stressed elegance and musicality, but the kids, who perhaps someday would dance more elegantly, didn't show a lot of it in the rondas. To me they looked as if they were gearing up for a stage career, not for dancing socially in the milongas where there was no room for that stuff. This contest was supposed to be about social dancing, Tango de Salon. There was a category for stage tango in the Mundial, the Tango Championships of the World.

A multitude of foreigners came to compete in the Mundial and to take back from BA the *Tango Para Turistas* that was wildly popular overseas and that was carried around the world by teachers on tour like the plague. Other countries only saw tango on TV and in big stage shows, and that was the tango they wanted to learn. So touring teachers provided athletic choreography, kicks and lifts and spectacular tricks and lots and lots of figures.

But that was not the tango as danced by the real people in the salons of Buenos Aires. That was probably not the tango that these same youngsters would be dancing when they were older. When their youthful exuberance faded, they would begin to look for the milonguero style of the close embrace, the connection to the music and their partner, the sensuality and improvisation that milongueros have always danced, and I hoped that would still exist.

In all the separate sections of the contest, it was the young and professional who won, whether they followed the written rules of the judges on how to dance or not. If rules were ignored with impunity, the rules would eventually change or be eliminated altogether. I thought it was ridiculous to have a 60-year- old milonguero competing with a 25-year-old professional stage dancer.

When a milonga was half-full of foreign dancers doing leg-wraps, *colgadas, volcadas,* and elaborate *adornos,* real "Dancing With the Stars" stuff, this made an impression on the Argentines. Certainly some of them would want to do it too. When the old milongueros were gone, would people be dancing stage-salon tango in dance halls to see who could *boleo* the highest and *gancho* the fastest? Just like when tango came back to Argentina from Paris in the '20s, it had become a different dance. So it would change again with all of the cross-pollination of the Campeonato Mundial and the travelling salesman/tango teachers who sold the buyers what they wanted.

CHAPTER 20

It is especially confusing to newbie women because they may very well think, 'Oh this is a cultural thing' or, 'Maybe he just got carried away with the passion of the dance.' Many visiting foreign women behave in ways they never would on their home turf. They go to bed with guys whose last names they don't even know, whose marital status should put them on notice, with guys who have no jobs and no money.

—Anonymous comment on my blog, tangocherie.blogspot

September 2006

Out on the streets, buckets of fragrant *jazmines* were for sale (called gardenias in the north). The professional dog walkers seemed to be working overtime; I saw one with 14 large breed dogs. BA had its recycling system of *cartoneros*—street kids who were trucked in every night around midnight to go through everyone's trash looking for bottles and cardboard. (No one knew how many there were in Buenos Aires, but estimates were in the five figures.) There were no such things as the large plastic garbage bins that were so familiar in the States, and people simply arranged their rubbish in market plastic bags around the nearest tree to wait for the kids, who sifted gloveless through the trash.

Spring finally had sprung. The weather, although recently stormy with exciting thunder, lightning, and even hail, now was sunny and warm. I planted seeds in pots on my balcony and hoped to have fresh herbs to cook with. I was having a local couple over at noon for a little Argentinian barbecue (meat, meat, and more meat) but I wasn't sure what else they would eat. People here only liked very plain food without much taste, and it always confounded me what to serve them. Once I had people over for dinner and served pasta and salad, but they didn't eat salad with pasta, I was informed, they ate bread with pasta. I had to throw out most of the delicious salad with different greens, herbs, artichoke hearts that I had searched all over Caballito to find.

The lack of variety of obtainable foods was bothering me. I was from Los Angeles, where everything was available year round, and enjoying what I ate was important to me. I preferred to eat nothing rather than something unappetizing just because I needed nourishment. Yes, I was what people call a foodie. The food was one huge reason I tried so hard to live in France after Jack died. Eating well just made life richer and more worth living. But here people ate beef, potatoes, iceberg lettuce, bread, and ice cream, with starters of cheese, salami, ham, and olives. Plus pasta (*fideos*) with tomato sauce and pizza with no spices. Going to the market was such a frustrating experience for me as there wasn't much I wanted to buy, let alone cook and eat.

When Ramon took me to Jumbo, a huge supermarket in Palermo, I was a kid in a candy store as I ran around dumping things into my cart that I'd never seen in BA markets before. Raspberries and goat cheese and Thai noodles and cans of curry sauces in three colors and ground coffee without sugar were impossible to find in neighborhood chain supermarkets like Disco, Coto, and Dia. I almost went into cardiac arrest though when I got to the check stand. Imported foods were taxed to the skies.

I was tired of my multi-colored red hair. Anyway I felt that frankly fake red was passé now. A friend from Pilates, who had a really cute haircut, suggested her hairdresser Abel in Pelo's Design, not far away in Caballito. Ramon took me and sat waiting for me the whole five hours it took to get all of the colors out. I told him to go get a coffee or something, but he sat there, making small talk with Abel and the other customers until I once again had a normal hair color and a good haircut.

After our success in the Tango Championships, and probably also because of our demonstration at Club Español on my birthday, many dancers approached us for lessons. Since my apartment had little furniture and a parquet floor, we were happy to oblige in my spacious living room. We were becoming well-known in the milongas.

People called Ramon and me *La Pareja Feliz* (the Happy Couple), *El Negro y La Novia* (the Blackie and the Girlfriend), and something not so nice, *La Dama y El Vagabundo* (The Lady and the Tramp). I was certain the gossip about us was that Ramon took advantage of me, the "rich American." Many of the expat women I knew did have money, often from successful divorces, and they purchased lavish houses and apartments in the best Buenos Aires neighborhoods. And it was true that Ramon didn't have a regular job and because of me and teaching with me, he had a better lifestyle than he otherwise would have had. There was a word for men who didn't work and danced tango and who accepted gifts from women, *atorrante,* and I supposed he was called that by some people.

My volunteer work with Judy at the church had led to a deepening friendship between us. We often went out to lunch in San Telmo and she frequently invited me to her lovely apartment for tea. Large and elegant, there were family portraits and paintings of Scotland everywhere. She had seven children and many grandchildren and loved sharing stories of their successes and adventures. Tea was just like I had experienced on my travels to England, with toast in a toast rack and jam, pate and cheese, and biscuits, little tea sandwiches with a cake she had baked, and of course embroidered napkins. She had a wonderful sense of humor and we laughed like sisters over our teacups.

Robyn Ash-Rose, an Australian who had moved to BA and bought an apartment, wrote a memoir about her tango experience, as many women did. But Robyn wrote as therapy, she told me one night at Club Español, because she was dying of kidney cancer. A beautiful, positive person, her memoir was inspired by British journalist Miranda France's book from the '90s, *Bad Times in Buenos Aires,* which contained accurate and interesting perceptions of the porteño life, traffic, sexism, huge contrast of the very rich and the very poor, rats outnumbering people, the *viveza criolla* (artful lying), still current so many years later. France wrote about the popularity of psychoanalysis in Argentina: After a year of living in BA, France wrote, "I felt I knew what it was like to be forgotten. I knew what it was like to live at the end of the world." Well, I felt exactly the same way ten years after she wrote that.

But Robyn didn't. She was happy living her new and chosen life "at the end of the world" in Argentina, even though she was so very sick. She wanted to counteract France's bad impressions of the chaos and melancholy that permeated BA with her happy ones, and so she titled her memoir *Better Times in Buenos Aires*. She put Ramon's and my photo on the cover because she said we looked so happy when we danced, that she couldn't stand all of the tragic "tango faces" that dancers often adopted. Sometimes the women even put on "orgasmic" expressions in order to get more dances.

We were honored to be her cover image, but terribly saddened that shortly after publication she passed away alone in her apartment and wasn't found for two weeks. That was an ending that I wanted to avoid, that I feared for myself, even though I now had a partner. When Ramon and I fought, we didn't communicate, he wasn't living with me, and was often at home with his family. I could imagine keeling over one day and no one knowing until it was too late. Certainly all older people living alone envisioned such an ending.

CHAPTER 21

Looks, but more particularly women's looks, were a persistent, urgent topic of conversation...Two-thirds of schoolgirls had ambitions to become, not lawyers, doctors, or scientists, but models...

—Miranda France, *Bad Times in Buenos Aires*

Winter 2006

Carolina, my Spanish teacher, the landlord's daughter, was pregnant, and I had a feeling that my comfortable life was soon to be over. Her apartment was so small and they would need more room for the baby. Sure enough, I was notified that when my two years were up in August, I had to find other digs, as Papa was giving the place to his daughter.

Nobody could believe that it was so hard to find somewhere to live. Sure, there were a million high-priced tourist apartments for short-term vacation living, but large, unfurnished places without a *garantia* from a property owner in the city of Buenos Aires, was almost impossible. Most real estate agents hung up on me when they heard my American accent. Even when Ramon called, when they heard the client was an "Americana," they hung up, even though I could pay one year in advance, two months realtor's commission, and two months deposit. I asked a couple of porteño friends if they would sign the garantia for me, but they all reneged, including Cristina, saying their properties were in someone else's name.

Studying the classifieds in Clarin on a daily basis, I learned about an open house in Boedo. When I first saw the great tiled terrace with a fabulous L-shaped view, and even a parrilla (barbecue) nine stories up, I knew I would be happy there. The view was breathtaking as there were no tall buildings nearby blocking the sky, and the panorama stretched forever in three directions. I knew Phoebe would also be content as she would have her own personal cat door to go in and out of the *quincho* at will. And I would be happy that finally I had a place to live again in BA where I could see the sky from every room. I hoped I wouldn't have to go through all of this again in two years.

Finally "my people" (I had asked a trusted couple from Toastmasters, both lawyers, to be there with me as I was learning that the *viveza criolla*–artful lying–of Argentina often left me holding the bag) and "their people" of real estate agents, lawyers, and landlord, culminated my four-month apartment search by sitting around a big conference table in an elegant lawyer's office in Puerto Madero, signing contracts and handling thousands of dollars in cash. No, I wasn't buying a six million dollar building, but simply renting an unfurnished two-bedroom apartment in Boedo—the ancient Barrio de Tango in Buenos Aires.

Moving day was an experience. Carolina advised me to order a *flete,* a pickup truck with wooden sides (there was even a tango called "El Flete" as there were tangos about every aspect of porteño life), and reserve *canastos* to put my things in. The flete driver dropped off the number of baskets I had ordered the day before the move, I filled them up, then he loaded them into his truck the next day and delivered them to my new apartment, collecting the empty canastos the third day. I thought it was a very efficient way to move—no buying boxes, tape, and wrapping paper, and then having to dispose of them. The canastos were recyclable in that they were used again and again until they wore out.

As there was only a tiny elevator, the only way to get my rented piano upstairs to the ninth floor would be to carry it up. The owner didn't want that, and so I sadly sent it back to her in Martinez.

After the move from Caballito, I set up a meeting with Dr. Landlord at the historic café Homero Manzi (a celebrated tango composer) at the corner of San Juan y Boedo (the name of another tango) in my new neighborhood. I arrived on time and ordered coffee. He was late. When he got there he didn't order anything and seemed to be in a rush. I had all my receipts and paperwork ready to prove how much I had invested in his apartment, upgrading plumbing, electrical, and heating. I expected to be reimbursed, and to get my security deposit back. He didn't even look at my papers, simply said, "In Argentina, nobody gets their deposit back." Then he left. I was so angry I could have spit nails. I paid for my coffee, embarrassed that Dr. Landlord had acted so rudely in front of the waiter. Where was the machismo that ruled the land? I supposed money and profit trumped being polite to women—or anyone else. La viveza criolla.

Juan, my new landlord, was very nice—an ex-football player who was now in medical school. I planned to stay in his apartment "forever" unless he kicked me out, but it would be a while until his ten-year-old daughter would have a family and need to live there herself. I crossed my fingers.

Sometimes I needed to run out of a milonga because of the smoke. At Lo de Celia's I sat at a table near a window so I could open it and stick my head out for air. Before I sat with Ramon, the hostess at Gricel always put me at a table of five local women who all smoked. Everyone seemed to smoke in Buenos Aires.

So my joy knew no bounds when in October a No Smoking ban was passed. I couldn't believe it. I thought it might turn out like it had in France—with a complete disregard for No Smoking signs. But the milonga organizers, restaurant owners, and taxi drivers throughout the city enforced the new law. I was ecstatic. Now my only complaint was that all the smokers stood outside by the front door smoking every chance they got, so I had to hold my breath walking in and out of the venues. But I would never complain—I was too comfortable breathing normally inside. I was grateful that Ramon was considerate about his smoking and was careful not to smell of smoke when I saw him. He never complained and never went outside on the sly to smoke.

After Jack's hopeless prognosis, I had been assigned a therapist whom I saw weekly, and for years after his death. Talk therapy had worked for me. But here in Argentina I didn't have anyone to talk frankly with, to bare my soul to, and to discuss the worries that often kept me up at night. Since Buenos Aires was the psychotherapy capital of the world—the joke was there were more psychologists than residents—I thought I should try to find one for me. Many advertised to expats online on the BANewcomers mailing list. I thought a bilingual Argentine woman would be a good fit for me and I found one, Laura, in Palermo, the "expat barrio." She insisted I go to her *consultorio* in her apartment twice a week for sessions, so I made a commitment. Maybe she could help me adjust.

I missed my family, old friends, and Los Angeles so much that this time I decided to return for a couple of weeks to get my passport stamped instead of Uruguay. Whenever I was sad or depressed, all I had to do to feel better was to buy an airplane ticket. So I had Thanksgiving at home in Los Angeles with son Jason, who took me to see the Nutcracker Ballet. I had so many memories of his dancing the Snow King, the Nutcracker, and the Grand Pas de Deux that now tore at my heart.

I was so happy in L.A. whenever I was there "on vacation." I stayed with Jason or Roy and Sheila nearby, old and dear friends I knew from the library, so I wasn't alone. I drove Jason's BMW everywhere I wanted to go and visited all of my favorite places, usually starting with IHOP and pancakes. I ate all the food that I never had in Argentina. I shopped at Ralph's, snapping photos of the displays of cheeses and produce, until Jason said I looked like a terrorist who might get arrested. I cooked dinners for Jason and his friends with all of his favorite foods like leg of lamb, shrimp and peppers with linguini, Texas-style chili con carne, and strawberry shortcake made from scratch like my grandma used to make. I went to my dentist to have my teeth cleaned, as they didn't do that in Argentina. (My Argentine dentist had told me when I requested a cleaning, "If it's not broke, don't fix it." He was amazed I still had all of my teeth!) Plus the super-fabulous surprising bonus was that I worked as a substitute librarian whenever I was in L.A., keeping my hand in but also making some extra money.

L.A. friends extended themselves, inviting me to events and restaurants. And once in a while my oldest son Adam, a musician who lived in the mountains near Sacramento and didn't get to L.A. very often, came down when I was in town. He was so wise, such an old soul. I really missed him and my grandson, Dominic, who I never really had gotten to spend time with. It was so unlike when I lived there by myself after Jack died and I felt isolated. During my brief L.A. trips from Argentina and before that from Mexico, I was truly happy, busy, and never lonely.

Like all vacations, my Thanksgiving visit galloped by. I flew around the freeways of L.A. I never drove in BA. But I had driven in L.A. since I was fifteen, and nothing could match the feeling of freedom and infinite possibility that I had on the 101 freeway with the radio blasting, the violet mountains to the north, the neon-peppered skyline of Hollywood on the south, the salty sea air blowing in from the west. I had missed the fact that I did my best thinking behind the wheel.

Before leaving, I filled my suitcase with spices, coffee, and goodies from Trader Joe's to make the bland Argentine food taste better. Argentines didn't even use garlic or black pepper. Their pepper was the mild white. I always returned with lemon pepper, pink Himalayan salt, and green Tabasco sauce. I even smuggled a pound of bacon.

After checking in to my flight, I staggered to an airport Mexican restaurant and had a margarita for the road—the last one before leaving the States. At the gate a grumpy employee grabbed my roller bag and said it had to be checked to Buenos Aires. I snatched it back and said it had passed muster downstairs. He argued that it was too wide, so I removed a book and put it in my purse, and got on the plane with my bag.

Eighteen hours later, I arrived on time at Ezeiza where Ramon was waiting for me. He had used my time away to paint my entire apartment knowing how I couldn't tolerate chemical odors.

Settled into my Boedo home, it was a hot beautiful day when I went to the supermarket. The only green things in the produce section were apples. Maybe I could find a lettuce in a little verduleria. What a crazy life.

Ramon had never had material possessions, except the occasional car. I didn't appreciate how important having a vehicle was to him. Like the Latinos in Los Angeles, it was a cliché that a car was the first thing they bought. It was almost like wheels equaled their power as men. Ramon felt more macho behind the wheel.

When he was working those twenty years for the TV station, Ramon had earned good money, owning a fancy white van and throwing a big quinceañera party for his oldest daughter. But otherwise he didn't care about what money could buy. He was the opposite of materialistic. He wanted to pay the utilities at his house, wanted to take care of his grandchildren and see that they had enough to eat, and wanted to take care of his car. But other things just passed through his life without notice.

I wasn't terribly materialistic myself. But I really valued the things I already had and took very good care of them. Some of my clothes I'd had for twenty years, and there were the Oriental scatter rugs I had brought in my suitcase, photos, books, my piano music, some little tchotkes from my travels that gave me pleasure. In my old life, I had taken pride in my big beautiful home and the things I filled it with. And even in my rented apartment I tried to preserve the few things I had.

But when it came to Ramon, I loved to see him looking good, and bought him cheap flashy rings from China to wear dancing. And other little trinkets I thought he would enjoy. Every return trip from Los Angeles I brought a suitcase stuffed with nice clothes for him that I had bought at the Goodwill. But nothing ever lasted—lost, broken by him or his grandchildren, or taken by his sons. It didn't seem to bother him, but it bothered me.

CHAPTER 22

The nature of catcalling is so embedded in Argentine culture and it, unfortunately, reinforces male dominance and the idea that women are property.

Men here perceive catcalling as their duty, their right, as the norm. They don't see it any other way; they are simply the dominant figures in society.

—Julia Sipos, *The Machista Culture Of Argentina: An Epidemic of Violence Against Women*

Summer 2006

One hot, scorching Sunday afternoon when the temperature topped 40°C (104F), Ramon and I went to the Bosque de Palermo, an old lovely park. Ramon knew the man at the boat rentals and he let us have a rowboat for free, so we toured the whole lake, followed by a stroll in the rose gardens and a *choripan* lunch from a food stand. After three years of living in BA, it was my first time in the Bosque, built over a century ago and recently restored. It was lovely to see the rollerbladers, runners, and families enjoying themselves in the park.

Boedo was a whole different world from Palermo. There wasn't even a park or grass area let alone a lake, no movie theater, and no imported foods. Boedo was an old blue-collar neighborhood with useful shops and businesses on the main street of Avenida Boedo—banks, bakeries, hardware stores, Chinese laundries, a couple of supermarkets, drug stores, shoe stores, and cheap Chinese import shops, along with a few inexpensive restaurants. I could see that, as is the case wherever you are in the world, the neighborhood where you live determines your impression of the whole city (and sometimes of the whole country.) Even though Boedo was the historic "barrio del tango," (and there was a tango called "Boedo"), there was very little tango going on there now. Nothing for tourists apart from the Homero Manzi Café where they had tango shows. No cobblestone streets, fancy boutiques, or elegant restaurants, and sadly, no trees. People on the street going about their business all wore jeans, shorts, or jogging clothes. I never saw anyone dressed up. My new neighborhood was so different from Congreso, with its government officials and lawyers going out to lunch in suits and ties, and from Recoleta and Palermo where the embassies, diplomats and palaces were, and where the expats who could afford it lived.

Judy had invited us for tea so after our day in the park, we enjoyed a British tea time. It was a new experience for Ramon certainly but it was nice that my good friend and my boyfriend could speak fluently with each other as I sat contentedly between them.

In early December Ramon got a job to perform with a woman at her birthday party at a Puerto Madero restaurant. He asked her if I could come along, so I did. A lovely venue on the water, the room was packed with guests. It was a true party, not only a tango party, and folks were circulating with drinks in their hands, chatting. There was a large buffet table in the next room piled with cold cuts, potato salad, breads, and olives. Ramon didn't eat but he was drinking one beer after another, which never seemed to affect him. When the time came for the performance, he put on his jacket and disappeared with Cynthia. Then a loud, fast rhythmical tango came on, "Ansiedad," and out they danced, grabbing everyone's attention with energy and personality. The crowd went crazy and demanded an encore so they danced a tango vals. I was very proud of Ramon, who was such a beautiful dancer. I loved watching him dance. We stayed a bit more for Ramon to receive compliments and to eat and drink a little more too. The restaurant was air-conditioned but outside the night was as steamy as a Turkish bath and the moon shone hotly on the river.

Afterwards, as we drove up the nearly empty streets towards Boedo and my apartment, a driver cut us off. Ramon suddenly turned into a raging bull. I couldn't believe it. He rolled down his window and yelled at the other driver, "Hey *pelotudo del orto*!" who yelled back, "*La puta que te parió!*" and then they both began a game of "chicken." They both slowed down and made to stop. I just knew they were going to get out of the cars and physically fight.

"*Baja un cambio!*" I told him. "Stop it, grow up! You're not a teenager." I was afraid of the portending violence, the drunken road rage that could end in tragedy.

He then yelled at me, "Don't tell me what to do! *No me rompas las bolas!*" Don't break my balls!

So I cried, "Que falta de respeto para mí! Don't you have any respect for me? Let me out! Let me out!" and moved to open the door, but he reached in front of me and slammed it shut, and then drove like a maniac straight to the apartment. Before he could park I jumped out and ran into the building, locking the door behind me, for all the good it might do. He had the keys. But now I could see how drunk he was. I hoped he would just go home.

But it wasn't long before he was upstairs and in the apartment, an enraged middle-aged man reeking of machismo and alcohol. "Get out! I don't want you here!" I yelled, backing into the kitchen. "*Boracho!* You're drunk and acting like a baby!"

And he hit me. I couldn't believe this was happening to me. He didn't hurt me, but he had hit me.

"Get out! *Dejame tranquila!* I never want to see you again! Go get some counseling. Just leave! Give me your keys!"

"If I had wanted to hurt you I would have," he said coldly, and then left, tossing the keys onto the floor. Even from the ninth floor, I could hear his old car roar off.

While I overlooked many things, I did have a line that could not be crossed: violence. No one had ever hit me before and no one would ever hit me again. It didn't matter if I were hurt or not, it was the intention behind the act.

He called countless times over the days that followed but I never answered. I knew his machismo would not let him apologize, but it didn't matter. I would not be abused.

After that night I went to the milongas I knew he didn't attend, like Canning and El Arranque. It wasn't fun, I didn't enjoy the dancing or being there. But I was stubborn and I had to live my life. Women flocked around me when they saw me alone and sad, and I told them the truth: he hit me so that was that. It was over. They hugged me and consoled me, and didn't seem the least surprised, but nothing helped. I felt stupid and so alone. The men avoided me. And of course, despite it all, I missed Ramon.

Laurence was again back in town, and he picked up on the fact that I was going to milongas alone. So we danced together, and when he asked me to meet him at a café the next night before going to El Beso, I agreed. We sat across from each other with our little cups of espresso with nothing to say. I didn't enjoy gazing and exploring his face like I did Ramon's, who had so many different expressions and was so very interesting to look at. But I was trying to find pleasure in doing other things, being with other people.

We walked across the street from the café to El Beso and sat separately. The old milongueros were lined up as usual in front of the bar. Now I noticed they periodically went to the men's room and came out rubbing their noses, like I had seen with Gavito at La Catedral, and frequently at another nearby milonga, Porteño y Bailarin. I had been oblivious for many years, but now I knew about the cocaine. Sometimes when I danced with one of them, they could hardly stand. Evidently in the milongas some dancers were addicted to more than the tango.

When the Pugliese tanda began, I stared at Laurence sitting across the floor in front of the mirrors, but he was looking elsewhere. He had talked so much about loving to dance Pugliese with me, and now he wasn't paying attention. So I left and went home.

Christmas Eve there was a party in La Cúpola, one of the distinctive red domes on the Plaza de Congreso that was often rented out to tourists. I had gone to a party there on my first BA trip, and with the invitation from a visiting New Yorker, Cristina and I made plans to go together. Luckily she had a car as otherwise there was no transportation until about 3am Christmas morning.

I had answered when Ramon called me earlier that day to wish me *Feliz Navidad.* He said he was going to counseling and would I meet him after midnight. He had to talk to me.

So I left Cristina and the party at the Cupola to meet Ramon in the dark Plaza. We walked up Rivadavia to the only café that was open and ordered espressos. He explained about the counseling and that he missed me. I was glad to see him, but I only said he should have thought of that before he acted like a wild drunken fool in the street. That I was sad and disappointed that he hadn't taken care of me at all—just the reverse. And I went back to Cristina and the party.

The day after Christmas I took the bus to my pilates class as usual. Because of the holidays the regular instructor wasn't there, and we had a substitute. I was glad the classes were continuing as I really enjoyed the workouts on the transformer and had been going three times a week for a year, even after I had moved to another barrio. And now, without my relationship or enjoyment at the milongas, I needed it more than ever.

The new teacher had us standing in a strange position on top of the table and I lost concentration and fell, hitting the legs of the table. I heard a loud crack, and all of a sudden I couldn't breathe. The pain was excruciating. The gym called an ambulance and one of the women in the class, María, went with me to the hospital. After the exam and tests, the doctor gave me my x-rays and told me I had two broken ribs and there was not much to do about it except wait for them to heal. He didn't recommend a "corset."

It hurt so much to talk, even to breathe, but I squeezed out, "Llama a Ramon," which María did. She took me home in a taxi and Ramon was there in a flash. He took total care of me—renting a walker, cooking, bathing me, taking me to the bathroom. I was completely helpless and in terrible pain. What would I have done without him? What would have happened to me? I supposed I would have had to hire someone I didn't know to live in and I would have worried about her stealing me blind while I was immobile in bed. But Ramon was there.

CHAPTER 23

I too hear stories of dancers who beat their dance partners. It's disgraceful!

—Tito Palumbo, Editor of *B.A. Tango*

January 2007

Ramon moved into the little second bedroom of the apartment. It was perfect for him because he brought in the TV and was happy just to be able to watch it from bed even though it was only a folding cot. And since he was a snorer and had a restless leg syndrome and I was such a light sleeper, we both could rest better in separate rooms, especially as I was in so much pain.

New Year's Eve Ramon went home to be with his family, but he was back with me by 2am, even though I told him I would be fine. I worried about him on the road New Year's with the drunks and maybe he would be one of them too. Other nights he went to dance as usual after preparing dinner, and I spent a lot of time sunning on the terrace. Phoebe was my constant companion. Was I jealous that Ramon went to milongas and came back smelling of other women's perfume? Absolutely not. I was grateful that he was taking on the burden of caring for me, and I wanted him to enjoy himself if he could.

During my homebound two months the priest from the Anglican Cathedral, St. John the Baptist, came to give me communion. My psychologist made weekly house calls and I demanded that Ramon sit in and participate to discuss his violence toward me. He said all of the right things, his body language was appropriate, he seemed to be listening, but I knew he would never take advice from a woman. When we talked about the sessions afterward, I could tell he had just gone through the motions. However I believed he understood he could never raise his hand against me again. I swore I would call the police although I knew the police wouldn't care about a man hitting a woman. In that macho culture it was routine. It was common to call a woman *histérica,* meaning she was crazy because she was a woman. I was surprised that no one else came to visit, no visiting foreign dancers I knew, or friends from the milonga. Maybe they were concerned about how Ramon and I were getting along, as they had all heard about the breakup.

Weirdly enough, once the pain eased, I was happy. I felt that this no-dancing time proved that my love for Ramon was more than merely loving to dance with him. I was glad, to see him every day, glad we were together again, and it didn't matter that he went dancing without me. Somehow, perhaps because I needed him, I forgave him for hitting me, or if not exactly pardoned, forgotten. (Deep down inside, and inadmissible even to myself, I wondered if my accident had been intentional on some level, a way for Ramon and me to get back together.)

I read a lot, grateful for my Kindle. Unfortunately Ramon didn't enjoy reading; he had never read a book. But it was amazing to me that for someone who had left school so young, he could read and write well and his spelling was perfect, as was his math (his memory for numbers was impressive). He had taught himself, and had learned much in the school of hard knocks, including literacy.

We watched some TV together, but mostly he watched sports—not just *fútbol* (Boca Juniors was his team), but tennis, boxing, golf, even fishing. He loved game shows that I couldn't abide. The only programs we enjoyed together were *Mr. Bean*, who made us laugh so hard it hurt my ribs, and *Bailando por un Sueño* (Dancing for a Dream). I originally thought that *Bailando* was the Argentine version of *Dancing with the Stars* but after a while it seemed like a parody. The judges looked like clowns and much screen time was spent in arguing. It was never about the dancing, but how scanty the women's costumes could be. The camera work was low to better show the bare buttocks of the *vedettes*, or starlets. Eventually I couldn't stand to watch it anymore.

When I watched TV alone, I enjoyed American programs like *Law and Order: SVU* and *Lost*. I especially looked for movies with scenes of L.A. and familiar locations and corners of Hollywood. Somehow it helped the homesickness. But I also appreciated Argentine programs that not only were entertaining, but that helped me understand the culture: musical broadcasts, cooking shows (Francis Malmann was my favorite), talk shows, and Argentine movies.

As soon as I could move around a bit on my own, I sat at my desk and tried to keep in touch with the rest of the world via the internet. And then I began to blog. I created *tangocherie* where I wrote posts about the tango and being an expat in BA.

There were quite a few bloggers in BA. I was amazed when I found them online. Some wrote about the tango, others about expat life, food, Buenos Aires and Argentina. One blogger, an American businessman, Frank Almeida, had married an Argentine woman and started a cookie business—Sugar and Spice. He invited all of the BA bloggers to his factory in Palermo to meet and sample his wares. I got lost getting there, and ended up climbing over the railroad tracks, but eventually I made it to his cheery orange-decorated showroom and met several of the bloggers I had only known virtually before. Most of them were American, but a few were British and there were local writers as well. Like volunteering at the church and going to milongas, blogging helped me to feel more connected to my adopted home.

Another blog called out for fellow bloggers to write about their ideal day in Buenos Aires. I had done with gusto all of the things he mentioned in his own description of a perfect day—but as a visitor. Now I lived in BA and my own "perfect day" would be less touristy: wake up without the alarm, stuff myself on fresh fruit and coffee, enjoy the gorgeous view from my terrace in Boedo while doing some herb gardening, teach a tango class or two, rest, pet my cat, clean up, go to a milonga with Ramon and dance and greet my friends, then come home and enjoy a good steak with a bottle of vino tinto. For variety, after the milonga I would relish a seafood dinner in a Spanish restaurant with champagne.

Writing the blog was excellent therapy for me. I found inspiration everywhere for posts, so although my body was housebound, my mind was active. I even wrote a post after being inspired by *CSI: Miami*, titled "Here's What I Want You to Do…"

C.S.I. Miami *is one of my favorite TV shows. I love the computer tweaked Miami colors, the interesting characters, and especially David Caruso's* Horatio Caine, *ex-homicide detective turned Crime Scene Investigator. Standing in a graceful slouch, he takes off his sunglasses, looks at you and says in a calm and compelling voice,*

"Here's what I want you to do." And you trust him and you're not afraid anymore. And you want to do exactly what he's going to tell you to do, and you do it.

That's what happens when someone calm and graceful, musical and confident takes a woman in his arms to dance tango. He doesn't say anything, but says everything. His body tells you what he wants you to do and you do it with pleasure. You feel safe, and free. And it's now that you can fully express yourself and the music because he has taken care of all the basics and you know he will take care of you, and of absolutely everything.

It took two months for me to mend, and by then I had a beautiful tan. By the time I returned to the milongas, I looked like I had spent the summer in Mar del Plata. Still, though my ribs were healed, I was not overdoing it, just Club Español on Thursdays and Los Consagrados on Saturdays. We had several students too, and I was back at Toastmasters. I put the difficulties of the past months behind me.

February 2007

Even though I had moved to BA to escape financial worries, I still had them. The inflation rate was so high in Argentina, and I didn't know how to reduce my expenses. I was frightened about the upcoming July when the rent would go up 25% and of having to pay twelve months in advance in cash.

I had wanted to buy a cheap used piano but when Ramon took me to the Salvation Army store to look at one, it was a ruin, missing keys, a complete disaster. While I was there I looked at men's clothes to buy to give away in the Ropería, but unlike in the States, all of the donated clothes were torn and stained as well as expensive. So we left empty-handed.

The real problem I realized was that I had lived longer than

I expected to—next month it would be ten years longer than Jack, ten years longer than my father, who had both died at 54. I had planned to be dead when my money ran out and I hadn't prepared for my own survival.

I thought about teaching English, but the problem was that even though the inflation was terrible, labor was cheap. The most I could make would be $5usd per hour, and getting around in this city really wore me out. Since I broke my ribs I couldn't take the bus because of the bumps and jostling, so I tried to stay home as much as possible. I did apply to a new magazine as a writer, but they wanted only young people, the hot new voices. There was plenty of discrimination in Argentina: ageism, sexism, racism.

Teaching tango and doing tango tours seemed the best idea, but the competition for students was intense. Anybody who had ten lessons looked for foreigners in order to "teach" them. There were tango classes in the lobbies of hotels, side rooms of tango shoe stores, basements of bookstores, back rooms of cafés. Argentina in fact was a kind of jungle, with everyone scratching and fighting for funds and a place in the pecking order, and a way to survive.

CHAPTER 24

I still love that man to this day. I believe we were soulmates. His life was troubled and he was burdened with having to live in the shadows. He never asked me for anything. I know, to this day, he is waiting for me to return.

—Anonymous, Milonguero online survey

March 2007

March 8 was the International Day of the Woman. Men on the street wished *Feliz Día* to women as they passed, and some milongas even handed out flowers to the ladies. In Argentina everyone had their day, including photographers, brewers, journalists, editors, sculptors, investigators, decorators, translators, taxi drivers, graphic designers, professors, football players, bankers, biologists, inventors, dentists, actors, pharmacists, psychologists, architects, and teachers—there's even an unofficial *Día del Boludo* (Day of the Asshole)—but this particular one for women made me mad. Women got one day and men got 364? Didn't Argentine women want more than a flower? To me this "holiday" just proved how unequal women were, how "special" we were, and we were half of the world.

Of course, there was an official Day of the Tango (December 11), but not of the tango teacher. Ramon and I loved teaching the tango; we loved that in our small way we were helping to maintain the beauty and profundity of the historical tango, the real tango of real people, along with the culture and the codigos.

We didn't do the common thing of dancing with beginners in order to convince them they needed our classes. We didn't paper the milonga with our cards as so many *profesores* did. We didn't search out foreign people to talk them into learning our milonguero style technique from us. We danced, and we waited for people to approach us because they liked how we danced. Watching the floor from our table in the milongas, we said, oh, if only we could just correct her knees or his head or their posture, their dancing would vastly improve. But we waited to be asked.

Many times locals pointed us out across the salon when people inquired about teachers. And so we followed an understated way of enlarging our student base—mostly by word of mouth and recommendations, and my blog helped too. We figured if they liked the way we danced, then what they wanted to learn was the music, rhythm, the walk, connection, and the embrace. And of course, in BA, it was so important for the man to learn to navigate a crowded floor. If someone wanted to learn the Dreaded 8-Count Basic that was a beginner's class staple, or flashy *boleos* and *ganchos,* we were not the teachers for them.

Our student base grew by leaps and bounds, boosted by the reviews on TripAdvisor. For several months we were the Number Two Attraction in Buenos Aires, just below horseback riding in the park. We had eighty-eight five-star reviews! I received many inquiring emails, and I spent a great deal of time answering them, explaining what the lessons consisted of and didn't consist of, and quoting prices for classes, tours, accompaniment, and how to pay. At least by the time the students booked with us they knew what they would get, and everyone loved what they received from us. It was very gratifying. Ramon had a saying as the students bid us farewell—"You came to us as students, and are leaving as friends." And sometimes they would even tear up when we said goodbye. I felt so lucky to be a part of that.

We had developed lesson plans for various types of classes that always included some tango history, a few of the most important codigos, explanation, and demonstration of the three rhythms—tango (2 x 4), vals (3 x 4), and milonga (4 x 4), as well as basic floorcraft. But the majority of the class time was spent on actual dancing. For advanced students the classes included musicality and how to dance differently to different orchestras. It was ideal that we were a teaching couple because that way the students always had a partner. If it were a private with a man, he danced with me and Ramon corrected while I gave feedback on the lead and how it felt. Ramon also danced with him so he could feel how to lead. If it were a private with a woman, the student danced with Ramon and I showed her fine points of following and the steps that only women did, like ochos. If it were a couple, we danced with both of them. If it were a group class, we had everyone dance with each other, but we always danced with each one of them too. We taught a large group of dancers from the Dominican Republic, a medium group from Russia, a small family group of adults and young children from Scotland, and a graduating class from Westpoint—we taught them all. We even taught regularly at the U.S. Embassy!

For many foreign students, this would be the only time they would spend time with a milonguero and get to know him a little, especially if they didn't know Spanish. I was busy teaching, explaining, translating, dancing. We took our classes very seriously, and I admired that Ramon wanted to share what he knew and had learned on his own during his forty years in the milongas. And since we had students from all over the world, he felt like they would take back what they'd learned from us and from dancing in BA and it would help to contradict the "tango gringo" that was overwhelmingly popular in other countries.

Meeting people from many nations, chatting (usually in English), often inviting them to a barbecue on my terrace—all helped me to feel less lonely and isolated living at the bottom of the world in another culture and language. My blog helped as well, because I was communicating with global folks who were interested in me and what I had to say about life in BA, and who usually left insightful comments. I felt a part of a community, despite the distance, and an international community thanks to the internet. Plus the librarian came out in me as on my blog I explained many aspects of tango only obvious in BA, such as the codigos, and how the milongas worked, tango happenings in town, what to wear, how to sit, how to gaze into the eyes of strangers.

Ramon worked like a Trojan during our Tango Tours to La Boca, the Mataderos Gaucho Fair, San Telmo, and milonga accompaniments or "taxi dancing." The term "taxi dancer" wasn't used in tango until recently, coming from the cabarets of the '20's and '30's where young women danced with strangers for tickets and encouraged the purchase of champagne. The popular torch song, "Ten Cents a Dance" was about this custom.

On my first trip to Buenos Aires in 1998, very astutely, the organizer hired local dancers, "teaching assistants," to dance with us during the classes and at the milongas. Not only were they paid a salary, they were also able to make separate deals with us, the tourists, for private lessons. One male assistant even went back to the States to marry one of the tourists from the group.

When big tango festivals began several years ago, people traveled all over the world to dance. But, as usual in social dancing, there were more women in attendance than men. These women were often unhappy about not having someone to dance with in the classes that they paid large sums of money for. So the organizers started bringing in young male dancers from the local community, and the women paid for them. Then at the festival milongas, where there were so many more women as well, it was a short jump to figure out taxi dancers were needed at night too. Soon the practice became highly organized, with the taxi dancers wearing special tee shirts and the women buying tickets and choosing whom they wanted to dance with. Sometimes there were also a few young women taxis as well.

When all of these tango dancing foreign women then descended on the milongas of Buenos Aires, where they were already more women than men, it wasn't hard to see that paying a taxi dancer to dance with you might be preferable to sitting planted in your chair all night, especially for the tourists who didn't know the codigos or how to carry off the cabeceo. So the profession of "milonga accompaniment" was born. There were now several websites devoted to the taxi dancer business in BA.

The problem was that, because they were cheaper, organizers hired (usually for 20 pesos). young twenty-something boys who were beginning dancers themselves. And most of the foreign women who requested this service were over fifty. You could spot these couples a kilometer away at the milongas: older bejeweled foreign lady/boy in a suit looking uncomfortable. The taxi was used to dancing in an open hold and Nuevo-style steps with fancy figures, the client wanted the close-embrace improvised milonguero style that she had traveled to Buenos Aires for. Everyone could see what the arrangement was, nobody else would ask the lady to dance, and it was all a bit awkward.

When women wrote to me asking about our "tango services," sometimes I suggested they might want Ramon to accompany them to milongas. Often they were horrified. "I don't need to pay someone to dance with me," they would say. "I have yet to stoop that low!" I felt like a pimp trying to explain the benefits of hiring Ramon, how the codigos worked, and how an unknown woman had to be seen dancing in order to be asked to dance by the locals, unless of course she were young and beautiful.

Ramon often was asked to be a taxi dancer, but he preferred the term, "milonga accompaniment." He always asked me to explain to the inquiring woman that he would sit with the men across the room, and the lady would sit with the women. He would cabeceo her at pre-arranged times (not every tanda), and she would have the chance to dance with others as well. Dancing several tandas with a great dancer like Ramon was a learning experience, and everyone watched whom Ramon danced with, so this helped the client to be seen and to get more dances later. Normally this arrangement was for three hours and the client also paid expenses (transportation, entrada, a soft drink).

Ramon did his very best to explain everything and to see that the students had a good time, the women he accompanied to milongas would dance a lot, and they all would leave with a greater understanding of tango dance, history, music, and culture. Plus they always had lots of fun. I myself learned a lot from his explanations too, about tango history and the music. Ramon could taxi dance a whole group of women and they all ended up pleased and satisfied.

People asked me if Ramon and the other milongueros were ashamed to be doing taxi dancing. It was honest work, Ramon needed the money, and it was helpful for the women to know what good tango was all about. Was I jealous when he went out to milongas to accompany foreign women who were paying him? I also did taxi dancing on occasion and it was true that I thought Ramon was jealous when I was seen dancing and sitting with other men. But when he was working, I went to bed with my computer and my cat and was happy.

Ramon also helped me around the house, did all the cooking, shopping, cleaning, and driving me everywhere. He found a discarded washing machine in the street that he fixed and installed in the quincho, and he refinished the parquet floor, haggled with the cable service; whatever needed doing, he did. Ramon really took such good care of me. He would scour the city to find the strawberries that I loved to put on my morning cereal. At the same time, he completely took care of himself—washing, ironing, mending his own clothes. I felt we were a partnership, a team. I did what I could, and he did what he could. Maybe his handiwork wasn't pretty, but the end result of using paper clips, super glue, and duct tape was that the item or problem in question was fixed. He was like a Cubano—making something out of nothing. Without him I couldn't have managed so many years in Buenos Aires.

We both worked hard, but I let Ramon keep the tuition and tour fees after the deduction of expenses (we always included admission fees, transportation, and lunch, which I fronted).

He never asked, but since I did have my small pension and he had no other income, I felt it was fair.

CHAPTER 25

I wish I were water to evaporate with the heat and rain on your skin to taste the sweetness of your body

—piropo

May 2007

Sometimes after the milonga we went to a buffet restaurant, a *tenedor libre*. Normally I didn't like to go to those: in the summer I worried that the food wasn't refrigerated properly and in the winter I worried that someone had sneezed or coughed on it. But one on Avenida San Juan was always packed with people and it seemed clean, and sometimes we went when I wanted to eat out. The buffets were cheap. Ramon and I always ate different things—I went for the Chinese dishes (the buffets were always Chinese-owned, just like the mini-supermarkets) and he ate Argentinian dishes—meat and cheese and jello. We couldn't afford to go often to restaurants, so usually we went shopping in the supermarket and he cooked. He preferred that anyway, and he was an excellent cook. Plus he always cleaned up the kitchen afterwards.

But when we did go out, he wasn't always a good dining companion. He was particular about the dishes he ordered, instructing the waiter about this or that. And if the food or the service wasn't to his liking, he made a scene. I often said, "Please don't make a big deal and ruin our time out together. Just relax and try to enjoy being with me in a nice place. It's my treat anyway." This happened a few times at our neighborhood hangout, Café Margot, a Bar Notable. Once he ordered sweetbreads with a green onion sauce, but there weren't enough onions in the sauce. But I see now that my reminding him that I was paying never helped the situation. But it got so that I didn't want to go out to eat anymore. Sometimes he liked to buy a pizza and faena (kind of a chick-pea mush cake that Argentines liked with pizza) on the way home from Los Consagrados, or once in a great while we would order delivery of little many-flavored empanadas from Homero's that we both liked. But the happiest meals were when Ramon cooked at home.

One dismal winter day he planned to drive me around to get various chores accomplished, but it was pouring rain and he didn't have windshield wipers so I didn't even want him to drive to his home to Banfield. We had students calling for classes and a tango tour scheduled for Sunday. Monday I had to pick up lab results from one place, and go to another for a kidney ultrasound, and then waited to see the gyno with all my papers to find out when one of my surgeries would be, and then we had a new couple in the afternoon for a private. Staying home was enough.

July 2007

Ramon was unwell. The Pepto Bismol I gave him came right back up. Ramon didn't take care of himself and he still hadn't got his gall bladder checked out. I was so frightened because of my memories of Jack being sick.

It was wet and freezing cold so I was grateful that the pharmacy delivered something he wanted that seemed to help a bit. When he did sleep, he was snoring. So I made plans to take him to TV Salud to get his gall bladder removed. We were being inundated with requests to perform and to teach, so apart from anything else, he needed to get into shape so he could dance and teach, his bread and butter.

Clínica San Camilo in Parque Centenario was a beautiful, old, extremely clean Catholic hospital complete with nuns and a Mother Superior. The usual hospital "chapel" was a large, glorious old church. Ramon had a private room and the couch was made into a bed for me. His sister came, as well as one of his sons and his daughter. Luckily it was caught just in time as his gall bladder was ready to burst. The surgery went a bit longer than expected, but it went well. Ramon had problems coming out of the anesthesia however, and I was glad I was allowed to stay the night and in fact was encouraged to do so. I was grateful to be there to calm his panic as he was waking up. The doctor assured us that many patients had difficulties from the anesthesia, more than from the surgery.

I was grateful that finally Ramon's digestive suffering would be over—as long as he changed his diet to less fat. I had bought him a plaque of his favorite saint—Sacred Heart of Jesus—at the Don Bosco shop in Boedo, and put it over his hospital bed. He was never without the Sacred Heart of Jesus prayer card in his wallet. He thought of it as his protector saint. When the Mother Superior came to visit, he proudly pointed out the Sacred Heart plaque, saying he was being watched over, and Mother said, "And so is San Camilo watching over you." I loved that, being there, and knowing Ramon was well taken care of spiritually as well as physically.

I liked the hospital, the beautiful grounds, and the order so much that when I found out they had an Alzheimer's wing, I made Ramon promise that when the time came for me, he would see to it that I was admitted there. With my mother and my mother's mother suffering and dying of that horrible, insidious disease, I felt better imagining living out my last days in the company of San Camilo, and the Daughters of San Camilo. Every time I forgot someone's name or what I did the previous week, I thought, uh-oh, this is the beginning of the end. Ramon swore that he would always take care of me if I became incapacitated like my mom and grandma, and I believed him. Each time we saw an old couple holding hands crossing the street, we both said, "There go Ramon and Cherie, if we're lucky. *Si tenemos suerte.*" And whenever we passed old folks' homes, I always pointed them out, commenting on how many stars they had on their signs, and he always promised only five stars for me. It was a comfort.

If I lived in Los Angeles there would be no one. I was sure my sons would see that I was in a "home" if necessary, but other than that I think I'd be on my own. I've always been independent and they are used to that. They have consistently been busy with their own lives. Maybe it's my fault, maybe I didn't bring them up right, maybe I should have had a daughter too.

CHAPTER 26

I'm building a pirate ship to sail through your lips and enter into your heart.

—piropo

August 2007

Soon I would be having minor surgery myself (a biopsy), so I spent a week doing pre-op tests, plus teaching students in town for the Campeonato. There was a magazine that wanted to interview me because I was the only foreigner in the Campeonato Finals the previous year and it was timely. God, I needed to get to the hairdresser.

A sign that I was indeed aging was my frozen shoulder. While I was exercising something sort of popped and the pain got worse with time. The doctor had me buy a syringe and a vial of zylocaine from the pharmacy and he injected it, which helped. Now I was going to physical therapy and doing the prescribed exercises half an hour a day. They wanted to use magnetic treatments on me, but couldn't because of my two breast cancers.

We went to Chiqué and I couldn't embrace with my left arm but we danced anyway. People went to dance in the milongas with disabilities, arms in casts, patches on eyes. Al Pacino's blind tango in "Scent of a Women" wasn't unlikely at all. Several dancers in the milonga had Parkinson's. Once hooked, tango dancers couldn't go very long without a fix.

One of my favorite partners used to be an old, fat, bald man a head shorter than I was. I loved to dance with him because of his feeling and sensitivity to the music, his secure balance, his musicality, his pure joy in the dance. But even though I had thought I was safe with him because of his age, that we were simply friends who enjoyed dancing together, he still wanted to seduce me. I guessed it was impossible in that macho environment to be friends with a man. He had told me he was in his middle seventies, but when he passed away, I learned he had been eight-eight.

I had the biopsy, a small part of my inside body was removed because it was pre-cancerous, and I was turned loose. Like an old friend had once said, after fifty, it's patch, patch, patch!

October 2007

In Los Angeles, since it's always "spring" year round, we used to talk about the four seasons we had: earthquake, fire, flood, and mudslide. The annual Santa Ana winds marked the season of fire. So if you included the wind, the L.A. seasons were the four basic elements: earth, fire, water, and air.

In the tango world of Buenos Aires, in which I'd lived for almost four years, there were only two seasons: tourist and "quiet." Right now we were moving into the highpoint of the first tango tourist season—October and November. It was springtime, the weather was beautiful, and tango tourists from all over the globe could hit the milongas for a month and then get home to enjoy the holidays with their families. The autumn of March and April was the same. During those times there were also tango conferences, festivals, and "tango weeks" put on to attract foreigners to BA. Many people I knew came for the two months of each season every year. And some even returned in August for the tango championships and the festivals that promoted tango tourism in Argentina.

There were good and bad reasons for visiting Buenos Aires at these times. The most obvious was the weather: Spring and fall had the best weather, winter was chilly and summer was blazing, humidly hot. And since our winter corresponded with the summer of most of the countries of the visiting dancers, it made sense that tourists didn't want to forgo summer at home to endure a nasty winter instead.

The other factor was that apart from the tourist seasons, the milongas were tranquil with only the locals attending. There was less energy, but also less competition to dance with porteños/as. And there was more space on the floor.

In spring and fall, the total character of most of the milongas was changed by the influx of outsiders and tourist groups. Some local people only went out to dance when the tourists were in town. Then there were more people to dance with—and more competition.

For me, personally, I enjoyed the visitors so much that I wished I could spread them throughout the year so that I would have more time to spend with each one. On the other hand, when everybody came at once, it was a reason to have a party. Since Ramon loved to cook and entertain, and he did it so well, we had many lunches and dinners on the terrace. If it rained, we just moved the tables indoors and kept on eating and having fun. We always danced afterwards.

One large party we had however, left a bad taste in my mouth because of how some of the Argentine guests behaved. We had invited a couple from the milonga—the man was married but he had a regular girlfriend whom he was always with. She couldn't come to the party and so he came alone. But during the entire evening he was trying to seduce a friend of mine from Australia who wasn't the least bit interested. She got very annoyed at him and I was disgusted. I asked Ramon to talk to him, to tell him to leave her alone as she felt harassed, but he wouldn't do it. Men only encouraged each other to go after women, not discouraged them. It wasn't macho. But it was embarrassing to me, that a guest was uncomfortable in my home.

Another couple, also tango teachers, were marketing themselves to our friends and students outside on the terrace. It was rude and ungracious that while accepting our hospitality, they were trying to take students from us on the sly. It was the viveza criolla; nothing at all mattered but personal gain—and you were admired for it.

Live orchestras rarely performed at the traditional milongas. The milongueros liked the music they were used to—the thousands of recordings of songs from the Golden Age by the great orchestras. But wisely some of the modern orchestras used the same arrangements of the old masters and it was often very exciting. I especially liked Los Reyes del Tango who played the music of Juan D'Arienzo.

One evening there was live music by Los Reyes at a milonga we attended. I was struck by how much like an acoustic piano the electronic one on stage sounded. It was amazing. So afterwards, I asked Ramon to talk to the pianist about the piano—make, model, where he got it, if he liked it.

I was lucky there was one for sale on eBay, as it was made

in Italy and no longer manufactured. It was fantastic, with a real touch of an acoustic piano and a full 88 key keyboard with three pedals. It had other bells and whistles too, but I didn't care about them. At last I had a piano I could play. And play I did.

I got out the same stack of music I had been carrying around all of my life—some scores had even belonged to my father and my grandmother—which I had dragged to France and Mexico too. I had always delighted in playing my beautiful Knabe parlor grand in the living room of my old house in Los Feliz while Jack was working in his study or reading in the family room. He always said how much he enjoyed listening to me play. And in those days I accompanied my boys playing solos on their horns, and singers at church, where I also played duets with the organist on occasion. But now I loved playing the many tangos I had collected over the years from the music store in El Centro. Sometimes Ramon sang along.

November 2007

In broad daylight two blocks from my apartment in quiet, blue collar Boedo, I was walking to church on Estados Unidos, and a kid of twelve or thirteen ran up behind me and grabbed my purse. I wouldn't let go, and he kicked me in the stomach to the ground and we struggled some more until the cheap plastic strap broke and he ran off down the street. I yelled and screamed, but only too late did neighbors come out of their houses.

Thank God I wasn't more hurt, and that my passport hadn't been in the bag. But my camera that I had waited five years for, with undownloaded videos of Ramon's performance the night before at La Ideal, was. I was lucky, that I wasn't badly hurt, that more wasn't lost—don't we always tell ourselves that? But I felt violated and so very frustrated and angry. And so helpless. But this wasn't an unusual occurrence—there were constant petty crimes of mugging and stealing, as in most places where the people have so little.

CHAPTER 27

I met my milonguero in London...I've learned a lot about the chamuyo and would strongly recommend that women did not have an affair with an Argentine milonguero.

—Anonymous, Milonguero online survey response

January 2008

A glamorous restaurant in Palermo, a group of over one hundred New Yorkers, a fabulous set menu with cocktails and wines—and Ramon y Cherie!

We were contacted months in advance about doing a "lecture-demo" performance for this high-end American tour group. The organizer of this very special tour had called us from the States to organize a presentation of the "real" tango Argentino. He wanted the group to see more of tango than the dinner show at the Faena Hotel in Puerto Madero, where they were going on their first night. We planned carefully to make it as instructive and entertaining as possible. We would have anyway, but they were paying us a lot of money. The tour leader completely won my admiration, not only for this educated and broad-minded point of view, but for finding and hiring us.

However the Casa Cruz venue, a large restaurant, left a lot to be desired in terms of presenting a show. It was too big and dark, with huge vases of massive flower arrangements ruining the sight lines. They built a little stage for us at one end, but with those flowers reaching almost to the high ceiling, many people would have blocked views. The ambiance was rather depressing, probably because it was trying to look expensive and elegant. Ramon called it a *velatorio,* a funeral parlor, especially because of the crosses—the motif due to the owner's name being Cruz.

We contracted another couple, Vilma y Osvaldo, and planned our presentation to include a little history of the tango, milonga codigos with demonstrations, and exhibitions. And then complete the show with a tango class for volunteers.

We had to be flexible about when and how long to do the various segments, but because we had done our homework and had DJ Dany make us two CDs with all of our music in order, including Tango Negro and La Chacarera, it went beautifully. And the mini-class was so popular we had to repeat it three times. I learned something about myself too. Our show was bilingual, but because the audience was American, I translated everything Ramon said, plus I contributed ideas and anecdotes that I knew the Americans would enjoy. So I had the microphone for the entire time. And I felt the power! It was amazing for me, who was so afraid of public speaking, I didn't want to relinquish the mic. Of course I was speaking about my favorite topic, the tango, but I could have gone on and on. Toastmasters worked! But luckily no one had to get the hook.

April 2008

I had been working for many years on my memoir, *The Church of Tango,* but I needed feedback. Many bad things had happened to me during the period I was writing about, but I was determined not to whine or complain. I had some exciting stories to tell of my life in several countries, and my goal was to offer an uplifting response to tragedy as well as a good read. And I just couldn't do it in a vacuum by myself.

I was grateful that I found a group of like-minded individuals from several countries to discuss writing in English. We met once a week in a café on Corrientes. How wonderful to have some support and to make friends with creative and sincere people who lived in BA year round and who didn't all dance tango.

I was grateful, too, for my blog, *tangocherie*. It had begun as just a casual thing, a hobby, an opportunity to express myself and to share information (as was my wont as a librarian) about BA and the tango, especially when I was housebound with my broken ribs. But after a while writing the three posts a week became important to me. Sometimes a topic would suddenly sprout from my fingers, but other times it was a challenge. I thought quite a bit about what I wanted to say. And then there had to be illustrations, and it was fun searching and finding the suitable ones. Occasionally I wrote about controversial topics and the writers' group would tell me if I had gone too far, although it was my blog and my opinions. No one had to read it, but thousands did. But the most wonderful part was the comments, which often led to real conversations. I felt connected to the world, at least the international world of the tango, and that helped to ease my loneliness and the knowledge that in truth, I lived so far away at the end of the world, a stranger in a strange land.

One night after the milonga, Ramon and I were interviewed for an article in a tango magazine. Rather Ramon was interviewed. The two men were just talking away and

I couldn't get a word in edgewise. I had to say, *espera espera espera, por favor.* Wait, wait! Because I had answers too, and I also had opinions and ideas, which no one was interested in as I was a woman, and even worse, a foreign woman.

Equally when Ramon and I went out to dinner, I didn't exist for the waiter. Often I didn't even get a menu, but that was okay, because I knew the extremely limited Argentine Master Menu by heart. But even if it was a restaurant where the waiter knew me and when I went alone we exchanged besitos and conversation, when a woman was with a man, she ceased to exist. Riding in a taxi with a man was just the same. The woman didn't dare to tell the driver where to go, or to have any kind of conversation with him if a man accompanied her. She was invisible. And middle-aged tango tourist women complained about being invisible to men in their home countries. But in Argentina they were only ignored when they were with a man.

CHAPTER 28

El Gaucho

My glory is to live as free as the bird of the sky, I do not nest in this soil where there is so much to suffer; and no one has to follow me when I take flight.

—verso gauchesco

May 2008

Sometimes we experience moments of grace, probably when we least expect them. But for me they always seemed to happen at the Feria de Mataderos. Part of our work with students was to offer tours to the Mataderos "gaucho fair" on the city limits where the cattle auctions and slaughter-houses used to be. Every fine Sunday except in summertime when it was too hot for the horses, a regional fair of foods and handicrafts from all over Argentina takes place in the little plaza surrounded by colonial arched buildings in various states of disrepair. These excursions were very popular with visiting tango dancers who weren't quite sure where or when to go and how to get there, especially if they didn't speak Spanish.

Anna, a tango student from Albuquerque, booked the day with us for one Sunday in May. The weather forecast was good, and we had checked several times that the fair was open despite the swine flu scare that had closed schools and had overrun the public hospitals.

We arrived early as usual; if you came too late, the restaurants would run out of meat! Before the live performances began on the stage, ordinary folks danced in the street to recorded music. I noticed a middle-aged woman beautifully dancing *La Zamba* by herself, swirling and twirling her handkerchief in a lovely flirtatious manner. Then suddenly, a tall, thin, handsome gray-goateed man bounded out of the crowd and became her partner, pulling a white handkerchief from his pocket. Their dance was so gorgeous and elegant, and so natural, like the tango should be danced. When the dance finished, he disappeared back into the crowd and was gone. It was magical.

Dark clouds were gathering, so the next stop was the *Criollo Museum*. Ramon knew much about gaucho history and living in the countryside, and he explained the exhibits interestingly and with humor, while I did my best to translate for Anna. We saw a recreation of a typical gaucho's simple *rancho*, a *pulperia* where he drank, and then, in the courtyard when heavy rain unexpectedly began to fall, a real gaucho brushing his horse, Rodrigo. The gaucho, dressed in traditional work clothes of *bombacha* (full pantaloons), cotton shirt, neck kerchief, wide belt, and *boina*, a type of beret cap, gave me a sugar lump so I could make friends with Rodrigo. After that, we didn't spend much time in the gallery displaying all the different meat cuts of Argentina, which disappointed Ramon because he loved to talk about beef. He could go on forever pointing out various cuts and how to cook them in front of the large poster of a side of beef. But I pulled him away probably to Anna's relief.

At the top of my list of things I loved about Argentina was the gaucho life and history, and especially as it related to the tango. I loved the mystique and above all, the outfits—the lace trimmings, colorful ponchos, and a beautiful *falcon*, or knife, tucked in the back of their wide belts embellished with coins.

Gauchos today correspond to the American cowboy, in that they still live life with their horses, which in the province of Buenos Aires, they keep at home. At Mataderos, when it wasn't raining, they rode on Sundays in a competition of the *sortija*, the winner earning a purse.

Outside the museum, it abruptly began to hail golf balls as musicians rushed under the arcades with their guitars and mandolins. Strumming turned into playing and humming became singing of traditional songs and folklore; the crowd, waiting for finer weather, joined in. Ramon belted out the familiar sad songs with gusto in his resonant baritone.

Booths were being dismantled in the downpour, the stage was wet and barren, there wasn't a gaucho or horse in sight, and it was freezing cold. We always included a parrilla lunch in our tours, and so we went to our favorite one where usually we sat outside and watched the gaucho games. But because of the weather we were happy to sit inside the old white-tiled workshop, cozy despite its history as a slaughterhouse. The huge hooks used for hanging beef carcasses years ago now had antique utensils, an old drum, an iron, a candle chandelier hanging from them, with a bin of hot coals in the middle of the floor to keep us warm.

Our lunch of vacio and asado and chorizos came in steamy hot from the parrilla outside, accompanied by scorching hot French fries. We had the two bottles of vino tinto from the nearby ArgenChino supermarket because it was superior to that sold in the restaurant, and no one minded. The waitress brought us jelly glasses and a corkscrew, and was relaxed and jovial, as there wasn't much work to do. All the people enjoying lunch in the comfortable and friendly room seemed content to be there.

Since the stands weren't able to sell their wares outside, some vendors came inside to us, and our student was thrilled to buy a beautiful pair of leather boots for only 40 pesos.

Since Mataderos was the old slaughterhouse district of BA, their social club was named Nuevo Chicago. All that the Argentines knew of Chicago, U.S.A., were the mafia and the stockyards. We thought of dropping in to dance at the club's weekly "baile" because at least it was dry and indoors, but as we peeked in the windows and saw the hundreds of empty tables and heard the loud cumbia music, we kept on going.

While Ramon went to look for a taxi, an old man descended from the bus and stared straight at Anna and me. With a gorgeous smile revealing only a few teeth, he proceeded to give us a heart-warming piropo: *Ah, at last I see the sun come out when I look at you two beautiful ladies!* We both looked like bundled up Esquimos, but as we got into the taxi, we had warm smiles on our faces.

The gaucho figures strongly in the history and life of Argentina. Centuries ago when there was wild cattle roaming the country, the gaucho made his living by herding and selling them, banding together with his comrades to get a job done, and then going off after his solitary life again. Each man was allowed to round up 12,000 heads. When a cow was killed, the gaucho threw the tongue on the fire and ate that, so as to not ruin the carcass he needed to sell. He lived on beef and mate (an herb tea), and had the company of a "china" (country girl) and his guitar.

When the pampas began to be fenced in and owned by grand estancias in the 19th century, the gauchos had to look for another type of work. Some took jobs at the estancias, and many came to Buenos Aires and had to wear closed toed shoes for the first time in their lives, as the gaucho boots left their toes free. It was at this time that the tango began, and first danced by gauchos, sailors, ex-slaves, street toughs, and dandies.

Aside from his skill on a horse, the gaucho prided himself on his skill with the asado, or barbecue, which was truly an art in Argentina. He didn't use charcoal, but wood, and kept moderating the temperature of the fire by adding and subtracting the coals. He added coarse salt during the slow cooking to keep the meat from drying out, right before he turned it over, bones down. All parts of the animal were eaten, including the fat. In Argentina only the men were asadores. Ramon thought of himself as a gaucho because of his childhood in Tucuman, growing up close to animals and the land. And he was a magnificent asador, always earning guests' applause at our rooftop barbecues.

CHAPTER 29

The true milonguero is a respectful gentleman in all respects. His counterpart, the imposter 'tango dancer' is the most despicable of reptiles and I believe BsAs is crawling with them.

—Anonymous, Milonguero online survey response

July 2008

The government raised export taxes and the country fell into even more chaos. Highways were blocked all over the country, people were stuck out in nowhere with no way to return. Not much food was arriving in BA and what there already was had jacked-up prices. Supermarkets put limits on the number of staples you could buy. The banks didn't have any cash, and I had to come up with enough cash to pay six months rent in advance, due soon. When the ATMs had cash, they only allowed you to take out $100usd at a time, and then charged an $18usd fee on top of that. Banks and offices were closed because of the stop in transportation and the huge mess made by demonstrators.

The city was once again covered in smoke from farmers burning their crops in protest and dissidents burning trash and tires in the streets. I was afraid to leave the apartment as I had been so sick in April from breathing the foul air. A girlfriend had her laptop stolen when she went out into the streets to record the civil disorder.

Phoebe passed away the same week, in a horrible, agonizing way. I loved her so much, I couldn't have made this journey without her. I didn't understand why she had to endure such agony, why the vet let her suffer so while I sat sobbing in the waiting room. I had to scream and beg for her to be put out of her misery. It wasn't right. And then I couldn't just leave her there to be thrown away. Ramon found a box and picked her up, and we took her to the country and buried her under a tree with a prayer. Life was indeed short, change inevitable, and love fleeting.

Ramon never had been around cats before, but he had fallen in love with Phoebe and had even found a rescue cat at the vet's to take home to his family. He named her Manchi, "Spotty," because she was a white cat with brown patches. He did the correct thing of having her spayed. The animal societies offered free spay clinics, but I was horrified to learn that Argentines didn't usually neuter male pets! Castration was too horrific to contemplate, I supposed, even for dogs and cats.

Ramon, however, a man with many responsibilities, was a responsible man. Even on the street with strangers, he was alert to help when help was needed and perhaps nobody else even noticed. If anyone fell on the street or in the milonga, he was the first person to offer help at their side. He had a wonderful way with children and animals and plants—a telling quality in my book. I totally trusted him—an honest man in a dishonest society. Without him I wouldn't have stayed in Argentina. I couldn't have done. Phoebe was gone, and now I needed Ramon.

With everyone knowing I had a partner, a man to "protect"

me, I felt freer to dress as I wanted. I don't think I ever went over the top, but I had no fear that something tight or low cut would give the wrong impression because it was obvious I was accompanied. I felt shielded from all of the cultural machismo that I had originally appreciated but which, once I could see it for what it was, began to bother me. Only Ramon's machismo affected me now—not that of every man I met.

But when he drank and the machismo came out…I wanted to run away. All the way home to Los Angeles.

What I did take personally was Ramon criticizing how I played the tango on my piano. Of course I didn't play like a "tango pianist." I played like I played the blues or other pieces I enjoyed playing. I was only playing for myself after all. But he was listening and didn't like it. I thought I might take lessons from a tango pianist but then I just was so hurt that I didn't decide, I just never touched the piano again. I covered it up with a shawl and put a vase of flowers on it, and that was the end of a lifetime, since the age of five, of playing for enjoyment. I didn't understand why I let his criticism turn my pleasure at making music sour, but I did.

I suppose I felt somewhat like I wasn't doing a good job of appropriating his culture. It was fine to dance it because I danced it very well, better than many porteñas. But I knew I didn't play tango very well—just the notes and the timing were right. Tango was played in a special way, it was so much more than the correct notes and rhythm. I guessed I thought Ramon owned the tango, and if I didn't play it appropriately I needed to stop. And so I suddenly stopped playing anything.

October 2008

Prices, including fuel, had gone up so high that flights were more expensive. People were canceling vacation plans and tourism was much less than normal during this springtime high season. Several dancers who had booked lessons/tango tours with Ramon and myself had completely cancelled their trips. And now the government was going to impose a tax on all foreigners entering Argentina. I hoped that wouldn't apply to my re-entering every three months.

Australian filmmakers received a grant from their government to make a documentary about an Australian couple who came to BA to compete in the Campeonato Mundial, the World Championships of Tango, and Ramon and I were in it, talking and dancing. Titled *One Tango Moment*, it would be shown on Australian TV, and who knew, maybe one day compete as the best documentary.

We also were invited to perform in a special exhibition honoring Miguel Caló at Club Argentina. Caló's orchestra was my favorite—the romantic tangos, the valses—I just loved dancing to his music. And now we could show our emotions for Caló to the public. Two other couples would also perform, and big posters were displayed around town with all our photos. I wore my teal Campeonato dress and I felt elated and satisfied about our performance.

We were interviewed for a podcast, and several magazines, and we participated in two other documentaries on the tango in BA. I felt like a celebrity. It seemed I was also the poster child for BA expats, so I was inundated with questions, requests for interviews, and information. This was especially gratifying because the librarian in me liked being helpful and providing information. It was what I was trained for.

CHAPTER 30

The truth is that every guy in BA will try to take you to bed as fast as possible. I think it is about culture, not about the tango.

—Anonymous, Milonguero online survey response

April 2009

Tango at sea! Ramon and I were asked to teach tango every afternoon on a two-week cruise on the Royal Caribbean Radiance of the Seas from Valparaíso, Chile to Buenos Aires!

Ramon worried about his grandchildren during the two weeks we would be gone, and stocked up on bread and yerba mate at the supermarket. He said he felt better to know that at least they would have that. I found this heartbreaking, but I didn't comment. He also took it upon himself to replace the weather-beaten fur on my green Land's End parka. He found some fake fur somewhere, and cut and sewed it around the hood, making it look new again for our voyage, the first cruise for both of us.

We took the bus to Mendoza from BA and then transferred to another bus to travel across the border through the Andes with spectacular scenery and into Chile and Viña del Mar where we spent the night before taxiing to Valparaíso and the ship the next morning.

After bad and wet weather at our Chilean ports, the ship took a detour early one morning in order to confront a glacier. Out on deck in the dark wee hours, dressed in our gloves and parkas, we saw the magnificence of the gigantic ancient blue ice looming before us. The sky turned white, the water gray, the glacier an otherworldly aquamarine blue. The size, the age, the grandeur moved me, allowing me to feel connected to the cosmos, to history, to life. Ramon felt awed too and hugged me. *La naturaleza!* he whispered into my ear. We watched as a small crew went out in a tender to gather ice to bring back to us on board. And then we had shots of bourbon chilled by ancient bits of glacier at 5am.

Another morning I set the alarm so I'd be awake as we navigated the Straits of Magellan and the Beagle Channel. We went around Cape Horn! So eerie to look at the ship's globe and to see exactly where we were at that moment on the map, at the very bottom of the world. Unfortunately we did not visit Las Malvinas, the rocky Falkland Islands that caused war and bloodshed between the UK and Argentina in 1982. But I experienced how very far away from the rest of the world we were. I wondered why the politicians thought it was worth lives? Bitter discord exists to this day.

We disembarked in Rio Grande and hobnobbed with the penguins. We visited the Tierra del Fuego (Land of Fire) and The End of the World National Parks. These were places I had only read about, learned about in school, or dreamed about. In Ushuaia I searched the dark skies (to no avail) for the Southern Lights, the Aurora Australis, that mirror the Northern Lights.

Being on the beautiful ship was spectacular too. Ramon

commented in the Atrium that he was amazed that all six elevators were working, and I replied that things generally functioned in the U.S. And what fun it was to teach the tango to South Americans and several Americans who had no idea what it really was like outside of television.

Originally we were seated at dinner with a very pleasant American couple who spoke no Spanish. Ramon and the couple wanted to chat, but I was frustrated trying to eat my meal while also translating the conversation between them. So I requested seating at a Spanish-speaking table. I was surprised to hear there were very few Spanish speakers on the cruise in South America, but they found us a table of Argentines, Chileans, and a French couple, which worked out perfectly.

During the voyage Ramon and I got along wonderfully because he couldn't drink very much. Alcohol was prohibitively expensive on board. It about killed us that we saved half a bottle of wine each night for the next dinner. And Ramon didn't guzzle the many bottles of beer every day he was used to. I did get annoyed at him though because he wouldn't try any of the dishes on the buffet except beef (with no sauce and well-done), hotdogs, French fries, bread, iceberg lettuce, and ice cream. But I made up for his fear of trying something new, and tasted all of the Indian, Mexican, Chinese, and other unusual dishes I could. I had gotten so tired of the Argentine beige food found at every BA restaurant.

On karaoke night, I encouraged Ramon to sign up, and he studied and studied the list of available songs. He wanted to sing, "My Way," or "Mi Manera," but all the songs were in English. He was shy anyway, despite his beautiful baritone voice. I'm sure he would have won the karaoke contest as the other candidates weren't very good. One woman had planned ahead and brought along her own karaoke disks, and she wasn't terrible. So she won the bottle of champagne.

Teaching our nightly class in the top-deck disco was sometimes quite challenging as the ship lurched and rocked, but it was fun nonetheless. Then we went to the large theater after class for a superb show every night. I slept so well in the cradle of our cabin. Ramon usually went to the Casino because he liked to watch the blackjack table, and he could smoke. When he returned, he showered, shampooed, and left all of his clothes in the bathroom so the tobacco smell wouldn't enter the bedroom. I was already asleep and so if he snored I wasn't bothered. I was moved and grateful to have experienced the wonders of nature that we saw during those two weeks. It was such a glorious trip that once we arrived back in Buenos Aires, I was ready to turn around, get back on and do it all again.

Arriving home without Phoebe to greet me with dirty looks and reproachful meows made me feel so lonely, especially after the camaraderie of the ship. I missed Phoebe so much. All my life I had had a cat, and so now it was time to get another one. The vet who had cared for Phoebe several times when I left town had a rescue cat that reminded me of Phoebe, a tortoiseshell color but with longer fur. Someone had tossed her in the street in front of the vet shop when she was pregnant and had complications. Dr. Isabella had operated on her and brought her back to health and now was looking for a new home for her. Because of her Phoebe-like coloring, and because I knew her story, I took her home. Ramon suggested

Mirasol, or Sunflower, for her name. And once again, home was where the cat was.

CHAPTER 31

There are gentlemen who showcase their skills dancing...Lately they devote themselves exclusively to the foreign ladies...The foreigners are eager for the tanguero 'macho'. They get carried away by the warm embrace, the 'precise' step between their legs, the innocent 'feeling up.' These women generally come from 'cold countries'...The tanguero then takes advantage. These men, backed by their experience and always ready for the conquest, have found a fertile ground to hand out 'affection.' And I emphasize from other countries because we natives don't buy their act."

—Beatriz Pozzi, Los Aguilas, *B. A. Tango*, April 2000.

December 2009

Many of the porteñas were very friendly to me because they wanted to meet our foreign students, or they thought I could rent their apartments for them, or sell our students tango shoes or fringed skirts. So in a way I had learned not to trust anybody because they probably had ulterior motives. Surely there was a way to profit from this friendly foreign woman, me. *La viveza criolla* at work.

Locals couldn't understand why Americans were so blunt and forthright, yes, honest too. In the English law tradition, our word was law and a handshake was a contract. At least that was the intent of the culture. But the Argentines thought we were crazy and simple, because their culture was completely the opposite. Maybe their way of interacting wasn't a lie, but it wasn't the truth either. Everything was sub-rosa, hidden, circular, and certainly not obvious. They liked to tell you what you wanted to hear in order to make you happy. So from the get-go there was a lack of understanding between me and the local people I was trying to forge relationships with. Americans were used to believing other people, to trusting what was said as a matter of course, and Argentines were accustomed to taking whatever was said with a grain of salt.

Argentine culture was melancholy—the roots of tango, and I was melancholy too. I so often got disappointed in people. Folks came to BA on vacation and thought that we expats did nothing but twiddle our thumbs all day, without knowing it took complete full days to pay our monthly bills, if not more. I wasn't a psychotherapist for all the people who couldn't get along at home and expected things would change just because they were in BA for a few weeks on vacation.

And in my case, for every hour I spent out in the world interacting with people, I needed several hours to recuperate. My old therapist in L.A. had told me I was a Highly Sensitive Person, which now apparently was a thing. Nobody understood that about me and I didn't like to explain. I expended a lot of energy when I was out with people, when I was teaching, when I was dancing, and I had fun doing so. Most folks found me extremely energetic and outgoing. However, for whatever I took out of my bank of energy and attention, I had to repay with quiet and no stimulation. I had always been secretly an introvert like that. Ramon understood that after a big day of socializing, I had to be quiet in my room with the door closed, replenishing my batteries. He cooked, cleaned, or watched television at those times and we both were content.

I continued volunteering at the church, teaching tango to the homeless often with Ramon's help, working with Judy in the Roparia, and helping at their annual fêtes in the Fellowship Hall. I was sure the fêtes were just like in England only indoors, with stands of books (run by me), white elephant items, and used clothing for sale, along with the handicrafts made by the women. There was a tea and cake stand too, which I loved. If you purchased a "tea" you were served in delicate china cups along with an assortment of finger sandwiches and biscuits, and were waited on by the ladies carrying brimming teapots. I always bought a cake to take home. I tried to encourage the handicraft women I had been teaching to show-off a little tango for the guests, but they were too shy. For several years Ramon and I were the entertainment and performed a couple of tangos to the wild enthusiasm of the fête attendees.

Ramon usually went with me to the Sunday service too, especially as I was so uneasy going downtown alone when there was no one around but indigents early on Sunday morning. He had been raised Catholic but was no longer practicing. He still remembered the Lord's Prayer and other ritual responses of the mass, but deep down he was more shamanic than catholic, believing in the mystical ways of country folklore mixed with the saints. He was superstitious as well, and refused to take the saltshaker from someone's hand because it foretold bad luck. His mother taught him some "curandismo" and he often tried to relieve my head and stomachaches with prayer and magic.

Judy's family threw her a surprise 80th birthday party. After a restaurant dinner with her sons and granddaughters, all of us guests shouted, "Surprise!" when she opened the door. Such a lovely, loving family, they had taken care of everything to make a happy evening of celebration for Judy. I was so proud to be there and enjoyed getting to know some of her children better. Ramon had nothing in common with any of them except for the language, but he was sociable and enjoyed the refreshments. When they insisted we dance a tango, we did our best in the center of the apartment crowded with her friends and family.

CHAPTER 32

The tango is composed of three sadnesses, three memories: that of the immigrant, the gaucho, and the black slave brought against his will.

—Tango Negro: The African Roots of Tango,
documentary film, 2013

January 2010

I couldn't take leaving the country every three months anymore and for many years I had collected documents to begin my application for a long-term visa. When I first arrived I had tried to start the arduous process on my own but I was uncomfortable alone in the sketchy area by the railroad tracks where Migraciones was located, and the procedures confounded me, so I gave up.

But once Ramon was a part of my life, like a stubborn mastiff he kept persevering, pushing me forward, sometimes literally dragging me in his old batata through the crowded smog-filled streets of downtown Buenos Aires to one government office after another to get the coveted DNI, *Documento Nacional de Identidad,* the official I.D. for my permanent residency.

Ramon was an excellent driver—after all driving had been has profession for twenty years. He drove defensively in the choked streets, marked for four lanes but often with five or six lanes of traffic, everyone leaning on their horns and aggressively straining to beat the other drivers. Women were more machista than the men when they were behind the wheel. Driving a car made them equal and suddenly powerful, and they used it to the max.

I was never a backseat driver with Ramon at the wheel. I thought he was a wonderful, safe driver, at least when he was sober. Still, the trips downtown always seemed like Mr. Toad's Wild Ride. And for some reason, the way I sat in the passenger seat really annoyed him. The car was old, the streets had many potholes and speed bumps, so a rider got jostled around a lot. But something about the way I "jostled" made him mad. He couldn't explain exactly what it was that irritated him, or how I could change the way I sat, and I in turn couldn't understand the problem. Why should he care how I shook with the bumps and turns? But he got visibly angry many times with me. "Why don't you just sit properly in the seat?" he asked every time my head snapped back during a rapid stop. I was stupefied. It may have been that my body movements felt to him like criticism of his driving, but I was simply shaken like a bean in a maraca.

Yet I was able to take the first step of my seven-year paper chase through many lines in government buildings, with Ramon pushing from behind. Over the years the lists of required documents changed, and so I never had all of the right ones. Every person I saw in Inmigración made a different list, sometimes noting on a scrap of paper in pencil a newly required certificate. Several times after going through the red tape to get a document, and paying for it, I was told that it wasn't needed after all. I finally had a five-pound box of papers that included photos, documents with golden apostilles, fingerprints, certificates, official translations, proof of spending my entire pension in Argentina, and a bank account, even though I legally couldn't have an account without a DNI (official resident papers).

One seemingly insurmountable hurdle was that the name on my birth certificate and the name on my passport were different. In the U.S. when a woman marries she often takes her husband's last name, unlike the more sensible custom in Latin America of just adding it to a woman's maiden name. In the U.S. you can call yourself anything you want and some of us did. So I needed to prove I was the same person. I called the U.S. Embassy for help, and Ramon and I took the bus there. Instead of walking the last three blocks to the Embassy, Ramon hired a horse-drawn carriage. I arrived at the ugly bunker of a building as if I were Cinderella attending the Embassy Ball. Only American citizens could enter so he waited for me across the street in the cold park.

There was a delay of several hours before my number was called and the Consulate was able to contact Social Security. I was happy that when I signed the document, I only had to raise my right hand and swear in front of the Consul that it was true, that all those names were mine and I was one and the same person. I liked that so much. Somehow it felt honest and American. Why couldn't I have done this in the first place?

A few weeks later we took the subte downtown and crossed Plaza de Mayo where there was a huge demonstration in front of the Casa Rosada (the official government palace), with tents and police and the media. There was also a large gathering of folks outside of the Registry office, a pushy-shovey crowd all trying, like I was, to just make an appointment. There was one official in attendance who told everybody quite rudely that all the turns were gone, and that they had to have lined up (it was more of a stampede than a line) before 6am to ask for an appointment.

So the next day we went to the *Registro Nacional de Personas Extranjeras* (Alien Registry) to make an appointment. We arrived just before the icy dawn and took our place in the line of bundled-up applicants, several with babies in their arms. If we hadn't been there that early, the numbers would be taken shortly after the office opened at 8am. The sun eventually rose over the river and shone weakly on the bleak surroundings, and we were glad to see a vendor with mate and coffee setting up his cart for business.

When the line finally turned into the building itself, the crowd jammed up the only doorway. There was no way people leaving with their documents could exit without shoving, pushing, and many "con permisos." Ahead of us were several people, waiting just as long and uncomfortably as I had, who learned that their documents weren't ready yet. Instead of screaming and yelling, inciting riots, beaten down by the cold waiting hours, they numbly said, "Gracias," and left the window, clutching the scraps of paper they would have to bring back on another day.

Ramon was patient yet insistent. He spoke for me to the officials in charge, identifying himself as my "bulldog Argentine." When I got confused and disoriented in the throngs, he took my hand and led me to the right place in line or window or waiting room. When I got angry at the chaos and confusion, he was calm and reasonable, accepting the bureaucracy that was life in Argentina. And so step-by-step he plowed ahead towards the goal of my permanent residency with me trailing behind him.

After seven years of trying, I finally received my first DNI but it would expire two months later! So Ramon and I returned to Migraciones to ask what to do. We grabbed a number from the machine, 457, and I took the only empty chair. They called 31.

Then across the hall I saw Ramon in the middle of a tightly pressed group crowded together, everyone waving their arms. I could hear his voice from where I sat reading my book. A lady in front of me vomited and fainted dead away. Security rushed over with a drink of water, a doctor came, and her *trámite* was hand-carried to her, who by now thankfully had miraculously recovered. The atmosphere in there was terrible; I completely understood anyone being overcome by the crowds, overheating, screaming babies. But I learned something too. Being the macho society that it was, a fainting sick woman had power.

Maybe God was trying to tell me something. Maybe they would send the police to my house to arrest me and toss me out of Argentina, but at that moment, I couldn't have cared less. I was ready to forget the whole thing and to just leave every three months like before, or just leave period. That thought had been lurking in the back of my mind of late.

If I had it all to do all over again, if I knew then what I knew now, I would pay a lawyer to do all the paper chasing I had done during these years. All of my expat friends had hired help. I was the only one I knew who was trying to do it "alone," even though I had Ramon to do it with me. I had been "en tramite" for seven years, and it wasn't over yet. It had taken its toll on my health and my nerves, as well as on my bank account. And now, I began to wonder if it all was worth it.

CHAPTER 33

...gender violence doesn't start with the first blow, it starts when the man begins to control the woman, to mistreat her, humiliate her publicly, to tell her what to wear.

There's a lot of work put into reducing her self-esteem, so by the time the blow arrives the behaviour has been naturalised.

—Jimena Aduriz, *The Guardian*

March 2010

I loved Ramon and he loved me, in his way. But although we got along, there was actually very little real understanding between us. Because we could not talk. It wasn't a language problem—my castellano was good enough now to converse about many subjects and ideas. It was Ramon's refusal to talk about emotional issues. He got mad at me all the time, often for little things about which I hadn't a clue. He also always took everything personally. I was sure it had to do with his machismo and with his underlying insecurity as well. It had always been this way from the beginning with Ramon, but now I was getting fed up. Love was not enough. A couple had to communicate.

I didn't enjoy his being around so much anymore. I preferred to be on my own—reading, writing, thinking—more than his constant criticism. Ramon had many wonderful qualities, but there were a few that I couldn't take any more. I was sure it could be different if we could just talk things over.

He felt it was his job to make me—and everyone he could—happy. But he thought he could make me "happy" his way, not in the way I wanted or needed. He thought he had all the answers and that I only needed to do as I was told to be sunny and satisfied. To Ramon, it was really my problem that I was a highly sensitive only child who needed quiet and calm. But how could I be myself if my partner were angry with me over something I had no idea about?

I felt better when we were dancing. A good tango is the best drug, a happy pill. Even though he never said he was sorry about anything, sometimes when we were dancing I felt the exact moment when his body apologized. It was uncanny. He was a very verbal person, always ready with an apropos comment or a joke or funny observation, but when it came to his inner self and his feelings, it was only his body that spoke to me.

No matter how tired I was at a milonga, if the DJ played folklore, especially if it were the recordings of Chaqueño Palavecino, I had energy to dance the chacarera. I loved it so much, it reinvigorated me, Ramon too, and we smiled during the whole dance. When Chaqueño gave a live concert at a theater on Corrientes, we sat in the third row until we were dancing in the aisles. Argentine folklore was one reason I always enjoyed so much the gaucho fair at Mataderos. DJs were more likely to play a tanda of tropical with cumbia, merengue, and paso doble, than la chacarera. But no matter what, whenever I heard Chaqueño begin to sing, I was up on my feet dancing.

Once after a lovely evening at Nuevo Chiqué at the Casa

Galicia, we walked to the corner in search of a taxi. Ramon was in between old cars at the moment. There was another older man on the corner also waiting for a cab, but after Ramon hailed one, the old man started to take it. Ramon, as usual at a milonga, had had a lot to drink, and he crossed the street ready to punch the guy. How ridiculous were two old white-haired men socking each other in the street over a taxi when there was one around every corner? I hung on to Ramon, shouted at him to grow up, got another taxi myself, and pushed him into it. I wouldn't speak to him all the way back to Boedo, or until he sobered up the next morning. Some of the trouble was that I couldn't tell when he was drunk, even as well as I knew him, because he often seemed normal and I expected him to be his usual self, but at those times he wasn't the Ramon I loved.

I banished him for three days, which was the only way we seemed to be able to scab over our problems. He would leave and go home, and eventually we both would forget what it had been all about. Then he would return and get busy cooking in the kitchen, and we would just never talk about it. We would eat, drink wine, kiss, and it was over, with nothing solved.

Was I glad to be with Ramon, even though sometimes he drove me crazy and there was nothing I could do about it? I supposed I was because I didn't end it or leave. It was all so very complicated. I couldn't even complain to girlfriends, and I didn't see my shrink Laura anymore. I no longer trusted her. I had gotten a strong feeling that she was on the mercenary side and also that she had a bias against Argentine men. I had hoped deep down to be convinced of the solidity of my relationship, of the quality of Ramon's affection for me, that underneath it all he was a good partner despite our cultural differences, that it was me who just didn't understand.

Saturday at Los Cons I got nervous from trying to do too much. While I was conversing with the newcomers at our table, Ramon constantly interrupted me. Then the *boludo* Guillermo monopolized me for half an hour talking about himself. I told Ramon later that he had to rescue me when he saw that Guillermo had me in a conversational straitjacket. One of our guests was also going on and on about which tango show to see, while slimy Carlos with the black mustache lurked behind our table, scouting our group for foreign women. A woman from our group ended up leaving with him and not paying her bar bill. I did. I would never forgive him for his abuse of Loretta, but there was no point in warning this lady as she wouldn't believe me. Women always think it will be different with them.

Laurence was back in BA. At Los Consagrados he would wait until Ramon was dancing with someone else and I was sitting alone at the table to cabeceo me. I would dance one tanda with him during the evening, never more. Ramon didn't know our history of sailing in the Mediterranean, but with his great powers of observation plus his witchy ways, he suspected something was between us. So after a few weeks of my dancing one tanda with Laurence each evening, he told me he didn't like it. I could dance with anyone else, but not him. Naturally his telling me what to do made me seethe.

But I realized I had two choices: I could dance with Laurence and then have a huge fight with Ramon, or I could not dance with Laurence. So the next time when Laurence came to my table, I told him that although I wanted to dance with him and I enjoyed dancing with him, the price of doing so was too high. He just said, "Well, it's your life," and turned on his heel.

But was it my life, when I wasn't "allowed" to dance with whomever I wanted? I could have chosen to anyway, but I wasn't up for the stressful scene, both Ramon and me getting sick from it, maybe even taking too much Ativan trying to calm down. I knew that I could always end the relationship with Ramon and live on my own. But I didn't think I could tolerate living in Argentina without him, without the teaching together I enjoyed so much, without our tango.

I think now that maybe I should have decided to leave at that moment, to pack up and return to Los Angeles where no one ordered me around. But I then would have lost the teaching and the tango of *Ramon y Cherie*.

I was home alone, writing one afternoon, when the phone rang. It was Santi, the handsome young waiter at several milongas whom I had known for years.

"Hola, Cherie? This is Santi, from the milonga. How are you, *querida*?"

"I'm fine, Santi. What's going on?"

"I was wondering if you'd like to go out with me, to be with me today."

"Santi, I am complimented that you think of me that way. I like you very much as a friend. But you know I am with Ramon."

"Bien, sí, but I just thought I would try."

"Okay then, see you at the milonga. Ciao!"

I hung up the phone in shock. Yes I was very flattered that a 28-year-old, tall and handsome young man would want to be with me. But didn't he feel disloyal to Ramon, his friend too? What if I had gone with him, would he have felt proud that I would cheat with him on Ramon? Was there no honor among thieves in this machista culture? Any woman was to be seduced, nothing else mattered. Another notch on the gun?

My little autobiographical vignette, *The Key*, from my memoir, *The Church of Tango*, won first prize in a competition to promote Maria Finn's new book, *Hold Me Close and Tango Me Home*. First prize was turning it into a tango song with words and music by Marian Barry.

Was it a good thing or a bad thing to win an essay contest called the *Heartbreak Competition*? Of course it wasn't about whose heartbreak was the biggest, but who wrote about it best in a tango way. Traditional tango songs were all about sad stories of broken hearts, death, loss, yearning, frequently disguised behind metaphors.

Life was full of heartbreak and ache of one kind or another and writing about it could be cathartic. I was thrilled that something I wrote was selected by a panel of judges to be the "best." The heartache of losing my husband, home, happy life, was still there, but winning anything was good medicine.

My life had had so much drama and loss and tragedy, it had always been a "tango," and now I thought here was the proof.

The Key

My old house sits under the full moon of Hollywood as I drive past where I lived so long ago. As always, the street's ancient cedar trees perfume the air, and in the

> *black night, the glimmering Observatory hovers above like a friendly space ship.*
>
> *The courtyard gates are locked, but the closed windows shine from within and beckon to my heart. The drawn draperies glow like a candle in the window lit for me, calling me home.*
>
> *Perhaps inside the wrought-iron gates and behind the cozy golden windows is my old lost life. Maybe if I stare long and hard enough, I can catch a shadow of a vanished time, the comings and goings of a happy family.*
>
> *What if I found the key and opened the door into another dimension, and came home?*

The spoken intro of the recording was an edited and greatly condensed version of my text, followed by a bland electronic "tango Nuevo," not in the traditional style at all. Naively I had hoped that my words would become actual song lyrics in the classical tango manner. I had imagined that Ramon and I could make a video dancing to the song and put it on my blog along with the author's book cover.

Ramon, traditionalist to the bone, said naturally it wouldn't be an "authentic" tango as it was not from Buenos Aires but New York City!

CHAPTER 34

Men don't live in a world where they will be constantly bombarded with sexually objectifying images of themselves...a constant reminder and reinforcement of the fact that our bodies are perceived by many to be public property.

—Emily Jensen

April 2010

We were approached again by the cruise line to teach tango on a trip from BA to Rio de Janeiro! All my life I had wanted to visit Rio—the land of the samba and Copacabana Beach. What made it even better was that Ramon had a friend in Rio who often came to BA to dance, and she invited us to stay with her for a week after the cruise. I had met Olga—a lovely person, an oral surgeon with her own practice, and a two-bedroom apartment in Niteroi, just outside of Rio.

Her boyfriend Gustavo was staying there too, and when Ramon and I arrived, being a foursome was nice. Olga drove us all around Rio, to the beach, and to the Brazilian milongas. The availability of many exotic and beautiful fruits and unusual dishes never seen in Argentina, the thrill of climbing up to the monumental, iconic Christ the Redeemer statue, seeing Sugar Loaf and the beach of Ipanema plus several milongas made the week in Rio a wish come true.

I had met Gustavo years ago on my early trips to BA. He was charming and nice-looking, but many people talked about his bad reputation with women and how dishonest he was. There were also rumors that he had been a drug mule from Spain or England, and also was a bigamist, so he had needed to leave the country before his legal problems caught up with him.

Janet, another longtime expat who wrote a tango blog, especially gossiped about how dishonest he was, that he stole cash from women, but I never noticed any of that. Cristina always vouched for his character, and she would have him over to make empanadas (but with store-bought dough, not like Ramon's) for her guests at her tango house, and that's how I met him. Years later I asked Cristina what ever happened to him and she told me he had met a Brazilian woman who loved him so much that she took him home with her and set him up teaching. That was Olga, I was pretty sure.

Olga worked very hard to get Gustavo's papers in order. However he kept cheating on her, and after a year, she kicked him out. He then went with an African woman with several children. Gustavo loaned his cell phone to one of her sons who mounted up incredible charges, and that led to him being locked out of his apartment with all of his clothes and belongings inside. So Olga felt sorry for him and ended up taking him back just a few weeks before our visit. She even fixed his teeth since he only had five by that time.

Gustavo worked three nights a week as a security guard in a nearby restaurant, making 500reals a month ($300usd). He didn't want to work as a taxi dancer because he felt it was demeaning. There was a huge market for taxi dancing in Rio—every older lady had her young stud.

I was one of the many foreign women Gustavo had seduced years ago, in the '90s, but I didn't see that as a problem now. We just had a one-time fling, even though he ended up calling me in L.A. I found his aggressiveness overwhelming. In Olga's apartment the four of us lived in close quarters during that week, but Ramon didn't know about the long-ago flirtation.

Olga asked him if he knew me, but he denied it, and also denied knowing Cristina. I didn't know why women stayed with such losers, but so many did. I was sure people talked about Ramon, and me too.

Whenever Olga and I had a chance to chat alone, she repeated that she loved him despite everything, at the same time complaining that he wouldn't help her around the house (women's work). I got the impression that she didn't have healthy relationships with men in general, that maybe to her any man was better than no man. That also was the point of view of macho men, and Brazil and Argentina had plenty of those. I even suggested counseling but nobody ever goes when a friend suggests it. Olga and I got along great, but I think she had eyes for Ramon too.

CHAPTER 35

I have been to BA over 20 times. Most of the milongueros want to find a lonely American woman. I have had many women friends run back to BA just because these milongueros give them sooooo much attention that they do not get in the States. I think these women do lots of favors for them.

—Anonymous, from online Milonguero Survey

May 2010

My son Jason and our mutual friend Connie came to visit! He had also gone to San Miguel de Allende for a week when I lived there, and now I was delighted to show and share my life in yet another country with my youngest son. I had enjoyed immensely being with Connie when she came to BA that Christmas in 2004.

The ten days of their trip were so much fun. Ramon and Jason were cut from the same boyish cloth and they were constantly laughing, making Connie and me laugh too.

The four of us went to the Delta de Tigre and stayed in a log cabin by the river and the guys went fishing and Connie and I went kayaking. Ramon made an elaborate and delicious asado on the beach, as well as cooking the other meals in the tiny kitchen. I teased him about being "Survivorman" who could make do in any situation (he had seen me watching the TV show). No matter where he was, he could fashion a barbecue out of whatever he found, and make a delicious meal.

We gave them tango lessons, took them tango shoe shopping, and then dancing to a milonga. We took them on all the tours we made a business doing, like San Telmo, Mataderos Gaucho Fair, and La Boca.

We even took them to a tango dinner show, because that's what tourists like to do, explaining that the many tango shows in BA were all basically alike: the bigger and more expensive shows just had more dancers, singers, and musicians. They all were choreographed, depicted a little of the tango history myths, had a comical piece, sexy costumes, and had nothing in common with the social tango the porteños danced every night in milongas. I warned them that show dancing always included the woman in poses of submission, which now that I lived in the everyday world of machismo, bothered me a lot: the woman in a deep back bend with the man in control, the woman on the floor in a split looking up at the man, the woman walking away and being grabbed from behind—the clichés that I used to enjoy until I lived them.

Ramon couldn't stop cooking all of his Argentine specialties for them. He was so happy for me that they were visiting, because he had known for years how much I missed my folks from home. He even insisted on sleeping on the floor to free up a bed. I was ecstatic to show "my people" my life and an "insider's view of BA," and I had never been happier in Buenos Aires.

After they left, I felt extra lonely so Ramon and I went to the Bird Fair, *La Feria de Pájaros,* in Pompeya and bought a baby Australian parakeet. We named him Coquito, after the bandoneon player I saw one night at a neighborhood milonga. Coquito was so cute—with a blue body and yellow head—and sweet. I was worried how Mirasol the cat would behave, but she just ignored him. He lived in his cage in my little office off the kitchen. Whenever we let him out to fly around, we put Mirasol in the bedroom. His happy chirping and sweet little voice was a lot of company.

June 2010

It seemed like I was constantly sick in BA. And Ramon frequently had digestive issues and/or the stomach flu as well. It was so disheartening that neither of us ever felt 100%. The worst time for me was spring and fall, full of allergies. I had a big jar of generic Benadryl I had bought from Amazon when I was last in L.A., and it was fantastic that in Argentina you could buy antibiotics without a prescription. But of course I didn't always know which one was for what, but my go-to was Cipro. I wasn't afraid of dying, only of being sick. After all that time being miserable from my cancer treatment, it made me crazy to lie in bed doing nothing, not living the life I had left to me.

I was furious that Ramon wouldn't go for his general medical checkup. After all, I was paying monthly for his health insurance. When it came to Ramon, I just swallowed everything and I felt it was killing me. I didn't have the little ways I used to cheer myself up like I did in L.A. or even France or Mexico—the nice lunch in a small restaurant where I was known, a walk with a girlfriend, some quiet time in the library, window shopping, or a drive in the country. I was afraid to leave the apartment alone lately. I was also afraid of becoming agoraphobic, afraid of being afraid.

Every once in a while a foreign friend and I would go out

for a meal when they came to town to dance. But the truth was, I would really have loved to have a conversation with my female friends that wasn't about this man or that man they danced with in the milonga. I was so sick of that I could scream. Now if they were to tell me they went to a love hotel or at least a man invited them to dinner and paid, or something interesting and new, yes then I would love to listen. But none of them ever told me those things, only about the tango.

So over time I had come to expect less from everybody and to protect myself more. Still, I could easily get hurt. Many people tossed you over in a second when it came to friendship, or money.

The problem was that I loved conversation, to debate and discuss. But with whom? Ramon didn't want to. He didn't have that kind of mind. He accepted the way things were and didn't see any point in complaining or discussing the state of things. He did criticize, though, but again it was enough to be negative and that was the end of it. He didn't want to go into why, what was in the other person's mind (if it were a person being disapproved of), or how things could be better. He criticized me—on no occasion how I looked or how I danced, but for some perceived slight that I was never aware of.

He also liked to put me down in front of other people, although it was done in a teasing manner. I was stunned the first time he did this. We had made friends with an Argentine couple on the ship in Chile and I couldn't believe that he said negative things about me in front of them. I had to tell him several times not to do that before he finally stopped. I didn't know if it was cultural to say cutting things about your partner as a kind of joke on yourself, or to make yourself seem higher in outsiders' esteem, or what it was. But I hated it and wouldn't put up with it. I had known couples in the past that only fought in front of other people—perhaps to have witnesses or to somehow keep it safe. I never understood this kind of behavior, and I always was so embarrassed to be a spectator.

But Ramon's remarks were different. They weren't meant to pick a fight, just to put me in a negative light. But if you're a couple each person's light shines on the other, so it didn't make any sense to me. I couldn't understand that reasoning, and the truth was that I probably didn't understand Ramon at all.

My friend Tina was leaving town, like so many of my expat friends, and so we made plans to meet at the old Confitería La Ideal for a *despedida*, a farewell. Coming back I was nervous on the subte as a gang of young toughs reeking of beer and BO crowded into the car right next to me. Somehow there was an "incident" requiring the conductor to ride in the train with us. Everyone was uneasy and I could just picture violence. When I got off at Boedo, I looked over my shoulder as I scurried away, only to see a bus crashed on my corner with stopped traffic in every direction. The evening's events felt ominous, portentous, and I was relieved to reach home and lock the door.

CHAPTER 36

I danced non-stop with one porteño after another. One lovely man said to me in broken English, 'Close your eyes and sleep.' And so I did, and in this dreamlike state felt as though my partner was telling me a poetic story through his body, his dancing, his tight embrace. I've never experienced anything like that in my life. My entire body felt it had just imbibed a glass of wine and thus was relaxed from its liquid in my veins. It was as though I'd been given passage to a secret world where senses collide in the form of tango.

—Carolina from Canada

July 2010

Ramon's sickness got worse until he had to go to the ER. He was having a liver attack due to no gall bladder. I was furious with him for not eating right, for not having his prostate exam, for being the stubborn fool that he was. He said he would rather die. Okay, fine, but did I have to watch him do it?

After the ER, Ramon's wreck of a batata broke down again and yet he was pushing it and working on it in the freezing cold when he was so unwell. We arrived back to the apartment in the nick of time to give a tango lesson.

The next day despite being ill, Ramon thought that his life would go on as usual: he was going to go work on the batata and then return to give three hours of classes and then take people to the Chiqué milonga.

Ramon was like a bull in a china shop that created messes wherever he went. But he then cleaned them up, ruining his clothes, scarring his body, bending over backward to help any and everyone. Yet he wouldn't do one thing for himself.

María Valle de Concepción, Ramon's teenaged granddaughter, was as beautiful as her name. She lived with her two brothers, her father and his new girlfriend, and Ramon, in Ramon's house outside of BA. I felt immediately that we were *simpatica*. Ramon brought her sometimes to visit, and occasionally she stayed several days with me to get a little break from the commotion at home. Although very shy, she was aware of her beauty and spent hours in front of the mirror arranging her long brown hair and elaborate makeup, and then posing for selfies for Facebook.

Once when she was fifteen she was with me for a week, and she slowly opened up about her life. She felt bad that she hadn't had a quinceañera party on her birthday but was philosophical about it—she knew there was no disposable income for such an event. Her whole story was sad to me. Her mother had left when the last baby, Franco, was only three months old. She just took off. Mari had no memories of her. The three kids were basically raised by their grandparents, Ramon and his ex, who Mari called Mamá. Her father was always off with other women. Mari had no privacy in the house.

One particular night when she was staying with me, she

began to cry as we finished up our simple dinner in the kitchen, because she had no secure place to keep her things at home. Her brothers had friends in and out of the house, her father had his various girlfriends, lots of cousins visit, and. her babysitting money had been stolen. This broke my heart. The only thing I could do was to embrace her and let her cry. When she left to go home, I gave her one of my suitcases and a padlock.

Ramon and I took her on various excursions out of town—a weekend in Lujan, a couple of nights in Gualeguaychu for the Carnival. But the poor little thing was sick both times with stomach issues. I guessed it was nerves.

From time to time I bought her cute little tops and fancy makeup kits, and tried to encourage her to think of her future, to finish school, and perhaps train as a hairdresser or makeup artist.

Public school was grim and trying. Her high school, or *colegio,* was on three sessions per day. Her session finished close to midnight! And the kids had to be picked up by an adult, but there wasn't always someone available. It was tough for everybody. Plus the teachers were often on strike. I didn't understand how anyone learned anything in such chaos.

When she was seventeen, instead of preparing to graduate, she became pregnant. Ramon was furious with her, especially because she left the house to live with the boy and was not in touch with her family for a while. Ramon refused to even talk about her with me he was so angry. But soon, as we all had predicted, she returned home with the baby boy and no boyfriend.

CHAPTER 37

I've had intimate relationships with men I met in BA milongas...the relationships started with an invitation for coffee after the milonga.

—Anonymous response to Milonguero online survey

October 2010

Many days I didn't dance tango, I didn't talk about tango, I didn't write about tango. What I did was wait in lines. That was life in Buenos Aires.

In Argentina you couldn't simply sign on to your online account and pay by clicking your keyboard. Nor could you write checks and drop them in the mail. Here you had to pay in cash and wait in lines to do so. Sometimes the ATM machines ran out of cash, and even when there was cash available, I had to do the operation three times in a row to get enough, paying a service charge for each withdrawal.

November 2010

Thanksgiving was my favorite holiday, and I really missed celebrating it. Since we had dinners and luncheons all the time at my apartment, this year I wanted to invite my American friends for a traditional Thanksgiving. I had a can of cranberry sauce in the cupboard and there were plenty of yams in the verdulerias. All we needed was a turkey.

Of course in Argentina the last Thursday of November was springtime, and the elusive fat and juicy American turkey was not to be found in the markets, as they had all recently hatched and were still chicks. I tried to order one but the butcher said it was impossible. Actually they rarely had them in the autumn either, as turkey wasn't a popular food in Argentina. So Ramon went out to a poultry farm in the country to see if he could find and tag one for us come the end of November. He said the only mature ones he saw were scrawny tough-looking old toms that didn't at all look like they would be tender and tasty. So I changed the plan. On Thanksgiving Day we would have an Argentine asado.

The day before Thanksgiving, at noon on Wednesday, Ramon and I walked to the Coto Supermarket to buy ingredients for the asado. When we returned one hour later, Ramon's car, which had been parked in front of my building, was gone. His third old jalopy had been stolen again. This time it was even worse as his son needed it for work. Ramon freaked out. "How can he go to work? What about my grandkids? How will they eat?"

Ramon said that if he ever got another car he would chain it to a tree, as removing the battery and using a steering wheel club hadn't worked. He also had learned in the past that he couldn't leave anything in the trunk. How sad that someone would break in to steal his tango shoes! I heard that Juan Carlos Copes, the extremely famous stage tango star, had been carjacked in his garage and everything in his apartment was stolen. But at least with him, it wasn't the poor stealing from the poorer.

When he went to report it to the police they accused Ramon

of stealing it himself! That he stole it for the insurance! And the car wasn't even insured.

Thanksgiving Day, twelve friends showed up for the asado on my beautiful terrace, with views to San Telmo on the south, and that followed the river to Recoleta in the east. It was a gorgeous late spring afternoon. We followed the American custom of going around the table to speak of what we were thankful for that day. When it was Ramon's turn, he stood up and explained about the stolen car and broke down in tears, ending by saying he was thankful to be surrounded by friends on that day. When it was my turn I silently thought that I was thankful in the knowledge that I was going home to L.A. for Christmas, but said something generally mundane entirely!

My two worst Thanksgivings ever:

The Thanksgiving From Hell #1 was in 1988, one month after Jack's diagnosis and terminal prognosis. Friends from England had just arrived in L.A. for a month's vacation—a brother and sister in their 20's. Sarah had MS, and they both drank like fish. I had told them by phone about Jack but they decided to come anyway as planned and I hoped, especially with the brother, they would just go about their business and leave us alone to figure out our tragedy. Jack's surgery for castration was scheduled for the week after Thanksgiving. I ordered all the Thanksgiving dishes from Gelson's gourmet foods, which cost a fortune, and nobody ate anything. Sarah was on some sort of special diet, and she and Richard just drank. I ended up throwing it all out. That night in Jason's old room, next to ours, Sarah kept falling out of bed. In a few days I gave them my credit card and car keys and told them to go to a hotel, as I couldn't handle their vacation and Jack's situation at the same time. Instead of understanding, it broke up a long relationship between our two families.

Thanksgiving from Hell #2 came in 1993. The Serrano house in Los Feliz, our family home since 1976, had been sold and I was scheduled to move out the Saturday after Thanksgiving into an apartment complex, Park LaBrea. I had the flu and just planned to pack boxes all day. Jason and Adam were supposed to go to their aunt's for dinner and bring me back a plate of food. On the Wednesday before, Jason was stopped on the freeway for not having license tags and then tossed into the slammer when they discovered a mountain of unpaid parking tickets. Adam was hysterical, saying Jason would be raped or worse, and demanded that I bail him out. Not only did I not have any cash, I thought maybe my son would learn something from this, since he had not behaved in a responsible way. He was in the downtown L.A. jail for more than 24 hours before he got bailed out. I had no car (Adam had it); I had no money, and no food at all because of the upcoming move. So I spent the day sick and so very hungry, but packing those damned boxes.

The Best Thanksgiving I ever had was in 1989 with another American couple in the little French village of Lugrin, the location of our beautiful apartment overlooking Lac Léman. Our favorite restaurant, Le Verniaz, spit roasted over the fire in the dining room a small free-range turkey from Bresse, with a sauce of something resembling cranberries poured over the bird. There was pumpkin tart flavored with lemon for dessert. The table was decorated with little American flags. From the cozy interior by the fire, we looked out the windows to see the snow covered peaks of the French Alps. It was unforgettably wonderful, even though I knew it would be one of our last Thanksgivings. I was still very grateful.

Ramon continued to teach while I was in L.A. for two weeks over Christmas. It didn't bother me at all that he was alone in my apartment with the students. He often Skyped me so I could talk to them during the lesson, explaining ideas in English that they didn't understand in castellano.

One student, Sabrina, had taken several classes from us last year, but now took some private lessons with Pedro, the old milonguero I had known for years and who I made the teaching video with when I first arrived. Sabrina was very conservative and completely shocked when Pedro felt her up during the class. When I returned to BA after New Year's, she took a class with us and confessed to me how upset she was. He had kissed her on the mouth! Usually her niece was with her to translate, but Pedro didn't want the niece around this time. Years ago, before Ramon, he had shown me his wallet full of Viagra—in order to turn me on, I supposed. But I was completely disgusted. Before that I had thought we were good friends. He lived at home in Boedo with his wife of decades and his daughters and grandchildren, but was a typical milonguero trying to seduce whatever woman came his way. After Sabrina's story and the Viagra, I no longer had any respect for him despite how wonderfully he danced. He was just another dirty old man.

Ramon arrived from his house nervous and exhausted and his hyper behavior made me crazy in the milonga. I just couldn't stand it when he was like that, but I didn't say anything. He had so many people to worry about and care for, how could

I blame him? He rarely shared what went on at home, but it was usually regarding his sons or cars.

At the milonga I was too tired and stressed to have fun, and I supposed Ramon was too. We gave a class first to a couple from San Diego and then took them with us to Los Consagrados. There was a group of strange women planted at the head of our table when we arrived, as there had been the week before, and so we just moved over to the next table. It turned out they were friends of a friend and after a time they introduced themselves. But I was already fuming—it didn't take much at that point. Foreigners didn't understand that one's table was yours, that you sat where the host seated you, and regulars had the same table week after week, year after year. Tango tourists often thought they could sit anywhere they liked, and do anything they liked in the traditional milongas of Buenos Aires.

Ramon ran around the salon trying to arrange things, and then went to dance with an Italiana he had told me he was going to dance with, (to Pugliese). A friend I had made, Natalie, had written me she didn't want to leave BA without a dance with Ramon, so he danced with her, and then his friend from La Plata wanted Ramon to dance with her friends who weren't dancing, so he scurried around looking for men they could pay as taxi dancers, and then he bustled about doing other things, I didn't know what. I was just getting more and more annoyed, sitting there. He asked the DJ to play a tanda of Caló that we always danced together, and then we danced but it wasn't the best Caló, and I really couldn't have cared less.

All that year, we had been working 24/7, at least it felt like it, which was fabulous but I was ready to drop dead from exhaustion and it wasn't over yet. I told Ramon if we worked like that in the States we would be wealthy! We had happy, contented students from South Africa, the Philippines, Hong Kong, London, Denmark—just too many places to remember. All of them extended invitations to us to visit and organize workshops. We would have loved to, but we just couldn't afford the expensive airfare.

CHAPTER 38

At some point most women come to the silent and terrible realization that the men in their lives—fathers, brothers, uncles, boyfriends and husbands—are not especially outraged by their experience of sexual harassment.

—Aminatta Formi

January 2011

After the New Year, cordoned-off streets all over BA's working class neighborhoods pulsed with drumbeats on weekend nights. My barrio's *murga* club, *Los Chiflados de Boedo,* practiced on Carlos Calvo—the street below my terrace. The rhythms of the *bombo con platillo* (bass drum with small cymbals on top), and the *silbato* (whistle) were hypnotic and exciting, and I loved feeling the energy as I got ready for the Saturday milonga.

Not related to carnival, except happening at the same time of year, the murgas had no religious overtones, although frequently there were political issues. The idea was to have fun and express yourself, and old and young flocked out into the streets to watch the murga clubs perform in their bedazzled satin top hats and tailcoats.

People armed themselves with cans of spray foam and attacked everybody, coming or going. I was afraid of being sprayed in the eyes, and so I tried to steer clear of groups of kids as I watched the dancers perform the same step over and over, jumping and kicking, and touching the ground with each beat of the *murgueros'* drums.

The *comparsas* were practicing for *Carnaval Porteño* citywide at the same time: floats and almost-naked girls adorned with feathers—what people tended to think of as Carnival, or Mardi Gras, with *batucada* Brazilian drum rhythms.

During the military dictatorship 1976-1981 of Jorge Rafael Videla, gatherings were forbidden. Tango went underground along with the murgas due to their political content, and Carnival as well. (I first knew about this at home in L.A. when I watched a bootlegged copy of "Tango Bar," with Raul Julia.) But recently the murgas and *corsos* were reinstated, along with declaring the four days before Lent legal holidays, the custom before 1956. Another four-day weekend with everything closed citywide and people drinking from morning to late at night. How wonderful, I thought.

We took Ramon's grandson, Franco, to Tigre, but just for the day. Franco's father never took him anyplace or spent time with him, so Franco really enjoyed fishing with his *abuelo* who also was trying to teach him to swim. Poor city children never had a chance to learn to swim.

Then the two of us drove up to Gueyleguaychu for *Carnaval*! We stayed four nights in a beautiful hotel by the river. Ramon went fishing and to the Casino; I read and relaxed. At night we played in the swimming pool, the warm dark waters reflecting the southern stars overhead. The Carnaval parade was unbelievable, something I would never forget—the floats, costumes, dancing, music, all such creative and artistic concepts. I loved it. It lasted until 3am but the time flew by. It was well worth it to do it that way, instead of that awful turnaround trip of years ago in a little van when Ramon was so sick with a gall bladder attack.

April 2011

It was autumn and we were working every day, trying to make hay while the sun shone. One week a marvelous Russian couple took several classes and a Tango Tour. They invited us for dinner at Fervor, an upscale expat restaurant in Palermo. It was a riot. Igor was wealthy and like to throw it around a bit, so he ordered every alcoholic beverage on the menu. At frequent intervals he and Ramon gave each other a big hug with emotional tears in their eyes. It was like watching a movie. I expected glasses to be thrown against the wall at any moment. I had tears in my eyes too because for the first time in ages, I had my favorite cocktail, a Cosmopolitan, and it brought back so many memories. They offered to sponsor us for workshops in Moscow, and offered to do the paperwork. We could stay with them. It was a nice fantasy.

June 2011

Timing is always everything. And fortunately, the timing for us to visit the spectacular scenic area of Argentina's Patagonia was perfect. Pristine waters, snow-capped mountains, fresh, clean air, piney forests—I had been imagining it for so long. But one week after our beautiful trip there, it was a disaster of volcanic ash, polluted water, dead animals, closed airports, and empty supermarkets. The Chilean volcano Puyehue erupted sending smoke, ash, sulfur fumes, and death around the globe

When Descuento City had a promotion for a week's excursion for two to Patagonia and the Lake District, including air, at half price, I snapped it up. Ramon had been there when he was working for the TV station, but I wanted to see as much of Argentina as I could. It was so much more than Buenos Aires.

Now ash fell like snow in BA. And I couldn't breathe.

"You need a Nebulizer treatment," Ramon said.

"What's that? I've never heard of it."

"They do it in the farmacias. Vamos," he commanded.

We went down the elevator and out into the street where I was struck with feeling like I would suffocate. It hurt to inhale. I had a handkerchief around my mouth and nose as we walked to the Farmacity one block away on Avenida Boedo. Ramon talked to the clerk in the pharmacy and paid a few pesos. Once in the small procedure room, a pharmacist brought in a little machine and gave me a plastic mask to put on. He filled the reservoir with a solution, and turned it on. I breathed through the mask for a few minutes and immediately felt better. So that was a nebulizer machine. I wished I could walk around hooked up to one.

I never worried before about Acts of God or natural disasters such as earthquakes. I was used to them in Los Angeles; severe shakes as I'd experienced in '71 and '94 never frightened me. However, after a big earthquake, I still had clean air to breathe even if my china and antique pottery suffered.

One thing about living in BA was that there were no earthquakes, tornadoes, hurricanes, floods, or volcanic eruptions. No Acts of God in particular, just lots of acts of people, for better but often for worse. But the winds of ash know no barriers.

When I saw the videos on the news, of cars buried in cinders in Bariloche, of day turned into night, with dead fish and sheep, of hospitals full of those who couldn't breathe—and with the week-old memory of the pristine skies and waters I had experienced, I was heartbroken. My mind filled with images of Pompeii. I had believed that scientists could tell when a volcano was about to erupt, and people could be warned to leave the area. I guessed not.

For nature, these events were not disasters, just things that happened in the scheme of the natural world. But for man—building his house on sand and damning the mudslides (as they do in Malibu, California), we needed to have more respect.

CHAPTER 39

I could see overseas women being overly flirtatious and they would get many dances. I wondered if more was involved. Certainly with Australian women a few of them have told me they have had sex with the men they danced with.

—Anonymous Milonguero online survey response

August 2011

The milonga was like a snapshot, a microcosm of Argentine life. Over the years I saw everything happen there, the ebb and flow, the yin and yang, the good and the evil. One Saturday night in Los Consagrados we witnessed an incident so terribly shocking I couldn't believe my eyes. We were dancing on the crowded floor close to the front of the hall, where Osvaldo and Coca Cartery were sitting at the edge of the pista. The Famous Milonguero (Osvaldo), the tango idol of many and Tango Champion from 2004, was walking (not dancing) along the floor to return to his table when a dancing woman accidentally stepped on his foot. He took her butt in two hands and shoved her, she slapped him, and then he slugged her face with his fist!

Blood streamed from her nose. She returned to her table, the waitress brought her some ice, and then she gathered her belongings and left the ballroom. Osvaldo sat looking smug, while Coca put her arm around him in comfort. Those of us who had been dancing nearby were rooted to the floor with our mouths open in shock watching this awful scene.

Osvaldo and Coca had been champions of the tango contest back at the beginning, in 2004, when requirements were few, and competition little. Ever since, butter wouldn't melt in his mouth. But the real Osvaldo was the opposite of humble. I had always heard that now because of the championships and teaching, his skinny fingers were all over his female students in inappropriate ways. I didn't know for a fact that he was a dirty old man, but now I saw with my own eyes what a violent misogynist he was. Hitting a woman in public—what a machista asshole! Poor Coca, I wonder what her married life had been like, but I could only imagine he had hit her too.

It was also around that time that Pablo Verón, who had become super-famous after starring in Sally Potter's movie, "The Tango Lesson," got into fisticuffs with a woman at a New York milonga.

These were men who had fans all over the world, who were tango idols to many. Osvaldo and Coca made a cute couple on the floor, Osvaldo so skinny and old, Coca short and round wearing stiletto heels and housewifey dresses. They had been married forever and once their children were raised, they went back to dance at the milonga. And somehow won that early championship. But I believed the power and fame—as well as the money from teaching—had gone to his head and made his machismo even more intolerable. I felt sorry for those who idolized him, because they had no idea what a bastard he was.

There was something a bit immoral to me about worshipping so-called heroes who behaved badly. We could admire their talent—the way they play football or golf, or the way they danced. And that was what should be appreciated, not the whole package of a low-down, rude, haughty, superior s.o.b. Famous tango dancers were famous mainly due to good luck and marketing. If a person liked the way someone danced, they should by all means study how they danced. But perhaps they shouldn't be "adored" otherwise.

CHAPTER 40

I hated the comments, the way men leaned into my space and whispered their relish of my anatomy.

—Miranda France, *Bad Times in Buenos Aires*

March 2012

How naïve I was to think I could get a round trip to L.A. on 30,000 miles. When I tried to book the ticket they said I needed 120,000 more. The regular price was $1800usd. I was very disappointed not to go home for my birthday. I had really been looking forward to the possibility. Ramon wanted to refinish the wood floor as all the dancing had removed the shine, and I couldn't be in the apartment because of the chemical odor. I never envisioned when I first moved to BA that one day I wouldn't be able to afford to buy a ticket for a visit home. I supposed I would just have to wait until I got my tax refund.

Ramon made empanadas to celebrate my birthday. We had more than twenty guests and only half as many forks and glasses. We borrowed stools from the portero. Ramon worked hard preparing the meal, serving, arranging the table and seating. Luckily when he cooked, especially the delicious empanadas that were his specialty, he hardly drank at all.

May 2012

I was proud and honored, as well as nervous, to have been invited by the U.S. Embassy to read from *The Church of Tango* at the Buenos Aires International Book Fair. The reading was Monday, April 30 (a holiday in BA). Following my presentation was Donigan Merritt reading from his novel, *Blossom*.

Like many writers who are used to working alone in silent rooms, it was a bit traumatic to read aloud one's own work especially if it was about yourself. I had always been afraid of public speaking, and even after joining *International Toastmasters* never completely conquered my fears. Still, It was a chance for personal growth, as they say.

My first book reading: a thrilling event for me. I became too emotional, so it wasn't as great as it should have been. But it was an extraordinary occasion anyway, especially because so many friends showed up in support.

The *International Book Fair* in Buenos Aires had grown to be second only to the Frankfurt Book Fair, and was the largest one of course in Latin America. It took place for three weeks every year in the huge Palermo fairgrounds, La Rural, where Ramon and I had danced in the tango championship finals in 2006. Four big pavilions housed the many stands of publishers and bookstores from all over the world. It was strange to see stands from Cuba and Paraguay, and not from the U.K., but politics played a part in everything, books and information as well. It was great to see so many people not only interested in books, but buying them too, even mine!

The U.S. Embassy stand was quite impressive with its sleek white curves and changing colors via spotlights. It was simple, elegant and clean at the same time. There were several iPads in the lobby area with games and puzzles having to do with the U.S. And then a circular room with white poofs as chairs for the presentations.

After my reading my friends wanted to celebrate, so we stood in line at one of the many cafés and ordered a bottle of champagne, and another of malbec, while Ramon and Daniel were trying to arrange a table for six in the crowded café. Every time I looked over at Ramon, he was carrying a plastic chair over his head through the crowd.

The young man at the register told us he couldn't seat us there, and we said, no problem, our guys are arranging it over in the corner. He called someone on his cell phone while we were anxious to order some snacks to go with the drinks. The line behind us got longer and longer, but he was unflappable. Finally all was paid for, and instead of letting us go to our corner table, a waitress appeared and, opening a velvet rope, ushered us upstairs to the VIP Salon! We sat on purple and cerise velvet chairs and had our wines served in appropriate crystal far away from the bustling and noisy crowd downstairs. If this was the author's life, then it was for me. Now I had to get back to work on my prequel, *Arabesque*.

July 2012

July was the time of year I annually feared: the apartment lease renewal. My rent went up \$100usd / month —and at that moment we had no students, being winter and off-season. Plus I had to pay \$200usd to stay in Argentina another twelve months.

I had actually thought of moving back to L.A., but the idea of another big international move was frightening. I honestly didn't think I had the strength not only to move 6,000 miles north but also to find a place to live and all that that entailed. I had done it so many times, with so many possessions and treasures, and, well...it was beyond unthinkable to do it again. I didn't even believe I could make the flight to L.A. from BA many more times. A lot had changed since I had moved twelve suitcases to Paris on Christmas Eve in 1994. And then to San Miguel de Allende on Christmas Eve in 2001. I wasn't getting any younger.

October 2012

Yet, despite all of these feelings, unconsciously I think I knew I would be leaving in the near future, so I splurged on a five-day trip to Ramon's childhood home. He was born in a little village in the Province of Tucuman in the northwest and he had never been back since he left at age fourteen to come to BA with his mother. I wanted to see where he was from. Maybe that would help me understand him better.

But our trip was a failure. I knew that the city was surrounded by sugarcane fields because Ramon had quit school as a child to cut cane. But I didn't know that periodically they were burned to regenerate the earth. They were burning the fields when we were there. It hadn't rained for months and everything was covered in dust and ashes, even the flowering trees. The air, plants, windows, cars, everything was gray with soot. I had to go to the hospital. Ramon got sick too. We did make it to his village and I got to see the house where he was born. Some of his cousins still lived there, and I was glad they could meet once more.

For the past few years I had survived my expat life in Buenos

Aires by being almost a recluse, hermit, a shut-in. I had never been agoraphobic before, but somehow in BA I was. With so many students and friends with tales of muggings, my own included, plus the polluted moist heavy air outside, I was most comfortable inside with Mirasol, Coquito, and my computer. Then I felt okay. Judy called me frequently and it was such a delight to hear her lovely cheerful voice when I answered. She was undergoing many difficulties lately, including the loss of her son, her own surgeries, and increasing forgetfulness, but she was always upbeat and positive despite it all. She provided a wonderful role model for me.

We planned to buy a baby female parakeet so that Coquito could have a family. Mirasol was as needy as ever but seemed to have mellowed some. I was grateful to have them both. But I still missed Phoebe my Expat Cat, and I guessed I always would. Poor Mirasol, the truth was, it was more fun to talk to Coquito because he answered me. I used to joke he was trilingual: English, Spanish, and Bird. He said all kinds of cute things, like "Dame un beso!" (Give me a kiss) and gave my lips a peck, and "Birdie Boy," "Okidoki," and "Te quiero, Mama!" I had to keep reminding Ramon to not use bad words around him!

CHAPTER 41

Do not call it piropos. If you walk the street of Buenos Aires and an unknown person talks or honk to you that is catcalling. I lived in Argentina for 30 years and as a regular woman you never feel flattered when that happen you always feel uncomfortable and humiliated. You can't dress the way you want, you can't walk freely wherever you want. I hope things would change, I know it is a cultural thing but we should educate men, they may think it's a compliment but it's harassment.

—Maria Victoria, Facebook

December 2012

For bloggers writing away a couple of times a week, the truth of an expat life is raw and naked—not perfumed and poetic or polished like the full-on memoirists who write in reflection. There was no time to edit one's life let alone one's daily blog posts plus research information or recipes. I noticed that many of the blogs I followed were shutting down. Most of the expats I knew in BA who didn't own local businesses or who were not married to a local with a business, had left or were planning to. And everyone I knew had been mugged or robbed. No wonder I was afraid to leave the apartment without Ramon.

The expat life was not easy. And whether I put myself out there when I was down or crawled into my home library, it was just survival. Even if I had a handsome local boyfriend, even if I managed the language, even if I had a nice place to live even if it wasn't mine, even if I could dance tango whenever I wanted, still I was so far from home at the end of the world.

Living in Mexico had been quite different, less foreign due to all of the U.S. and Canadian expats who lived there, and certainly less far away. San Miguel was a town of 140,000, not a capital city like BA of 3,000,000 people, and I could walk the whole town, meeting friends everywhere. From Leon, the airport closest to San Miguel de Allende, I could be in Los Angeles in two and a half hours. The Texans I knew could even drive home or take the bus to the border. And Mexican life was full of spiritual events and wonderful holiday customs, and there was always something to see and do.

I had become more and more unhappy, nervous, and sad, particularly at the thought of having to be in BA over Christmas. I would have loved to go home but I couldn't. And I didn't know how to make things better. I didn't want to spend my last years like this, even though that was what I had planned when I moved to BA nine years ago.

January 2013

I was feeling trapped in the sweltering city. Neither Ramon nor I even wanted to go dancing, and if we didn't have the tango, what did we have?

One Saturday night we decided finally to get out, maybe it would cheer us up to dance and see people, but we returned from the milonga with both of us in a bad mood. Ramon had had way too much to drink—champagne and beer at the milonga, and when we got home a lot more beer. He started to argue with me, I wasn't quite sure about what, but he kept talking over me. I got more and more irritated, and retaliated in all of the foul castellano I knew, and I knew a lot of awful words. I had always felt that Jack brought out the best in me, helped me to be a better mother and a better person. But I was my vilest self with Ramon. He brought out the worst in me and I hated that. I didn't like the woman I had become. Finally I went into my room with Mirasol and my computer and slammed the door.

But I was nervous and couldn't sleep. Instead of one Ativan I took two, and then several hours later, I took two more. In the morning it all started over again, with Ramon's critical attitude and my frustration, so I took another one, and then a few hours later, another one. Ramon fixed lunch and we drank red wine, but I still didn't feel relaxed. And then I blanked out. I remembered nothing about the whole afternoon and evening, except vague memories of my taking all my books out of the étagère. Ramon said I took down the Mexican cross that was over my bed and tried to hit him with it. He said I tried to jump off the balcony. I didn't remember any of that. He took me to the ER, but I didn't know what happened there. It was a lost 24 hours. The next morning I got up and got ready to teach a class, but I was certainly a zombie teacher, although I really couldn't remember.

I tried hard to recall what had happened. I knew the episode was brought on by too much Ativan combined with alcohol. I was hurting so much inside, so frenzied in my brain and body with nerves, each pill I took I expected to relax me and to make me feel better, but it never happened. Then the wine with the meals just pushed me into a blackout. I recalled pulling all of my books down to the floor, and maybe even my clothes out of the closet. I mostly remembered seeing Ramon watching me with such sad, mournful eyes.

I didn't remember at all trying to climb over the terrace railing to my death. But I had been briefly suicidal at age nineteen when I was a student and had been hospitalized for it. So I guess the "suicidal tendencies" were there. It was true that over the years with Ramon in BA, when we were fighting—almost always about something I didn't understand—sometimes when I tried to sleep I imagined myself swallowing a bottle of Ativan and jumping into the Rio de la Plata (I couldn't swim), just anything to stop the pain.

The next morning everything was in order, except I couldn't comprehend why my books were all rearranged. I had had them in a particular order and, after I had taken them down, Ramon just put them back in any way on the shelves. My clothes in the closet were also shuffled and willy-nilly. After our return from the hospital, Ramon had worked to clean up all the messes I had made.

The fact of it being a lost day was very scary. Who knew what I might have done when completely out of my mind? I never suspected I was capable of violence, but if I could attempt to hurl myself off the terrace maybe I could hurt someone else too? What kind of life was this? I didn't recognize myself. Was this why I had worked so hard to build a life in Argentina? Was this what loving Ramon had made of me? Was this the result of my tango addiction?

CHAPTER 42

I've seen lots of beaten women. Once in a make-up class, the teacher was touching up a woman's black eye to cover it up. But I've seen plenty since: the wife of the vegetable seller on the corner, who sat around on boxes on the sidewalk drinking with his drunk buddies all day everyday, while his wife ran the verduleria and looked after their tiny kids at the same time. She got beaten up pretty bad. I've seen women on the subway with black eyes. Once you've seen one you start noticing more and more.

Then of course there's worse news: men killing their wives, ex-wives, ex-girlfriends, and even their ex-partners and their whole family. It happens daily. It's on the news daily. Beaten women are beaten into submission.

—Marilyn, an expat in Buenos Aires

February 2013

A wealthy American milonga friend invited us and another couple for a visit to her condo in Punta del Este in Uruguay. Unfortunately the weather was bad most of the week. Ramon just went fishing once and never saw any signs of a fish. He said he kept changing the bait out of boredom. There wasn't much to do, especially in bad weather. He barbecued a lavish meal on the terrace, and made empanadas. I was surprised he was restless as all it took usually was beer and TV to make him happy.

A huge resort area, there were only big condo buildings dotting the shoreline, fancy designer shops in town, and beautiful beaches. Uruguay was more progressive than Argentina, but also more expensive; still, there were all sorts of imported foods in the markets, which delighted me. I loaded up several items to take home to Buenos Aires.

We went to a milonga that was part of the tango festival that was going on—it was difficult to get ready to go out at 10:30 pm, especially after a big asado, but we did it and found our way there through the dark streets. Without a reservation the five of us ended up at a bad table, but everyone was dancing Nuevo anyway, which meant non-traditional music, fancy show-off steps, no embrace but a "hold," poor floorcraft. We stuck it out for a couple of hours and then all agreed to leave.

The night before we returned to BA, Ramon couldn't sleep, and he was extra nervous on the flight. When we got to Boedo in the taxi, he looked up at the apartment in fear. It was then he told me he had a premonition that something awful had happened. Perhaps all of my furniture would have disappeared, or Mirasol the cat would have fallen off the terrace, or he didn't know, but something was missing, gone. I knew he was part *brujo*, a witch, from his mother's side, and his frequent psychic moments would often frighten him if they were horrific. I somewhat believed in his prescient ability, especially after one night when he woke up from a deep sleep and ran to the terrace to look into the street. That roused me, so I followed him. "Que pasó? A nightmare?"

"I dreamed someone stole my car!"

He got dressed and went downstairs, and sure enough, his car was gone! It had indeed been stolen.

And now he had dreamed that I was gone. He had read my subconscious mind and seen the future.

March 2013

I hadn't been writing on my blog much lately. For a few years I posted three times per week. I had always wanted to be a columnist, as I felt the personal essay was my forte, and the blog was a perfect way to express myself, especially as Ramon and I didn't really converse except to exchange information. Most of my posts received many comments, and so it was like a conversation and I felt a bit less lonely because of it. But I was getting tired of all the tango questions. I told Ramon that although I had used to enjoy it, I couldn't stand anymore being the "go to" person for tango advice in BA. And of being the hostess for whomever felt like dropping by our table, with no warning and expecting to sit with us and to dance with us, and talking about whatever, assuming I would translate for them. Then when they took lessons they went elsewhere, sometimes leaving me with their bar bill, and I was fed up.

The previous night there had been five unknown women at our table. Ramon was exhausted, and yet these women demanded, cajoled, cried for attention, insisted on help communicating with the waitress, and complained to me about everything.

I wanted a table for two from now on, maybe we would even wear disguises. When I was at a milonga I wanted to listen to the music, watch the dancing, greet friends (briefly), and dance with Ramon. But of course that couldn't happen in BA. When we were out of town we did that, as we had in

Mar del Plata, but the milongas outside of the capital were never the same, never the great salons, with the wonderful dancers and fabulous music we were used to. But at least where we were relative unknowns, we could just be ourselves. The funny thing, though, was that Ramon, underneath it all, was shy. It took me a long time to realize that. So when he was in a social situation where he didn't know people, he was quiet and reserved, just the opposite of his usual outgoing self. He went with me to many events and gatherings where English was mainly spoken. He was a good sport, but he never had a good time. (And sometimes he took it out on me afterwards.)

I had offered to teach him basic English numerous times, but aside from a few useful phrases, especially those he could use in tango classes, he wasn't interested. He peppered his speech with a few favorite English words that sounded very charming and cute. He could say, "What is your name?" and "Where are you from?" in several languages, but he communicated best with body language.

And while I just wanted to dance with him, part of the milonga fun for him was to dance and impress other women, show off his flirtation skills as well as his dancing. I understood that and didn't mind, because I wanted him to enjoy himself and be happy. What I did mind, though, was when these foreign women (the locals never went outside of the codigos) came over to our table, ostensibly to greet me as if we were friends, and then turn to Ramon and ask him to dance, even though he often kept his hand on my leg in a proprietary manner when we sat next to each other. Sometimes these aggressive women massaged his shoulders and neck, and if there were an empty chair next to him they would sit and try to talk to him in pigeon Spanish, often asking me to translate, hoping eventually he would dance with them. It was extremely rude, I would become annoyed but I never let on. Those tactics usually never worked anyway, because Ramon was very traditional and wanted to be the asker, as the codigos required, the *conquistador*. One woman from L.A. was especially aggressive with him, and the final straw came when she pointed her finger at him and said, "You owe me a dance!" And that was it. He never danced with her again.

You couldn't keep on giving to people who only take. It had to be reciprocal. I've had the same issues in my life, and when I was down, I finally learned to avoid the life-suckers. I learned not to give mercy dances, mercy fucks, mercy time if there was nothing in it for me. Reciprocity was key. That was what friendship and love were all about. People may have thought Ramon was only taking from me, but I felt he gave to me all that he could as well.

I lost the friendship of several American women during my years in Buenos Aires. One I had been a friend with in Los Angeles cut me cold one night in Gricel. Later on I tried again to greet her and once again she turned her head away. I had no idea why, but the truth was, I didn't care enough to make a big deal about it, inquiring why she was angry with me. And then there was a woman from Toronto who I thought was a bit ditzy and over the top, but whose company I enjoyed anyway. When she asked Ramon to dance and he said no, she wrote me a letter saying that because of that, she would no longer speak to me. And then one friend I had been especially close with, the one who had invited us to Punta del Este, the one we took to the hospital instead of attending our favorite milonga because she couldn't explain in Spanish that she had hurt her hand, wrote me an email to say because she heard about something on Facebook that I hadn't previously told her, I was not the type of friend she wanted so she was cutting all ties.

I didn't understand any of these women, just wished they had talked to me personally about the problems they had had with me. I began to wonder about my own defects and annoying qualities that I didn't know I possessed or how to correct, and to think that maybe that was why Ramon was so frequently mad at me. He never explained either.

A milonguero named Horacio had a heart attack and died on the floor of Canning. What a way to go. I envied him a little bit.

The U.S. Embassy invited me again to give a book talk and reading in their booth at the Buenos Aires Book Fair. What an honor. This time I would read from my new memoir, *Arabesque: Dancing on the Edge in Los Angeles,* the prequel to *The Church of Tango,* part of my eventual memoir trilogy, Death Dance Destiny. Arabesque was a kind of love letter to L.A., the Los Angeles that didn't exist anymore, and to the depressed teenaged girl who wanted to dance and be loved more than anything else in the world.

Instead of having a birthday lunch or dinner like usual, this year I wanted a St. Patrick's empanada fest, with no mention of my special day. I joked to Ramon that he should make the empanada dough green, and he almost choked. I went to every party shop I could find looking for green party favors, paper plates, napkins, and surprisingly I only could find three green balloons. But along with silver ones, they made the terrace festive for our shamrock luncheon.

On my actual birthday, we were invited to lunch at the

Club de Pescadores (Fisherman's Club). I had wanted to go there ever since I first saw it sitting out on the pier in the river in all of its Victorian splendor. And of course I assumed they served fish, something I didn't get enough of in Buenos Aires. I also assumed, being in Argentina, that there would be beef somewhere on the menu for Ramon.

CHAPTER 43

I witnessed a young woman rolling up her skirt at a milonga almost revealing her underwear to get men's attention. She would otherwise be a normal person outside of the milonga...Foreign women new to tango often misinterpret Argentine men's embrace and the body connection.

—Anonymous comment on my blog:
tangocherie.blogspot.com

June 2013

One of the foreign women who regularly visited BA to dance was a wealthy Chinese woman from California. Lala was beautiful, tiny, and looked twenty years younger than her age of 55, which she used to her advantage—dressing like a teenager and wearing her hair waist-length. The Argentine men were crazy about her. She said she was turned off of men after her divorce, but that didn't stop her from coming round to our table at the milongas to ask Ramon to dance.

Roberto, an Argentine, regularly visited the capital about once a month from the city of Colon outside of BA. He taught tango and organized a milonga there. His birthday was coming up and he invited Ramon and me to perform at a big celebration in his town. I wasn't keen on it until he said that he hired the Reyes de Tango Orchestra to play too. I loved them, the way they played the same arrangements of Juan D'Arienzo's music from the Golden Age. We had previously performed "Loca" to their music one night at a local milonga. He also invited Lala to attend the party, as he had a crush on her. Naturally he was married, but his wife knew Lala too, and it all sounded like a fun weekend. I always enjoyed going someplace new.

We asked Lala to ride with us and I explained that Ramon's car was an old jalopy, hoping somehow that she would ask her chauffeur to drive all of us. But we made the three-hour journey in Ramon's batata.

We arrived on time, which in Argentina meant that we were early. In all these years I had never learned how not to be on time. Even though I tried, I was always the first at any gathering. The Reyes showed up and played their first set, and a couple of preteens danced a choreographed number. However no one had done a sound check and there were loud pops like gunshots every so often and I screamed at each one due to my sensitive startle reflex.

A lavish buffet was served on the dance floor that was soon covered in grease and crud, impossible to dance on. Then there was lots of cumbia from the DJ. The sound exploded again. I thought my ears would bleed. The Reyes hadn't returned. Guests began to smoke. Ramon said he knew it would be like that, that the fiestas in the countryside were always like that. He thought it would be hours yet before we would perform.

"Ramon, I'm sorry but I have to get out of here. You can stay if you want but I'm walking back to the hotel."

Lala said, "Me too."

Ramon was pissed off. "I drove three hours not to honor my commitment to perform?"

"Sorry, Ramon, I can't take it anymore. If you knew it would be like this, you should have told me. Blame it on me. Tell Roberto I'm sick."

I was aggravated that this out-of-town weekend had been a disaster from beginning to end and seemed to encapsulate the unhappiness and loneliness I felt. No matter what I did or how hard I tried, my way of doing things, my expectations, were different from the Argentinian reality. After living and trying for ten years, I didn't want to be a misfit foreigner anymore, although I supposed I already was; I just never realized it before.

CHAPTER 44

I have a beautiful hacienda. I can show it to you.

—piropo

July 2013

I had my annual round-a-bout with Juan, my landlord, over his desired 25% rent increase. The building fees also went up 25%. Juan thought I could trade my pension dollars on the black market to get more pesos. It was illegal to exchange money anyplace but at banks and casas de cambio for official rates, but nobody did that. Even people in the government did the same thing. The official exchange rate was complete fiction. There was a website where you could check the fluctuating prices of all the various dollar exchanges. The illegal dollars were called "blue" to differentiate them from the cheaper black dollars, and of course the black market dollars, which were the cheapest of all.

Exchanging dollars for pesos became a series of whispers, back alleys, fortified doors, and passwords to enter *cuevas*. The savings were substantial, but it was so against my grain to deal under the table or against the law that it made my stomach hurt each time I had to do it. But of course I did it like everyone else. We even advised our students where to go for the best blue dollar deals.

Money fears put me over the top and I knew my reactions and anxieties were a little extreme. I thought every year at this time of my lease renewal that I might be dead and then wouldn't have to worry about it anymore. I panicked about having to pay more—not only for the apartment but also in building fees and utilities as well as general cost of living. Argentine inflation was endless but my income was finite and fixed, although because it was in dollars I was a little better off. But any time you change foreign money into local currency, you pay, and in Argentina you pay a lot. So that is why I rather hoped my time would be up before the obligations of each new year terrorized me anew with sleepless nights and dread. I was at the age now that I could realistically pass away of natural causes and no one would be shocked. People would just say, "Well she had a good life."

As a distraction I did a lot of sky gazing out on my terrace. Frequently the moon was breathtakingly beautiful, and I would call for Ramon to come out and look at it with me, but he wasn't interested in the moon. It was frightening that it was magnificently full so very often—it seemed like every week. The moon's rapid waxing and waning appeared to illustrate my recent life. Time was circling swiftly past me, like the shooting stars or the Milky Way moving across the sky with the Southern Cross. Even the sky was unrecognizable to me at "the end of the world": no North Star, and the familiar northern constellations appeared "upside down" and difficult to find to my eyes used to the heavens above the Equator. It was eerily strange and lovely on a clear night, even with the light pollution of BA. I imagined the same moon in Los Angeles shining on the Griffith Observatory, on the Hollywood Bowl, on the Santa Monica Pier, on the people I loved.

Those moments out on the terrace almost made me wish

I smoked because I wanted to stay outside, but with nothing to do I usually went in after only a few minutes. It would be nice to sit looking at the sky with someone in the dark and talk intimately about thoughts and feelings and ideas, but Ramon stayed inside with the television. I did love it though when he was watching football. Boca Juniors was his team, and he would excitedly shout "GOL!" all by himself. I was happy he was happy. Out on the terrace I could hear the same jubilation echo around the barrio. "GOL!" came from the four corners.

Earlier I had taken a student to the Bellas Artes Museum, where we saw Van Gogh's *Le Moulin de la Galette* from 1886. There had been a Van Gogh exhibition there in 2003, and now we saw some works by local artists inspired by his painting. Looking at the night sky often made me think of Van Gogh and his "Starry Night." He wrote to his brother Theo, "I know nothing with any certainty but the sight of the stars makes me dream." Yes, me too, Vince.

In the daytime I took hundreds of photos of the skyline and rooftops on my corner of Carlos Calvo and Maza, with the resplendent skies as a backdrop. Due to the pollution the sunsets were gloriously colored works of celestial art, and black clouds rolling in from the river or breaking up after a storm were dramatic punctuation marks.

After a while I specialized in shots of laundry hanging out to dry on the rooftops. I don't know why it fascinated me to see week after week the same clothes hanging on the same lines but always looking different depending on the light. Because parrillas were often on roofs, there were asados and parties almost every Sunday with fragrant smoke perfuming the barrio, and I took photos of those too with a telephoto lens, peering into other people's lives.

Even though it was a stretch financially for me, I sent

Ramon to Rio de Janeiro to get his teeth fixed. Our tanguera friend in Rio, Olga, the dental surgeon, offered to do it for free. I just had to pay any lab costs as well as his airfare and expenses. He would be there for two weeks. I couldn't go along because of the cost, even though I certainly could have used some beach time with a caipiroska in my hand. It was freezing and damp in BA, and the possibility of snow was being discussed on the news.

I was nervous about his being gone for two weeks because I depended on him for everything. Now I was really suffering from agoraphobia and didn't want to leave the apartment alone. I was lucky to have a *dispensa,* a little grocery shop, on the ground floor of my building that had not much selection but still a little of everything. So when I didn't want to take the granny cart to the big supermarket or even the smaller "ArgenChino" markets, I could pick up basic supplies downstairs. It was owned by Giovanni, who we called "Tano" because he was Italian, and his sociable wife, Blanca. They were so nice to me and it was comforting to know they were just downstairs in an emergency. Blanca gave me her home number and told me to call her anytime if I needed anything.

Ramon was nervous too about Rio because he didn't like travelling or flying, and this would be his first flight alone. Tooth infections could lead to brain damage and loss of sight. But I told him I couldn't be with a man with few teeth.

He Skyped me every night with Olga sitting in the corner of the room. He was unhappy, although it seemed she tried her best to entertain him between dental sessions. They went to the beach and to milongas. He shopped at the market while she was at work and did the cooking. How bad could it have been?

He returned with a couple of healthier teeth, a small bridge, and a prosthetic tooth he put in on special occasions. And with a completely different opinion of Olga. Previously he couldn't say enough good things about her, but now he didn't even want to mention her name. I let it go.

CHAPTER 45

You dropped a paper... the one that was wrapped around you, sweetie.

—piropo

August 2013

My gynecologist at TV Salud always wrote the Ativan prescriptions for me. She knew me through the years and trusted that I had some sense. But this time when I ran out she was on vacation, and I had to see a psychiatrist to get the script. He was tall, handsome, and very young—and he freaked out when I told him I'd been taking one milligram every night to sleep ever since Jack was diagnosed. "New studies show that with verbal therapy along with an antidepressant, you can get off of the lorazapam."

"No, doctor, I'm fine just as long as I can get it. I only take one tablet at night." (I didn't mention the lost weekend of the Ativan and wine disaster.)

"But taking it so many years is not healthy. I must insist you try to get off of it as I suggested. You don't have to quit taking the Ativan, you take it along with the other drug I will prescribe. And then see me every other week for therapy."

I didn't want to agree. I was afraid. Over the years I had tried various types of antidepressants that all had given me terrible side effects. But maybe this new study would prove to be helpful. It would be great not to have to take anything or to be dependent on a pill to sleep. Like now, when my doctor was on vacation, it could be a crisis if I couldn't get a refill.

I filled the prescription—I didn't know what it was in English—Xanax, Lexapro?—and started taking it once a day and still took the Ativan at night. After a month, Dr. Morales upped the dosage of the antidepressant to two, one in the morning and one at night. But after a couple of weeks I felt like I couldn't move, as if I were nailed to the bed. I had no interest or energy for anything. Even on Saturday, I didn't want to go to the milonga.

On Sunday I didn't take it, and I felt normal. Of course I still took the 1 mg of Ativan to sleep.

On Monday I felt awful, nauseous, and then all of a sudden that night I started to heave from both ends of my body. It was violent. I fainted on the kitchen floor. Somehow Ramon got me to the hospital; I didn't remember going or anything at all for days. Ramon said I looked green and dead, like a zombie again. It took more than a week to recover.

When I did recover I had to take stock. I told Dr. Morales I would never again take an antidepressant, I was done even though I knew the depression seemed to be getting worse. Memories of my hospitalization with depression for six weeks when I was nineteen came back to me, especially as I had been thinking and writing about those years in *Arabesque,* my new memoir. And now I was seriously agoraphobic too, afraid to leave my apartment without Ramon.

What kind of existence was this? Everything got worse with time and age, I knew that. What would my life be like in a few years? What if something should happen to Ramon, my lifeline? I had no other support system in Argentina now that Judy had gone to the British Care Home. All of my friends came and went, left and returned. Sure I knew folks in BA, but did I have anyone to call on in an emergency? Basically I didn't have anyone to call on for socializing either, as everyone worked and had families who needed them. I socialized at the milonga and sometimes went to parties. When visiting friends came on holiday we had lunch or met for a drink, and then they went back to their lives in other countries.

I came to see that ever since Jack had died in 1991, I had tried to trade devastating grief for a productive life with international moves, relationships, adventures, speaking new languages, and dancing. But now I felt ready for an easier and simpler life. And one in which a man, however helpful and responsible, didn't try to control me.

CHAPTER 46

The first time I went to Argentina I was overwhelmed. Men had no problem telling me I was "hermosa," or that I had beautiful eyes (code for breasts). Once I was walking out of my apartment and a man stopped in front of me and clutched his chest. 'I'm dying!' he said. "I'm dying, I know that I am dying because an angel with golden hair just dropped out of the sky!' He laughed and continued walking. At my age it felt good! It is nice to hear that you look good, smell good, are attractive. However not all piropos are nice. Sometimes they are about your body parts and what the man wants to do with them.

—Deby, Tango Spam

September 2013

My baby son was pregnant! I had just about given up on Jason at 44, but finally he met the perfect woman and was in love. I was so happy for him, and for me. Although being far away I was torn. All I could do for the baby shower was to send a baby gaucho outfit back with a student to mail to Jason in L.A. There was no one from my side of the family left, no one to represent his mother at the shower.

We had few students but Ramon had no other work. He had hopes of working as a *remisero*, but the transmission broke on his batata and he was trying to fix it. I was so sick of the worry and stress, I was at the point of despair, where I had been for some time. I didn't even want to go to a milonga; I just wanted to stay home. Alone.

I realized that because of my age I was nearing the end of my life, something that made me more anxious than ever about living it "well," enjoying it, having fun occasionally. Lots of expat folks were trying to figure out how to leave Argentina, but without tons of money, it was difficult. The crazy inflation, the constant strikes, the crime, the insecurity caused many people to reconsider their lives in Argentina, me among them. Now the prospect of a wedding, baby showers, and a baby, made me yearn for "home" more than ever. Soon my little blood family of two sons and one grandson would be enlarged to four. And I wanted to be there.

I had never planned to leave Argentina. I had built a life in Buenos Aires, I had a partner whom I cared about, I had students—although many less than before. I also had the best tango in the world, and I had a reputation and a kind of "fame." I had my pets, I had my few treasured belongings brought over little-by-little on airplanes, I had an apartment that I loved. But the 25% yearly increase scared me. I was constantly worried about money. I missed my family, few though they were. And the extremely difficult Argentine way of life was getting me down the older I got. I wanted to go home, like Dorothy. But it took quite a bit more than clicking my ruby heels together to leave everything behind and start a new life again in Los Angeles.

If I left would that mean I had failed? Would I be giving up? I wasn't a giver-upper. I honored my commitments, even to myself. I had planned to live in Argentina until I died. I didn't have a Plan B. When I worried about getting Alzheimer's,

Ramon promised no matter what, he would take care of me. No one wanted to do that in L.A. How could I turn my back on all that I had built during the past eleven years?

I had joked for many years that Ramon's list of priorities was Family, Car, the Tango, and Cherie, in that order. I always laughed when I said that to people. But now I thought, do I really want to be Fourth on his priority list? Or maybe it was just my imagination, maybe that wasn't his list at all. But that was how it felt, and now I didn't like feeling last. Aside from my family so far away, he was my Number 1. I always knew I was Number 1 to Jack, as he was mine, because I knew I was the most important thing in his life. But with Ramon, I did feel like Number 4, and perhaps there were others on his list ahead of me. I had no idea, because we never talked about emotional things. Although he did so much for me and was consistently reliable, I felt more and more like I was his "job." He showed up, did what he was supposed to do, and went home when the job—teaching, cooking, dancing—was done. Wasn't that work? Was I his *work*? I was getting tired of perceiving myself as an outsider in my relationship as well as being the perpetual outsider in a foreign country at the bottom of the world.

CHAPTER 47

In Argentine cities, piropos, or catcalls, are as common a *sound as honks and sirens. They can be as subtle as the pop of a kiss from a lorry driver or as menacing as a shout of, 'Oh God, if I got my hands on you…' Some men think these are compliments. Mauricio Macri, Buenos Aires's mayor said not long ago that 'secretly, all women like it when you catcall them.'*

—The Economist

December 2013

The hottest holiday season ever! BA was a concrete jungle with few shade trees. Christmas Eve the polar bear in the Buenos Aires Zoo died of heat exhaustion and stress from the fireworks. I knew just how he felt.

Furthermore, because of all the air conditioners working overtime, Boedo suffered a blackout. Without electricity the water pump on the roof couldn't work so there was no water. Ramon carried up buckets of water nine flights of stairs so we could bathe and flush the toilet. We had to cancel our scheduled tango classes because of no elevator and no music. All the food in the refrigerator spoiled. The blackout ended after ten days only when all of us neighbors congregated on the street corner below my terrace and banged pots and pans, a *cacerolazo,* the traditional way to protest in Buenos Aires. And soon, electricity was restored. But my blood pressure dropped so low I had to go to the hospital with heat stroke and be on an IV for several hours.

In the middle of the terrible heat wave, Edith from France arrived. She and her travelling companion's cruise ship had docked in Retiro, and they were staying a few days in a hotel near the Obelisco. I couldn't believe it, since she had never travelled much, as she only spoke French, and good food and eating well was a priority. But now here she was in Buenos Aires!

She invited me and Ramon to a restaurant in Recoleta, saying she wanted to taste the best food Argentina had to offer. Maybe her hotel concierge had suggested it, but it was German, of all cuisines. We met there, right across from the famous Recoleta Cemetery, and I was so happy to see her, although I had to dig very deep for my French. I wanted to tell her everything, but I couldn't find all the French words. She insisted I suggest the most typical and tasty Argentine dishes on the menu, as being a chef, and French, food really interested her, but because it was German, I couldn't. It was a very boring menu with the typical Argentine Master Menu dishes plus a few German ones of pork and cabbage. I think they were disappointed.

Her friend, François, was in a wheelchair and I felt bad because BA was not set up for the handicapped. Even their hotel room was difficult, with no easy access into the bathtub. I tried to talk to the manager who wasn't at all accommodating.

Ramon of course wanted to cook for them, so they came over the next day for an asado. Ramon prepared different cuts of beef, some sausages, chicken, and a variety of vegetables on the barbecue. He wanted to give a good impression of Argentine cuisine—especially after the German restaurant. I made salads and chimichurri, the national sauce for meat. And then after he cleared away the lunch (it had been too oppressive to eat outside on the terrace), he insisted on giving them a tango lesson. He even got François up out of his chair and had him dancing a simple walk with Edith in just a few minutes. It was rather breathtaking to see.

Naturally we wanted to take them to a milonga that afternoon, and Ramon danced with her while I took lots of photos. I was so happy to entertain them, as Edith had done so very much for me. I continued being frustrated that my French was buried so deep. I wanted to tell her countless things. I needed to confide in my long-loved friend. But I couldn't.

True to form, she had brought me a large Tomme de Chevre cheese, my favorite, almost melted in the horrible heat. I felt sad that the weather was so disgusting during their visit. I could hardly breathe outside, and they weren't used to this December heat, humidity and pollution. They both were very good sports about it. I hoped they enjoyed Buenos Aires, because I realized I no longer could.

It seemed that Buenos Aires was having a meltdown along with me. There was a fire of toxic chemicals on a Chinese ship in the port that filled the city with a poisonous cloud, a colossal electric rainstorm that flooded the streets enough that people who had them used canoes, and a tornado a little ways out of town. Plus it was a "regular" day to close the subway, so the traffic was insane. My barrio again lost electricity for several hours, so we had to cancel a programmed tango class. I didn't think I could take another BA summer. And I was so sick of being sick.

Especially as Jason was now the father of Greyson James! I was thrilled to see the beautiful little family when we Skyped, and ached to take baby Greyson in my arms. Maybe I should have left Argentina a couple of years ago, but now I had the best reason in the world to return to Los Angeles and my precious little family. I was already a grandmother to Adam's son Dominic, but had missed out entirely on getting to know him as a child because I was out of the country his whole life. I vowed that this wasn't going to happen with Greyson, let the chips fall where they might.

I never especially wanted to be a mother, it just happened, and I was glad. But I had always wanted to be a grandmother—a kind of kooky Auntie Mame type who would have a wonderful relationship with the grandkids and introduce them to the extra lovely things in life like classical music, exotic food, and Paris. And now was my chance. I had waited long enough: Jason was in his mid-forties, and I wasn't getting any younger. I had lived for ten years with the fact that family was everything in Argentina, and now I wanted my own.

February 2014

Jason Skyped me holding the most adorable baby, my grandson."Mom, I need you here, I want you here. You will love little Greyson so much!" And that was the impetus to tell Ramon my plans: that I was going to leave Buenos Aires and return to Los Angeles to be with my little family. He took it calmly and very quietly. Although he was sad on the surface, who knew what he felt underneath since he never talked about his feelings. Certainly he could understand, being the family man he was, how it was important to me to be with my new grandson. But sure enough, according to form, he got sick, and was in bed for several days suffering with a cough and congestion.

I had worked hard to build a life in Argentina. I had done my absolute best. The idea of another international move was nearly inconceivable. I had no strength left. I had moved "definitively" to France, to Mexico, to Argentina, and now I had to face the reality that none had been the "forever home" I had yearned for. My beautiful apartment, the perfect furnishings and decorations, my books and possessions, my pets and plants, the people I knew, and most of all, Ramon, would have to stay behind. When I made my final Equator crossing north to Los Angeles all I would have on arrival would be my sons and grandsons, two suitcases, and my Mexican "shoes in a suitcase" painting.

I had been granted more life than I had expected after having cancer twice, and many more years than Jack had lived. That meant another chance at happiness. I was ready to move on, to take risks once again on a new life with all the work and uncertainty that entailed. And yes, with more loss.

CHAPTER 48

By saying the most beautiful words, it's the same as dancing the tango—maybe you're ugly, but if you are a beautiful dancer, you have a chance.

—Oscar, street artist and tango dancer, in an article by Kaitland Quistgaard.

May 2014

We took Mirasol to the vet for some nodules on her belly, and the doctor just shook her head. It was a kind of sarcoma. She was terminal.

My time in Argentina was coming to an end also. Ramon was taking it like a champ, at least on the surface. He was under the illusion that I would come back to visit in November. He wanted me to keep the apartment and rent it out for profit to tourists, not a bad idea, but I couldn't afford to maintain an "income" residence in a foreign country—I couldn't even afford to rent a garage apartment in Los Angeles. I was hoping I could work again at the library to make ends meet.

He was wounded though, and occasionally comments escaped him. He danced with someone to Miguel Caló, my favorite orchestra, and almost always we danced that tanda together. When he sat down afterward, I said, "So how was dancing Caló with someone else?" And he said, "I didn't realize it was Caló until too late, but anyway, we have to get used to it, don't we?"

Yes, I would have to get used to no more fabulous tandas with Ramon, my partner of so many years. No more milonguero warm, cozy, and safe embrace. No more surrender to the music and a man who always danced me well. Maybe I would also have to get used to living without the satisfying and thrilling tango that fed my addiction, the emotional and spiritual tango that had sustained me since my first trip to BA so long ago. The tango had always been different outside of Buenos Aires–less musicality, emotion, sensuality, connection, soulfulness—everything I was addicted to.

Could there be awe-inspiring, sensuous, emotional, mystical tango without the machismo that kept it from being just another ballroom dance? Could the tango be the same without the macho man holding me in a tight embrace, leading me to do beautiful movements I didn't know I could do? Maybe in order to live as a happy, free, independent woman there was no place in my life for the tango that I loved so much, for the macho man who made me feel like a desirable woman, a man who danced me well.

It was a different tango world now in Buenos Aires. Like everything else in life, all was in flux. Nothing could ever stay the same, no matter how much we wanted it to. I knew that better than anyone. So many of the famous milongas where I used to dance had closed: Sunderland, Pavadita, Sin Rumbo, Almagro, Italia Unita, Galeria, Viejo Correo, Maracaibo, Glamour, Glorias Argentinas, Porteño y Bailerin, Niño Bien, Los Andes, Plaza Bohemia, Maipu 444, and the biggest loss of all, Club Español. So many milongueros had passed away too.

I recognized that it wasn't the same for me anymore, not

even the holy tango that had brought me here. That now perhaps it was the time to move on, even though it was so difficult to imagine leaving the life I had built with so much effort.

Still, I was looking forward to living without the chauvinism that determined how women should lead their lives, the toxic masculinity that caused the man I loved to be frustrated and angry when he couldn't order me around, or when I didn't understand or care what machismo demanded of me.

Ramon was finally scheduled to have the hernia surgery that he had needed and avoided for years, and I was grateful that I would be there to take care of him afterwards. Unfortunately it wasn't at the same lovely hospital, San Camilo in Parque Centenario, but was on a dark side street in Constitución, a sketchy part of town. I didn't like it from the beginning. It felt like the Black Hole of Calcutta. Trying to be admitted at the appointed time, there were not enough seats and many patients and their families had to sit on the floor in the hall, including us. And then once checked into his small and sad double room, the nurse told him to shower with a special antiseptic soap, but there wasn't any and the shower wasn't even working. I couldn't believe it. The nurses and the doctor seemed competent and were kind, but the facility was abysmal.

I waited in the depressing room during the surgery, and just like after his gall bladder operation, the anesthesia had a bad effect on him and he was a bit delirious. There was no cafeteria or food available for visitors, or a place for me to stay as there had been at San Camilo. So once I got him calmed down and a bit more relaxed, much as I hated to leave him,

I went outside and looked for a taxi to take home. It was a scary neighborhood and there were no cafés or restaurants anywhere near and I had to eat.

So I taxied home, ate something, tried to rest but couldn't. I went out on the terrace and stared at the blood moon shining down, and then took another taxi back to the dark scary hospital to sit by his bed and hold his hand, trying not to worry about his wellbeing once his healthcare and I were both gone.

I put ads online and asked friends if they were interested in buying any of my antiques, which hurt Ramon. He helped me pack, boxing up books to donate to the English Library in El Centro. He lugged my beautiful glass and iron étagère down the stairs and up the stairs of the girl in San Telmo who bought it. He carried framed posters to the homes of friends who wanted them. He carted bags of clothes home to his granddaughters to sell or give away. He heaved my old appliances and gigantic tube TV down the elevator and took them home in his batata.

His friends at the milonga harangued me with pleas not to leave—that I would fight with my son and/or my daughter-in-law and then I would be sorry I had left Ramon.

It would get much worse than this, I knew. I looked at Ramon and saw the future. Mirasol the cat would pass away, our relationship would be over, my Argentine life would end. It felt like when I had looked at Jack and saw the tragic conclusion waiting for us, could see it in his face and feel it in my heart. The sad finale was ahead.

Mirasol became sicker, sadder and more pathetic. The ulcers all over her body were infected, leaking pus, blood, and foul odors. As my time to leave BA got closer, I panicked about what to do with her. I had taken her to the vet several times (unfortunately the veterinarian who had rescued her was no longer practicing), explaining that I was leaving the country, she was obviously terminal, and she needed to be put down. Each time the doctor said as long as she eats, shits, and walks, she would not be put down.

"What am I to do then?" I cried. "No one will take her, will you take her?" The doctor took a step backward. "I'm leaving Argentina. She is suffering, in pain and misery. What do you want me to do?"

"I'm sorry, but at this point there is nothing I can do."

I was panic-stricken. "I am moving from my apartment, I have a plane ticket to fly back to Los Angeles, no one will take a dying cat. Please help her go in peace!" I was begging. But it was no use.

"Come back when she is closer to death," the doctor said.

Oh God in heaven!

CHAPTER 49

The Argentine male treats the woman badly, the woman leaves him and then he cries, drinks and sings a tango. He is always a weeping male, singing and crying. And why? Because he treated the woman badly. Treat her well, crazy guy, for then all is well and you do not cry anymore.

—Luca Prodan, 1953-1987, Italian-Scottish musician and singer, leader of rock band Sumo

June 2014

The very last milonga I would attend in BA was at La Nacional, the elegant Italian club on Calle Alsina in El Centro. As we walked up the marble stairs to the salon on the second floor, I felt nostalgic and sad that tonight would be my last tango in Buenos Aires. I wore my prettiest dress, an orange silk, with orange and gold suede *Comme Il Faut* stiletto heels. We had made a reservation with Dany y Lucy and a *frappero* of champagne was waiting for us on our table. Also at our table was an unfamiliar young blond woman who had asked Dany for us at the door and he sat her there. She was from Los Angeles but I didn't know her. Wearing white jeans and sneakers she didn't speak castellano or know how to dance. She just sought the real tango experience like many tourists do. I wanted my last milonga to be for me. But years and years of hospitality to tango tourists prevented me from just asking her to go sit somewhere else. Anyway it was very difficult for me to be rude. So she sat next to me asking me all the usual questions about tango, the milonga, the people, the codigos.

Then Ramon got up and went to sit at a front table with a striking curly-haired brunette woman I didn't know. He actually sat down with her at her table! This wasn't done. I felt like an abandoned old shoe. Everyone knew this was my last milonga and was watching the drama. My partner of ten years had left me to sit with another woman in front of everyone. I felt sick, shaky, and I broke out in a cold sweat.

The stranger next to me was quite lovely so I told her to look at the men in order to get her up and possibly away from me, but she was too shy to stare. And without the "mirada," a woman didn't dance. We drank the champagne. The time dragged. I kept staring at Ramon and his Argentine "amiga." I didn't know who she was, thinking surely he would return at any minute. I was stuck. Women didn't wander around the dance hall. We only got up to visit the restroom, and then returned to our table.

But finally when a rhythmic tanda of Juan D'Arienzo began and since Ramon and I always danced to D'Arienzo, shaking with nerves and anger I did go over to Ramon and the woman. "Ramon, are you coming back to sit with me? We haven't even danced yet." I stared at the woman next to him but she looked like she couldn't have cared less.

"When I'm ready," he said. "You have someone to talk to," tossing his head towards our table and the uninvited guest.

"This is our last chance to dance. Why should I sit in a corner?" I was hoping to embarrass him.

"I'll come back when I'm ready. My friend and I are just

catching up," he said calmly, draining his beer. I wondered who was paying for it.

"You can catch up when I'm long gone. Or now. I don't care. I'm leaving. *No me lo banco más*. You can fuck yourself." Maybe Ramon wasn't ashamed but I was.

I returned to my table, left some money for the champagne, and made an excuse to the young woman. She had said she wanted tango lessons from Ramon, but I told her he was unavailable.

Grabbing my jacket and bag, I bolted. I was so humiliated and, as is my way, just wanted to remove myself from a bad and uncomfortable scene. I ran down the marble stairs and stood under the art nouveau glass and iron canopy outside hoping to snag a taxi, but Ramon came right after me and led me firmly by the arm to his batata. He seemed discomfited maybe but certainly angry. I guessed I hadn't realized how very angry and hurt he was at my leaving. This was his way of expressing it, of acting it out because he wasn't capable of talking about his feelings. Or maybe rude behavior was just more macho.

He drove back to the apartment like a maniac, both of us silent, just the roar of the engine tearing through the night. I was afraid we'd have an accident but luckily the streets were empty at that late hour. Still it was a wonder we didn't crash into something. When we arrived, I told him to go home, I had had enough. The tango that didn't happen was my last tango in Buenos Aires. I didn't want to see Ramon again until I went to the airport.

At the last possible moment, with my suitcases loaded into

Ramon's batata, we took Mirasol to the vet, where finally she was put out of her, and my, misery. There was no time to drive to the country to bury her as we had done with Phoebe. I was holding her towel-wrapped body in my lap in the front seat of the car, crying hysterically. Ramon, ever practical if not sentimental, stopped at some trashcans on the way to the airport, and we put her inside, my heart breaking. We said a prayer as we laid her body into a dumpster along with my aspirations, effort, heart-longings, love, and regret, as well as my tango obsession. I supposed my addiction was cured. Tango Heaven seemed oh so far away now.

I would never, ever, understand this country, and Lord knows, I had tried. Now I had to start over in another country—my own. Somewhere I had to find new courage and desires. Somehow I would drag some hopes and dreams out of my sad soul. I just had to begin, once more, by getting on an airplane.

> *I already feel that it has done me good to go South, the better to see the North.*
>
> —Van Gogh, letter to his brother, May 1890

GLOSSARY

MILONGUERO

My definition of a "milonguero" is an old tanguero. He has grown up in the milongas, never taken a tango lesson, probably learned by watching and with help from his dad, uncle, or brother, never had a regular job or profession and worked part-time in some menial field, and went every night to the milongas where he danced until dawn. He had to wear a suit and his shoes had to be polished or he wasn't allowed in. Therefore by this definition there is no such thing as a "young milonguero" or even a "milonguera." In the olden days women just didn't hang out alone every night at milongas unless they were working girls.

Previously "milonguero" was a term of disparagement. "Oh, he's nothing but a milonguero!" implied that the man had no regular job, hung out in the milongas dancing every night looking for women, and had no money. He was almost always married.

But recently "milonguero" has become a complimentary term, indicating that a man had danced all of his life, knew the music and the codigos, and probably danced very well. Alas, milongueros are quickly disappearing and so the word has taken on a more simple and modern meaning a man who frequently dances in milongas.

ABUELO

Grandfather

AGASAJO
entertainment

AMIGO/A
a friend

ASADO
the food that is barbecued

ATORRANTE
a man who doesn't work

BAILARÍN
a dancer

BÁRBARO
great, interesting

BATATA
literally a "yam," an old car or jalopy

BATUCADA
a substyle of samba and refers to an African-influenced Brazilian percussive style, usually performed by an ensemble, known as a bateria. Batucada is characterized by its repetitive style and fast pace.

BESITO
cheek kiss

BESO
kiss

BOLICHE
a nightclub

BOLUDEAR
to joke around

BOLUDO
a jerk

BORRACHO
drunk

BRONCA
anger

CABECEO
a nod of the head in order to invite or accept a dance

CALLEJON
alley

CACEROLAZO
a protest in the streets featuring the banging of pots and pans

CHABON
a guy

CHAMUYERO
a man who chats up women

CHAMUYO
sweet talk, pick-up lines

CHORIPAN
sausage sandwich

CODIGÓS
unwritten etiquette rules of how to behave in a traditional milonga

CONFITERÍA
a tea and pastry shop

CONSULTORIO
Doctor's office, examining room

CORTINA
literally a "curtain" of different music played between sets so it's obvious when the tanda is over. Everyone returns to their seats.

DALE
do it!

DAR BOLA
to pay attention

DEPENDENCIAS
maid's quarters

DESPENSA
convenience store

EXTRANJERO/A
foreigner

FACTURA
breakfast pastries

FIACA
feeling lazy

FRAPPERO
ice bucket

HINCHA PELOTAS
annoying

JODA
wild party

LINDO/A
nice, pretty

LUCA
money

MIGA
very thin small sandwiches

MILONGA
a place where social tango is danced; also one of the three rhythms of tango.

MANGO
money

MINA
girl

MIRADA
look, stare, glance

NI EN PEDO
not even drunk

NOVIO/A
boyfriend, girlfriend

OCHO
a figure eight, one of the basic steps of tango

OJO!
(with hand gesture under eye) Watch out! Careful!

PALADAR
private restaurant in Cuba, usually in someone's home

PARRILLA
a physical barbecue of brick or metal

PIBE
a kid

PLATA
money

PIROPO
compliment

PORTEÑO/A
A person who lives in Buenos Aires

PORTERO
porter or super

QUE SE YO?
what do I know?

QUERIDO/A
sweetheart

QUILOMBO
a total mess, a disaster

QUINCHO
back porch, garden hut

REMISE
a private taxi

RONDA
the counter-clockwise line of dance

TAL CUAL
exactly

TANDA
a set of three or four songs usually by the same orchestra, all danced with the same partner

TANGUERO
a man who dances tango

TELO
a "love" hotel

TENER GANAS
to want to, to be in the mood

TRÁMITE
official document, bureaucratic paperwork

TRUCHO
fake

VALS
waltz, one of the three tango rhythms

VERDULERIA
fruit and vegetable shop

VINO TINTO
red wine

VIVEZA CRIOLLA
artful lying

VISTE?
you see?

CHERIE MAGNUS

Death Dance Destiny memoir series:

#1 Arabesque: Dancing on the Edge in Los Angeles

#2 The Church of Tango: a Memoir

#3 Intoxicating Tango: My Years in Buenos Aires

Made in the
USA
Lexington, KY

Harvard Historical Studies • 189

Published under the auspices
of the Department of History
from the income of the
Paul Revere Frothingham Bequest
Robert Louis Stroock Fund
Henry Warren Torrey Fund

DISCIPLINING THE EMPIRE

Politics, Governance, and the Rise of the British Navy

SARAH KINKEL

Harvard University Press
Cambridge, Massachusetts
London, England
2018

Printed in the United States of America

First printing

Library of Congress Cataloging-in-Publication Data
Names: Kinkel, Sarah, 1982– author.
Title: Disciplining the empire : politics, governance, and the rise of the British navy / Sarah Kinkel.
Other titles: Harvard historical studies ; v. 189.
Description: Cambridge, Massachusetts : Harvard University Press, 2018. | Series: Harvard historical studies ; v. 189 | Includes bibliographical references and index.
Identifiers: LCCN 2017051034 | ISBN 9780674976207 (alk. paper)
Subjects: LCSH: Great Britain. Royal Navy—History—17th century. | Great Britain. Royal Navy—History—18th century. | Great Britain—History, Naval—17th century. | Great Britain—History, Naval—18th century. | Great Britain—Politics and government—1603–1714. | Great Britain—Politics and government—18th century. | Civil–military relations—Great Britain—History—17th century. | Civil–military relations—Great Britain—History—18th century. | Great Britain—Colonies—America—Administration.
Classification: LCC VA454 .K49 2018 | DDC 359.00941 / 0903—dc23
LC record available at https://lccn.loc.gov/2017051034

To Dad, for all the lessons, historical and otherwise

CONTENTS

DISCIPLINING THE EMPIRE

INTRODUCTION

THIS IS THE STORY of not how, but why Britain became the world's greatest naval power. It explains why the ascension of the British navy was inseparable from the modernization of the British Empire and the fracturing of that empire in the American Revolution. This book is intended neither as a complete history of naval administration and operations during the eighteenth century nor as a comprehensive discussion of eighteenth-century British imperial politics. These have been ably accomplished elsewhere. Rather, this is a consideration of where the two intersect and an explanation of why the nexus between the Royal Navy and the popular political sphere—particularly in the Atlantic world—was crucial both to the course of the future empire and to the development of the future navy.

Naval power exemplified British imperial might and made possible the empire that Britain became. Britain's naval ships carried its empire to the far corners of the world. They bombarded and blockaded foreign ports. They transported armies and administrators. They ensured the safe passage of imperial trade. They attempted to suppress and control imperial discontent. The British Empire as we know it could not have existed without such a commanding naval force. Its naval heroes are the stuff of legend and ongoing adulation. There is a strand of English national myth that holds that this tradition of naval triumph and fearlessness dates back to the Elizabethan era and the victory against the Spanish Armada. In reality, the majority of the fleet sent to face the invading Amanda was a cobbled-together force of merchant ships and privateers, not a royal or national force at all. There is another strand of myth that argues that the importance of naval power was something on which all

Britons agreed. The chorus of "Rule Britannia" seems to suggest as much: "Rule Britannia, Britannia rule the waves; Britons never, never, never shall be slaves." This unofficial national anthem depicts a nation unified by liberty, commerce, and the freedom of the seas and guarded by a benevolent navy. However, this song was actually popularized by people who criticized the existing navy as a tool of tyranny—it was propaganda about the way the British Empire and its navy should be, rather than the way they were. In comparison with their foreign competitors, Horatio Nelson and his fellow captains did indeed display distinctive qualities that contributed substantially to British naval victories—such as a duty-bound commitment to seeking out decisive battles and the willingness to engage in combat in extremely disciplined, and personally dangerous, ways—but those qualities would have been alien to British naval commanders of a hundred years earlier, when caution and prudence were rewarded over aggression and risk.

This overview highlights three questions that go to the core of our understanding of Britain's rise to naval glory and concomitant imperial power. If naval success was not a foregone conclusion, then when did Britain's naval ascendency begin? If there was not consensus over the form and function of the British navy, then what were the lines of rupture, and what were the political stakes? If much of Britain's eventual success on the seas can be traced to the actions of committed, disciplined, and aggressive sea officers, then where did those qualities come from, and why were those same officers reviled by some contemporaries as pirates? In short, why did Britain become the world's most dominant naval power?

The British Empire's rise to naval greatness was located firmly in the eighteenth century. These were the years which saw Britain's transformation from being just one amongst several competitive sea powers to being the acknowledged ruler of the waves. They were also the years that saw the global explosion of British imperial rule, the emergence of new, more socially challenging forms of political radicalism, and the eventual fracturing of the British Atlantic in a civil war. Each of these developments was linked to the others. Reintegrating the navy back into broader political, social, and cultural histories shows that the creation of a dominant naval force was neither inevitable nor consensual: it was the outcome of fierce debates within the Anglo-imperial world over the shape of the empire and the bonds of political authority.

✧ ✧ ✧

Did the British Empire have a maritime destiny? If so, it was not obvious before the eighteenth century, when there were clear transformations in both quantitative and qualitative assessments of British naval power. By the early nineteenth century, British ships were likely—though not certain—to force decisive battles and to be victorious, even when outnumbered. Battle was only a means to an end, however: the real goal was to be able to control sea lanes and protect imperial commerce, territories, and populations. In that regard, the navy also became increasingly successful at blockading enemy fleets and protecting trade. This was what naval dominance came to mean for British policy makers.

A variety of quantitative indicators point to England's growing power in relation to its external competitors. In the seventeenth century, control of the largest fleet shifted back and forth between England, France, and the Netherlands.[1] In 1675 the French navy outnumbered the English by a 3 to 2 ratio.[2] In 1691 the French naval secretary casually dismissed the English navy as being composed of ships that were "very poorly equipped and break down every day."[3] In contrast, by 1800 Britain controlled two to three times as many warships as each of its closest competitors, and Prussian field marshal August Neidhardt von Gneisenau admitted in 1815 that the British were the "lords of the sea, and neither in this dominion nor in world trade have they any rivals left to fear."[4] Based on total tonnage displacement (the aggregate size of all ships), Britain controlled fully 50 percent of the world's naval power in 1810. This was the only time between 1500 and 1850 that any country displayed such dominance.[5] The manpower of the wartime Royal Navy increased by more than 250 percent, while the manpower of the royal dockyards increased faster still. Britain's global reach expanded. Whereas in the seventeenth century the vast majority of English naval ships were deployed in the waters surrounding the British Isles, by the beginning of the nineteenth century, Britain had established a permanent peacetime presence around the globe, buttressed by dockyards in the Mediterranean, Canada, the West Indies, South Africa, and Asia. British sea officers and sailors became more effective at the mechanics of naval warfare. In Admiral Edward Vernon's 1739 capture of Porto Bello, British ships fired about once every two minutes. By the end of the eighteenth century, that rate of fire had doubled in many ships, owing to officers' emphasis on training their crews.[6] Britain became better able to protect its merchant ships in wartime. French privateers from the hub of Saint-Malo captured 858 British ships in the wars of 1695–1713, but only 41 in the Seven Years' War of 1756–1763. By the time of the French Revolutionary Wars, the Admiralty organized convoys protecting up to a thousand ships; as a consequence, during those wars the number of British merchant ships actually increased.[7] Taken together, these factors indicate a clear transformation in the reach, power, and behavior of the British navy over the course of the eighteenth century.

In attempting to explain Britain's naval dominance, historians generally emphasize several major factors: geography, economy, administrative institutions, and the culture of battle. All of these played some role in facilitating Britain's naval rise. However, all are missing the crucial component of political contestation, without which neither the true nature of the Royal Navy nor its development can be understood.

One factor that has formed the core of some explanations is Britain's natural geographic advantage. In this view, Britain was the power most geographically suited for warfare in the Atlantic world. While some older interpretations rested on the innately commercial characteristics that supposedly arose from Britain's island condition—suggesting that the superiority of Britain's navy was preordained because it was an island nation with a well-distributed population—other factors that should also be taken into account include the direction of trade winds and the location of natural harbors. British naval efforts had to accommodate these natural dynamics. At the end of the seventeenth century, as naval warfare began to shift from the English Channel to the Atlantic, William III ordered a new dockyard built at Plymouth to help victual and refit ships coming in from Ireland and other western approaches. As naval warfare moved south and west, natural factors had a role in dictating where and how naval power could be exercised. Geography was not a pure advantage, however: in many ways the French were actually better positioned to attack the English by sea than vice versa.[8]

A second major factor that historians have drawn on to contextualize Britain's naval rise is the nation's increasing economic power:

Britain's dynamic economy permitted the financial outlay a great navy required. During the eighteenth century, Britain experienced an economic explosion especially in overseas trade, which this interpretation suggests contributed to an increase in naval power in two ways.[9] First, maritime trade provided a nursery for seamen, giving the Royal Navy a pool from which to draw experienced recruits. Second, the increase in national wealth permitted Britain's governments to spend more on warfare. The British were able to use their expanding economy to field the numerically largest and therefore most successful navy.[10]

The third set of factors are the institutional and administrative, both of which build on the economic: Britain became the world's greatest naval power, some historians argue, not because of an expanding economy but because of the ability of Parliament to tap into national wealth and the development of a capable bureaucracy able to administer those funds effectively. This explanation rests on the establishment of Parliament as a permanent, trusted political institution following the Glorious Revolution of 1688–1689, which enabled greater extraction of wealth in the form of taxes and also enabled a greater loan of private wealth through the creation of a national debt. The British populace trusted parliamentary power in ways they had not trusted their kings previously and were therefore willing to give the state greater access to their wealth. The British government became increasingly effective at extracting resources from its population, assisted in part by its willingness—or obligation—to act in partnership with the private sector, which gave rise to a state particularly in tune with the desires of the mercantile world. Moreover, the fact that the navy came under parliamentary authority while the army remained a royal prerogative meant that the navy was perceived to be a symbol of national liberty rather than a symbol of authoritarian central power. The Glorious Revolution meant that Parliament was able to access the wealth of the nation and the nation was willing to allow its wealth to be spent on the navy, because it represented the liberty of the nation. During the eighteenth century Britain also developed significant naval administrative capabilities. Among these were the ability to manage large quantities of stores, to reliably victual ships so that their crews would remain healthier and the ships would be able to stay at sea longer, and to repair and maintain large numbers of ships of a variety of sizes, all of which were facilitated by a relatively meritocratic Admiralty secretariat that preserved institutional memory.[11]

Finally, there is the question of the particular tactics and the institutional culture of service embraced by the British navy: British officers were more aggressive and, simply put, better at actual naval warfare. Proponents of this view argue that in the latter half of the eighteenth century, a clear pattern appeared in how the British conducted maritime warfare. British officers demonstrated that pattern at Trafalgar: a highly aggressive form of combat even in the face of superior numbers that relied on trained, disciplined commanders and sailors for success, and a naval culture in which officers and men alike were encouraged to believe in the importance of personal abnegation in deference to national duty. The British institutionalized aggression in ways that required high levels of discipline from officers and sailors, such as Admiral Richard Howe's orders at the 1794 Battle of the Glorious First of June that his ships approach the enemy's close enough to lock yardarms, or about twenty feet apart. This ultimately allowed the British to unleash devastating broadsides from close range—which because of training, they could fire faster than their enemies—but exposed them to continual enemy fire while they approached and put the captain in the most exposed position of all.[12] This attitude was not shared by other navies.[13] French sea officers frequently tried to avoid combat unless necessary—not irrationally, since if a strategic goal could be accomplished without combat, then it was an unnecessary risk. British sea officers deliberately sought out decisive battles. The fact that the British were more aggressive in combat has been well documented by a variety of naval historians, who suggest that this difference was particularly visible from the late 1740s and 1750s. Daniel Baugh notes that "successful British fleet battles in the eighteenth century were fought by commanders who either issued special instructions and signals designed beforehand to deal with the inevitable problems or took a chance on success, knowing that a combat victory would vindicate them."[14] Ruddock Mackay and Michael Duffy suggest that "British fleet tactics and blockade strategy in the middle of the eighteenth century reached a level of sustained aggression and decisiveness in their outcome that had never been achieved before."[15] J. R. Jones agrees, maintaining that from midcentury, "aggressive leadership . . . brought devastating successes."[16]

Each of these factors—the geographic, the economic, the institutional, and the tactical—was an important component of British naval power. A landlocked country is an unlikely candidate for a naval power, as is a bankrupt one. A regime unable to incorporate the interests of its elites, in order to win their acquiescence and secure their investment in its projects, is also unlikely to be successful.

But are these factors alone sufficient to explain Britain's choice of and success in a naval path to power? A comparative context suggests that they are not. At a minimum, there have been many examples of countries whose historical experience did not correlate with Britain's and yet became naval powers, as well as of countries whose historical experience did correlate with Britain's and yet did not become naval powers. In terms of geography, France, the Ottoman Empire, Russia, and in the modern era Germany and the United States have each had powerful navies without being islands; if being an island is not a necessary precondition to being a naval power, perhaps it is insufficient in and of itself to explain that trajectory. Neither does a high volume of maritime trade automatically correlate with a country's likelihood of becoming a naval power. In the early modern period, Russia built a competitive navy without having a strong foundation of maritime trade. In contrast, Prussia had a large volume of maritime trade but no naval power to speak of. The independent United States quickly established global patterns of maritime trade but had no permanent naval force until the latter part of the nineteenth century.[17]

Moving away from maritime trade toward the question of overall economic power, France had a larger economy than Britain during the eighteenth century but was no longer the superior naval power. The explanation generally given by historians—and certainly believed by contemporaries—was that France had too many continental commitments to devote the full power of its economic or administrative might to fighting on the seas. This reasoning, that France had other political priorities besides naval power, is persuasive but raises another question. In the eighteenth century, Britain was ruled by German kings with German lands and therefore had a European foothold from which to base European conquest. Why did Britain not take its national wealth and create a continental army? What the French case illustrates is that political commitments matter. Britain was constrained by geographic and economic realities, but political considerations shaped which ones were significant. At any given moment, there were multiple paths forward for those who wished to see British power aggrandized on the world stage, and politicians as well as citizens engaged in heated debates over which to follow.

In short, each of the above factors is an important precondition for the development of naval power, but they are not sufficient. The major missing element is that of conscious choice and political struggle. Historians have detailed political spats over the British navy, but have interpreted these conflicts as operating at what might be termed a "surface" level, one in which participants still accepted the same fundamental underlying principles. For example, N. A. M. Rodger's magisterial *Command of the Ocean* outlines parliamentary conflict over victualing in the 1690s and over the conduct of naval affairs in the 1770s, among other moments of tension covered in the book's 166-year span, but explains both events as "partisan"—intended to attack ministers rather than the basis of naval policy. Rodger explains that there was "strong, consistent and broad-based political support" for the navy throughout the period; although "few [Britons] knew much about the Navy . . . they knew that they needed it" and "Parliament supported the Navy essentially because it was the physical embodiment of England's political and religious freedom."[18] Historians have shown that there were tensions over naval manning[19] and over the distribution of naval resources,[20] that the needs of the navy were at times in an uncomfortable balance with the government's other financial priorities,[21] that interest groups could influence naval policy,[22] and that individual sea officers could become objects of public adoration or condemnation.[23] However, these types of conflict were not about the essential form or purpose of the Royal Navy, nor have they been described as such. Rather, John Brewer terms the eighteenth-century navy a "virtually incontestable shibboleth." Jeremy Black argues that the navy was "one of the few fields in which opposition criticism was not directed at the fundamental bases of government policy."[24] Mackay and Duffy assert that "the British taxpayer" "believed in the navy's essential role"; Patrick O'Brien and Xavier Duran conclude, "Almost nobody inside or outside Parliament questioned the need to spend ever increasing sums of money to construct, man and maintain warships"; and Margarette Lincoln claims, "There was parliamentary consensus about the value of the Navy as opposed to the value of a standing army."[25]

A framework of "fundamental consensus" does not, however, explain why an English newspaper might warn that recodifying punishments for sea officers would lead "the reason, end, and intention of all law" to be "annihilated," why a pastor might give a sermon in Boston that classed officers as "pirate[s], who took away [American] property without their consent, by violence, by arms, by guns, by oaths and damnations," or why some parliamentarians argued that building defensive structures for the dockyards would lead to the downfall, rather than the support, of a maritime empire.[26] Even supposing that there was consensus within the walls of Parliament—which there was not—must parliamentary consensus automatically have reflected the opinions of the millions of people in the British Empire who had not cast votes for representatives? Can the political world of the empire be legitimately constrained to "Parliament" when the past thirty years of scholarship have shown us the dynamic and engaged nature of the public sphere on both sides of the British Atlantic?[27]

And yet, if there was deeper conflict at a fundamental level over naval affairs, why has it not been more fully recognized? One possible explanation is that the use of similar language has obscured the extent to which there was conceptual discord. For example, all eighteenth-century British politicians agreed that there should be an institution called "Parliament," though they did not necessarily agree about how often that institution should meet, who should be permitted to be a part of it, what its role should be, or what its relationship of authority was with regard to other political institutions. One could therefore make the argument that "Parliament" was a foundation of eighteenth-century British political culture, and there would be truth to this, but one could equally make the argument that "Parliament" was a concept that could divide as much as it united. I argue that the concept of "the navy" functioned similarly: on the surface, it might appear that politicians agreed, but in many ways this was a linguistic mirage that concealed genuine conflict.

This book focuses on the relationship between the political ideologies of the eighteenth-century British Empire, the form and function of the British navy, and the structure of imperial governance. Questioning political commitments is crucial to assessing Britain's changing naval fortunes during the eighteenth century. As Alan James has suggested, militaries can only truly be comprehended within an ideological context: "Perceptions, or ideas, in other words are important because that is what lies behind the decisions to build ships, guns, sails and complex organizations."[28] Understanding the relationship between politics and the navy requires taking the ideological content of eighteenth-century politics seriously. Contemporaries believed that changes in the governance of the navy not only reflected changes in their society but also had the power to shape that society. In this period, British sea officers suddenly began behaving differently both from their European counterparts and their predecessors of a generation earlier. While some welcomed this transformation as heralding a resurgence in Britain's imperial fortunes, others worried its consequences would undermine the foundations of the empire itself. These perceptions were validated as an increasingly disciplined and hierarchical navy became one of the primary means by which imperial administrators attempted to reshape imperial governance into increasingly disciplined and hierarchical patterns following the Seven Years' War.

✦ ✦ ✦

The political classes of the British Empire were divided about the feasibility or desirability of naval power. In the connected debates over the shape of Britain's empire, society, and military, several distinctive viewpoints emerged over the course of the long eighteenth century. The chapters that follow center on the primary moments of change and challenge to the Royal Navy in the years between the Stuart Restoration in 1660 and the aftermath of the American Revolutionary War in the 1780s, focusing particularly on the importance of the years between 1745 and 1775. They explain why different viewpoints came to dominate naval policy making at different moments and why British naval culture looked very different by the end of the century than it had at the beginning.

A word needs to be said here about the power structures that governed political and naval decision making in eighteenth-century Britain. There was no single authority in charge of all matters that touched on the navy. The Admiralty Board was the political face of the navy. As such, its members—normally seven commissioners, of whom the First Lord was the head—were political appointees. At least one commissioner and generally two or three were sea officers themselves; the rest might have little prior experience in naval affairs. Unlike some political appointments in the eighteenth century, a place on the Admiralty Board was no sinecure. Commissioners of the Admiralty Board met regularly and nearly every day of the week during wartime. The First Lord of the Admiralty was the liaison between the naval and political worlds: ultimately, he was the one responsible for ensuring that the navy could carry out the tasks politicians set for it. The Admiralty could enact some policies on its own but needed parliamentary or Privy Council approval for others. Some areas of policy were not clearly in the remit of one department or another, which meant that a minister who felt strongly about an issue or who had more political capital could annex it to his domain. The Admiralty Board shared responsibility for naval infrastructure, provisioning, and care for the members of the service with four other boards: the Navy, the Victualling, the Ordnance, and the Sick and Hurt Boards. In theory, these boards were parallel in authority and had independent spheres of authority; however, in practice the Admiralty increasingly monopolized authority and dictated overall policy to the other boards.[29]

Parliament had limited control over what happened within the navy. Members of Parliament could directly influence the yearly size of the fleet, or at least the amount of money earmarked for it. Any naval matters previously enacted by parliamentary law—such as the pay scale or the definition of what crimes were justiciable by court-martial—could only be altered by Parliament. Members of Parliament could express their ex post facto displeasure at events by launching an inquiry into naval expeditions, the behavior of officers, or the orders given to them by the Admiralty or the secretaries of state. Much of parliamentary influence on naval affairs ran through informal rather than official channels, relying on patronage, the public shaming of an inquiry, or pressure on leading ministers, who could in turn pressure the Admiralty. Ministers both in the Admiralty and in Parliament had to be sensitive to the opinions of the monarch, which still mattered.

Parliament, ministers, and the Admiralty were also increasingly influenced by popular politics. Even those who could not vote were often invested in national and imperial matters and could voice their opinions through formal petitions, informal protests, or other means. The shift of taxation away from land toward excise (consumption) taxes meant that the tax burden was now shared far more widely than it had been previously. Parliament enacted a greater number of public laws every year, which meant that national governance became steadily more prominent in the lives of people at every level. Popular discussion of major political and imperial issues happened across the country through newspapers, pamphlets, coffeehouses, and ballads. As the largest organization in the British world, which employed—voluntarily and involuntarily—many tens of thousands of people in war and in peace, the navy had a particular impact on many people's lives.[30]

In the connected debates over the shape of Britain's empire, society, and military, several major political groups emerged over the course of the eighteenth century.[31] These parties did not have rigid boundaries. Individuals sometimes changed from one affiliation to another. Groups collaborated on some issues and opposed each other on others. As in modern multiparty political systems, coalitions were sometimes formed between parties that did not agree on all issues. Some parties had concerns that overlapped with those of other parties, and some individuals held beliefs that defied easy categorization or changed over time. What identified each group was its particular constellation of concerns; voters perceived parties to act in ideologically consistent ways.[32] Though there were changes in the political terrain during this period, there were also coherent political genealogies from one generation to the next.

Chapter 1 argues that the navy was one arena within which the Stuarts and their opponents contested the nature of English governance in the years following the Restoration. It played an important role in debates over foreign policy, the political and social leadership of aristocrats versus the middling sorts, the expansion of royal authority, and the threat of Catholicism. During this period, the English navy was inferior to those of continental rivals. The navy continued to be a point of conflict following the Glorious Revolution of 1688–1689, particularly in debates over political economy, the shape of the empire, and the expansion of the state which mapped onto the new whig and tory political parties. Whigs stood for the increased role of Parliament, increased religious toleration for Protestant sects outside the Church of England, a political economy based on trade and manufacturers, and a foreign policy based on engagement with and intervention in continental European affairs. The tory worldview was hierarchical, with a high church ecclesiastical structure and strong monarchical authority, including some support for the divine right of kings. These were complemented by a land-based political economy in which wealth was inherently finite. Although the relative strength of the navy increased at the end of the century, English naval tactics remained primarily defensive.

Chapter 2 explores the naval policy of the "establishment," "court," or "Walpolean" whigs, who evolved from the seventeenth-century whigs. They believed the Glorious Revolution had gone far enough in changing Britain's constitution, imperial outlook, and general political settlement. Their primary concern was stability, which they attempted to maintain politically (by discouraging public participation in politics), economically (by reducing the national debt, avoiding expensive wars, and supporting the financial elites who funded the national debt), and religiously (by walking a fine line between supporting the established Anglican church without eliminating the liberties of Dissenters). This chapter argues that with the support of the first two Hanoverian monarchs, Prime Minister Robert Walpole pursued a continentally focused foreign policy that prioritized maintaining the balance of power through alliances and that equally prioritized restraint in government expenditure. To complement these policies, Walpole and his associates pursued a restrained naval policy, which was intended as far as possible to be inexpensive, passive, and useful in negotiating alliances. They saw little point in building up an expensive or aggressive naval force—a Royal Navy structured on those lines would only undermine the balance of power by making Britain appear aggrandizing, would be too expensive, and would be irrelevant regardless, because the establishment whigs did not want to expand the empire. The navy under Walpole was intended as a passive deterrent—large enough to dissuade other countries from going to war but used forcefully only as a last resort, if alliances and negotiations broke down. This policy of restraint and passivity was deeply unsatisfactory to the opposition that was beginning to emerge against Walpole's species of whiggery. One of the first major eighteenth-century moments of public debate over the role of the navy came in 1727, when Britain fought an abortive war against Spain and the Holy Roman Empire. Walpole's naval policy continued to be a central component of opposition critiques of his regime until his fall from power in 1742.

Chapter 3 looks at the alternative naval model put forward in the 1740s by the authoritarian whigs, one of the major opposition groups to Walpolean whiggery.[33] The authoritarian whigs perceived a growing disorder in British society and in the British Empire; they believed order, discipline, and hierarchy would prevent impending anarchy. Politically, they strongly opposed the reformers of the latter half of the century and believed that the current political system needed to be buttressed rather than broken down; economically, they supported taxing certain types of consumables, which they thought encouraged luxury and decadence; religiously, they tended to support the Anglican Church though they also were beginning to envision an empire that could accommodate Catholics; and in foreign policy, they strongly pushed to bring Britain's empire under centralized, rationalized control, so that colonies would become ordered, disciplined, and obedient. Leading authoritarian whigs negotiated their way into the Admiralty Board and enacted a series of professionalizing naval reforms they hoped would mold it into a disciplined, ordered force—one that mirrored the changes they hoped to see in British imperial society at large. The professionalization of the navy in the 1740s transformed it into a dedicated military force in which personal glory mattered less than commitment to duty—or rather, glory could only be achieved through obedience to duty. The authoritarian whig Admiralty inculcated the values of aggression against foreign enemies and obedience to superiors within the service. These reforms culminated in the 1749 Navy Bill, intended to strengthen and rationalize naval court-martial law and the second of the major eighteenth-century moments of public debate over military governance. The bill passed despite opposition that characterized it as an attempt to impose on Britain a despotic military system comparable to that of France or the Ottoman Empire. The authoritarian whigs were successful in implementing new systems of both reward and punishment in their attempts to discipline the fleet.

Chapter 4 looks at the alternative naval model put forward by the patriots, the second of the major opposition groups to Walpolean whiggery. The patriots perceived a growing constitutional corruption in British imperial society and believed that the solution to this was greater popular participation in forms of power, whether that power was political, economic, religious, or military. They protested oligarchy and supported the autonomy of local imperial assemblies, emphasized the importance of consumption as the basis of wealth and opposed monopolies, advocated for the expansion of more civil and political rights to Dissenters, and argued for an expanded empire based on trade rather than coercive control, from which more people would be able to benefit. The patriots distrusted a professionalized navy and proposed instead an ad hoc force in times of war, complemented by privateering at sea and a militia on land. Both privateering and militias were means of incorporating greater numbers of citizens into military endeavors without necessarily placing them under direct military oversight. Although the patriots had some success—the militia was formally reestablished in 1757—they did not have the influence to remove the naval system put in place by the authoritarian whig Admiralty. The Seven Years' War demonstrated the efficacy of naval professionalization as officers began to fight in tactically more aggressive ways and became less willing to back down from an open battle, even when outnumbered or when the risks were high. The execution of the rich and well-connected Admiral Byng for failing to obey his orders, a third major moment of debate over naval governance, cemented adherence within the naval service to disciplined aggression.

Chapter 5 argues that in the years between the Seven Years' War and the American Revolution, the navy was tasked with shaping imperial society into the same disciplined, ordered system that the naval service now embodied. Authoritarian whigs—buttressed by George III's sympathy to their cause—were now in positions of authority throughout the central British imperial administration. As they attempted to implement new systems of political and economic control throughout the empire, sea officers were their most reliable representatives in the colonies. This chapter argues that their reliability was a direct consequence of the navy's prior professionalization. As the patriots had feared, the professionalized authoritarian whig navy enabled the expansion of executive power, supported by military force, over civilians. While this could be seen throughout the empire from the Americas to India, it generated the most conflict in North America. Colonial resistance to what was perceived as military governance was a contributing factor to the American Revolution.

The Conclusion explores the navy's experience in the American Revolutionary War and argues that although the war is often described as a naval failure, British capitulation in 1782 in fact represented a political rather than naval defeat. As colonists had feared in the 1760s, the navy was able to exercise a significant stranglehold on American trade but was overstretched by a confused and disjointed strategy. When the public was forced to confront the question of why Britain had lost the majority of its North American colonies, few directly blamed the conduct of the Royal Navy, but many asserted that the administration should have directed the navy to abandon its despotic war against the colonies and focused instead on the empire's true enemy: the French.

The culture within the navy went from one that rewarded caution, restraint, and defense in 1700 to one that lauded risk taking, commitment of resources, and aggression in 1800. This shift was a direct consequence of the ideological struggles over the shape of the Anglo-imperial world that took place in London, Philadelphia, Boston, Madras, and beyond during the course of the century. Throughout this period, arguments over naval governance were intimately linked to arguments over political governance at home and abroad. Contemporaries believed not only that the navy was a necessary foundation for a variety of imperial aspirations, but also that its size, structure, and governance had the potential to impact land-based society.

The story of Britain's naval rise is not one of a military hermetically sealed from societal aspirations or fears. Instead, it is a story that is deeply embedded in the context of wider battles over Britain's imperial future and over the nature of the sociopolitical realm at home: arguments over the navy were integral to much wider disagreements and debates about the structure and governance of Britain's empire. Differing visions of Britain's imperial future and differing visions of that empire's social relations made arguments over war (the political goals of Britain's elites) and warfare (the culturally determined ways in which violence was carried out, when it was carried out) inevitable. The outcome of those arguments had real consequences for how Britain chose to project its power on the world stage and to what ends.

A politically aware history of the navy sheds new light on the common bonds, boundaries, and fractures of the Atlantic world. The historiography of the early modern Atlantic has in recent years extensively discussed the movement of people, goods, letters, and news from one shore to another. Re-creating these networks has been an important historical task, but equally as important is understanding the ideological world in which they operated. As the single largest organization of people and resources in the empire, contemporaries understandably believed the navy had a role to play in the future of that empire. Reintroducing the navy to these political debates is not just about bringing back a forgotten historical actor; it reorients our perspective on why some in London wanted to change the rules of the empire and how they thought they could accomplish that. The story of the eighteenth-century navy allows us to see the frictions along the boundaries of the British world, precisely because the navy was policing those boundaries both against imperial competitors and against imperial citizens. Thinking about the navy in this context brings together the complexities of the Atlantic system in a new, organic way. It allows us to connect the highest levels of parliamentary argument and the popular pamphlets that crossed the Atlantic with the actual face of imperial enforcement and the realities of imperial resistance.

Over the past thirty years, there has been a vibrant resurgence in interest in the political culture of eighteenth-century Britain. Although these histories often emphasize conflict in the political arena, they have followed in the footsteps of naval histories in accepting naval power as a point of universal consensus within British society, suggesting that there were no arguments over the basic premise of naval aspirations.[34] In fact, arguments over the form and function of the British navy played out not only in Parliament and in pamphlets but also in much wider displays, which in Britain involved burning admirals in effigy and in the North American colonies involved burning actual ships as well. This realization adds further support to the growing body of literature that argues for the politically and socially tumultuous nature of early modern and Augustan Britain. It challenges the still persistent though less dominant view that politics in eighteenth-century Britain was a matter of factional struggle rather than a matter of ideological principle. If even the navy—supposedly the bulwark of liberty—was open to question and contestation, then the British Empire was a divided society indeed. Debates over the navy were intimately connected with questions of imperial governance and the nature of the British constitution, two of the most divisive issues of the eighteenth century.

These debates played out throughout the empire and demonstrate the importance of connecting both British and American histories with those of the wider world. An insular British perspective blinds us to the possibilities a powerful standing navy represented elsewhere in its empire, even in white settler colonies. An American history that stops at the coastline likewise obscures one of the most powerful tools of governance that the imperial British state deployed against those colonies. Conversations over the proper form and function of the military took place in Britain, North America, the Caribbean, and India. Nor was this simply a case of the periphery repeating without thought the arguments of the center: individuals and groups in all parts of the empire made their own contributions to the conversation, which were absorbed and reflected in turn. Pamphlets were reprinted in multiple places, newspapers were copied and distributed throughout the empire, and across the empire, individuals were part of widespread networks, whether familial, commercial, or otherwise. Radical North American colonists laid claim to an authentic interpretation of "Britishness" every bit as much as a Norfolk clergyman, a London tailor, or an East India Company factor. The ideological divide was not predicated upon a monolithic British political culture in opposition to a monolithic American one. Colonial radicalism resonated within British society, just as the emphasis of some Britons on loyalty to existing hierarchical authority resonated with some American colonists. Moreover, many individuals and political groups saw the empire as unified in another way and believed that events in one part of the empire would inevitably affect their own. How India was governed signaled to American colonists how they might be governed in the future; whether the Church of England was established in America signaled to Protestant sects outside the church how they might expect to be treated on British shores. Eighteenth-century British history should not be confined by the waters around Britain's edge; rather, discussions of the British experience should be placed in this broader imperial world. This was how contemporaries understood the boundaries of their society, and I therefore use the phrase "Anglo-imperial world" deliberately.

Reintegrating political choice and contingency into the history of the navy also provides insight into issues of change and continuity in the British Empire. The historiography of both domestic and imperial Britain has long noted an increasingly authoritarian trend toward the end of the eighteenth century. On the domestic front, historians have pointed to the resurgence of loyalism based around a monarchical, hierarchical nationalism and the acts of William Pitt the Younger (such as arresting the leaders of reforming societies and suspending habeas corpus) as evidence of increased repression.[35] Within the imperial context, the American Revolution marked the shift from the eighteenth-century empire—Atlantic, mercantile, populated by white Protestant settlers, and with a large degree of local autonomy, or in other words, "Protestant, commercial, maritime, and free"—to that of the nineteenth-century—African and Asian, militarized, based on resource extraction from nonwhite subordinated peoples, and centrally controlled.[36] Historians generally attribute these changes to one of several exogenous forces: the debt of the Seven Years' War obligated a financial restructuring of the empire,[37] the territorial expansion of the Seven Years' War brought in new subject populations necessitating new forms of governance,[38] the American Revolution showed the fragility of existing imperial control,[39] or the French Revolution sparked fears of internal discontent and in turn efforts to contain that discontent.[40] However, the commitment of the same individuals and political groups to the same principles in each of multiple arenas suggests that rather than being separate phenomena, these authoritarian developments were all part of the same project. The authoritarian whigs supported an obedient empire, a hierarchical political society within Britain, and an ordered, disciplined military. The patriots and later the radicals promoted a more open political sphere, a less centralized and hierarchical empire, and a less professional and more civilian-driven military. These battles did not originate with the French Revolution or the Seven Years' War, which suggests an internal logic rather than an external catalyst. The authoritarian whig naval reforms of the 1740s embodied a model of society that was every bit as obedient and hierarchical as the one the authoritarian whigs of the 1760s or 1780s attempted to enforce. They were accompanied at the time by imperial reforms that mirrored those imposed in the 1760s, including reducing autonomy for colonial assemblies, reinforcing the role of colonial governors, and bringing colonial laws into greater compliance with British laws. Though unsuccessful at the time, the same individuals attempted to reassert similar principles of governance twenty years later, when the political parameters within Britain had changed. This suggests that the authoritarian shift historians have identified as taking place in British society and the empire during the latter half of the eighteenth century must be redated from the 1780s or 1760s to the 1740s. The push to reassert a more obedient, hierarchical society came from within. The so-called second British Empire based on territorial acquisition, central control, and stricter governance was not simply a contingent response to the accession of George III or to the outcome of the Seven Years' War, but a preexisting ideological strand in British imperial thought, waiting to be unleashed.

Arguments regarding imperial policy displayed continuities between the first and second British Empires rather than a sharp, definitive rupture, but the policies *implemented* changed. The late eighteenth-century authoritarian impulse described by scholars was real, though it was not new. One of its first and most immediate consequences was the revolt of the North American colonies, in which the newly professionalized navy played a central role. Just as it is time to reintegrate the navy back into the story of Britain's politically turbulent eighteenth century, so it is also time to reintegrate the navy into the story of the American Revolution. Port cities were central to disseminating revolutionary sentiment; waterfront workers were major catalysts in sparking revolutionary action.[41] The navy was remarkably efficient in disrupting the American economy during the Revolution, which it accomplished both by preventing waterborne trade and by capturing port cities, thereby interrupting the regional economies of which they were the hubs.[42] What is still missing is an understanding of what the navy *meant* to American radicals, who were largely located in the very port cities the navy was most able to affect directly. The navy embodied a very specific form of governance—centralized, authoritarian, hierarchical, with common law and civilian liberties subordinated to military law. Radical colonists critiqued the navy as an exemplar of arbitrary, militarized policies, as the naval force that previously faced outward against *guarda costas*, privateers, and men of war now turned inward on its own people. Sea officers searched and seized ships carrying illicit goods, enforced the Stamp Act even after colonial governors had backed down, and closed harbors in retribution for disobedience. Although the Seven Years' War changed the stakes for politicians within Britain, it was in large part the naval reforms of the 1740s that made the restructuring of imperial relationships possible. The navy was not simply a weapon to be used against foreign competitors; it was a means of exerting authority internally and a more effective tool than the army in policing trade and enforcing revenue measures. The professional navy proved to be a crucial tool in the hands of administrators in London as they attempted to force the modernization of their empire.

Third and finally, there is the question of what the professionalization of the British navy can tell us about the nexus between war, society, and state building. In the famous formulation of sociologist Charles Tilly, "War made the state, and the state made war."[43] This argument draws on technological changes in early modern warfare within the context of the highly competitive European system to explain the rise of modern states. In the early modern arms race, European rulers spent ever-greater sums on fielding ever-larger armies, which required ever-larger bureaucracies to manage both the armies and the taxation needed to fund them. Rulers were unable to opt out of these escalating military commitments because if they were to be defeated in battle, their regime would face annihilation. Technological changes led to changes in warfare, which in turn led to changes in society.[44]

War was certainly an important component in British state building. John Brewer's seminal *Sinews of Power* has shown how transformative the Second Hundred Years' War (1689–1815) was for the development of the fiscal-military state (characterized by a large military, a large bureaucracy, a large debt, and high taxes) in Britain. The series of French wars required an increased and more effective extraction of resources from the population, a bureaucracy with which to do that, and an administration that could likewise supply the military with manpower and supplies. The state in Britain became one that was strong (capable of exercising its allotted power very effectively) but that had a relatively small purview.[45] Rather than fiscal-*military*, however, a better term for Britain might be a "fiscal-*naval* state." The navy was not only one of the British government's largest expenditures; it was also one of its largest bureaucracies and in the eighteenth century employed a wartime population that exceeded that of every British town with the exception of London. The navy was at the heart of the state. As N. A. M. Rodger has suggested, "The industrial, technical and managerial resources required to build and operate warships vastly exceeded in kind and quality anything needed by an early modern army." In comparison to other European states, the British state was "distinguished by its commitment to a capital-intensive, high-technology mode of warfare demanding long-term state investment."[46]

But war did not make the state in a vacuum. France was an equal participant in the Second Hundred Years' War, but a very different state emerged. Culture and political choices mattered. These were always contested. Despite Britain's identity as a "maritime nation," the character of its navy was far from preordained. If a different political group had been able to control the formulation of naval policy as the authoritarian whigs did for much of the latter half of the eighteenth century, the Royal Navy—in size, in purpose, in culture—would have looked very different. It might or might not have played a role in sparking an imperial rebellion. It might or might not have been able to hold off Napoleonic France. Understanding the transformations that enabled Britain's rise to naval glory requires a return to two Clausewitzian principles: first, that war is the continuation of politics by other means; and second, that military organization is intrinsically linked to social organization. Why states declare war is political; how societies carry out violence is sociocultural. Understanding Britain's military development during the eighteenth century requires understanding both war and warfare.

In the case of Britain, the empire made the state as much or more than war did, and empire was a choice. Between the mid-seventeenth century and the beginning of the nineteenth, we can see the tandem development of a centrally ruled empire and the state apparatus within Britain. Under Oliver Cromwell, the capacity of the state in England expanded dramatically and the state also embarked on its first attempt at directly ruled empire in Jamaica. James II used the colonies as a laboratory for practices of governance that he wished, but was currently unable, to use in England. By the end of the eighteenth century, customs duties generated by colonial trade had become an important part of the state's fiscal foundation. Some hoped to use the navy as a part of that state apparatus. Its role in customs enforcement was intended to maintain the viability of one particular vision of the imperial state. Politicians and administrators attempted to develop new ways of tracking, shaping, and intervening in the lives of subjects in large part owing to the challenges of ruling imperial populations.

The professional navy was indeed implicated in and associated with the rise of the modern Weberian state in the British Empire—that is to say, with the monopolization by the state of legitimate violence, the emergence of an effective extractive fiscal system, and the creation of a bureaucratized administration.[47] However, the triumph of this system was not predetermined. The patriots who opposed professionalization were far from pacifist, but they abhorred the idea of a state monopoly on violence and emphasized instead militias and privateering endeavors which would remain in the hands of civilians. They likewise opposed the creation of bureaucratic "placemen," and there were vehement debates over exactly where, when, and in what ways the administration should be able to tap the purses of its citizens. The creation of a professional navy was a political choice, negotiated within the Anglo-imperial world rather than necessitated by international warfare. Likewise the creation of the particular British state that emerged—one with a monopoly on legitimate violence, an extractive fiscal system, and a large bureaucracy—was linked to the rise of a professional military, but by choice, negotiation, and struggle rather than by obligation. War did not make the state; political choices did.

This book demonstrates that debates over the nature and role of the navy allow us to understand the ideological texture and conflicts at the heart of the eighteenth-century British Empire and the development of the British state. Parliamentarians and coffeehouse politicians debated political goals, the ends to which the empire should direct war. They also debated modes of warfare. Some argued about how to harness and control the forces of anarchy and entropy they feared lurked behind every unregulated, undisciplined individual. Others argued about how to unleash Britain's power onto the world in a manner befitting its constitution and liberties. These debates mattered because contemporaries understood, in implicit and explicit ways, that the spheres of public life reinforced one another. Hierarchy established in one area was not always easy to break down in another, and power gained in one sphere could be applied in others. The creation of a professional Royal Navy based on order, authority, and central control thus foreshadowed and facilitated the modernization of the Anglo-imperial world.

1

SEVENTEENTH-CENTURY FOUNDATIONS

By the end of the seventeenth century, contemporaries had convinced themselves that they had a glorious naval past to live up to. The vision was heroic: Elizabethan ships facing down the Spanish Armada and swashbuckling adventurers sailing off to plunder far-flung imperial possessions (hopefully someone else's). However, the Elizabethan navy was largely composed of private ships temporarily united in national service, rather than a corps of royal ships intended for permanent standing service.[1] Elizabethan adventurers likewise embarked on private endeavors, at times given official sanction by the state, at times an unofficial wink, and other times crossing the line into piracy. There was not yet a tradition of having a permanent English naval force that could be considered comparable to a standing army. During the seventeenth century, the naval forces mustered by England were substantial—battle fleets could outnumber their eighteenth-century counterparts several times over—but the sea corps was still less than permanent and less than professional, although toward the end of the century there were changes in the recruitment and promotion of officers as well as in shipbuilding. During this period, English sea officers were often unreliable in carrying out their orders, and many naval expeditions failed to come to fruition. Politicians and the naval administration at times rewarded passivity in sea officers rather than risky aggression.

Nevertheless, the Royal Navy played a significant role both practically and symbolically in discussions over foreign policy and the domestic social and political order. Contemporaries debated the structure of the navy (who its officers should be, how many ships of what types it should comprise), the purpose of sea power (whether it was the primary theater of warfare or an auxiliary one, whether it was meant to plunder or protect), and the tactics of naval battles (should they be offensive or defensive). As was the case later in the eighteenth century, changes in the composition of the sea officer corps and in naval governance were taken to be a bellwether of wider sociopolitical changes: one commentator observed, "Our Navy is the soul of our government."[2] Opponents of government policy expressed concern that an expanded or more professional naval force would mean a concomitant expansion of executive power, threatening to unbalance the constitution. Throughout the Restoration and Glorious Revolution eras, the sea service was linked in the public mind to the most important divisions in English society.

The Seventeenth-Century Navy in Focus

During the seventeenth century, naval warfare changed fundamentally in character. While previously it had been standard for merchant ships to be involved in naval battles, they became increasingly obsolete for purposes of warfare as naval ships increased their firepower. In 1650 naval battles tended to include massive numbers of ships of a variety of origins and sizes, but by 1710 the trend was to deploy fewer, larger ships with more guns. In the seventeenth century, the English navy was substantial in numbers but existed in rough parity with its primary rivals, the French and the Dutch. By 1710, however, the British navy had increased in size to outstrip both, though it was still far from being able to exert unquestioned dominance over its competitors. During this period, most naval actions took place within the waters around the British Isles, expanding to include the Mediterranean during the War of the Spanish Succession.

John Guilmartin Jr. identifies a series of "revolutions" at sea during the early modern era, beginning with the first transoceanic sailing vessels in the fifteenth century, adapting to the use of gunpowder, and culminating in the ship of the line of the seventeenth century.[3] This ship of the line—capable of carrying heavy cannons and sustaining their fire—for the first time permitted potentially global warfare.[4] It also spurred two further important and related developments. The first was the invention of the "line of battle" as a combat tactic. In earlier naval warfare, battles were melees, with individual ships swarming and engaging other individual ships, frequently in an attempt to board the enemy ship and carry out hand-to-hand combat. They were land battles fought on floating platforms. In contrast, "line of battle" formation, which the English adopted in 1653, involved ships sailing one after another in a line, allowing them to discharge full broadsides of cannon fire at the enemy's parallel line. Previously, merchants had been encouraged to build ships that were suitable for war, which were then frequently hired or coopted into royal fleets.[5] The line of battle and the fact that ships would now have to be able to withstand direct cannon fire meant that there was less of a place for merchant ships in war fleets.

Although nowhere near as large in terms of manpower as the eighteenth-century navy, the navy was of considerable size even in the seventeenth century, at least during wartime. In September 1672, during the Third Anglo-Dutch War (1672–1674), the 238 ships in active service held just under 30,000 men—a population larger than all English towns with the exception of London and Norwich. The English fleets at both the 1653 Battle of the Gabbard and the 1665 Battle of Lowestoft were each composed of one hundred ships. As a point of comparison, Nelson's fleet at the Battle of Trafalgar in 1805 was composed of twenty-seven ships.[6] While the number of ships involved in individual battles did dramatically decrease, this reflected a tightening of control and an increasingly focused form of warfare. In terms of thinking about professionalization, merchant ships hired into royal fleets were naval mercenaries: private bearers of legitimate violence temporarily co-opted into a larger force. While they certainly contributed to the overall force a country could bring to bear on its enemies, they cannot be taken as evidence of a state's ability to control naval warfare, when it was forced to contract that warfare out. The commissioning of merchant ships faded after the 1660s.[7]

The English navy was not the unchallenged ruler of the seas during these years. As Table 1.1 illustrates, control of the largest fleet shifted back and forth between the English, French, and Dutch, all of whom displayed acute awareness of the policies other countries were pursuing. Louis XIV and his ministers repeatedly dismissed the idea that the English navy posed a real threat. In 1666 Louis XIV claimed "the English by themselves were not to be feared." Under the direction of Jean-

Table 1.1. Relative strength of major naval fleets, 1660–1710.

	England		*France*		*Dutch Republic*	
Year	*Ships of the line*	*Cruisers*	*Ships of the line*	*Cruisers*	*Ships of the line*	*Cruisers*
1660	76	55	21	5	64	33
1675	73	37	102	32	80	30
1690	83	26	89	32	52	21
1695	112	46	119	30	72	42
1710	123	57	94	24	86	33

Technically a cruiser was any ship sent to patrol on its own; however, here I am following Rodger's usage of the term to refer to ships of less than five hundred tons displacement (before 1680) and fifth- and sixth-rate ships (from 1680 to 1790)—in other words, smaller warships like frigates that could be used in combat but were not considered sturdy enough to survive line of battle warfare. There are no reliable numbers for Spain before 1715. The only other major European naval power at this time was Denmark, which increased its numbers from twenty to forty ships of the line and maintained around ten cruisers during this period. During the 1710s, Russia began its own naval building program and would soon have numbers comparable to Denmark's. These figures are drawn from Rodger, *The Command of the Ocean*, 607–608; see also the comparative chapters in Davies, *Pepys's Navy*.

Baptiste Colbert—Louis XIV's minister of finance and the secretary of the navy—France embarked on a massive building program in the 1670s, which meant that by 1675, the French navy outnumbered that of the English by a 3 to 2 ratio. At that time, Colbert was confident that French ships were "better equipped, better armed, and better commanded."[8] The Dutch fleet also outnumbered that of the English. In response to this—at Charles II's urging, for reasons explained below—Parliament voted the funds for an English building campaign to match, known as "thirty new ships." While the Dutch's relative naval strength dropped over the following twenty-five years, those of the English and the French stayed in relative parity. In 1690, the French fleet was generally larger and better armed than that of the English. Although the English destroyed a number of French ships at the Battle of la Hogue in 1692, the French added 100,000 tons of warships between 1691 and 1693, offsetting those losses. During the Nine Years' War (1688–1697) and the War of the Spanish Succession (1701–1714), the English also added substantially to their fleet, building 159 ships of the line and 113 cruisers, for a net increase of 31 ships of the line and 58 cruisers. By the end of the War of the Spanish Succession, England had taken the lead, though France and the Netherlands continued to maintain substantial fleets of their own.[9]

What complements this picture of England as simply one among several top-rate naval powers is the fact that the English navy experienced only mixed success during these years. English failures like the Dutch raid on the Medway (1667), the Battle of Beachy Head (1690), and the Caribbean and North American campaign of 1702–1703 were counterbalanced by successes in the Battles of Barfleur and la Hogue (1692), the Battle of Vigo (1702), and the capture of Gibraltar (1704) and Minorca (1708). The navy's track record was haphazard.

A further major difference between the seventeenth-century and eighteenth-century navies consisted of their spheres of action. In the latter half of the seventeenth and early eighteenth centuries, the English navy was relatively limited in range. The majority of English naval warfare in the seventeenth century was concentrated in the waters around England.[10] With the Dutch as the primary adversary, many seventeenth-century battles were fought in the North Sea and could be heard more than a hundred miles inland. In 1666, for example, Charles II, his brother James, and Samuel Pepys went to St. James's Park in London to listen to the St. James's Day Battle taking place off the coast of Kent. The English fleet did for the first time begin to conduct more sustained campaigns in the Mediterranean, though most of the burden of defense still fell on individual merchants.[11] In June 1666 only two of England's warships were out of the waters around the British Isles, both on convoy to Barbados. In July 1696 during the Nine Years' War with France, more than 70 percent of England's warships were in the English Channel, the Bay of Biscay, or other waters immediately around the British Isles; an additional 10 percent were stationed or on convoy to the Mediterranean. Only 7 percent of the ships were stationed in the Americas, with an additional 8 percent convoying trade there. The remaining 4 percent were in the East Indies. In June 1707, during the War of the Spanish Succession, roughly 50 percent of warships were in home waters or in the Bay of Biscay, while another 30 percent were in the Mediterranean, one of the war's major naval theaters. Roughly 17 percent were in the Americas. As a point of comparison, in July 1757, during the Seven Years' War, the percentage of warships in home waters had fallen to roughly 20 percent with an additional 12 percent in the Mediterranean; 30 percent of warships were in the Americas, 7 percent in the East Indies, and 30 percent on convoy duty to a variety of locations. In 1778 during the American Revolutionary War, the number of ships kept at home increased to 45 percent to protect against invasion from France, but the proportion of ships stationed in the Americas also increased to 50 percent, with 2 percent in the East Indies and 3 percent in the Mediterranean.[12] While it is not surprising that the navy would be deployed to North America in a war against North American colonists, this brief snapshot suggests the extent to which the navy's sphere of action expanded away from European waters to become much more global by the end of the eighteenth century. Britain established permanent peacetime naval presences in both North America and the Caribbean, with a large proportion of ships on active duty there during wartime.

This is reflected in the spread of naval dockyards around the globe. In 1711 the navy had eight dockyards within the British Isles and essentially no docking facilities elsewhere. Naval ships used Port Royal in Jamaica from the mid-seventeenth century for limited refits and Britain acquired Port Mahon in the Balearic Islands in the first decade of the eighteenth century, but neither site really had the ability to accommodate ships of war. By 1815 there were seven domestic royal dockyards, as well as dockyards overseas at Gibraltar, Malta, Halifax, Bermuda, Jamaica, Antigua, Barbados, the Cape of Good Hope, Madras, and Bombay (although the latter two technically belonged to the East India Company).

The eighteenth-century expansion of British naval power can also be seen relative to internal markers of growth. Between 1700 and 1800, the population of the British Isles doubled, from about 7.3 million in 1695 to about 14.7 million in 1800, but the growth in the manpower of the wartime navy exceeded that, expanding from about 48,500 men in 1695 to about 125,000 in 1800. Between 1695 and 1760 the percentage of the overall populace serving in the navy increased from 0.66 percent to 0.92 percent, before declining slightly toward the end of the century to 0.85 percent.[13] The manpower of the royal dockyards quadrupled, from 4,000 in 1697 to more than 17,000 in 1815.[14]

These numbers and statistics are potential indicators of relative strength, though they are suggestive rather than conclusive. To make sense of them, we need to place them in their larger imperial and social context, to ask what aspirations seventeenth-century Englishmen and -women had for their navy, as well as what threats they believed it embodied.

The Stuart Restoration: Politics and the Navy

The English Civil War ushered in a new era in English state building. During the course of the 1640s, the size of the warring armies increased tenfold; one in ten men was now in arms, and the parliamentary government doubled the percentage of national wealth it controlled.[15] The financial innovations introduced during the war years and the Interregnum—policies like the abolition of feudal land tenure and the introduction of land and excise taxes—were maintained as contemporaries came to terms with the realization that funding a state bureaucracy out of the king's ordinary revenues, without parliamentary support, was no longer a reasonable expectation.[16]

Although Charles II seems to have been welcomed back by the majority of the English people in the Restoration of 1660, it soon became apparent that the Restoration had restored not just the monarchy but also pre–Civil War tensions about the direction of English society. By the 1680s two major parties in English political society had developed in response to these tensions: the whigs and the tories.[17] These factions were split over a variety of issues, including the distribution of authority in society, the nature of England's religious settlement, the relative power of English political institutions, and English foreign and imperial policy. Each of these issues was reflected in debates about the Restoration navy. The typical whig supported parliamentary rather than monarchical government, a "low church" vision of the Church of England, and a vision of political economy which emphasized the importance of manufacturing, labor, and economic consumption as a path to potentially infinite wealth. The typical tory supported royal authority, "high church" Anglicanism, and a zero-sum political economy based on finite natural resources like land and the products of the land (for example, tobacco, sugar, and the slaves needed to produce them). The tories were the party of Charles and James, who favored an alliance with Catholic absolutist France.[18]

One of the first major areas in which the broader divisions of Restoration society could be seen in the navy was in the question of who could be an officer—or in other words, over the social distribution of military power and authority. The recent civil war, royal execution, and decadelong exile gave Charles a keen sense of the stakes and the importance of having people with the right political and social loyalties leading his kingdom's military forces. Charles's initial inclinations were to pursue conciliatory policies—in the 1660 Declaration of Breda, he promised indemnity for those who had fought against him, agreed to pay the arrears owed to Commonwealth soldiers and sailors, guaranteed property rights, and promised religious toleration. The navy, however, presented Charles with a conundrum. He did not want to pursue a clean sweep of sea officers or naval administration because that might upset those within England who had helped him regain the throne, weakening his position. On the other hand, he owed something to those who had joined him in exile and now expected rewards for their loyalty. More problematic still, the sea officers he inherited from the Commonwealth were a bastion of radicalism. Following a naval revolt in favor of royalists in 1648, the Rump Parliament instituted a purge of both sea and dockyard officers, frequently replacing them with merchant captains known to be sympathetic to the radical cause. An individual's ideological sympathies became an important factor in promotion, meaning that in 1660 there was extensive political and religious radicalism among sea officers.[19] From Charles's perspective, both the navy and the dockyards were largely in the hands of his enemies. He had to somehow remove the threat they posed while still being able to draw on the expertise represented by the officer corps.

Charles's first step was to replace the Commonwealth's Admiralty and Navy Commissioners with a Navy Board headed by his brother James, Duke of York, as Lord High Admiral. Both Charles and James were extremely interested in and knowledgeable about naval affairs, so James was in some ways a reasonable choice. This was not a complete purge: Charles included some of the previous commissioners and other individuals who had been prominent during the Commonwealth but whom Charles believed he could trust, such as Edward Montagu, Earl of Sandwich. The next step was to ask all sea and dockyard officers to take the Oaths of Allegiance and Supremacy, swearing allegiance to Charles as the head of the Church of England, which religious radicals like Quakers and Anabaptists could not do (either because of their hostility toward the Church of England or because they refused to take oaths in general). In the dockyards, this removed several senior officers and at least twenty-six more minor officials and workmen. Fewer than 1 percent of sea officers refused to take the oaths, but Sandwich and his associate Samuel Pepys, who had been appointed Secretary to the Admiralty, began to comb through the corps more systematically, removing "known enemies" among both commissioned and warrant officers, down to the level of cooks.[20]

While previous service under the Commonwealth was not an automatic barrier to service in Charles II's navy, Charles did not fully trust these ex-parliamentary sea officers. The Tonge Plot of 1662, for example, involved a number of sea officers and seamen. Plotters intended to kill Charles, James, and General George Monck, who had helped to engineer the Restoration, and reestablish England as a republic with annual parliaments and religious freedom. During the Second Anglo-Dutch War (1665–1667), there were claims that Anabaptists had corrupted the navy and that there might be widespread defections to the Dutch. This did happen in at least some cases: Philip Holland commanded an English warship in 1666 but defected to the Dutch Admiral Michiel de Ruyter in 1667. Other sea officers like Sandes Temple promised Dutch republicans that they would engineer a mutiny among the fleet. During the Exclusion Crisis, some whigs believed they would be able to sway the navy away from loyalty to Charles.[21] William Goodson, who had been a vice admiral under Cromwell, allegedly attempted to recruit seamen in the maritime districts of London and reported that he had promises from many that "they will be right and true Protestants, and will throw their officers overboard."[22] Neither the Tonge Plot nor Goodson's conspiracy eventuated, but Charles had reason to believe that many former parliamentary sea officers were less than loyal to his restored regime. Charles, James, and their naval administration hoped to slowly supplant the ex-parliamentary officers with men they believed were more trustworthy.

There was a class dimension to this decision: the Stuarts preferred gentlemen rather than the merchant captains or soldiers who had dominated the Commonwealth navy. Men of aristocratic or gentry birth were largely excluded as sea officers during the Interregnum in favor either of generals-at-sea (who had proved their loyalty to the Commonwealth) or tarpaulins ("true" seamen who had been essentially raised on board ship).[23] Charles and James introduced new methods of bringing young gentlemen, particularly the younger sons of Cavalier royalists, into what they hoped would be an increasingly royalist navy.[24] This process was not instantaneous, but its progress can be seen over time.

Although Charles recommissioned a number of Commonwealth sea officers, that did not necessarily mean he intended to employ them: at least thirty-six officers recommissioned in 1660 saw no employment in the next three years and roughly half of those officers were never employed again. Of the ninety-one new commissions made between 1661 and 1663, roughly 40 percent had been parliamentarians during the Civil War, but included in the remaining 60 percent were many men with clear royalist loyalties.[25] In 1661 Charles created a new category of naval service, the "volunteer-per-order"—nicknamed the "King's Letter Boys" because they entered under royal patronage—to "give encouragement to such young gentlemen as are willing to apply themselves to the learning of navigation, and fitting themselves for the service of the sea." A further regulation in 1676 increased their numbers to encourage "families of better sort . . . to breed up their younger sons to the art and practice of navigation" and established that the boys could not be older than sixteen, young enough to become "true" seamen.[26] In 1665–1667 approximately three-quarters of officers were either tarpaulins or veterans of the Interregnum—though again religious nonconformists were scrupulously excluded—but ten years later approximately half of officers were gentlemen. It became increasingly rare for men to work their way up to commissioned commands from the lower ranks of seamen or warrant officers.[27]

"Gentlemen" sea officers were attacked for their perceived lack of competence and for their allegedly corrupting influence. Men like John Birch, who had fought for the Commonwealth, believed the Restoration navy was inferior to that of the Interregnum and blamed the promotion of "gentlemen captains" rather than men "who are bred betwixt London & Blackwall" (that is to say, were born in the Docklands and therefore were "true" seamen).[28] Those who disliked gentlemen captains tended to admire men like the Dutch Admiral de Ruyter, whom they characterized as an honest, simple, apolitical man with his country's best interests at heart. This stood in contrast to the English commanders—like Prince Rupert of the Rhine, the Earl of Sandwich, or the Duke of Albemarle—who were closely connected to the court but boasted only haphazard naval experience.[29] One anonymous treatise claimed that the sole reason gentlemen officers had been created was to increase royal influence in the navy by promoting men who had "expectancies of employments at court as well as at sea." The author admitted that although not all gentlemen were bad sea officers, there was no way to get rid of those who were; the lack of discipline exhibited by gentlemen who "loved loitering in port, and hated the toils of the profession" had turned the navy into a "slut's corner."[30] Pamphlets like *An Inquiry into the Causes of Our Naval Miscarriages* questioned the morality of gentleman officers, claiming that "instead of the good morals and harmless conversation of our seamen in the Parliament-times, there was [now] nothing but cursing, swearing, damning, sinking, and obscene nasty language to be heard on board our fleet; so that it looked more like the suburbs of Hell, than a Christian navy."[31] In the words of Robert Glass, aristocratic men appointed as sea officers were "regarded by many not only as a giant step backwards in terms of seamanship and fighting efficiency, but also as a symbol of the corruption and decadence of the restored monarchy."[32] They were court favorites rather than men who understood or had earned their privileges.

Charles and James hoped to slowly create a new officer corps that combined the experience of "true" seamen with the loyalty and trustworthiness of gentlemen. This was one probable motivation behind a major innovation in naval administration during this period. In 1677 Samuel Pepys, then secretary of the Admiralty, proposed a system of examinations for individuals who wished to be commissioned as lieutenants. For the first time in the English navy, sons of aristocrats and sons of fishmongers would—at least in theory—have to fulfill similar requirements based on training, practical skills, and merit rather than connection in order to be promoted.[33] This would allow Charles to continue to encourage the rise of young gentlemen through the ranks of sea officers without having to sacrifice the benefit of experience.

Charles's encouragement to sea officers of higher social background was interpreted by whigs as a signal of his broader intentions to replace governance by the honest gentry and merchants who had held power during the Commonwealth with governance by degenerate aristocratic elites. As J. D. Davies has explained, disproportionately appointing members of the nobility to positions of authority in the military "could be interpreted all too easily as an attempt to make the navy a more effective instrument of royal absolutism."[34] Charles hoped to create a corps of officers on whom he could rely, whose social and political interests would align with his own, but critics believed that the appointment of gentlemen sea officers signaled the re-hierarchicalization of English society. It left the navy in tory-leaning hands.

A second major issue of contention in Restoration England was the question of the relationship between church and state and what religious denominations would be "tolerated." James publicly converted to Catholicism in 1673. This was particularly upsetting to ex-parliamentarians and proto-whigs, who tended to believe that the forces of the Catholic Church were trying to establish universal monarchy over the world and to eliminate all Protestantism. James's conversion raised two sets of concerns about the presence of Catholicism in the navy. One was whether Catholics could be trusted to serve national interests rather than religious ones—if Catholics controlled the waters around England, what force would stop a Catholic invasion? Beyond that, allowing Catholics to embody military authority enhanced their social and political authority, which was a frightening thought to those who believed Catholics were constantly trying to undermine the Protestant English nation. The year of James's conversion, the proto-whig Sir Nicholas Carew warned that Catholics should be excluded from the sea service, saying, "If they may command our ships, they may command us also."[35] This resulted in a parliamentary inquiry into the religious affiliations of sea officers. Most chose to take the Oaths of Allegiance and Supremacy and to fulfill the conditions of the new 1673 Test Act, which required would-be officeholders to reject the Catholic religious doctrine of transubstantiation. The Test Act forced James to relinquish his position as Lord High Admiral, though both he and Charles continued to regularly attend meetings of the Admiralty Commission, now headed by their cousin Prince Rupert. Within the anti-Catholic hysteria generated by the (fictional) Popish Plot of 1678, many in English society believed that James had used his position as Lord High Admiral to promote Catholicism in the navy. With his influence over naval patronage, he had the opportunity to build up his client network, putting young gentlemen—who might be French or papal agents—into positions of power and authority.[36] In the immediate aftermath of the plot, Sir John Bennet expressed his desire for "an account [of] how popery came to be planted in the Navy." In another debate, Bennet pushed his point further, claiming that "I will prove popery in your fleet, at the bar. There is not a man in the fleet, that has served in the fleet since the King came in, but was made by the Duke of York." Pepys attempted to defend his patron, arguing "by all the care and inspection that could be taken in the Navy, there was no one Catholic in it from top to bottom" and claiming it was ridiculous "that a general reproach should be cast upon the Navy, because the Duke of York named officers!"[37] In response to these concerns, Pepys ordered a new inquiry into the religious beliefs of sea officers, most of whom again took the oaths they had taken in 1673. The concerns over Catholics in the sea service continued into the eighteenth century; in theory, they were not supposed to serve on naval ships even as sailors. In 1706 one Protestant Irish nobleman argued that employing Catholics in naval ships would be of more "dangerous consequence" than if the ships were manned by "land soldiers."[38] The navy was thus one arena where the religious tensions of the day were embodied.

The question of how large the fleet should be was also contentious, in large part because it was enmeshed with two other major debates in Restoration England, over foreign policy and over the balance of power between executive and legislative political institutions. Charles, James, and their proto-tory supporters pursued a pro-France foreign policy, arguing that the Dutch were England's true rivals because they were attempting to engross all the trade of the world to themselves. They envisioned an alliance with Louis XIV in which the French might conquer Europe, but England would rule the seas and face down the Dutch on that element. Maintaining a large navy was central to these ideas about England's role in European politics. However, proto-whigs perceived the absolutism and religious intolerance that they believed Louis XIV represented as the true threats to English society. They hoped the Protestant Dutch would be an ally in the fight against France and claimed that the French had secretly planned the Anglo-Dutch wars as a means of undermining their two major rivals to sea power in an effort to establish universal monarchy over both land *and* sea. They thought that combatting France would require substantial military engagement on land.[39]

Building warships, as the tories wanted, was also seen as a way for the Stuart monarchy to establish its independence from Parliament. In 1675, representing the concerns of Charles II, Pepys presented a report to Parliament that noted that both France and the Netherlands were involved in naval building programs that would outstrip the navy of England. He estimated that England would need to build thirty ships of

60–100 guns to keep up—the large, powerful warships which tory foreign policy required. Whigs saw this "thirty ships" program as a ploy by tories to sidestep Parliament. Since the Restoration, Charles had ultimately been dependent on Parliament to vote funds; one of the goals of those advancing a royalist agenda was to remove this check on royal power and give Charles better access to funds outside Parliament's control. Naval ships were expensive investments: some claimed that if Parliament voted the extensive funds Charles was requesting, there would be no reason for further Parliaments. The money voted for ships might be diverted to some other, presumably despotic, purpose. In 1678 Thomas Osborne, Earl of Danby and Lord Treasurer, requested £108,840 a month to maintain the fleet—more than double the money needed for the army—in case of a war with France, a proposal which received substantial support in Parliament from proto-tories. Given that the whigs were the party who actually wanted war with France, it was a decent strategy on the part of the tories to use that hawkishness to their own ends. Joseph Williamson, one of the king's spokesmen in the Commons, warned, "In case we are not at sea, the French will certainly be at sea." However, the whigs were not convinced. The staunchly whiggish William Sacheverell, who supported a variety of anti-Catholic bills, claimed that the possible war was a mere pretext (as it was) and that "when money is once got, we may not have a Parliament ever after." Henry Powle, another long-standing critic of what he perceived as pro-Catholic and arbitrary policies, agreed: "there will be an end of all Parliaments by giving at the rate some Gentlemen propose." Thomas Lee suggested he would be willing to vote the money, but not until the fleet was "actually at sea; lest, by the temptation of so much money, we have again no fleet at all."[40] After Danby's fall from power in early 1679, Sir John Bennet returned to this matter, reiterating that the Stuarts wanted to build such a large fleet that "the necessity of the Navy will make you all beggars" and he admonished his listeners, "let us never give supply to be cozened of it by these villains."[41] The large warships favored by the Stuarts and the tories were more expensive, meaning funds might be misdirected, and required more officers, meaning the Stuarts had more opportunities to promote their own clients to positions of command. To quote J. D. Davies, "For all the evocative language used by some MPs and pamphleteers to describe the 'wooden walls' which guarded England's liberty, religion, and trade, the navy was just as evocatively portrayed by others as one of the likeliest harbingers of Stuart absolutism."[42] The debate over Charles's navy in the 1670s echoed that which would take place over James's standing army in the 1680s.

The Restoration navy thus held symbolic significance, both for the social class and religion of its officers and for the way the size of the fleet was connected to foreign policy debates and the struggle between the executive and legislature for control over the English state. Despite this extensive symbolic resonance, officership was not seen as a career, actual administration over the navy was frequently haphazard, and the state-owned navy was not a dominant force in battle. This was not the professional, permanent standing Royal Navy it would later become.

One marker of military professionalization is the extent to which officers are careerists. In the Stuart navy, men did not view officership as their profession. For a variety of reasons, officers were in and out of service and often combined employment in the Royal Navy with other roles. In the St. James's Day Battle, the English fleet was led by Prince Rupert and George Monck, both of whom had served as land-based generals during the English Civil War (though on opposing sides) and neither of whom had been trained as a sea officer.[43] For most of the period between 1660 and 1688, England was at peace with major European powers. The navy was largely demobilized in peacetime, meaning that it was in practice relatively small and for that reason was manned primarily with volunteers rather than impressed men.[44] However, this meant that officers often lacked experience in naval warfare, though they might have had other forms of maritime experience, and they were routinely obligated to find other means of financial support. This frequently meant purchasing a commission in the army, captaining a merchant ship, or taking a lower paid position in the navy—one captain even became a dockyard shipwright.[45] Between 1668 and 1675, various classes of officers were offered a stipend of half their normal pay during times when they were not currently commissioned. Some began to construe half pay as a retainer for future service—in other words, began to envision officership in the navy as something permanent rather than ad hoc. In 1672 warrant (noncommissioned) officers were granted superannuation, or pensions, for the first time.[46] Nevertheless, the routine decommissioning and downsizing of the fleet in peacetime contributed to a lack of experience among both officers and crew and to a lack of continuity in service. It also meant that there was an incentive for sea officers to make the financial best of their short periods in employment, regardless of what "duty" required.[47] There was a perception among sea officers that promotion depended more on political patronage and influence than on attention to duty.[48]

Another marker of military professionalization is the bureaucratization of administration. Naval administration under Charles and James was personal rather than institutionalized. Charles wanted to retain as much control over naval policy within his own family's hands as possible. During a few moments of crisis—after James's public conversion to Catholicism, for example, and during the Popish Plot and Exclusion Crisis—Charles offered up some cosmetic gestures to make the Admiralty appear less under direct royal control. Once his political position had strengthened in 1684, he dismissed the board and resumed personal oversight of naval affairs, with Pepys as Secretary of the Marine.[49] Such administrative oversight as existed was not especially effective in ensuring compliance from subordinates. The Admiralty attempted to enforce some accountability through the system of courts-martial. The judicial panels of those courts were, however, composed of fellow officers who seemed to feel a greater sense of resentment against bureaucratic administration for attempting to interfere with their independence than they did a duty to punish offenders, thus refusing to convict the accused.[50] The Navy Board likewise exercised little effective oversight over shipwrights, for example, who built vessels according to their own secret plans.[51] While they resisted governance from above, officers also tended to monopolize authority less than their eighteenth-century successors would do: captains frequently consulted lower-ranking officers and sometimes even crew members before taking an important decision.[52]

Finally, if we look at outcomes, the English fleet experienced very mixed success during the Second and Third Anglo-Dutch Wars, including seeing the Dutch burn the English fleet at anchor in the Medway in 1667. Three of England's five major flagships were destroyed while a fourth was captured as a prize. Although the navy provided some convoys primarily in the waters around the British Isles and increasingly to the Mediterranean, Dutch privateers were very successful in raiding English trade. At least 360 English ships were taken as prizes in the Second Anglo-Dutch War, and of the at least 648 ships the Dutch captured during the Third War, most were English, nearly destroying English trade in the Mediterranean. The fact that at least some captains did not take convoy duty seriously may not have helped. One Dutch captain captured a convoy in 1665 without having to fire a single shot; apparently, this was because the English captain was "so overtaken with drink when they did take him that he should have been 2 hours aboard of the vice admiral's ship before he knew where he was." The Dutch also raided the Chesapeake and recaptured the colony of New York. The vast majority of English naval warfare in the Caribbean was not state controlled; it was carried out by privateers and buccaneers like Henry Morgan. When the Admiralty sent a warship to restrain this private naval warfare, Morgan seized it and repurposed it as his own flagship. In 1679 the navy removed its final two frigates from the Caribbean.[53]

The navy was thus implicated in the most explosive political debates of the 1660s–1680s. Contemporaries believed that the structure of the navy and the character of its officers mattered in part because they reflected wider societal divisions but also because they could be used to tip the scales. Whiggish critics accused Charles and James of trying to build a navy that would strengthen the aristocracy's hold on English society, allow for Catholic subversion, and undermine the role of Parliament, all in the name of pursuing a misguided foreign policy against the Protestant Dutch and in favor of Catholic, absolutist France. In the fleet itself, officers tended not to be continuously employed or at least not necessarily at the same rank or in the same capacity, they had little guarantee of what type of behavior would secure them promotion, and they were unlikely to be successfully called to account for their actions by the Admiralty. The navy's record during these years was mixed and a large percentage of warfare was still being carried out by private adventurers like Morgan.

The Glorious Revolution and the Second Hundred Years' War

In 1688 James II's son-in-law and nephew, the Protestant Dutch prince William of Orange, invaded England. James fled; William and James's daughter Mary were declared joint monarchs in early 1689. During the Williamite regime, whigs and tories continued to argue over familiar issues but with a twist: whigs were now the party closer to royal favor, while tories found themselves in opposition. The Glorious Revolution did not transform the navy structurally. What it did transform, immediately and dramatically, was English foreign and imperial policy. Debates over the navy shifted accordingly to reflect tensions over its purpose on a broader global stage.

In some ways, the Glorious Revolution forced political decision makers to confront similar questions about the navy as the Restoration had. With the regime change, the navy's loyalty was again suspect in the 1690s. William made efforts early in his reign to balance whig and tory appointments to high-level positions, but perhaps one out of six sea officers was purged out of fear they were Jacobites (supporters of the deposed James II). There were times such as at the Battle of Barfleur (1692) when French admirals expected the English fleet to be disloyal to William and possibly to stand aside. Ministers also began once again to promote "tarpaulins" rather than "gentlemen." This was more of a political statement than the genuine distinction it had been in the 1660s, as lieutenants had been required since 1677 to prove their experience and understanding of seafaring, regardless of their birth.[54] In terms of professionalization, the navy was still viewed as more of an ad hoc service than a permanent standing one. There was still no clear path of professional development: an officer who on one ship had held the position of captain might on another ship be placed in the position of lieutenant, or an officer who had previously been appointed a lieutenant might serve elsewhere as a gunner. An individual was an officer so long as they served on a particular ship in that particular role—the rank was not something they carried with them in and of themselves. The overlap between the navy and the army continued. George Forbes, for example, was a naval post-captain as well as an officer in the marines and in the Horse Guards. Education was haphazard. Upon joining the navy, future sea officer James Spelman reported that the clerk instructed to teach him navigation had in fact never been at sea before "and therefore doe[s] not understand the practical part."[55] Perhaps for that reason combined with a lack of long-term experience, sea officers were not universally reliable. In one instance, Admiral Peregrine Osborne, Marquis of Carmarthen, fled from his own fleet after mistaking them for the French.[56]

Naval administration under William and his successor Queen Anne remained largely haphazard. Unlike Charles and James, William had no interest in the navy and unlike the Stuarts' tory-leaning administrations, the whigs saw little purpose for a large, aggressive navy. William treated the Admiralty as if it were a committee of Parliament rather than an independent body in its own right, and in turn Parliament showed little respect for naval administration. In 1689 the entire Victualling Board was put into the Tower of London by the House of Commons for failing to find sufficient credit to support the navy's war efforts, though the board could reasonably have pointed to the lack of funds voted by Parliament as a root cause of its troubles. During the 1690s, there were "ten persons or organizations claiming some responsibility for the operations of the Navy, without considering administration at all: the king, the Lords Justices, the Privy Council, the two Secretaries of State, two Houses of Parliament, the commander-in-chief of the main fleet, the Admiralty and the Board of Trade."[57] Naval affairs were frequently delegated to the secretaries of state or occasionally to the commanders in chief of various fleets. Sea officers at times acted without reference to the Admiralty at all, though generally in conjunction with other ministers. In 1693 someone reported that Sir John Lowther of the Admiralty said "nobody could tell to this day whither our fleet's last orders were to carry them . . . none could know less of it than they of the Admiralty."[58] When Admiral Edward Russell and Sir John Trenchard, as Secretary of State, planned an assault on Brest in 1694, they did so without consulting the Admiralty. Between 1702 and 1709 there was no Admiralty Board at all; between 1704 and 1709 there was no one individual who could clearly be held accountable for the state or actions of the navy.[59]

Despite this, there was some investment in naval affairs. A new dockyard was founded at Plymouth in the early 1690s because all currently existing dockyards were better located to fight the Dutch rather than the French. England embarked on a new building program that increased the number of their warships by thirty-one ships of the line and fifty-eight cruisers. Primarily, these were smaller ships intended to engage in trade protection or to pick off lone enemy merchant ships, rather than to engage in full naval battles. By 1696 both England and France were running low on money for naval maintenance, and both increasingly turned to privateering instead. At least on the French side, there were some doubts about the quality of English shipbuilding. In 1691 the secretary of the French navy, Louis Phélypeaux, Marquis de Phélypeaux, had "certain information" that English ships were "very poorly equipped and break down every day."[60] In a noteworthy development, Parliament did not vote any money at all for new shipbuilding between 1696 and 1745. Instead, existing ships were taken apart and "rebuilt."[61]

Under Charles and James, contemporaries had argued over the structure of the navy because they saw it as linked to domestic concerns regarding hierarchy, religion, and the distribution of power in government. Under the later Stuarts, the most visible arguments over the navy were about its purpose. William's regime largely embraced whiggish foreign and imperial policy, directed against Catholic France, and many colonial merchants eagerly welcomed him in return for his support of whiggish economic policies. Whigs believed that trade should be free to all to participate in—because the wealth that could be generated by labor and trade was potentially infinite, there was little reason to limit it to the king's political favorites. Whigs expected state intervention in the protection of manufacturing and overseas trade; they encouraged imperial endeavors that either created or opened new markets of consumers or that permitted the manufacture of trade goods that could then be sold on to Europe. Whigs complained that economic monopolies like the Stuart-sponsored Royal African Company restricted trade from reaching its full potential, as did other restrictions like the Navigation Acts. These arguments were buttressed by the dynamism of colonial markets and colonial demand. Exports to the colonies, particularly English manufactures, were an especially dynamic part of the English economy. Whigs generally supported leaving the direction of colonial trade to merchant-planter elites rather than enforcing central oversight.[62]

The tory vision of empire built on a zero-sum understanding of wealth and therefore advocated control of territory, the extraction of natural resources, and sometimes the plundering of enemy empires. Both Charles II and James II had drawn on royally sanctioned forms of property, such as licensing monopoly trading companies, which created alliances between the monarchy and mercantile interests, filled royal coffers, and left those interests dependent upon royal favor for their own profits. Tories were also more likely to advocate central imperial control. Under the later Stuarts, tory foreign policy shifted to emphasize the importance of staying out of European continental conflicts and instead relying on the English Channel as a barrier.[63]

The different ideas held by whigs and tories about what imperial development should look like also meant they envisioned different roles for the navy in policing and protecting that empire. Although the navy held some resonance in both tory and whig conceptions of foreign policy, it was the primary realm of engagement for tories and a more peripheral one for whigs. Essentially, a tory empire would require the use of the navy to *police* waterborne trade, in terms of keeping interlopers out of monopoly trades. It would also use naval power to *plunder* rival empires. Whig theorists emphasized the importance of using the navy to *protect* trade from foreign predation. These different purposes required different types of ships: tory naval policy emphasized large, powerful warships (as in Charles's "thirty ships" program) while whig naval policy relied on small, fast cruisers.[64] During the whiggish Nine Years' War, the bulk of combat was focused on land maneuvers and battles in Europe. The navy played an auxiliary role by trying to block Jacobites in Ireland and protecting trade. Whigs also encouraged private engagement in national warfare by supporting and providing incentives for colonial privateering. The War of the Spanish Succession opened the possibility of a more proactive naval policy. It strengthened the tory belief that the navy was the central component of proper foreign policy, that maritime wars would be more cost effective, and that together these measures would reduce England's reliance on potentially treacherous allies like the Dutch, whom tories still mistrusted. While whigs initially argued that a maritime war carried out in conjunction with the Dutch was an important part of the War of the Spanish Succession, they responded to tory attacks by increasingly emphasizing the centrality of land war in countering French power.[65]

Because the whigs envisioned the navy as a primarily defensive force, they encouraged defensive behavior in officers and discouraged risk taking. Sea officers followed these expectations. The career of Admiral Arthur Herbert is an example of the hold the defensive approach exercised on the naval community. On 1 May 1689 he commanded the English fleet against a relatively evenly matched French counterpart in Bantry Bay on the southwestern coast of Ireland. The French were attempting to land troops and supplies to support James II as he fought to reclaim the British Isles. An inconclusive battle followed. Both sides claimed victory: the French lost control of the Irish Sea but were able to land their reinforcements. When he withdrew, Herbert's fleet had not lost a single ship. Nor did he regroup and reengage: the fleet waited for reinforcements and, when none arrived, returned to England. Writing to Secretary of State Daniel Finch, Earl of Nottingham, Herbert claimed success in "bringing off the fleet without loss of a ship," justified his behavior, and expressed the hope that he would be "able to encounter the enemy upon some sort of equality," though the English had had twenty-two ships in opposition to twenty-four.[66] Rather than being punished for allowing the French to reinforce Jacobite troops in Ireland, Herbert was promoted to the peerage as the Earl of Torrington.

A year later, Torrington followed similar protocol in the Battle of Beachy Head. On 30 June 1690, fifty-six English and Dutch ships of the line (plus twenty fireships) confronted seventy French ships of the line (plus thirty fireships). As the commander of the allied fleet, Torrington had been ordered to give battle no matter what. Although a subordinate admiral, Ralph Delaval, engaged as ordered, Torrington held back and allowed Delaval and the Dutch to bear the brunt of the French attack. The French destroyed fifteen ships before the battle was over, though only one of them English, and gained temporary control of the English Channel. In December 1690 Torrington was court-martialed for failure to obey orders, to engage the enemy with vigor, or to assist the Dutch as English allies. He justified his behavior, claiming that "if the government were just to him, they must not only not punish him, but thank and reward him" because if he had engaged, the Anglo-Dutch fleet would have been destroyed—only his reticence had saved any of the ships.[67] Torrington was acquitted. Accounts of the court-martial vary: some observers claimed that the court-martial was stacked in Torrington's favor all along and that only witnesses who would support Torrington were allowed to speak.[68] Regardless of whether this was an unbiased trial, the outcome demonstrates the same point. If the court-martial was biased in Torrington's favor, the administration was willing to condone this lack of verve and protected it. If the court-martial was in fact unbiased, then Torrington's peers were equally ready to condone the behavior. There was no question about what Torrington had done or not done—accounts of the battle were in agreement that he had kept back and had not engaged the enemy. Torrington's own justification of his behavior admitted as much and the opposing French admiral also observed that "Only Herbert [i.e., Torrington] and his seconds assuredly did not fight at close quarters, but chose only [to fight] particular vessels of the squadron of the Marquis d'Amfreville."[69] In Torrington's division, only a third of the ships' powder was used, whereas both the Dutch and French fleets nearly exhausted their powder supplies. The commissioners charged with investigating the affair concluded that "it seems to be a general opinion, that if [Torrington] and the Rear Admiral of the Red had bore down and pressed the enemy, equally with the rest of the fleet, the French probably would not have had the success as to be able to keep the sea; and many officers of these two divisions wished they might have been nearer the enemy."[70] For Torrington, it was better to preserve ships than to risk them in battle, and his promotion and subsequent acquittal demonstrated that a substantial percentage of the naval and political worlds agreed with him.

The Nine Years' War ended more or less in a stalemate. In terms of what the English navy actually accomplished, there were few victories. Bantry Bay (1689) was largely inconclusive, but the French were able to land their supplies for James. Beachy Head (1690) was a disaster for the Anglo-Dutch fleet. Barfleur and La Hogue (1692) did result in the destruction or capture of many French ships, but the losses were made up within two years. The attack on Brest (1694) was a defeat, and the English suffered heavy losses. Naval bombardment of French coastal towns, such as Saint-Malo, Dieppe, Le Havre, Dunkirk, and Calais, served little military purpose, though it did send a message. In the meantime, England suffered heavy privateering losses. In 1693 the French captured an allied merchant fleet en route to the Mediterranean. Although the majority of the merchant ships escaped, English mercantile losses were still as great as in the 1666 Great Fire of London. The French sold the captured prizes for a total of thirty million livres, which was as much as they had spent on their entire naval budget in 1692.[71] The tory bishop Thomas Wagstaffe complained that "the French privateers have been more busy and bold than ever." The navy had been "rigged at incredible expense, and all for nothing else but to furl their sails . . . we think a pasteboard ship at my Lord Mayor's show might do as well as any in the ports." He added that while "our ships and our seamen are as good as ever . . . our want is more honest and able ministers."[72] The Nine Years' War was successful in solidifying William's position on the English throne, but offered little evidence of English naval superiority.

At the outbreak of the War of the Spanish Succession a few years later, tories were hopeful that it would be a very different type of war.

Because of concerns over the growing national debt and higher taxes, as well as their suspicion of the newly prominent financial (rather than landed) elites, tories suggested that the war should be primarily maritime. One tory pamphlet argued that the Nine Years' War "left us abominably in debt, with an Army upon our hands, from which we are not yet wholly freed." The throne of Spain was no business of England's: "If the people of Spain complain not of any hardship, but are willing to take the Duke of Anjou for their king, I know no reason why [we] should complain for them." In the meantime, "If France attack us, if the Lords of the Admiralty please, we know how to defend ourselves without the assistance of a land force, or turning knights errant in seeking dangerous enterprises, and broken bones abroad, because we are weary of peace at home."[73] However, much of the early war effort was run under whig auspices, meaning that it again involved English armies on the continent as well as alliances and subsidies to those allies.

Whig visions of the war involved a role for naval power, but one subordinate to that of land forces. Rather than using the navy as an active and aggressive component of warfare, they intended to use it to protect English trade; much of the plundering of foreign trade was left to individual privateers. A whiggish pamphlet, *A Debate between Three Ministers of State*, argued that "the prizes to be got at sea, may, if well managed, largely contribute to discharge the expenses both of the naval, and the land forces," but if England did not "vigorously, and speedily join with Holland, and the Emperor, all this expense will be without glory or hopes to obtain any advantage."[74] Whig Daniel Defoe warned that "If the French get the Spanish Crown, we are beaten out of the field as to trade, and are besieged in our own island, and never let us flatter ourselves with our safety consisting so much in our fleet." Once the French had control of the trade to Spanish America, they would "have the most money, will have the most ships, the best fleet, and the best armies"; a brief historical perspective on the past few decades would "tell you that all our English [ships] was not able to look them in the face, if we had no Dutch on our side, and hardly with the Dutch and us together."[75] Whig Joseph Addison agreed that a French appropriation of Spanish trade would encourage the French to become superior to England at sea, leaving England with no protection. Sea power was important to Addison in that regard, but he still maintained that "an enterprise that carries in it the fate of Europe, should not turn upon the uncertainty of winds and waves, and be liable to all the accidents that may befall a naval expedition."[76] As the tories put increasing pressure on the whig administration for a more maritime war, the whigs pushed back by arguing that the very idea of a maritime war against France was so foolish that it brought into question the tories' loyalties. Daniel Defoe's periodical *Review of the State of the British Nation* criticized the "new notion . . . of our fighting France at sea, being the chief part of our business" as a treacherous ploy: "I know, those people, that would not have us beat France at all, mightily fall in with such a notion." He admitted that naval power "may help, but by land is the main stroke to be struck." Even such naval victories as England had had in the war thus far were due to the deployment of land forces: "you had never ruined the ships at Vigo, and taken the booty there, tho' they were 60 sail to 22, but for the land-forces that beat them from their batteries; you had ruined the naval power of France at Toulon, had your land-forces been sufficient, but that failing, the fleet was obliged to give it over, so that this war must be chiefly carried on by land."[77] Pamphlets like *Division Our Destruction: Or, a Short History of the French Faction in England* argued that the navy was a distraction from the more important parts of the war efforts. According to the author, the tories "voted a great fleet, which was a prodigious expense, and signified no more than to impoverish us, France having (as they well knew) no designs at sea at that time" when they should have been asking William to put the country in a proper state of defense and to form necessary alliances.[78]

Whigs drew on lessons from the Nine Years' War to make what they hoped would be better policy in the War of the Spanish Succession. The manpower necessary to supply an increase in naval ships was drawn largely from merchant ships; deploying ships away from home left home-bound trade more exposed to privateers. During the Nine Years' War, merchant fleets were depleted by the large-scale hirings necessary to man the fleet guarding Ireland in 1689–1691 and the one involved in the amphibious descent upon Brest in 1694. Parliament passed restrictions on trade that limited long-distance trades to only half their normal manpower and tonnage in comparison to the 1680s; ships were allowed to sail only between the end of May and the beginning of the following February, pushing trading voyages into unseasonable times of year, which threatened profits. Additionally, many of England's European markets were disrupted by the war. This led to a collapse in trade revenues at the same time as England was sending vast quantities of bullion overseas to support the land forces, culminating in a crisis in the value of England's coin and contributing to the Great Recoinage of 1696. During the War of the Spanish Succession, the whig Parliament did not repeat this error. There were still some restrictions on trade, but not such extensive ones. Ministers steered clear of amphibious expeditions, and the presence of more naval ships near the Iberian Peninsula and the Mediterranean meant they were in position to be better able to protect trade even if not technically on convoy duty.[79]

Aside from roles in transporting troops and supporting land forces, the primary role of naval power in the whig military vision was as cruisers and convoy protectors, as laid out in the whig-sponsored 1708 "Act for the Better Securing the Trade of this Kingdom, by Cruisers and Convoys." This act removed forty-three ships from Admiralty control and specifically designated them as intended to protect trade in home waters. With some exceptions, the majority of Royal Naval presence in the western Atlantic was in the form of small ships convoying trade rather than large men of war; the naval presence was defensive rather than aggressive.[80] Another whig-sponsored naval act of 1708 was the "Act for the Encouragement of Trade to America," which displaced aggressive maritime warfare from the navy to individual privateers. The act gave captors the right to the profits of the entire prize and prohibited impressment from privateers in American waters. An earlier failed bill, the West-Indies Bill of 1703, would have offered certain privileges to anyone who was willing to capture French or Spanish ships or territories in the Americas. West Indian merchants like Gilbert Heathcote supported the idea of capturing a Spanish port to use as a gateway for trade; for whigs, capturing a port was not about plunder, but about creating permanent access to a colonial market. Once access to Spanish markets was open again after 1704, West Indian merchants instead tended to turn against privateers whom they perceived as threatening good relations with Spain.[81]

The whig dominance of policy making in the early years of the war did not stop tory-leaning individuals from pitching plans for expeditions that would fulfill tory ideals of empire. Thomas Ekines, who was so enthusiastic about naval endeavors that he served in the navy as a volunteer without pay, repeatedly pitched naval expeditions to the colonies. One involved sacking Buenos Aires, another was to destroy every enemy port except Lima and Panama and seize the Spanish silver fleet, and another to seize Spanish Cartagena and Vera Cruz in Central America and French Placentia in Canada, along with their treasure ships. Although Sidney Godolphin, Earl of Godolphin and Lord Treasurer, was interested in the plan—Godolphin was himself tory leaning, though serving in a whig administration—John Churchill, the Duke of Marlborough, a whig and Queen Anne's favorite, dismissed it, noting that campaigns of that sort always served as "a pretext to plunder."[82] Toward the end of the war, tory Charles Davenant wistfully agreed that the war should have been carried out as a series of raids on the West Indies. He claimed that "the reign of Queen Elizabeth shows how easy and profitable those expeditions were, and what masses of gold and silver were brought from thence. And considering how much weaker the Spaniards are now, than they were in that age, 'tis more than probable, that an attempt there would have paid its own charges."[83] There was no shortage of proposals for more aggressive naval and colonial expeditions, but very few of them came to fruition, primarily because for the Marlborough-Godolphin ministry, the continental war was always more pressing. Additionally, England's allies, the Dutch and the Holy Roman Empire, were not willing to support expeditions to Spanish America. Although the Dutch promised their support for a proposed expedition to the West Indies under the leadership of Charles Mordaunt, Earl of Peterborough, in 1702, they did not follow through on their part of the military commitment in time, leading English ministers to call off the mission. These types of failures left the tories even more convinced of the inadvisability of relying upon allies.[84]

The tories came to power following the election of 1710 and continued to make their opinions of the war clear. Davenant argued that supplying land armies in Europe went against Britain's interests. It drained capital out of the country because armies had to be paid abroad, whereas "the chief expenses of our fleet are at home among ourselves, and keep our treasure within the kingdom." Rather than intervening in a land war, Britain should have "carried on an extended war by sea, and to have distressed the enemy in all their ports at home, and on their West-Indian coast; and we should, in a larger degree, have left to the confederates the care of their own defense by land." Properly deployed, Britain's navy would "protect our trade from the insults of our enemies, and from the encroachments of our allies and friends."[85] Tory Jonathan

Swift argued that alliances diverted the navy from its national purposes. In the alliance with Portugal, for example, "the same care, in almost the same words, is taken for our fleet to attend their coasts and foreign dominions, and to be under the same obedience." Britain's other allies the Dutch "never once furnished their quota either of ships or men; or if some few of their fleet now and then appeared, it was no more than appearing, for they immediately separated to look to their merchants and protect their trade." He regretted that "instead of being employed on some enterprise for the good of the nation, or even for the protection of our trade," the British fleet was instead "wholly taken up in transporting soldiers."[86] For Swift, "protection of trade" was not encompassed in "enterprises for the good of the nation," but it was still better than facilitating a land war. The tories returned naval decision makers to a central role in the administration; the Admiralty Board had been restored in 1709, and from 1712 onward the First Lord of the Admiralty was recognized as having a cabinet position.

The War of the Spanish Succession was a victory for England, but one without major naval accomplishments. The attack on Cadiz (1702) achieved little other than to accidentally put the English in the right place to capture the Spanish silver fleets at Vigo, though most of the silver had been unloaded and in fact the greatest losers were English and Dutch merchants whose assets in Spain were seized in retaliation. In 1704 the English successfully captured Gibraltar, which the tories trumpeted as an example of the power of the navy. In 1707 Anglo-Dutch sea forces in combination with land forces from Savoy assaulted Toulon in an attempt to capture a Mediterranean base. They were unsuccessful, but they did frighten the French enough to scuttle their own ships to prevent their capture, meaning that the Anglo-Dutch navies now had control of the Mediterranean. In 1708 they captured Mahon on the island of Minorca. There were thus some successes to point to, primarily in the Mediterranean. Privateering losses were reduced, in part owing to fewer French privateers and in part owing to a different distribution of naval forces, but they were far from eliminated. One contemporary estimated that the French had captured 3,600 ships, which was probably an overestimate but not one too far from the mark. This prompted John Thompson, Baron Haversham, to observe in Parliament that England's "disasters at sea have been so many, that a man scarce knows where to begin. Your ships have been taken by your enemies as the

Dutch take your herrings, by shoals, upon your own coasts."[87] Royal Naval expeditions to the colonies remained relatively rare, though there were some; maritime warfare in colonial waters was more likely to be carried out by colonial naval forces or by privateers and buccaneers. Rather than support expensive and risky expeditions to the West Indies, most whig efforts in the Caribbean between 1702 and 1707 focused on persuading Spanish colonists of the benefits of commercial intercourse with England. That said, though, after 1713 there were generally at least a few naval ships stationed in the Caribbean, primarily to protect against pirates.[88]

Perhaps the most important consequence of the Glorious Revolution for the navy, however, happened off the seas. The long-term fiscal and state-building consequences of the Glorious Revolution are well known and well rehearsed at this point. The appearance of a parliamentary guarantee of government debt enabled extensive levels of government borrowing and the creation of a true national debt to fund Britain's many wars. This encouraged the development of a state bureaucracy that became increasingly adept at reaching into the pockets of citizens, who largely granted their consent to this development. Britain developed what has been termed a fiscal-military state.[89] To a certain extent, however, this was less a fiscal-military state than a fiscal-naval one. Whereas funds for the army were frequently spent overseas on items of immediate consumption, funds for the navy could be spent locally, both for shipbuilding supplies and for victuals, and could be invested in capital rather than consumption.[90] As economic historian Patrick O'Brien contends, "Without sustained support from the most efficient fiscal and financial system in Europe, hegemony at sea that prevailed for two centuries after 1713 could never have been sustained."[91]

In the late seventeenth and early eighteenth centuries, the structure of the English navy, how its ships should be deployed strategically, and what tactics its officers should use once in battle were all up for debate. These various dimensions of sea power were points of contention not for purely military reasons, but because they were seen as representing and influencing other aspects of English life. By the end of the seventeenth century, the navy was strongly associated with tory policy, including hostility to the Protestant and republican Dutch, the elevation of the privileged nobility over more proficient and "deserving" middling sorts, and executive authority strengthened at the expense of the legislature. The events of the Nine Years' War and the War of the Spanish Succession strengthened these perceived connections. Whigs portrayed themselves as defenders of international Protestantism and for that reason tasked with defeating French aspirations for universal Catholic monarchy. They pointed to the tory reluctance to accept this land-based warfare and the types of financial innovations necessary to fund it as proof that tories did not have the nation's best interests at heart. The value of the navy was not obvious to "objective" viewers; it was based on the perceived needs of the foreign policy situation and the observer's own desires and fears regarding domestic English society. Depending on the perspective of the observer, the navy could easily be a threat to English liberty rather than its protector.

Despite claims from some that England was the ruler of the seas, this was wishful thinking rather than an accurate reflection of reality. For most of the seventeenth century, both France and the Netherlands challenged and possibly surpassed the English in naval power. Moreover, one of the signal attributes that would later help bring the British success was not yet present: the aggressive pursuit of decisive battle in nearly any circumstances. There were certainly some who believed in the power of the wooden walls, but equally there was debate, contestation, and fear about what else might be required to make those walls truly secure, what other sacrifices of liberty might be demanded. By 1710 British ships did indeed outnumber those of their rivals, but as contemporaries were quick to point out, ships alone meant little without capable men to sail them and ministers willing to use them the "right" way. From 1714 onward, the accession of the first Hanoverian monarch, George I, began a long period of whig monopolization of the highest levels of politics. Although those whigs continued to express a commitment to trade, the expansion of British commerce to the Caribbean that followed the War of the Spanish Succession meant that some interpreted the protection of those interests as requiring naval restraint, passivity rather than action. Britain's naval future was far from clear in the early decades of the eighteenth century.

✦ 2 ✦

WALPOLEAN IMPERIAL AND NAVAL POLICY

IN 1729 MORE THAN two dozen British ships were mustered at Spithead—a major anchorage south of Portsmouth—where they were joined by fourteen Dutch ships. This fleet, which became known as the "Spithead expedition," sat for three months before the Dutch sailed home and the British were paid off. In many ways, the Spithead expedition was an appropriate symbol of the 1727 Anglo-Spanish conflict of which it was a part. Between the declaration of war in early 1727 and the signing of peace at Seville in 1729, nothing really happened. No major battles were fought, nor was the face of Europe or the overseas empires changed. The conflict was a response to an alliance signed in 1725 by the Holy Roman Emperor, Charles VI, and the Spanish king, Philip V, in the Treaty of Vienna. Britain in turn formed a counter-alliance with France and Prussia via the Treaty of Hanover.[1] By early 1727 the two sides were poised for war, a prospect that was embraced with remarkable unanimity in Britain. Representatives of the House of Commons waited on George I with "a vigorous resolution" promising their support for "any measures he shall think convenient."[2] Parliament's example was "followed in a very singular manner by the City of London; the Lord Mayor, Aldermen and Common Council having unanimously agreed upon a most dutiful & loyal address to his Majesty, full of assurances of approbation, and support." Thomas Pelham-Holles, Duke of Newcastle and Secretary of State for the Southern Department, noted that this address was "the more remarkable" as it was the first time the representatives of London had unanimously addressed George I since his accession to the throne.[3] It was the only time they would do so during his reign. The diplomat Thomas Robinson reinforced the singularity of this event to the ministers of the French court, noting that this address had been "proposed by those who are known for being the principal members of the opposition party." Since London "gives the lead to all other cities in the Kingdom, it is to be imagined that all the nation will soon follow its example."[4] Public confidence and interest in the looming war was high; stocks were rising, and "the first question in all conversation is, peace or war?"[5]

Within one interpretation of British history, this unanimity requires no explanation. Of all the periods of the eighteenth century, the two decades under Robert Walpole's administration (1721–1742) are often described as the most stable. The major issues of the seventeenth century—religion, the constitution, and their attendant dynastic struggles—had been laid to rest. The foundations of this stability were the existence of a common identity and common aspirations among elites, strong ministerial control by Walpole, his use of patronage to secure his administration, and the consequent proscription of the tories from office. The political realm was not completely quiescent, but it operated within clearly delineated parameters and on a relatively narrow range of issues. Political competition was primarily factional rather than ideological, because conflict took place within a wider context of social consensus.[6] If the major issues of the seventeenth century had been settled, the major issues of the eighteenth century—imperial and, once again, constitutional struggles—had not yet raised their ugly heads.[7]

Yet despite their seeming unanimity before the war, Britain's political classes continued to rehash the 1727 conflict with increasing acrimony until Britain and Spain formally declared war once again in 1739. In particular, members of the opposition returned over and over again to Walpole's handling of naval affairs as evidence of his administration's flaws. One ballad scathingly suggested that although the Spithead expedition had never sailed, keeping so many sailors in port for so long would leave a large crop of illegitimate children who could be raised as sailors in the future, so "the scheme for the public was very well laid" despite the expense of outfitting the fleet. A second ballad agreed that at least the ships "had plenty of guns, tho' they use none at all." A third pamphlet compared the expedition to Caligula's campaign against the Britons, in which (according to Suetonius) he mustered his forces on the

Gallic shore facing the English Channel, ordered them to gather seashells, and then declared victory. Being likened to one of the more insane Roman emperors was not especially flattering for Walpole.[8] His ministry tried to cut off the criticism—the ministerial newspaper the *Daily Courant* said as early as 1730 that the "whole kingdom, or all who are worth convincing, must now be convinced, that the clamour without doors has been unjust; and that the invidious reflections . . . have been detestable, undeserved, and base" and George II criticized those responsible for such "libels" in a speech to Parliament—but the opposition refused to be diverted.[9]

Rather than being considered in the context of stability or consensus, the Anglo-Spanish conflict of 1727 and its aftermath need to be evaluated within the context of a strongly contested political realm, one in which significant public discourse was generated by imperial questions.[10] The major political sides in this particular episode of imperial struggle were the establishment whigs—also known as the court whigs—led by Walpole, and what is often referred to as simply "the opposition." It would be incorrect to say that the establishment whigs opposed Britain's current empire or wanted to see its dismantlement. However, they were not committed to its expansion. Walpole had risen to the role of leading minister in the wake of the 1720 South Sea Bubble financial crisis, which shook not only the British economy but also public confidence in the government. One of his primary concerns was, as H. T. Dickinson has explained, "to stabilize the nation's finances so that the landed, moneyed, and merchant interests, or at least large parts of them, would support his administration."[11] In Walpole's opinion, restoring public faith in national finances required avoiding unnecessary public expenditures. He allied himself with the remaining monopoly trading companies, the South Sea Company and the East India Company, both of which were used to finance the national debt.[12] Lord John Hervey recorded in his memoirs that Walpole was "hated by the city of London, because he never did anything for the trading part of it, nor aimed any interest of theirs but a corrupt influence over the directors and governors of the great moneyed companies."[13] Walpolean establishment whiggery had thus shifted away from some of the tenets of turn of the century whiggism.

In turn, during the 1720s the whig-tory binary began to break down as some whigs grew increasingly discontented with Walpole's administration for reasons of both foreign and domestic policy.[14] These dissident whigs—who by the 1740s would diverge into authoritarian and patriot strands—believed that Walpole had abandoned the Glorious Revolution, that domestically he restrained the civil and political liberties secured following the Revolution, and that overseas he no longer supported British trade and manufactures.[15] The opposition became a collection of different ideological strands, both tory and dissident whig. Both groups wanted imperial expansion, though within different parameters. The tories were interested in easy colonial plunder or territories that would pay for themselves in natural resources. Pro-colonial dissident whigs were committed to the expansion of British colonial trade, which possibly entailed the removal of Spanish sovereignty over their American colonies but certainly required a change in Spanish colonial policy. George I and Walpole's political and financial priorities encouraged them to focus on the Holy Roman Empire and seek accommodation with Spain. Tories and dissident whigs considered a war with the Holy Roman Empire to be at best a distraction, at worst un-British; Spain was their main target.

The apparent unanimity leading up to the outbreak of war in 1727 in fact rested on several temporarily congruent goals, rather than being a product of genuine agreement. On one side stood the Hanoverian kings, Walpole, and the establishment whigs, all of whom were primarily focused on the European dimensions of the conflict and especially on the Holy Roman Empire, rather than on Spain. On the other side stood the opposition—tories and dissident whigs—who were primarily focused on the colonial dimensions of the conflict and especially on Spain. The hasty resolution of the conflict brought this divergence in objectives into stark focus: the peace satisfied those prioritizing European stability but was deeply disappointing to those who prioritized imperial expansion.

The 1727 conflict was a formative moment in solidifying the opposition ideologies of the 1730s and 1740s, particularly with regard to imperial affairs. For the next decade, Walpole's handling of the war was one of the main critiques slung at his administration by the opposition. The naval policy of the establishment whigs formed an important part of this critique: Walpole and his associates conceived of a navy in line with their own priorities of stability and economy. Under Walpole's administration, the Royal Navy was a passive force focused on deterrence rather than an aggressive, active one. It was undermanned, underofficered, and with insufficient infrastructure to maintain unquestioned dominance even in the waters around Britain. It was not a naval force intended to be dominant in battle, but this was a deliberate and rational choice in terms of the goals held by the administration. Understanding the naval system favored by the establishment whigs is important in order to be able to understand later arguments over naval power and naval governance; both the authoritarian whig and patriot military systems were reactions to establishment whig military governance. Based on the accounts of British and foreign politicians and naval officers, it would be inaccurate to depict the Walpolean Royal Navy as a maritime hegemon. Both France and Spain believed at points during this period that they could legitimately challenge British naval power. While Britain's expanding economy opened possibilities for military power, Walpole deliberately sidestepped them.

The 1727 Anglo-Spanish Conflict

In April 1725 Spain and the Holy Roman Empire signed a treaty of alliance at Vienna. Publicly, this treaty secured Spain's agreement to the Holy Roman Emperor's Pragmatic Sanction—which permitted the Austrian throne to be inherited by a female heir—and in return the Hapsburgs gave up their claim to the Spanish throne. The Spanish prince Don Carlos was given the succession to the duchies of Parma and Tuscany, and Austria promised to try to persuade Britain to restore Gibraltar and Minorca back to Spain. Emperor Charles VI had chartered an Austrian overseas trading venture in 1722 to compete with the English, Dutch, and French companies trading to the East Indies; Spain agreed to allow this Ostend Company equal access to its overseas territories on the same terms as the Dutch and English companies. There were rumors as well of an additional secret treaty. British ministers could not say with certainty that they knew the terms, but they believed they knew the gist. First, there was the possibility that the alliance was to be solidified by the marriage of Don Carlos to the eldest daughter of the emperor. Second, they believed that the secret treaty represented an offensive rather than a merely defensive commitment, and that Austria promised to help Spain regain Gibraltar and Minorca through force of arms if persuasion failed. Third, George I and his ministers believed that the secret treaty contained plans to restore the Stuarts to the British throne.[16] Political interests in Britain perceived two primary sets of threats from these provisions. One set of threats, sensed by George I and the establishment whigs, were primarily continental; the other set of threats, identified by the tory and dissident whig opposition, were primarily colonial. Different types of naval action would be required depending on which of these hazards was to be addressed.

George I's understanding of the treaty and the subsequent conflict was inseparable from his role as Elector of Hanover, a position that gave him prominent political standing in the Holy Roman Empire. George claimed the treaty was retaliation for his alliance with France and contestation of certain policies within the empire.[17] Charles VI allegedly insinuated that if George did not accept the Treaty of Vienna, it would negatively affect his Electoral dominions.[18] As John Perceval, closely associated with the Hanoverians and Walpole, wrote, the cause of the treaty was that "the Emperor is grown jealous of the power of Prussia and Hanover in Germany, and would fain bring them lower that he may settle the Empire his own way, and dispose of all affairs in Germany at his pleasure."[19] From this perspective, the Treaty of Vienna was intended to undermine George I as King of Britain in order to bring him into line as Elector of Hanover. Spain was only a tool being manipulated by the emperor, who was the real adversary.[20]

Accordingly, George repeatedly made it clear—at least to his ministers, though not necessarily to the public—that his primary concern was Emperor Charles VI.[21] The French court, Britain's major ally in the conflict, agreed. The British ambassador told Cardinal de Fleury, the leading French minister, that George I believed "our chief efforts should be leveled against the Emperor, as being the more formidable power, and indeed the author of the troubles that had broken the tranquility of Europe, that Spain might be considered only as the dupe and tool of the Imperial Court."[22] The two courts together hoped to "take such measures as might separate Spain from the Emperor, or making the Emperor appear to be the aggressor in the eye of Europe, give us an opportunity of turning our main force with success against him."[23] If they were successful in separating the two allies, Britain and France "would be immediately justified to turn their main strength against [Charles VI], without distressing or reducing Spain any farther."[24] For George, the British navy thus had two purposes: to protect his continental position, including his allies, and to undermine and isolate his main rival, the Holy Roman Emperor. For example, when a British squadron was sent to the Baltic in 1727, the official reason was to shield the Danish coast so that the Danish king could send troops against Charles. Protecting British trade to the region was also listed as a reason, but a subsidiary one.[25] The navy was also sent to blockade Spanish treasure fleets in the Americas, in hopes of leaving Spain unable to fulfill its financial obligations to Charles and leaving him in turn unable to pay his troops.[26]

As the king's leading minister, Robert Walpole and his political contingent were bound to support this policy to a certain extent. Their faith in balance of power politics enhanced this commitment. The establishment whigs believed the Holy Roman Empire's alliance with Spain threatened continental stability by upsetting the balance of power and their propaganda highlighted the hazards of an unbalanced Europe, along with emphasizing the value of alliances in maintaining stability.[27] One of the dangers of the Treaty of Vienna was the possible marriage contract between the Spanish prince Don Carlos and the Austrian archduchess Maria Teresa, a marriage that would in time lead to the resurrection of the sixteenth-century Hapsburg Empire: Spain and Austria reunited, along with the Spanish overseas territories and parts of the Netherlands and Italy.[28] The ministerial newspaper the *British Journal* argued that the Holy Roman Emperor's ambition required intervention—not only Britain, but "all the powers of Europe were consequently jealous of Germany, and opposed its rising greatness."[29] Breaking the Spanish alliance with Charles would remove the threat of their combined power and restore the European balance of power. By planning with France "to take such measures as might separate Spain from the Emperor," Walpole's ministry accomplished its goal of preventing the creation of a power bloc, as well as George I's goal of focusing actual violent hostilities on Charles VI alone.[30]

Establishment whigs also believed the treaty threatened colonial stability by providing competition for Britain's monopoly trading companies. Horatio Walpole, Robert Walpole's brother, cited the Ostend Company as one of the primary problems of the Treaty of Vienna, one which "visibly tended to the entire ruin of many valuable branches of our trade."[31] The Ostend Company created more competition for the English East India Company. Its authorization to establish a factory in Cadiz would also undermine Britain's trade to Spain and Spanish

America.[32] More specifically, it would damage the trade of the South Sea Company, the only British entity allowed to trade directly to the Spanish West Indies. The South Sea Company theoretically traded primarily in slaves, but was also permitted to sell other goods once a year at the major South American fair. Investors in this trade therefore hoped to block the Ostend Company without damaging relations with Spain. If true war with Spain commenced, the legal trade to the Spanish colonies would be lost. The South Sea Company might also bear significant financial losses when their goods in various Spanish ports were seized.

The establishment whigs neither needed nor wanted to come to a full break with Spain, nor did they necessarily need to come to full war with Charles VI, either. They only needed to break the Spanish-Imperial alliance and force the emperor to back down on the Ostend Company in order to achieve their ends in the war, which was the restoration of the status quo ante bellum. As John Perceval acknowledged, "Neither France nor England desire better than that things should remain as they are (the Ostend Company in some points to be restrained excepted)."[33] Establishment whigs rejected the idea of conquest or colonial expansion, as Perceval explained in a later letter: "we have done what we could to have peace . . . we affect no conquests."[34] Establishment whig concerns over the financial implications of war a made them eager to find a solution through negotiation. One pamphlet that defended the French alliance also claimed that the "business of England was to prevent the new allies from being able to begin a war, not to begin a war ourselves, which was to be avoided if possible."[35] Using the navy aggressively was counterproductive; instead, establishment whigs hoped to use the navy as a deterrent to dissuade their enemies from escalating the situation. Sending the navy to the Caribbean to cut Spain off from its monetary resources also made sense, as a means of undermining the Spanish-Imperial alliance. The establishment whigs' goals could be achieved through deterrence and negotiation. The official opening of hostilities was intended more as a rattling of the saber than a genuine commitment to dismantling either the Spanish or Imperial regimes.

These continental preoccupations can be seen in how George I and Walpole tried to sell the impending conflict to the public. They emphasized the pact they believed Spain and the Holy Roman Empire had made in favor of James Stuart, the so-called Pretender to the British throne.[36] In his address to Parliament in January 1727, George I cited "an invasion in favour of the Pretender" as the reason why Britain needed to be put in a state of defense. Robert and Horatio Walpole added that "the Treaty entered into between the Emperor and Spain could not take effect unless the Pretender were on this throne and therefore it was one of the first Articles agreed between them."[37] When the French found out that there was no immediate plan for a Jacobite invasion, they warned Walpole not to let the British public know, in case it dampened popular fervor.[38] However, the French ministers misunderstood the situation. As one observer noted, following George's speech to Parliament, "If the disposition of the Kingdom were to be understood by the Huzzas of the mob as the King went and returned from the House, you would think us all impatient for war, they were above 3000 crying out God save King George who protects our trade down with the Jack Spaniards No Pretender &c."[39] Although George was more focused on the Pretender, for many people the Spaniards outweighed the Stuart threat. Newcastle noted as much, writing to the British embassy in Paris that the even if the public knew there was no immediate threat of a Stuart invasion, that "would not abate the spirit here; what has inflamed the nation, is the repeated indignities & injuries put upon us by the Spaniards."[40]

The tories and dissident whigs prioritized Spain over the Holy Roman Emperor or the Pretender. The tories believed the Spanish colonies were rich in natural resources and might be ripe for plunder; the dissident whigs believed Spain fundamentally threatened the survival of British trade in the Caribbean. Since the Treaty of Utrecht in 1713, Spanish *guarda costas* (coast guard ships) increasingly stopped and searched British merchant ships, seizing them if they carried any goods which indicated they had been illegally trading with Spanish colonies. It was certainly true that some British traders smuggled. However, it was also true that some of the items the Spanish used to "prove" smuggling were circulated throughout trading networks in the Caribbean and could be legally acquired outside the Spanish colonies.[41] This meant that even a ship that had not engaged in illegal trading could be subject to seizure, according to the Spanish standards. Acknowledging the right of the Spanish to search British ships using these criteria might severely limit independent British trade to the Caribbean.

The tory commitment to war was not unshakeable, mostly because they feared it becoming a continental land war. The tory William Shippen criticized the Treaty of Hanover in Parliament because "it would engage the British nation in a war, for the defence of his Majesty's dominions in Germany."[42] A fellow tory, William Wyndham, condemned Walpole's balance of power politics, saying, "Penelope-like, we were continually weaving and unraveling the same web; at one time raising up the Emperor to depress France, and now we were for depressing the Emperor, which could not be done without aggrandizing France, which in the end, may make the latter too powerful: so that at this rate, under pretence of holding the balance of Europe, we should be engaged in continental wars."[43] Instead, tories hoped for an American maritime war in which the navy would be used aggressively to take and hold imperial territories. They voiced their concern, as the tory Lord Bolingbroke did in a *Craftsman* essay, that in this regard they were being surpassed by the Spanish, French, and Dutch.[44] Taking territories allowed for the development and exploitation of the natural resources found in the colonies, and it also played to the tory desire to benefit from plundering Spanish riches.[45] Both Shippen and Wyndham spoke in Parliament in favor of a war in which Britain's ships could have "rifled the galleons at Cartagena, and plundered Portobello."[46]

While the tories were fixated on easy plunder, the dissident whigs wanted to secure and expand British trade to the Americas. They faced two separate problems, but with potentially one solution. The first problem was that the independent traders whose interests they reflected believed their trade to the British Caribbean was increasingly under siege from Spanish *guarda costas*. In June 1724 alone, the Spanish took three ships off the coast of Virginia and another one in the Bahamas.[47] One list counted forty-eight ships taken by the Spanish in the Americas between 1712 and 1725.[48] The Admiralty Board warned Newcastle that according to the representations coming from the Caribbean, "his Majesty's trading subjects are more prejudiced by the aforesaid Spanish ships, than by the pirates which have infested those seas" and that the problem was only increasing.[49] Merchants from Bristol and Liverpool, cities known for their involvement in the slave and West Indian trades, were especially insistent about the toll the depredations were taking. When war opened in 1727, Bristol merchants were among the first to request letters of marque to make good their losses on the Spanish.[50] Those two cities later specifically petitioned Parliament against the continued depredations. Ministerial apologists singled them out as especially vocal troublemakers.[51]

The second problem was that these independent traders felt excluded from the full benefits of trade to the Spanish Americas. The 1670 Treaty of Madrid forbade British merchants from trading with Spanish colonies; the 1713 Treaty of Utrecht reiterated this prohibition, with the exception of the South Sea Company. Elites profited through the monopoly trading company, but smaller traders were prohibited from participating legally. The South Sea Company monopolized not just the legal trade but the illegal smuggling trade as well. Classical whig economic theory already argued against monopoly trading companies.[52] Beyond that, the company's actions generated a variety of complaints from independent traders and planters in the Caribbean. These ranged from accusations that the company and the *asiento* had stopped British trade to Spanish settlements, as the Jamaican Assembly declared in 1732, to complaints that the company drove up the price of slaves and thus hindered the British planter from being able to cultivate his land, as Bolingbroke wrote in the *Craftsman*.[53]

These two problems could share the same solution if the Spanish trade were opened to all British subjects or if the Spanish no longer held sovereignty over their American colonies. Either of these options would require using the navy aggressively, either to counter Spanish attempts to prevent British trade or to support rebellions in Spanish colonies. As the whig Daniel Defoe argued in a pro-war pamphlet of 1727, "if our neighbours pretend to shut the door against our commerce, we must open it; and that by force, if no other means will procure it."[54] Another pro-war pamphlet argued that Britain ought to encourage Spain's imperial subjects to rebel, set up an independent government, and open a free trade with Britain.[55] If the territories no longer belonged to the Spanish, the South Sea Company no longer held a monopoly and anyone would be able to participate: it would hurt the company but would benefit the other merchants. Defoe explained that the point of the war was to take over Spanish trade in the West Indies, "not only to break in upon their trade by all such methods as we find practicable, but to make such gaps and openings in it, as it shall never be in the power of the Spaniards to close and make up again."[56] The merchants of London and other trading cities hoped that this impending war with Spain would address Caribbean concerns, making the region more fruitful for British trade.

Although the Treaty of Vienna created a momentary overlap in the continental concerns of George I and the establishment whigs and the colonial concerns of the opposition, the reality was that once war broke out, these goals were likely to become incompatible. In the end, the 1727 Anglo-Spanish conflict delivered no actual hostilities. No major battles were fought, on land or sea, and no territories were captured. The Spanish besieged Gibraltar—a siege that largely consisted of digging trenches while the British fleet sat on the coast and watched. A British squadron was sent to the Caribbean under Admiral Francis Hosier with orders to stop the Spanish treasure fleet from sailing; the treasure fleet slipped away home anyway and a vast percentage of Hosier's sailors died. Although the establishment whig Thomas Robinson observed in January 1727 that peace "was more to be wished for, than expected," in fact less than a month later the Holy Roman Emperor indicated he was ready to negotiate. Spain was forced to follow his lead and the preliminaries of peace were signed in Paris in May 1727.[57] The terms proposed by Charles VI were largely what the establishment whigs hoped for: the emperor backed down from supporting the Ostend Company, Spain backed down from its claims to Gibraltar, and peace was restored in Europe and abroad, assuming Britain withdrew its ships from the West Indies. Newcastle immediately agreed that "Nothing can be more reasonable than . . . bringing matters back upon the foot on which they were established by the treaties of Utrecht & Baden and the Quadruple Alliance." As far as British trade was concerned, "settling the commerce to Spain and the West Indies upon the foot that it was established by treaties antecedent to those of Vienna & Hanover can meet with no objection" as long as the Holy Roman Emperor and Spain disavowed the Ostend Company.[58] The goal was to restore the balance that existed prior to the Treaty of Vienna, but no extension of British trade was deemed necessary. The 1729 Treaty of Seville formalized the peace and largely reiterated these points. Those who hoped to see an aggressive colonial war were quickly disappointed.

Establishment Whig Naval Policy

There were thus a variety of interests in Britain in 1727 with different imperial and foreign policy aspirations; the naval policies they would have required were mutually incompatible. Instead, the 1727 Anglo-Spanish conflict embodied establishment whig naval policy: a passive force focused on deterrence.[59] This passivity was not an accident or a failure of imagination on the part of the establishment whigs. They created a navy that complemented their other priorities, such as fiscal restraint and maintaining the balance of power—both by ensuring that other countries were dissuaded from upsetting it and also by ensuring that Britain itself did not appear too ambitious or aggressive. The establishment whigs were reluctant to commit Britain to the expenditure of war and had no desire to expand Britain's colonial holdings. Embracing a large, aggressive navy was seen as counter-productive. The opposition latched on to Walpole's naval policy as a means of highlighting his administration's failures; their imperial aspirations would have required a very different navy. Under Walpole's leadership, the Royal Navy was far from reaching the potential which Britain's economic growth might hypothetically have unlocked—not by accident but by political choice.

One concept, more than any other, defined the establishment whigs' naval policy: restraint. In conversation with French ministers, Horatio Walpole cited as confirmation of Great Britain's moderation the fact that "the powers of the Admiral now before Gibraltar were so restrained, that he suffered the embarkation of provisions and ammunitions to pass unmolested by him, that were destined for the Army assembled and preparing to besiege Gibraltar."[60] This was true: in 1727 Admiral Charles Wager had allowed provisions to reach the Spanish army besieging Gibraltar, a choice that Walpole's administration gave its approbation.[61] The *British Journal* defended this policy: "I cannot see any reason we had to begin hostilities, or to seize their ships or stores, before they broke the cessation of arms."[62] Establishment whig pamphlets argued Britain "had before eminently suffered, by a rash and undue exertion of national prowess and valour; and we have not now been less gainers, by the prudent restraining of it," because by inhibiting active hostilities they had regained Spanish friendship.[63] The members of Walpole's administration were aware that what they characterized as a positive feature of their policy others decried as a negative. One pamphlet that defended the negotiations of 1729 observed that the administration had "been censured with such uncommon virulence . . . upon the supposed inactivity of our squadrons." The opposition suggested that "the commanders of our men of war have been restrained from protecting our trade, and from resenting the injuries and insults which our merchants have suffered from the Spaniards." The pamphlet referred to the Bastimentos expedition of 1726–1727, which led to the death of Admiral Hosier and more than 3,000 seamen as they blockaded the Spanish galleons in port. The pamphlet argued that if the ministry had ordered Hosier "to have committed open hostilities by attacking the galleons in the harbor of Porto Bello, it was impossible for the Admiral to have taken any thing, but the empty hulks of the ships," which "could not have had much influence on the counsels of Spain." On the contrary, the author questioned who would have "sacrificed so fair a prospect of establishing a general tranquility" as negotiations represented "to the distant and uncertain views of obtaining it by a bloody and expensive war." He concluded that those who argued for a war did so in order "to reap some private advantage from the calamities into which they endeavour to plunge their country."[64] The establishment whigs embraced restraint as a marker of moderation, which they equated with wisdom and public (as opposed to private) interest. The "idle popularity arising from bombarding a sea port, and bringing home a few cargoes of snuff and trinkets, was justly despised by those, who were the guardians of our welfare," suggested their pamphlets.[65]

Restraint was likewise seen in Walpole's approach to privateers. Walpole's ministry was decidedly unenthusiastic about issuing letters of marque and both publicly and privately questioned the advisability of a pro-privateering approach. Ministerial pamphlets refuted the opposition's claim that George II absolutely refused to grant letters of marque, but admitted that since the Spanish were ready to come to terms so quickly, allowing privateering was not prudent. They praised the king and his ministers, saying their "caution was very commendable, and even necessary."[66] Another pamphlet asked, rhetorically, what more Britain could have done to Spain than it had already: "Shall we make a piratic war, and burn their coasts? This may indeed ruin a great many miserable people, at a great expense on our part, but without being at all nearer to the end of the war, or to a good peace."[67] Publicly, establishment whigs countered the pressure in favor of privateers by arguing that they were simply not effective in gaining Britain's goals. Privately, the argument was slightly different. Establishment whigs believed the average British subject was not capable of acting with restraint: men who were permitted to become privateers in time of war would quickly become pirates in time of peace. Admiral Wager repeatedly commented that the reason no letters of marque had been granted, although they had been "so often demanded," was because the ministry believed "our seamen who are too much addicted to such a kind of life would swarm in the West Indies, and do inconceivable mischief to the Spaniards (as they formerly did) as well as to others, before they could be restrained."[68] He explained that privateers, like *guarda costas,* "must rob & plunder or they can not live, and they will be so used to it, that [the government] will not be able to restrain them." The British ministry knew "it would be the same thing with our West Indians, if once commissions were given them, and that is the reason that we have not given letters of reprisals."[69]

The navy did not play an aggressive or offensive role in establishment whig foreign policy, but it did have a more passive role as a deterrent. Simply putting the navy on view might be enough to accomplish the administration's ends. As Wager put it, "The Spaniards have a proverb, that every man shows, what he has; that is, if he has white teeth, he keep his mouth open, if he has a white hand, he keeps his glove off; if he has land armies, he brings them most in sight; if he has ships & navies? Let us show them, that being our case, wherein we exceed our neighbours."[70] One pamphlet that defended the use of Hosier's squadron acknowledged that "some people indeed find fault with the sending this squadron [to the Caribbean] . . . because they did not do more." The author countered that deploying the squadron "produced the preliminaries, which suspended a war, though it did not immediately produce a peace."[71] The *British Journal* asked, "If securing Gibraltar, if protecting our colonies and merchants, if suspending the Ostend Company, and procuring again our ships and effects in the South Seas; if these have not accrued by distressing the Spaniards in blocking up the galleons, I would desire to know some other causes."[72] Establishment whig pamphlets returned to the argument that it was necessary to restore friendship with Spain, and asked, "Was this to be done, by reducing Spain by force of arms to a faithless, temporary compliance?" They argued that, on the contrary, "blustering violence, and the pomp and terror of naval armaments, were methods the most opposite to this great and desirable end."[73] British naval maneuvers in 1727–1729 were intended more to strike fear into the hearts of the Spanish and show them what they had to lose in a war with Britain than to fight real battles or make real conquests. This was the reasoning behind the "Spithead expedition" of 1729. For Walpole, the purpose of mustering the combined British and Dutch fleets was to overawe the Spanish and force them to sign the final peace treaty. Establishment whigs defended the Spithead expedition: "to this very fleet, pacific as it was, it is probable, our country owes the accomplishment, at least the so speedy accomplishment of its desires . . . [it] carried as much terror into the bosoms of our enemies, as if those preparations had been prosecuted."[74] The establishment whigs used the British navy as a successful deterrent against the opening of wider hostilities between European powers.

For the opposition, this policy of naval restraint was unsatisfactory. The tories envisioned the navy as Britain's first, best, and only proper military force, its "great and natural strength."[75] It was a bastion between the British Isles and Britain's continental foes, as well as the necessary force to snatch overseas territories without expensive land campaigns. The dissident whigs likewise advocated aggressive naval warfare in order to protect and expand overseas trade. Although these whigs had not completely abandoned the support of continental engagement that characterized whiggish foreign policy at the end of the seventeenth century, their eyes were increasingly turned to the Americas rather than to Europe.[76] In part this may have been owing to the increasing importance of American trade to British manufactures. Though this trade had not yet supplanted European commerce in terms of absolute value, as it would by the end of the century, it provided much of the *expansion* of trade.[77]

The opposition used the perceived naval failures of the Bastimentos expedition, the Spithead expedition, and Wager's inactivity during the siege of Gibraltar to challenge ministerial competence, undermining the argument that the establishment whigs were acting in the best interests of the nation. A variety of opposition ballads mocked the very idea of passive deterrence as an effective means to Britain's ends. One sang, "Come you Whig and you Tory, / Attend to my story, / For you ne'er heard the like, nor your fathers before you; / How Britain, Great Britain! is Queen of the Main, / And her navies in port are the terror of Spain." Another popular ballad referred to the Spithead expedition as "the pacific fleet" and claimed that Walpole and his allies thought "the same end we fulfill, / If we bear the expense, tho' the fleet do lie still / For we so frighten Spain, they will do what we will."[78] These ballads were right: the establishment whigs did think that. Though the opposition disagreed, they did not misunderstand. *Fog's Weekly Journal* mockingly proposed a bill for "for supplying our Navy Royal, with all manner of sailing tackle, to enable 'em to go out of port the next summer."[79]

Whereas the establishment whigs wished to avoid privateering as much as possible, many dissident whigs pushed for privateering. The pro-war pamphlet *Great Britain's Speediest Sinking Fund is a Maritime War, Rightly Manag'd* argued, " 'Tis highly requisite that the private adventurers in the ensuing war should be many" and " 'Tis to private adventurers that Great Britain may be said to owe all that she has to boast of." It encouraged the nobility, gentlemen, and trading parts of Britain to outfit privateers.[80] The merchants of Bristol petitioned the Admiralty for letters of marque; the West Indian merchants "desire nothing more, than to be let loose upon the Spaniards, they say, that they will do themselves justice."[81] A pro-war screed of the late 1730s argued that Britain's merchants "desir[ed] nothing more ardently than an occasion to assist their friends in those countries both with ships and money and desire no other recompense than the plunder they may get and the future security of their trade."[82]

Both tories and pro-colonial whigs found Walpole's establishment whig foreign policy to be deeply disappointing. In particular they critiqued the administration by stressing the defensive nature of the Walpolean navy. For establishment whigs, using the navy as a deterrent made sense both diplomatically and financially. Why bear the costs of fully escalated naval warfare if the same ends could be accomplished another way? The opposition, however, envisioned an active and aggressive navy. These same arguments continued to resonate throughout the 1730s, and the opposition continued to draw on specifically naval examples to persuade the public of Walpole's misunderstanding of the true interests of the nation.

The Peace of 1729 and Its Legacies

The 1729 Treaty of Seville largely reinstated the status quo ante bellum. In doing so, it satisfied the establishment whigs but not the tories and whigs of the opposition, who found themselves in exactly the same position they had been in in 1727. Accordingly, they continued to advocate for a more aggressive imperial policy. As Walpole instead persisted in using the navy as a means to cement alliances and prevent warfare—

deploying it to ferry Spanish troops to their new Italian territories in 1731 and to discourage hostilities between Spain and Portugal in 1735—rather than to prevent Spanish *guarda costas* from taking British merchant ships in the Caribbean, members of the opposition became increasingly incensed. As their anger escalated, they repeatedly cited naval episodes from the 1727 conflict as confirmation of the failings of Walpole's administration. Naval policy thus acted as a rallying point around which opposition parties cohered.

The Treaty of Seville restored all former treaties and conventions, voided all Spain's commitments in the Treaty of Vienna that were prejudicial to previous treaties between Spain and England, and returned commerce in Europe, the East Indies, and the West Indies to its former footing. As in the Treaty of Vienna, Spain's prince Don Carlos was guaranteed the succession of the duchies of Parma and Tuscany, which were to be secured by Spanish garrisons; Britain promised to "persuade" the current dukes of Parma and Tuscany to accept those garrisons. The Spanish king Philip V guaranteed the safety of the British kingdom, thus implicitly turning his back on any promises to the Pretender. Spain and the Holy Roman Emperor went their separate ways. This broke the power bloc which, Walpole and the establishment whigs believed, threatened the balance of power and cleared the way for Britain to make alliances with both parties.[83]

The treaty thus decided many of the European issues, but critics believed it asked more of Britain than it did of Spain. One pamphlet complained that "nothing [was] granted to Britain but what [the Spanish] had previously consented to," and warned that Spanish promises meant little.[84] In 1731 Spanish ministers denied that the Treaty of Seville even existed because, they claimed, Britain had not upheld its obligations; the British ambassador in Madrid, Benjamin Keene, thought that insisting that the treaty did exist would lead to an immediate rupture between the two countries. At the same time, the Spanish were rebuilding threatening engineering works in front of Gibraltar.[85] When the opposition, including the tories William Wyndham and James Oglethorpe and the dissident whigs William and Daniel Pulteney, Thomas Saunderson, and Sir John Rushout, pointed out in Parliament that this was bordering on openly hostile, Robert Walpole countered by saying he was "surprised at some gentlemen's aim: when we were well with France then they would have us break with her, now we are well with Spain, they would have us break with her."[86] Shortly after the Spanish denied the Treaty of Seville existed and were rebuilding their fortifications around Gibraltar, the British fleet escorted Spanish troops to secure Don Carlos's new territories in Tuscany.[87]

The Treaty of Seville largely left undecided the colonial issues which many believed were the war's true purpose. Throughout the 1730s, the establishment whigs' policy of colonial and naval restraint remained a central feature of opposition criticism. The treaty did not resolve the question of whether the Spanish had the right to search British ships in American seas and it did not secure Spanish repayments for merchants who claimed they had been the victims of unlawful seizure. Instead, commissioners were appointed, ordered to evaluate the various claims on both sides, and negotiate reimbursement where appropriate.[88] By 1733 the commissioners had not yet finished this task. Sir Wilfrid Lawson, a leading opposition whig, claimed, "I cannot hear of any one of our merchants who has met with any redress." William Pulteney, another leading opposition whig, added, "It is a little surprising, that in so long a time there should have been nothing done."[89] The one exception to this was the South Sea Company: the treaty specifically reiterated the right of the company to the *asiento* and demanded by name the restoration of the company ship *Prince Frederick*.[90]

What was more frustrating to independent Caribbean traders than the fact that the treaty did not explicitly address past depredations was the fact that it also failed to stop *guarda costas* from seizing British ships in the future. In 1730 the merchants of Kingston wrote to the naval commander in chief based at Jamaica, Rear Admiral Charles Stewart, that they had "constant & repeated advices that several Spanish sloops & vessels are now actually cruising in these seas in order to take, plunder and destroy the ships & vessels" belonging to British merchants. The merchants concluded that without intervention, Jamaica "must (by the continual losses and the difficulties of coming to or going from it in safety) be reduced to a most deplorable condition."[91] A pro-ministerial pamphlet counted twenty-six ships by the Spanish taken between 1725 and 1729; a later list counted fifty-three merchant ships taken between 1725 and 1731.[92] The merchants of Bristol and Liverpool petitioned Parliament again in 1731 regarding the ongoing depredations, but seizures continued through the 1730s.[93] In one sense, the numbers were negligible. As one critic estimated in 1731, perhaps 200 British ships went to

Africa and then on to the Caribbean in a year, but only two had been taken the previous year and only two plundered, leaving 98 percent of the British ships untouched.[94] This was, to his mind, hardly a crisis of national proportions. However, the merchants had a different perspective: given increased risk, their insurances rose regardless of whether their own ships were taken or not.[95] Moreover, they did not necessarily have the ability to absorb the loss if their ship were one of the unlucky 2 percent; they were not big companies with large reserves of capital.

Part of what was at stake here was the question of who would benefit from British trade to the Caribbean: a monopoly like the South Sea Company, which would limit profits to relatively few wealthy investors, or a larger number of independent traders? The company was unwilling to risk its good relations with Spain by allowing its competitors to argue over a few ships of comparatively little worth. Sea officers were forced to decide whether to passively protect the company by trying to prevent a new war, or to actively escalate the situation in an attempt to secure the commerce of smaller traders. One incident will serve to illustrate this dynamic. In 1731 the snow *Mary* of Liverpool was seized and carried into Puerto Rico with its cargo and crew. Independent Jamaican merchants and the representatives of the company called a meeting and argued strenuously over whether or not to request Admiral Stewart to commence reprisals. The independent merchants argued that Stewart should "seize & detain all Spanish effects by way of reprisal for the great losses and injuries we have sustained."[96] The company factors accused the independent merchants of thinking themselves "of consequence sufficient to cause a war in the West Indies" and warned Stewart that by "endeavouring to right one person" for a cargo of little value, "you will endanger the trading part of the British nation in the loss of many hundred thousand pounds sterling."[97] The South Sea Company argued that war helped only the few whose ships had actually been seized. The independent merchants argued that peace helped only the few who were protected by the company's name. The early Hanoverian kings and Walpole sided with the company. Naval commanders in the Caribbean were ordered to "act cautiously . . . so as not to give just cause of complaint to the Spaniards," and to seize only *guarda costas* they were certain had committed depredations.[98] This certainty was difficult to come by: the Spanish claimed the seized merchant ships were smugglers, while British merchants claimed the *guarda costas* were essentially pirates. The

Admiralty Board hinted that if captains were to proceed only when they were certain, they would simply not proceed at all. Despite a timid inquiry from the Admiralty regarding the wisdom of altering the orders, the official line of Walpole's administration was to maintain restraint.[99] The British ministry refused to authorize reprisals in the West Indies.[100]

Unsurprisingly, the treaty was deeply unsatisfactory to those who had hoped for an aggressive maritime Caribbean war to establish the security of British trade in the region. It was widely criticized by opposition newspapers and pamphlets, which characterized Walpole as favoring drawn-out and ineffectual negotiation over concrete action. One popular ballad claimed that in Walpole's peace with Spain, "You shall find nothing here, of a musty old right, / Of a free navigation, and shittle come shite; / As well might a school boy cry—Doctor no birch, / As England but name to proud Spaniards—No search."[101] Admiral Charles Wager advised Keene of the increasing resentment British mercantile communities felt against the Spanish. He remarked that he had "seen more than once, both in the House of Commons & in the City, the violent resentments of number of people, against the K[ing] & his ministers, for so patiently bearing such affronts & abuses."[102] The *Craftsman* observed in 1729 that its editors "hope[d] the Spaniards are not to be always thus in a state of hostility with us, in America, and we always at peace with them, though at the same time under all the inconveniencies and at all the expenses of a war."[103] What was missing throughout all of this, at least for the opposition, was the presence of an active navy.

The Walpole administration's reluctance to fall out with Spain over colonial matters was further evidenced by its actions in the Spanish-Portuguese quarrel of 1735. The dispute first erupted over an alleged insult to the Portuguese ambassador by the Spanish court, but there were hints that the incident in reality stemmed from colonial friction in South America. The question of where the southern border of Portuguese Brazil ended and the northern border of Spanish Uruguay began had been a long-standing one, but was given new life at the end of the War of the Spanish Succession.[104] British ministers thought that perhaps the Portuguese were exaggerating the seriousness of the insult in order to start an actual war, which would allow them to resolve the issue of the border between Brazil and the Spanish colonies to the south. Portuguese ministers argued that, on the contrary, it was the Spanish who had bellicose plans and their insult to the Portuguese minister was a sign of it.[105] Portuguese claims about Spanish behavior in South America bore remarkable resemblance to the recent experiences of British merchants.[106] Nevertheless, although Walpole chose to secure Portugal against actual invasion, his ambassadors warned the Portuguese that they would have no British support should they choose to escalate hostilities rather than reconcile, nor would British military forces offer any provocation to Spain. Admiral John Norris, who was sent with a squadron to the Portuguese coast, was ordered to use his "utmost endeavours to dissuade" the Portuguese king from opening actual hostilities.[107] The role of the fleet was not to intervene on Portugal's behalf, but to ensure that the Spanish did not escalate the matter. To some extent, this strategy was successful. British ambassador Benjamin Keene reported that George II's decision to send the fleet to Portugal had created "great alarm" at the Spanish court, and that the leading Spanish minister, Don José Patiño, had tried to persuade him to have the fleet recalled. Newcastle asked British representatives in Portugal to use these statements as proof of "how great an effect his Majesty's fleet, has already had, in procuring these assurances from the Court of Spain" that the matter at hand would be negotiated rather than fought over.[108] Despite the experience of British merchants in the West Indies over the last decade, the establishment whigs refused to take the opportunity to reduce or restrain Spanish power in South America, even for the benefit of a longtime ally.

By the late 1730s, resentment to what the opposition perceived as Caribbean insults and threats finally broke out again in new cries for war. London and West India merchants petitioned for war in 1739, saying that without immediate intervention, British trade "will become so precarious, as to depend in a great measure, upon the indulgence and justice of the Spaniards."[109] The *Craftsman* asserted, "If the Spaniards should be allowed to search our ships . . . it will be giving up the sovereignty of those seas, and in effect the Sugar Islands."[110] As John Carteret, a leader of the opposition whigs, noted in Parliament, "The Spanish court says, 'We have a right to search your ships': but 'no search' are the words that echo from shore to shore of this island."[111] The opposition believed the situation between Britain and Spain had reached the point where negotiation could not resolve the issue. As a treatise entitled "Reasons for a war against Spain" explained, "Spain must either be content to give up half of their yearly treasure from the West Indies at once; or that the English must give up their plantations, and entirely lose their whole West India trade. Therefore it is clear, that this dispute can never be determined but by a war."[112] Carteret agreed that there were only two possibilities left: either Britain would enjoy "the quiet and uninterrupted exercise of navigation and commerce" or Spain would have "an absolute and uncontrollable sovereignty of these seas."[113]

In many ways, the discussions of 1738–1739 mirrored those of 1727–1729. Walpole and the establishment whigs argued that "a war with Spain ought to be avoided if possible" until the king and ministry have "given over all hopes of obtaining redress by negotiation."[114] Walpole tried to accomplish this by negotiating the Convention of Pardo in 1739. This convention actually reduced British claims for merchant compensation from £200,000 to £95,000 (while owing the Spanish £68,000 for the years when the South Sea Company had not fulfilled the *asiento* because of war) and maintained the Spanish right to search ships within specified geographic limits. Ministerial pamphlets and newspapers such as the *Daily Gazetteer* reiterated their claims from a decade before that only a minority supported the war, that entering into a war with Spain hurt the nation more than it helped it, and that in all likelihood, the merchants complaining were in fact guilty of what they had been accused of. One pamphlet that asserted, "War is never to be tried till treaties prove ineffectual," also claimed, "Some of our colonies are known to have been hives of smugglers, or illicit traders; all men know it."[115] The *Gazetteer* asked, "Supposing the whole rumor is true of the Spanish Depredations (which by the way I am sure it is not in any degree)," was it right that Britain should "put an end to a beneficial commerce, which would . . . be the ruin of many."[116] The Duke of Newcastle warned the House of Lords, "In the end, we may find ourselves losers by our conquests" as the French gained more trade through neutrality and British trade suffered through enemy privateering.[117]

The opposition reasserted that allowing the Spanish the right to search gave them a potential chokehold on British trade in the West Indies. Thomas Sanderson observed that Britain had come "at last [to] a war, unless we have a mind to give up our plantations and West India trade."[118] William Pitt observed that according to the terms of the Convention, British trade to the Caribbean was "to be given up and sacrificed; for it must cease to be any thing, from the moment it is submitted to limits." Walpole countered that what the opposition really meant by "no search" was "that the trade to the Spanish West Indies ought to be open to every interloper of ours. . . . This, Sir, is the plain English of what the gentlemen who are for a war with Spain advance."[119] The merchants of Bristol, Liverpool, and Glasgow again petitioned Parliament regarding the Spanish depredations in 1738, as they had in 1729 and 1731.[120] The *Craftsman* admitted that not all the merchants of London were completely ruined by the Spanish actions, but they asked questions about the ones who remained unscathed. "Do they consist of honest merchants and fair adventurers, who endeavour to enrich the nation, as well as themselves, by exporting our manufactures, and turning the balance of trade in our favour? Or are they composed of usurers, stockjobbers, and managers of great moneyed Companies?" The writers of the paper asserted, "If we descend to the inferior class of traders, and ask them, how business goes on; I am afraid they will answer, never worse."[121]

The dissident whigs argued that the reason to make war in the Americas rather than in Europe was "what we take on the continent of New Spain we may keep, & improve: thereby very greatly enlarge our trade the support of the British nation." Regarding concerns that France might intervene on Spain's behalf, one pro-war advocate noted that he hoped they did, as "it would give us a very proper occasion to destroy those great branches of trade which they have got into since the last war" and the British "should be able to possess ourselves of their settlements in Newfoundland, Mississippi and Hispaniola and render them incapable of ever pretending to cope with us in trade."[122] As David Campbell explained while advocating an attack on Vera Cruz in 1741, "from this expedition will result not only signal vengeance for the insults upon, and ruin of [British] trade, which for these many years past it has suffered, but also that we shall take, conquer and hold, a country, port, or strong place." This conquest would be a stepping stone to "a new beneficial and extensive trade for all her subjects"—*all* British subjects, not just those who were investors in a monopoly company.[123] In May 1738 the leading patriot, William Pulteney, introduced a bill that would have given prize money for captured Spanish ships and allowed private individuals or corporations of individuals to keep what they could conquer from the Spanish.[124] Establishment whigs responded to these arguments by emphasizing the danger that Britain itself might upset the balance of power in Europe. They accused the authors of opposition newspapers such as the *Craftsman* and *Fog's Weekly Journal* and "and the whole club of people calling themselves patriots" of being "men who intend to conquer and trample upon the whole world."[125] Walpole's supporters implied that

Britain had a proper place in the existing system—as did other powers—and that the allegedly untrammeled belligerence of the opposition threatened to undermine the system itself.

The opposition explicitly referenced acts of naval restraint from the 1727 conflict as evidence that the Walpole administration could not be trusted to carry out this renewed war effectively. The ministerial newspaper the *Gazetteer* claimed in 1738 that expensive preparations were underway to equip a naval squadron to force the Spanish to give the nation justice. The *Craftsman*'s response was that "the famous expeditions to the Bastimentos and Spithead convince us, by experience, that the mere equipment of expensive and formidable squadrons is no sure sign of their being intended for compulsive service, even when persuasive arguments will not prevail."[126] When establishment whigs fought down a request to place orders given to Admiral Edward Vernon in front of the House of Lords, the Lords of the opposition noted that since Walpole's accession to power, "instructions began to be of such a nature that we do not wonder their authors desired to conceal 'em." Given the "instructions by which our fleet lay in shameful inaction before Gibraltar when besieged, & suffered the enemy's ships to bring provisions & ammunition to their army & those by which three admirals above thirty captains above 100 lieutenants & 400 private seamen perished most ingloriously at the Bastimentos," the opposition had "a just suspicion of all subsequent instructions flowing from the same source."[127]

The new war with Spain, which broke out in 1739, was very much a continuation of the 1727 conflict. Its supporters envisioned an aggressive colonial war in which the navy—unleashed from the constraints placed on its actions by George I, George II, and the establishment whigs—would play a major role. There remained deep distrust over whether Walpole could really be trusted to carry on a war known to go against his own foreign policy beliefs. His previous naval policy was frequently deployed by the opposition to demonstrate his administration's failures.

Naval Supremacy?

A naval policy of deterrence and restraint fit in rationally with the goals of a party that claimed those "who know well the state of the nation, the load of the public debt, the difficulty of laying new taxes, and the expense of a war, will readily be of opinion, a war should if possible be prevented."[128] However, it raises the question of whether, given these priorities and this policy, Britain's Royal Navy was in fact "the leading sea power, without a rival" and "the acknowledged mistress of the seas," having achieved a position of "naval supremacy" during the early part of the eighteenth century, as it has been described.[129] Although Britain's fleets were at times numerically superior to those of their opponents, this was contingent on the time, the place, and the context. If the navy was to be a deterrent and a selling point in alliance negotiations, it had to command some level of respect. But it did not necessarily have to be a great fighting force, as combat was more likely to be a last choice than a first choice. Britain could certainly claim a greater absolute number of ships than its rivals, but ships laid up in storage did not win many battles. There was often a lack of resources—either in terms of physical commodities, manpower, or political commitment—to move ships from storage to the seas. Opinions regarding British naval power varied, both among domestic and foreign observers, and occasionally more in accordance with the observer's wishes than with reality. It was telling that many of the domestic observers who questioned Britain's naval superiority were those who should theoretically have understood the situation best: the sea officers themselves.

There was no consensus, either within Britain or among European observers, about relative British naval strength during this time. Dissident whigs and tories alternated between applauding the strength of the navy and decrying its weakness, which they inevitably blamed on Walpole's neglect. One tory pamphlet of 1732 did both, claiming, "We have had no rivals at least of late years, not one of any the most formidable Maritime Powers hath pretended to rivalship with us in the dominion of the seas," but Britain had also seen the "ill management" of "maritime affairs, and the remarkable neglect of them" by "some ill-judging and vain politicians."[130] The establishment whigs vacillated between defending their care of the navy and claiming that it could not stand alone against the rival navies of the world, which justified their decisions to seek allies and avoid open warfare. A 1739 pamphlet defending the Convention of Pardo argued that what "chiefly protects Spain is her low condition and weakness. She furnishes nothing to lay hold of, and we can make no suitable reprisals," and explained that therefore naval war would be ineffective. However, a 1742 pamphlet maintained that

Spain was not the impotent enemy the opposition characterized it as being: "Spain has now near fifty stout ships of the line, besides frigates, &c, actually equipped; and France, upwards of thirty, which is a force superior to any the united Crowns ever had at sea, any one year, during the last war." Walpole claimed in Parliament in 1738, "I am far from thinking that we are not a sufficient match for the Spaniards . . . [but] we are not a match for the Spaniards and French too."[131] The propaganda needs of the moment influenced publicly declared opinions regarding the relative strength of the British navy.

Opinions of foreign observers were perhaps slightly more reliable but still subject to wishful thinking. It is possible, however, to deduce from rival powers' policy decisions whether they thought they had a chance of competing with Britain in the naval realm. Cardinal de Fleury, the leading French minister, had a high opinion of Britain's naval capabilities throughout the 1730s. The British ambassador reported in 1735 that it was likely neither of the French fleets at Brest or Toulon would "stir out this year. The Cardinal is so prepossessed that their ships could not stand a fight with ours, that he thinks it ten to one they would be beat." The Cardinal held the same opinion four years later when he seemed to believe that "fifteen of our [British] ships in good order would beat thirty Spanish of equal strength."[132] There were others who thought that France could equal Britain in naval power. One French memo obtained by British ministers explained how, in a step by step process. France did decide to contest British naval superiority in the 1740s after all.[133] Spanish opinion likewise held British naval power to be fallible. Don Patiño embarked on a building campaign in Catalonia, Andalusia, and the Bay of Biscay; he also ordered ships from foreign builders in Genoa, Venice, and Saint-Malo. He "sent commissaries to all the sea coasts of Spain to number all the seafaring men & to enroll them in classes as is practiced in France." The British ambassador to Spain, William Stanhope, warned the Duke of Newcastle, "If it be possible for any man to succeed in such an undertaking in this country, Patiño most certainly will."[134] The Spanish also thought that the British could be beaten by other countries. When word came in 1726 that the Russian fleet had put to sea in the Baltic, the general prediction of the Spanish court was that "his Majesty's fleet in the Baltic has been destroyed . . . and that his Majesty will in a few months lose his dominions in Germany and the Pretender be settled upon the throne of Great Britain."[135] While Stanhope dismissed these ideas as mere fantasy, as is clear from the tone of his letter, it is equally clear that they must have held some genuine purchase among the Spanish, or he would have had nothing to mock. One advantage the French and Spanish had was that they did not necessarily need to win an outright naval battle in order to accomplish their objectives. At times they only had to evade Britain's ships, as when the Spanish successfully brought their American treasure fleets home despite Hosier being stationed in the Caribbean and two other admirals off the coast of Spain.[136] Both France and Spain were also aware of the efficacy of privateering against British merchant ships—privateers did not have to be superior to the naval ships of Britain, but only able to evade them, which they did with success in the early years of the War of Jenkins' Ear.[137]

When it came to preparations for actual combat, propaganda fell by the wayside, at least in private correspondence. Whatever they might say in public, British ministers were aware that their fleets were far from invincible. The Duke of Newcastle wrote to a fellow establishment whig in 1740, "We shall not be too strong in the West Indies and the event will show I am in the right." Admiral Edward Vernon, stationed in the West Indies, admitted to Wager his relief that "neither His Majesty's forces have yet met any misfortunes from the superior power of the Spaniards, and the more powerful squadrons of their auxiliaries."[138] It was not that the British necessarily had an inferior fleet, but merely that the outcome of a naval conflict was perceived to be unpredictable.

Being able to field an effective fighting force was also a question of personnel and infrastructure. In this regard Walpole's administration of naval affairs appeared to fall short. Many ships, though still present in lists of naval strength, were in such a condition as to be essentially worthless, as Admiral Norris recorded in his journal in 1740: "it has been the highest neglect in the government of the Commissioners of the Admiralty to have from forty to forty-five ships from fifty guns upward unfit to be put to sea; when the whole of the fleet from fifty guns upward is but a hundred and twenty."[139] Nearly a third of Britain's theoretical naval strength was on paper only. Not only were many ships relatively derelict, but there were difficulties in equipping and manning those that were in repair. The Admiralty admitted in 1740 that it would be unable to field enough ships to prevent a Spanish invasion of either Ireland or the West Indies, should one materialize. When outfitting Norris's squadron later that year, twenty-five ships had originally been planned, but only fifteen ships could actually be equipped and manned.[140] This was not simply a question of a wartime manning shortage: the same difficulty in manning had been experienced in 1735 when Norris had been sent to Portugal. As the naval captain Francis Holburne observed, the fleet under Norris was "to be sure the best ships and the best manned that ever went out of England but they pretty well stripped the ships here to complete them"; the ships that were left behind were "in a very bad condition as ever ships were for men." Holburne asked his correspondent not to spread this information too widely, "for I should be the last man that should tell our distress we are in."[141]

Ordinary sailors were not the only manning problem; qualified officers were also in short supply. When outfitting a squadron to counter a possible French threat in 1734, the Admiralty found itself "calling upon our old captains & lieutenants many of which we find to be 3/4 worn and some more"; although Britain would "put a large fleet into commission" it would "take up most of the captains, & all the lieutenants we have, and [we] shall be forced to make more."[142] At around the same time, Admiral Wager pointed out that British sailors and officers were not necessarily better trained or braver than their continental counterparts. Despite the "many people who seem to continue in an error, (which contrary to all experience) has long prevailed that one Englishman can beat two Frenchmen, and the same, I suppose, of any other nation," Wager believed that "the French squadron will doubtless be very strong; and if we think of meeting them, ours ought to be so too."[143] The quality of officers was compromised by the establishment whigs' tendency to manage the navy as they did political matters on shore, where they disbursed offices and sinecures as rewards for political support. The navy to them was a source of patronage, and they went to elaborate lengths to use it effectively for those ends. They frequently played a system of naval musical chairs in order to ensure all friends and connections a claim to promotion. Norris explained to Wager in 1737 that he had been requested by Vice Admiral Stewart to promote one Captain Forbes by declaring his fireship to be a frigate—which would give him the rank of post-captain, entitling him to rise on the basis of seniority—but had also been requested by Sir Robert Walpole to provide for (future admiral) Edward Boscawen, still only a lieutenant. Norris's solution was to "prevail" upon a current captain to resign his ship so that Boscawen could be promoted; that captain would be promised another employment upon his return to England. Norris also politely indicated his concern for Wager's own interests: "I hope you will have made your own nephew, Mr. Watson, a captain."[144] Norris later observed that "interest would get the better of merit always."[145]

Upon the opening of the 1739 war with Spain, advocates of naval warfare quickly found reason to criticize the navy's performance. One 1741 pamphlet questioned the bravery and competence of the sea officers, asking, "In this war can it be said, that any of our squadrons, except that under the direction of Admiral Vernon, who is supposed not to be under the same influence with others, have performed glorious exploits?"[146] If, as Wager believed and opponents complained, there was nothing inherently superior about British seamanship or officership at this time, then the British did have to rely on numerical superiority, an advantage that was not necessarily secure. As Norris observed, Britain could not be superior in all theaters of the war and was therefore required to station its ships strategically; however, even a numerical superiority did not mean that the enemy would be prevented from accomplishing its own naval goals.[147] Numerical superiority was only ever relative—it was contingent upon the choices of other countries. This was a fact that preyed heavily on Norris's mind. He several times used ominous stories from his younger days as warnings in ministerial meetings. One he repeated was that of the 1692 Battle of Barfleur. Admiral Edward Russell destroyed sixteen to eighteen of France's major ships, and yet the very next year, the French regained numerical superiority, having (as Norris recalled) seventy to eighty ships laying off the Portuguese coast, not including around twenty that were still at Toulon.[148] Norris used this story to illustrate how quickly the tide could turn against Britain if France turned its attention to a naval war.

In the 1720s and 1730s, Britain could rightfully claim some of the foundations of naval power. It had a growing economy and political institutions that were highly effective at tapping into that national wealth. It also had, from a significant part of the population, the popular will to use naval force and, on paper, substantial numbers of ships. However, these factors alone were not enough. In a 1742 Parliamentary inquiry into the conduct of the War of Jenkins' Ear thus far, twenty separate merchants were brought in to testify to their own experiences of naval negligence. There simply were not enough ships to cover all the trade routes, which might perhaps have been the case regardless of whether Walpole was at the head of the administration or not—but what would have been different was the ministerial attitude. When the merchant Henry Lascelles went to the Admiralty to ask for a ship to protect the African trade, one of the commissioners, the establishment whig Lord Vere Beauclerk, responded, "You would have a war and you see the consequences, you must take what follows."[149] The ministry was uncommitted to the idea of a superior fighting force, because their goals simply did not require one. The lack of political will to commit the nation to the type of navy which would be able to carry out an aggressive war was one area where Britain fell short, but not the only one. Naval infrastructure was insufficient to maintain all the ships Britain technically owned on paper and the officer corps was out of practice from disuse. Thus, although Britain could still field a Royal Navy that forced other nations to take notice, whatever "superiority" it had was at best ephemeral, based on momentary conditions and easily lost. There were no systemic reasons to for the British nation to believe it could not be challenged on the oceans, as its sea officers—Wager, Norris, Vernon, Holburne, and others—were aware.

The 1727 Anglo-Spanish conflict and its aftermath revealed a multiplicity of divisions within British society over political, economic, and imperial issues. Later, contemporaries would link the outbreak of the Seven Years' War to the failures of the 1739 War of Jenkins' Ear (or War of the Austrian Succession, as its continental theater was known), but the 1739 war was itself linked to the failures of the 1727 conflict, creating a long chain of frustrated imperial ambition throughout the eighteenth century. The opposition paid Walpole's naval policy special attention in their critiques of his fitness to lead the British nation, as their excoriation of the conduct of Admiral Wager during the siege of Gibraltar, Admiral Hosier's failed expedition to Bastimentos, and the inactivity of the "Spithead expedition" indicated.

Imperial policy crucially exacerbated the developing schism within the whig tradition. For those in Britain who wanted to see imperial expansion, having a military that was capable of securing those imperial goals was essential. Empires did not acquire themselves. In this, however, they were thwarted by the establishment whigs' commitment to a policy of naval restraint. This was not a matter of incompetence on the part of Walpole's administration, but a rational move toward achieving its foreign and domestic policy goals. Those goals included maintaining stability in Europe through alliances and balance of power politics, preserving colonial stability by preventing expansion, and protecting domestic political stability through a cautious financial program that aligned with the interests of elites. Naval restraint veered into the realm of neglect only from the point of view of the opposition; from the point of view of the establishment whigs, there was little sense in investing in what they viewed as an unreliable tool. They did not believe the navy alone was a sufficient defense against foreign powers, making alliances and continental engagement obligatory. Moreover, under Walpole's foreign policy, the navy did not need to be especially competent because the Hanoverian kings and establishment whigs did not need it to conquer and did not necessarily even need it to fight—Britain's naval force would only be put to the test when all their other diplomatic safety valves had failed. The main purpose of the establishment whig navy was to be a deterrent against other countries developing ideas of expansion. It represented the threat of power rather than its actual exertion.

Despite Britain's wealth, despite its ever-increasing overseas trade, and despite the belief many of its citizens had in its strong naval tradition, the early Augustan navy was not the undisputed powerhouse that some contemporaries and historians have claimed it to be. Nor was there a reason why it should have been: having a large, active, aggressive navy did not fit with Hanoverian or establishment whig foreign policy. A small standing fleet which could be expanded in time of need and could be used to avoid wars rather than to fight them did fit with their priorities. It was a rational choice. This relatively inactive force led to issues in the qualities of the officer corps, as did the use of the navy as a patronage farm—many officers were old or inexperienced, but there was no real need to ensure they were anything else. There was little reason to put money and political capital into an organization that was unable to achieve the goals the establishment whigs wanted, especially when they distrusted its capabilities to boot. But as events of the following decade were to show, the navy was also unreliable under Walpole because of his lack of investment in it. Under different leadership, and with different goals in mind, the navy had the potential to become quite formidable indeed.

✧ 3 ✧

DISORDER, DISCIPLINE, AND THE POLITICS OF NAVAL REFORM

BRITAIN WAS EMBROILED IN two connected conflicts in the 1740s: the War of Jenkins' Ear (1739–1748), incited by colonial concerns, and the War of the Austrian Succession (1742–1748), sparked by European power dynamics. Between 1739 and the mid-1740s, Britain's navy could claim few true successes. The widely lauded success of Admiral Edward Vernon in capturing Porto Bello in November 1739 was followed by the abortive siege of St. Augustine (1740), the destructive and counterproductive attacks on Cartagena (1741) and Cuba (1741), and the battles of La Guaira (1743) and Puerto Cabello (1743), all in the Spanish Caribbean and all of which resulted in either the defeat or withdrawal of British naval forces. These were followed by the Battle of Toulon (1744), during which the British Mediterranean fleet allowed blockaded French forces to escape, and the Battle of Negapatam (1744), by which France conquered the British colony of Madras in India. In contrast to these early disappointments, the naval engagements of the later years of the war included the capture of Louisburg (1745), decisive victories at the First and Second Battles of Finisterre (1747), a defeat at the Second Battle of Santiago de Cuba (1748), and a more limited victory at the Battle of Havana (1748). Britain's naval success was even more pronounced in the Seven Years' War, which followed a decade later, when the navy supported the capture by British forces of French Canada, many Caribbean islands, parts of French Africa, French Indian ports, and Spanish Manila, as well as achieving definitive victories on the seas in battles such as those at Quiberon Bay and Lagos (both 1759). Beginning in the late 1740s, Britain's navy was much more successful in achieving its own priorities—forcing decisive battles and protecting trade—than it had been in previous years. The question for historians is, why?

To explain this reversal of fortunes, historians have often cited a series of reforms enacted by the Admiralty Board in 1745–1749. Changes implemented during this time included modifications in dockyard infrastructure, revised systems of promotion and retirement, the first naval uniform, new ship designs, and an increased emphasis on training. The Admiralty Board consisted of a combination of political figures and high-ranking sea officers. The primary members of the Board during these years were John Russell, the fourth Duke of Bedford; John Montagu, the fourth Earl of Sandwich; and Admiral George Anson. All three came into power at the Board in December 1744, with Bedford as First Lord of the Admiralty and head of the Board. When Bedford moved on to become Secretary of State for the Southern Department in 1748, Sandwich succeeded him; Anson succeeded Sandwich in turn in 1751. A variety of other members of the Board, both sea officers and politicians, also came and went during these years. Although the Admiralty Board consisted of seven members at any given time, much of the historical literature has suggested that, in the words of Daniel Baugh, "the improvements of leadership at sea after 1744 came largely through the efforts of a single, dedicated officer," namely, George Anson.[1] "By the middle of the century," agrees Clive Wilkinson, "George Anson had transformed the Navy, both as a fighting force and as a civil department of the State." The Admiralty embraced "a more system-based management attitude" and exerted "increasing influence."[2] N. A. M. Rodger also argues that "the transformation in a dozen years from the humiliating failures of the early 1740s to the triumphs of the Seven Years' War" was the consequence of Anson's "rigorous devotion to high standards of training and conduct" and that Anson was "one of the key figures in the creation of a distinctive naval ethos . . . the ingrained assumption that a man's first duty was to the good of the Service." He concludes that "the Navy of the Seven Years' War was what Anson had made it, and the list of its virtues is to a great extent the list of his achievements."[3]

Historians describe these reforms as uncontroversial and essentially "rational," in part because they perceive the navy itself to have been apolitical. They suggest that any officer of Anson's generation would have implemented these reforms, but Anson happened to be the first one in a position of power to do so. As Brian Lavery writes, "At forty-seven he was much younger than any of his recent predecessors, and able to view the problems with a fresh eye."[4] The reforms were, G. S. Smith asserts, a matter of "common sense:" Anson's experience led him naturally to see that the Royal Navy was inefficient, factional, and out-of-date.[5] This account of unproblematic modernization fits in with an understanding of the navy as a point of consensus in eighteenth-century British society. Rodger describes the "strong, consistent and broad-based political support" that surrounded the navy.[6] This consensus was based on the vision of the navy as a bastion of liberty: unlike a professional standing army, a navy would be confined to the seas, could not enter civilians' homes, and therefore could not crush civilian liberties.

What is absent from these narratives is an awareness of the important roles played by the two other principal members of the Admiralty Board—the Duke of Bedford and the Earl of Sandwich—in developing the reform program. Omitting the politicians from the narrative precludes a full understanding of the imperatives that made naval reform a priority; in particular, it obscures a crucial component of Britain's naval resurgence, which is the connection between these politicians' actions at the Admiralty Board and their other political projects. Undoubtedly Anson's experience as an officer did indeed contribute to his conception of how to remedy the perceived problems, but experience is filtered through ideology: different individuals may perceive the same problems, but propose very different solutions. Indeed, some officers with just as much experience as Anson—such as the celebrated Admiral Vernon—opposed the majority of the Admiralty Board reforms, some of which also generated widespread discontent within the sea service at large. Contrary to historians' consensus, the reforms were neither uncontroversial within the service nor were they apolitical. One element of the reforms, a recodification of court-martial law, spawned an intense parliamentary debate and a series of pamphlets and newspaper articles, in which opponents denounced the bill as, in their words, initiating oriental despotism in Britain. Some claimed the bill was intended to "make [sea officers] the cut-throats of the state . . . to make them the Admiralty Janissaries."[7] Others compared sea officers to mamelukes. The Janissaries were the household troops and bodyguards of the Ottoman sultans; the mamelukes were the slave soldiers of Egypt. One Londoner remarked at the time that the "affairs of the Navy have lately much engaged the thought and conversation of this Town," adding that "matters have been carried on with much warmth."[8] Thus, though the naval reforms might seem to be of small interest in and of themselves, they had a much greater significance for contemporaries.

The naval reforms of the 1740s were linked to both imperial and constitutional debates. Observers viewed the attempted reforms in the context of the other actions and preoccupations of the political members of the Board and thus interpreted them through an ideological prism. Bedford and Sandwich were at least as influential in pushing the reform of the navy as Anson; in fact, some of the reforms instituted during their First Lordships fell by the wayside during that of Anson. Bedford and Sandwich believed the primary flaws undermining the navy's performance were disorder and disobedience; this disorder threatened the navy's capacity to expand and secure an American empire. Their solution was to impose discipline and hierarchy, and thereby to create order and enable success. Discipline and hierarchy were the same tools that Bedford, Sandwich, and their associates deployed for the next three decades when faced with disorder in either imperial or domestic society. In contrast, resistance to the naval reforms came overwhelmingly from the patriot opposition. The patriots valued liberty and civic participation; they resisted the expansion of ministerial power because of the corrupting consequences it was believed to have for political virtue. Their interpretation of Britain's naval failures lay in the restraints that the long-serving Prime Minister Robert Walpole had placed on the navy; success would come once the navy was permitted to fight aggressively, under a free and virtuous leadership. According to these patriots, the sea service did not need to be changed; it only needed to be unleashed. Creating a naval force bound by discipline and strict hierarchy both infringed on the liberties of those in the service and created an extraordinarily dangerous weapon in the hands of ministers: a professional military capable of subverting the constitution. For them, naval reform raised the specter of despotism.

The naval reforms of the 1740s created, for the first time, a professionalized naval force. The Admiralty Board did not simply attempt to streamline the service; they intended to create a new culture of naval service, the "distinctive naval ethos" referred to by Rodger. This new ethos was, however, politically controversial: the importance of unquestioning obedience was not a universally accepted value. It was divisive because the subordination of individuals (including those with honor and personal reputations) to ministerial authority was seen as emblematic of other wider concerns over the decay of British society and the country's political future. Thus, the naval reforms provide a window into the early stages of wider sociopolitical tensions that would harden and escalate during the following decades. These tensions were sometimes still inchoate and the lines of debate were not yet ossified, but their existence suggests that there were deeper roots to the arguments over disorder, empire, obedience, and the constitution that shook the Anglo-imperial world in the 1760s and 1770s. Only by contextualizing the reforms within the political worldview of the members of the Admiralty Board—and that of their opponents—can we truly understand the contemporary implications of the alterations in naval culture that occurred during this period.

The Authoritarian Whigs, the Admiralty, and the Americas

The 1740s were a period of political flux in Britain. Having risen to power as First Lord of the Treasury in 1721, Robert Walpole fell from grace in 1742 in the face of vocal opposition to his pacifist foreign policy. He was succeeded by William Pulteney and John Carteret, both of whom had hitherto been leaders and darlings of the patriot opposition that had helped to force Walpole out. Once in office, Pulteney and Carteret appeared to abandon their patriot principles and lost their popular support; moreover, George II remained attached to the establishment whiggery embodied by Walpole's regime and in 1744 moved to replace Pulteney and Carteret with Walpole's designated successors, Henry Pelham and his brother Thomas Pelham-Holles, Duke of Newcastle.[9] Pelham and Newcastle did not have sufficient support in Parliament to form an administration and needed to form a coalition with members of the opposition to buttress their authority. They were willing to grant authority over certain government departments to these oppositional allies in return for their overall support of the government's policies. Bedford and Sandwich were among those who agreed to participate in what became known as the "broadbottom" coalition. They had their conditions, however: they demanded to be placed in the Admiralty. Controlling this Board had been a goal of members of the opposition for several years, and although other members of the administration resisted this placement, they eventually gave in.[10]

This was not mere political maneuvering: there were real principles at stake. During his long two decades in power, and with the support of first George I and then George II, Walpole had maintained relatively strong control over the highest levels of the administration, though popular political divisions had continued to exist. Walpole's regime represented the zenith of establishment whiggery, which was committed to maintaining the balance of power in Europe and stability in imperial affairs and was content to allow autonomy in the colonies so long as they made an economic contribution. For the establishment whigs, public debt served as a means of preserving stability. Walpole repeatedly borrowed from the sinking fund during the 1730s in order to maintain a low land tax, in hopes of preserving the support of the landed classes for his regime, and he built a mutually beneficial relationship with the "moneyed men" of the City.[11] The pressures of Walpole's long-lived administration combined with other external events led to a series of party realignments, as a consequence of which the strict binary division between whig and tory began to break down.[12] Although this volatility at times erased easily detectable party lines, it did not obliterate coherent ideologies, nor did it prevent individuals from acting in ways consistent with those ideologies.[13]

There were three major groups left in opposition following Pulteney and Carteret's union with the administration, but in the debates over naval professionalization only two of these ideologies took center stage, both in opposition to Walpole's establishment whiggery.[14] Each was supported by a group of individuals with affiliations with one another, who looked to a common leadership and acted in ideologically consistent ways in the 1740s and continued to do so for the following several decades. Whether or not the adherents to these ideologies therefore constituted formal political parties is a valid question, though not one that is relevant to understanding the political currents surrounding naval professionalization, because a party is not a necessary prerequisite of coherent political action. These two competing ideologies—not the only ones that existed at the time, but those that were most invested in arguments over professionalization—were authoritarian whiggery and patriotism. The adherents of authoritarian whiggery were led primarily by Bedford and Sandwich. The adherents of patriotism were at this time largely centered around Frederick, Prince of Wales, the eldest son of George II and heir to the British throne. Their ranks included William Pitt and his Grenville and Lyttleton cousins.

The decay of British society was a common preoccupation of both authoritarian whigs and patriots. Walpole's oligarchic regime had created concerns over the corruption of politics; when his fall did not bring about a demonstrable shift in policies, many found the explanation in a "broader problem, with deep roots in society. Gin drinking, gaming, irreligion, and immorality were increasingly emphasized as both symptoms and causes of general social disorder." As Bob Harris has explained, many concerns such as "poverty, luxury, immorality, and irreligion" were "not narrowly party-political."[15] The patriots tended to view these concerns in terms of corruption, and they saw the threat to British society as coming from above, from power-hungry ministers intent on monopolizing power. In contrast, they believed that popular involvement in the exercise of power mediated its corrupting effects and restored virtue. They therefore called for an expansion of access to power politically (by demanding more frequent elections, fewer ministerial placemen in Parliament, and by supporting the autonomy of local imperial assemblies), economically (by emphasizing the importance of consumption as the basis of wealth, actively participating in the expanding commercial sphere, and opposing monopolies), religiously (by advocating for the expansion of more civil and political rights to Dissenters), and in foreign policy (by arguing for an expanded libertarian empire based on trade rather than coercive control, which more people would be able to benefit from). In addition, they called for the militia to replace the professional standing army. Much of the popular support for patriotism came from the commercial strata of society such as artisans and the middling sorts, as well as from merchant centers.[16] Frederick, Prince of Wales, one of the primary patrons of patriotism at this time, began to present himself as a putative "Patriot King" on the basis of his "rigorous personal virtue" and "virtuous political leadership" which would bring about "moral revival." "Rule Britannia" was first performed at his country house.[17] From the 1760s, radicals who had no direct affiliates in Parliament took up the patriot positions and expanded on them. They put forward a more far-reaching agenda than the patriots of the 1740s did,

but they continued to perceive many of the same problems and their solutions were based on similar rationales. Both patriots and radicals argued in favor of a more egalitarian society in which authority was more widely vested and in which larger numbers of independent individuals would be able to participate in commercial opportunities.

Like patriotism, authoritarian whiggery also identified a decay in British society; unlike the patriots, the authoritarian whigs tended to see that breakdown in terms of disorder, which came from below rather than above. The *Protester,* a newspaper founded by Bedford, warned in its second issue that "the great disorder of the nation" lay in "a suppression, if not an extinction, of morality and the shame of doing ill."[18] Their solution was to advocate policies that emphasized hierarchy and discipline, which they hoped would prevent society from descending into anarchy. Authoritarian whiggery differed from Walpole's establishment whiggery in two principal ways: one was its approach to imperial and foreign policy; the other was its attitudes toward public debt. Whereas establishment whiggery embraced stability based on the balance of power, and permitted colonial autonomy, authoritarian whiggery advocated a more expansive imperial policy and a more centrally organized empire. Establishment whigs saw a positive role for the public debt in preserving stability, while authoritarian whigs opposed relying on public debt, which they believed led to higher taxes and higher wages, which in turn allowed the laboring classes to live above their station.[19]

Although the tenets of authoritarian whiggery became more explicit in the 1760s and 1770s, they did not come out of nowhere. In the 1740s the Bedford circle was on the rise, and those associated with its leaders—Bedford, Sandwich, and George Montagu-Dunk, second Earl of Halifax—in that decade acted as consistently in favor of order and hierarchy as those associated with the same individuals did in the 1760s. The Bedford circle of authoritarian whiggery had little following in the Commons at the election of 1741—having the support of only five MPs—but this increased to sixteen by 1747, among them Thomas Brand, Charles Fane, Richard Neville Aldworth, Richard Rigby, and a number of members of the Leveson-Gower family; in the Lords, they also had the support of John Egerton, Duke of Bridgewater, and John Leveson-Gower, Lord Gower, an ex-tory leader.[20] By 1748 Bedford's circle of association controlled four major offices (First Lord of the Board of Trade, First Lord of the Admiralty, Secretary of State for the Southern Department, and

Lord Privy Seal) and four lesser ones. Authoritarian whig concerns over disorder were increasingly clearly articulated during the 1750s and 1760s, but these concerns were also apparent during the 1740s and authoritarian whig actions during that decade were consistent with their later declarations. Within the domestic sphere, they believed that changing dynamics of consumption threatened stability. They claimed the poor were "idle and licentious" and that easy access to consumer goods had destroyed social order.[21] The conservative-leaning *Gentleman's Magazine* called in 1734 for the reinstatement of sumptuary laws governing dress, noting that "Pride in dress is one of the epidemic evils of the present age. . . . This vice has inverted all order, and destroyed distinction," creating a world in which servants passed for gentlemen.[22] Bedford and Sandwich argued in a 1743 parliamentary protest that "the opulence and power of a nation" depended on the "industry of its people; and its liberty and happiness on their temperance and morality"; therefore, steps should be taken to keep the poor working hard by ensuring temptation remained out of their financial reach.[23] Authoritarian whig economic thinkers proposed a wide variety of schemes for taxing consumer goods, as a method of reining in independence by constricting the prosperity that seemed to fuel it.[24] Nor were the threats solely social. The 1745 Jacobite rebellion threatened political instability and suggested that the current regime still had domestic enemies. A Jacobite supporter assaulted Bedford at the Lichfield races in 1747, so he had personal experience with the dangers of political disorder.[25] In the face of these threats, authoritarian whiggery advocated a unified society under hierarchical leadership. The *Protester*'s first issue asked "whether the English monarchy answers to the image exhibited in the frontispiece of Hobbes's *Leviathan,* of a community united under and directed by one superior intelligence, and concurring with all their powers and faculties in one and the same act; or whether the people, as a people, resembles a shapeless, helpless, heartless body?"[26]

In the 1740s both the patriots and the authoritarian whigs argued for a more aggressive imperial policy than that advocated by Walpole, but where the two ideologies differed was in how they thought an expanded empire should be governed. The events of the 1740s appeared to provide ample examples of imperial disorder. There was unrest among enslaved peoples in Antigua, Jamaica, New York, and South Carolina. Boston exploded in the Knowles anti-impressment riots of 1747, and the governors of nearly all of the royal colonies claimed to be unable to carry out their orders. Ireland likewise gave cause for alarm during Charles Lucas's electoral campaign in 1748–1749, in which he publicly accused the English government of treating the Irish like conquered slaves.[27] Authoritarian whigs wanted to rationalize British law throughout the empire, and believed that Britain should assert stronger governance over its colonies. Bedford argued in 1759 that the intention of legislature should be "uniform and consistent"; he informed the Irish parliament the following year that the "greatest happiness and prosperity, a free nation, can enjoy, is only attainable, by a thorough submission to the laws, and a veneration for them."[28] In both the 1740s and 1760s, authoritarian whigs such as Halifax repeatedly attempted to bring Britain's empire under centralized, rationalized control, so that colonies would become ordered, disciplined, and obedient. As First Lord of the Board of Trade, Halifax tried to strengthen central control over the colonies by making governors financially independent from colonial assemblies but directly obedient to central ministerial authority. He attempted to improve communications between London and America, which theoretically enabled a further reduction of colonial autonomy. He intended to create a comprehensive collection of colonial laws and to revoke them where necessary in order to "form a body of new and well digested laws in lieu thereof," laws that would emanate from London toward the colonies rather than originate in the colonies themselves.[29] Halifax's imperial policy prioritized standardization, the central monopolization of authority, and the submission of inferior colonies to the hierarchically superior mother country.

Authoritarian whig foreign policy shifted attention from Europe to the colonies. Though they did believe in the importance of manufactures, commanding trade alone was not sufficient: territory and people needed to be controlled, as well. They feared the colonies' growing sense of autonomy. But in addition to securing the colonies against the colonists, the authoritarian whigs also believed that they needed to be secured against imperial competitors, to some extent the Spanish but especially the French. The authoritarian whigs played a role in the agitation for war against Spain during the 1730s, but they were more concerned with the northern colonies than they were with the southern colonies.[30] The British colonists in the mainland colonies of North America were, they claimed, under serious threat of being "pushed into the sea" by the French and their Native American allies.[31] Sandwich explained in 1743 that although France was the real threat to Britain, it was so powerful that entering a European war would be a mistake. Instead, reducing its territories and impairing its trade outside of Europe would break France's backbone and its hopes of universal monarchy.[32] Even before war officially broke out with Spain, some pro-war advocates expressed their hope that France might also enter the conflict, as it would create an opportunity to secure forcibly the northern colonies by conquering France's territories in "Newfoundland, Mississippi, and Hispaniola," which would render them "incapable of ever pretending to cope with us in trade."[33] Canada and Cape Breton, off its coast, were particular targets. As sea officer Peter Warren—a protégé of Bedford, Sandwich, and Anson—wrote in 1743, "Dispossessing [the French] of Canada and Cape Breton would be of greater consequence to Great Britain than any other conquest that we hope to make in a Spanish or French war."[34] Supporters of the effort explained that capturing coastal Canada would protect the existing North American colonies from French incursions and would secure access to naval resources like timber and seamen (who would be trained in the coastal fisheries).[35] Within Britain, an attack on Cape Breton was reported to be "a popular attempt," and between 1743 and 1744 the *Westminster Journal,* an opposition newspaper, repeatedly agitated for the removal of the French from North America.[36] The authoritarian whigs made the acquisition of Cape Breton and Canada a central goal of their war aims; they were not the only ones to emphasize the importance of those conquests, but the value they placed on Canada explains why naval affairs became an important arena for them.

The Problem: Naval Incompetence and Public Critique

In the years leading up to the authoritarian whigs' assumption of Admiralty power, the navy had demonstrated itself to be an unreliable weapon—at least for their ends. By 1745 the navy had delivered quite a number of failures and gained quite a number of increasingly vocal public critics. Winning Canada and reliably exerting central authority in the American colonies would be impossible without a dependable navy, but the navy that existed in December 1744 did not fulfill this requirement. Under the guidance of Robert Walpole and George II,

Britain's navy was not directed at pursuing an aggressive foreign policy.[37] Rather than aggression, Walpole's administration urged restraint upon the navy and used it as a deterrent to dissuade other countries from contemplating belligerence of their own. Although Britain could deploy more ships than its neighbors, these ships were meant for display rather than use. The Duke of Bedford critiqued the Walpolean navy as "a fleet which only floats upon the ocean" rather than pursuing any active course.[38]

In compliance with Walpole's foreign policy, sea officers were not conditioned to pursue aggressive warfare to its full extent. Merchants alleged that Admiral Davers had abandoned his convoy to privateers, and Captain Hardy was reported to have done the same.[39] Commodore Mitchell fled before an inferior force of French ships.[40] Bedford had noted in 1742 that there was "too much reason to believe, that some [sea captains] have . . . deserted the traders in places where they have known them most exposed to the incursions of the enemy."[41] Pamphlets claimed that the typical sea captain had "no mortal aversion for the French; it is not their blood he thirsts after, but their claret; 'tis unvoluntary, to be sure, if he spill of the one, or the other." Although "every old woman knows, that the end of war-ships, is fighting," sea officers seemed "to believe them built and maintained purely for sailing, and wearing out canvas."[42] An anonymous letter sent to Bedford soon after he became First Lord argued that, if he examined the character of Britain's admirals, "it may not be difficult to gather the reasons, why we have made so indifferent a figure in our marine affairs."[43] The public was increasingly disgusted with naval failures and with captains who seemed afraid to fight; observers in London noted that "the present spirit of the nation is full of resentment, against all the commanders of the men of war, who in general have behaved with great want of courage & discipline."[44] The conclusion arrived at by one pamphleteer was that until Britain's "ships of war come to be better commanded, and better officered in general, vainly do we talk of our mighty squadrons, and vainly boast of our expert and gallant seamen."[45] In April 1740 three British ships required six hours to overwhelm only one Spanish ship.[46] Failures such as this encouraged public criticism of the navy and its officers. One naval captain admitted, "We are at a low ebb as to character of bravery."[47]

Inequities within the naval infrastructure exacerbated this lack of zeal. Captain Francis Holburne complained in 1740, "I lay three weeks in the dock and not a nail drove, because Sir John Norris's son's ship must be first served."[48] This same son, Captain Richard Norris, was later tried at a court-martial that refused to find him guilty, despite what members saw as obvious dereliction of duty, because they believed his father would be the next First Lord of the Admiralty.[49] Given that resources, commands, and promotions were often distributed with regard solely to connection, young officers had few reasons to strive for merit but many reasons to think of the navy as a political game. The debacle following the 1744 Battle of Toulon further exposed sea officers to open scrutiny. Two admirals were court-martialed. Rather than trusting in the highly publicized courts-martial to run their course, Parliament instigated an official enquiry and public interrogation into the defeat.[50] In the end Admiral Richard Lestock, who held back from fighting during the battle but had better political connections, was acquitted of any wrongdoing; in contrast, his superior Admiral Thomas Mathews, who had engaged the French, was cashiered from the navy. There was much public concern over both this naval failure and the politically influenced outcome to the inquiry.[51] With little reward for merit and little punishment for negligence (given the right connections), it was no wonder that merchants such as Michael Lee Dicker of Exeter complained, "Our sea captains . . . for the most part seem to act more like privateers than men fitted out and maintained at the public charge."[52] Sandwich wrote that he feared "it is too true what is the general opinion of mankind," that sea officers "have been led away by their private prejudices or narrow principles, to the discredit of themselves, & to the ruin of their profession."[53] The navy appeared rife with disorder.

In addition to the issues within the British fleet, the Spanish and French fleets were in the midst of a resurgence and therefore posed a renewed threat. From the early eighteenth century both British and French agreed that British ships were inferior to those of the French, which were faster and had more firepower.[54] A British admiral said in 1745, "I have never seen or heard . . . that one of our ships alone, singly opposed to one of the enemy's of equal force, has taken her, and I have been in almost every action and skirmish since the year 1718."[55] Now both the Spanish and French governments were committing new financial resources to their fleets, as well as giving them other marks of prestige and official favor.[56]

The Solution: Professionalization and the First Four Years of Reform

The opportunity for Bedford and Sandwich to rectify this situation came in December 1744, when they offered their support to Pelham and Newcastle's coalition government in exchange for control of the Admiralty. With them, Bedford and Sandwich brought in Captain (soon to be Admiral) George Anson, a sea officer who had recently become a hero for capturing the rich annual Spanish Acapulco galleon in the Pacific. Their bureaucratic coup set the stage for the ideological battle over the future of the navy that was to follow. The authoritarian whigs recognized that simply putting more ships on the sea meant nothing if the officers and crews of those ships would not or could not fight, or if they were so corrupt or incompetent that they lost public support. They had to somehow create a Royal Navy that would be capable of the goals they had set out for it. Moreover, they had to create a navy that would appear to be worth the sacrifices it demanded of the nation.[57] If the navy could not prove itself to be successful, it would not continue to receive political support.[58] To solve their naval problem, to create a force capable of taking and holding an empire, and to remedy the disorder they believed undermined the navy's efficacy, the authoritarian whigs decided to mold the navy into the same social model they advocated for Britain and for the empire at large: a disciplined, hierarchical one.

The Admiralty Board did not control all elements of British naval policy. It shared responsibility for naval affairs with four other bureaucratic boards: for example, decisions about where ships would be sent were made by the Privy Council (of which the First Lord was a member). But it did have unilateral control of the officers and the men—their recruitment, their training, their promotion, the distribution of commands—and what happened on board ship.[59] Although there were seven commissioners on the Admiralty Board at any one time, the First Lord was the unquestioned head. Subordinate commissioners were there to share the workload, not to challenge the First Lord, although a weak First Lord might hand decision making over to a subordinate or to the leading minister. Bedford was not a weak First Lord: "The Duke of Bedford governed the Admiralty absolutely, was very obstinate, and would not be spoken to," recalled the tory Earl of Marchmont, adding, "the

Ministers knew no more of what he was doing there than I."[60] Bedford was capable of intense engagement on issues he cared about. The Duke of Newcastle—who generally had little good to say about Bedford—noted when the administration was planning the invasion of Canada in 1746 that "the Duke of Bedford works night and day, and so must every body do that would be well with him."[61] Although both historians and contemporaries chastised Bedford for his often poor attendance at Board meetings, he had Sandwich as his deputy to represent their shared viewpoints. The correspondence between Bedford, Sandwich, and Anson reveals that the two lords were deeply invested in the affairs of the Board; Anson may have provided practical experience, but Bedford and Sandwich provided the political ends to which that experience would be applied.[62] Upon the appointment of Bedford as First Lord of the Admiralty in late 1744, there was an immediate and clear shift in the types of positions the Admiralty Board took toward training, duty, discipline, and naval preparedness. It is clear that these changes came from the creation of a new regime at the Admiralty Board.

The authoritarian whigs visualized a professional navy. Their navy would be a permanent, standing force, just like a professional army.[63] Just as crucially, its officers would be primarily careerists.[64] It would fulfill each of the criteria that distinguish professions from occupations: high social prestige, specialized and advanced education, competency tests, autonomy in professional affairs, a code of conduct, and the monopolization of the market for the service provided.[65] Though not all of these were new innovations—for example, lieutenants' exams had existed since 1677—those not created from scratch were strengthened or altered. Naval commanders in chief could not always be strictly constrained to follow precise and detailed orders. Being often so far away from the center of command, they necessarily had to use their own judgment in assessing situations and soothing or escalating conflicts. This was why it was so important that men of good judgment rose to positions of command. However, subordinate captains in a fleet and subordinate officers on a ship were expected to fulfill their orders without deviation. The authoritarian whigs worked to create a system in which, at all levels of command, failure to behave appropriately would be punished without mitigation for place or connection. They formalized, codified, and rationalized naval organization; monopolized authority over naval affairs; and instilled a sense of duty, of belonging to an actual corps separated from civilians, which they strongly reinforced through a system of regimented discipline. Few of their reforms were uncontroversial; nearly all attracted opposition either from their fellow ministers, Parliament, and the public sphere, or from within the naval service itself.

All of the authoritarian whig naval reforms fitted into the larger framework of instilling discipline. As Bedford's Admiralty explained to George II, "Nothing but discipline will effectually answer and make good every expectation which your Majesty and the public can found upon the behaviour of the fleet of Great Britain."[66] Military systems may be characterized as being based on either internal or external discipline. Internal discipline can be thought of as self-discipline—in a system based on internal discipline, individuals can make their own decisions, because they are trustworthy, rational, capable beings. External discipline is forced on an individual from a higher authority, through drilling, hierarchy, and punitive correction. It is not necessarily draconian, but it does assume the individual needs to be shaped and constrained to fit the system. The authoritarian whig system was primarily based on external discipline. Some of the reforms focused on prestige; some on standardization and ordering of resources, processes, and infrastructure; others focused on training, education, and promotion based on competence; a third set focused on obedience and punitive discipline; and many of the reforms overlapped these categories. Each of these sets of reforms involved rationalization, standardization, and ordering, all of which reinforced discipline in different ways.

A central focus of the reforms was the state of naval infrastructure. To be an effective fighting force, the navy needed both a sufficient number of quality ships and dockyards capable of keeping them in repair. Given that neither one of these areas was directly under Admiralty control—falling instead under the authority of the Navy Board—they achieved only partial success.[67] The commissioners of the Navy Board were chosen for long experience, either in the dockyards, on board ship, or as clerks in the naval service, and therefore had far more experience with naval infrastructure than most Admiralty Board commissioners. Their repeated resistance to Admiralty Board attempts at reform throughout the eighteenth century again suggests that the reform program was political in character rather than based purely on objective experience.[68] In 1745 Bedford's Admiralty proposed building French-style two-decked seventy-four-gunships, which would have been able to face off against their French counterparts and stay at sea in rough weather. The new design increased the firepower of the seventy-gunships with which Britain began the war by nearly 50 percent.[69] The Admiralty also proposed a new standardization of ship design. Given the current haphazard nature of building and acquisition, many ships were of such different dimensions that very little of their rigging or stores were interchangeable. This absence of uniformity increased the difficulty of outfitting the fleet—as one officer noted, it led to ships being "obliged to take promiscuously such stores as were at hand, whether they were suited to the size of the ship or not"—and also meant that the capabilities of an individual ship could be unpredictable.[70] These two propositions met with recalcitrance from the Navy Board and the Surveyor of the Navy Jacob Acworth. Acworth had been Surveyor since 1715 and had the power to forestall changes in government ship design; the Admiralty had to wait until his death in 1749 to revise frigate design substantially.[71] At around the same time, Sandwich's Board again requested the Navy Board to build the two-decked seventy-four-gunships it had proposed in 1745, and the Navy Board again refused to comply. It was not until the middle of the 1750s, with the death of another Surveyor and the installation of an authoritarian whig protégé as co-Surveyor, that the redesigned ships of the line were built.[72] The authoritarian whig Admiralty also concerned itself with the rational and orderly functioning of the dockyards. Convinced that the Navy Board was not running the dockyards efficiently, the members of the Admiralty Board personally visited every dockyard in England in 1749. This was an unprecedented step—even the Navy Board had only visited the dockyards once before, in 1686.[73] One Admiralty commissioner asserted that without direct intervention, there would be "the same laziness, the same want of economy, the same aversion & discouragement to ingenuity."[74] During these inspections, the Admiralty Board paid close attention to opportunities for standardization: for example, they corrected the stacking of timber at Woolwich and rationalized its storage so that the most seasoned wood would always be used first. They standardized the frequency of pay at Sheerness. They informed artificers at Deptford and Woolwich that they would no longer be able to have a separate breakfast time, because it was not standard practice at the other yards. They recommended to the Navy Board the implementation of task work in all the yards, as it had been shown to improve efficiency in the yards in which it was currently used; the Navy Board refused.[75] Inspections of the dockyards commenced under Sandwich's First Lordship; Anson allowed them to lapse, but Sandwich restored annual inspections upon his resumption of the office in 1771.[76] It was not therefore the man with the greatest naval experience who most valued the imposition of standard and orderly practice under the central authority of direct Admiralty scrutiny.

As their actions in the dockyards bore witness, the authoritarian whigs wanted to expand Admiralty authority to encompass all naval affairs—in other words, to create a single, central governing body for the sea service with a monopoly on authority. In an attempt to expand the authority of sea officers, Bedford's Admiralty lobbied heavily for the standardization of rank with land officers. This would improve the effectiveness of amphibious expeditions by clarifying the chain of command and would also raise the status of sea officers at home and abroad.[77] Sandwich argued that this step "will do great good to the service."[78] This simple reform was not granted without an argument from opponents on the Privy Council.[79] Sandwich jumped at an opportunity to bring marines—who previously were under the authority of the army—within the purview of the Admiralty Board, arguing that if they could make the first step "it will be impracticable for any ministry afterwards to change it . . . an opportunity ought never to be lost."[80] This desire to monopolize authority brought the authoritarian whig Admiralty into conflict with some of its high-ranking admirals, who were not accustomed to being strictly subordinated.[81] In 1746 the Board clashed with Edward Vernon over his determination to maintain his own authority and dismissed the wildly popular admiral from his command.[82] These decisions reflected the authoritarian whig belief that strengthening order required strengthening hierarchy. Accordingly, they also took steps to reinforce the chain of command and hierarchy on board ship. Upon hearing that Rear Admiral Henry Medley was ignoring the orders of his superior, the Board informed him that they would "never countenance any carriage in junior officers, tending to independence of their superiors, or want of respect and obedience to them."[83]

The authoritarian whigs introduced the first naval uniform in 1748, which created order by standardizing dress. It also reinforced hierarchy. The Board insisted that officers wore it especially in circumstances where they most needed visible authority, as for example when on those areas of the ships restricted to officers or when sitting in judgment in a court-martial.[84] Seaman William Spavens described an incident when a lieutenant arrived on board the ship of a superior officer without wearing his uniform or his sword. When asked by his superior officer "why he came on duty without those badges of his office," the lieutenant replied, "I am as good a man without them as with them." The lieutenant was arrested, tried at a court-martial, and thrown out of the service.[85] Uniforms created a feeling of unity among the corps, while reinforcing a sense that obedience was owed to the position, not the man.[86] One pamphlet endorsing the use of a uniform argued that it would ensure "an entire subordination [would] be paid not only from seamen to officers, and from officers to superior ones in the same ship, but also from all seamen in general to all officers, and all officers in general to their superiors."[87] The establishment of uniform dress stressed obedience to the system rather than personal honor or loyalty. Uniforms also separated sea officers from civilians and gave the impression of increased public authority. In taking these steps, the authoritarian whigs standardized and rationalized the source of authority, making sure it descended in a strictly ordered way from high to low.[88]

Bedford's Admiralty Board sought to enable a more aggressive form of warfare by ordering regular training exercises for officers and crew.[89] Training standardized behavior and ensured that the same process was performed in the same way on every occasion, making ships more reliable in battle. A subordinate captain noted of Anson that "in my life I never . . . saw half such pains to discipline the fleet"; this discipline paid off at the 1747 First Battle of Finisterre, when Anson observed that "the enemy's ships behaved well; but I could plainly perceive that my ships made a much hotter fire, and much more regular than theirs."[90] This training continued until some late eighteenth-century crews had doubled the rate of fire of their midcentury peers. Having a well-trained, disciplined crew was necessary to support the shift in the style of naval combat that the authoritarian whig Admiralty also supported. From the mid-seventeenth century, the standard form of naval combat had been for each fleet to form one long line of battle, with ships following prow to stern; enemy fleets thus sailed and fought in parallel lines. This was an essentially defensive formation which made winning definitive victories difficult, but it was one which previous Admiralty Boards had supported. From the mid-1740s onward, British fleets increasingly began to break the line of battle in order to pursue more aggressive, more definitive victories. Anson first employed this more aggressive tactic at Finisterre in 1747. British fleets began to sail closer to the enemy before engaging; this enabled them to inflict more damage, but it also exposed sailors and officers alike to continuous enemy fire while they approached, and put the captain in the most exposed position of all.[91] Discipline in training coupled with obedience to authority—standardized, orderly behavior—enabled more aggressive warfare. These riskier tactics were often successful, though not always. In 1747 the young Augustus Keppel was so intent on chasing a French ship that he accidentally ran his own ship aground, destroying it. Both Anson and the Admiralty's protégé Peter Warren approved Keppel's "eagerness to come at the enemy," and the Admiralty promised Keppel a newly built ship as soon as his obligatory court-martial cleared him.[92] For the authoritarian whig Admiralty, the potential rewards of aggressive warfare outweighed the risks.

There were several strategic shifts in naval deployment under the authoritarian whig Admiralty. The first was the creation of the Western Squadron, which one Admiralty commissioner described as leading to "revolutions . . . in the disposition of the marine."[93] The Western Squadron entailed keeping the home fleet to windward of the English Channel rather than in the Channel itself, thereby guarding Ireland, deterring invasion, protecting trade convoys, and watching the French naval port of Brest. This squadron was not a new idea in the 1740s, but it had not been made a permanent part of naval strategy before.[94] An Admiralty commissioner described the Western Squadron as having been originally supported by Bedford and congratulated him on the defense of the idea against its critics in the administration.[95] In 1746 Bedford wrote to Anson, "You know my opinion has long been that we ought to unite all the ships cruising to the Westward" and approved Anson advocating the change to George II. His reasoning was revealing, as he added, "I am the more strongly confirmed in that opinion at present, because, [of] the sending away [of] so great a force, to America."[96] The year 1745 marked the first time there was a specific North American squadron under a designated commander in chief.[97] Thus, this shift did not result solely from the straightforward naval expertise of Anson but also from the wider imperial commitments of the authoritarian whigs. It was intended both to defend East India ships and compensate for the diversion of so much naval force to the Americas.

Of course, simply because the Admiralty ordered changes in dress, behavior, and training did not necessarily mean that captains obeyed. To an extent, the authoritarian whig Admiralty was caught in a trap: the very difficulties of directly overseeing what happened on board ship were exactly the reasons why they believed it was so important to develop officers who would obey orders. For example, although the Admiralty's 1745 instructions to its captains ordered them to train and discipline their crews in gunnery more frequently, the Admiralty found it necessary to reinforce those orders with an additional regulation in 1756, suggesting that the practice was not as regular as they would have hoped. Certainly there was variation in how diligently captains followed their orders. However, the Admiralty had several methods at its disposal to encourage or coerce obedience. One of these was surveillance: the 1745 regulations, for example, required captains to record in logbooks how frequently they trained their seamen. These logbooks—documenting everything from ships' locations, the weather, orders given, and disciplinary action to monies spent—were required to be submitted to the Admiralty upon the end of a cruise; if the logs and accounts were not accurately maintained, neither the captain nor the crew might be paid for months. Captains were not the only ones required to maintain logs. Noncommissioned officers like pursers maintained their own records regarding their areas of oversight, but more important, lieutenants were also required to keep logs that were later submitted to the Admiralty. In the case of a court-martial or other concern, the lieutenant's log could be cross-examined with the captain's to check for discrepancies.[98] Aside from correspondence with officers and their own observations, the members of the Admiralty Board did therefore have a means to assess how thoroughly their orders were followed.

Another major means of controlling the behavior of officers was through promotion. The Admiralty was already the center of promotion and patronage within the navy.[99] The authoritarian whig Admiralty introduced a reform that would permit it even greater control over which officers were promoted to higher levels by finding a way around the tradition of promoting on the basis of pure seniority.[100] The Admiralty explained in a memorial to George II that as "the war, we are now engaged in calls for the service of the most able and most active officers" it would be a "danger to the public" to promote on seniority alone. Rather than allowing officers to move inexorably up the ladder of rank until they died or became admirals, the Admiralty invented a new rank: admiral without distinction of colors, which meant an admiral without a command.[101] Now anyone the Admiralty thought unfit to serve could be put on half pay and retired with a pension, but it would technically be a promotion. This allowed the Admiralty to reach as far down the captains' list as it liked in order to promote the most deserving and, as one lesser member of the Board rather unfeelingly put it, would permit "the discharge of all that immense load of rubbish."[102] This strengthened the Admiralty's hand in its dealings with its officers; officers had a strong incentive to stay on its good side, especially because there were always more officers than there were active positions. Economic historians have described promotion within the navy as a hierarchical tournament: given a limited number of places and the significantly higher financial compensation that came with promotion (including better cruises at sea and a greater chance at prize money), officers were in direct competition with one another for promotion, strongly incentivizing their performance. At the end of the War of the Austrian Succession, Anson informed a captain that continued employment during peacetime would go to "those who had behaved well."[103] The threat, whether articulated or not, of being unemployed was a constant presence. The authoritarian whig Admiralty showed its willingness to follow through on that threat by cashiering Edward Vernon for attempting to maintain too much individual authority, despite his popularity. The message was clear: even the well-connected would not be permitted to disobey.[104] Because there were more commissioned officers than there were active positions, the Admiralty did not need to actively coerce or convince every officer to follow their new regulations. They needed only to monitor which did or did not and promote or sideline accordingly. Officers' own financial incentives would help bring them into line. Self-interest manifested itself in other ways, as well. Senior officers generally had a following of more junior officers on whom they bestowed patronage in turn; they, too, were increasingly incentivized to consider an individual's merit, as "it was very much against an officer's interest to weaken his following and damage his reputation by advancing incompetents."[105] The authoritarian whig Admiralty's willingness to promote officers of lesser seniority but whom it deemed more capable was satirized in a variety of places, including in the 1750 print *The Naval Nurse, or Modern Commander* (Figure 3.1), in which "Boy Captains just wean'd from the Breast" command Britain's warships.

The authoritarian whig reforms encouraged the discipline of training, regularity, and systematically ordered behavior. Bedford told one would-be admiral that when he was considering a man for promotion, he looked

Figure 3.1. R. Attwold, *The Naval Nurse, or Modern Commander,* etching, 1750. Reproduction courtesy of The Lewis Walpole Library, Yale University (Image ID: lwlpr 00074).

for "a constant assiduity in his naval service either at home or abroad, and a ready willingness to undertake any service that shall be thought proper for them."[106] This sense of a more abstract duty to the service or the nation contrasted with the more personal sense of honor which had previously prevailed.[107] To ensure compliance with their new system of hierarchical obedience within the service and aggressive warfare against enemies, the authoritarian whigs created further encouragements to and constraints on the behavior of their officers. They instituted a system of promotion that allowed the Board greater flexibility in choosing commanders, ensuring that the officers promoted were those willing to adhere to the newly aggressive system.[108] This was supplemented by a system of punitive discipline intended to root out the causes of failure and prevent them from reoccurring in the future. Before he became First Lord of the Admiralty, Bedford had argued that although "neglect of duty is, in the present state of our naval establishment, considered as disreputable and irregular, yet it does not appear that it has been censured with the detestation which it deserves, or punished with the severity necessary to its prevention."[109] In particular, the authoritarian whig Admiralty instituted a rationalization and expansion of the existing law of court-martial. They believed sailors and officers would be less likely to risk punishment if they knew it would be certain, despite whatever political connections they might have. The majority of their previous reforms had been carried out under the immediate authority of the Admiralty, but to recodify naval law required an act of Parliament, which was introduced as the 1749 Navy Bill. This was to be the most publicly contested of the authoritarian whig reforms.

The 1749 Navy Bill and the Patriot Opposition

Neither the authoritarian whigs' imperial goals nor their sociopolitical model were universally accepted, but it was the sociopolitical implications of their naval reforms that led to the greatest opposition to their program. The emphasis on constructing a system of external discipline and their monopolization of authority over the navy created a division between the authoritarian whigs and the adherents of patriotism. Although patriots also supported aggressive naval warfare in the imperial sphere, their fears regarding strong executive government and consequent corruption in the body politic meant that their military model relied on the honorable, virtuous participation of the citizen, such as in the militia and privateering models—both of which were nonprofessional, less hierarchical means of conducting warfare. Popular participation would, as in the political sphere, cleanse the military of the dangerously corrupting potential it would have were it to be permanent and professional.[110]

The initial reforms primarily concerned internal naval matters and did not require parliamentary approval; although they sometimes occasioned public notice, they did not generate public debate. The Navy Bill of 1749 changed that. During the course of debates over the bill, many opposition commentators cited previous reforms as proof of the ill intentions of the authoritarian whigs. In Parliament, opponents of the bill noted that the authoritarian whig Admiralty had been "possessed with the spirit of lawgiving" since 1745 and had "discover[ed] several defects, never before thought of in our laws for regulating the government of the navy." The *London Evening Post,* a patriot paper, reminded readers that the 1749 Navy Bill was set into motion by the same Admiralty who "introduced regimentals [uniforms] into the Sea Service, not only in imitation of the French, but with the addition of the colour white, which . . . is the common badge of French slavery." *Old England,* also a patriot newspaper, warned its readers that this was the same Admiralty who had fought over the centralization of authority with Vernon, arguing that Vernon had been "arbitrarily cashiered" out of jealousy of his popularity.[111]

Pro–Navy Bill pamphlets and newspaper articles, some published by the Admiralty, justified the bill as simply rationalizing preexisting naval law.[112] It specified more clearly where and when a sea officer could call a court-martial. It explicitly laid out which punishments were applicable to which crimes, and removed leeway from courts-martial in how they applied those punishments. The bill also stated that the power of courts-martial applied to officers on half pay as well as to actively serving officers.[113] In the Battle of Toulon courts-martial, clear political influence had been used to attack and defend those involved, as had happened in other cases. They had not been the only courts-martial in recent memory to be subjected to parliamentary interference: the court-martial of Sir John Norris's son, Richard Norris—which had been dismissed by the president of the court when it became apparent Norris would be found guilty—was declared by parliamentary resolution to be "partial, arbitrary, and illegal."[114] Pamphlets supporting the Navy Bill hoped that "as little room as possible may be left for men of interest, who have offended, either wholly to escape, or to meet with a slight punishment, where the crime has been great and notorious."[115] This was consistent with Bedford's later statements emphasizing the importance of "uniform and consistent" legislature.[116] "Had this been done after the infamous battle of Toulon, what a trouble and expence would it have saved the nation," exclaimed one pamphleteer. "And from what a load of ignominy and contempt would it have preserved the fleet? And what an advantage a strict and impartial enquiry would have been to the service."[117] As Daniel Baugh has noted, an increased role for courts-martial would have given the Admiralty greater control over the officer corps.[118]

In contrast, the arguments against the Navy Bill centered on the fear that a professional military would enhance state power to the point of overwhelming the rights of the civilian. The parliamentary and popular opposition against the bill was led by the patriots, particularly by those surrounding Frederick, Prince of Wales. The *Remembrancer,* a newspaper closely linked to Frederick's patriot circle, claimed that "since the passing of the Septennial Bill . . . no point so much deserved the notice of the public, as the attempt to establish a military system, under the forms, and with the sanction of law."[119] One pamphlet published during the debate suggested to those unhappy with the bill that "if those masters now presiding over you will not bend to your just petitions," then "in the Heir Apparent you'll ever find the pure certain balm."[120] There were three principal objections to the overall thrust of the bill. The first was that it imposed too much external discipline on those in the sea service and took away their liberties. A second objection was that officers unable or unwilling to disobey could be used against a civilian population. Even without the use of force, sea officers would become nothing better than placemen and could be used to subvert the constitution through electoral or other means. The third objection was that several clauses raised military law above the common law.

The first argument, that the Navy Bill infringed on the liberties and challenged the honor of the sea officers, was the one most often put forward by the sea officers themselves, though it also appeared in wider public discourse. The thirty-fourth article of the bill stipulated that half-pay officers could also be subject to courts-martial—in other words, even during peacetime or if they were not on active service. When sea officers petitioned the Admiralty against the 1749 Navy Bill, they cited as their major complaint the fact that the bill "subject[s] the half pay officers to a greater degree of discipline & command" and that such "methods of compulsion dishonour the service." They requested that the thirty-fourth article be removed from the Bill, and that other articles that "serve to put officers . . . under an improper & servile subjection" be altered.[121] The *Remembrancer* claimed that the authoritarian whigs were trying "to establish all that tyrannical rigor of discipline, in time of peace, which nothing but the exigencies of an actual war could excuse; to expand it to the sea service, as well as to the land; to those on half pay, as well as to those who have the full profits of their commissions . . . and thereby to convert two orders of subjects into slaves."[122]

Opponents of the bill also suggested that officers under the strict discipline of a professional military might threaten civilian society. They might, for example, undermine the legitimacy of political institutions. Patriots critiqued many positions subject to government patronage as being "placements," where loyalty was bought and sold in return for employment. They claimed that placemen, as these officeholders were known, were then obligated to vote in favor of the government in elections and in Parliament. Pamphlets hostile to the Navy Bill argued that it would turn sea officers into a similar category of political dependents. They warned that the Admiralty already had more power than was good for it: "Has not the Admiralty then the power already of influencing every officer, as far as he regards his half-pay, to make such interest as they shall direct at any election?"[123] Professionalizing sea officers would further undermine the legitimacy of British representative government. There was a darker possibility, as well: that sea officers might destabilize civilian society through violence. A callused, desensitized military cut off from civilian society might follow orders of any kind, especially if they owed their livelihood to the state, as professional officers did, and especially if they faced severe punishment for disobedience. As Captain Augustus Hervey explained, professionalized officers might be unable to consider the legality of the orders they were given: " 'Tis no time to consider whether 'tis consistent with the law of the land, and if it was not, you are to murder the law, or they to murder you." Hervey warned that sea officers were being put in a position where they would be forced to "obey command, or else, 'tis disobedience! That's mutiny!

And mutiny is present death when on service: how melancholy, how arbitrary, how tyrannical."[124] Hervey was closely affiliated with George Grenville, still at this time acting within the patriot coalition; he coordinated the opposition to the bill with members of the Prince of Wales's inner circle.[125]

Linked to these arguments was the third major objection to the bill: the way in which it seemed to elevate martial law over common law. In framing their response to the offensive clauses, the opponents of the Navy Bill drew on an incident that had occurred three years prior earlier, in which the Admiralty, in the words of *Old England,* had "presumptuously vot[ed] themselves superior privileges above the control of law."[126] In 1746 the Admiralty had fought successfully against an attempt to establish civil jurisdiction over courts-martial, saying, "It is easy to foresee, what scenes of riot and disorder his Majesty's ships of war may come to be, and what fatal consequences may be apprehended from such a failure of discipline" should civil courts be able to interfere in courts-martial.[127] Bedford had claimed that unless the government "debar[red] the Courts of Westminster Hall from interfering in affairs of a military nature," there "must inevitably be an end of all discipline in his Majesty's sea service."[128] In the eyes of patriotism, this was "an open attempt to raise the military above the civil, to give the Admiralty jurisdiction pre-eminence over the common law, and to vest absolute power in the hands of a few."[129] The 1749 Navy Bill seemed to continue this trend toward establishing military jurisdiction over the civilian population. One article removed some criminal cases previously within the jurisdiction of colonial courts into the realm of courts-martial; another declared that anyone who was found trying to corrupt the loyalty of any sailor would be tried by a court-martial and, if found guilty, put to death. This applied to sailors and civilians alike, leading the opposition to claim in parliamentary debate that "every man in the kingdom seems to be subjected to the jurisdiction of a court-martial."[130] The *London Evening Post* warned that the bill unbalanced the constitution, saying that "if the Admiralty jurisdiction, or the power of land court-martials be extended, so much ground will be gained on the civil government . . . the checks that deter men from abuse of power will be lessened."[131] When the opposition accused the Admiralty Board of being "possessed with the spirit of lawgiving," they implied that the Admiralty wanted to be able to give the law not only to the navy but to the nation. They also criticized the entire program of professionalization, saying that if the Admiralty "had confined their Bill to the repealing of all the laws made since 1661, for the government of his Majesty's Navy, we should have consented to it; because every alteration since, has made the case worse instead of better."[132]

Patriots claimed that a professionalized military required a dangerous alienation from civilian life. The *Remembrancer* argued that the goal of the bill was "to separate the half-pay officers from the body of the people."[133] Removed from the bounds of civil protection, officers became hardened; since they were subject to martial law, they became unconcerned at imposing harsh, unconstitutional rule on others. Patriots argued that the whigs in administration had picked up where the old tories had left off in trying to turn the nation into slaves, that "both [parties] want to constitute power where it should not be; neither of them likes that the law should reign supreme . . . they will first dictate to the theatres, next to the Army and Navy, next to the press, and at last command our persons and properties." The fact that the bill solely concerned the navy rather than the army was irrelevant, and many opposition newspapers included them in the same breath. *Old England* claimed it "is incumbent upon us to keep the Army and Navy as free as we can: too much already are they under [ministerial] control," and that "such an Army, or such a Navy, under such restrictions, must inevitably degenerate and become in the end composed of cut-throats or cowards, or both." The *London Evening Post* cautioned that "if the military by land and sea should be ever reduced, by arbitrary discipline, from brave servants to the public, to be the abject slaves of their heads or leaders, our laws, which are now so good a check on their vicious and daring presumption, will become utterly useless."[134]

The division between authoritarian whiggery and patriotism was not based on a misunderstanding—the authoritarian whigs were in fact trying to do what their opponents claimed they were. They were trying to separate sea officers from the civilian population and they were trying to establish martial law as a separate rather than subordinate sphere from civil law. Captain Hervey, in a pamphlet published against the bill, argued that it would lead to sea officers "being enslaved under such a banner, fettered with such steel, & lashed with such rods of iron, as this makes every inferior officer liable to from every superior he meets," and, indeed, the authoritarian whigs did want to make inferior officers subject to the orders of their superiors, regardless of claims of honor or independence.[135] This was exactly what pamphlets claimed the implementation of uniforms would achieve; it was exactly how the authoritarian whig Admiralty had explained their attitude toward discipline in 1745. The difference came in what each side thought the consequences of these changes would be. To authoritarian whigs, such reforms would result in a highly effective war-making machine, capable of taking on and turning back external threats in order to secure Britain's colonial empire. To patriots, these reforms would result in a dangerous expansion of government power. The *London Gazetteer* newspaper summed up the criticism of these reforms by saying, "The error that principally blinds and misleads their minds consists in their not distinguishing between discipline and despotism," because when "men [are] made to dance to the pipe of absolute will, discipline loses its name, and is changed to despotism."[136]

Despite opposition from patriots, Parliament passed the 1749 Navy Bill into law, although the clause regarding half-pay officers was dropped. However, the argument was not over. Only four days after the Navy Bill was finally sent from the Commons to the Lords, the Admiralty proposed a manning bill to ameliorate the dearth of seamen Britain suffered at the beginning of every war. The proposal was to keep 20,000 sailors on the navy's payroll even in peacetime—some upon half rather than full pay—so that upon the commencement of the next war there would be less need to impress sailors from merchant ships. Again, the patriots surrounding Frederick, Prince of Wales, opposed the bill; the Earl of Egmont, the prince's leader in the Commons, declared that the plan to institute a standing navy in peacetime was "a new attempt for introducing a military government amongst us."[137] In this case, the opposition was successful and no law was passed.

As we will see in Chapter 4, patriotism offered an alternative vision of the military organization and culture appropriate for a free society such as Britain. This did involve roles for both an army and a navy, but there were two major differences from the vision of authoritarian whiggery. Rather than a large standing military, patriots supported smaller, more ad hoc organizations of forces which were mobilized only when necessary. Rather than militaries composed of professionals, they believed strongly that military power should remain in the hands of civilian citizens. William Pulteney, before he fell from patriot grace, proposed a bill in Parliament that would have allowed private citizens to keep whatever they could conquer from the enemy in their own names.[138] Widespread military participation would ensure a virile and invested population as well as protecting the political virtue of the community. More people invested in and able to control the military would act as a safeguard against the corrupting nature of military power, much as Parliament acted as a safeguard against the dangers of executive power. Patriotism's military was based on the quality of the men involved rather than the nature of the discipline imposed on them—in other words, on internal rather than external discipline. In practical terms, these preferences manifested themselves through support for a militia on land and privateers on the sea. Frederick, Prince of Wales, repeatedly promised to establish a militia, to reduce the size of both the professional army and the navy, and to prohibit both land and sea officers under the rank of colonel or rear admiral from sitting in the House of Commons.[139] Proposals for a reinvigorated militia received sustained support from the urban, mercantile communities that were the bastion of patriotism, and these same communities similarly supported patriot ideas by investing in privateering endeavors.

The very idea of a professional, standing navy, characterized by subordination to external discipline and in which large numbers of individuals were to be kept in the government's pay outside wartime, was anathema to the patriots. They looked at the authoritarian whigs' attempts to separate sea officers from civilians, to bend them to the Admiralty will, to remove their independence, and to eliminate parliamentary oversight, and saw in them a tool of tyranny. A professional navy was thus not immune from the types of fears that surrounded a professional army. In both cases, a professional military moved out of the control of civilians and into the hands of the executive.

In the years between 1745 and 1749, Bedford and Sandwich, as leading proponents of authoritarian whiggery, drew on a combination of their own political priorities and the experience of Anson to make significant moves toward professionalizing the Royal Navy. They formalized, codified, and rationalized its structures. They supported the social prestige of naval officers, by putting them on an equal footing with army officers and attempting to repair their public reputation. They promoted the education necessary for good seamanship in their officers and sailors. Competency tests leading to licensing were already in place, but the authoritarian whigs made competency more of a central component in promotion. They pushed for a code of conduct based around commitment to duty, reinforced by discipline and hierarchy. The Admiralty Board took more autonomy in the conduct of their own professional affairs—lessening the control of Parliament, ministers, admirals, and the other naval boards. The fact that the majority of these reforms focused on officers rather than sailors was indicative of the authoritarian whigs' top-down approach to naval governance: the sailors they merely wanted to control, rather than to professionalize.

The reforms did indeed create the duty-bound officers, trained and disciplined crews, and increasingly well-organized infrastructure necessary to support a navy capable of winning battles, as was demonstrated during the later campaigns of the War of the Austrian Succession and in the Seven Years' War. Both domestic and foreign observers credited the policies of authoritarian whigs with improving the success of the Royal Navy. In both Paris and The Hague, commentators noted the "different figure that the English fleet has made in the last years, from what it did at the beginning of the war" and attributed the improvement to the Admiralty Board.[140] The authoritarian whig reforms did more than streamline the infrastructure of the navy, though they did that, too: they created a change in how officers were expected to conduct themselves in war. They transformed naval culture away from the passive restraint advocated by Walpole, but also away from the model of the virtuous citizen-sailor, responsive to his own honor, which patriotism supported and which was embodied in the navy by Admiral Vernon. Instead, naval service now implied the aggressive pursuit of combat and the subordination of personal priorities such as honor to the duty of obedience to the service. Authoritarian whig naval culture centralized authority and, accordingly, reinforced hierarchy. This combined with a visible strengthening of military power and the desire to establish what was seen as a standing navy in peacetime—as opposed to one on call in times of war—that would be strictly obedient to the administration led to the outcry from patriots regarding the undermining of the constitution.

There was a concomitant change in imperial priorities which was clear from the moment the authoritarian whigs took over the Admiralty. Having the Duke of Bedford in the Privy Council gave the authoritarian whigs a voice in the decision-making process and in the commitments that Britain made overseas, though these efforts still had to be negotiated with others in the Council. Authoritarian whig supporters had spoken before of the war of a desire to attack the French in Canada; one of the first acts of the authoritarian whig Admiralty was to support the capture of the French Canadian island of Cape Breton.[141] Although it was carried out without substantial logistical support from London—and, indeed, could not have had official support from the authoritarian whigs, as it was happening in America only weeks after they had taken office in London—the conquest received sustained ex post facto support from the authoritarian whigs. As a first round of peace negotiations were being made in 1745, the Duke of Newcastle predicted that "the great[est] point of all will be the restitution of Cape Breton in return for the restitution of all, or the great part of, the towns in Flanders" but worried that "there the Duke of Bedford and his friends will be immoveable."[142] Negotiations fell through in that year, meaning that the authoritarian whigs were free to propose and support plans for further attacks on French Canada, which Bedford did in March 1746.[143] This expedition failed to materialize, and Bedford feared Britain had let down the American colonists, who "justly looked upon as their only security . . . the entire expulsion of the French out of the Northern continent of America."[144] At the time, William Pitt believed that all American plans "as far as they have gone or are to go, we owe to your Grace alone."[145] Authoritarian whig supporters continued to argue into 1747 about the importance of capturing Canada.[146] After the return of Louisbourg and Cape Breton to the French at the Peace of Aix-la-Chapelle, the authoritarian whigs supported colonizing Nova Scotia instead. They planned to build it into a military and trading center that would rival Louisbourg.[147] These efforts were coordinated through Halifax at the head of the Board of Trade.

Authoritarian whiggery was not the only ideology concerned with disorder, nor was it the only one to advocate imperial expansion or support naval warfare. What differentiated authoritarian whiggery from patriotism or from the whiggery supported by Walpole was its particular constellation of concerns and the tools that authoritarian whigs used to solve perceived problems. When authoritarian whigs saw disorder in the navy, they relied on the same solution they later attempted to use in Ireland, in the North American colonies, and against domestic political reformers: strengthening order from above rather than depending on virtue from below.

The reforms of the authoritarian whigs significantly changed British naval fighting culture for the remainder of the century. The public controversy indicated the importance that eighteenth-century British society attributed to matters of military governance: the navy was not immune from political ideology or popular debate. Historians have increasingly recognized that there were attempts at imperial reform prior to the Seven Years' War, reforms that—though they largely failed at the time—mirrored those imposed following that war.[148] The congruency of the imperial and naval reforms of the 1740s—both based on centralized authority, hierarchical obedience, and the creation of a standardized unitary whole—and their implementation by political allies with a similar set of aspirations for domestic British society suggest that rather than Halifax's imperial reforms being seen as an isolated or pragmatic attempt at remaking British imperial relations, they were part of a coherent vision of what the British world should look like and consequently formed an attempt to reshape the bonds of authority accordingly. The form and function of the navy were highly contentious because contemporaries believed that the navy represented a microcosm of the social order, and they projected their idealized versions of the Anglo-imperial polity onto naval debates. For authoritarian whigs, this polity was one of ordered submission to central authority—whether that authority was imperial and based in London, social and vested in the upper levels of society, or naval and located in the Admiralty. For patriots, in contrast, this polity was one of independence for virtuous citizens. Through its connection with these wider questions of imperial governance and the nature of the British constitution, the controversy over naval reform therefore presaged two of the most divisive issues of the later eighteenth century.

✦ 4 ✦

THE SEVEN YEARS' WAR AND THE PATRIOT ALTERNATIVE TO PROFESSIONALIZATION

THE SEVEN YEARS' WAR (1756–1763) was a period of intense political turmoil across the British Empire. Some Britons both in the British Isles and in North America desperately wanted imperial expansion, leading to renewed warfare with the French and Spanish empires. This in turn raised the stakes of imperial politics: over the course of the war, innumerable British subjects went into the streets to make clear their anger with decisions made at the highest levels of government. Some, particularly urban commercial sorts, did so to insist that the war be fought as aggressively as possible on the imperial stage; others, like rural laborers, did so to protest the demands the war placed on their pocketbooks and their bodies. The war was a testing ground for the newly professionalized navy: had the authoritarian whig reforms actually created a naval force that was more reliable in battle and in protecting imperial trade and territories? The first years of the war suggested that the answer was no. One event in particular sent shock waves throughout the empire and led not only to riots but to the fall of a ministry: the defeat of Admiral John Byng off Minorca in the summer of 1756. The government had sent Byng to relieve the besieged Mediterranean island; following a poorly managed and inconclusive engagement with the French fleet, Byng sailed back to Gibraltar and Minorca surrendered to the French. When confirmation of these events reached Britain, people burned Byng in effigy in the streets. "The Ministers rave, the K[ing] swooned, the mob swears, the Navy hang their heads & the merchants despair. This is the true account," wrote one Londoner.[1] Some claimed Byng was an incompetent coward and warned that there might be a revolution if he were not executed. Others portrayed Byng as the patsy of an establishment whig administration that cared too little about imperial warfare to bother carrying on the war with any kind of commitment; they could have sent Byng to Minorca in time to relieve the island but did not.[2] One observer reported that there was more spirit of rebellion among the people over Minorca than there had been during the Jacobite uprising of 1745.[3] Another "heard the whole city of Westminster disturbed by the song of a hundred ballad-singers, the [chorus] of which was, 'to the block with Newcastle, and the yard-arm with Byng,'" suggesting that the Duke of Newcastle, acting as prime minister, should be beheaded and Admiral Byng hanged from a mast.[4] Byng was court-martialed on the charge that he, for reasons of "cowardice, negligence, or disaffection," had "not do[ne] his utmost" for His Majesty's service.[5]

Although at first Newcastle and other leading ministers tried to brazen out the crisis, they eventually resigned, opening the door for the patriots to enter government as part of a coalition administration and giving them the opportunity to try to implement their own military agenda. This agenda included attempting to undo the foundations of the professionalized standing navy in favor of supporting civilian participation in warfare through privateering and the militia. The patriots believed these measures would make Britain better able to carry out aggressive imperial warfare, but also that they would address other sociopolitical issues by encouraging virtuous engagement in the affairs of the nation. They met with mixed success. Establishment whigs succeeded in drawing legal limits around privateering. Although the patriots won the parliamentary battle over the militia, they found themselves forced to defend it against those who failed to see the value of imperial warfare.

In the midst of this, Byng's court-martial opened the door for onlookers to once again use the navy and its officers as a means of debating the potential strengths and weaknesses of the British Empire—politically, militarily, and to some extent, in terms of social structure. More than eighty published works of political literature, many of which were reprinted in multiple editions owing to their popularity, and a similar number of political prints responded to the trial in some way.

Newspapers throughout the country discussed Byng's court-martial, such as the *Bath Advertiser, Belfast News-Letter, Derby Mercury, Ipswich Journal, Newcastle Courant, Salisbury Journal,* and *York Courant,* among others. The topic also proved to be fertile ground for ballad singers, whose wares were one genre of political literature authored and embraced by all levels of society.[6] The battle lines on Byng were clearly politically delineated. The establishment whigs pushed for his trial and punishment; the Pitt-led patriots pushed for his pardon (though not, perhaps, for his complete exoneration). What is intriguing is that the Pitt-led opposition were also those who had been most vocal in promoting the war, those who were most committed to supporting it, and therefore those who should have been the most outraged at the setback of the loss of Minorca, and yet they were the most active in trying to prevent Byng's execution. Why did the war's biggest supporters try to protect the war's biggest villain thus far, at a time when people called for his blood in the streets? Considered as a discrete incident, the Byng affair appears relatively straightforward: the combination of a disliked administration and a military setback encouraged malcontents to take the opportunity to cast the ministry in the worst light possible. However, considered in the wider context of previous wars and the naval professionalization which had taken place a decade earlier, it becomes clear that the patriots acted on ideological rather than purely partisan motives. Patriots interpreted the loss of Minorca in the context of the establishment whig resistance to expansive imperial projects. They continued to push back against strict military discipline by protesting Byng's court-martial at every turn, but without success. The Navy Bill of 1749 left little leeway for the judges of the court-martial, who found Byng guilty. His execution in March 1757 was an unambiguous warning to all other sea officers of the dangers of disobedience. Thus buttressed, the authoritarian whig system of warfare and discipline seems to have taken a stronger hold in the later years of the war, which became the most successful naval war Britain had yet fought.

Tensions in the Buildup to War

One traditional explanation has held that the Seven Years' War was the outcome of unauthorized skirmishing on the peripheries and a reaction to French aggression in the colonies, compounded by a diplomatic revolution on the continent.[7] Though certainly both of these factors contributed to the precise ways in which the war developed, they must be supplemented with an understanding of the deep and long-term commitment from metropolitan traders to imperial expansion, which they had demonstrated both in 1727 and in 1739. The Seven Years' War was an outgrowth of both the 1727 Anglo-Spanish conflict and the 1739–1748 Wars of Jenkins' Ear and the Austrian Succession. The British did not suddenly discover they wanted an empire in the middle of the eighteenth century, nor did they accidentally discover they had acquired one after the war. Sections of British society had hoped to secure imperial territories and expand imperial trade for many years. Thwarted in their earlier aspirations for an aggressive imperial war, the patriot supporters of the Seven Years' War were even more fervent in their hopes for this iteration. Their disappointments at the many early setbacks of the war were colored by their fears that, as in previous conflicts, the war would be aborted before their ambitions could be realized. In this view, the Treaty of Aix-la-Chapelle represented a mere hiatus.[8]

The political divisions of the past decades continued to hold true. The establishment whigs continued to favor using continental alliances to avoid war. As their leader, the Duke of Newcastle, said in 1755, "Nothing is so much to be wished, as a peace."[9] If the alliances failed and war broke out regardless, these continental engagements meant it would be a land war, which required an army. As had been true in the past, this was not to say that the establishment whigs believed Britain should have no navy or no colonies, but they believed the navy was unreliable and insufficient for defense, and they did not support colonial expansion. The authoritarian whigs continued to advocate a pro-war strategy focused on the Americas, the linchpin of which was the professionalized navy the Duke of Bedford and his followers had built as Lords of the Admiralty. The tories for decades had been arguing for a complete disengagement with the continent in favor of a purely maritime foreign policy. The pamphlet *Some remarks on the Royal Navy* expressed this view, saying "whether the Queen of Hungary or the King of Prussia get the better of one another, what is it to us? . . . by making ourselves principals on the Continent . . . we must inevitably draw ruin on our own heads."[10] However, as had been the case in the mid-1740s, the tories found themselves without substantial parliamentary leadership and diminishing in numbers. The patriots led by William Pitt wanted a more expansive global war than the authoritarian whigs, one designed to cripple France's economic power permanently. The ideological tenets and social bases of patriotism have played a prominent role in discussions of eighteenth-century Britain's political landscape. Broadly speaking, patriots believed that British society and the British constitution were being undermined by corruption, particularly generated by power being concentrated in too few hands. Greater popular involvement—whether in the political process, economic endeavors, or the military sphere—would cleanse this corruption. For patriots, this was the rationale behind having regular parliamentary elections, for example. In England as well as Ireland and the American colonies, patriot rhetoric focused on the need to defend traditional liberties from the threat of encroaching executive power and to protect the people's virtue by protecting their independence. Socially, patriots tended to be drawn from the urban, commercial middling sorts. There was also correlation between patriotism and members of Dissenting religious groups—religious organizations that were less hierarchical than the Church of England and placed a greater emphasis on the individual worshippers.[11] Pitt's primary political base was composed of merchants who were outside the dominant trading companies, who participated in American or West Indian trade, and who were especially concentrated in the City of London.[12] His political allies and affiliates included his cousins (the Grenvilles, the Lytteltons, Lord Temple, and Admiral Temple West); the Jamaican sugar planter William Beckford, representative of the City interest; and many of those who had previously been connected with the Prince of Wales and Leicester House, such as Lord Egmont, George Dodington, and the naval officers Admiral Edward Vernon and Captain Augustus Hervey.

The difference in how patriots and authoritarian whigs approached issues of governance could be seen during Bedford's time as Lord Lieutenant of Ireland, 1757–1761. During his tenure, he was involved in a series of clashes with the Irish parliament over whether the local legislative assembly or the representative of royal executive authority would hold the reins of power. He quarreled with Pitt—then Secretary of State for the Southern Department—in turn over how to handle these disagreements; Bedford pushed for a stronger reassertion of authority, while Pitt was sympathetic to the concerns of the lower sorts.[13] Bedford believed that without some kind of more effective control from above, "the unbridled licentiousness of the lower class of people" meant that "Ireland will soon degenerate into its ancient barbarism."[14] He hoped to be able to "properly dispens[e] rewards and punishments to put a stop to this spirit of faction," much as he had done in the navy, and demanded that Pitt allow him to dismiss anyone who was disloyal in an effort to "make the people here look up to their governor." Pitt refused, arguing that instead Bedford should practice the "softening and healing arts of Government" in an attempt to reassure the people that the government did not intend to take away their rights.[15] In 1759 there were a series of anti-English riots in Dublin, which Bedford believed local Irish authorities did little to quell. Bedford warned Pitt that Ireland had become "a country where laws had lost all energy, magistracy all authority, and even Parliament itself all reverence, and that nothing but military force" could "restrain the subject within due obedience." Bedford insisted that the instigators had been Irish Dissenters, who were "totally republican, and averse to English government, & therefore, they are at least equally with the Papists to be guarded against."[16] Pitt countered that if they were Protestant weavers, as Bedford claimed, then they had probably been rightfully upset at a recent banking corruption scandal; Dissenters, he added, could not possibly have been the true source of the riots because they were "a very valuable branch of the Reformation" and "firm and zealous supporters" of the Glorious Revolution and the Hanoverian monarchy. Pitt placed the blame repeatedly on Catholic French agents.[17] Despite the fact that the riots took place in broad daylight, only a handful of people involved were ever identified. Bedford's chief secretary Richard Rigby concluded, "These mobs and Parliaments are damned troublesome to be sure." But the real problem, he believed, was that those who "ought to have the power of governing [Ireland] . . . from timidity or unpopularity, are afraid to exert that power. The time is come when it is necessary for me to speak to them here, and believe me I do not mince matters with them. I am cramming a Riot Act down their throats."[18] This was not the patriot model of governance.

At the opening of the war, William Pitt's pro-war contingent was a coalition comprising tories and patriots, with the patriots more prominent. Just as the failures of 1727–1729 served as a focal point for the pro-war opposition in 1739, the 1748 Treaty of Aix-la-Chapelle ending the

War of the Austrian Succession was the subject of sustained criticism in the 1750s. The opposition condemned it as having been left "unfinished," meaning that the war was left unfinished: Britain had not come away with the continent of North America in hand, nor had they secured their position in India. Vice Admiral Peter Warren, who had abandoned his previous authoritarian whig patrons for the patriots, proclaimed in Parliament that the treaty had solved nothing, "as the Spaniards . . . continue their insults, and the French their encroachments, in America . . . an open war will be the certain consequence, unless our ministers are resolved to bear with all the injuries and indignities that can be offered."[19] In 1756 one pro-war pamphlet asserted that "the unavoidable necessity of a French war has subsisted ever since that strange patchwork, and inglorious peace made at Aix la Chapelle, where . . . our right and title to all Nova Scotia, and the settlements upon the river Ohio, were left . . . vague and unsettled."[20] The French tried to raise Spanish support by distributing a pamphlet that reminded them, "It is known that there are many people of the first rank in England, who were very little satisfied with the success of the last war in Europe, having wanted their nation to employ all its forces against Spanish and French America, and for this consideration, have objected to those who completed the Treaty of Aix la Chapelle."[21] After the Seven Years' War was over, both Hans Stanley, the British ambassador to France, and the Duc de Choiseul, the French foreign minister, "agreed, that the real sources of that war, had been the leaving the treaty of peace at Aix la Chapelle imperfect, and incomplete."[22] Thus in 1756, just as in 1727 and in 1739, pro-colonial groups forced the administration into a conflict that the party in power, the establishment whigs, wanted quickly patched up or diverted to the continent. In July 1756 Newcastle was very unhappy at the part Britain had been forced into playing. He wrote to one continental correspondent, "Never had this country so hard, and so difficult, a part to act as at present. . . . The silly notion of a maritime war, and the advantages to this country from it, prevailed to a degree, to prevent our entering into any measures for a diversion on the continent."[23] Other establishment whigs agreed with him, the ambassador to The Hague writing, "I defy . . . any body . . . to invent any other way of going on, than in concert with Prussia."[24]

The American colonies were the initial focus of those advocating war, though Pitt would later support carrying the war to the French in

Europe as well. Newcastle advised a correspondent in 1755 that "we are like to have a troublesome [parliamentary] Session, this winter. Great zeal for an American, and maritime war; and great apprehension of & dislike to a war upon the Continent . . . may create us trouble."[25] He encouraged Philip Yorke, first Earl of Hardwicke, to try to avoid patriot parliamentary attacks by being "a little more particular in describing our measures; our fleets, our forces in N[orth] America, & our encouragements to the colonies; I would also hint at the avoiding a continent war," but this advice was to no avail, as the patriots did indeed launch an attack on the first day of the parliamentary session on the basis of American versus continental foreign policy.[26] As one patriot wrote, "It would not be difficult to prove that it would be more for the interest of G[reat] Britain & her colonies, to give France Minorca, Gibraltar, Jersey, Guernsey & (I don't exaggerate) Ireland also, than even the navigation of St. John's River," in Canada.[27] Both patriots and authoritarian whigs had already argued in the 1740s that taking Canada was a necessity.[28] The patriot-tory newspaper the *London Evening Post* informed its readers there were "certain accounts" that the French were encroaching on British territory in America, building new forts, and encouraging their Native American allies to attack British settlers. The paper concluded by warning that "if there is not a vigorous and united opposition effectually to prevent it, they will, in a few years, lay a solid and lasting foundation for making themselves in time masters of all America."[29] American correspondents reinforced these fears.

Although the pro-war supporters claimed that they only wanted to secure their trading interests, they believed that security required expansion. They wrote of "the long wished for opportunity of employing our fleets & armies abroad . . . for annoying, if not conquering, some of the plantations of our enemies."[30] Throughout the 1720s and 1730s, patriots had argued that the only way to prevent future wars with rival empires was to divest them of their imperial territories, thus cutting them off from their riches and from their pretensions at universal monarchy. This argument had not lost its persuasiveness in the 1750s. The Antiguan sugar planter Samuel Martin suggested in 1755 that Britain's best move would be to use its fleet to "sweep away all [French] trade," while at the same time "turning a large army of the Boston men well paid & provided loose upon the French in America, where by act of Parliament they should keep all they can conquer. This is the only way to treat with France, which no other treaty can bind." During the peace negotiations, he continued to argue for expansion both on the mainland and in the Caribbean, saying he hoped "the Jamaica politics of not extending our sugar colonies for fear of depreciating the lands of that island, are laid aside . . . and that the prosperity of our country, will now be promoted by the extensions of our sugar colonies."[31]

The French also perceived the main focus of the war to be the colonies. A 1755 letter written from the French Canadian fort of Louisbourg informed its metropolitan recipient that "we know that there is no war in France, but it is furious in this country."[32] A pamphlet distributed by the French in Spain argued that "the project of universal monarchy, and of a general influence through wealth, will come to be reality, if one country comes to be the absolute master of all the commerce of America" and accused Britain of trying to become that country.[33] France's representatives tried to convince the Spanish court that a British war against the French would only be a prelude to an attempt to undermine the Spanish empire, as well.[34] During previous conflicts, establishment whig propaganda warned that imperial expansion would cause Europe to see Britain as a threat to the balance of power and lead Europe to become united against it, and indeed France now turned to that argument. The French minister Rouillé suggested that "Europe cannot but see with extreme surprise . . . that the English, to satisfy their ambitious goals of conquest, are trying to destroy the balance of power in the New World, which it is no less important to maintain there than in Europe, and in which all commercial nations are essentially interested."[35]

Though some within Britain thought of conquered acquisitions as bargaining chips for the negotiating table, more agreed that there was no point in going to war if everything was going to return to the status quo ante when it was over. As the 1762 pamphlet *Considerations on the Approaching Peace* asked, "Where then is the benefit of making war if we are to return almost all that we take?"[36] During the peace negotiations that ended the Seven Years' War, both British and French sources acknowledged that the permanent gain of American territories and trade—Canada, the neutral Caribbean islands, the fishery, the cutting of logwood—had been the point of the war.[37] Those same interests which had been most loudly pro-war—primarily located in the City of London—were also the most vocal about keeping what Britain had conquered. The *Monitor* newspaper, which represented the trading interests of the City, argued for continuing the war rather than giving up any territories, as did the *North Briton* and the *Court Magazine*. The tories were more amenable to returning certain captures.[38] This was not expansion for solely expansion's sake, but was intended to secure trade and the existing American colonies.

In the first years of the 1750s, a variety of groups, but especially the patriots, expressed their support for a war in the Americas against France. They had come to see France's colonies as a greater threat to the empire than the Spanish colonies that had previously drawn their attention. A war against France also seemed to promise greater opportunities for the expansion of British trade. Freeing French colonial territory from French rule would turn the trade of those territories toward Britain, they hoped, and would weaken France to the point where it could no longer threaten British power. This idea of expanding American trade, for the patriots, and securing the control of the existing colonies, for the authoritarian whigs, followed coherently from their plans for American war earlier in the century. The establishment whigs continued to oppose American expansion. They mustered a variety of arguments in support of their position, among them that no imperial expansion was necessary, that attempting such a campaign would disrupt the balance of power and turn Europe against Britain, and that Britain was incapable of successfully standing against France without allies, let alone the rest of Europe. Contemporary newspapers, pamphlets, ballads, and printed materials all depicted a lively and at times unruly debate about these positions on foreign policy. Although a significant proportion of the population—especially the urban, commercial population—wanted this war against France, they were all too conscious that many of the highest ministers would prevent its realization if given the opportunity, for the third time in three decades. This was the volatile environment in which news of Byng's retreat from Minorca was received.

Byng's Court-Martial

Admiral Byng's retreat to Gibraltar and the subsequent loss of Minorca were accompanied by serious losses in the North American theater of the war. Two-thirds of the British troops under General Jeffrey Amherst were annihilated in 1755 on a campaign to take Fort Duquesne; the

British lost Fort Bull and Fort Oswego in 1756 and Fort William Henry in 1757, and failed to take Louisbourg from the French in 1757. The British public was therefore aware that not only were there ideological struggles over the fate of the war at the highest levels of the administration, but that there appeared to be something systematically flawed with Britain's war efforts thus far.[39] Within this context, there appeared to be two primary explanations for Byng's failure to defend Britain's Mediterranean bastions. One explanation, seized on by the establishment whigs, was that this defeat was the navy's fault: either Byng was personally responsible or, more worrisome, Byng was representative of the quality of the Royal Navy, which was inadequate for the task of taking and holding a colonial empire. The other major explanation, voiced by the patriots, was that this humiliation was the government's fault: there was a cohort in the administration which, having previously betrayed Britain's true interests by not aggressively pursuing colonial war, were now taking their betrayal one step further by deliberately sabotaging Britain's overseas possessions.

The establishment whigs argued that Byng was to blame, and Newcastle quickly took steps to prosecute him. The administration also published and circulated printed materials attacking Byng.[40] In part this was self-defense: if Byng were at fault, the administration would be exonerated.[41] Underlying this self-serving hope was the establishment whigs' belief that the navy was an unreliable tool, which needed to be buttressed with other forms of diplomatic and military engagement. Newcastle wrote to a fellow establishment whig that "if Byng had done his duty, it is as certain as anything of that kind can be, that the French fleet, would have been beat, and the siege of Port Mahon raised."[42] A pamphlet entitled *An Appeal to Reason and Common Sense* argued, "It is evident, that had the A[dmiral] engaged the whole squadron, with the same ardour, with the same British courage and love of glory that the Rear A[dmiral] engaged his part of it, Minorca had been still our own, the French fleet entirely defeated . . . and the French King, probably not able by this time to send even a fishing boat to sea."[43] One poem aimed to expose Byng's cowardice and self-interest by speaking in his voice: "Had I expired in feats of glory, / And been recorded oft in story. . . . What gain from that accrues to me, / When in the bowels of the sea? . . . No, Gentlemen, you quite mistook me, / For all my brains had not forsook me; / I therefore chose, as prudence taught, / To sail away as quick as thought." This writer consoled himself with the fact that Byng's soul had surely gone straight to hell upon his execution.[44] Some sea officers—who can be assumed to have been capable of understanding the technicalities of naval engagement—agreed that the fault was Byng's.[45] As this view gained traction in the public sphere, Byng's effigy was ceremonially burned, hanged, or both in more than two dozen towns.[46]

Aside from Byng's personal failings, some drew wider lessons about the feasibility of a maritime war and the capabilities of the Royal Navy. Even before Minorca, establishment whigs had doubted Britain's naval strength. Newcastle wrote in 1755 that "the notion of obliging France to confine the war to the sea & to America, I always thought difficult, if not impracticable . . . [the French] are, or I am afraid will very soon be, superior to us at sea."[47] He believed Minorca confirmed these fears, saying, "We have undertaken, the nation has forced us to it, more than we can go thro'; we are not, we never were a match *alone,* for France . . . they will soon be more than a match for us at sea. They can attack us, where they please, we cannot defend all places."[48] One of Newcastle's correspondents informed him that "the ill conduct of our fleet in the Mediterranean . . . has had such an effect on people's minds" that "the conduct of the Navy is lately much censured" and the public believed "that the enemy with half our number of ships are superior to us in most parts."[49] When Newcastle ordered preparations to be made for the "immediate trial, & condemnation of Admiral Byng, if as I think there can be no doubt, he deserves it," he added, "the sea officers should be learnt to talk in this manner, & not to think to fling the blame upon civil ministers."[50] When Byng's court-martial found him guilty, some admirals sitting in judgment recommended mercy, explaining that although they were "unanimously of opinion, that he did not do his utmost to relieve St. Philips Castle, and also that during the engagement . . . he did not do his utmost to take, seize, and destroy the ships of the French king, which it was his duty to have engaged, & to assist such of his Majesty's ships as were engaged in fight with the French ships, which it was his duty to have assisted," they did not believe Byng was criminally negligent. This was an "an error in judgment" rather than a sign of disaffection or cowardice.[51] This distinction was publicly criticized, with one poem explaining that of course Byng "ne'er showed any tokens of fear"; the author asked, "How the Dev'l should he, so far in the rear?"—out of harm's way. This poem suggested that the reason for the admirals' mercy was their perception that "Let his case be our case, for likely it may"—in other words, that these admirals also were likely to fail the public.[52] Newcastle and other establishment whigs wanted to defend their administration against charges of negligence, but they were also predisposed to believe that the navy was likely to fail. In Daniel Baugh's assessment, Byng was indeed at fault. He displayed some defeatism even before he left Great Britain. The administration could possibly have gotten him to Minorca a week earlier, but not soon enough to prevent the French army from landing. No matter what, Byng would have had to fight. The administration believed the fort of St. Philip's was strong enough to withstand the siege if its troops had been bolstered as Byng was ordered to facilitate, but he did not even take the additional troops from Gibraltar which might have supported the garrison.[53] From the establishment whig vantage point, the navy deserved to be blamed for its inadequacies; any attacks on the administration were ploys intended to distract from that truth.

The reactions of the authoritarian whigs and the patriot-tory coalition were more complicated. The loss of Minorca was particularly thorny for the authoritarian whigs because it brought into question whether their reforms of the 1740s had actually solved Britain's naval problem. Byng's retreat was reminiscent of the 1744 Battle of Toulon, which also generated widespread accusations of cowardice. The authoritarian whig reforms did not prevent Byng's abandonment of Minorca, but they did determine what happened to Byng on his return to England. Court-martialing a disappointing officer was precisely in accordance with the authoritarian whig solution to inadequate performance, which was punitive and corrective discipline. Moreover, one of the changes the 1749 Navy Bill made to the Articles of War was to strengthen the punishment for officers found guilty of not doing their utmost for His Majesty's service, through cowardice, negligence, or disaffection. Whereas previously a court-martial was able to exercise discretion, after 1749 the only possible punishment for that offense was death. Publicly, the authoritarian whigs were silent on the issue of Byng's punishment. They distrusted the establishment whig administration and its imperial policy, but they could not or would not say anything against Byng facing the punishment they had outlined seven years earlier for just such an eventuality.[54] Privately, they complained about both the administration and Byng. Bedford expressed to Secretary of State Henry Fox his opinion that while

Byng should have been sent sooner, he "cannot justify his conduct," and that "the officer who has not done his duty to the utmost in the day of battle cannot be too severely punished."[55]

The patriot-tory coalition sought to turn the blame for the loss of Minorca away from Byng toward the administration instead. Many actively sought to reprieve him, citing his court-martial as an example of the dangers of a professional military. Some of London's patriot aldermen applied to the Lord Mayor to summon the Common Council for the purpose of recommending Byng to the king's mercy.[56] Pitt participated in a parliamentary effort to have Byng's sentence overturned.[57] Patriot pamphlets loudly proclaimed that Byng was a mere scapegoat.[58] One version of this theme was that the administration had, through negligence or accident, sent Byng either too late or with insufficient forces to properly aid Minorca.[59] The tory periodical *Critical Review* argued that Byng's actions hadn't directly led to the fall of Minorca; rather, the ministerial lack of preparation did that.[60] One pamphlet suggested, "Upon the effects of any fatal mismanagement, you are sensible, it is no unusual State-Trick, for those in power, to devote some sacrifice (however innocent) to the popular resentment, and thus . . . divert the public attention from a *real* to an *ideal* offender." The same pamphlet concluded, "Whatever loss or dishonour the nation may have sustained from this unfortunate affair, it is not owing at least to any deficiency of Naval Spirit, on which the wealth and glory of this Kingdom so essentially depend."[61] If Minorca's loss were the fault of politicians in government, then the war effort itself would not be invalidated; in that case, the war could and should continue, preferably under patriot leadership.

A second version of the patriot-tory attack on the administration was to suggest that the ministry had deliberately failed to save Minorca. Admiral Edward Vernon, who had been associated with the patriots for the past decade and a half, referenced "the dubious state, that our affairs have been transacted with of late years leaving us in a doubtful state, whether we are to attribute many of them either to stupidity or T[reache]ry."[62] The experiences of 1727 and 1739 predisposed the patriots to believe that the establishment whig administration was looking for an opportunity to end the war. William Pitt openly asserted that ministers wanted Minorca to fall so that they would have a reason to stop the war.[63] An address from "the Citizens of Bristol" published in the *London Evening Post* referred to the administration's "design in giving up Minorca, and their reluctance to succour North America, by which Oswego, and several other unnecessary fortresses were got rid of."[64] Some claimed Newcastle had sold Minorca to the French out of personal greed. One anonymous bulletin posted in London read, "Now selling by auction, by order of Thomas Holles of Newcastle: Great Britain and the dominions belonging thereto. Gibraltar and Port Mahon were disposed of the first day and the latter is already delivered. Tomorrow comes on the sale of the King and Royal Family."[65] The patriots judged, accurately, that the establishment whigs preferred peace and believed that they would sacrifice nearly anything to achieve it. These fears were not entirely unfounded. Vernon asked, "Should our timid ministers clap up a peace, might not the terms of it, be giving up our stolen provinces on one side, and our returning captures taken by reprisal on the other," and in fact this was exactly what Newcastle was negotiating.[66] Newcastle believed that France "show[s] certainly a desire to make up & I think, considering our circumstances, that we should not neglect them . . . there is then a promise to restore the effects seized, and I own, I can have no doubt, but we should do it."[67] Hardwicke, the Lord Chancellor, agreed, saying, "I cannot help wishing that his Majesty would seriously look towards a peace, tho' at a distance, & be endeavouring to lay some scheme & put things in train for that purpose; for that this war is hopeless, & may be ruinous, I have been for some time convinced."[68] The French minister Rouillé was thus accurately informed when he wrote to his ambassador in London that he was "persuaded of the pacific intentions of the London court."[69] The threat of an establishment whig administration to the imperial plans of the patriot opposition was very real.

The stakes were high as the establishment whig administration and the patriot opposition attempted to convince the public of the validity of their own particular interpretations of the loss of Minorca, using pamphlets, ballads, newspaper reports, satires, and plays to communicate their arguments. The establishment whigs worried that entering this war, especially with a navy insufficient to perform the tasks required of it, would be Britain's downfall. British informants in France reported that "increasing the [French] fleet . . . is the favourite point at present of the King, court, and nation."[70] On the other hand, the patriots were convinced that the future of the nation lay in the security and expansion of its colonies. These ends could not be attained through negotiation; the only way to achieve them was war. Members of the public thus had options in what they chose to believe. Despite the establishment whig efforts to prove their commitment to the war by prosecuting Byng for his failures, the story of government betrayal resonated with the public. Resentment was widespread across the country: thirty-seven towns and boroughs addressed the government, calling for an inquiry into the loss of Minorca.[71] Warwickshire rioted. One concerned citizen wrote to the secretary of state that he "never knew the spirit of discontent . . . so great in itself; 'twas nothing like it the last rebellion, I mean the people in this part of England are more discontented now than at that time."[72] One politician observed to Newcastle that "matters were brought to such a crisis, & the national ferment wrought up to such a height that it was impossible for your Grace to stand it; that therefore he thought it more advisable for your Grace to persuade the King to permit you to resign . . . whether it would or would not allay the present uneasiness and clamour he could not guess."[73]

In the end, Newcastle did resign and Byng was executed. If one were to look at only the events that took place between June 1756, when word of Byng's retreat from Minorca first reached Britain, and March 1757, when he was executed, it would seem that the frustration the patriots felt at seeing their imperial plans thwarted once again was the sole cause of aggression toward the administration and leniency toward Byng. However, if one looks at a longer time frame—backward toward the 1749 Navy Bill and forward toward the 1757 Militia Act—it becomes clear that there was another factor at work, too. That factor was the way in which the patriots' ideas about political virtue and the importance of independency from state control affected their ideas about military governance. The patriots did not want the war to be discredited; they believed that Britain was a match for France and believed an aggressive wartime navy would be essential to damaging France's trade and carrying the war to the far corners of the world. But the patriots did not want to see a permanent standing naval force, the type of professionalized military that Byng's court-martial represented. The 1749 Navy Bill, which the patriots opposed so vigorously, directly led to Byng's execution in 1757. Byng's defenders made this same connection between the 1749 Navy Bill and what they perceived to be Byng's excessive punishment. One pamphlet by "an old sea officer" noted that in the past, courts-martial had more discretion in their judgments and claimed that the rigidity that marked Byng's trial was something new. He warned that few would follow in his footsteps as an officer given the current situation, in which "whoever shall be lucky enough to escape the broadsides of the enemy, must now, according to the modern interpretation of our law, be exposed to a still more dangerous artillery."[74]

To a large extent, the same individuals comprised the opposition to both the 1749 Navy Bill and Byng's court-martial. In the 1740s patriots affiliated with the Prince of Wales and Leicester House claimed the Navy Bill was a move toward an unfree society. Major opponents included Lord Egmont, George Dodington, Thomas Potter, Sir Francis Dashwood, and the Prince of Wales himself, who expressed his belief that the bill made slaves of naval officers.[75] In the 1750s, now led by William Pitt, patriots continued to resist the consequences of the Navy Bill even as they also advocated for imperial war. In 1755 Egmont, Dodington, Potter, and Dashwood all spoke in Parliament in favor of an American and maritime war.[76] Dodington was one of the few people to speak in Parliament in support of a pardon for Byng. Potter and Dashwood introduced a bill into Parliament that would have led to Byng's reprieve.[77] Among naval officers, two of the Navy Bill's chief opponents were Augustus Hervey and Temple West. Hervey described the bill as "pernicious, ill designed," presented the naval officers' petitions against it, and wrote at least four anonymous pamphlets suggesting that all those discontented with the bill should turn to Leicester House and the patriot opposition.[78] Hervey also wrote at least five pamphlets in support of Byng. Describing his questioning by Byng's court-martial, Hervey claimed, "Nor did I ever fail to throw in everything in my power that I could to prove I thought that the failure of that day's success should have ALL laid at the doors of those infamous ministers who sent such a weak squadron out."[79] When the court's judgment was passed down, Hervey "went to Lord Temple, to Lord Egmont, Mr. Dodington, in short to everyone I could to stir up all the assistance I could to show a face against such an infamous violation of justice."[80] Temple West, William Pitt's cousin, had also written a pamphlet against the Navy Bill; he resigned in protest from the Admiralty Board rather than be involved with Byng's execution. Admiral Edward Vernon, William Pitt, William Beckford, and Lord Temple were all pro-war and defenders of Byng.[81]

For the authoritarian whigs, Byng's court-martial represented positive progress in the navy; their reforms had not prevented the lapse in duty, but at least the incompetence would be punished and an example made. For the patriots, however, Byng's court-martial represented everything wrong with the Royal Navy of the mid-eighteenth century. Though the authoritarian whigs believed the standardization and discipline of their system encouraged skill and dedication to duty, the patriots believed it led to despotism and punishment that did not fit the crime.

The Patriot Alternative: Privateers and Militia

The patriots lost the battle over Byng's court-martial, but as Parliament debated the value of both privateering and the militia, they had other opportunities to make an impact on Britain's military policies. Patriots were not inherently opposed to military forces during wartime—they did not generally call for the complete dissolution of the Royal Navy or formal military regiments, for example—but they maintained that civilians also had an essential role to play in a nation's military institutions. Patriots defended privateering in Parliament and supported the principle with their pocketbooks. They also attempted to revive the militia in England as part of their efforts to revitalize virtue and the ideal of the citizen-soldier. Both of these issues generated their own arguments, discord, and clamor.

In privateering, private individuals or incorporated groups funded and outfitted their own ships to cruise in search of the enemy, which they were permitted to do by a government-granted letter of marque. The spoils of war went to those same private individuals. Privateering was thus both an investment made with expectation of financial return and a means of supporting the public cause through private violence. Sailors on privateering ships did not receive wages; their compensation came from whatever prizes they could take. In that sense, they were as much shareholders in the expedition as the original investors, contributing to the participatory nature of the endeavor.[82] Engagement in privateering was especially widespread among exactly the same community that tended to support patriotism: the urban and commercial middling sorts. Nicholas Rogers has noted that "virtually every sector of the London business community appears to have speculated in privateering," from aldermen to ironmongers.[83] One pro-privateering pamphlet addressed to the Anti-Gallican Society, an organization created in support of

British manufactures, compared the "truly valuable subjects (that is to say) merchants, common tradesmen, &c. [who] . . . fit out private ships of war to cruize against France" with the country's gentlemen, who instead spent their money in the "purchasing of lottery tickets, betting at cock-matches, horse-races, or other delusive games of chance."[84] Patriotism portrayed merchants and manufacturers as investing in the nation's future while gentlemen frittered away their wealth. The *Monitor* newspaper, headed by Pitt's ally William Beckford and representing the trading interests of the City of London, complained that the establishment whig administration had not warned the colonies about the official outbreak of the war. Had they done so, the *Monitor* claimed, "our trade would have been less exposed, and our American privateers sooner let loose. A measure, which infancy might suggest."[85] Meanwhile, patriots continued to express their opposition to a standing navy through measures such as the Habeas Corpus Bill of 1758. This bill, prepared by Pitt's ally Attorney-General Charles Pratt (later Earl Camden and a supporter of the American colonists) and encouraged by Pitt, would have partially demobilized the navy even during wartime because it extended habeas corpus rights to impressed seamen.[86] This opposition to a standing navy was not purely partisan; it was grounded in a coherent worldview that valued virtuous participation and feared power.

In contrast to the support given to privateering by patriotism, the establishment whig administration expressed concern that unfettered individual participation in warfare led to disorder.[87] These concerns were similar to the ones voiced by the authoritarian whigs. In 1758 the Customs Commissioners complained to the Treasury that too many letters of marque were being granted to small ships. The commissioners protested that smaller ships were unable to annoy the enemy effectively but were perfectly suited for smuggling goods. Their small size made them manageable in coastal waters and their letters of marque gave them an excuse to be close to enemy territory. The commissioners further claimed that, aside from smuggling, "it is notorious that many of them have committed acts of piracy in the Channel against his Majesty's subjects, and also those of neutral powers."[88] Neutral powers such as Spain and the Netherlands did complain vociferously about being attacked by British privateers. These grievances left Beckford unimpressed; he suggested via the *Monitor* that "an open war with such a nation is much more eligible, in our circumstances, than peace with such an ally."[89]

Elizabeth Anson wrote to her admiral husband that if he were unable to find any other enemies, he "could do justice" by "hanging up almost all the captains [of privateers] you met, & making a better use of the men; indeed they are at present the enemies of all mankind, & make all mankind ours. There seems to be a resolution of regulating them in some new way next Session, if some worthy Patriot (as Mr. Beckford I suppose) does not prevent it."[90] Anti-privateering forces introduced the Privateers Act in the following parliamentary session, intended to eliminate smaller privateers and to regulate more strictly those that were licensed by requiring greater sureties.[91] Aside from their concerns over disorder, supporters of the professional navy had other reasons to resent advocates of privateering, as they competed with naval ships for sailors and for prizes.[92]

The second branch of the patriots' ideal military was the militia, an institution they envisioned as equal in importance to the army and independent from the command of professional officers.[93] As one militia supporter pointed out in Parliament, "A well regulated and well disciplined militia is as much a standing army as any sort of army can be" and "What is now called a standing army of regular troops ought to be called a standing army of mercenary troops."[94] William Pitt and George Townshend introduced the Militia Bill in 1756; it passed the House of Commons but the establishment whigs defeated the bill in the House of Lords. Horatio Walpole warned Chancellor Hardwicke against challenging the bill, telling him that it was "become a very popular and plausible object" and that should it be defeated it would "occasion a great deal of ill humour and clamour, industriously fomented and propagated."[95] Once again, a similar roster of political players were involved in supporting a militia as had been in opposing the Navy Bill and defending Byng. Thomas Potter and Sir Francis Dashwood, who had tried to have Byng reprieved in Parliament, both also advocated a militia.[96] Edward Vernon, Pitt, Beckford, and Lord Temple had all defended Byng and were also pro-militia.[97] Politically, the militia represented civic virtue for the patriots, but the threat of democracy for its opponents. Imperially, a militia guarding the homeland freed the navy for more aggressive maneuvers abroad and also opened the possibility of less-regulated guerrilla warfare on the imperial frontiers. As the patriots generally favored the most aggressive war possible against France, this appealed to them. However, the imperial dimensions of the Seven Years'

War also generated some of the most dramatic opposition to the militia, as rural people who felt alienated from the goals of the war rioted against being enlisted in the militia.

For the patriots, a militia represented both a belief in the trustworthiness of the wider population and a guarantee of civic virtue. The importance of the former consideration—of the militia as a symbol of trust and participation in the life of the nation—should not be underestimated. The *London Chronicle*, an opposition newspaper, claimed that the only reason the English Militia Bill could have been rejected by the Lords was because they believed "Englishmen were not fit to be entrusted with the care of their own liberties."[98] Between 1760 and 1762 the Scottish politician George Elliot, backed by the majority of Scottish parliamentarians, twice embarked on "rash and hazardous" campaigns to restore the militia to Scotland. He did so from a desire to publicly demonstrate Scotland's political rehabilitation following the 1745 Jacobite Rebellion.[99] However, advocates of a militia primarily emphasized the role that a militia would play in guaranteeing the civic virtue of the political community. If privateering was a way to ensure private citizens shared in the perceived benefits of warfare, the patriots believed that the militia was a way to insure against the perceived harms of it. This guarantee was twofold. First, a militia would lessen the power of the executive by diluting its control over the military. Ministers cited their fear of a French invasion to justify maintaining a standing army; a militia would deal with both those issues in one fell swoop. The pro-militia pamphlet *A Modest Address to the Commons of Great Britain, and in Particular the Free Citizens of London* reminded its readers that "as there is no danger so great to contend against, as the exorbitant power of a standing army too numerous, let every Briton therefore dispassionately consider the necessity there is, to oppose all farther extension of mercenaries and foreigners at home; and . . . to encourage every laudable proposal for a militia."[100] Professional officers, as the patriots had made clear in the debates over the 1749 Navy Bill, could too easily be used to subjugate a civilian population. Because they were accountable only to the executive power, they would not hesitate to carry out illegal orders. Because they were segregated from civilian society, they had no investment in it. Creating a militia system restored military investment in society. Being under the ministerial thumb, professional officers acted as placemen and degraded Britain's constitutional system that way, too. A rather scathing address from the opposition in Bristol to the city's MPs suggested the reason for establishment whig resistance to a militia was that "if once a national militia came to be established . . . there would then be no further occasion for so large a standing army in times of peace, by which means many of our young noblemen and gentlemen would be deprived of very genteel sinecures."[101] A militia thus protected civic society from the dangers of professional officers, who had little to gain by protecting liberties but much to lose by disobeying orders.

In addition to restoring military investment in society, a militia also restored society's investment in the political fabric of the community. Individuals who might be called to serve in the militia by a lottery draft system had more reason to feel engaged in political debates and in the affairs of the nation. Decisions made by Parliament were more likely to affect individuals in concrete ways. Individuals would thus be reminded that their well-being relied on the good of the commonwealth as much as on their private interests. Participating in the public life of the nation was the birthright of Englishmen, as the patriot Admiral Vernon expressed in a letter to Pitt: "with our people generally armed, I am persuaded France would never dream of invading us; kept as we are the most generally disarmed nation in the world, is their greatest encouragement to undertake it, from the dissatisfaction it must give to a nation, who know they have paid dear for a liberty they ought to possess."[102] Participation in the nation's military affairs would restore Britain's men to the Roman ideal of the military prowess of the citizen-soldier; it would bolster the masculine virtue some feared Britain's men were losing.[103] Men with something to lose, men who were invested in society, would be better fighters. The patriots characterized professional soldiers as being slaves regardless of who their master was; what was it to them if they served a British monarch or a French one? The Antiguan sugar planter Samuel Martin, who had connections to Leicester House, suggested that when Britain's people were "well formed into a regular militia, all the potentates of Europe will court the British monarch; and even the wise King of Prussia will think himself honored by an alliance with a King, who commands an army of two millions of soldiers, who are freemen; & many of them people of great property."[104] Supporters believed the effect of the Militia Bill would be to place more power and authority in the hands of local leaders rather than in the central government; positions of military authority would go to men of responsibility, not to the sons of political supporters. A militia would free the country from the threat of French tyranny as well as the threat of ministerial tyranny.

The militia had imperial as well as domestic implications. Supporters claimed that having a militia to guard the British Isles would permit a greater proportion of resources to be turned toward the war in America. The patriot leader Lord Temple attributed early defeats in American campaigns to the lack of a militia at home: "By the want of such a militia we have been prevented from sending such succours to our countrymen in America, as we ought to have done." The *London Evening Post* emphasized that passing the Militia Bill would free naval ships from coastguard duties, a measure it claimed would have prevented the setbacks at Minorca and in America.[105] Samuel Martin believed that equipping an American militia would encourage more aggressive guerilla warfare against the French. He argued that Britain should "turn the North Americans loose upon the French" and that "by a militia all over the continent . . . I dare say the French may be exterminated." Martin's plan suggested that men who served in the militia should be given frontier lands exempt from taxes or other obligations, "except the personal defence of their own possessions upon the frontiers, in the way of a military tenure."[106] Settling ex-soldiers on frontier land accomplished a number of goals at once: it secured the frontiers, gave the men involved a viable alternative to being lifelong professional soldiers, and the independence necessary to becoming virtuous members of civic society.

Despite the patriot-tory coalition and the occasional characterization of the militia as a tory issue, the tories were at best ambivalent. Tories might use the militia for partisan purposes and to embarrass the administration, but the patriots were genuinely committed to the endeavor. The 1757 Militia Bill did not receive strong support from the midlands, an area with strong tory leanings. Areas like Norfolk, which tended toward political radicalism, were more supportive. Many of the militia reformers were, in the words of J. R. Western, "deists and admirers of republics"; tories who were firm champions of royal authority tended to stay away from the militia issue.[107] Just as the commercial interests had been most active in promoting the war and in promoting privateering, they were also linked with the promotion of the militia. One poem addressed to the ladies of Great Britain referred to merchants as "These god-like men, to whose industrious care / You owe the gem that sparkles in your ear." These merchants were "Not only patriots but heroes too. . . . Those men who round us happiness dispense, / Now brandish th' awful sword in its defence." Like in the pro-privateering discourse, these virtuous merchants were compared with the self-interested aristocrat, whose "only care is, how to serve his ends."[108] Aristocrats were blamed for the game laws, both for their monopolization of resources—in this case, wild game—to the detriment of the wider British community and because these game laws had, in the words of Western, "brought to an end the acquaintance of the people with firearms and the cultivation of marksmanship as a popular country sport. Their repeal was a necessary step in any general revival of military prowess."[109] This tension could be seen in prints like *The English Lion Dismember'd* (Figure 4.1), which bemoaned the loss of Minorca while simultaneously juxtaposing the poorly armed but honest English militia with the German soldiers imported to secure the nation (rather than relying on the English people themselves) and with the French soldier plotting again British North America. In this image, one militiaman announces, "Whores and cards, hunting & horse-racing are more their concern than commerce or glory," while another complains, "Our enemies have guns. Our arms are only rakes and flails. The gentry are more concerned to preserve the game than their country."

Although the majority of militia supporters were opponents of the professional navy, the authoritarian whig coalition did not have a unified position in return. While there was frequently a general bundle of ideas that most authoritarian whigs or patriots might agree on, individuals did not always align with every single element of the broader ideology. George Townshend, who introduced the 1756 bill with Pitt, was an example. In many other ways—his own career as a military officer, statements he made about the way ideas of equality appealed to the "vanity of the inferior orders of men," the role he later played in expanding central oversight to Ireland in the 1760s—he fit the model of an authoritarian whig.[110] But he also believed deeply in the importance of a militia, in part because he seemed to be concerned about whether the army alone was enough to defend the British Isles but also because he imagined the militia to "grow naturally out of the soil" to "act with the principle of the landed interest."[111] The Duke of Bedford also supported a militia in England, for practical reasons rather than ideological ones. Having a militia to defend British shores would permit the navy to cease its coastguard duties and pursue more aggressive endeavors. Bedford critiqued "our incapacity of making the proper use of our fleet

Figure 4.1. The English Lion Dismember'd or the Voice of the Public for an Enquiry into the Loss of Minorca with Adl. B—g's Plea before His Examiners, etching with engraving, 1756. Reproduction courtesy of the National Maritime Museum, Greenwich, London (Object ID: PAF3986).

for want of an internal force" and informed the House of Lords that "this [Militia] Bill will relieve our ships from their sentry duty, will weigh their anchors & wash them to distant parts for the recovery of the territories we have lost, & the conquest of the enemy's possessions."[112] On the other hand, Bedford opposed the use of the militia in Ireland during his tenure as Lord Lieutenant and encouraged enrollment in the regular army instead, a point on which again he and Pitt disagreed.[113] When Bedford's son, Lord Tavistock, became involved with the militia in Bedfordshire and announced himself "more militia mad than ever," Bedford scolded him for being too enthusiastic about keeping low company.[114] In contrast, Bedford's normally stalwart ideological compatriot the Earl of Sandwich opposed the Militia Bill, informing the Duke of Cumberland, "I did all I could against the Bill during the whole progress of it, & am really sorry it was to no purpose."[115] The desire of the authoritarian whigs to allow the navy they had constructed to operate at full capacity clashed with their belief in the importance of a professional military and the dangers of unleashing unregulated individuals in the military sphere. To a certain extent, the interests of the authoritarian whigs and the patriots overlapped on the question of the militia, but not because they were necessarily committed to the same principles.

In Parliament the bulk of the opposition to the Militia Bill came from the establishment whigs, who feared the degradation of executive authority and the move toward democracy. Baron Sandys expressed the establishment whig fear that the militia would empower the untrustworthy by claiming that "every man of property who happens to be chosen by lot, will pick up some loose, abandoned fellow to serve as his substitute; and of such only all the common men of our modern militia will always consist," adding that although the standing army was composed of those people, as well, at least "there the officers have, by the military law, power enough to hold them to their duty, and to prevent their being riotous or seditious."[116] Chancellor Hardwicke justified his opposition to the Militia Bill by saying, "The scale of power, in this government, has long been growing heavier on the democratical side. I think this would throw a great deal of weight into it." He also pointed out the lack of martial law over the militia as another objection.[117] As one correspondent had informed then-Prime Minister Henry Pelham during the 1745 Jacobite rebellion, "the government has two parties in this Kingdom, the Jacobite & the Republican to guard against. . . . I am humbly of opinion it would be prudent in the government to avoid, as much as possible, the arming the people, and the teaching them military exercise, lest we should thereby experience the Revolution of 41," referring to the English Civil War.[118] The establishment whigs were only willing to permit the common population to be involved in military endeavors insofar as they could be controlled.

There was a marked contrast in the types of people who opposed the Militia Bill outside Parliament; rather than the aristocratic, oligarchic establishment whigs, the majority of popular resistance to the militia came from poor, rural people. After its initial defeat in the House of Lords in 1756, patriots reintroduced the Militia Bill a second time; the Lords passed this second bill after a fierce struggle. The act called for a census of able-bodied men between eighteen and fifty years old; those chosen by ballot would be in the militia for three years, but could find a substitute or pay ten pounds to be exempted. The militia was to be paid for by general taxation, not the Land Tax, meaning the financial burdens would be felt beyond the landed gentry.[119] Beginning in late August 1757, reports started to reach London of widespread rioting in Northamptonshire, Hertfordshire, and Bedfordshire in reaction to the passing of the Militia Bill. In Hemel Hempstead, "a great number of people, armed with hedgestakes, woodbills, &c assembled in a riotous manner . . . and proceeded to Berkhamstead to meet the magistrates, who were there assembled to ballot for the militia men . . . swearing all the way they went, they would stick by each other, and rather die than serve."[120] A mob of a thousand was reported in Bedfordshire.[121] By the middle of September swaths of Yorkshire, Derbyshire, and Nottinghamshire were also in arms. Upon hearing that the constables were assembling lists from which would be drawn the names of the men to be enlisted in the militia, mobs threatened government representatives, tore down houses where militia meetings were due to take place, and demanded and confiscated the lists from the constables. The sheriff of Yorkshire reported, "Forty parishes came to my house armed with guns, scythes & other weapons, and forced me to promise that I would not act in this Militia Bill in the manner it now stands."[122] In Yorkshire, as elsewhere, the extent of the feeling against the act led magistrates and royal officials to announce publicly that they would not enforce it.[123] By October and November the disturbances had spread farther still.

The patriots and the establishment whigs each had their own interpretations of why these riots happened, based on their different understandings of the trustworthiness of the common people. The measure's supporters tended to argue that people simply misunderstood the bill and the true reason for its failure lay in the resistance of the Lords Lieutenant of the counties, who were responsible for its local implementation.[124] In contrast, Lord Holdernesse, who voted against the bill, believed that the Militia Bill was an excuse for rioting, burglary, and other felonies.[125] The Lord Lieutenant of Yorkshire agreed, saying that the Militia Bill "can only be a handle for their violences" and adding that he believed the disturbances were being stirred up by Catholics (who were presumably Jacobites).[126]

According to statements made by the rioters themselves, they had not been manipulated by anti-militia forces nor were they necessarily unhappy with Hanoverian rule. Instead, they emphasized their feelings of disassociation from the causes and perceived benefits of the Seven Years' War. The terms of military service mattered to them, as did their perception of what sacrifices they were being asked to make in comparison with other parts of society. Although the patriots wanted a more inclusive sociopolitical system and wider engagement in public sphere, support for these measures were still largely limited to more urban, commercial social groups—merchants, artisans, tradesmen—not to more rural, agrarian groups. The anti–Militia Bill rioters were consistently described as country people, farmers, or sometimes pitmen from the coal mines. They disagreed with how the militia was to be funded, which they thought fell too hard on them and not enough on the people of property. In Derbyshire, one person made a speech to the effect that "the expence of national preservation is the duty of the proprietors of the soil, and that 'tis enough of them (the poor) to hazard their persons in defence of the rich."[127] The mayor of York reported, "The necessitous who are by much the majority are endeavouring to promote a levelling principle (which is constantly made use of in their meetings) which would prove fatal to the peace & happiness of our constitution, & they think by the Militia Act the poor are to defend the rich."[128] One anonymous letter written to militia commissioners informed them that if the gentry and merchants "would have men raised you may raise them by the assistance of your long green purses and be da[m]ned if you will . . . they swear they will not fight for your estates, they will fight for their own lives first and so begin at home, for they have had loss enough by the rot last year and no consideration from the landlord at rent day," reminding the commissioners that "tis the farmers that maintains both the poor and such as they too."[129] Lord Poulett observed to Pitt that although "the middle rate of people seem much disposed towards carrying the act into execution, the lower rank of people seem afraid only of being sent abroad."[130] These small farmers did not necessarily feel connected to the goal of civic virtue which the patriots embraced, nor did they feel connected to the imperial ideals of the Seven Years' War.

The Seven Years' War was a popular war to many, but was still far from being universally approved. The war's biggest supporters were trading communities populated by individuals who believed themselves to be capable of full participation in the public sphere, both politically and militarily. For them, there was a clear connection between the case of Admiral Byng and the need for a militia. Addresses from various constituencies to the government on the loss of Minorca linked a more popular military system with a better-executed war. In the City of London's address to George II, they requested "the authors of our late losses and disappointments to be enquired into and punished" and additionally "lament[ed] the want of a constitutional and well-regulated militia."[131] The towns of Tavistock and Southwark, along with others, linked their demands for an inquiry into the fall of Minorca with requests for the establishment of a national militia. Coventry, Ipswich, Lichfield, Nottingham, Salisbury, and Wells and the counties of Kent and Staffordshire made similar addresses. These petitions sometimes included requests for triennial parliaments or place bills, two other favorite measures against ministerial corruption.[132] The failure of Minorca and the solution of a militia were clearly linked in many imaginations: the government could not be trusted to execute the war properly because it was uncommitted to the war, but bringing in a more widely based, popular administration of military affairs would rectify that.

The Seven Years' War was in many ways the war the patriots had wanted to fight for the previous thirty years. However, in its early days, victory seemed distant. The public was far from united on what the goals of the war should be, or how it should be conducted. The administration was actively negotiating for peace with France. The navy seemed like a failure, and the first engagements of the war had been defeats and setbacks. There were interest groups within Britain that dearly wanted a colonial war to secure territory, trade, and resources for manufactures, which had tried twice before to force Britain to fight a colonial war and had been denied each time. These groups believed they were faced with a third chance to secure Britain's place as a colonial power—a place that if Britain did not take, France or Spain would. In 1756 and 1757 Britain's imperial future appeared precariously fragile. But within time, the war became what the patriots hoped it would be: aggressive, imperial, worldwide, and—eventually—successful. By 1763 British forces had captured Canada, a variety of French and Spanish Caribbean islands, the strongholds at Senegal and Gorée on the West African coast, large swaths of India, and Manila in the Philippines.

Despite ongoing patriot opposition, the professionalized navy proved its worth. One naval captain reported after engaging with a French privateer that the enemy "hardly fired a gun for my ten."[133] Describing his victory over the French off Lagos, Portugal, Edward Boscawen wrote to the Admiralty that "most of his Majesty's ships under my command sailed better than those of the enemy."[134] In another action with the French fleet off India, George Pocock—an officer amenable to the authoritarian whig system of discipline and hierarchy—was pleased that the British seamen "by the vigour and constancy of their fire, obliged the enemy to retreat; notwithstanding their great superiority."[135] One 1759 ballad, so taken with Admiral Sir Edward Hawke's victory at Quiberon Bay and other naval glories, declared that Neptune must have resigned his throne to George II.[136] This victory—along with later major victories of the French Revolutionary and Napoleonic Wars—relied on the aggressive tactic of breaking the line of battle that the authoritarian whig Admiralty under the leadership of Bedford, Sandwich, and Anson had been the first to support.[137] These successes were not simply based on the number of ships at sea or upon diplomatic changes: the Seven Years' War was indeed fought in a different diplomatic alignment, but continental diplomacy could not force officers to fight when previously they had not.[138] Commanders increasingly risked their fleets against superior forces and chased enemies into dangerous shoals, rocky bays, or uncharted waters rather than back down. Officers found themselves subjected to the authoritarian whig system of punishment and reward based on their successes or failures. In a later battle, Pocock was less pleased with the conduct of three of his captains, whom he believed had failed to engage the enemy with sufficient aggression; he ordered a court-martial to judge their behavior. Two were dismissed from the service and the third was put ashore, "sentenced to lose one year's rank as a post-captain." Pocock characterized aggression in battle as "the most material part of the duty [officers] owe to his Majesty and their country."[139] In contrast to this punishment for failure, Henry Osborn—another authoritarian whig officer—granted Lieutenant Carkett the command of a ship for his bravery, as an example to others.[140] As Clive Wilkinson has explained, not just officers but also "administrators at all levels found themselves working within an environment . . . in which they were increasingly accountable, to the Admiralty, for the discharging of their various duties."[141]

Historians of the navy have identified this commitment to aggressive leadership as a hallmark of British naval culture from midcentury. J. R. Jones argues that the navy became "a decisive instrument of power" in British warfare in the years 1757–1763, "when aggressive leadership (above all, that of Hawke) brought devastating successes."[142] N. A. M. Rodger argues, "It is an undoubted fact that British ships, collectively and individually, were during the Seven Years' War conspicuously better handled and better fought than their enemies'."[143] He highlights "developments in professional competence" as an explanation for Britain's "triumph in the Seven Years' War, after so many disappointments before," though he believes these came from uncontroversial practical experience.[144] Brian Lavery concurs that a "new spirit had been produced among naval officers, which had induced Hawke to place his fleet in great hazard in following the French into Quiberon Bay, whereas one of his predecessors would probably have waited outside, or abandoned the chase." Lavery suggests that these were the years when the Navy was transformed "into a devastating fighting force, which Nelson was to use even more effectively." Byng's court-martial and execution acted as a stark reminder to naval officers that real consequences might await them at home should they fail to fight the war aggressively abroad. It warned that "failure would not be tolerated or excused."[145] Byng was the son of a war hero himself. He was rich and well connected. If he could be executed, anyone could be. Byng's court-martial certainly left a lasting impression on sea officers and on the political world more generally: after being a frequent reference point in the 1778 debates over whether Augustus Keppel had done his utmost against the French in the Battle of Ushant, Byng continued to surface in parliamentary debate years later. In a 1788 debate over the promotion of sea officers, many in the opposition accused the authoritarian whig Admiralty of corruption; Edward Loveden suggested that Admiral Howe, the First Lord of the Admiralty, might not have been corrupt but certainly had exercised bad judgment, and "begged to know if error in judgment was nothing? For what was admiral Byng condemned and executed?"[146] Later histories continued to remind readers of his execution.[147] Byng surfaced again in 1808, when General John Whitelocke was court-martialed and found guilty of not having done his utmost to retake Buenos Aires. In Isaac Cruikshank's print *The Ghost of Byng* (Figure 4.2), Byng protests that Whitelocke, who has "caused the death of thousands," has been "suffered to escape."

The patriots did not give up the fight against professional, disciplined militaries following their defeat on the issue of the 1749 Navy Bill. Their opposition to Byng's court-martial was evidence of that, as were their serious and genuine attempts to create a legitimate alternative to a standing army via the militia. Though the patriots failed to roll back the professionalizing reforms taking place in the navy, they did find opportunities during the Seven Years' War to advocate for their own military systems. Patriotism argued that citizens should have the right to participate in the military life of the nation as free men, not just as externally controlled and disciplined soldiers. Likewise, citizens should have the right to participate in the political life of the nation as free men, not just as ministerial lackeys and sycophants. The patriots' opposition to naval professionalization and discipline, their support of a militia, and their support of and engagement in privateering were military issues, but they were also entangled with domestic political matters. The more control the public had over the military, the more they could use it for their own aggressive war aims and the less opportunity an unfriendly administration would have to suppress that war. The patriots hoped to win an overseas empire that would crush French power forever. This empire would be based on a citizenry that, because the people were internally regulated and disciplined, had no need of external regulation or disciplining.

The Seven Years' War was an opportunity for the patriots, finally in the ascendant, to offer their military alternative. The war resulted from

Figure 4.2. Isaac Cruikshank, *The Ghost of Byng,* etching, 1808. Reproduction © The Trustees of the British Museum (Museum Number: 1868,0808.7631).

a long-term ongoing commitment from those interested in colonial expansion, but the reactions in the public imagination to Byng's court-martial revealed the rifts and uncertainties that lay at the heart of Britain's imperial project. These questions would become more visible still during discussions over how the expanded empire would be governed in the years before the American Revolution.

5

THE AUTHORITARIAN NAVY AND THE CRISIS OF EMPIRE

IN 1732 THE *New England Weekly Journal* informed its readers that "It is a just and a laudable thing for the people to contribute largely and voluntarily to the public necessities, such as the improving and supporting their fortifications, the supplying of their magazines with arms, ammunition and all the necessary implements of war, and the augmenting and keeping in good order their Navy."[1] By the mid-1760s, this feeling of goodwill had largely evaporated. Merchants in Rhode Island and Boston entered into agreements not to employ sailors who had previously enlisted on naval ships, and crowds often abused local American pilots who cooperated with the Royal Navy. Sea officers were arrested and at times assaulted for carrying out their orders; a Rhode Island mob took over Fort George in Narragansett Bay and fired on a naval ship engaged in policing revenue laws.[2] In the words of Congregationalist minister John Lathrop, the officers of the Royal Navy were no better than "the King's pirates."[3] In the East Indies, a similar shift took place, while in contrast Caribbean planters began to beg for a permanent naval presence.

Why did the Royal Navy become a source of resentment in some parts of the colonial periphery after the Seven Years' War, at the same time as its ships were becoming perceived as essential in other regions? In both imperial and domestic British historiography, historians describe a transformation toward the end of the eighteenth century from a more relaxed, hands-off approach to governance to a more restrictive and hierarchical model. What has not been agreed on is when the turning point occurred. One argument is that conflict motivated the move to a more disciplined, hierarchical empire: the shift toward authoritarianism happened in the 1780s or later, as a reaction either to the loss of the American colonies or to the stresses of the French Revolutionary wars.[4] A variant of this argument suggests that the move toward a more authoritarian imperial relationship did take place during the 1760s, but it was a reaction to the actions of the American colonists rather than a cause of it.[5] In contrast, a second school of thought argues that the move to a more centrally controlled empire and more strictly controlled domestic sphere predated eighteenth-century imperial conflict, rather than being its outcome. One interpretation identifies the Seven Years' War as the transformative moment for the empire, either by creating new problems—whether of governance or finance—that necessitated new solutions,[6] or by creating a consensus among the political classes that there was a preexisting problem of authority in the empire.[7] The second variation of this focuses on the accession of George III to the throne in 1760. Unlike his Hanoverian predecessors, George III offered a sympathetic ear to authoritarian, paternalist language and attitudes, which was visible in religious doctrine, political theory, the law, and other areas of society.[8] George III's accession changed which political groups had access to power and which methods of governance were deemed acceptable at the highest levels.

The ascension of George III made possible a fundamental shift in domestic politics and instigated a new attempt to reshape the nature of British imperial relations. However, neither George III's accession nor the Seven Years' War created the impulse toward tighter imperial control from scratch. Some of the most important groundwork had been laid in the 1740s by authoritarian whigs in the Admiralty, at the same time as an authoritarian whig in the Board of Trade commenced serious efforts to restructure imperial relationships along more centralized, hierarchical lines. Changing circumstances—new political priorities at the top and the perception of a growing threat of radicalism both at home and abroad—allowed the authoritarian impulse to reach full fruition in the 1760s. The naval professionalization of the 1740s made this imperial reform actually possible. For the first time Britain had the coercive power to exert itself effectively in the colonies. Many of the same people who supported the original professionalization project also supported the restructuring of imperial relationships, which operated along similar lines: more rationalization, less room for discretion, more obedience, greater hierarchy. In the 1740s the Earl of Halifax, an authoritarian whig, tried to tighten imperial governance at the same time as authoritarian whigs tightened governance over the navy, but he was unsuccessful owing to a lack of coercive power in the colonies and a lack of political commitment to the project at home. Now that political will existed and the coercive power had been created. This coercive power included an army in the American colonies, but it also included the Royal Navy. The navy was in many ways a more effective tool than the army in terms of policing trade and enforcing revenue measures, as so much of American trade was waterborne.

The shifting dynamics of Britain's imperial relationships in the 1760s cannot be understood without understanding the role of the Royal Navy. The navy was at the forefront of the struggle to impose greater governance over the imperial world. Additionally, it was implicated in many of the constitutional debates that echoed throughout the empire. The British ministry began to use the navy in exactly the ways that patriots had warned, for purposes that were (some argued) intended to extend the power of the executive government over civilian liberties. The navy became the representative of the central government's increasingly visible policy in the North American colonies and in India; radical colonists critiqued it as being an exemplar of the arbitrary, militarized policies they claimed the central administration wanted to impose. The Seven Years' War tested the reformed navy, proved its efficacy, and provided a surfeit of service-hardened officers at the Admiralty's disposal. Throughout the empire, imperial subjects recognized sea officers as some of the foremost representatives of centralized state power, while ministers depended on officers' loyalty and mobility to carry their authority to the far corners of the world.

The Political Divide in the Anglo-Imperial World

Authoritarian whiggery and patriotism maintained their positions at the center of the ideological battleground in late eighteenth-century Anglo-imperial politics.[9] Although both underwent changes in the years after the Seven Years' War, the fundamental bases underpinning each remained consistent from the 1740s through the American Revolution. Authoritarian whigs became increasingly convinced that many parts of global British society were barely one step removed from open rebellion and took increasingly strong stances against disorder for that reason. Patriotism's call to cleanse the political system of corruption morphed into Wilkite radicalism's demand for genuine reform of the structures of political authority. As is to be expected over a span of thirty years, some of the individuals involved changed and some changed sides. The authoritarian whiggery of the 1770s was not identical to that of the 1740s, nor was 1770s radicalism identical to 1740s patriotism, but in both cases there were strong ideological continuities.

Between the 1740s and the 1760s, some proponents of patriotism became increasingly radical and found a voice both in John Wilkes and in the Dissenting pulpit. Radicals were drawn from similar sectors of society as the patriots—smaller merchants, tradespeople, and Dissenters.[10] They were generally invested in commerce and increasingly taking part in the consumer revolution which swept Britain.[11] Though the Wilkite radicals put forward a more extreme agenda than the patriots of the 1740s, they continued to perceive similar problems and their solutions were based on similar rationales. As John Brewer has argued, "Fear of a powerful and corrupt government, fear for the rights of dissenting Protestants, a desire to harness or apprehend the powerful economic forces in the Anglophone world were the mainsprings of radical politics," just as they were for the patriotism of the 1740s.[12] Radicals took the patriot idea that the people needed to be regularly involved in Parliament one step further, arguing that MPs were not just representatives using their best judgment but factotums directly answerable to the electorate. Like patriots, radicals opposed placemen and advocated for more frequent elections, but they emphasized to an even greater degree the importance of popular participation, contractarian government, and the independence of the elector.[13] The radicalism of the 1760s and 1770s was not a fundamentally different ideology from the patriotism of the 1740s: radicalism followed the same logic as patriot reasoning and rhetoric but pushed that logic further. What distinguished these radicals from previous reformers was "their ruthless determination that the old shibboleth, that all Englishmen enjoyed certain rights and liberties under the law . . . should be more than a hoary cliché"; their readiness to try to force these reforms "made them radical and threatening."[14] Throughout the middle decades of the eighteenth century, patriots and radicals argued in favor of a more egalitarian society in which authority was more widely vested and a greater number of independent individuals were able to participate in commercial opportunities.

This radical critique of a government perceived to be nonrepresentative and inexorably encroaching on liberties and rights spanned the Atlantic.[15] Bernard Bailyn argues that a large part of colonial American society was educated in the Commonwealth Whig tradition, in which Parliament's rights were limited by common law and the customary rights of the people. Liberty naturally resided in the people, while power naturally resided in the government and inevitably attempted to expand its bounds. Thus, government was inherently a threat to liberty.[16] American radicals found few consistent friends in Parliament. The followers of William Pitt (now the Earl of Chatham) and Lord Temple were the most sympathetic to the radical cause. They opposed the use of general warrants, the Stamp Act, and the use of force in the American colonies.[17] If they had few allies in the British Parliament, however, Americans nevertheless found many in wider global British society: there was significant division within the British population over whether to treat the Americans with coercion or conciliation. Many patriots and radicals believed they were joined in a struggle that stretched across the empire and offered their allegiances accordingly. For example, James Kelly describes Irish patriot and MP Edward Newenham as "a keen supporter of Wilkes and the American colonists, whose wordy commentaries proffered an idealized vision of the balanced Protestant constitution in which the liberties of the people were protected by responsive MPs."[18] Americans acknowledged this perceived common cause by continuing to import Irish goods in the 1760s even when they were boycotting goods from the rest of Britain.[19]

In the 1760s authoritarian whiggery became more clearly articulated and more widely persuasive. Outside Parliament, the majority of its support continued to come from gentlemen, clergy, and the professional class.[20] Leaders such as Bedford, Sandwich, and Halifax were joined by a new generation such as Thomas Thynne, Third Viscount Weymouth, Wills Hill, Earl of Hillsborough, Charles Townshend, and Lord Frederick North, as well as by previous opponents such as George Grenville, who split with William Pitt over the issues of debt, disorder, and growing radicalism. Authoritarian whigs were emboldened by the sympathetic ear of George III to take ever-stronger stances in favor of hierarchical obedience as a bulwark against disorder.[21] They believed, for example, that the repeal of the Stamp Act would end the British Empire in America, by not only rewarding "open rebellion" but allowing the colonies to overthrow their hierarchical relationship with the British parliament.[22] Their experiences within Britain and the wider empire helped convince them that the breakdown of societal order was upon them. Bedford had already seen Dublin erupt in riots in 1759. In 1765 he found his house in Bloomsbury besieged by disgruntled silk weavers, which he declared to be "open rebellion"; Secretaries of State Sandwich and Halifax supported using the military to quell the disturbance.[23] Richard Rigby, Bedford's manager in the House of Commons, claimed the British "are become a disgrace to civil society. Would to God! the government of it was in such hands as would risk anything rather than permit the mob to lord it over us in this manner"; he thought he would live to see the mob "[kick] both Houses of Parliament down stairs."[24] William Knox articulated some of the perceived remedies for this disorder. Knox had spent five years in colonial government in Georgia and returned convinced that the democratic nature of colonial constitutions "excluded all Ideas of Subordination and Dependance," threatening to bring the entire imperial system crashing down. His solutions entailed creating a colonial aristocracy, establishing the hierarchical Church of England in North America (because as long as "Every Man [is] allowed to be his own Pope, he becomes disposed to wish to be his own King"), and eliminating the colonial militias in favor of relying on the "King's Troops, Ships & Forts" for protection. He promoted policies like these as undersecretary of state for the colonies in North's administration from 1770 to 1782.[25]

Authoritarian whigs were among the most vocal opponents of domestic political reform; in return, radicals burned Sandwich and Halifax in effigy.[26] Responding to petitions for political and economic reform, North declared that he could "never acquiesce in the absurd opinion that all men are equal."[27] Grenville and Townshend were the architects of Britain's new imperial program of political and financial control following the Seven Years' War. Bedford, Sandwich, Halifax, and Grenville formed an alliance on the American question, and both Bedford and Grenville reiterated in negotiations with other politicians that they were unwilling to compromise on a strong American policy.[28] From the 1740s to the 1770s, authoritarian whiggery called for restoring order in the Anglo-Atlantic politically, economically, and imperially by reinforcing a more strictly hierarchical society in which fewer people had access to authority or could participate in the rituals and structures of society at the higher levels.

Naval Regulation of Trade and the Policing of the American Colonies

Following the peace of 1763, ministers in London enacted a new program of imperial legislation—characterized by but not limited to the Stamp Act of 1765, the Townshend Acts of 1767, and the Coercive Acts of 1774—designed to bring the American colonies into a more obedient, financially extractive relationship with the metropole. That many American colonists felt increasingly angry with the central British administration on the basis of this legislation is hardly news, but why was the navy targeted? Two broad understandings of the causes of the American Revolution can be extracted from the wealth of writing on the subject. One major strand of interpretation, which might be labeled the whig account, argues that the conflict was about constitutional issues and the development of two mutually incompatible political cultures on either side of the Atlantic. The navy, however, was constitutionally unassailable as the defender of the nation's liberties.[29] A second major strand of interpretation, which might be labeled the progressive account, privileges economic self-interest over ideology. In one variation of this view, the catalysts for revolution were economic change and local socioeconomic clashes. In a second variation, colonists mustered constitutional arguments to disguise basic self-interest: they simply did not want to pay more taxes. After 1763 the navy enforced customs collection, drawing it into the imperial crisis, but the colonists would have resented whatever organization collected taxes—they had no particular animus against the navy for its own sake. This is the argument put forward by Neil R. Stout in the most comprehensive work discussing the navy's role in the American colonies after the Seven Years' War, as well as by James Volo.[30] In both of these broadly grouped interpretations, the navy was peripheral to the real sources of the dispute; it was implicated in a wider imperial struggle but not a source of resentment in and of itself.

In recent years some historians have moved beyond the whig and progressive paradigms to consider other aspects of the Revolution, such as the role of the military or, more specifically, the role of the military in connection with emotions or cities in the movement toward open conflict.[31] Each of these accounts adds something important to any understanding of the role of the British military in the outbreak of the Revolution, but each also has a crucial oversight: the military is represented only by the army.[32] The importance of port cities in the development of revolutionary sentiment and the coercive influence the navy was able to exercise over those cities and their hinterlands suggest a potential connection between this naval coercion and the development of American radicalism which needs to be taken seriously.

The Royal Navy was on the front lines of the imperial conflict between Britain and its American colonists. Its officers took on an increasingly large role in the implementation of new customs and revenue laws and in supporting faltering civil authority. There had been conflicts between colonists and the sea service prior to 1763—impressment was frequently contentious, for example—but resentment and resistance were local and occasional rather than sustained or systemic, largely because when a bureau of the colonial administration enacted an unpopular provision, neither the higher levels of the ministry nor the Hanoverian kings had the willpower to enforce the measure.[33] In 1763 that situation changed because, for the first time, sea officers were disciplined enough to carry out their orders regardless of resistance and the imperial administration was unwilling, at the highest levels, to back down. The navy was at the heart of the imperial maelstrom because it benefited financially from resurrected commercial regulations; it represented, in the very character and spirit of its officers, a sociopolitical system that both American and British radicals rejected; and it policed the contested endeavors of waterborne trade and smuggling.

One example of the navy's involvement in the imperial crisis of the 1760s was as an intended beneficiary of regulation. Stephen Conway has recently argued that one of the key provisions in the Navigation Acts—that goods be carried on British ships, thus creating a pool of experienced seamen on which the navy could draw—was perceived as so central to maintaining British naval power that Grenville, North, and their associates believed it was worth going to war with the colonies to uphold the acts.[34] During his ministerial leadership, Grenville passed several controversial measures, including the expansion of the customs service and the vice admiralty courts in the colonies, new taxes such as the Stamp Act, and also revitalized old measures that had long lain dormant, such as the 1733 Molasses Act. The revenues resulting from these measures were intended to pay off the debt from the Seven Years' War—including the costs of naval warfare—but they would also pay for the very military forces used to enforce their collection. One example was the resurrection of the Six Penny Duty, which Parliament enacted in a series of laws between 1696 and 1711 and expanded to the American colonies in 1729; it obligated every sailor on a British-owned vessel to pay sixpence monthly for the benefit of Greenwich Hospital, which cared for elderly and infirm sailors of the Royal Navy. Massachusetts fishermen protested against the 1729 act and by the 1760s it often went uncollected.[35] Henry Hulton, the principal deputy receiver of the Six Penny Duty, advocated using naval ships to inspect merchant vessels on the high seas for proof of their payment of the duty. Those working under his supervision expanded the range of the duty to include new classes of people, such as enslaved sailors in the south and fishermen in the north.[36] Hulton received a petition from the fishermen of Salem, Marblehead, and other Massachusetts towns that warned that "the revival of this demand, which may be said to be in some measure obsolete, tends to increase the discontents in the minds of his Majesty's subjects in America." Hulton dismissed their concerns, arguing that if these fishermen were exempted then customs would be obligated to exempt others who had already acquiesced. Moreover, he believed the colonists "do not seem to question its authority, but plead long indulgence, and are persuaded that it is the intention of Government that they should be winked at."[37] He believed imperial administrators had spent too long asking "How shall we extend our commerce?" rather than "How shall we support our authority?," but the time had come to reverse that.[38] The Six Penny Duty was not a new creation, but it was one which had not been possible to collect effectively previously. A professional naval presence changed that.

Like the Six Penny Duty, the White Pines Act was another old law intended for the support of the navy revived by the Grenville administration. Shipwrights used white pines for masts on naval ships. Originally enacted in 1711, the White Pines Act created a crown monopoly on all white pine trees, preventing individuals from logging the American forests. Even if the land did move into private hands, the trees still could not be cut down without a royal license.[39] Violations of the act were tried in courts of vice admiralty. Colonists claimed that this was an unnecessary monopoly, as there were more than enough white pines to satisfy the needs of both the navy and private enterprise, and they ignored and resisted the act. Given this initial colonial resistance and a lack of dependable officers in the American colonies, administrators did not regularly enforce the White Pines Act until after the Seven Years' War. The shift of naval forces to American waters increased dependence on American masts as opposed to Baltic naval stores. This new need for American-grown masts combined with the Grenville administration's desire to bring the empire into greater compliance with British law spurred the resurgence in enforcement.[40] The costs of naval upkeep were part of the financial burden the central administration asked colonists to share.

The navy was also involved in the imperial crisis as a point of constitutional debate, particularly in regard to the dangers of overextending the power of the executive branch and, as a corollary, about to what extent it was appropriate for the executive to intervene in the everyday lives of citizens. Colonists did not resist the navy purely because they resented taxation, which is clear given that arguments against a professional navy began as early as the end of the seventeenth century and continued into the new American Republic. American newspapers across the mainland colonies published the writings of libertarians John Trenchard and Thomas Gordon, who emphasized the dangerously corrupting nature of power. Trenchard argued in the late seventeenth century that nations could only remain free if they did not arm "any who had not an interest in preserving the public peace, who fought *pro aris & focis* [for hearth and home], and thought themselves sufficiently paid by repelling invaders"—in other words, by not arming any who fought for money. He acknowledged the argument that "the officers of our fleet may be corrupted" and offered the militia as an alternative solution to a standing army or navy.[41] Captain Peter Warren's 1745 comment regarding New England colonists indicates the extent to which these ideas had gained currency in colonial society: "as they have the highest notions of the rights and liberties of Englishmen, and indeed are almost Levellers, they must . . . be treated in a manner that few military-bred gentlemen would condescend to."[42] Twenty years later, the radical newspaper *Newport Mercury* called sea officers "this set of Myrmedons," a classical reference to the followers of Achilles that by the eighteenth century had come to mean not just a loyal entourage but also hired ruffians.[43] Radicals strongly emphasized the importance of independence from another's control, which a professional officer could not have.[44] The rigid hierarchical structure of a professional military, in which all inferiors owed obedience to all superiors and a coercive discipline was implemented from above, was antithetical to the sociopolitical views of radicals on both sides of the Atlantic. As the authoritarian whigs removed the navy from parliamentary interference and thus placed the sea force more in the hands of the ministerial executive than ever, they fulfilled radicals' preexisting fears about a professional military: divorced from civilian life, slavishly obedient, subordinated to power.

Moreover, the navy's new role as the police force of colonial trade implicated it in a number of other ongoing constitutional battles. "An Act for the further Improvement of His Majesty's Revenue of Customs," instigated while Grenville was First Lord of the Admiralty, recognized the Royal Navy as an acceptable branch of customs enforcement.[45] This act was received with "consternation" in Boston, and the *Boston Gazette* immediately challenged the use of the navy to police civilians, asking, "Are the gentlemen of the Navy judges of the nature of commerce and the liberty of the subject?"[46] Merchants assumed the involvement of sea officers meant customs laws would be more strictly enforced and this rigor of enforcement more than the actual financial burden inspired resentment in many.[47] Indeed, Alexander Colvill, Lord Colville, the naval commander in chief of the North American station, immediately informed his subordinate captains that "the prevention of illicit trade is one of the principal duties of your station."[48] British administrators and colonial radicals held different definitions of "illicit," however. Many radicals argued that restricting trade violated the rights of personal property by limiting where and how people could dispose of their property.[49] A Boston town meeting of June 1768 argued that the "fresh arrival of ships of war" would be "a still severer restraint upon our trade," and a published message to Massachusetts governor Francis Bernard listed the presence of a ship of war in Boston Harbor as one of the town's two major grievances.[50] The radical *Massachusetts Spy* called naval ships "p–r–t–c–l [piratical]" and suggested it was "a little below his [Britannic] Majesty to keep men of war employed in robbing some of the poorest subjects."[51] Several radical papers printed a piece in 1773 that, after reporting the movements of several ships of war, concluded, "What a pity it is, that a certain class of mankind can't find better employ, than that of Preying on the *industrious* part of their fellow-creatures!!!"[52]

Aside from the question of whether the central administration had the right to regulate American trade, there was also the question of the specific methods it employed in doing so. General warrants, which allowed searches and arrests to be made without having to specify the individuals to whom the warrant applied, became a major issue in Britain following the arrest of John Wilkes as the author of *North Briton* no. 45. These general warrants were also granted to sea officers to search and seize ships and smuggled goods; in some cases, American lawyers used the issue of general warrants to discredit sea officers in court. After a ship's seizure, its owners were tried without a jury in vice admiralty courts—courts technically under the authority of the Admiralty, with equal rather than subordinate jurisdiction to common-law courts.[53] Thus, from the point of view of radicals, the navy used illegal warrants to try civilians in unconstitutional courts in the name of illegitimately enacted trade laws.[54] This state of affairs seemed to validate the belief that a professional standing military would lead to the extension of military justice over civilians, as patriots alleged against the authoritarian whig Admiralty in the 1740s. Arthur Lee, an American in Britain, published a pamphlet arguing that naval regulation of trade led to smuggling far more than it prevented it. He claimed that "every officer of the Navy having a revenue commission subjects trading vessels to be perpetually stopped, searched, insulted, and sometimes plundered, so as to distress and impede trade as much as human invention or malignity can contrive"; the "inevitable consequence of these severities and restraints is, to compel the people to turn smugglers."[55] But it was not simply an economic matter: he also protested that the military had been elevated above the civil in the colonies, that naval commanders in chief were superior to civil governments in peacetime, and that the military interfered in the everyday affairs of civilians. Lee compared the current situation in the American colonies with the extraction of ship money in the 1630s, which spurred discontent in the years prior to the English Civil War. This reference clearly implied that open warfare was nearly at hand and that it would be justified against an encroaching executive power.[56]

These fears regarding the undermining of common law were reiterated in the context of the 1773 royal commission created to investigate the burning of the *Gaspee*. In 1772 a mob headed by the leading merchants of Providence lured the *Gaspee* aground, burning it and shooting its commander, Lieutenant William Dudingston, before arresting him.[57] A letter published in the *Providence Gazette* claimed that Dudingston's behavior "was so *piratical* and provoking, that Englishmen could not patiently bear it."[58] British colonial officials agreed that this attack had been prompted by Dudingston's commitment to regulating smuggling.[59] The ministry response to the incident was shaped by John Pownall, co-undersecretary of state for the colonies alongside Knox and also closely associated with the authoritarian whigs. He later was influential in closing Boston Harbor following the Tea Party. Distrusting local American magistrates, the British ministry appointed a royal commission of inquiry that consisted of the governor of Rhode Island, several chief justices from neighboring colonies, a judge of the Admiralty, and Admiral John Montagu (by virtue of his position as naval commander in chief of North America). Montagu was a cousin of the Earl of Sandwich and had overseen Admiral John Byng's execution; Sandwich, from 1770 once again First Lord of the Admiralty, had chosen Montagu for the position of commander in chief, possibly in part because Sandwich disapproved of the previous commander's conciliatory efforts toward colonists and expected Montagu to take a harder line.[60] Radical colonists alleged that this commission, combined with the threat that the involved parties would be transported to London for trial, violated their constitutional liberties by bypassing the right to a trial by a jury of their peers. The *Massachusetts Spy* asked, "Can any one hear of troops and ships of war posting from one part of the continent to the other—Governors, Admirals and Custom-House Officers parading from colony to colony, subjecting the inhabitants to trial, without Juries . . . or what is worse, if possible, transporting them beyond the seas, and think himself secure in the enjoyment of his natural and constitutional rights!"[61] Samuel Adams called the commission a "court of inquisition, more horrid than that of Spain and Portugal," adding that the current methods of trade policing were "more unjustifiable than highway robbery."[62] The *Newport Mercury* claimed the commission was "a general warrant of the worst kind."[63] Similar sentiments were voiced from other sources across New England.

For both administrators in London and radicals in the colonies, the burning of the *Gaspee* helped crystallize what was at stake. One of the best-selling pamphlets of the prerevolutionary era justified the attack on the ship: "if there is any law broke, it is this, that the Gaspee Schooner, by the power of the English ministry and admiralty have broke the laws, and taken away the rights of the Americans." The author continued, "The King's Ministry and Parliament must be rebels, to God and mankind, in attempting to overthrow, (by guns, by swords, by the power of war) the laws, and government of Rhode-Island."[64] John Adams, in discussing the *Gaspee* commission, concluded that "there was no more justice left in Britain than there was in Hell" and that he "wished for war."[65] Though some pamphlets and newspapers justified the attack—colonists defending disorder frequently claimed that military or naval forces deliberately provoked them in order to justify a draconian reaction—official statements from colonial councils usually did not.[66] They generally disavowed the attack while still claiming it had been provoked and that the response was unwarranted. Newport pastor Ezra Stiles, previously accused of inciting violence against the local stamp collector, wrote to a correspondent that "no one justifies the burning of the Gaspee. But no one ever thought of such a thing as being treason."[67] One of the commissioners in the inquiry later claimed that the "whole continent was alarmed" at the reaction to the burning of the *Gaspee* and that they nearly "rushed into rebellion 3 years before they did."[68] *Gaspee* became a watchword for the colonial struggle. The *Essex Gazette* asserted that if the ministry tried to land tea in Boston in 1773, "it will be reshipped on board the LIBERTY, and sent to GASPEE, the first favourable wind and weather," referring to the *Liberty* as another royal ship (previously seized from Boston merchant John Hancock and repurposed as a customs vessel) that colonists attacked and burned.[69] The ministerial response to the *Gaspee* incident used the same tactics—sidestepping common-law courts, issuing general warrants, and giving military officers authority over civilians—that already agitated radicals.

The *Gaspee* incident was the most widely publicized attack on a naval vessel, but not the only one. At a minimum, vessels, officers, or sailors were also attacked in Massachusetts, New York, and South Carolina, as well as on previous occasions in Rhode Island.[70] The *Newport Mercury* called sea officers "those pimping R[oya]ls, those locusts of America" and encouraged its readers to "receive them in such a manner as they shall think the nature of their errand demands."[71] At least some American radicals heeded this call, especially in Rhode Island, which was consistently hostile to sea officers. Since it was also one of the most democratic colonies—the governor was elected on a yearly basis rather than being appointed by the Crown—Rhode Islanders' resentment only seemed to confirm suspicions that lack of hierarchy led to anarchy. One sea officer associated with the authoritarian whigs called the Rhode Islanders "cunning, deceitful, and selfish" and their magistrates "partial and corrupt" and concluded that this was "principally owing to their form of government."[72] Chief Justice of New Jersey Frederick Smyth, a loyalist, agreed that popular government was undermining justice and order in Rhode Island, as did Daniel Horsmanden, Chief Justice of New York. Horsmanden asserted that Rhode Island's "government (if it deserves that name), it is a downright democracy; the Governor a mere nominal one."[73]

The radicals' frequent use of the word "pirate" was in and of itself significant. Before the authoritarian whig reforms reestablished naval discipline, one frequent criticism was that the officers of the navy "seem to act more like privateers" than like military officers interested in the public good.[74] Though the difference between a pirate and a privateer may seem negligible to a modern sensibility, in the eighteenth century it was much more significant. Privateers, licensed by their home governments, acted with legitimate authority; pirates did not. American colonists privateered extensively and certainly understood the difference.[75] Censuring sea officers as pirates rather than privateers, as earlier criticisms had done, made the claim that sea officers acted without legitimate authority for their actions. For radical colonists, the military became inherently illegitimate once it attempted to enforce governance on civilians.

What quickly became clear was that the Royal Navy was one of the most effective mechanisms the central imperial government had for attempting to impose its will on the colonies. Naval enforcement of imperial legislation continued even in the face of colonial resistance, which made it both a crucial support of central authority and an impetus for colonial unification. Of the twenty largest cities in British America in 1775, nineteen were port cities, dependent on commerce, sustenance, and communication from the seas: the easiest way to influence those populations was likewise from the sea.[76] A 1763 Treasury memo to the Privy Council explained the importance of naval involvement to Grenville's American plans, arguing that it was "the likeliest means for accomplishing these great purposes" and adding that the Treasury "earnestly wish, that the same may not only be continued, but even extended and strengthened as far as the naval establishment will allow."[77] These hopes proved to be justified, as the navy was crucial in enforcing the Sugar Act. In New York, for example, it intercepted all incoming vessels, forcing merchant vessels to unload at the customhouse or not at all. Later, a little more than half of all American seizures made from September 1767 to January 1775 came from the Royal Navy. Ships could be more mobile than a regiment, their occupants did not need to be quartered, and they presented a more impregnable front (though individual sailors and officers still offered vulnerable targets). The navy was far better suited for the task of trade regulation than any regiment, and some merchants believed it to be more effective than the customs in preventing illicit trade. Those who sided with London in the colonial dispute often called for greater naval intervention as a solution to perceived problems. As the situation worsened in the Americas, the navy acted as a bastion of civil and central authority. The qualities radicals feared in a professional military were indeed what made the navy more effective than other means of exerting colonial authority.[78] Unlike the previous authoritarian whig imperial reforms of the 1740s, which failed in part because of a lack of coercive power in the colonies, the reforms of the 1760s actually succeeded in threatening colonial autonomy. In part this effectiveness stemmed from new parameters within British politics, but it also depended on the new coercive power that sea officers wielded. Without the tools to actually implement new policies, no philosophical shift could have been realized.

Both merchants and customs officials recognized the navy's potency in shutting down illicit trade. In 1773 the merchants of Dartmouth claimed that "the seizures made [in Newfoundland] for 3 or 4 years past . . . were mostly made by the Governor [who in Newfoundland was always a sea officer] or other commanders of the ships of war, and not by the Customhouse officers."[79] In 1764 Lieutenant Thomas Allen arrived in Casco Bay, Maine, to find "the business of the Customhouse in the greatest confusion, vessels arriving & sailing daily without paying any regard to the regulations lately established." The customs officer either could not or would not stop these vessels, but Allen did.[80] The navy offered more authority and more firepower than customs in trying to overawe colonists, leading some customs officials to request naval support in their efforts.[81] Naval ships had a physical range that customs vessels did not. Smuggling vessels could no longer count on being able to slip in and out of the coast unregulated but would also have to be lucky enough to evade all of His Majesty's ships at sea.[82]

The navy also supported imperial authority by deploying the threat of violence. The ships of the Royal Navy had often been described as floating fortresses, but there was nothing to say that their guns would always be pointed outward toward the open sea. The imposition of the Townshend Acts in 1767 caused serious unrest in Boston. At that time, Governor Francis Bernard said "he believe[d] the *Romney* prevented rebellion," and Joseph Harrison, the Boston collector of customs, thought the town had been brought back into line more by the presence of ships of war than by the eventual presence of soldiers.[83] Colonists were conscious that harbors with naval ships could quickly transform from fortresses to prisons, and the emphasis on imprisonment or garrisoning was clear in accounts of naval ships in American harbors. In his celebration of the burning of the *Gaspee,* preacher John Allen explained that colonists had "burnt their prison."[84] During the unrest over the Townshend Acts, one correspondent reported, "We now behold Boston surrounded at a time of profound peace, with about 14 ships of war, with springs on their cables, and their broad sides to the town!"[85] In June 1768 the *Romney* assisted in seizing a vessel belonging to Boston patriot John Hancock and in doing so sparked a riot. In the aftermath a Boston town meeting claimed that the *Romney,* in order "to over-awe and terrify the inhabitants of this town into base compliances and unlimited submission, has been anchored within a cable's length of the wharves."[86] In January 1773 two radical newspapers reported that the harbor of Newport "is now *guarded* by the Mercury man of war, Capt. Keeler, of 24 guns, the Arethusa frigate, Captain Hammond, of 26 guns, the Lizard frigate, Capt. English, of 28 guns, the ship Swan, Capt. Ayscough, of 20 guns; and the Halifax schooner, Capt. Crispin."[87] The same ironic emphasis was given to an account from Boston in 1773: "We have now, *only* his Majesty's Ships Fowey, Swan, Tartar, Gaspee and Halifax armed Vessels in this Harbour, to protect us from—*ourselves.*"[88] A similar message was conveyed in Paul Revere's 1774 engraving *A View of the Town of Boston with Several Ships of War in the Harbour* (Figure 5.1), which depicted Boston surrounded by armed warships. This image served as the frontispiece to the January 1774 issue of the *Royal American Magazine,* a radical periodical published by Isaiah Thomas, who also published the *Massachusetts Spy.* British radicals shared this perspective on the activities of the navy; the 1774 print *The Able Doctor, or America Swallowing the Bitter Draught* (Figure 5.2) showed authoritarian whigs attempting to force America into compliance. North holds America down and forces tea into her mouth, while the Boston Port Bill peeks out of his pocket. Sandwich is looking up America's skirt, hinting that the navy was less enforcing commercial regulations than it was prying into colonial affairs and forcibly imposing itself on colonial bodies. A man to the right—possibly the Earl of Bute—holds a sword with the inscription "Military Law," while in the background the viewer can see "Boston cannonaded" by naval ships. The navy was a crucial support for ministerial authority in the colonies: colonists believed the ships were present not to maintain legitimate order but to intimidate the unruly into submission. At one point, Montagu wrote to the Admiralty that the colonists were "almost ripe for independence" and that "nothing but the ships prevents their going to greater lengths."[89] Charles Townshend received a proposal suggesting the stationing of a permanent naval force in the Great Lakes to better control Native American communities; one reason why the authoritarian whig Earl of Hillsborough was believed to oppose a new settlement in the Ohio Valley was because he feared that naval ships would no longer be able to regulate colonists once they were too far from the water's edge.[90] Ships could be more mobile than a regiment; they did not need accommodation to be found for them; and they presented a more impregnable front (though individual sailors and officers could still offer vulnerable targets).

Whereas many colonial officials were willing to back down in clashes over imperial legislation, sea officers were less obliging. During the Stamp Act crisis, New York's customhouse, with the knowledge of the governor, decided it was unable to enforce the act. Captain Archibald

Figure 5.1. Paul Revere, *A View of the Town of Boston with Several Ships of War in the Harbour*, engraving, 1774. *Royal American Magazine*, January 1774, opp. 7. Reproduction from The New York Public Library (Image ID: 54194).

Figure 5.2. The Able Doctor, or America Swallowing the Bitter Draught, etching, 1774. Reproduction © The Trustees of the British Museum (Museum Number: 1855,0609.1926).

Kennedy, on the other hand, informed merchants that he would seize any ships that tried to sail with unstamped papers, despite customs officials turning a blind eye. Alexander Lord Colville supported him in this stand, arguing that "a sea officer must be justifiable in endeavouring to defeat the purposes of all such who break the laws on the element he occupies."[91] A similar situation played out in North Carolina.[92] In a parliamentary debate, Halifax declared, "Instead of sending 10,000 men to enforce [the Stamp Act] I've always [believed that] two or three 20 gun-ships properly stationed would enforce it."[93] Beyond New York and North Carolina, sea officers were involved in Stamp Act unrest in Georgia, Maryland, Massachusetts, New Jersey, and Pennsylvania, but no stamps under naval protection were ever destroyed anywhere in America.[94]

In contrast to this reliability, many customs officials were willing to ignore certain practices in return for bribes or gifts. Judges of vice admiralty courts sometimes looked for legal ways to acquit accused merchants. Elected governors, as in Rhode Island, were certainly influenced by the will of their constituents, but even royally appointed governors could collude to protect smugglers. From the beginning, Colville believed the connection of colonial administrators with American society would make the navy's job more difficult. He warned the Secretary of the Admiralty, "Should we prove successful in our pursuit of these enemies to fair trade, it will be very difficult to get the prizes condemned in the Admiralty Courts of New York and New England" because the "judges are generally supposed to be too much interested in the welfare of their neighbours; and the practice of smuggling has become so common, that it almost ceases to be looked upon as criminal or unfair."[95] At times, customs officials and judges of vice admiralty courts actively tried to prevent the navy from carrying out its orders. The judges of the vice admiralty courts refused to accept a parliamentary act that granted a ship's crew a portion of the prize money from a seized vessel, or the subsequent royal proclamation that affirmed it.[96]

Sea officers' steadfastness rested on their independence from the bonds of family, patronage, or salary that tied others to colonial society and on the professionalization carefully cultivated by the Admiralty. This professionalization transformed unreliable and undisciplined officers into officers inculcated with a sense of duty and who had a clear sense of the penalties that awaited them should they fail in that duty.

Indeed, despite his efforts in the Stamp Act crisis, Captain Kennedy found himself accused of not having done his utmost to uphold the law. The Admiralty promptly recalled him to Britain on account of his "lack of zeal for His Majesty's service," where he was court-martialed on the same charge as John Byng had faced a decade earlier: that he, for reason of "cowardice, negligence, or disaffection," did "not do his utmost" for His Majesty's service.[97] Unlike Byng, Kennedy was able to demonstrate his commitment to his duty to the court's satisfaction; he was found innocent and returned to his station. Had he been found guilty, he could have faced the same fate as Byng. Neil Stout suggests that sea officers were not the most rapacious of customs enforcers because if a sea officer behaved badly, that behavior would have a greater negative effect on his career than it would on the career of a customs officer, meaning a sea officer had greater incentive to toe the line. But allowing laws to go unenforced would have negatively affected their futures every bit as much. In contrast, there were no similar clear consequences for failed colonial governors or customs collectors.[98] Colville had an accurate sense of the situation when he observed that "a majority of our provincial councils being either themselves engaged in trade, or nearly connected with others that are, we could expect but little relief from an application to the Governors & Councils even in cases of the greatest exigence."[99]The central colonial administration gave professionalized sea officers the task of policing a civilian population for which they did not necessarily feel an affinity. Psychological and physical distance protected them, as opponents of professionalization originally argued would be the case.

The separation of sea officers from civilian society went hand in hand with naval professionalization, as did the commitment to duty. In the 1720s and 1730s, the British and American public perceived sea officers as lackadaisical in their duty and reluctant to engage in conflict with foreign enemies.[100] The sea officer of the 1760s was made of sterner stuff: the efforts toward professionalization had been ongoing for two decades, and lieutenants and younger captains had been brought up in this culture. Many sea officers and their crews were assaulted in the course of their duties in the colonies, and yet they persisted.[101] The 1757 execution of Admiral Byng for negligence of duty sharply illuminated the consequences of disregarding orders. In response, sea officers took their orders seriously. It was exactly this unwavering commitment that had alarmed opponents of naval reform in the 1740s: they warned of sea officers being compelled to obedience, even if given illegal orders. When the crew of a trading vessel stopped near Boston attacked the naval ship that stopped it, beating and throwing the naval sailors and several officers overboard, one Lieutenant Thompson was obligated to defend himself with his sword against a civilian who had attacked him with a broadax. A warrant was issued for Thompson's arrest, and he fled to England; however, as soon he found out that the man had lived, Thompson "embarked immediately onboard a merchant vessel in order to return to his duty."[102] Patriots had claimed that the naval reforms were intended to "establish a blind and slavish obedience" among sea officers, and argued that officers under the strict discipline of a professional military were unable to consider the legality of the orders they were given: "you are to murder the law, or they to murder you."[103] The consequences of naval professionalization thus linked the 1760s with earlier trends from the 1740s, when the creation of a more authoritarian, obedient navy laid the groundwork for a more authoritarian, obedient empire.

Colonists were fully aware of the navy's frontline role in increasing central governance in the colonies and enforcing greater regulation of trade. They complained that the navy was interrupting legitimate trade, either from overzealousness or as a part of deliberate policy. West India merchants complained to the Treasury in 1763 that "our men of war under the orders they had received from hence to prevent contraband trade, had interrupted our commerce with the Spanish Main" and requested that the Admiralty's orders be reworded so as not to include that legitimate branch of trade.[104] Some viewed the situation in a more sinister fashion than a simple oversight in wording orders. One pamphlet published in the midst of the Stamp Act debates claimed that, fearful of the American colonies' growing strength, Britain had determined to "keep the colonies in that kind of dependence which is occasioned by weakness and poverty, and not in that subordination and obedience which arises from gratitude and the voluntary duties of children to parents." Deliberately disrupting trade was a part of this policy, and it was to this that the American colonists "impute the ruin of the Spanish trade, by the royal navy of Great Britain acting in the spirit of the guarda costas of Spain."[105] The Royal Navy was thus equated with the hated *guarda costas,* whose seizing of British merchant ships had been declared little better than piracy for decades.

The navy's role in enforcing the internal governance of the North American colonies did not bring them into conflict with all colonists, but it did exacerbate the matter with those who were already predisposed to expect tyranny from the government.[106] It would be far too simplistic to suggest that all colonists agreed on what issues were at stake in the arguments with the British ministry or on what the proper solutions were. Just as in Britain, there were divisions within American society, both before and after the Revolution, about what the proper relationship between military and society was. Lawrence Cress argues that American colonists, even the rebellious ones, did not oppose a professional military. They opposed a professional military that was not under the control of their own colonial assemblies.[107] This is partly correct. What this argument ignores, however, are the disputes over military form and service that took place during the Revolution and in the early Republic. For example, in Virginia the minuteman militia failed significantly to attract volunteers, because it was a more ordered, hierarchical replacement for the independent, egalitarian companies that previously existed. Small Virginian farmers cared about the terms on which they would fight the British. In the words of Michael McDonnell, "They desired a more egalitarian distribution of the burden of war, a more democratic and consensual military organization, and equality within the service. When policy makers did not take these considerations into account, ordinary Virginians refused to serve."[108] After the war, there was serious debate over the composition and purpose of the new United States Navy, which broke down along Federalist versus Anti-Federalist lines. The Navalists (who were also the Federalists and included Alexander Hamilton and John Adams) wanted a larger navy that could influence European policy and force Europe to take the United States seriously. The Antinavalists (who were also the Anti-Federalists and included Thomas Jefferson) wanted a "militiaman concept: a few small and relatively weak vessels patrolled far-flung stations while citizens in the homeland remained blissfully confident that, in case of an overt threat, citizen sailors would volunteer in droves to serve aboard makeshift warships or to work the coastal artillery." One Anti-Federalist, William Grayson, argued in the 1788 Virginia ratifying convention that a flaw of the proposed Constitution was that it did not limit the size of the navy to ensure it did not threaten civilian liberties.[109] In the 1790s the clash over naval policy was intense enough that Alexander Hamilton suggested his replacement as Secretary of the Treasury use clandestine extralegal means to appropriate the money to build frigates as a way of circumventing those opposed to a standing navy. The head shipbuilder at the Philadelphia yard feared the frigates already under construction there would be burned by Antinavalists.[110] Clearly, the debate was not simply over whether the American colonists or the British ministry controlled the military force (though having control over the professional military did sway some). The argument was over whether to have a standing, professional navy, and on how that choice might influence the relationship between government and society.

From 1763 the navy was implicated in a series of arguably unconstitutional acts—searching and seizing based on general warrants, trying civilians in courts without a jury, upholding central revenue measures such as the Stamp Act, enforcing authoritarian acts such as the Boston Port Act, and acting as a key foundation of the increasingly challenged central authority in the colonies. Tensions escalated in the American colonies not because this was the first time London had tried to bring them under greater central control but because this was the first time resistance on the part of the colonists did not bring surrender from the representatives of central authority. The obedience of sea officers, inculcated by the authoritarian whigs in the 1740s, now served as a linchpin of the authoritarian whig strategies to bring the American colonies to heel. Because of its central role in the reshaping of imperial relationships into a more disciplined, obedient model, the navy was a focal point of resistance for radical colonists. Stout argues that "violence might have been avoided if the sea guard had been a Royal Navy monopoly" because the customs vessels that earned most of the bad reputation dogging revenue enforcers were in fact private contractors, but that statement does not take into consideration the long ideological tradition holding that the military had no legitimate role in governing civilian affairs.[111] Benjamin Franklin's suggestion illustrates as much: one useful step to encourage rebellion in colonies, he wrote, would be to "convert the brave honest Officers of your Navy into pimping tide-waiters and colony officers of the customs. Let those who in time of war fought gallantly in defense of the commerce of their countrymen, in peace be taught to prey upon it."[112] A professionalized navy did not follow the major commandment for political virtue in the eyes of radicals: by definition, the individuals in it could not act independently. It embodied a model of society, one of unbending hierarchy in which every inferior owed obedience to every superior—a model that British and American radicals rejected.

The very idea of a professional navy, one characterized by subordination to external discipline and, if necessary, coercion, was challenged in the 1740s both in Parliament and the public sphere. In the 1760s the fact of a peacetime navy being deployed against British subjects, in the service of the executive power, to bring them into conformity with a sociopolitical system which they believed was equally characterized by hierarchy and coercive power, was also protested against in pamphlets and on the seas. Radicals in the Anglo-imperial world saw this as the natural fulfillment of a professional navy's destiny, one which they anticipated when they saw the groundwork being laid in the 1740s. A professional military moved out of the control of civilians and into the hands of the executive.

India, the Caribbean, and Ireland

The North American colonies were not the only parts of the empire where the Royal Navy was used to buttress imperial authority and control unruly populations. Sea officers and naval ships were being asked to perform similar roles in India and the Caribbean. Ireland was placed under increased central oversight in part because authoritarian whigs perceived ongoing disorder there as well, but also perhaps in part because of its importance to maintaining naval power.

In India some East India Company servants saw sea officers as the representatives of central authority and resisted their presence on that account. Rather than a long series of contested encounters with sea officers, as the American colonists had, the EIC's complaints centered around one officer, Sir John Lindsay. Lindsay was sent to the East Indies in 1769 as part of a force originally requested by the company.[113] The company's General Court believed that the presence of royal men of war would give the company added weight in its (armed) negotiations with a local rival in the Persian Gulf and would protect a newly claimed settlement near Borneo.[114] Though a majority of voting stockholders in the General Court supported sending naval frigates to the East Indies, they were not pleased when they discovered that the ministry intended to send Lindsay as a royal officer, rather than one under EIC authority. The General Court wanted the appearance of official ministerial approbation, not the actual presence of central authority. After many days' debate, the General Court concluded that they would not permit Lindsay to participate in the company's councils in the East Indies, even on matters of war and peace. They refused direct government intervention in their negotiations and were entitled to issue their own orders to Lindsay. On the surface, Lindsay was to act in the East Indies under company direction.[115]

Lindsay did not meet with a warm welcome in India. The governing council of the EIC factory at Madras believed that Lindsay was the tip of the wedge in creating a direct link between the local Indian powers and the British ministry, one unmediated by the EIC. Previously, negotiations with local powers and ritual marks of honor would have been carried out by representatives of the EIC. Upon discovering that Lindsay had been granted plenary powers to negotiate with the local powers in his own name, rather than that of the company's, the members of Madras's council refused to aid him or to attend such meetings, noting this as a "remarkable deviation from former custom, in sending his Majesty's letters and presents immediately from his Majesty, and not thro' the Company's representatives."[116] When Lindsay requested information regarding the company's affairs in order to be better able to assist them, they refused to give him the information he asked for.[117] Lindsay was still in the East Indies a year later, when the council announced "the apprehensions which deeply affect us of the danger with which the Company's rights and privileges are threatened by powers from the Crown sent out to India."[118]

The council at Madras was correct in believing that Lindsay was sent to the East Indies to circumvent the company. Viscount Weymouth's assumption of the duties of Secretary of State for the Southern Department in 1768 signaled a shift in ministerial willingness to intervene directly in East Indian affairs.[119] Weymouth, an authoritarian whig, was frustrated at the company's unwillingness or inability to give accurate information to the government regarding the situation in the

East Indies.[120] For Weymouth and others, matters in India were now too important for the company to be permitted to mismanage them. Britain might be forced to become involved should the EIC instigate a war, regardless of whether it was for private profit or the national interest. The ministry needed more reliable information to be able to make effective decisions. Lindsay had secret orders from Weymouth to survey the situation and evaluate the company's position, as well as to provide direct lines of communication between ministers in London and local powers in India. Weymouth informed Lindsay that "the servants of the Company, both at home and abroad, are too much taken up with partial and selfish schemes." The EIC had asked the British government to include East Indian articles in the Treaty of Paris, which ended the Seven Years' War, making the crown a guarantor of the East Indian peace. According to Weymouth, however, the EIC then ignored the provisions they themselves had asked for, both with regard to the French as well as local powers. Weymouth believed the company had "trifled with, and eluded" the terms of the treaty, mistreating the Nabob of Arcot. If true, this dishonored George III. Lindsay was ordered to make direct contact with the Nabob if necessary and reassure him that George would stand by his promises and act as an impartial adjudicator rather than unquestioningly support the claims of the EIC. Thus, Lindsay's public orders were to support the EIC in their negotiations in the Persian Gulf, protect their new settlement, and guard against encroachment from the French. His secret orders were to provide the ministry with a set of eyes they considered to be reliable and to open a direct line of royal authority over those within the sphere of British power in India.[121]

Lindsay found as much evidence of EIC malfeasance as Weymouth and others had feared he would. He informed Weymouth, "the Company's servants were determined to oppose every endeavour of mine to fulfill my commission." Lindsay stated that the EIC did not fulfill its treaties, in part because they had a habit of making contradictory treaties and thus leaving themselves in the position of being unable to fulfill all of them, they were pushy and demanding with him as a sea officer, and they would soon lead themselves (and the nation) into real trouble. Lindsay concluded that a more permanent representative of official authority should be sent to the East Indies with powers such as his own, and spoke of the necessity of "extending the Royal Protection" to the East Indies.[122] Lindsay's report offered ammunition to those who would have liked to assert greater central control over East Indian affairs. Perhaps for that reason, when the Earl of Sandwich returned to the Admiralty Board in January 1771, his new program of repair and expansion included a proposed permanent peacetime detachment in the East Indies.[123] His Admiralty Board also brought into Parliament a bill intended to restrict the shipping tonnage of the East India Company on the grounds that the EIC was using timber the navy needed more.[124] When the bill came to a vote in April 1772, voting was split not just along the lines of division regarding the need for greater government control of East Indian affairs, but also along the lines of division regarding the need for a larger, more active navy. The opposition claimed the timber bill was "full of the most dangerous doctrines," which would lead to the wealth of the East Indies falling into the hands of the executive—which would then be freed from parliamentary oversight.[125] On multiple levels, the expansion of the official naval presence in India raised similar issues to those present in the North American colonies.

In the Caribbean, naval ships were not deployed to provide backbone to reluctant imperial officials, as they were in North America and India. Rather, their actions frequently mirrored a different dimension of their North American presence: controlling unruly imperial populations. Naval ships were used with increasing frequency to suppress rebellions by enslaved populations. Uprisings were not a new phenomenon—enslaved people had periodically turned to violent means to regain their freedom ever since Caribbean colonies had first become dependent on enslaved labor—but they were becoming more frequent as enslaved laborers increasingly outnumbered white residents.[126] In the early eighteenth century, however, those rebellions did not seem to lead white planters to call for naval assistance. For example, there were uprisings in Antigua in 1701, 1728–1729, and 1736, and in the Bahamas in 1734, but no requests seem to have been made at those times for naval ships to help quell unrest among the enslaved.[127] That began to change in the 1730s, accelerated around the time of the Seven Years' War, and by the end of the century the navy was a regular presence in suppressing slave revolts.

Naval ships could be useful in stifling slave rebellions in a variety of ways. First, they could provide support in combat. This might entail lending sailors, arms, ammunition, or other provisions to slave owners. During the First Maroon War in the 1730s, the Speaker of the Council of Jamaica wrote to Admiral Sir Chaloner Ogle to ask for his assistance, explaining that "the present ill situation & defenseless condition of the country" prevented the council from thinking of "any other effectual [measure], than by making this application to you for some assistance from the Navy." Ogle sent 200 sailors ashore to fight the maroons. White Jamaicans received other assistance from naval commanders during that conflict, as well.[128] During Tacky's Revolt (1760–1761), Jamaican slaveholders again found themselves supported by sea officers. Admiral Charles Holmes transported land troops, loaned about 400 sailors and marines, and supplied the troops with ammunition as well as provisions. Even captains of smaller ships, like Captain John Lewis Gidoin of the *Antonio,* sent sailors ashore to help fight escaped slaves when requested.[129] In the First Carib War on St. Vincent (1769–1773), Admiral William Parry loaned marines from naval ships, helped to transport troops, used his ships to scout the coastline for the safest place to land those troops, then ordered his captains to fire on Carib forces on shore.[130] Sam Willis has written persuasively of the many ways in which sea officers and naval manpower, guns, and provisions contributed to land-based war efforts in the American Revolution, sometimes far away from oceans.[131] The same dynamics could be seen in naval warfare with enslaved people in the Caribbean, who were fighting for their freedom just as colonists believed they were fighting for theirs.

As in the North American colonies, naval ships in the Caribbean did not always have to engage in open combat to make their presence felt. Some nervous planters believed that simply the presence of a naval ship would help dissuade enslaved laborers from trying their luck. During the 1770–1772 slave uprising on Tobago, Robert Stewart, president of the island, wrote to Admiral Robert Man to request the ongoing presence of a naval ship. He explained, "The appearance of a ship of war, and the report of her being here, to assist us when necessary, must certainly be of the utmost benefit, not only with respect to assistance which she may actually afford upon an emergency, but also may have a good effect in overawing & intimidating such negroes, as may be disposed to join those desperate wretches already in arms."[132] During a 1773 slave revolt in the British settlement on the Bay of Honduras, leaders again pled with the naval commander-in-chief not to withdraw the ship currently in the area. The chairman of the settlement wrote to Admiral George Rodney that "we cannot help expressing our fears, that should the *Diligence* leave this place, before some other of his Majesty's ships is sent by you to our relief, this insurrection may become so general, as to . . . be productive of the total ruin and destruction of this settlement." He concluded, "The fate of this settlement will in a great measure depend on the answer we receive from you."[133] Another way naval ships could help forestall rebellions was by cutting off access to potential allies. In 1762 the governing elites of Bermuda expressed their belief that the French intended to send military aid to "our disaffected negroes, who have been lately detected in a dangerous conspiracy & intended massacre of the white inhabitants." They requested that a naval ship be stationed at the island to prevent communication between escaped slaves and the French.[134] In 1769 Admiral Man informed the secretary of the Admiralty that at the request of the local governor, he had sent a ship to cruise between St. Vincent and St. Lucia "to prevent the intercourse between the black Caribs of St Vincent, & the French inhabitants of the latter island; upon an apprehension, that the black Caribs, who have of late been very troublesome to the British inhabitants, have been instigated thereto by the neighboring French from whom they get arms and ammunition."[135] Finally, naval ships in the Caribbean also reprised their roles as both fortresses and prisons. During Tacky's Revolt, Admiral Holmes ordered his subordinate captains to "give the best accommodation on board of their ships, to all the ladies and the wounded, who might stand in need of their protection & succour." In that same conflict, naval ships also acted as jails for recaptured enslaved laborers.[136]

Having a naval ship in the area could be a comforting sight for plantation elites. Many island colonies wrote to the Admiralty at various points to request a greater naval presence. Toward the later end of Tacky's Revolt, several Jamaican planters and merchants wrote to the Admiralty to express their pleasure at the "brisk and impetuous attack of seamen, at which the negroes are so much intimidated" and to request that a naval ship be permanently stationed in Port Antonio harbor. However, not all sea officers were convinced of the wisdom of allowing planter elites to use the Royal Navy as their own personal security force—not because they were concerned about the effectiveness of naval ships in suppressing slave rebellions, but because they thought acting as a stationary floating battery in port might distract them from their other duties. When Holmes was informed of this request, his response was that he believed "the brisk and impetuous attacks of seamen should be confined to their own element, except in cases of real extremity." The gentlemen who had requested this intended to "make the squadron a machine to operate and serve them every way, when, in truth, it can only serve well, when properly put in motion in its own natural way."[137] Nevertheless, in those moments of "real extremity," the officers of the Royal Navy provided adept at helping local elites maintain control over vastly larger enslaved populations. The maroons of Jamaica, Caribs of St. Vincent, or any of the other hundreds of thousands enslaved people in the Caribbean would not have assumed that the navy was a bastion of liberty.[138]

The navy was less directly involved in maintaining imperial control over Ireland; instead, Ireland played an important role as hub of naval infrastructure and resources. Similar transformations in governance were under way there as in other parts of the empire, including a stamp act, all in an attempt to make the representatives of central administration independent of the Irish Parliament.[139] Bedford had argued that Ireland needed a constant representative of central authority; by the late 1760s, that had become the case as a newly permanently resident Lord Lieutenant stripped local politicians of their power.[140] As Lord Lieutenant, George Townshend argued for increasing the military presence in Ireland. He hoped to establish new lines of revenue, such as the direct importation of rum into Ireland, which would lessen the governor's financial reliance on the Irish Parliament.[141] He was also deeply critical of the idea that "all men are equal," spoke disparagingly of the "the low arts of these pettyfogging patriots," and referred to the actions of North American colonists as "rebellion."[142] Ireland had long been useful to England as the nation's barracks: the place where soldiers were stationed when they weren't immediately wanted, far enough out of sight that English voters could pretend they did not maintain a standing army. It was also significant geographically. Trade from North America and the East Indies came through Irish shipping lanes and much of the time sea officers spent stationed in Irish waters was therefore dedicated to protecting trade or suppressing smuggling. Because of its geography—and its Catholic population—Ireland was a potential staging ground for invasion, meaning that during wartime ships had to guard against incursions like the one at Carrickfergus in 1760. In the latter part of the eighteenth century, Ireland also became important to naval resources, specifically manpower. By the time of the American Revolution, Dublin was the second single largest source of sailors after London; overall, Ireland supplied about 17 percent of the sailors in that war.[143] Authoritarian whig William Knox thought it should be encouraged to do more.[144] Like the North American colonies, Ireland was increasingly asked to bear a larger share of the costs of maintaining a standing navy, financially and in other ways, as well. Throughout the empire, the officers of the Royal Navy played crucial roles in maintaining order and expanding central authority, but at a cost.

✧ ✧ ✧

The officers of the Royal Navy were essential agents in making the more centralized, authoritarian empire possible in the years between the Seven Years' War and the American Revolution. They were on the frontlines of the growing imperial conflict. The needs of a professional navy—its costs in war and peace—made the redistribution of control over certain types of resources more imperative. Because of its implication in other constitutional issues, the navy's use for internal policing by the central administration exacerbated the conflict with the American radicals, for whom the navy became a focal point of resistance. Without the navy's previous transformation into a disciplined, professionalized force, the attempts at imperial restructuring in the 1760s would have been far more difficult and perhaps impossible.

The Seven Years' War and the accession of George III were not negligible events in the British imperial world. Both affected the dynamics of British imperial politics, but regardless of how many in the political classes came to agree that bringing the American colonies into line was important, these efforts would have been futile without an effective means of coercion. When the authoritarian whig Earl of Halifax tried to bring the colonies into greater compliance with central imperial governance in the 1740s, his efforts failed both because others higher in the administration did not support his efforts and because no effective means of coercion existed. The naval reforms of the authoritarian whig Admiralty, enacted at the same time as Halifax's imperial reforms, changed that by creating a disciplined military force capable of regulating that most supreme of British imperial concerns: trade. The imposition of authoritarian government in the British Empire was the fruition of a longer trend rather than a postwar innovation. At a minimum, reintegrating the navy back into the story of the British Empire in the 1760s supports P. J. Marshall's argument that a sharp dichotomy between the first and second British Empires is misleading.[145] A similar form of government was pushed onto both America and Asia at the same time; it provoked rebellion in one but succeeded in the other. The role played by the navy in the imperial periphery in the 1760s and 1770s complicates our understanding of how free the first British Empire really was.

This story also indicates the extent of ideological political conflict within the Anglo-imperial world. At the very height of the political era Lewis Namier identifies as consisting of factions devoid of principle or belief, political groups across the Atlantic clashed and coalesced over imperial questions of authority, revenue, representation, and ensuring military power did not overwhelm the civilian sphere.[146] Within Britain, imperial questions sparked the rise and fall of ministries, and made or broke political alliances. They provoked petitions and demonstrations from tradesmen and artisans. Imperial issues mattered deeply in the British eighteenth century.

This was an imperial crisis, not one in which separate causes created coincidentally concurrent problems. Both radicals and supporters of central authority believed events in the empire and Britain were linked. The authoritarian whig commitment to upholding their empire in Asia caused the administration to refuse to back down on the duty on tea when they backtracked on the rest of the Townshend Duties.[147] They expected the American colonies to maintain the profitability of the eastern empire; moreover, they intended the profits from the duty to make colonial governors independent of colonial assemblies by giving them assured salaries, making them capable of being more responsive to the wishes of the central administration. The authoritarian whigs approved bringing both Asian and American colonies into greater compliance with central authority, and supported using a professional military to do so. The Wilkites supported the American cause as being their own, which seemed to further threaten political stability at home. In Britain, both those who supported the American cause, such as Richard Campion and Richard Price, and those who supported central authority, such as William Knox, argued that the fights were one and the same. Price claimed that the Quebec Act, which established episcopacy in Canada, was proof of "the sort of government they wish for in this country [Britain]." One Irish patriot declared, "We are all Americans here." Knox argued the war against the colonists was part of the fight against "the republican disposition, which is gaining ground in this island and in Ireland, under the mask of free thinking and philosophy."[148] In America, both those who supported independence and those who opposed it claimed the rights of Englishmen. Josiah Quincy Jr. defended the Tea Party by declaring, "It was not difficult for Englishmen in Britain to tell how Englishmen in America would conduct on such occasions." On the other hand, the author of the loyalist pamphlet *Free Thoughts on the Proceedings of the Continental Congress* encouraged his readers to set aside the nonimportation agreements and realize "that you are Englishmen, and will maintain your rights and privileges, and will eat, and drink, and wear, whatever the public laws of your country permit, without asking leave of any illegal, tyrannical Congress or Committee on earth."[149]

Both sides agreed that what was at stake was more than just the collection of revenue. Authoritarian whigs believed colonists resisted imperial governance because of "Ideas of imaginary independency," which led them to be in "direct Contempt to all Government." Because they refused to show "that ready Obedience and Deference which ought to be paid to Acts of the British Parliament," military force was necessary.[150] Appreciating the changes enacted on and through the navy indicates just how deep the divisions really were between the authoritarian whig view, embodied by the Duke of Bedford, the Earl of Sandwich, George III, and others, and that of their opponents. The transformation the authoritarian whigs tried to effect on Anglo-imperial society was vast, spanning many spheres of public life. The use of a professional, disciplined military to regulate and govern civilian society was not the only point that angered radicals, but it was linked to and representative of many others. The rise of a professional standing navy based on order, authority, and central control foreshadowed and facilitated attempts to restructure the British Empire into a more coherent, hierarchical whole. It is striking, as Denver Brunsman has pointed out, that a Victorian-era observer like John Ruskin could describe his ideal colonies as "motionless navies."[151] The authoritarian whigs first built a navy that reflected the social relationships they wanted to see—hierarchical, disciplined, and obedient to centralized authority—and then used that navy to enforce a similar imperial relationship on recalcitrant imperial subjects. Given the widespread prevalence throughout the colonies of libertarian arguments that warned against professional militaries whose members fought for pay rather than in defense of their own liberties, given colonists' repeated emphasis on the illegitimate authority of sea officers, and given the ongoing arguments in the early Republic about the dangers of a standing navy, the most persuasive conclusion is that radical colonists accurately realized that a professional navy had the potential to be far more than just a conduit for revenue extraction. The professional navy embodied a strictly hierarchical sociopolitical system that radicals feared, and it supplied the means by which authoritarian whigs in London attempted to force that system on the colonies. Although the existence of a professional navy led to victories on the sea for Britain, it also led to the fracturing of the very empire it had helped acquire.

CONCLUSION

The American Revolutionary War

BRITAIN LOST THE AMERICAN Revolutionary War. Some historians have laid the blame for this at the feet of the navy. At the basic level of the naval conflict, there was an element of outmaneuvering: the Royal Navy could not consistently maintain local superiority along the North American coast. As John Derry points out, "If a British fleet had been in Chesapeake Bay, as Cornwallis had expected, there would have been no surrender at Yorktown" in 1781.[1] For the purposes of this book, what is more important is why those facts were true. Does the outcome of the American Revolution challenge the assertion that the professionalizing reforms of the 1740s created the bedrock on which the future success of the Royal Navy was founded? Is the argument that the navy had a sustained impact on colonial trade in the years leading up to the revolution—or that it was seen as a threat to colonial freedom—undermined if the war that followed proved naval weakness?

In fact, the American Revolution was less a naval defeat than it was the result of poor strategic choices and the loss of political will. Rather than being taken as an indication of British military or naval feebleness, the outcome of the American Revolution signaled the extent to which Britain was itself politically divided over the war and its aims. Despite setbacks, the British navy was gaining ground over its competitors in the waning days of the war, before the political will to continue the fight crumbled. A variety of factors hemmed in commanders and contributed to the eventual British surrender, among them the failure to establish a coherent strategy, the navy's lack of a clear target in the beginning of the war followed by being almost immediately overstretched from the moment France entered the fray, and the deeply divisive domestic political landscape. In the years following American independence, contemporaries asked themselves where they had gone wrong and settled on similar answers. The men who from 1784 were largely ensconced as the new whig opposition—led by politicians like William Henry Cavendish Cavendish-Bentinck, Third Duke of Portland, Charles James Fox, and Richard Brinsley Sheridan—blamed ministerial partisanship during the war years for driving away honest naval commanders, who were thereby prevented from serving their country as they wished to. Though this opposition was itself divided between the heirs of aristocratic establishment whigs, like Portland, and more radical and populist elements, like Sheridan, their public rhetoric fixated on the common ground of ministerial corruption. In contrast, William Pitt the Younger and his supporters emphasized the need for the navy to be able to act more freely than it had during the Revolution. They proposed a system of dockyard fortification, which they argued would help guard against French invasion and would permit the navy to act more aggressively in defense of Britain's overseas territories.

The British loss in the American Revolutionary War was not inevitable, but commanders and politicians were faced with a series of challenges which they failed to address adequately. Among these challenges were the lack of strategic coherency, the lack of a clear naval target in the early years of the war followed by the overstretching of forces once official hostilities broke out with France, and the incredibly damaging bitter partisanship that created a rift in the public political sphere. The outcome of the Revolutionary War did not indicate that the authoritarian whig professionalizing reforms had failed to alter the culture of service in the navy, though it did outline some of the limits of usefulness of that system.

Strategic Confusion and Overstretch

From the beginning, British politicians could not agree on what type of war they were fighting or what its strategic objectives should be. Could the war be won in one quick campaign which would shatter the illusion of American unity? Should they slowly starve the continent out? Were colonists enemies to be crushed or brethren to be reconciled? Recent scholarship has heavily emphasized the extent to which the absence of one single overriding understanding of the war's aims hindered military and naval commanders attempting to follow orders from London. Andrew Jackson O'Shaughnessy blames "a political system in Britain that frustrated the formulation of clear strategic priorities" and the "absence of a central command system to provide essential coordination between the various departments of government responsible for the war effort."[2] Peter Whiteley highlights "inadequate long-term planning" and the "strategic failure to identify clear objectives and to concentrate on them to the exclusion of sideshows."[3] David Syrett explains, "Because of divisions of responsibility and lack of leadership within the North government, British policy vacillated between objectives, depending on which minister or group of ministers prevailed in the cabinet. There was no overarching strategy for the conduct of the American war."[4]

At first it was unclear what the role of the Royal Navy would be once open warfare had erupted. Despite being dependent on the sea in many ways, the American colonies did not have a regular fleet for the Royal Navy to combat. Although some revolutionaries feared the navy could not be overcome, other believed they could face the British on the high seas: in Silas Deane's analysis, "It is evident if [the British] cruise in a fleet they will not be formidable to trade, and if single they will be liable to be attacked by an equal if not superior force of the Continental fleet . . . for they dream as little of our meeting them, on the sea as of our invading Canada."[5] Christopher Gadsden, a South Carolinian delegate to the Continental Congress, believed that Americans could begin by capturing a few smaller ships with privateers, then eat their way up the line to bigger ships. Gadsden had previously served in the Royal Navy and, like many radical colonists, believed that bigger ships would be more likely to be manned by unwillingly impressed sailors held in line with strict discipline, who would greet American captors as liberators.[6] The Continental Congress initially planned thirteen frigates, along with a variety of other ships. Many of these ships were never built; none of the frigates survived until Yorktown. By the end of 1778, all of the Continental Navy's major ships were out of the picture. Some states manned a ship or two on their own, but the overwhelming majority of American ships on the seas from that point onward were privateers.[7]

What the Royal Navy could do was continue the role it had played in the 1760s and 1770s: to patrol and control the coasts, but now as a blockading force. Sandwich's preferred policy was to rely upon a naval blockade to slowly starve out the rebels.[8] Observers in the colonies like Henry Hulton agreed that "reducing the colonies to obedience by a naval war" was the more "sure" way to proceed, by which Hulton intended a combination of blockade and naval capture of port cities.[9] During the winter of 1776–1777, the blockade's impact was felt in American markets as prices of foreign goods rose; at points, the navy may have been intercepting as many as 40 percent of American merchant and commercial fishing ships. Its presence certainly discouraged many more from even making the attempt to get to sea.[10] Over the course of the war, the navy also proved effective at capturing every major port city on the continent for at least some period of time, seriously disrupting the regional economies of which they were the hubs.[11] Jeremy Black suggests that not taking further advantage of this capability earlier in the war was one missed opportunity for the British.[12] Although North's cabinet believed that a naval blockade might be effective in the long run, they feared that the navy would not be able to protect loyalists, who would suffer in a drawn-out conflict. Furthermore, a lengthy war might only increase the opportunities and temptation for France to become involved. George Sackville Germain, Secretary of State for the Colonies, urged a more aggressive military approach.[13] The naval blockade became subordinated to land-based military campaigns and between 1775 and 1777, the Admiralty was given little influence in calculating strategy. However, once the navy was withdrawn from supporting army operations, it imposed a very successful blockade, as it would do again in the War of 1812.[14]

Preventing the French from entering the war as active participants continued to be a major concern of the North administration. Despite Sandwich's protestations that the navy needed to be augmented, others worried that a full naval mobilization might provoke France or Spain into likewise mobilizing. Although the navy was increased to roughly 45,000 men over the autumn and early winter of 1776, Sandwich still warned that this would not be enough if European enemies formally joined the war.[15] Aside from those within the administration who disagreed, in 1777 Edmund Burke, opposition MP, spoke out against augmenting the navy to 60,000 men because it was a time of ostensible peace (apparently the war against the colonies did not count with him).[16] This gamble—that the war with the colonists could be resolved before the Bourbon powers intervened—failed. From 1778, when France declared war (Spain officially followed in 1779 and the Netherlands in 1780), the Royal Navy, which had not been put on a full wartime footing, was simply stretched too thin. As Sandwich had warned previously and as he explained again in 1779, Britain now faced the united Bourbon powers with "no one friend or ally."[17] There were not sufficient ships to simultaneously defend Britain from invasion at home, protect trade, blockade the North American coast, and prevent French and Spanish fleets from reinforcing enemy troops. As O'Shaughnessy points out, "After 1778, the British army and navy were engaged not only in the war for America but in the protection of the British possessions in the West Indies, the Mediterranean, Africa, and India. . . . The last battle of the American Revolutionary War was fought in India."[18] Aside from the new worldwide dimension of the war, there was no longer a unified opinion about whether the primary enemies were the rebel colonists or Britain's European imperial rivals. According to both Syrett and N. A. M. Rodger, once the Bourbon powers had entered the war, Britain should have abandoned the fight for the colonies and focused on Europe instead. By being so overstretched, the navy was forced to act passively and reactively rather than aggressively.[19] This was a failure of strategic foresight rather than an inherent flaw in the infrastructure, administration, or men of the navy.

Partisanship

Another factor impeding the navy's ability to fight the war effectively was the politically divided nature of Britain itself. This made itself felt in the cabinet where ministers disagreed about what the war's aims were, in Parliament where opposition MPs regularly harangued ministers about their conduct of the war, and in the navy itself where captains and admirals refused to serve. James Bradley has ably shown how popular the American cause was in some sectors of British society; as argued in Chapter 5, radicals on both sides of the Atlantic believed that the war was not just about imperial governance, but about the battle between liberty and corruption throughout Anglo-imperial society.[20]

Owing to a combination of factors—the emotive resonance of the navy, the nation's disappointed expectations for it, and Sandwich's own well-known political views—Sandwich became a particular target for the opposition. In Parliament, Fox claimed, "it was the first lord of the Admiralty, the earl of Sandwich, who was alone to blame, who ought to be made the subject of inquiry."[21] Temple Luttrell repeatedly accused Sandwich of deliberately misleading the nation about its naval strength. He linked these accusations to denunciations both of the administration's American policy and its naval governance, suggesting that Sandwich had "suffer[ed] the most useful of the ships, and the flower of your seamen, to be sent 3,000 miles off, on a fruitless, romantic attempt, to reduce the vast continent of America to unconditional submission" and warning his fellow parliamentarians that "if the people of England knew the real state of our marine power and resources, and the great superiority of our natural enemies in these seas, they would scarce suffer so many ships and men to be dispatched to the further quarter of the globe, even on a more rational and profitable pursuit than the reduction of our American colonies to despotism."[22] Luttrell later bemoaned Parliament's diminishing authority over naval matters and cautioned that if Britain were to best its Bourbon rivals, "I am confident it cannot be done by the present commissioners of the Admiralty with their press-warrants and never-ending servitude."[23] In March 1778 the Duke of Bolton moved in the Lords for an inquiry into naval matters; Charles James Fox did likewise in the Commons. Unsatisfied by the outcome of the first two motions, later that month the Earl of Effingham tried again, claiming that naval expenses from 1770 onward far outstripped what they had been in 1727 and alleging ministerial malfeasance. The clear implication of this assertion was that what Britain needed was a return to the small, defensive Walpolean navy.[24]

The fallout from the Battle of Ushant (July 1778) exacerbated this already poisonous atmosphere. The British fleet was commanded by Augustus Keppel, who had long been associated with the establishment whigs; he had been an Admiralty commissioner during the Marquess of Rockingham's administration in the 1760s and continued to be connected with the opposition. In contrast, his subordinate admiral, Sir Hugh Palliser, was closely allied with Sandwich and an Admiralty commissioner himself; he received repeated marks of favor from the authoritarian whig Admiralty. The battle, between roughly equal French and British fleets, was inconclusive; both sides claimed that they won. The matter rested there until October 1778, when the *General Advertiser* printed a letter, claiming to be from an officer who was present, which asserted that the reason why Keppel had not more aggressively pursued the French was because Palliser had not brought his ship back into line following a skirmish. Palliser's honor was affronted and he demanded that Keppel publicly repudiate the newspaper's account. Keppel refused and Palliser published his own version of the events, claiming his ship had been disabled and accusing Keppel of misconduct in action.[25] The Admiralty ordered a court-martial on Keppel for "misconduct and neglect of duty"; Keppel was acquitted and Palliser demanded a court-martial in turn in order to clear his own name, which the opposition tried to block—or at least discredit—at every turn so that Palliser would not have a chance to be exonerated of professional misconduct himself.[26]

The Keppel-Palliser controversy became a considerable public debacle. The opposition claimed that Keppel had been sent out with an insufficient fleet, for which the Admiralty and particularly Sandwich was to blame. In a debate on the Admiralty's right to court-martial officers, Colonel Isaac Barré, a stalwart of the opposition, "compared his Majesty's ministers to a knot of midnight conspirators, plotting their country's ruin, and proscribing the lives, fortunes and reputations of every man who was likely to stand in the way of the accomplishment of their deep-laid but weak and nefarious system; a system every way calculated to ruin the nation, to render parliament shamefully servile and contemptible."[27] The opposition claimed that Sandwich was deliberately scapegoating Keppel for his known opposition to government policy. Thomas Townshend (later Viscount Sydney) claimed, "Every step taken by administration afforded the most unequivocal proofs that the same system had been uniformly pursued, which was a proscription of every officer who professed to be a Whig, or acted independently, or dared, upon any occasion, to differ from the King's servants."[28] Fox demanded a parliamentary censure of the Admiralty and the removal of Sandwich as First Lord, claiming the "great waste of public money, the promises of the noble lord, our inadequate state of defence in June, the neglect of reinforcing the noble lord [Admiral Richard Howe] over the way, when the fate almost of America depended upon it; the abandoning the trade and fortresses in the Mediterranean" as his reasons, added to the "partiality of the Admiralty-board, which he considered to be entirely influenced, or rather directed by the noble earl."[29] Augustus Hervey, now Earl of Bristol, made a similar motion in the Lords.[30] The matter continued to be debated in Parliament into 1781. Two and a half years after the original battle, Fox continued to attack Palliser personally as "one great cause of those calamities under which this country was now suffering, and therefore he felt against him all that public enmity which such a just sense of his conduct ought to inspire."[31]

The administration defended itself by arguing that the navy was in a better state than it had been in the years leading up to the war and that the opposition was trying to build political capital by fomenting disaffection in the service. Constantine Phipps, Second Baron Musgrave as well as a sea officer and Admiralty commissioner, asserted, "When [Sandwich] came to the presidency at the Admiralty, there was not a year's timber in any one of our yards, no stores in our arsenals, and the whole navy in a perishing state . . . now there was at least timber enough for three years consumption in every one of our yards; our arsenals were also full of stores; our navy had a greater number of large ships than ever, and was not only in a respectable but in a flourishing state."[32] Moreover, he added that "it was utterly impossible to provide a suitable defence to possessions so widely extended as those belonging to Great Britain, that some must be neglected; and that in exercising the discretion inherent in ministers, no blame could be imputed to them for having directed their attention to places of the greatest consequence, in respect that they were more vulnerable, and, of course, more likely to invite an attack."[33] While Sandwich vindicated Keppel's decisions during the battle, he also subtly suggested that other truer British naval heroes would have done otherwise. Keppel returned to Britain before the battle for reinforcements, which Sandwich said had been permitted in his instructions, "yet lord Hawke, upon similar orders, acted in a different manner: his instructions were to cruize 14 days off Brest with an inferior force; he out-stayed his time, and on his return gave for answer, that he did not regard a small superiority."[34] Palliser was in turn exonerated by his own court-martial, though the opposition claimed this "no better than a mock trial" and that there were "the strongest grounds to suspect a collusion in [his] favour."[35]

The Keppel-Palliser controversy was not limited to Parliament: it attracted vast public attention. The constant subtext of the Keppel-Palliser controversy was the memory of the Byng trial. Like Byng, supporters of Keppel claimed he was a scapegoat intended to hide government failures. Like Byng, the issues at stake were not merely naval. As Nicholas Rogers explains, newspapers framed the controversy "within the larger struggle over domestic and imperial politics," implying that "the battle between naval commanders was really a synecdoche for larger struggles within domestic politics over the conduct and necessity of the war with America." He concludes, "the Keppelian affair, as represented in the press, was well, not thinly contextualized, framed by the ongoing disagreements over the American war, the future of the empire, and the political stalemate of an increasingly sclerotic electoral system."[36] In Fox's March 1778 motion of censure on the Admiralty, "not a single seat was unoccupied in any part of [the House of Commons], and upwards of fifty members, for whom there was no room in the body of the House, were obliged to sit in the side galleries."[37] Rogers estimates that perhaps one in six adults read about the Keppel court-martial in a newspaper, not counting others who discussed it orally; the coverage "more or less monopolized the news in late January and early February [1779], consuming anywhere from three to ten columns of a 16-column paper" and included regional papers outside of London, such as the *Bath Chronicle, Derby Mercury, Jackson's Oxford Journal, Leeds Mercury, Northampton Mercury,* and *Sussex Weekly Advertiser.*[38] Keppel's eventual acquittal was celebrated in sixty-three boroughs, and he was voted the freedom of the City of London, supported by opposition leaders such as Rockingham, the Duke of Portland, and John Wilkes.[39]

The Keppel-Palliser controversy further undermined confidence, both within the public and within the navy, in the Admiralty and its policies. Admiral George Rodney informed Sandwich that "The unhappy difference between Mr Keppel and Sir Hugh Palliser has almost ruined the Navy. Discipline in a very great measure is lost . . . and officers presume to find fault and think, when their duty is implicit obedience."[40] Sandwich agreed that faction in the navy was the "bane of our discipline."[41] Mulgrave accused the opposition of "employ[ing] their factious emissaries, their little officers, to insinuate themselves among their brethren of the profession, and in unguarded moments, attempt[ing] to seduce them from the duty they owed their country."[42] North rebuked sea officers who had signed a remonstrance in Keppel's favor, warning that their action "was in its nature subversive of all discipline and subordination. If appeals of such a kind were promoted or encouraged, no person could say where they might end, or whether in time they might not be extended to every subordinate rank and class of seamen, and . . . be productive of mutiny and disobedience."[43] In the early years of the war, when the American colonists were the only targets, some sea officers refused to serve against them, including Keppel and George Johnstone (a position both reversed once the conflict included France).[44] Now the opposition claimed that others were likewise driven from the service on political grounds. Sheridan stated, "All the world knew and felt the treatment which the veteran commanders of the fleet had experienced . . . their country had, in its worst moments, lost the benefit of assistance from such distinguished characters as a Keppel, a Howe, a Barrington, a Parker, a Harland, a Pigot, a Byron, and all the others whom they had driven into retirement."[45] Edmund Burke made similar claims; sea officer Hugh Pigot maintained that he was no longer offered employment after having refused to vote as Sandwich wanted in East India Company affairs.[46] Keppel was accused of persuading other captains not to serve, which he denied.[47] As it happened, the opposition accusing Sandwich of partisanship in the navy was the pot calling the kettle black—one of the first acts of Keppel as First Lord of the Admiralty once the North administration fell in 1782 was to recall Rodney, an associate of Sandwich, and replace him with Pigot, who had not been in active service for nineteen years but professed the right beliefs. Awkwardly, Rodney had just won a major victory of which the administration was yet unaware, making the political motivations for his dismissal appear even starker.[48]

Naval Resurgence

Despite being overstretched, Britain's naval position was strengthening in the later years of the war. In terms of infrastructure, Sandwich began an extensive new building program. Sandwich asked his critics to make a comparison between the shipbuilding programs of 1759 and 1781; Baugh notes, "Never in the course of British naval events had so many ships been ordered to be built in such great numbers by so unpopular a set of ministers."[49] Administratively, Sandwich continued to protect naval appointments from promotion based purely on interest without accompanying merit; he often clashed with officers or aristocrats who thought that interest alone would suffice.[50] We can see this in records drawn from Sandwich's third tenure at the Admiralty, between 1771 and 1782. On land, R. J. B. Knight notes that out of the approximately 300 applications for dockyard posts, only thirteen listed political usefulness as a qualification and only four of these were successful. On sea, N. A. M. Rodger calculates that approximately 40 percent of officers promoted during that period had any sort of patronage behind them—meaning that the majority did not—and concludes that "there can have been very few if any areas of eighteenth-century public life in which well-connected candidates would not have fared better."[51] Although patronage continued to play a role in promotion, patronage for naval positions came primarily from within the navy rather than from other politicians. As a variety of naval historians have documented, captains had an incentive to bestow their patronage on young men who would validate their good judgment by performing well.[52] Patronage was not divorced from the concept of "merit."

In the fleet as well, the authoritarian whig model of officership was taking root. George Brydges Rodney certainly embodied the authoritarian whig officer, if anything possibly going too far in his views on hierarchy. He informed one subordinate that the "painful task of thinking" was for the commander-in-chief alone, repeatedly emphasized the importance of "implicit obedience," and ordered every lieutenant under his command to sign the logbook at the end of his shift, "that he may know whose fault it is that his signals are not obeyed." He was also known for being sympathetic to "making a stand against the encroachments of republicanism and restor[ing] to the Crown its constitutional independence of the House of Commons."[53] Despite his statements that under his command "every opportunity shall be taken, to bring [the Bourbon powers] to a general battle," and despite actually winning several resounding victories, at the Moonlight Battle in 1780, the capture of St. Eustatius in 1781, and the Battle of the Saintes in 1782, some of his subordinate officers thought he could have been more aggressive still. One of these was Samuel Hood, who also embodied the model. Allied with Pitt politically, Hood believed Americans were full of "rancorous & dangerous principles"; he warned against officers "depart[ing] from the great line of service, on the score of private considerations." In his conduct of warfare, he brought his own ship within point blank range at the Battle of the Saintes before firing a shot; he then recalled that he "opened such a tremendous fire, as [the enemy] could not stand for more than ten minutes." Although the British captured four French ships, destroyed a fifth, and took a large number of prisoners, Hood regretted that the entire fleet had not been captured. He did later capture two of the escaped French ships.[54]

During Palliser's court-martial, George Johnstone, also a sea officer and the former governor of Florida, gave testimony that sheds light on the accepted norms of behavior for a sea officer. Johnstone explained, "When a commander of a ship did not join his commander in chief, as ordered, by signal, it was a matter immediately complained of; all the officers took notice of it, and there was scarcely a ship in which it was not said, publicly, 'Good God! What's that fellow about? Why does not he come up?' "[55] Officers were aware of and commented upon the behavior of other officers; there was pressure from within the group to conform to expectation. Ruddock Mackay and Michael Duffy assert that the majority of admirals at this time wanted to improve their ability to closely engage and "believed greater control and direction by the commander was essential for this"; they looked to Frederick's Prussian models for inspiration.[56] Rear Admiral Richard Kempenfelt claimed that "fleets as well as armies require rules for the execution of their movements, and that the one stands in need of tactics as well as the other; without which both are unwieldy masses, where force is lost for want of form and order." He added, "The men who are best disciplined, of whatever country they are, will always fight the best," and also endorsed uniforms, regular training, and routine surveillance by superior officers.[57] After the Battle of the Saintes, the French admiral de Grasse allegedly said, "were we not enemies, he should have been charmed with the superior discipline, neatness, and order, that prevailed in our ships of war."[58]

This was not to say that the British navy had thus reached a pinnacle of modernization or professionalization and would undergo no further changes. Would-be disciplinarians like Rodney and Kempenfelt continued to complain that the navy had not gone far enough and that yet more discipline would crush the slovenliness and disorder they still saw lurking in the fleet; in Kempenfelt's words, "We want in the navy such a discipline which should be general; and all commanders, &c., required to put it strictly in practice. It has been for want of this that such a spirit of insolence and licentiousness has so daringly showed itself of late upon so many occasions . . . disorders arise from a defect in discipline."[59] But it still was a vastly different force, in composition and behavior, from that which had existed under Walpole. If this had not been the case, people like Effingham would not have needed to express a wish for a return to 1727.

Contemporary Interpretations

In the immediate aftermath of the loss of the American colonies, there was intensive debate and introspection about the cause of Britain's misfortune. Some contemporaries did blame the Royal Navy for the war's lack of success. A letter published in the *Public Advertiser* from "Candidus," for example, explained that "in the course of the last miserably conducted war, both by sea and land, it was evidently discovered that a great falling off from our former excellence of conduct both by sea and land, took place." Far more frequently, however, contemporaries on both sides of the ideological divide professed an observed improvement in the French and Spanish fleets rather than an actual degeneration of the British one—the Royal Navy was perceived to have suffered a relative decline rather than an absolute one. Candidus continued, "In particular our ancient opposers, the French, had gained new and very considerable advantages, both in the manner of their fighting and manoeuvring at sea."[60] Thomas Fitzherbert noted in 1782, "Such powerful strides had been made by the House of Bourbon, towards having a superiority in their marine, that . . . had astonished all Europe."[61] Rear Admiral Hood agreed in 1786 that "France and other maritime powers of Europe had of late much increased their naval force."[62] One pamphlet from that same year observed that the French were "full of exertion, in putting their navy upon the most respectable footing." They had "reversed their system of politics; and wisely perceiving, that, without a formidable navy, they could never protect their trade, nor support the honour of their country, they . . . devoted their whole attention to the establishing [of] a numerous navy, which they so successfully effected, that we have it but too recent in our memories, not to admit of the manifold advantages which accrued to them, and on various occasions brought everlasting disgrace upon the arms of Great Britain."[63] This perception of French naval resurgence has been validated by modern historians.[64]

The vast majority of contemporaries focused on political or strategic choices to explain the outcome of the war. The opposition under Fox and Sheridan, who had largely been unenthusiastic about the war against the American colonies, continued to place the blame at the feet of the North administration, specifically for its alleged partisanship, corruption, and mistreatment of sea officers. They asserted that the administration had embraced flawed policies—that the war was despotic from the beginning—which it only exacerbated by attacking virtuous men who attempted to point out the error of its ways. The ideological implications of the American war therefore hampered Britain's efforts against the French. When Fox moved for the removal of Sandwich from the king's councils in 1782, he argued that the administration should have realized when it commenced open warfare against the colonies that France would inevitably become involved. Rather than prepare for war with France in 1776, however, "They sent all the frigates of England to the American seas, for the great national purpose of destroying the American trade . . . even in the very moment when the treaty was signing between France and America, were the large ships of Britain tossing about in the seas, encountering all the dangers and injuries of winter storms, for the sake of pillaging American craft."[65] During the war, sea officer James Luttrell warned, "How far the resources of this country, its sea and land forces, are equal to contend with France, Spain, and America, ministers, who have made the task inevitable, must answer to the nation." He made the rest of his political commitments clear by continuing, "I glory in opposing arbitrary power, and never wish to see despotic principles established in the constitution of Great Britain, whether by the arms of our enemies, or through the treachery of our ministers."[66] The opposition argued that this lack of effective leadership was also evident in the administration's treatment of sea officers. In 1779 Burke claimed that the "successive resignation of three great [sea] officers was not a matter that should be passed over in silence or lightly treated." Barré agreed with him, suggesting that the disunity in the navy stemmed from disunion and incompetence in the cabinet itself: "There he would behold one minister contending for unconditional submission; another for the terms proposed by the commissioners to the American Congress; a third haranguing on public profusion and corrupt contracts; and a fourth defending both public and private contracts."[67] A more virtuous administration would not have pursued a despotic war against the colonies—would not, in fact, have provoked them to rebellion in the first place—and if the war had been a just one, the nation would have been able to depend on the service of all of its military leaders.

In contrast, authoritarian whigs also blamed the American war for hampering the war with the Bourbon powers, but for practical rather than ideological reasons. It was not that the war against the rebellious colonies was inherently unjust, they explained, but that British forces had been spread too thin. This was the position taken up by the administration that emerged under William Pitt the Younger in 1784. Pitt explained the outcome of the American Revolutionary War by asserting that the Royal Navy had not been enabled to do its utmost. It was tethered to the British Isles and forced into a defensive rather than an aggressive role, because the islands lacked sufficient defense of their own. One solution proposed by the Pitt administration in February 1786 was to build a series of fortifications around Plymouth and Portsmouth dockyards, on the premise that better defense at home would enable a more active and aggressive naval presence elsewhere.[68] In Pitt's account, during the American Revolutionary War, "A considerable part of our fleet was confined to our ports, in order to protect our dock-yards; and thus we were obliged to do what Great Britain had never done before—to carry on a mere defensive war; a war in which, as in every other war merely defensive, we were under the necessity of wasting our resources, and impairing our strength, without any prospect of benefiting ourselves but at the loss of a great and valuable part of our possessions." Securing the dockyards would help secure the islands as a whole, which "would enable our whole fleet to go on remote services, and carry on the operations of war at a distance, without endangering the materials and seeds of future navies from being liable to destruction by the invasion of an enemy."[69] George Berkeley—a sea officer who was related to both Pitt and Fox but who supported Pitt—reminded listeners in the Commons that in the next war, Britain would not want to find itself again in the situation of the American Revolution. The nation would want to "see the fleet properly employed in war in annoying the enemy . . . the proposed fortifications would be of essential use, as, instead of cramping the operations of the fleet, it must assist them, because the commander-in-chief would act with more vigour against the enemy when he knew our coasts and our dock-yards to be safe and protected."[70] Pitt added that although the money could in theory be given directly to the navy instead, it would not do as much good there: at some point, Britain simply could not man any more ships, but this project would enable those ships it did have to be more aggressive.[71]

These proposed fortifications sparked yet another iteration of the debate over how militarized Britain was to become. John Burgoyne—despite being an army officer himself—"considered the idea of defending the kingdom by fortifications as inconsonant to the genius of our constitution, and irreconcilable with the security of the liberties of the people."[72] John Courtenay asked, "Where was this system to end? Who could set bounds to it? If Portsmouth and Plymouth were to be covered with military works to preserve the naval stores, London should be fortified on the same principle," along with Newcastle, Sunderland, and many other places. Soon "country gentlemen would fine their terraces converted into bastions, their slopes into glaces, their pleasure-grounds and shrubberies into horn-works and crown-works." He suggested the Commons should consider the possibility of a future despotic regime, noting that if Portsmouth had been fortified in the English Civil War, the parliamentarians would have been unable to capture it.[73] Sir William Lemon declared that the system had an "unconstitutional tendency" and appeared to be "a design of abandoning the cultivation of our marine, and relying rather on the army and military erections for security. . . . Were the proposed system of fortification adopted, it should be considered as the fatal era from whence the decline and ruin of our navy might be dated."[74] The fortification debate was widely reported in the press. The *General Advertiser, London Chronicle, Morning Chronicle and London Advertiser, Morning Herald, Morning Post and Daily Advertiser, Public Advertiser, St. James's Chronicle,* and *Whitehall Evening Post* all published extensive accounts of the parliamentary debates on the issue in February and March 1786. Other elements of the same debate, including questions of military law, parliamentary oversight over naval promotions, and the electoral privileges of men belonging to military and naval administration, continued to rage throughout the 1780s.[75]

Political divisions in Britain severely hampered the navy's efforts during the early years of the American Revolutionary War. Disagreements about the war's goals made defining a clear strategy difficult, prevented a timely mobilization before the French officially entered the conflict, and encouraged distrust and disaffection in the navy, reducing the number of officers on whom the Admiralty could rely. Despite these factors, by the later years of the war the British navy was gaining ground against its competitors. Even the opposition was willing to acknowledge this, once the North administration had fallen from office. When John Luttrell accused Fox in December 1782 of having exaggerated the poor state of the navy previously, given its victories in the later years of the war, Fox claimed that Keppel, First Lord of the Admiralty for a whole eight months, had turned the entire situation around.[76] In fact the building program and the turnaround had begun much earlier. Sam Willis has gone so far as to ponder whether the British surrender at Yorktown was a foregone conclusion, even given the navy's defeat in the Chesapeake. He observes that Cornwallis in fact had at least sixty-eight ships of varying sizes with him, which he could have used differently to evacuate his own troops or forestall the American boats ferrying soldiers to the peninsula. In his interpretation, Yorktown may have been less a failure of sea power than a failure on the part of a land-based general to understand how to use the sea power at his disposal.[77] In the larger picture, as Baugh explains, although the navy faced the combined fleets of Spain, France, and the Netherlands as well as predation by American privateers, "By 1782 British general superiority at sea was established. And all evidence indicates that it was the Franco-Spanish naval effort, not the British, that was nearing exhaustion toward the end of the war."[78] Britain went into the French Revolutionary War in a strong position.

Britain's ability to fight a naval war might have been increasing, but its political will to do so was plummeting. As Thomas Lyttelton, Second Baron Lyttelton, concluded as early as 1779, the war against the American colonies had been fought on constitutional principles and he had supported it for that reason, but it had quickly become "one black era, pregnant with the most dire mischiefs, the most cruel fortune, the bitterest calamities and the most inexpiable evils, that this country ever endured. . . . America, he contended, never would be ours by conquest." The proposals put forward by the commissioners attempting to resolve the situation with the colonists were so liberal that they made even Lord Chatham appear to have embraced "a Tory system of government" in comparison, so there was little left to fight for when the original principles had been abandoned.[79] John Derry suggests, "Since the war was going badly it seemed to confirm the mythology of a crisis in the Constitution."[80] Baugh reasonably proposes that "peace came because the Yorktown disaster brought Opposition politicians into power who were disposed to end the war—to the great relief of the French government."[81] These same politicians had opposed the war from the beginning; little surprise now that they ended it when they had the chance, especially given that even erstwhile enthusiastic supporters of subordinating the colonies, like Lyttelton, had concluded that the war was over.

By the 1780s some of the boundaries between what had clearly been distinct ideological positions had become blurred, just as between the political groups themselves. William Pitt the Younger held positions on many matters that were congruent with the authoritarian whig ideology, but he was not an implacable enemy to political reform. Similarly, he supported an active standing navy, but was willing to tolerate, at least rhetorically, the existence of the militia. Despite their strident opposition to the expansion of executive power, which they asserted was still growing, radicals like Sheridan also expressed support for a larger standing navy. In 1786 Sheridan claimed that the money granted to the navy for the following year was too little, "even for a year of peace: he reminded the House that our situation was different now from what it had been at the end of the war before the last . . . we required therefore a stronger Navy than was before deemed necessary."[82] Whereas patriots in the 1750s would likely have continued to push for an active navy in wartime but a much smaller fleet in peace, Sheridan was willing to make the compromise—despite his far more radical positions on many political matters. This suggests that the authoritarian whig naval system was "settling," becoming incrementally more acceptable to radicals as it appeared less of an innovation. The well-documented reversion toward hierarchical loyalism in the years following the American Revolution may have contributed to this.[83] Few of these ideological positions were immalleable: as Britain faced new challenges within new parameters, the dynamics of debate likewise evolved over time. No one can reasonably expect that a political position staked out within a particular historical moment will still inevitably resonate fifty or one hundred years later, when the historical moment has changed. Broadly, however, the navy continued to function as a microcosm of wider political debates, symbolic of the moral health of the nation, and politicians continued to have conflicting views of what it should accomplish. Even in peace, Pitt advocated a strong, active navy specifically structured to be able to cruise worldwide and defend the global empire. Even in war, opposition figures like Burke and the Earl of Effingham attempted to reduce the navy to Walpolean levels, to ensure it was a defensive rather than offensive force.

The current historiographical consensus is that naval weakness was not the cause of Britain's defeat in the American Revolutionary War, though naval overstretch certainly played a role. The North administration fought the war poorly, because it was divided about what the goals of the war were and achieved neither internal nor national consensus. Political partisanship split the navy and poisoned its operations. Strategic miscalculations, over Sandwich's objections, left naval mobilization too late to be effective once the Bourbon powers were also involved in the war. The navy was asked to do too many things at once: blockade the colonies, protect British trade, defend against invasion, and counteract Bourbon fleets in the Americas. Once the French entered the war in 1778, abandoning the colonies and focusing on the European conflict would likely have changed the naval outcome, but the North administration—and certainly George III—were unwilling to make this political compromise. The war did highlight some of the strategic shortcomings of the authoritarian whig naval model: as Keppel pointed out regarding the Battle of Ushant, British commanders could not force an enemy to stay and fight a decisive battle if they did not want to. The navy was successful in taking many American merchant ships, but American privateers also preyed on British trade; the professionalized navy could not prevent a *guerre de course*.

Disciplined and obedient officers could not compensate for a lack of strategic coherence or for a deeply divided national political landscape. If British society was unclear about whether the true enemies were the rebellious American colonists or the Bourbon imperial rivals, a professional navy could not settle the matter. Although some of the parameters of the debates were shifting alongside Britain's political landscape, what remained constant was the fact that the navy mattered in a significant way to arguments about imperial governance and the constitution at home. To that extent, the navy was not merely a tool of foreign policy—though it was that, too—it was also a prism through which social values could be reflected. The fleet, along with its officers and ships, continued to be a battleground for Britain's imperial future.

EPILOGUE

OVER THE COURSE OF the eighteenth century, the British navy increased its size and global reach and became more successful in battle against foreign competitors. Britain's naval fortunes were in part connected to the nation's similar economic transformations, its political institutions, and the capacity of its administrative bureaucracy. However, they were also in part due to the changing culture of naval warfare among sea officers: by the end of the century—in contrast both to other European naval corps and to their own predecessors—they had, to paraphrase Admiral John Jervis, rubbed out "can't" and put in "try."[1] This metamorphosis was not a foregone conclusion. Britain became the world's greatest naval power in the eighteenth century because of the convergence of a particular set of imperial and societal goals, a set of goals to which not all in British society subscribed.

In comparison to later incarnations, the seventeenth-century navy was more geographically restrained, less aggressive, and more deliberately defensive. Its officer corps was less cohesive and acted more independently of Admiralty control. In the early eighteenth century, the navy was used primarily as a tool of stability to build alliances and maintain the balance of power. From the mid-eighteenth century, however, the navy began to be deployed more aggressively, both in terms of foreign policy and in terms of battle tactics. This trend intensified through the end of the century. Again, the difference in conduct, attitude, and tactics between British sea officers and those of other European fleets has been long noted by a wide variety of naval historians and widely attributed to be first perceptible from midcentury. The origin of this difference, however, has not been explained. I have argued that there was clear overlap between the way the authoritarian whigs who came into the Admiralty in midcentury conceptualized order in wider society—whether political, economic, or imperial—and how they conceptualized order within the navy. Likewise, I have argued that their renewed emphasis on hierarchical discipline within the navy was the genesis for the aggressive, risk-taking, duty-bound behavior that officers exhibited later in the century.

The authoritarian whigs in the Admiralty were able to accomplish this transformation through applying a combination of pressures and through longevity of administration. While the Admiralty was of course not able to control everything that happened on board its ships, it did have significant influence over its officers and a variety of incentives at its disposal to encourage or coerce compliance, from surveillance to courts-martial to, most especially, promotion and the financial incentives of salary and prize money. The Admiralty did not need to compel every officer to embrace their value system or to personally enforce the reforms that were intended to buttress it; they could promote those who did and punish or ignore those who did not. Over the course of several decades, officers who did not wish to be relegated to the ranks of half pay would be likely to fall into line voluntarily. The longevity of their regime at the Admiralty gave the authoritarian whigs the time necessary to allow this system to come to fruition. Between Bedford, Sandwich, and Anson, the Admiralty Board of December 1744 was responsible for representing and shaping naval policy for thirty of the next thirty-seven years, until the fall of the North administration in 1782. It is also worth remembering that although traditionally Anson has enjoyed by far the highest profile in the development of these naval reforms, the majority of the initial reforms took place under Bedford or Sandwich's leadership in the 1740s and 1750s. Although some reforms were allowed to fade during Anson's tenure, many were resurrected once Sandwich regained the Admiralty in the 1770s. The politics of these First Lords are an important prism through which to try to understand how they believed society and the empire worked and how the navy fit into that relationship.

This book has traced a series of public crises regarding the navy and the ordering of military authority in relation to society: from concerns over the navy's ability to secure or undermine the Restoration, to its role in protecting trade in the Caribbean in the 1720s, to professionalization and punishment in the 1749 Navy Bill, to the public outcry over Byng and the militia in the 1750s, to increasing resistance to naval enforcement of imperial authority in the 1760s and 1770s, to open civil war. This is not to suggest that arguments over the appropriate relationship between military authority and the governance of civilian society stopped in the 1790s; on the contrary, those debates went on and the navy continued to change in response to social and political pressures.

Nor do I mean to argue that the navy of Trafalgar in 1805 was then somehow completely "modern." There were elements of naval service at the end of the eighteenth century that remained decidedly early modern in character and there were later developments that altered naval governance. As examples of the latter, both steam power and the telegraph changed the way the Admiralty was able to govern its ships, while the Naval Discipline Act of 1866 enlarged the powers of land-based naval administration over the day-to-day activities on board ship. As an example of the former, one could point to the continued role of patronage in promotion as one of a variety of remaining early modern aspects of naval service. However, it is important not to invest the early modern dimensions of military service with too much symbolic weight, which can underestimate the extent to which what we might term "early modern" and "modern" understandings of social and political relationships can and do coexist. Eighteenth-century patronage, for example, was not divorced from merit. Captains had an incentive to bestow their patronage on young men who would validate their good judgment by performing well.[2] The concept of merit had a significant hold in the late eighteenth-century navy and the Admiralty, as the source of promotion, was able to establish what "merit" meant.[3] Nor must merit be divorced from patronage. Patronage still exists, as any job applicant who has ever had to request a letter of recommendation can attest. In many industries, it has been renamed "networking." Picking through the various dimensions of naval service in 1805 to identify what was "modern" and what was not is not a very fruitful or illuminating exercise. The argument I have made here is not that the navy of the later eighteenth century was the permanent culmination of a teleological process, but rather that it was fundamentally different from what preceded it in the scale of organization, in the ethos of military service, and in the discipline of training.

Throughout the long eighteenth century, the navy resonated in political debates both for the role it could play in foreign policy and for the wider implications it was seen to have for imperial society, either as a harbinger of changes to come or as an enforcer of those same changes. While the majority of eighteenth-century British subjects seemed to envision that the empire would put some ships on the sea, their notions of how those ships would be ordered, who would be permitted to hold authority on board them, how they would be manned, how they would interact with the rest of society, and what they would do against enemies varied widely. Contemporaries were well aware that "enemies of the state" could conceivably be domestic as well as foreign. As in the 1780s debates over the fortification of the dockyards, some opposed increasing the navy's power and scope precisely because they feared that it might also inherently expand the power and reach of the executive government, perhaps someday permitting the state to turn that power on its own citizens. If we think of a British navy that operated solely within the British Isles, this allegation perhaps sounds partisan, intended to score political points but not truly believed. However, if we extend our historical lens outward and include the empire as a legitimate part of British society, as contemporaries did, and view the American Revolution as the civil war that it was, we see a much more complicated perspective on what the navy was capable of and how it functioned in eighteenth-century British imperial society. The navy's role in the North American colonies in the 1760s and 1770s validated the assertion that sea power could be used to enforce an arguably illegitimate central authority against civilians; its assistance in maintaining the white plantation regime in the Caribbean was another demonstration of the importance of ships on land. When we think about "empire," we should think not just about the projection of British power overseas, but also about a genuinely global but especially transatlantic British society. The fact that this was not a geographically contiguous society did not negate the commercial, political, and intellectual ties that bound it.

The divergence of British and American military culture following the American Revolution shows the importance of ideology in shaping warfare. Although the early American Republic did not lack for conflict, its experience suggests that warfare did not automatically lead to the creation of the modern state, or at least not to any one type of state model in particular. The United States did not establish a permanent standing navy in the British model until well into the nineteenth century.[4] Instead, early Republican naval efforts relied heavily on privateers, with a minimal number of government-funded warships. In

1776 one contemporary calculated that perhaps 10,000 New Englanders were involved in privateering.[5] In 1781 there were probably around 500 American privateers in comparison to fewer than ten naval ships controlled by the Continental Congress; George Washington ordered that the Continental Congress's naval ammunition be made available to the public, further legitimizing privateering as a national endeavor. The officers of the Continental Congress's navy and those of the early Republic were "fiercely independent" of the orders of their superiors and their crews behaved likewise: John Paul Jones once had to face down a mutiny led by a lieutenant who "held up to the crew that being Americans fighting for liberty the voice of the people should be taken before the Captain's orders."[6] The debate in the Republic over the standing navy broke down along the same cleavages that divided people over questions of central authority versus personal liberty. In the immediate aftermath of the Revolution, the American Republic and Great Britain embodied the two different visions of military force current in Anglo-imperial society: one reliant on the virtue of its citizens to take up arms in times of national need and the other dependent on a professional, disciplined military force, kept separate from the civilian world.

This is not a story of heroes and villains. All those involved, from Walpole, Pitt, and Bedford to Franklin and the attackers of the *Gaspee*, believed they were acting in the best interests of British imperial society as a whole. They perceived different threats and acted accordingly. Virtue and vice was in the eye of the beholder. To acknowledge that the navy was capable of acting coercively is not to say that we should wholeheartedly agree with those who have cast it as a floating prison.[7] Rather, it is a recognition of the fact that many of the tools the state has at its disposal to protect and policy society, to maintain order, can be used against its citizens as well as on their behalf. This is one of the tensions inherent in the modern state; the eighteenth-century navy was not immune to that contradiction.

The role of the navy in enforcing a new imperial system also suggests that, despite their modern cultural resonance, redcoats alone might not have been sufficient to spark the American Revolution. The navy was a second dimension to London's attempts to discipline the colonies back into order, which contemporaries believed was at the heart of the conflict but which has surprisingly dropped out of modern memory of the period. Yet the navy is central to understanding how the conflict developed and why the Revolution happened when it did: it was the navy that formed the vanguard of imperial control and it was the navy that attracted much of the consequent resentment. When the Grenville administration wanted to restructure economic and imperial relationships, it deputized the navy rather than the army. Waterborne trade was a crucial component of the colonial economy and all the major cities of the North American colonies were port cities, as well as regional economic hubs. Any effective trade regulation would have had to involve a maritime component. Without an effective coercive maritime force, the administration would have found itself in much the same position as in the 1740s: able to pass laws but not able to enforce them. Without unrest caused by naval enforcement of acts like the Sugar and Stamp Acts, there would have been far less reason to station army regiments in cities and more reason to distribute them along the frontier, as many advocated, so if there had been less anti-naval sentiment, there might have been less anti-army sentiment, as well. It is also worth noting that the navy's regulation of trade brought it particularly into contact with maritime traders who were frequently based in exactly the types of urban commercial centers with strong Dissenting religious traditions which corresponded to more libertarian ideologies, in both Britain and its colonies. These were exactly the types of people whose ideological inheritance predisposed them to perceive corruption and expanding executive power; they had predicted it from the 1620s, which was precisely why many of them moved to North American colonies in the first place. An inland army presence would have been far less likely to come face to face as frequently with that particular ideological powder keg. That is not to suggest that the Revolution was only sparked by New Englanders' constitutional concerns; there were of course other issues at stake, one of which was the desire of some colonists for greater inland expansion and the resistance of the authoritarian whig regime to that idea. But it is also important to recognize that part of the reason why authoritarian whig administrations opposed inland expansion was precisely because they feared that naval ships would no longer be able to regulate colonists once they were too far from the water's edge. This is also not to suggest that had there not been a professionalized, disciplined, and obedient navy, there would never have been an American Revolution. Yet if we want to understand why the Revolution happened when it did—not in the 1740s with the earlier wave of imperial reform and not at a later date—we should look closely at the fact that for the first time, there was a coercive power in the colonies that did not back down in the face of colonial resistance. The navy's new role brought it particularly into conflict with colonists predisposed to fear the military governance of civilian life; its use as an arm of imperial governance appeared to fulfill every concern patriots, radicals, and libertarians already had about the outcome of too much concentration of power in executive hands.

The navy was not exempt from the ongoing political ferment taking place across the British Empire. A generation ago, eighteenth-century British society was described as having an adamantine stability; more recent political histories have shown us how inaccurate that description is. Although Walpolean oligarchy obscured some of the underlying political debate for the twenty years of his tenure as prime minister, that rapidly ceased to be true after his fall. During the 1760s, George III could barely keep an administration in office, reflecting tensions among the political elite that were mirrored in the public both in Britain and elsewhere in the empire. Pro-Wilkite mobs encircled Parliament, the Duke of Bedford's house was besieged in London, and naval ships were attacked and burned in the colonies. These were not the mindless acts of a deranged populace high on violence: they reflected genuine discontent with the existing political system and a genuine threat to the existing political order. Whether change would be positive or negative for the empire was, again, in the eye of the beholder, but nearly everyone at the time agreed that what they were faced with were drastically different visions of the type of society the British Empire could or should be.

The Royal Navy was a mirror for imperial society. Although the parameters of the debates changed over the course of the eighteenth century, what remained the same was that there *was* a debate. Questions about to what ends naval power should be turned and about the impact it might have on civilian society continued to resonate: the structure of the military and the tasks it was given were taken as symbols both of particular modes of governance and of the nature of the wider empire itself. Contemporaries projected both their hopes and their fears onto sea officers and their floating fortresses.

NOTES

Abbreviations

BL	British Library
CUL	Cambridge University Library
ESRO	East Sussex Record Office
HSP	Historical Society of Pennsylvania
NAS	National Archives of Scotland
NLS	National Library of Scotland
NMM	National Maritime Museum
PRONI	Public Record Office of Northern Ireland
Staff. RO	Staffordshire Record Office
Suff. RO	Suffolk Record Office, Bury St. Edmunds Branch
TNA	The National Archives, Kew
UNott	University of Nottingham Library
WA	Woburn Abbey
WCL	William L. Clements Library, University of Michigan

Introduction

1. See the general discussion in N. A. M. Rodger, *The Command of the Ocean* (New York: W. W. Norton, 2004), 1–163, 606–609, as well as Jan Glete, *Navies and Nations: Warships, Navies and State Building in Europe and America, 1500–1860*, 2 vols. (Stockholm: Almqvist & Wiksell International, 1993).
2. J. D. Davies, *Pepys's Navy: The Ships, Men and Organisation, 1649–89* (Barnsley, UK: Seaforth Publishing, 2008), 24.

3. Qtd. in Patrick Villiers, *Marine Royale, Corsaires, et Trafic dans l'Atlantique de Louis XIV à Louis XVI* (Villeneuve-d'Ascq: Presses universitaires du septentrion, 2002), 78.
4. August Neidhardt von Gneisenau to Gen. F. C. F. von Müffling, 29 June 1815, qtd. in Rodger, *Command of the Ocean,* 574.
5. Glete, *Navies and Nations,* 2:376.
6. Rodger, *Command of the Ocean,* 540; Brian Lavery, *The Ship of the Line,* 2 vols. (Annapolis, MD: Naval Institute Press, 1983), 1:128.
7. Patrick Crowhurst, *The Defence of British Trade, 1689–1815* (Folkstone, UK: Dawson, 1977), 28, 71–80.
8. For an explanation in which geography determines Britain's national character and naval destiny, see, for example, A. T. Mahan, *The Influence of Sea Power upon History 1660–1789* (Boston: Little, Brown, 1918); for foreign policy changes leading to geographic adaptations, see, for example, Michael Duffy, "The Establishment of the Western Squadron as the Linchpin of British Naval Strategy," in *Parameters of British Naval Power, 1650–1850,* ed. Michael Duffy (Exeter, UK: University of Exeter Press, 1992), 60–81. Daniel Baugh has also explored how French and British coastal geography determined the chances of successful invasion and interception of enemy ships in "The Atlantic of the Rival Navies, 1714–1783," in *English Atlantics Revisited: Essays Honouring Professor Ian K. Steele,* ed. Nancy Rhoden (Montreal: McGill–Queen's University Press, 2007), 206–231. He concludes that although the English were better positioned than the Dutch, the French were better positioned, geographically, than the English.
9. For the role of overseas trade in Britain's eighteenth-century economic expansion, see P. K. O'Brien and S. L. Engerman, "Exports and the Growth of the British Economy from the Glorious Revolution to the Peace of Amiens," in *Slavery and the Rise of the Atlantic System,* ed. B. Solow and S. L. Engerman (Cambridge: Cambridge University Press, 1991), 177–209.
10. For accounts of the importance of growing economic power, see Paul Kennedy, *The Rise and Fall of British Naval Mastery* (London: Allen Lane, 1976); Glete, *Navies and Nations;* Jonathan R. Dull, *The Age of the Ship of the Line: The British & French Navies, 1650–1815* (Lincoln: University of Nebraska Press, 2009).
11. For accounts of institutional and administrative factors, see Daniel A. Baugh, *British Naval Administration in the Age of Walpole* (Princeton, NJ: Princeton University Press, 1965); Daniel Baugh, "Naval Power: What Gave the British Naval Superiority?," in *Exceptionalism and Industrialisation: Britain and Its European Rivals, 1688–1815,* ed. Leandro Prados de la Escosura (Cambridge: Cambridge University Press, 2004), 235–257; Daniel Baugh, *The Global Seven Years' War, 1754–1763: Britain and France in a Great Power Contest* (Harlow, UK: Pearson, 2011); John Brewer, *The Sinews of Power: War, Money, and the English State, 1688–1783* (Cambridge, MA: Harvard University Press, 1988); Rodger, *Command of the Ocean;* N. A. M. Rodger, "From the 'Military

Revolution' to the 'Fiscal-Naval State,'" *Journal for Maritime Research* 13, no. 2 (2011): 119–128; Roger Morriss, *The Foundations of British Maritime Ascendancy: Resources, Logistics and the State, 1755–1815* (Cambridge: Cambridge University Press, 2011); Clive Wilkinson, *The British Navy and the State in the Eighteenth Century* (Woodbridge, UK: Boydell, in association with the National Maritime Museum, 2004). See also Ruddock Mackay and Michael Duffy, *Hawke, Nelson and British Naval Leadership, 1747–1805* (Woodbridge, UK: Boydell, 2009), 2–3; Patrick K. O'Brien and Xavier Duran, "Total Factor Productivity for the Royal Navy from Victory at Texel (1653) to Triumph at Trafalgar (1805)," in *Shipping and Economic Growth, 1350–1850,* ed. Richard W. Unger (Leiden: Brill, 2011), 302.

12. Rodger, *Command of the Ocean,* 540.
13. Baugh, *British Naval Administration,* 145; Jeremy Black, *The British Seaborne Empire* (New Haven, CT: Yale University Press, 2004), 121, 160; Lavery, *Ship of the Line,* 1:118; Sam Willis, *Fighting at Sea in the Eighteenth Century: The Art of Sailing Warfare* (Woodbridge, UK: Boydell, 2008), 140–141; N. A. M. Rodger, "The Nature of Victory at Sea," *Journal for Maritime Research* 7, no. 1 (2005): 114–115.
14. Daniel Baugh, "'Too Much Mixed in This Affair': The Impact of Ministerial Politics in the Eighteenth-Century Royal Navy," in *New Interpretations in Naval History: Selected Papers from the Fourteenth Naval History Symposium,* ed. Randy Carol Balano and Craig L. Symonds (Annapolis, MD: Naval Institute Press, 2001), 31.
15. Mackay and Duffy, *Hawke, Nelson and British Naval Leadership,* 217.
16. J. R. Jones, "Limitations of British Sea Power in the French Wars, 1689–1815," in *The British Navy and the Use of Naval Power in the Eighteenth Century,* ed. Jeremy Black and Philip Woodfine (Leicester: Leicester University Press, 1988), 47.
17. Glete, *Navies and Nations,* 2:482.
18. Rodger, *Command of the Ocean,* 183, 186, 193, 339, 577. See also Rodger's biography of the Earl of Sandwich ("All politicians agreed that [the navy] was the principal and essential means of national defence, and all opposition politicians agreed, whatever the circumstances of the moment, that the Navy and naval policy were being shamefully neglected"): *The Insatiable Earl: A Life of John Montagu, Fourth Earl of Sandwich, 1718–1792* (London: HarperCollins, 1991), 12, and his administrative history of the Admiralty ("the politics of Georgian England were based on fundamental agreement, among other things on the need of a navy"): *The Admiralty* (Lavenham, UK: Terence Dalton, 1979), 55.
19. See the extensive literature on impressment, including Denver Brunsman, *The Evil Necessity: British Naval Impressment in the Eighteenth-Century Atlantic World* (Charlottesville: University of Virginia Press, 2013); Daniel James Ennis, *Enter the Press-Gang: Naval Impressment in Eighteenth-Century British Literature* (Newark: University of Delaware Press, 2002); Roger Knight,

"From Impressment to Task Work: Strikes and Disruption in the Royal Dockyards, 1688–1788," in *History of Work and Labour Relations in the Royal Dockyards,* ed. K. Lunn and A. Day (London: Mansell, 1999), 1–21; Nicholas Rogers, *The Press Gang: Naval Impressment and Its Opponents in Georgian Britain* (London: Continuum, 2007).

20. Michael R. Snyder, "A Victim of Circumstance: The Timber Bill of 1772 and the East India Company," *Past Imperfect* 1 (1992): 27–47.

21. Nicholas Tracy, *Navies, Deterrence, and American Independence: Britain and Seapower in the 1760s and 1770s* (Vancouver: University of British Columbia Press, 1988), 8–28; Clive Wilkinson, "The Earl of Egmont and the Navy, 1763–6," *Mariner's Mirror* 84, no. 4 (1998): 418–433; Wilkinson, *British Navy and the State,* 35–65.

22. Philip Woodfine, "Ideas of Naval Power and the Conflict with Spain, 1737–1742," in *The British Navy and the Use of Naval Power in the Eighteenth Century,* ed. Jeremy Black and Philip Woodfine (Leicester: Leicester University Press, 1988), 75.

23. See Nicholas Rogers, "The Dynamic of News in Britain during the American War: The Case of Admiral Keppel," *Parliamentary History* 25, no. 1 (2006): 49–67; Kathleen Wilson, "Empire, Trade and Popular Politics in Mid-Hanoverian Britain: The Case of Admiral. Vernon," *Past & Present* 121 (November 1988): 74–109, as well as the discussions of Admiral Byng in M. John Cardwell, *Art and Arms: Literature, Politics and Patriotism during the Seven Years' War* (Manchester: Manchester University Press, 2004), 46–102, 175–177; Marie Peters, *Pitt and Popularity: The Patriot Minister and London Opinion during the Seven Years' War* (Oxford: Clarendon Press, 1980), 46–57, 69–71; Nicholas Rogers, *Whigs and Cities: Popular Politics in the Age of Walpole and Pitt* (Oxford: Clarendon Press, 1989), 347–389; Nicholas Rogers, *Crowds, Culture, and Politics in Georgian Britain* (Oxford: Clarendon Press, 1998), 58–84; Robert Donald Spector, *English Literary Periodicals and the Climate of Opinion during the Seven Years' War* (The Hague: Mouton & Co., 1966), 13–61; Brian Tunstall, *Admiral Byng and the Loss of Minorca* (London: Philip Allan & Co., 1928).

24. Brewer, *Sinews of Power,* 33; Jeremy Black, "Introduction," in *The British Navy and the Use of Naval Power in the Eighteenth Century,* ed. Jeremy Black and Philip Woodfine (Leicester: Leicester University Press, 1988), 3.

25. Mackay and Duffy, *Hawke, Nelson and British Naval Leadership,* 2; O'Brien and Duran, "Total Factor Productivity," 299; Margarette Lincoln, *Representing the Royal Navy: British Sea Power, 1750–1815* (Aldershot, UK: Ashgate, 2002), 41.

26. *London Gazetteer,* 4 March 1749; [John Allen], *An Oration, upon the Beauties of Liberty, or the Essential Rights of the Americans* (Boston, 1773), xi; Debate on Mr. Pitt's Motion for fortifying the Dock Yards, 27 February 1786, in *Cobbett's Parliamentary History of England,* 36 vols. (London, 1806–1820), 25:1096–157.

27. For scholarship on the British political sphere, see note 30; for the proliferation of newspapers in the colonies, see, for example, Edwin Emery and Michael Emery, *The Press and America,* 5th ed. (Englewood Cliffs, NJ: Prentice Hall, 1984), 51. Although the majority of these newspapers lasted less than two years and were of unreliable profitability, the urge to found new papers is nevertheless illuminating.
28. Alan James, "Raising the Profile of Naval History: An International Perspective on Early Modern Navies," *Mariner's Mirror* 97, no. 1 (February 2011): 201.
29. N. A. M. Rodger, *The Wooden World: An Anatomy of the Georgian Navy* (New York: Norton, 1996), 29–36; N. A. M. Rodger, *The Admiralty* (Lavenham, UK: Terence Dalton, 1979), 61–65; J. C. Sainty, *Admiralty Officials, 1660–1870* (London: Athlone Press for the University of London, Institute of Historical Research, 1975). For an account that demonstrates how complex the bureaucratic overlap between these boards could be, see, for example, David Syrett, *Shipping and Military Power in the Seven Years' War: The Sails of Victory* (Exeter, UK: University of Exeter Press, 2008).
30. The many ways in which popular politics responded to and influenced high politics has been a major theme in literature on eighteenth-century Britain. See, for example, Stephen Botein, Jack R. Censer, and Harriet Ritvo, "The Periodical Press in Eighteenth-Century English and French Society: A Cross-Cultural Approach," *Comparative Studies in Society and History* 23, no. 3 (1981): 464–490; James Bradley, *Popular Politics and the American Revolution in England: Petitions, the Crown, and Public Opinion* (Mason, GA: Mercer University Press, 1986); John Brewer, *Party Ideology and Popular Politics at the Accession of George III* (Cambridge: Cambridge University Press, 1976); Cardwell, *Arts and Arms;* G. A. Granfield, *The Development of the Provincial Newspaper, 1700–1760* (Oxford: Clarendon Press, 1962); Robert Harris, *A Patriot Press: National Politics and the London Press in the 1740s* (Oxford: Clarendon Press, 1993); Rogers, *Crowds, Culture, and Politics;* Kathleen Wilson, *The Sense of the People: Politics, Culture, and Imperialism in England, 1715–1785* (Cambridge: Cambridge University Press, 1995).
31. For an excellent discussion of the major ideologies of mid-eighteenth-century British imperial politics, see Justin du Rivage, *Revolution against Empire: Taxes, Politics, and the Origins of American Independence* (New Haven, CT: Yale University Press, 2017), 24–52.
32. See, for example, the accounts of voter consistency in Rogers, *Whigs and Cities,* 228; Bradley, *Popular Politics,* 152–154.
33. Contemporaries sometimes called these people "skeptical whigs" or "the Bedford party" (for one of their primary leaders, the Duke of Bedford), while other scholars have labeled them "authoritarian reformers" or "neo-Tories" to indicate, accurately, that their appeal crossed party lines. However, they would all likely have identified themselves as whigs, and thus "authoritarian whigs" is the imperfect label I have chosen.

34. Black, *British Seaborne Empire;* Brewer, *Sinews of Power;* Linda Colley, *Britons: Forging the Nation, 1707–1837* (New Haven, CT: Yale University Press, 1992); Harris, *Patriot Press;* Bob Harris, *Politics and the Nation: Britain in the Mid-Eighteenth Century* (Oxford: Oxford University Press, 2002); Rogers, *Whigs and Cities;* Rogers, *Crowds, Culture, and Politics;* Wilson, *The Sense of the People.*
35. E. P. Thompson, *The Making of the English Working Class* (New York: Pantheon Books, 1963), 102–186; Linda Colley, "The Apotheosis of George III: Loyalty, Royalty and the British Nation 1760–1820," *Past & Present* 102 (February 1984): 99–111; Henry P. Ippel, "British Sermons and the American Revolution," *Journal of Religious History* 12 (1982): 197.
36. David Armitage, *The Ideological Origins of the British Empire* (Cambridge: Cambridge University Press, 2000), 8; Vincent T. Harlow, *The Founding of the Second British Empire, 1763–93*, 2 vols. (London: Longmans, Green, 1952–1964), 1:62.
37. James Vaughn, "The Politics of Empire: Metropolitan Socio-Political Development and the Imperial Transformation of the British East India Company, 1675–1775" (PhD diss., University of Chicago, 2009), 444–450, 507–540, 516–522.
38. P. J. Marshall, *The Making and Unmaking of Empires: Britain, India, and America c. 1750–1783* (Oxford: Oxford University Press, 2005), 7, 183–206; Robert Travers, *Ideology and Empire in Eighteenth-Century India: The British in Bengal* (Cambridge: Cambridge University Press, 2007), 49–50.
39. C. A. Bayly, *Imperial Meridian: The British Empire and the World 1780–1830* (London: Longman, 1989), 8–9; Paul Langford, "Old Whigs, Old Tories and the American Revolution," *Journal of Imperial and Commonwealth History* 8 (January 1980): 121–127.
40. Michael Duffy, "World-Wide War and British Expansion, 1793–1815," in *The Oxford History of the British Empire*, ed. William Roger Louis, 5 vols. (Oxford: Oxford University Press, 1998), 2:184–207.
41. Benjamin L. Carp, *Rebels Rising: Cities and the American Revolution* (Oxford: Oxford University Press, 2007); Paul A. Gilje, *Liberty on the Waterfront: American Maritime Culture in the Age of Revolution* (Philadelphia: University of Pennsylvania Press, 2004); Peter Linebaugh and Marcus Rediker, *Many-Headed Hydra: Sailors, Slaves, Commoners, and the Hidden History of the Revolutionary Atlantic* (Boston: Beacon Press, 2000).
42. Richard Buel Jr., *In Irons: Britain's Naval Supremacy and the American Revolutionary Economy* (New Haven, CT: Yale University Press, 1998).
43. Charles Tilly, "Reflections on the History of European State Making," in *The Formation of National States in Western Europe*, ed. Charles Tilly (Princeton, NJ: Princeton University Press, 1975), 42. See also Timothy Besley and Torsten Persson, "The Origins of State Capacity: Property Rights, Taxation, and Politics," *American Economic Review* 99, no. 4 (2009): 1218–1244; Richard Bonney and W. M. Ormrod, "Introduction," in *Crises, Revolutions and Self-Sustained Growth: Essays in European Fiscal History, 1130–1830*, ed.

W. M. Ormrod, Margaret Bonney, and Richard Bonney (Stamford, UK: Shaun Tyas, 1999), 1–22; Anthony Giddens, *The Nation State and Violence* (Berkeley: University of California Press, 1985); Jan Glete, *War and the State in Early Modern Europe* (London: Routledge, 2002); John A. Hall and G. John Ikenberry, *The State* (Minneapolis: University of Minnesota Press, 1989); Philip T. Hoffman and Jean-Laurent Rosenthal, "The Political Economy of Warfare and Taxation in Early Modern Europe," in *The Frontiers of the New Institutional Economics,* ed. John N. Drobak and John V. C. Nye (San Diego, CA: Academic Press, 1997), 31–55; Hendrik Spruyt, "War, Trade, and State Formation," in *The Oxford Handbook of Comparative Politics,* ed. Carles Boix and Susan Stokes (Oxford: Oxford University Press, 2007), 211–235; Charles Tilly, *Coercion, Capital, and European States, AD 990–1992* (Cambridge, MA: Blackwell, 1990).

44. For discussions of the contribution of military revolutions to state formation and other forms of social change, see especially Geoffrey Parker, *The Military Revolution: Military Innovation and the Rise of the West, 1500–1800* (Cambridge: Cambridge University Press, 1996). See also Andrew F. Krepinevich, "Cavalry to Computer: The Pattern of Military Revolutions," *National Interest* 37 (1994): 30–42; Robert L. O'Connell, *Of Arms and Men: A History of War, Weapons and Aggression* (Oxford: Oxford University Press, 1989); Clifford J. Rogers, "'Military Revolutions' and 'Revolutions in Military Affairs': A Historian's Perspective," in *Towards a Revolution in Military Affairs?,* ed. Thierry Gongora and Harald von Riekoff (Westport, CT: Greenwood Press, 2000), 21–36; Lynn White, *Medieval Technology and Social Change* (Oxford: Clarendon Press, 1962).
45. Brewer, *Sinews of Power.*
46. N. A. M. Rodger, "From the 'Military Revolution' to the 'Fiscal-Naval State,'" *Journal for Maritime Research* 13, no. 2 (2011): 122, 123. See also Patrick K. O'Brien, "Contentions of the Purse between England and Its European Rivals from Henry V to George IV: A Conversation with Michael Mann," *Journal of Historical Sociology* 19, no. 4 (2006): 341–363.
47. As discussed by Rodger in "From the 'Military Revolution,'" 119–128.

1. Seventeenth-Century Foundations

1. For both the nonstate nature of the Elizabethan navy and the persistence of Elizabethan naval myth, see N. A. M. Rodger, "Queen Elizabeth and the Myth of Sea-Power in English History," *Transactions of the Royal Historical Society,* 6th ser., 14 (2004): 153–174.
2. New York Public Library, Great Britain Box—Navy, "Reflections on Navall Discipline" [ca. 1685–1690?].
3. John F. Guilmartin Jr., "The Military Revolution in Warfare at Sea during the Early Modern Era: Technological Origins, Operational Outcomes and

Strategic Consequences," *Journal for Maritime Research* 13, no. 2 (2011): 129–137.

4. M. A. J. Palmer, "The 'Military Revolution' Afloat: The Era of the Anglo-Dutch Wars and the Transition to Modern Warfare at Sea," *War in History* 4 (1997): 123–149.
5. Kenneth R. Andrews, *Ships, Money and Politics: Seafaring and Naval Enterprise in the Reign of Charles I* (Cambridge: Cambridge University Press, 1991); Frank L. Fox, "Hired Men-of-War, 1664–67 (Part I)," *Mariner's Mirror* 84 (1998): 13; Andrew Thrust, "Naval Finance and the Origins and Development of Ship Money," in *War and Government in Britain, 1598–1650*, ed. Mark Charles Fissel (Manchester: Manchester University Press, 1991), 133–162.
6. J. D. Davies, *Pepys's Navy: The Ships, Men and Organisation, 1649–89* (Barnsley, UK: Seaforth, 2008), 33, 36, 229.
7. Ibid., 88.
8. Louis XIV, *Mémoires for the Instruction of the Dauphin*, trans. Paul Sonnino (New York: Free Press, 1970), 123; Patrick Villiers, *Marine Royale, Corsaires, et Trafic dans l'Atlantique de Louis XIV à Louis XVI* (Villeneuve-d'Ascq: Presses universitaires du septentrion, 2002), 74.
9. Davies, *Pepys's Navy*, 24; D. W. Jones, "Defending the Revolution: The Economics, Logistics, and Finance of England's War Effort, 1688–1712," in *The World of William and Mary: Anglo-Dutch Perspectives on the Revolution of 1688–89*, ed. Dale Hoak and Mordechai Feingold (Stanford, CA: Stanford University Press, 1996), 59; N. A. M. Rodger, *The Command of the Ocean: A Naval History of Britain, 1649–1815* (New York: Norton, 2004), 106–109, 142, 152, 188.
10. There were exceptions to this, of course, including Oliver Cromwell's Caribbean campaign of the 1650s.
11. See Sari R. Hornstein, *The Restoration Navy and English Foreign Trade 1674–1688: A Study in the Peacetime Use of Sea Power* (Aldershot, UK: Scolar Press, 1991).
12. By "warships," I mean sixth-rate ships and larger. Generally speaking, first- to fourth-rate ships were considered "ships of the line"; fifth- and sixth-rate ships were considered cruisers or frigates. There were also other smaller ships of war that fell outside these classifications—including but not limited to sloops, ketches, fireships, and occasionally xebecs—but my point here is simply to give a general overview of how the ships most likely to see combat were distributed. These figures are drawn from Rodger, *Command of the Ocean*, 612–615, but regular abstracts of ship distribution can be found in the Admiralty papers in the National Archives, Kew (hereafter TNA). For example, see TNA SP 42/29, f. 221. Admiralty, "A List of his Majesty's Ships & Sloops . . . ," 1 October 1745; TNA SP 42/34, f. 251. Admiralty, "List of his Majesty's ships & vessels, in sea pay," 30 April 1750; TNA PRO 30/8/79, f. 185. Admiralty, "Abstract of the Ships of the Line in Commission," 20 February 1760.

13. Rodger, *Command of the Ocean,* 636–639; E. A. Wrigley and R. S. Schofield, *The Population History of England 1541–1871: A Reconstruction* (Cambridge, MA: Harvard University Press, 1981), 528–529; Michael Flinn, ed., *Scottish Population History: From the 17th Century to the 1930s* (Cambridge: Cambridge University Press, 1977), 198–199, 302; L. A. Clarkson, "Irish Population Revisited, 1687–1821," in *Irish Population, Economy, and Society: Essays in Honour of the Late K. H. Connell,* ed. J. M. Coldstrom and L. A. Clarkson (Oxford: Clarendon Press, 1981), 26.
14. Philip MacDougall, *Royal Dockyards* (London: David and Charles, 1982); Jonathan Coad, *The Royal Dockyards 1690–1850: Architecture and Engineering Works of the Sailing Navy* (Brookfield, VT: Gower, 1989), 3.
15. On this point, see Michael J. Braddick, *State Formation in Early Modern England, c. 1550–1700* (Cambridge: Cambridge University Press, 2000), esp. part III; Bernard Capp, *Cromwell's Navy: The Fleet and the English Revolution, 1648–1660* (Oxford: Clarendon Press, 1989); John Morrill, *The Revolt of the Provinces: Conservatives and Radicals in the English Civil War, 1630–1650* (London: Longman, 1980).
16. Mark Kishlansky, *A Monarchy Transformed: Britain, 1603–1714* (London: Penguin, 1997), 230. The period between the execution of Charles I in 1649 and the restoration to the English throne of Charles II in 1660 is alternately known as the Commonwealth, the Protectorate, and the Interregnum.
17. These parties solidified in the Exclusion Crisis (1679–1681), during which England's political classes debated whether to exclude James from the line of succession because of his Catholicism, along lines of division emerged throughout the 1660s and 1670s. In other words, the Exclusion Crisis encouraged people of similar political ideology to organize in more coherent ways but did not necessarily create those ideologies out of nowhere. It would therefore not be strictly accurate to label someone as a whig in 1670, though that person could be referred to as a proto-whig or as holding whiggish ideas.
18. For more on the ideological content of these parties, see Richard L. Greaves, *Enemies under His Feet: Radicals and Nonconformists in Britain, 1664–1677* (Stanford, CA: Stanford University Press, 1990); Richard L. Greaves, *Secrets of the Kingdom: British Radicals from the Popish Plot to the Revolution of 1688–89* (Stanford, CA: Stanford University Press, 1992); Tim Harris, *London Crowds in the Reign of Charles II: Propaganda and Politics from the Restoration until the Exclusion Crisis* (Cambridge: Cambridge University Press, 1987); Tim Harris, *Politics under the Later Stuarts: Party Conflict in a Divided Society, 1660–1715* (London: Longman, 1993); Mark Knights, *Politics and Opinion in the Exclusion Crisis, 1678–81* (Cambridge: Cambridge University Press, 1994); Gary De Krey, "The London Whigs and the Exclusion Crisis Reconsidered," in *The First Modern Society: Essays in English History in Honour of Lawrence Stone,* ed. Lee Beier, David Cannadine, and James Rosenheim (Cambridge: Cambridge University Press, 1989), 457–482; John Miller, "Public Opinion in

Charles II's England," *History* 80 (1995): 359–381; Steven Pincus, "'Coffee Politicians Does Create': Coffeehouses and Restoration Political Culture," *Journal of Modern History* 67 (1995): 807–834; Steve Pincus, *1688: The First Modern Revolution* (New Haven, CT: Yale University Press, 2009). On the way that debates over imperial policy displayed continuity through the Exclusion Crisis, see, for example, Abigail L. Swingen, *Competing Visions of Empire: Labor, Slavery, and the Origins of the British Atlantic Empire* (New Haven, CT: Yale University Press, 2015); Leslie Theibert, "Making an English Caribbean, 1650–1688" (PhD diss., Yale University, 2013).

19. Capp, *Cromwell's Navy,* 15–72, 396–397. For the breakdown in support within the mercantile community for the royalist versus parliamentary causes, see Robert Brenner, *Merchants and Revolution: Commercial Change, Political Conflict, and London's Overseas Traders, 1550–1653* (London: Verso, 2003).
20. Capp, *Cromwell's Navy,* 371–378.
21. Ibid., 381–389.
22. TNA SP 44/62, f. 101. Sir Leoline Jenkins to [Sidney Godolphin, Earl of Godolphin], 30 September 1680, reprinted in *Calendar of State Papers Domestic, 1680–81,* 28 vols. (London: His Majesty's Stationery Office, 1921), 22:44.
23. The Civil War was not exclusively the class-based revolution of the bourgeoisie against the aristocracy that Marxist historians like Christopher Hill have portrayed it to be, but the events of the war did encourage the undermining and levelling of a wide variety of hierarchies. The king was executed and a republic declared, overturning political hierarchies; the Church of England was disestablished, leaving no clear religious hierarchy; merchants rose to places of prominence in the new government they had not had before, challenging social hierarchies; and the collapse of censorship during the Interregnum encouraged a proliferation of ideas, undermining central control over the public perception of all of these arenas.
24. Davies, *Pepys's Navy,* 94–96.
25. Capp, *Cromwell's Navy,* 375–378.
26. John Hattendorf et al., eds., *British Naval Documents, 1204–1960* (Aldershot, UK: Scolar Press for the Navy Records Society, 1993), 283, 293, qtd. in Rodger, *Command of the Ocean,* 120–121.
27. One list from the 1690s did include twenty men who had done so, but fourteen of them (70 percent) had commissions from before the Restoration. Capp, *Cromwell's Navy,* 384–387; J. D. Davies, "The Navy, Parliament and Political Crisis in the Reign of Charles II," *Historical Journal* 36, no. 2 (1993): 280; Davies, *Pepys's Navy,* 96.
28. Davies, "Navy, Parliament and Political Crisis," 276.
29. J. D. Davies, "The Good Enemy: British Perceptions of Michiel de Ruyter and the Anglo-Dutch wars," in *De Ruyter: Dutch Admiral,* ed. Jaap R. Bruijn (Rotterdam: Karwansaray BV, 2011), 120–139.

30. New York Public Library, Great Britain Box—Navy. "Reflections on Navall Discipline," [ca. 1685–1690?].
31. *An Inquiry into the Causes of Our Naval Miscarriages*, 2nd ed. (London, 1707), 13.
32. Robert E. Glass, "The Image of the Sea Officer in English Literature, 1660–1710," *Albion* 26, no. 4 (1994): 585.
33. For more on late seventeenth-century naval reforms, see particularly Davies, *Pepys's Navy*, chaps. 13 and 14; Celina Fox, "The Ingenious Mr Dummer: Rationalizing the Royal Navy in Late Seventeenth-Century England," *Electronic British Library Journal* 10 (2007), Article 10.
34. Davies, "Navy, Parliament and Political Crisis," 277.
35. Carew wanted to allow nonconformists to hold office in England but to exclude all Catholics, including James; he also supported bills that encouraged English manufactures and the militia instead of a standing army. "Carew, Nicholas (1635–88), of Beddington, Surr.," in *The History of Parliament: The House of Commons 1660–1690*, ed. B. D. Henning, online version: http://www.historyofparliamentonline.org/volume/1660-1690/member/carew-sir-nicholas-1635-88; 3 March 1673, *Debates of the House of Commons, from the year 1667 to the year 1694 . . .* , ed. Anchitell Grey, 10 vols. (London, 1769), 2:86.
36. Though the accusations do not appear to have a solid foundation in fact, they were not out of the realm of possibility. James did have a liking for Irish officers, as Pepys had noted in the 1660s, and once he became king in 1685, he certainly promoted a variety of Catholics into office. Charles, as well, had secretly promised to convert to Catholicism and had issued a Declaration of Indulgence in 1672 that permitted both nonconformist Dissenters and Catholics to worship privately, though Parliament forced him to withdraw it.
37. 16 November 1678, 22 March 1679, and 14 April 1679, *Debates of the House of Commons, from the year 1667 to the year 1694 . . .* , 6:207, 7:20, 7:112.
38. In reality, however, most captains were desperate enough for manpower that they were willing to turn a blind eye. British Library (hereafter BL) Add. MSS 38153, f. 162, Lord Chancellor Richard Cox to Edward Southwell, 21 February 1706, qtd. in Patrick Walsh, "Ireland and the Royal Navy in the Eighteenth Century," in *The Royal Navy and the British Atlantic World, c. 1750–1820*, ed. Christer Petley and John McAleer (London: Palgrave Macmillan, 2016), 64.
39. On (proto-)whig and (proto-)tory debates over foreign and imperial policy, see particularly Pincus, *1688;* Swingen, *Competing Visions of Empire;* and Theibert, "Making an English Caribbean." For an account of the Stuart monarchy's attempt to tighten control over the empire, see Stephen Saunders Webb, *Governors-General: The English Army and the Definition of the Empire, 1569–1681* (Chapel Hill: University of North Carolina Press, 1979). For further accounts of the relationship between commerce and imperial

governance, see Brenner, *Merchants and Revolution;* Nuala Zahedieh, *The Capital and the Colonies: London and the Atlantic Economy, 1660–1700* (Cambridge: Cambridge University Press, 2010).

40. 6–8 February 1678, Grey's *Debates,* 5:95–122; Davies, "The Navy, Parliament and Political Crisis," 271–288.
41. 14 April 1769, Grey's *Debates,* 7:111–112.
42. Davies, "Navy, Parliament and Political Crisis," 288.
43. Generals-at-sea during the Interregnum also included Robert Blake, Richard Deane, Edward Montagu, William Penn, and Edward Popham. Individuals holding both army and navy positions following the Restoration also included Richard Kirby, George Legge, and Charles Skelton. Davies, *Pepys's Navy,* 16–18.
44. There are no reliable statistics on naval manpower before 1688 or on exactly how much was spent on naval affairs, meaning that it is difficult to reconstruct the exact size of peacetime fleets. Rodger, *Command of the Ocean,* 130, 636–641.
45. Davies, *Pepys's Navy,* 143.
46. For more on late seventeenth-century naval reforms, see particularly ibid., chaps. 13 and 14; Fox, "The Ingenious Mr Dummer."
47. During this period Pepys did reform the purser system, the means by which individual ships were victualed, to eliminate incentives for dishonesty and private emolument. David Davies, "The Birth of the Imperial Navy? Aspects of English Naval Strategy c. 1650–90," in *Parameters of British Naval Power, 1650–1850,* ed. Michael Duffy (Exeter, UK: University of Exeter Press, 1992), 14–38; Rodger, *Command of the Ocean,* 120.
48. Capp, *Cromwell's Navy,* 386; Davies, *Pepys's Navy,* 98.
49. Rodger, *Command of the Ocean,* 33, 95–111.
50. Robert E. Glass, "Naval Courts-Martial in Seventeenth-Century England," in *New Interpretations in Naval History: Selected Papers from the Twelfth Naval History Symposium Held at the United States Naval Academy, 26–27 October 1995,* ed. William B. Cobar (Annapolis, MD: Naval Institute Press, 1997), 53, 62; Glass, "Image of the Sea Officer," 599.
51. Frank Fox, "The English Naval Ship-Building Programme of 1664," *Mariner's Mirror* 78 (1992): 282.
52. Davies, *Pepys's Navy,* 230–232.
53. Rodger, *Command of the Ocean,* 77–92; Capp, *Cromwell's Navy,* 386.
54. Rodger, *Command of the Ocean,* 148–149; Davies, *Pepys's Navy,* 275.
55. William L. Clements Library, University of Michigan (hereafter WCL), James Spelman Collection, Small Collections, Box 23, Folder 4. James Spelman to James Vanden Bempde, 8 October 1701.
56. Rodger, *Command of the Ocean,* 202–204.
57. Ibid., 184.
58. Samuel Pepys, *Samuel Pepys's Naval Minutes,* ed. J. R. Tanner (London: Navy Records Society, 1926), 319–320, qtd. in ibid., 183.

59. Rodger, *Command of the Ocean*, 181–185, 193.
60. Qtd. in Villiers, *Marine Royale*, 78.
61. Rodger, *Command of the Ocean*, 156–157, 188, 197, 220; Davies, *Pepys's Navy*, 275–276.
62. Whereas England's overseas colonial population was around 140,000 in 1660, by 1700 that had increased to 400,000. Imports from these markets were important—tripling during that period so that by 1700 they were about 20 percent of the import trade—but exports to these markets (in other words, colonial consumption) were even more important. Zahedieh, *Capital and the Colonies*, 52, 238–292.
63. To explore these debates in far more detail, see Pincus, *1688;* Swingen, *Competing Visions of Empire;* Theibert, "Making an English Caribbean"; Zahedieh, *Capital and the Colonies.*
64. Very few of these cruisers were built until the 1690s, when whigs came to power. Davies, "The Navy, Parliament and Political Crisis," 287–288; Rodger, *Command of the Ocean*, 222.
65. Shinsuke Satsuma, *Britain and Colonial Maritime War in the Early Eighteenth Century: Silver, Seapower and the Atlantic* (Woodbridge, UK: Boydell, 2013), discusses these different conceptions in extensive detail.
66. Peter Le Fevre, "The Battle of Bantry Bay, 1 May 1689," *Irish Sword* 18 (1990): 10–12.
67. Dr. Williams's Library, Morrice MS R p. 223, qtd. in Peter Le Fevre, "The Earl of Torrington's Court-Martial, 10 December 1690," *Mariner's Mirror* 76 (1990): 247.
68. For accounts of the court-martial, see Brian Lavery, *The Ship of the Line*, vol. 1, *The Development of the Battlefleet 1650–1850* (Annapolis, MD: Naval Institute Press, 1983), 53–56; Le Fevre, "The Earl of Torrington's Court-Martial," 243–249; C. D. Lee, "The Battle of Beachy Head: Lord Torrington's Conduct," *Mariner's Mirror* 80 (1994): 270–289; Peter Le Fevre, "'Meer Laziness' or Incompetence: The Earl of Torrington and the Battle of Beachy Head," *Mariner's Mirror* 80 (1994): 290–297.
69. Etienne Taillemite and Pierre Guillaume, *Tourville et Beveziers* (Paris: Economica, 1991), 78, qtd. in Lee, "Battle of Beachy Head," 275.
70. *The Account Given by Sir John Ashby, Vice-Admiral, and Reere-Admiral Rooke to the Lords Commissioners of the Engagement at Sea between the English, Dutch, and French Fleets, June the 30th, 1690 . . .* (London, 1691), 8; Lee, "Battle of Beachy Head," 273–274.
71. Rodger, *Command of the Ocean*, 153.
72. Thomas Wagstaffe, *Supplement to His Majesty's Most Gracious Speech to the Honourable House of Commons* ([London?], 1693), 6.
73. *Remarks upon a Late Pamphlet Intitul'd, The Two Great Questions Consider'd* (London, 1700), 8, 13.
74. *A Debate between Three Ministers of State on the Present Affairs of England . . .* (London, 1702), 18.

75. Daniel Defoe, *The Two Great Questions Consider'd,* republished in *The Genuine Works of Mr. Daniel D'Foe,* 2 vols. (London, 1721), 1:364.
76. Joseph Addison, *The Present State of the War, and the Necessity of an Augmentation, Consider'd* (London, 1708), 17.
77. *Review of the State of the British Nation,* 8 January 1708.
78. *Division Our Destruction: Or, a Short History of the French Faction in England* (London, 1702), 5.
79. Jones, "Defending the Revolution," 62–71.
80. I. R. Mather, "The Role of the Royal Navy in the English Atlantic Empire, 1660–1720" (PhD diss., University of Oxford, 1995).
81. Satsuma, *Britain and Colonial Maritime War,* 134–151; Rodger, *Command of the Ocean,* 177–178.
82. J. D. Alsop, "The Age of the Projectors: British Imperial Strategy in the North Atlantic in the War of Spanish Succession," *Acadiensis* 21, no. 1 (1991): 37–39; Satsuma, *Britain and Colonial Maritime War,* 130.
83. Charles Davenant, *Sir Thomas Double at Court, and in High Preferments. In Two Dialogues . . .* (London, 1710), 73–74.
84. Satsuma, *Britain and Colonial Maritime War,* 126–129.
85. Charles Davenant, *A report to the Honourable the Commissioners for putting in execution the act . . .* (London, 1712), part I, 67, part II, 61. The 1707 Act of Union created the political entity of Great Britain; from that point onward, it is appropriate to refer to the British navy rather than the English navy.
86. Jonathan Swift, *The Conduct of the Allies, and of the Late Ministry, in Beginning and Carrying on the Present War,* 2nd ed. (London, 1711), 35–36, 45, 54–55.
87. John Haversham, *Memoirs of . . . John Lord Haversham, from the Year 1640 to 1710* (London, 1711), 28; Rodger, *Command of the Ocean,* 151–153, 177; Jones, "Defending the Revolution," 71.
88. Jones, "Defending the Revolution," 59–74; Rodger, *Command of the Ocean,* 136–180, 232; Satsuma, *Britain and Colonial Maritime War,* 103–125.
89. On this point, see the extensive literature on the Financial Revolution, including John Brewer, *The Sinews of Power: War, Money, and the English State, 1688–1783* (Cambridge, MA: Harvard University Press, 1988); Bruce G. Carruthers, *City of Capital: Politics and Markets in the English Financial Revolution* (Princeton, NJ: Princeton University Press, 1996); P. G. M. Dickson, *The Financial Revolution in England: A Study in the Development of Public Credit, 1688–1756* (London: Macmillan, 1967); Douglass C. North and Barry R. Weingast, "Constitutions and Commitment: The Evolution of Institutions Governing Public Choice in Seventeenth-Century England," *Journal of Economic History* 46, no. 4 (1989): 803–832.
90. N. A. M. Rodger, "From the 'Military Revolution' to the 'Fiscal-Naval State,'" *Journal for Maritime Research* 13, no. 2 (2011): 123.
91. Patrick K. O'Brien, "Contentions of the Purse between England and Its European Rivals from Henry V to George IV: A Conversation with Michael Mann," *Journal of Historical Sociology* 19, no. 4 (2006): 341–363.

2. Walpolean Imperial and Naval Policy

1. The Dutch also later acceded to the treaty, while Prussia dropped out.
2. BL Add. MSS 47031, ff. 125v–26v. Daniel Dering to John Lord Perceval, 28 March 1726.
3. BL Add. MSS 32749, f. 94. Thomas Pelham-Holles, Duke of Newcastle, to Thomas Robinson, 30 January 1727.
4. BL Add. MSS 32749, f. 112. Robinson to André-Hercule de Fleury, Cardinal de Fleury, 16 February 1727.
5. BL Add. MSS 47031, ff. 125v–126v. Dering to Lord Perceval, 28 March 1726; BL Add. MSS 32749, ff. 83–84. Newcastle to Robinson, 26 January 1727; [Daniel Defoe], *The Evident Approach of a War; and Something of the Necessity of It, in Order to Establish Peace, and Preserve Trade* (London, 1727), 1.
6. See, for example, Jeremy Black, "Introduction," in *Britain in the Age of Walpole,* ed. Jeremy Black (London: Macmillan, 1984), 22; Jeremy Black, *Robert Walpole and the Nature of Politics in Early Eighteenth-Century Britain* (New York: St. Martin's Press, 1990), 120–122; Linda Colley, *In Defiance of Oligarchy: The Tory Party, 1714–60* (Cambridge: Cambridge University Press, 1982), 12; J. H. Plumb, *The Growth of Political Stability in England, 1675–1725* (London: Macmillan, 1967), xviii, 189; W. A. Speck, *Stability and Strife: England 1714–1760* (London: Edward Arnold, 1977), 4.
7. James Henretta, *"Salutary Neglect": Colonial Administration under the Duke of Newcastle* (Princeton, NJ: Princeton University Press, 1972), vii; Brendan Simms, *Three Victories and a Defeat: The Rise and Fall of the First British Empire, 1714–1783* (London: Allen Lane, 2007), 2, 672.
8. *The Pacifick Fleet* ([Dublin?], 1729); *Great Britain's Glory: or, the Stay-at-home Fleet* (London, 1729), 3; *An essay upon Rewards and Punishments, According to the Practice of the Present Times. With a Scheme for Immortalizing the Actions of a Certain Great Man . . .* (London, [1732?]), 34.
9. *Daily Courant,* 25 March 1730; *The Craftsman,* 17 February 1739 and 1 November 1729.
10. Nicholas Rogers, *Whigs and Cities: Popular Politics in the Age of Walpole and Pitt* (Oxford: Clarendon Press, 1989), 5; Kathleen Wilson, *The Sense of the People: Politics, Culture, and Imperialism in England, 1715–1785* (Cambridge: Cambridge University Press, 1995), 129; Kathleen Wilson, "Empire of Virtue: The Imperial Project and Hanoverian Culture c. 1720–1785," in *An Imperial State at War: Britain from 1689 to 1815,* ed. Lawrence Stone (London: Routledge, 1994), 123.
11. H. T. Dickinson, *Walpole and the Whig Supremacy* (London: English Universities Press, 1973), 93–94.
12. Motion for appointing a Committee of Twelve to inquire into the Proceedings of the South-Sea Company, 1 June 1733. *Cobbett's Parliamentary History of England,* 36 vols. (London, 1806–1820), 9:151; *Daily Courant,* 28

February 1730. The alliance between monopoly companies and the central government was a long-standing one: the Crown secured the companies' right to exclusive property and in return the companies offered political and financial support. Robert Brenner, *Merchants and Revolution: Commercial Change, Political Conflict, and London's Overseas Traders, 1550–1653* (London: Verso, 2003), 54–56, 83, 199–204; Dickinson, *Walpole and the Whig Supremacy*, 99, 109; Bruce Carruthers, *City of Capital: Politics and Markets in the English Financial Revolution* (Princeton, NJ: Princeton University Press, 1996), 138.

13. Lord John Hervey, *Some Materials towards Memoirs of the Reign of George II*, ed. Romney Sedgwick, 3 vols. (London: Eyre and Spottiswoode, 1931), 1:138, qtd. in John Sainsbury, *Disaffected Patriots: London Supporters of Revolutionary America, 1769–1782* (Kingston, ON: McGill–Queen's University Press, 1987), 14.

14. The primary strand of dissident whiggism at this point was patriotism. Although in the near future a second major strand of dissident whiggism—that of authoritarian whiggery—would coalesce into a coherent political voice, this had not happened yet. Nevertheless, during this time period, I refer to those whigs in opposition as "dissident whigs" to acknowledge that the eventual adherents of authoritarian whiggery could be found in the opposition alongside patriots. Despite this, the opposition largely expressed patriot viewpoints; it would be difficult to highlight a specifically authoritarian whig perspective until the late 1730s.

15. The alliance between the monopoly companies and Walpole's administration ran counter to the whig impulses of the 1680s and 1690s—evidence, along with the Riot Act, the Registration Act, the Constructive Recusancy Act, the Septennial Act, the Smuggling Act, the Peerage Bill, and the Black Act, of Walpole's retreat from the whig ideals of the Glorious Revolution. Paul Monod, *Jacobitism and the English People, 1688–1788* (Cambridge: Cambridge University Press, 1989), 347.

16. BL Add. MSS 32687, ff. 155–159. Newcastle to [Charles Townshend, second Viscount Townshend?], 9 September 1725; Cambridge University Library (hereafter CUL) Ch(H) Political Papers 26/32. Sicilian Abbots to Horatio Walpole, 10 October 1727; TNA SP 94/94, ff. 27–28. William Stanhope to Newcastle, 4 February 1726 NS; BL Add. MSS 47032, ff. 1–2. Lord Perceval to Philip Perceval, 19 January 1727.

17. BL Add. MSS 32687, ff. 155–159. Newcastle to [Townshend?], 9 September 1725. Since 1719 George had wanted to be formally invested with the territories of Bremen and Verden; Charles VI was withholding that investiture until George agreed to the Pragmatic Sanction, the existence of the Ostend Company, and to argue the emperor's case regarding some Italian territories at the Congress of Cambrai. George read the threats contained in the Treaty of Vienna within the context of this ongoing power struggle within the Holy Roman Empire. For more on the imperial dimensions of

this conflict and particularly on George's interpretation of them, see Jeremy Black, *Politics and Foreign Policy in the Age of George I, 1714–1727* (Farnham, UK: Ashgate, 2014), 171–240.

18. Ragnhild Hatton, *George I: Elector and King* (London: Thames and Hudson, 1978), 269–270; H. Walpole, Debate in the Commons on the Treaties of Hanover and Vienna, 10 February 1726. *Cobbett's Parliamentary History,* 8:504.
19. BL Add. MSS 47031, ff. 114v–118. Lord Perceval to Edward Southwell, 12 March 1726.
20. TNA SP 94 / 94, f. 57. Stanhope to Newcastle, 15 March 1726 NS; TNA SP 94 / 94, f. 301v. Stanhope to Newcastle, 31 July 1726 NS.
21. Jeremy Black, *British Foreign Policy in the Age of Walpole* (Edinburgh: John Donald, 1985), 33.
22. BL Add. MSS 32749, f. 216v. H. Walpole to Newcastle, 10 March 1727 NS.
23. Ibid., f. 217v.
24. Ibid., f. 218.
25. BL Add. MSS 28146, ff. 120–121v. George I to Admiral John Norris, 24 April 1727.
26. TNA SP 94 / 94, f. 57v. Stanhope to Newcastle, 15 March 1726 NS; see also BL Add. MSS 32749, ff. 120v–121. Newcastle to Robinson, 2 February 1727.
27. In pamphlets such as CUL Ch(H) Political Papers 73 / 9. "To the author of &c Vindication of the Alliance with France," 1727; *The Treaty of Seville, and the Measures that have been taken for the Four Last Years, Impartially Considered* (London, 1730).
28. H. Walpole, Debate in the Commons on the Treaties of Hanover and Vienna, 10 February 1726. *Cobbett's Parliamentary History,* 8:504–505; *Some Remarks upon a Pamphlet, entitled, A Short View of the State of Affairs, with relation to Great Britain for Four Years past* (London, 1730), 11.
29. *British Journal,* 4 January 1729; *A Defence of the Measures of the Present Administration* (London, 1731), 16–19, 25; *A Letter from the Patriots of Great Britain to the Emperor* (London, 1730), 6.
30. BL Add. MSS 32749, f. 217v. H. Walpole to Newcastle, 10 March 1727 NS.
31. H. Walpole, Debate in the Commons on the Treaties of Hanover and Vienna, 10 February 1726. *Cobbett's Parliamentary History,* 8:504.
32. CUL Ch(H) Political Papers 73 / 11 / 1–6. MSS of undated pamphlet in Walpole's political papers.
33. BL Add. MSS 47031, ff. 114v–118. Lord Perceval to Southwell, 12 March 1726.
34. BL Add. MSS 47032, f. 121. Lord Perceval to Capt. John Worth, 19 June 1729.
35. *Treaty of Seville,* 13.
36. This fit with George's personal approach to the war, as he had the most to lose if the Pretender should indeed be restored to the British throne. However, it also fit with Walpole's ongoing practice of using the threat of

Jacobitism to demonize political opposition and to solidify his own administration. See G. V. Bennett, "Jacobitism and the Rise of Walpole," in *Historical Perspectives: Studies in English Thought and Society in Honour of J. H. Plumb*, ed. Neil McKendrick (London: Europa, 1974), 71; Colley, *In Defiance of Oligarchy*, 45.

37. BL Add. MSS 47032, ff. 1–2. Lord Perceval to Philip Perceval, 19 January 1727.
38. BL Add. MSS 32749, ff. 96–97. Robinson to Newcastle, 11 February 1727 NS.
39. BL Add. MSS 47032, ff. 1–2. Lord Perceval to Philip Perceval, 19 January 1727.
40. BL Add. MSS 32749, ff. 122v–123. Newcastle to Robinson, 2 February 1727.
41. Spanish pieces of eight were widely traded throughout the Caribbean (especially as British colonists there were routinely short on specie). Another item the Spanish routinely claimed must have been acquired illegally was logwood, a dyewood the British claimed they had a right to cut legally in the Bay of Campeche courtesy of the 1670 Treaty of Madrid. This right was contested, and was an ongoing source of friction between Britain and Spain.
42. William Shippen, Debate in the Commons on the Treaties of Hanover and Vienna, 10 February 1726. *Cobbett's Parliamentary History*, 8:506.
43. William Wyndham, Debate in the Commons on the Address of Thanks, 17 January 1727. *Cobbett's Parliamentary History*, 8:530. This skepticism about the conflict becoming a continental land war could also be seen in tory publications like *Mist's Weekly Journal*, 11 February 1727 and 25 February 1727.
44. *The Craftsman*, 18 January 1729.
45. Rogers, *Whigs and Cities*, 16–23.
46. Shippen, Wyndham, The Commons' Address of Thanks, 2 February 1728. *Cobbett's Parliamentary History*, 8:639.
47. University of Nottingham Library (hereafter UNott) Ne C 37. Newcastle to Stanhope, 23 September 1725; TNA SP 42/18, f. 299. George Anson to Josiah Burchett, 15 September 1725.
48. CUL Ch(H) Political Papers 20/43/2. List of British ships taken by Spanish 1712–1725, compiled by Mr. Harris, 11 March [1731].
49. TNA SP 42/18, ff. 172–173. Admiralty to Newcastle, 14 April 1725.
50. TNA SP 42/18, ff. 220–221. Admiralty to Newcastle, 29 June 1725; TNA SP 42/18, f. 429. Admiralty to Newcastle, 7 March 1727.
51. A Petition from several Bristol Merchants trading to America, complaining of the Spanish Depredations, 6 February 1731. *Cobbett's Parliamentary History*, 8:242–260; BL Add. MSS 32687, ff. 395–396. Crookshanks to Newcastle, 10 March 1731.
52. See, for example, *Observations on the Conduct of Great Britain, with Regard to the Negotiations and other Transactions Abroad* (London, 1729), 6; A Petition against the Renewal of the East India Company's Charter rejected, 26 Feb-

ruary 1730. *Cobbett's Parliamentary History*, 8:800–801; *Mist's Weekly Journal*, 12 February 1726; Steve Pincus, *1668: The First Modern Revolution* (New Haven, CT: Yale University Press, 2009), 356–389.

53. The South Sea Company carried on a large contraband trade with the Spanish colonies—shipping merchandise in ships that they claimed contained only slaves, exporting silver, expanding the size of their annual ship beyond its permitted dimensions, among other offenses—and actively tried to preserve this contraband trade to themselves by seizing the ships of any independent merchants it found smuggling. George H. Nelson, "Contraband Trade under the Asiento, 1730–1739," *American Historical Review* 51, no. 1 (1945): 55–67; Vera Lee Brown, "The South Sea Company and Contraband Trade," *American Historical Review* 31, no. 4 (1926): 662–678; Colin Palmer, *Human Cargoes: The British Slave Trade to Spanish America, 1700–1739* (Urbana: University of Illinois Press, 1981), 65–67, 86–87; *The Craftsman*, 11 November 1727.
54. [Defoe], *Evident Approach of a War*, 32.
55. *Great Britain's Speediest Sinking Fund is a Powerful Maritime War, Rightly Manag'd, and especially in the West Indies* (London, 1727), 1, 13–15.
56. [Daniel Defoe], *Evident Advantages to Great Britain and its Allies from the Approaching War: Especially in Matters of Trade* (London, 1727), 15, 27.
57. BL Add. MSS 32749, f. 59. Robinson to Newcastle, 29 January 1727 NS; BL Add. MSS 47032, ff. 11v–12v. Dering to Lord Perceval, 17 April 1727.
58. BL Add. MSS 32749, ff. 114–116. Robinson to Newcastle, 16 February 1727 NS; BL Add. MSS 32749, f. 164. Newcastle to Robinson, 16 February 1727.
59. See Daniel Baugh, "Naval Power: What Gave the British Naval Superiority?," in *Exceptionalism and Industrialisation: Britain and Its European Rivals, 1688–1815*, ed. Leandro Prados de la Escosura (Cambridge: Cambridge University Press, 2004), 249; Philip Woodfine, "Ideas of Naval Power and the Conflict with Spain, 1737–1742," in *The British Navy and the Use of Naval Power in the Eighteenth Century*, ed. Jeremy Black and Philip Woodfine (Leicester: Leicester University Press, 1988), 79, 84–85.
60. BL Add. MSS 32749, f. 217. H. Walpole to Newcastle, 10 March 1727 NS.
61. Ibid.; BL Add. MSS 32749, f. 249v. Newcastle to H. Walpole, 4 March 1727.
62. *British Journal*, 25 January 1729.
63. *Defence of the Measures*, 15.
64. *Observations on the Conduct of Great Britain*, 4, 7, 18–19, 54–56.
65. *Defence of the Measures*, 18.
66. *Observations on the Conduct of Great Britain*, 37.
67. *Treaty of Seville*, 17.
68. BL Add. MSS 19030, ff. 24v–25. Admiral Charles Wager to Benjamin Keene, 2 January 1732.
69. BL Add. MSS 19030, f. 149. Wager to [Arthur] Stert, 30 September 1732.
70. BL Add. MSS 19028, part 2, p. 1. Wager to Charles Delafaye, 4 July 1731.
71. *Treaty of Seville*, 12.

72. *British Journal,* 11 January 1729.
73. *Defence of the Measures,* 19.
74. *Letter from the Patriots,* 11–12.
75. *Reasons Shewing the Necessity of Reducing the Army, and Proving That the Navy of England Is Her Only, and Natural Strength and Security,* 2nd ed. (London, 1732), 26.
76. Rogers, *Whigs and Cities,* 5, 85; Pincus, *1688,* 206, 351, 355.
77. P. K. O'Brien and S. L. Engerman, "Exports and the Growth of the British Economy from the Glorious Revolution to the Peace of Amiens," in *Slavery and the Rise of the Atlantic System,* ed. B. Solow and S. L. Engerman (Cambridge: Cambridge University Press, 1991), 186–193.
78. *Great Britain's Glory,* 3; *Pacifick Fleet.*
79. It was suggested that the blame for this inactivity could be laid at Cardinal de Fleury's feet. Thus, British failures in the 1727–1729 conflict were also linked with the accusation that Walpole was too ready to cater to continental allies. N. A. M. Rodger, *The Command of the Ocean: A Naval History of Britain, 1649–1815* (New York; London: Norton, 2004), 232; *Pacifick Fleet; Fog's Weekly Journal,* 27 September 1729; *The Craftsman,* 1 November 1729.
80. *Great Britain's Speediest Sinking Fund,* 18–25.
81. TNA SP 42 / 18, p. 429. Admiralty to Newcastle, 7 March 1727; BL Add. MSS 19028, part 3, pp. 61–63. Wager to Keene, 1 November 1731.
82. BL Add. MSS 19036, f. 17. "Reasons for a War against Spain," June 1738.
83. Alliances were made with the Spanish in the Treaty of Seville and with the Holy Roman Emperor in the Treaty of Vienna, 1731, at which point the Hanoverian claims were also decided.
84. *Articles of the Treaty Signed at Seville in Spain . . . with Remarks on the Said Treaty* (London, 1729), 16, 25–27.
85. CUL Ch(H) Political Papers 26 / 40, 26 / 44. Marquis de Castelar, 28 January 1731 NS; TNA SP 94 / 107 [unfoliated]. Keene to Newcastle, 28 April 1731; TNA SP 94 / 107 [unfoliated]. Keene to Newcastle, 2 May 1731; TNA SP 94 / 107 [unfoliated]. Keene to Newcastle, 20 May 1731; TNA SP 94 / 107 [unfoliated]. Keene to Newcastle, 10 January 1731.
86. BL Add. MSS 47033, ff. 59–64v. Notes of Lord Perceval on the "Debate in the House of Commons touching the Spanish Works before Gibraltar," 5 April 1731.
87. BL Add. MSS 19028, part 1, p. 49. Wager to Burchett, 11 August 1731; BL Add. MSS 19028, part 2, p. 10. Wager's speech to Philip V, King of Spain, 7 August 1731.
88. The very existence of commissioners, rather than a firm, stated right by treaty, was widely criticized in publications like *The Craftsman.*
89. Debate in the Commons on the Spanish Depredations, 13 February 1733. *Cobbett's Parliamentary History,* 8:1190–1192.

90. *Cobbett's Parliamentary History,* 8:762–764.
91. TNA SP 42 / 20, f. 170. Admiralty to Newcastle, 21 August 1730; TNA SP 42 / 20, ff. 180–181. Merchants of Kingston to Charles Stewart, 28 May 1730; TNA SP 42 / 20, f. 243; Stewart to Burchett, 5 July 1730.
92. UNott Ne C 101 / 3. Keene to Don Sebastian de la Quadra, Marqués de la Quadra, 28 February 1738; *Observations on the Conduct of Great Britain,* 29; CUL Ch(H) Political Papers 20 / 43 / 1. Mr. Harris, "A List of Ships and Vessels taken by the Spaniards in the West Indies since the Peace 1725," 6 March [1731]. For accounts of individual ships, see also TNA SP 42 / 20, f. 321. Admiralty to Newcastle, 18 February 1731; TNA SP 42 / 20, f. 425. Newcastle to Admiralty, 3 June 1731.
93. For the petitions, see A Petition from several Bristol Merchants trading to America, complaining of the Spanish Depredations, 6 February 1731. *Cobbett's Parliamentary History,* 8:842–843; Petition from Liverpool Merchants, 25 February 1731. *Cobbett's Parliamentary History,* 8:857. For accounts of other seizures, see, for example, TNA SP 42 / 21, f. 424. Admiralty to Newcastle, 28 August 1733; TNA SP 42 / 22, f. 331. Benjamin Way to Edward Manning, 26 August 1737; TNA SP 42 / 22, f. 335. Anthony Weldon to Digby Dent, 7 September 1737; TNA SP 42 / 22, ff. 280–282. Wager to Newcastle, 8 October 1737; TNA SP 42 / 22, ff. 329–330. Peter and Organ Furnell to Thomas Fox, 12 November 1737; UNott Ne C 101 / 3. Keene to Marqués de la Quadra, 28 February 1738.
94. BL Add. MSS 32687, ff. 395–396. Crookshanks to Newcastle, 10 March 1731.
95. Proceedings in the Commons on the Petitions relating to the Spanish Depredations, 3 March 1738. *Cobbett's Parliamentary History,* 10:569; Debate in the Lords and Commons on the Address of Thanks, 1 February 1739. *Cobbett's Parliamentary History,* 10:904.
96. TNA SP 42 / 21, ff. 19–20. Merchants of Kingston to Stewart, 24 September 1731.
97. CUL Ch(H) Political Papers 16 / 4. Edward Pratter and James Rigby to Stewart, 3 March 1731; TNA SP 42 / 21, f. 11. Pratter to Stewart, 4 March 1731; TNA SP 42 / 21, ff. 19–20. Merchants of Kingston to Stewart, 24 September 1731; TNA SP 42 / 21, f. 25v. Pratter and Rigby to Stewart, 25 September 1731. Admiral Wager also commented on this tension and pointed out that while the British could begin seizing Spanish ships in retribution, the ships they could take might be worth "3 or 4000 dollars, and the Spaniards would immediately seize the South Sea ship (then at Portobello) worth half a million sterling." BL Add. MSS 19028, part 3, pp. 76–78. Wager to Stert, 2 January 1732.
98. UNott Ne C 41. Newcastle to Admiralty, 26 April 1725.
99. TNA SP 42 / 18, ff. 220–221. Admiralty to Newcastle, 29 June 1725.
100. Another example was the *Woolball,* captured by the Spanish in June 1731; the naval ship *Deal Castle* was ordered to demand its restitution from the

Spanish governor at Campeche, who refused. In retaliation, the *Deal Castle* captured a Spanish register ship, *La Dichosa,* in May 1732. However, this capture had come after Philip V had issued a cedula ordering his governors and *guarda costas* to be better behaved. Admiral Chaloner Ogle was ordered to restore *La Dichosa* to the Spanish, not because the *Woolball* had been restored—it was still a matter of contention in 1738—but because the Spanish king had made possibly empty promises that the situation would improve in the future. UNott Ne C 74. Series of letters and Privy Council minutes regarding the restoration of *La Dichosa,* October 1732; UNott Ne C 101 / 3. Keene to Marqués de la Quadra, 28 February 1738.

101. BL Add. MSS 20095, f. 18. "Sir R__t's Speech upon the Peace with Spain," [1729–1734].
102. BL Add. MSS 19028, part 3, pp. 61–63. Wager to Keene, 1 November 1731.
103. *The Craftsman,* 18 January 1729.
104. Portugal was granted the right to the Colônia do Sacramento on the River Plate, but Spain founded the town of Montevideo at the mouth of the river to monitor Portuguese expansion. Stanley G. Payne, *A History of Spain and Portugal,* 2 vols. (Madison: University of Wisconsin Press, 1973), 2:404; J. H. Elliott, *Empires of the Atlantic World: Britain and Spain in America, 1492–1830* (New Haven, CT: Yale University Press, 2006), 268; Anthony McFarlane, *The British in the Americas, 1480–1815* (London: Longman, 1994), 220–221.
105. BL Add. MSS 28130, ff. 169–170. Journal of Norris, 17 February 1736; BL Add. MSS 28146, f. 270. Newcastle to James O'Hara, second Baron Tyrawley, and Norris, 10 February 1736; BL Add. MSS 28130, ff. 117–118. Journal of Norris, 27 August 1735; BL Add. MSS 28130, f. 181. Mendoza to Norris, 6 March 1736.
106. According to the Portuguese, the Spanish governor at Buenos Aires had given a naval ship orders to cruise off of the mouth of the river and to search Portuguese ships; they had actually seized at least two Portuguese merchant ships and refused to give up the right to do so. BL Add. MSS 28146, ff. 154–158. Marco António de Azevedo Coutinho, Envoy Extraordinary of Portugal to Great Britain, to George II, 4 March 1736.
107. BL Add. MSS 28146, f. 140v. George II to Norris, 16 May 1735; BL Add. MSS 28146, f. 145. Newcastle to Norris, 28 May 1735.
108. BL Add. MSS 28146, ff. 146–147. Newcastle to Tyrawley and Norris, 12 June 1735.
109. Debate in the Lords on the Petitions against the Convention with Spain, 23 February 1739. *Cobbett's Parliamentary History,* 10:1140–1149; Petition of London merchants, 23 February 1739, reprinted in *Pennsylvania Gazette,* 19 April–26 April 1739.
110. *The Craftsman,* 28 January 1738.
111. John Carteret, Debate in the Lords on the Depredations of the Spaniards, 2 May 1738. *Cobbett's Parliamentary History,* 10:745.

112. Petition of London merchants, 23 February 1739, reprinted in *Pennsylvania Gazette,* 19 April–26 April 1739; BL Add. MSS 19036, f. 9. "Reasons for a war against Spain," June 1738.
113. John Carteret, Debate in the Lords on the Depredations of the Spaniards, 2 May 1738. *Cobbett's Parliamentary History,* 10:745.
114. R. Walpole, Proceedings in the Commons on the Petitions relating to the Spanish Depredations, 3 March 1738. *Cobbett's Parliamentary History,* 10:585.
115. *Popular prejudices against the convention and treaty with Spain, examin'd and answer'd* (London, 1739), 3, 18.
116. *The Daily Gazetteer,* 7 January 1739.
117. Newcastle, Debate in the Lords on the Depredations of the Spaniards, 2 May 1738. *Cobbett's Parliamentary History,* 10:773.
118. Thomas Sanderson, Debate in the Commons on the Convention with Spain, 8 March 1739. *Cobbett's Parliamentary History,* 10:1267.
119. William Pitt, R. Walpole, Debate in the Commons on the Convention with Spain, 8 March 1739. *Cobbett's Parliamentary History,* 10:1281, 1292.
120. Proceedings in the Commons on the Petitions relating to the Spanish Depredations, 3 March 1738; 16 March 1738. *Cobbett's Parliamentary History,* 10:572–576.
121. *The Craftsman,* 19 February 1737.
122. BL Add. MSS 35586, f. 262. A. B. to Philip Yorke, first Earl of Hardwicke, 23 July 1740; BL Add. MSS 19036, ff. 14v–15. "Reasons for a war against Spain," June 1738.
123. BL Add. MSS 40827 ff. 75v–69 [reverse paginated]; David Campbell to General Wentworth, 12 January 1741[/2?].
124. Wyndham, Debate in the Commons on the Bill for securing the Trade to America, 5 May 1738. *Cobbett's Parliamentary History,* 10:817.
125. *Letter from the Patriots,* 5, 18.
126. *The Daily Gazetteer,* 25 September 1738 and 29 September 1738; *The Craftsman,* 23 September 1738.
127. BL Add. MSS 61479, f. 55. Debate in the House of Lords that the instructions given to Vernon be placed before the House, 1 December 1740. According to a modern calculation, it was not 400 sailors, but 3,000 who died on the expedition, though only eight captains rather than the 30 quoted here. See Rodger, *Command of the Ocean,* 232.
128. *Treaty of Seville,* 9.
129. Paul Kennedy, *The Rise and Fall of British Naval Mastery* (London: Allen Lane, 1976), 87; Daniel Baugh, *British Naval Administration in the Age of Walpole* (Princeton, NJ: Princeton University Press, 1965), 505; John Brewer, *The Sinews of Power: War, Money, and the English State, 1688–1783* (Cambridge, MA: Harvard University Press, 1988), 172.
130. *Reasons Shewing the Necessity of Reducing the Army,* 26, 34–35.
131. *Popular Prejudices against the Convention and Treaty with Spain,* 9; *The Profit and Loss of Great-Britain and Spain from the Commencement of the Present War to*

This Time, Impartially Stated (London, 1742), 47; R. Walpole, Debate in the Commons on the bill for securing the Trade to America, 5 May 1738. *Cobbett's Parliamentary History,* 10:827.

132. BL Add. MSS 28146, f. 169v. Waldegrave to Newcastle, 6 June 1735 NS; TNA SP 78 / 220, f. 257v. Waldegrave to Newcastle, 26 June 1739 NS.
133. TNA SP 36 / 44 / 202. "Memoire pour faire connoitre que la France peut facilement augmenter la navigation et la rendre en peu d'annés egale et même plus puissante que celle d' Angleterre," 1737; Rodger, *Command of the Ocean,* 232–234.
134. TNA SP 94 / 95, ff. 93–102. Stanhope to Newcastle, 30 October 1726 NS.
135. TNA SP 94 / 95, ff. 2v–3. Stanhope to Newcastle, 18 September 1726 NS.
136. BL Add. MSS 32749, f. 45. Newcastle to Robinson, 17 January 1727; BL Add. MSS 32749, f. 294. H. Walpole to Newcastle, 21 March 1727 NS; TNA SP 94 / 95, ff. 183v–184. Stanhope to Newcastle, 9 December 1726 NS.
137. *The General Evening Post,* 29 September–2 October 1739; TNA SP 78 / 220, f. 258. Waldegrave to Newcastle, 26 June 1739 NS; Thomas Winnington, Debate in the Commons on the bill for securing the Trade to America, 5 May 1738. *Cobbett's Parliamentary History,* 10:864; *Hireling Artifice Detected: Or, the Profit and Loss of Great Britain, in the Present War with Spain, set in its true light* (London, 1741), 47, 57.
138. BL Add. MSS 34524, f. 8. Newcastle to Hardwicke, 3 October 1740; BL Add. MSS. 19332, f. 104. Edward Vernon to Wager, 5 January 1741.
139. It is worth noting that Norris, though at times disappointed by Walpole, was not a member of the opposition and his calculations were unlikely to have been politically motivated. BL Add. MSS 28132, f. 140. Journal of Norris, 24 January 1740.
140. BL Add. MSS 28132, f. 191. Journal of Norris, 20 May 1740; UNott Ne C 103. Stone and Newcastle to Henry Pelham, 14 June 1740.
141. National Archives of Scotland (hereafter NAS) GD18 / 4163. Francis Holburne to Sir John Clerk, 5 June 1735.
142. BL Add. MSS 19030, f. 230. Wager to [unknown], 9 February 1734.
143. BL Add. MSS 19030, f. 200. Wager to Newcastle, 18 July 1733.
144. BL Add. MSS 28150, ff. 60v–62. Norris to Wager, 9 March 1737.
145. East Sussex Record Office (hereafter ESRO) SAS / G / AM / 7(1). Samuel and William Baker to Peter Warren, 4 January 1745.
146. *Hireling Artifice Detected,* 65.
147. BL Add. MSS 28132, ff. 98–99. Journal of Norris, 14 December 1739.
148. BL Add. MSS 28132 ff. 37–38. Journal of Norris, 21 September 1739; BL Add. MSS 28132, f. 140. Journal of Norris, 24 January 1740; BL Add. MSS 28133 Part 1, f. 60. Journal of Norris, 22 September 1740. Rodger agrees that France's losses were made up within two years: Rodger, *Command of the Ocean,* 152.

149. BL Add. MSS 19034, f. 62v. "Extracts of Evidence given at the Bar of the House of Commons the 24th February 1741, in relation to the Trade of this Kingdom."

3. Disorder, Discipline, and the Politics of Naval Reform

1. Daniel Baugh, *British Naval Administration in the Age of Walpole* (Princeton, NJ: Princeton University Press, 1965), 504; Daniel Baugh, "'Too Much Mixed in This Affair': The Impact of Ministerial Politics in the Eighteenth-Century Royal Navy," in *New Interpretations in Naval History: Selected Papers from the Fourteenth Naval History Symposium*, ed. Randy Carol Balano and Craig L. Symonds (Annapolis, MD: Naval Institute Press, 2001), 33.
2. Clive Wilkinson, *The British Navy and the State in the Eighteenth Century* (Woodbridge, UK: Boydell, 2004), 103, 211.
3. N. A. M. Rodger, *The Wooden World: An Anatomy of the Georgian Navy* (New York: Norton, 1996), 31.
4. Walter Vernon Anson, *The Life of Admiral Lord Anson, the Father of the British Navy, 1697–1762* (London: J. Murray, 1912); Sir John Barrow, *The life of George, Lord Anson, admiral of the fleet, Vice-Admiral of Great Britain, and First Lord Commissioner of the Admiralty, Previous to, and during, the Seven Years' War* (London, 1839); Brian Lavery, *The Ship of the Line*, 2 vols. (Annapolis, MD: Naval Institute Press, 1983), 1:90; N. A. M. Rodger, *The Command of the Ocean: A Naval History of Britain 1649–1815* (New York: Norton, 2004).
5. G. S. Graham, "The Naval Defence of British North America 1739–1763," *Transactions of the Royal Historical Society* 30 (1948): 108.
6. Rodger, *Command of the Ocean*, 178, 577.
7. Seaman [Augustus Hervey], *A Detection of the Considerations on the Navy-Bill* (London, 1749), 15; John Perceval, Second Earl Egmont, Debate in the Commons on the Bill for subjecting Half-Pay Naval Officers to Martial Law, 1 February 1749. *Cobbett's Parliamentary History of England*, 36 vols. (London, 1806–1820), 14:542, 550.
8. Staffordshire Record Office (hereafter Staff. RO) D1798/HMDrakeford/22, J. Ayscough to Richard Drakeford, 11 March 1749.
9. Robert Harris, *A Patriot Press: National Politics and the London Press in the 1740s* (Oxford: Clarendon Press, 1993), 122–177.
10. John Perceval, First Earl Egmont, *Manuscripts of the Earl of Egmont*, 3 vols. (London: His Majesty's Stationery Office, 1920–1923), 3:260; William Coxe, *Memoirs of the life and administration of Sir Robert Walpole, Earl of Oxford*, 3 vols. (London, 1800), 3:266; N. A. M Rodger, *The Insatiable Earl: A Life of John Montagu, Fourth Earl of Sandwich, 1718–1792* (London: HarperCollins, 1993), 20.
11. Nicholas Rogers, *Whigs and Cities: Popular Politics in the Age of Walpole and Pitt* (Oxford: Clarendon Press, 1989), 15–51.

12. Walpole's two decades of administration meant that tories and those whigs left in opposition began to make common cause with one another, and in fact they did share some points of common critique. The 1745 Jacobite rebellion laid another blow upon the respectability of old-school toryism. Gabriel Glickman, "Parliament, the Tories and Frederick, Prince of Wales," *Parliamentary History* 30, no. 2 (2011): 120–141; Harris, *Patriot Press;* Bob Harris, "The *London Evening Post* and Mid-Eighteenth-Century British Politics," *English Historical Review* 110 (1995): 1132–1156.
13. For discussions of ideological consistency in mid-Georgian Britain, see, for example, Linda Colley, *In Defiance of Oligarchy: The Tory Party, 1714–60* (Cambridge: Cambridge University Press, 1982); Christine Gerrard, *The Patriot Opposition to Walpole: Politics, Poetry, and National Myth, 1725–1742* (Oxford: Clarendon Press, 1994); Harris, *Patriot Press;* Rogers, *Whigs and Cities;* Nicholas Rogers, *Crowds, Culture, and Politics in Georgian Britain* (Oxford: Clarendon Press, 1998); Kathleen Wilson, *The Sense of the People: Politics, Culture, and Imperialism in England, 1715–1785* (Cambridge: Cambridge University Press, 1995).
14. The third of the groups left in opposition were the tories, who supported a purely maritime foreign policy, but only if it could be carried out without major expenditure. They were in the process of splintering as a coherent party and former tories could be found associated with both the patriot whigs and the authoritarian whigs. TNA PRO 30/29/1/11/11. Philip Dormer Stanhope, Earl of Chesterfield, to John Leveson-Gower, Earl Gower, 13 April 1745 NS; BL Add. MSS 32804, f. 290. Chesterfield to Thomas Pelham-Holles, Duke of Newcastle, 13 April 1745 NS; Colley, *In Defiance of Oligarchy,* 57–81.
15. Harris, *"London Evening Post,"* 1144, 1155–1156.
16. For a more thorough discussion of the ideological content of patriotism, see Gerrard, *Patriot Opposition;* Rogers, *Whigs and Cities;* and Wilson, *Sense of the People.* For a discussion of how patriot ideology fed into late eighteenth-century radicalism, see James Bradley, *Religion, Revolution, and English Radicalism: Nonconformity in Eighteenth-Century Politics and Society* (Cambridge: Cambridge University Press, 1990); John Brewer, "English Radicalism in the Age of George III," in *Three British Revolutions: 1641, 1688, 1776,* ed. J. G. A. Pocock (Princeton, NJ: Princeton University Press, 1980), 324–331, 342–351; H. T. Dickinson, "Introduction," in *Britain and the American Revolution,* ed. H. T. Dickinson (London: Longman, 1998), 10–12; Harris, *"London Evening Post,"* 1134, 1151–1153. James Bradley has discussed extensively the links between Dissent and political radicalism throughout the eighteenth century; for more on the social and religious background of patriots, see Bradley, *Religion, Revolution,* 4–17, 133–147, 174–184; Brewer, "English Radicalism," 331–351; John Brewer, "The Wilkites and the Law, 1763–4: A Study of Radical Notions of Governance," in *An Ungovernable*

People: The English and Their Law in the Seventeenth and Eighteenth Centuries, ed. John Brewer and John Styles (New Brunswick, NJ: Rutgers University Press, 1980), 137–138; Rogers, *Whigs and Cities*, 46–129, 391–403; Wilson, *Sense of the People*, 152.

17. Aside from the Pitts, Grenvilles, and Lyttletons, other leading advocates of patriot ideology and associates of the prince included the Hon. Henry Bathurst; Charles Calvert, Lord Baltimore; George Bubb Dodington; John Perceval, the Earl of Egmont; Lord Thomas Gage; and Dr. George Lee. Gabriel Glickman argues that Frederick's support of naval warfare and attempts to position himself as a Patriot King drew on explicitly Jacobite tropes. Rather, any overlap is more likely evidence of how exiled Stuart promises shifted toward oppositional common ground, in this case libertarianism, in an attempt to win support. Though there was convergence between Frederick and the tories, any ideology that could be successfully appropriated by the heir to the throne cannot be termed Jacobite, and the shared language of patriotism nevertheless hid real divisions. Glickman, "Parliament, the Tories and Frederick, Prince of Wales," 125–126, 133–136; Harris, *Patriot Press*, 3–6, 255–256; Daniel Szechi, *The Jacobites: Britain and Europe, 1688–1788* (Manchester: Manchester University Press, 1994), 29–40.
18. *Protester*, 9 June 1753.
19. On their differing ideas about debt in relation to broader imperial policy, see Justin du Rivage, *Revolution against Empire: Taxes, Politics, and the Origins of American Independence* (New Haven, CT: Yale University Press, 2017).
20. Many of the authoritarian whig MPs were landed gentry, a few were lawyers, one was the grandson of a linen draper, and one was a London grocer and future Lord Mayor. Many were elected based on the interest of Bedford or one of his allies, but some were elected in large independent boroughs, at times in preference to official Treasury candidates. Few were outstanding speakers, though most were active members and served on committees. James M. Haas, "The Rise of the Bedfords, 1741–1757: A Study in the Politics of the Reign of George II" (PhD diss., University of Illinois, 1960), 76, 105–106, 170–182.
21. Charles Townshend, *National Thoughts, Recommended to the Serious Attention of the Public* (London, 1751), 1–3; see also writings by Matthew Decker, John Shebbeare, and Josiah Tucker. Du Rivage, *Revolution against Empire*, 24–52.
22. *The Gentleman's Magazine* (January 1734), 13–14.
23. Protest Again Passing the Spirituous Liquors Bill, 25 February 1743. *Cobbett's Parliamentary History*, 12:1439–1440.
24. See, for example, Matthew Decker, *An Essay on the Causes of the Decline of the Foreign Trade, Consequently of the Value of the Lands of Britain, and on the Means to Restore Both* (London, 1744); Josiah Tucker, *The Elements of Commerce, and Theory of Taxes* (Bristol, 1755).

25. Staff. RO D615 / P(S) / 4 / 3, T. Hinton to George Anson, 26 September 1747; Eveline Cruickshanks, *Political Untouchables: The Tories and the '45* (London: Duckworth, 1979), 107.
26. *Protester,* 2 June 1753.
27. Denver Alexander Brunsman, "The Knowles Atlantic Impressment Riots of the 1740s," *Early American Studies: An Interdisciplinary Journal* 5, no. 2 (2007): 324–366; David Dickson, *New Foundations: Ireland 1660–1800* (Dublin: Irish Academic Press, 2000), 99–101, 144–145; Jack P. Greene, "An Uneasy Connection: An Analysis of the Preconditions of the American Revolution," in *Essays on the American Revolution,* ed. Stephen G. Kurtz and James H. Hutson (Chapel Hill: Published for the Institute of Early American History and Culture, Williamsburg, VA, by the University of North Carolina Press, 1973), 65–68; Ian McBride, *Eighteenth-Century Ireland: The Isle of Slaves* (Dublin: Gill and Macmillan, 2009), 280–311; Charles Ivar McGrath, *Ireland and Empire, 1692–1770* (London: Pickering and Chatto, 2012), 64–65.
28. As in England and the Americas, Irish patriots argued that the Irish parliament needed to be strengthened to resist central English administration. Woburn Abbey (hereafter WA) HMC 8, vol. XXXIX, p. 166. Bedford to Sir Richard Bampfylde, 1 May 1759; WA HMC 8, vol. XLI, p. 202. Bedford, draft speech to Irish parliament, 17 May 1760.
29. TNA CO 5 / 21, vol. III, f. 238. Orders in Council, 14 April 1752, qtd. in Andrew D. M. Beaumont, *Colonial America and the Earl of Halifax* (Oxford: Oxford University Press, 2015), 10. For more on Halifax and the Board of Trade's repeated attempts to discipline the colonies into obedience, see Beaumont, *Colonial America;* Chris Beneke, "The Critical Turn: Jonathan Mayhew, the British Empire, and the Idea of Resistance in Mid-Eighteenth-Century Boston," *Massachusetts Historical Review* 10 (2008): 23–56; T. R. Clayton, "The Duke of Newcastle, the Earl of Halifax, and the American Origins of the Seven Years' War," *Historical Journal* 24, no. 3 (September 1981): 578–580; Greene "An Uneasy Connection," 72–74; P. J. Marshall, "Empire and Authority in Later Eighteenth Century Britain," *Journal of Imperial and Commonwealth History* 15 (1987): 105–122; Keith Mason, "Britain and the Administration of the American Colonies," in *Britain and the American Revolution,* ed. H. T. Dickinson (London: Longman, 1998), 37; Alison Gilbert Olson, "Parliament, Empire, and Parliamentary Law, 1776," in *Three British Revolutions: 1641, 1688, 1776,* ed. J. G. A. Pocock (Princeton, NJ: Princeton University Press, 1980), 291–311.
30. Bedford presented the petition of the City of London against the Convention of Pardo, which tried to preserve peace with Spain, and spoke against the Convention in the House of Lords, saying that the time had come for an end to negotiations. Debate in the Lords on the Petitions against the Convention with Spain, 23 February 1739. *Cobbett's Parliamentary History,*

10:1040–1041; Debate in the Lords and Commons on the Address of Thanks, 1 February 1739. *Cobbett's Parliamentary History,* 10:897–898; Debate in the Lords on a Motion for an Address against the Augmentation of the Army, 3 February 1741. *Cobbett's Parliamentary History,* 11:1028–1032; Debate in the Lords on taking the Hanoverian Troops into British Pay, 1 February 1743. *Cobbett's Parliamentary History,* 12:1073–1088.

31. Both Bedford and Sandwich agreed later in the war that Britain should isolate France by making a separate peace with Spain, and even give up Gibraltar if necessary, because Bedford thought that Britain could gain enough from Spain in the West Indies to make it worthwhile. TNA PRO 30/47/14/2, f. 37, William Drake to Charles Pinckney, 20 July 1736; Peter Warren to Stephen Corbett, 8 September 1744. Julian Gwyn, ed., *The Royal Navy and North America: The Warren Papers, 1736–1752* (London: Navy Records Society, 1973), 35–39; Warren to Anson, 2 April 1745, ibid., 70–75; Haas, "Rise of the Bedfords," 55.
32. Sandwich, Debate in the Lords on taking the Hanoverian Troops into British Pay, 1 February 1743. *Cobbett's Parliamentary History,* 12:1073.
33. BL Add. MSS 19036, f. 15, anonymous, June 1738.
34. Warren would later defect to the patriot opposition. Warren to Corbett, 6 February 1742/3, *Warren Papers,* 31–32.
35. See, for example, BL Add. MSS 32702, f. 320, Robert Auchmuty to Newcastle, 18 April 1744; BL Add. MSS 32702, f. 283. Christopher Kilby to Newcastle, 3 April 1744; TNA ADM 1/3817. William Shirley, Governor of Massachusetts, to the Admiralty, 27 March 1745; Charles W. Tuttle, "Christopher Kilby, of Boston," *The New England Historical and Genealogical Register* 26, no. 1 (1872): 43–46; Joseph J. Malone, *Pine Trees and Politics: The Naval Stores and Forest Policy in Colonial New England 1691–1775* (New York: Arno Press, 1979), 130.
36. ESRO SAS/G/AM/7(3), Samuel and William Baker to Warren, 30 April 1745; Harris, *Patriot Press,* 53–55.
37. These views were put forward both in public propaganda and in private correspondence. See, for example: CUL Ch(H) Political Papers 73/9, "To the Author of &c Vindication of the Alliance with France," 1727; *The Treaty of Seville, and the Measures That Have Been Taken for the Four Last Years, Impartially Considered* (London, 1730); *A Letter from the Patriots of Great Britain to the Emperor* (London, 1730); BL Add. MS 32749, ff. 114–116, Thomas Robinson to Newcastle, 16 February 1727 NS; BL Add. MSS 32749, ff. 164. Newcastle to Robinson, 16 February 1727.
38. Bedford, Debate in the Lords on taking the Hanoverian Troops into British Pay, 1 February 1743. *Cobbett's Parliamentary History,* 12:1088.
39. ESRO SAS/G/AM/7(4). Samuel and William Baker to Warren, 3 May 1745; UNott Ne C 241. John Masters to Michael Lee Dicker, 10 November 1744.

40. Warren to Charles Knowles, 6 October 1746. *Warren Papers,* 338–340.
41. Bedford, Debate in the Lords on the Bill for Securing Trade and Navigation in times of War, 1 June 1742. *Cobbett's Parliamentary History,* 12:767.
42. Edward Ward, *The Wooden World Dissected, in the Character of a Ship of War,* 3rd ed. (London, 1744), 16, 21; *The Plain Reasoner* (London, 1745), 8.
43. WA HMC 8, vol. IX, pp. 98–100, [anonymous] to Bedford, 7 February 1745.
44. ESRO SAS/G/AM/7(2), Samuel and William Baker to Warren, 23 March 1745.
45. John Moncreiff, *Galba. A Dialogue on the Navy* (London, 1748), 56–57.
46. Lavery, *Ship of the Line,* 1:85.
47. BL Add. MSS 19040, f. 67. Charles Windham to [William] Scobie, 14 April 1745.
48. NAS GD18/4177. Francis Holburne to Sir John Clerk, 17 April 1740.
49. ESRO SAS/G/AM/7(4). Samuel and William Baker to Warren, 3 May 1745; TNA SP 42/28, f. 262. Admiralty Board to [Lords Justices], 29 May 1745.
50. Debate in the Commons on appointing a Committee to enquire into the Miscarriages of the British Fleet in the Mediterranean, 26 February 1745. *Cobbett's Parliamentary History,* 13:1202–1237.
51. See, for example, *A Letter to a Friend in the Country, Occasioned by the Late Naval Engagement in the Mediterranean* (London, 1744); *An Impartial Review of the Conduct of the Admirals M__ws and L__k* (London, 1745); *A Just, Genuine, and Impartial History of the Memorable Sea-fight, in the Mediterranean* (London, 1745); BL Add. MSS 40776, ff. 143–144, [An officer onboard the *Namur*] to [Edward Vernon?], 24 February 1744; BL Add. MSS 19040, f. 65, Windham to Scobie, 26 March 1744; ESRO SAS/G/AM/7(2), Samuel and William Baker to Warren, 23 March 1745.
52. UNott Ne C 243. Dicker to Henry Pelham, 24 November 1744.
53. WA HMC 8, vol. X, pp. 110–112, Sandwich to Bedford, 22 October [1745].
54. In 1745 a British ship of 70 guns fired 918 pounds of shot and one of 80 guns fired 1,312 pounds, while a French ship of 64 guns fired 1,103 pounds of shot and one of 74 guns fired 1,705 pounds. A British admiral said in 1745, "I have never seen or heard . . . that one of our ships alone, singly opposed to one of the enemy's of equal force, has taken her, and I have been in almost every action and skirmish since the year 1718." BL Add. MSS. 15956, f. 119. Knowles to Anson, 6 January 1745; James Pritchard, "From Shipwright to Naval Constructor: The Professionalization of 18th-Century French Naval Shipbuilders," *Technology and Culture* 28, no. 1 (1987): 1, 5, 12; N. A. M. Rodger, "George, Lord Anson, 1697–1762," in *Precursors of Nelson: British Admirals of the Eighteenth Century,* ed. Peter Le Fevre and Richard Harding (London: Chatham Publishing, 2000), 188; Lavery, *Ship of the Line,* 1:90.
55. BL Add. MSS. 15956, f. 119. Knowles to Anson, 6 January 1745.

56. Miguel Alía Plana and Jesús María Alía Plana, *Historia de los uniformes de la Armada Española (1717–1814)* (Madrid: Ministerio de Defensa, Secretaría General Técnica, 1996), 21–22; Fernando González de Canales y López-Obrero and Manuel González de Canales y Moyano, "Tres siglos de empleos y divisas en el cuerpo general de la Armada Española (1717–2000) (III): Divisas de los oficiales generals," *Revista General de Marina* 258 (2009): 376–378; John D. Harbron, *Trafalgar and the Spanish Navy* (Annapolis, MD: Naval Institute Press, 1988), 23–29, 33; Henry Kamen, *Spain's Road to Empire* (London: Penguin, 2002), 452; Lavery, *Ship of the Line,* 1:81; Francisco de Sousa Congosto, *Introducción a la historia de la indumentaria en España* (Madrid: Ediciones Istmo, 2007), 350–353; Rodger, *Command of the Ocean,* 232–234; Marine Nationale, Prefecture Maritime Mediterranée, France, *L'étoffe des Marins,* http://www.dailymotion.com/video/xgusul_l-etoffe-des-Marins_news.
57. These included financial sacrifices, but could also entail much more personal sacrifices, such as the impressment of sailors, always a potential source of conflict. The navy could generally count on a base of support from overseas traders, whose ships and goods the navy was intended to protect, but it was these same traders whose vessels were scoured by impress gangs looking for men. At best, merchants' resentment at losing sailors was kept in a tense balance by their desire for protection on the high seas. If they felt that protection was lacking, whatever toleration they had offered for impressment would quickly evaporate. Nicholas Rogers, *Press Gang: Naval Impressment and Its Opponents in Georgian Britain* (London: Continuum, 2007).
58. For example, when the British presence in the Caribbean was scaled back in the middle of 1742, the reason given in the orders to Admiral Vernon was the "ill success" and "miscarriages" of the fleet.
59. Rodger, *Wooden World,* 29–36; N. A. M. Rodger, *The Admiralty* (Lavenham, UK: Terence Dalton, 1979), 64.
60. G. H. Rose, ed., *Selection from the Papers of the Earls of Marchmont,* 3 vols. (London, 1831), 1:213, qtd. in John Russell, *Correspondence of John, Fourth Duke of Bedford: Selected from the Originals at Woburn Abbey,* 3 vols. (London, 1842–46), 1:xl. For an account of the role of the First Lord, see Clive Wilkinson, *The British Navy and the State in the Eighteenth Century* (Woodbridge, UK: Boydell, 2004), 27–28.
61. Newcastle to Chesterfield, 6 April 1746. *Private Correspondence of Chesterfield and Newcastle, 1744–46,* ed. Sir Richard Lodge (London: Royal Historical Society, 1930), 134.
62. Unlike the Duke of Newcastle, Bedford did not retain copies of all correspondence received or sent, but an examination of the remaining correspondence at Woburn Abbey reveals that commissioners in London corresponded with Bedford even regarding minute details, Bedford frequently responded by return post, and there were at least some occasions

when he was better informed regarding the state of a naval matter than commissioners in London. Likewise, while Sandwich was on the continent negotiating the peace treaty that ended the War of the Austrian Succession, he remained in regular contact with Anson in London and they discussed Admiralty Board matters. See, for example, WA HMC 8, vol. XIII, p. 41. Lord Vere Beauclerk to Bedford, 2 September 1746; WA HMC 8, vol. XIII, p. 66. Same to same, 16 September 1746; BL Add. MSS. 15957, f. 28. Sandwich to Anson, 14 November 1747 NS. Moreover, as Daniel Baugh has noted with regard to Newcastle and Hardwicke, networks of transportation and communication in eighteenth-century Britain were certainly sufficient to permit statesmen to go to their country houses and yet remain in close and regular contact with politicians and ministerial duties in London. See Daniel Baugh, *The Global Seven Years War, 1754–1763: Britain and France in a Great Power Contest* (Harlow, UK: Pearson, 2011), 21.

63. Armies began to be professionalized in Europe in the seventeenth century, as they grew larger, more expensive, and as campaigns lasted longer. More advanced weaponry—especially artillery—meant that more technical knowledge was required to manage an army successfully. A professional army also implies centralized control by the ruler and this centralized control differentiates what are termed professional militaries from the professional mercenary forces which preceded them. Centralized control created more unified standards, in terms of dress, equipment, hygiene, victualling, and discipline. Finally, it was also crucial to the professional military that it be a sphere apart from the civilian world: it required the subjugation of social hierarchy to military hierarchy. This implied an abnegation of the amateur's quest for honor and glory in favor of the state's political and military goals. The aristocracy remained a crucial component of nearly every early modern military, but within military contexts, their rank and authority came from their military position rather than their social one. Jean-Paul Bertaud, *Guerre et société en France de Louis XIV à Napoléon Ier* (Paris: A. Colin, 1998), 10; Hervé Drévillon, "Courtilz de Sandras et les valeurs militaires de la noblesse à la fin du règne de Louis XIV," in *Combattre, Gouverner, Écrire: Études Réunies en l'honneur de Jean Chagniot*, ed. André Corvisier et al. (Paris: Institut de stratégie comparée, 2003), 359; John A. Lynn, *Giant of the* Grand Siècle: *The French Army, 1610–1715* (Cambridge: Cambridge University Press, 1997), 7; Roger B. Manning, *An Apprenticeship in Arms: The Origins of the British Army, 1585–1702* (Oxford: Oxford University Press, 2006), viii–ix, 432–433; Geoffrey Parker, "The 'Military Revolution, 1560–1660'—a Myth?," in *The Military Revolution Debate: Readings on the Military Transformation of Early Modern Europe*, ed. Clifford J. Rogers (Boulder, CO: Westview Press, 1995), 48; David Parrott, "War, State, and Society in Western Europe, 1600–1700," in *European Warfare, 1350–1750*, ed. Frank Tallett and D. J. B. Trim (Cambridge: Cambridge University Press, 2010), 74–95.

64. Historians have sometimes described the British Navy as having been professionalized from the seventeenth century. As described in Chapter 1, it had indeed made steps during that time period from being an ad hoc organization reliant on commandeered merchant ships to having a greater number of royally owned ships at the state's disposal; half pay was introduced, first as a reward for service but later as a retainer for trained officers; and some basic level of competence was necessary to become an officer. Yet in many ways, the Royal Navy was still more the collection of the king's ships than a true "corps." In the seventeenth century, rank was often determined on a ship-to-ship basis rather than being fleet-wide. In the 1740s, there still were few marks of special cohesion among sea officers. In the day-to-day workings of the navy as well as in constitutional theory, a sailor was first and foremost a member of an individual ship's company rather than of a larger naval organization. A seaman was only in naval service insofar as his name appeared in a particular ship's books; when he ceased to be listed, he ceased to be part of the navy. This was less true for officers, whose names would likely be on half-pay lists regardless of whether they were currently onboard ship, and who could expect to be recalled to service when a new conflict broke out. Rodger, *Wooden World,* 113.
65. Svante Beckman, "Professionalization: Borderline Authority and Autonomy in Work," in *Professions in Theory and History,* ed. Michael Burrage and Rolf Torstendahl (London: Sage, 1990), 125; Thomas Broman, "Rethinking Professionalization: Theory, Practice, and Professional Ideology in Eighteenth-Century German Medicine," *Journal of Modern History* 67, no. 4 (1995): 835; Randall Collins, "Market Closure and the Conflict Theory of the Professions," in Burrage and Torstendahl, *Professions in Theory and History,* 36.
66. TNA SP 42 / 30, f. 83, Admiralty Board to George II, 31 January 1746.
67. In theory, the Admiralty had a "clear-cut constitutional supremacy" over naval affairs; in reality, the relationship was more complicated: the "Admiralty was the centre of the naval system rather than its head." The Admiralty and Navy Boards had different spheres of responsibility, and the Admiralty was not able to compel Navy Board officials to obey orders because they were not subject to dismissal. See Baugh, *British Naval Administration,* 83–92; Rodger, *Command of the Ocean,* 295–300; Wilkinson, *British Navy and the State,* 19–25.
68. Baugh, *British Naval Administration,* 32–44; J. M. Haas, "The Royal Dockyards: The Earliest Visitations and Reform 1749–1778," *Historical Journal* 13 (1970): 192, 203, 208.
69. TNA ADM 3 / 49 / 243, Admiralty Board minutes, 8 February 1745; R. Middleton, "Naval Administration in the Age of Pitt and Anson, 1755–1763," in *British Navy and the Use of Naval Power,* 114; Lavery, *Ship of the Line,* 1:90–94; Pritchard, "From Shipwright to Naval Constructor," 1, 5, 12; Rodger, "George, Lord Anson," 188.

70. Some ships were built in royal dockyards, some built by merchants on government contract, and some foreign built and purchased as prizes. BL Add. MSS. 15956, f. 119. Knowles to Anson, 6 January 1745; Edward Vernon, *Adm. V__n's Opinion upon the Present State of the British Navy* (London, 1744), 7. For more on shipbuilding and the standardizations known as "the Establishments," see Baugh, *British Naval Administration,* 241–261; Daniel Baugh, ed., *Naval Administration, 1715–1750* (London: Printed for the Navy Records Society, 1977), 191–236; John Hattendorf et al., eds., *British Naval Documents, 1204–1960* (London: Printed for the Navy Records Society, 1993), 477–511; Peter Hemingway, "Sir Jacob Acworth and Experimental Ship Design during the Period of the Establishments," *Mariner's Mirror* 96, no. 2 (2010): 149–160; Lavery, *Ship of the Line,* 1:75–118; Middleton, "Naval Administration," 114–118.
71. Vernon, *Adm. V__n's Opinion,* 11–12; William Horsley, *A Treatise on Maritime Affairs: Or a Comparison between the Commerce and Naval Power of England and France. With a View to Some Paradoxes Advanced by M. Deslandes* (London, 1744), 7–8.
72. This protégé was Thomas Slade, who rose extremely quickly under the authoritarian whig Admiralty; in 1742 he was only a naval overseer to contract-built ships, but by 1750 he was the master shipwright at Plymouth dockyard. In 1747 it was Slade whom Anson and Bedford trusted to break down a captured French ship in order to study its construction and build two frigates on its model. WA HMC 8, vol. XI, p. 34, Henry Legge to Bedford, 6 March 1746; WA HMC 8, vol. XVI, p. 73, Anson to Bedford, 17 April 1747; Middleton, "Naval Administration," 114; Lavery, *Ship of the Line,* 1:96–102.
73. Haas, "Royal Dockyards," 193.
74. BL Add. MSS. 15956, f. 119. Knowles to Anson, 6 January 1745; TNA ADM 3 / 50 / 181. Admiralty Board minutes, 25 April 1745; WA HMC 8, vol. XVI: 53. Anson to Bedford, 3 April 1747; WA HMC 8, vol. XI: 34. Legge to Bedford, 6 March 1746.
75. TNA ADM 7 / 658, "Minutes of Visitation to the Dock Yards &c 1749"; Middleton, "Naval Administration," 110.
76. Middleton, "Naval Administration," 110; Haas, "Royal Dockyards," 193.
77. Full admirals would be equal to full generals; captains of post-ships to be equal to lieutenant colonels; lieutenants in the navy to be equal to captains in the army; and all other ranks were given an equivalent, as well. TNA SP 42 / 32, f. 306, Admiralty Board memorial to George II, 13 November 1747.
78. As a point of comparison, the Spanish court had explicitly made naval officers equivalent in command and prestige to army officers as early as 1714, at the same time as it further professionalized its navy by establishing a firm hierarchy of naval ranks. BL Add. MSS. 15957, f. 16. Sandwich to Anson, 20 July 1747; BL Add. MSS. 15957, f. 28. Sandwich to Anson, 14

November 1747 NS; Kamen, *Spain's Road to Empire,* 452; González de Canales y López-Obrero and González de Canales y Moyano, "Tres siglos de empleos," 376–378.

79. BL Add. MSS 15957, f. 260, Warren to Anson, 2 December 1747; TNA PC 2 / 100, f. 472, Privy Council minutes, 10 December 1747; TNA ADM 7 / 678, no. 9, Order in Council, 10 February 1748.
80. BL Add. MSS 15957, f. 77, Sandwich to Anson, 7 August 1748 NS; BL Add. MSS 15955, f. 270, Henry Fox to Anson, 25 October 1748.
81. For example, George II "abridg[ed]" the authority of the previous Admiralty Board and "transfer[red] [it] to a subordinate officer" by granting Admiral Sir John Norris authority over all the ships in home waters; consequently that Board could not directly give orders to any ship in the waters around England. TNA SP 42 / 27, f. 114, Admiralty Board to George II, 17 March 1744.
82. Vernon published a pseudo-anonymous pamphlet entitled *Some Seasonable Advice from an Honest Sailor* (London, 1746) in which he printed large sections of his correspondence with the Board. He complained that his command was too limited for his honor as an Admiral and that he did not have sufficient autonomy. Bedford personally delivered Vernon's dressing down in front of the entire Board. National Maritime Museum (hereafter NMM) VER / 1 / 4 / A, Stephen Corbett to Vernon, 11 April 1746; NMM VER / 1 / 4 / A, Journal of Vernon, April 1746.
83. TNA ADM 3 / 50 / 15, Admiralty Board minutes, 21 February 1745.
84. TNA ADM 7 / 658, ff. 65–78, "Minutes of Visitation to the Dock Yards &c 1749"; Edward Hawke to the Captains of the Guardships, 14 November 1749, in *The Hawke Papers: A Selection, 1743–1771,* ed. Ruddock F. MacKay (London: Navy Records Society, 1990), 106.
85. William Spavens, *The Narrative of William Spavens, a Chatham Pensioner* (London: Chatham, 1998), 68.
86. Jennifer Craik, *Uniforms Exposed: From Conformity to Transgression* (Oxford: Berg, 2005), 13; Lawrence Langner, "Clothes and Government," in *Dress, Adornment, and the Social Order,* ed. Mary Ellen Roach and Joanne Bubolz Eicher (New York: Wiley, 1965), 127.
87. *Observations and Proposals Concerning the Navy: With an Enquiry into its Condition, and Insufficiency Oftentimes to Defend us from a Sudden Attack of the French. . . . And a Remedy Proposed* (London, 1745), 66.
88. As a point of comparison, both commissioned and warrant Spanish officers had been given a uniform in 1717; the officers of the Spanish army and navy wore the same uniforms until 1761, when the navy was given a uniform of its own. Louis XIV had introduced some guidelines for the marking of hierarchy in French sea officers in 1665, though the first true French naval uniform was not regulated until 1764. See de Sousa Congosto, *Introducción a la historia,* 350–53; Alía Plana and Alía Plana, *Historia de los uniformes,* 21–22; González de Canales y Lopez-Obrero and González

de Canales y Moyano, "Tres siglos de empleos," 376–378; Marine Nationale, Prefecture Maritime Mediterranée, France, *L'étoffe des Marins*, http://www.dailymotion.com/video/xgusul_l-etoffe-des-Marins_news.

89. There was a tension between theoretical and applied knowledge in contemporary discussions of how to train good officers. The trend in public discussion was to push officers to undergo more scientific and theoretical training at an institution like Portsmouth Academy, which taught boys the skills thought necessary to be naval officers. These skills included most importantly mathematics (sailing by dead reckoning was still a key ability), but also writing, the study of fortifications, French, fencing, and gunnery. In contrast, there was uneasiness among sea officers over whether seamanship could really be learned in an academy. The authoritarian whig Admiralty's emphasis was more on practical training and on using theory to complement applied experience. When the Admiralty Board visited Portsmouth dockyard in 1749, they ordered a yacht to be fitted for the academy students with masts and yards, "such as they could rig and unrig upon occasion," and someone to "instruct them in sailing about the harbour that they might attain some knowledge in practice as well as theory." Practical training continued for Academy graduates once serving in the fleet. TNA ADM 3/49/259, Admiralty Board minutes, 14 February 1745. For public discussion of naval education see, for example, Horsley, *A Treatise on Maritime Affairs*, 4; Moncreiff, *Galba*, 13, 16, 56; *An Oration Spoke at Will's Coffee House, in Scotland-Yard* (London, 1744), 9–11; H. W. Dickinson, *Educating the Royal Navy: Eighteenth and Nineteenth-Century Education for Officers* (London: Routledge, 2007), 34, 45; Rodger, *Wooden World*, 263–266.
90. Warren to Bedford, 18 May 1747. Bedford, *Correspondence*, 1:217–219; Anson to Bedford, 11 May 1747. Ibid., 1:213–215.
91. Lavery, *Ship of the Line*, 1:9, 53–54, 127–128; Rodger, *Command of the Ocean*, 540.
92. Thomas Keppel, *The Life of Augustus Viscount Keppel*, 2 vols. (London, 1842), 1:102–103.
93. WA HMC 8, vol. X, p. 45, Legge to Bedford, 15 August 1745.
94. Michael Duffy, "The Establishment of the Western Squadron as the Linchpin of British Naval Strategy," in *Parameters of British Naval Power, 1650–1850*, ed. Michael Duffy (Exeter, UK: University of Exeter Press, 1992), 60–81; see also Daniel Baugh, "Naval Power: What Gave the British Naval Superiority?," in *Exceptionalism and Industrialisation: Britain and Its European Rivals, 1688–1815*, ed. Leandro Prados de la Escosura (Cambridge: Cambridge University Press, 2004), 249–251.
95. Rodger, *Insatiable Earl*, 35.
96. BL Add. MSS 15955, f. 133, Bedford to Anson, 18 July 1746.
97. Julian Gwyn, "The Royal Navy in North America, 1712–1776," in *The British Navy and the Use of Naval Power in the Eighteenth Century*, ed. Jeremy Black and Philip Woodfine (Leicester: Leicester University Press, 1988), 135.

98. Douglas W. Allen, "The British Navy Rules: Monitoring and Incompatible Incentives in the Age of Fighting Sail," *Explorations in Economic History* 39 (2002): 222–228.
99. At this time, the Admiralty had the de jure power of appointment of all officers on board all of its ships. While the Admiralty controlled who was able to become a lieutenant, in practice captains were frequently responsible for unofficially promoting lieutenants to more responsible posts while overseas. Thus the Admiralty's authority over promotion was sometimes de facto exercised as a veto power over those replacement appointments. However, as others have discussed, captains had incentives to promote lieutenants who would meet with the Admiralty's approval. A. B. McLeod, *British Naval Captains of the Seven Years' War: The View from the Quarterdeck* (Woodbridge, UK: Boydell, 2012), 21–23, 229; Daniel K. Benjamin and Anca Tifrea, "Learning by Dying: Combat Performance in the Age of Sail," *Journal of Economic History* 67, no. 4 (2007): 991; Rodger, *Wooden World*, 273–303.
100. As an anonymous letter writer put it to Bedford, it had become customary for "captains in the sea service to expect the honour of being created a flag officer according to their *length of service*" which meant that when a promotion became available, a captain immediately summoned "all his relations" and "parliamentary acquaintance" who insisted that "he must be made an Admiral because he is next in the list." This expectation of promotion and the mustering of political interest in support of it was "the reason, why several of our present Admirals have been so ill chose." WA HMC 8, vol. IX, pp. 108–110. [Anonymous] to Bedford, 16 March 1745.
101. NMM SAN / F / 1 / 2. Admiralty Board memorial to George II, 7 March 1747; TNA ADM 3 / 57. Admiralty Board minutes, 15 July 1747; TNA PC 2 / 100, f. 233. Privy Council minutes, 27 May 1747.
102. BL Add. MSS 15956, f. 195. Legge to Anson, 16 May 1747.
103. WCL, Thomas Smith Papers, Box 1. John Barker to Thomas Smith, 17 July 1748.
104. Several economic historians have studied the incentive structure of the Royal Navy, shedding light on the problem of implementation. See particularly Allen, "The British Navy Rules," 204–231; Daniel K. Benjamin and Christopher Thornberg, "Comment: Rules, Monitoring, and Incentives in the Age of Sail," *Explorations in Economic History* 40, no. 2 (2003): 195–211; Daniel K. Benjamin and Christopher Thornberg, "Organization and Incentives in the Age of Sail," *Explorations in Economic History* 44, no. 2 (2007): 317–341; also Brian Lavery, ed., *Shipboard Life and Organisation 1731–1815* (Aldershot, UK: Ashgate, 1998), 13, 45, 213–214; Ruddock Mackay and Michael Duffy, *Hawke, Nelson and British Naval Leadership, 1747–1805* (Woodbridge, UK: Boydell, 2009), 6–10; McLeod, *British Naval Captains*, 187–208; Tom Wareham, *The Star Captains: Frigate Command in the Napoleonic Wars* (Annapolis, MD: United States Naval Institute Press, 2001), 123–151.
105. Rodger, *Command of the Ocean*, 389.

106. WA HMC 8, vol. XI, f. 48. Bedford to Captain Mead, 7 April 1746, qtd. in Mackay and Duffy, *Hawke, Nelson and British Naval Leadership,* 90.

107. This shift in ethos is comparable with that which took place in other military professionalizations. N. A. M. Rodger describes it in more detail for the navy, though he suggests that it does not take place until later in the century. N. A. M. Rodger, "Honour and Duty at Sea, 1660–1815," *Historical Research* 75 (2002): 425–447; David Parrott, "Cultures of Combat in the Ancien Régime: Linear Warfare, Noble Values, and Entrepreneurship," *International History Review* 27, no. 3 (2005): 518–533.

108. NMM SAN / F / 1 / 2, Admiralty Board memorial to George II, 7 March 1747; TNA ADM 3 / 57, Admiralty Board minutes, 15 July 1747; TNA PC 2 / 100, f. 233, Privy Council minutes, 27 May 1747; BL Add. MSS 15956, f. 195. Legge to Anson, 16 May 1747.

109. Bedford, Debate in the Lords on the Bill for Securing Trade and Navigation in times of War, 1 June 1742. *Cobbett's Parliamentary History,* 12:766.

110. As Frederick would be king, there was necessarily a role for the executive within patriot ideology, but it was a limited executive, as demonstrated for example by Frederick's repeated promises to forgo Crown revenues for a limited Civil List of £800,000 per annum. A. N. Newman, "Leicester House Politics, 1748–1751," *English Historical Review* 76 (1961): 587–588.

111. Debate in the Commons on the Bill for subjecting Half-Pay Naval Officers to Martial Law, 5 April 1749. *Cobbett's Parliamentary History,* 14:410–411; *London Evening Post,* 16 February–18 February 1749; *Old England,* 11 March 1749; Harris, *Patriot Press,* 40–50; Harris, "*London Evening Post*"; Michael Harris, *London Newspapers in the Age of Walpole: A Study of the Origins of the Modern English Press* (London: Associated University Press, 1987), 70.

112. *General Advertiser,* 3 March 1749; *Considerations on the Bill for the Better Government of the Navy* (London, 1749); *The antient and present state of Military Law in Great Britain Consider'd: With a Review of the Debates of the Army and Navy Bills* (London, 1749); Debate in the Commons on the Bill for subjecting Half-Pay Naval Officers to Martial Law, 7 February 1749. *Cobbett's Parliamentary History,* 14:419–421.

113. This ensured that officers who had accepted a pension would report for duty when called for once more and also that officers who had committed a crime could not simply resign their commission to avoid punishment. As was the case with sailors, up until this point sea officers were not—in law or practice—members of a permanent corps. They held specific commissions for specific ships; resigning that commission in effect put an officer out of the reach of military justice. N. A. M. Rodger, *Articles of War: The Statutes Which Governed Our Fighting Navies 1661, 1749, and 1886* (Homewell, UK: Kenneth Mason, 1982), 8–9.

114. BL Add. MSS 28150, ff. 22–23v. John Norris to Wager, 8 November 1735; ESRO SAS / G / AM / 7(4). Samuel and William Baker to Warren, 3 May 1745; TNA SP 42 / 28, f. 262. Admiralty to [Secretaries of State], 29 May 1745;

Debate in the Commons for the Address for Courts-Martial on Matthews, Lestock, &c, 30 April 1745. *Cobbett's Parliamentary History,* 13:1300.

115. James Lind, *Three Letters Relating to the Navy, Gibraltar, and Portmahon* (London, 1757), 61–62, 66. Lind claimed he wrote this pamphlet in 1749, but only published it following the 1756 Battle of Minorca debacle.
116. WA HMC 8, vol. XXXIX, p. 166. Bedford to Bampfylde, 1 May 1759.
117. Lind, *Three Letters Relating to the Navy,* 61–62, 66.
118. Baugh, "Too Much Mixed in This Affair," 34. Whereas Baugh suggests that this would have increased the impact of ministerial politics in the navy, I would suggest that the Admiralty and the public were concerned that ministerial politics already played too great a role in exempting disobedient officers from punishment; reinforcing the power of courts-martial was in fact intended to exclude this outside influence.
119. The Septennial Bill changed parliamentary elections from every three years to every seven; the opposition claimed that this change infringed on the liberty of British elections. *The Remembrancer,* 8 April 1749; Harris, *Patriot Press,* 44.
120. The "heir apparent," of course, was Frederick. Suffolk Record Office, Bury St. Edmunds Branch (hereafter Suff. RO) 941 / 50 / 5, pp. 120–121. Augustus Hervey, draft of pamphlet published 18 February 1749.
121. TNA ADM 3 / 60, Admiralty Board minutes, 20 February 1749.
122. *The Remembrancer,* 25 February 1749.
123. Sea Officer, *Remarks on a Pamphlet called, Considerations on the Bill for the Better Government of the Navy* (London, 1749), 12.
124. Suff. RO 941 / 50 / 5, p. 115, Hervey, draft of pamphlet published 18 February 1749.
125. Hervey named as his collaborators Egmont; Hon. Henry Bathurst; Daniel Boone; Charles Calvert, Lord Baltimore; John Cust; Lord Thomas Gage; Colonel Richard Lyttleton; Richard Nugent; Thomas Pitt; Arthur Mohun St. Leger, Lord Doneraile; and Edmund Thomas. Many of these people had been associated with Frederick from the 1730s; almost all were officeholders in Frederick's household or would hold major government positions upon his future accession; several had spoken out in support of traditional whig topics such as maintaining British troops on the continent. This strongly suggests that despite the patriot-tory alliance, the opposition to the Navy Bill was still more a whig than a tory one, or at a minimum drew more on left-wing strands of patriotism than right-wing. Augustus Hervey, *Augustus Hervey's Journal: The Adventures Afloat and Ashore of a Naval Casanova,* ed. D. Erskine (London: Chatham, 2002), 79–83.
126. *Old England,* 11 March 1749; also referenced in *The Remembrancer,* 8 April 1749.
127. TNA SP 42 / 30, f. 361, Admiralty Board to Newcastle, 16 May 1746; TNA SP 42 / 30, f. 365, Corbett to Dr. Paul, Advocate General, and Heneage Legge, Counsel to the Admiralty, 16 May 1746.

128. TNA SP 42/30, f. 389, Bedford to Newcastle, 18 May 1746.
129. [Hervey], *Detection of the Considerations,* 3.
130. Debate in the Commons on the Bill for subjecting Half-Pay Naval Officers to Martial Law, 5 April 1749. *Cobbett's Parliamentary History,* 14:418–419.
131. *London Evening Post,* 28 February–2 March 1749.
132. Debate in the Commons on the Bill for subjecting Half-Pay Naval Officers to Martial Law, 5 April 1749. *Cobbett's Parliamentary History,* 14:410–411.
133. *The Remembrancer,* 8 April 1749.
134. The army and navy were at that moment linked in patriot rhetoric not just as the two branches of the British military but also because there was a concurrent struggle over reforms in the army which paralleled those imposed on the navy. The army reforms, embodied in the Mutiny Bill of 1749, were the brainchild of Prince William Augustus, the Duke of Cumberland and George II's second son, who had been politically linked with Bedford and Sandwich. Both the Navy and the Mutiny Bills were concerned with discipline and with increasing the ability of the military hierarchy to govern their subordinates; the patriots opposed both. If in part this may have been owing to a rivalry between George II's two sons, it was also true that the two princes embodied very different ideological positions and that therefore opposition was to be expected on this issue: Frederick hoped to be the "patriot king," and Cumberland was the head of the army. *London Evening Post,* 28 February–2 March 1749, 2 March–4 March 1749; *Old England,* 18 March 1749; [Hervey], *Detection of the Considerations,* 4; Glickman, "Parliament, the Tories and Frederick, Prince of Wales."
135. Suff. RO 941/50/5, p. 112, Hervey, draft of pamphlet published 18 February 1749.
136. The *Gazetteer* had previously been a ministerial newspaper during the regime of Walpole, but since his fall in 1742 had become independent. *London Gazetteer,* 4 March 1749; Robert Louis Haig, *The Gazetteer, 1735–1797: A Study in the Eighteenth-Century English Newspaper* (Carbondale: Southern Illinois University Press, 1960), 15.
137. Egmont, Debate in the Commons on a Plan for speedily Manning the Navy, without distressing Trade, 14 April 1749. *Cobbett's Parliamentary History,* 14:542.
138. Debate in the Commons on the bill for securing the Trade to America, 5 May 1738. *Cobbett's Parliamentary History,* 10:812–867.
139. Again, the fear was that professional officers, land or sea, were little better than placemen. UNott Ne C 127, Frederick, Prince of Wales, to Hon. William Talbot, Lord Talbot; Charles Calvert, Lord Baltimore; Dr. George Lee; Sir Francis Dashwood, 4 June 1747; Newman, "Leicester House Politics," 581–582, 587–588. William Pitt made similar demands when Pelham and Newcastle approached him about joining their administration in 1745. See Newcastle to Chesterfield, 20 November 1745. *Private Correspondence of Chesterfield and Newcastle,* 78–86.

140. BL Add. MSS 57820, f. 25, Edward Legge to Thomas Grenville, 7 December 1745; UNott Ne C 249, Dicker to Pelham, 28 August 1745; BL Add. MSS 15957, f. 338, Joseph Yorke to Anson, 8 March 1749 NS; BL Add. MSS 15957, f. 28, Sandwich to Anson, 14 November 1747 NS.
141. The initial attack on the fortress of Louisbourg was planned and executed primarily by the New England colonies with the support of the Royal Navy in the form of Peter Warren, at this time still affiliated with the authoritarian whigs. Francis Parkman, *France and England in North America* (London: Faber and Faber, 1956), 391–402.
142. Newcastle to Chesterfield, 9 October 1745. *Private Correspondence of Chesterfield and Newcastle,* 75. That same year, London merchants called for Cape Breton to be annexed to Britain by Act of Parliament so that the administration would be unable to restore it. Robert Harris, *Patriot Press,* 227.
143. Newcastle to Bedford and others, 28 March 1746. Bedford, *Correspondence,* 1:64.
144. Bedford to Andrew Stone, 10 November 1746. Ibid., 1:182–185.
145. William Pitt to Bedford, 19 July 1746. Ibid., 1:132.
146. WA HMC 8, vol. XVI, p. 19. William Bollan to Bedford, 20 January 1746/7.
147. WA HMC 8, vol. XXIII, p. 40. Halifax to Bedford, 24 February 1748/9; WA HMC 8, vol. XXIII, p. 79. Halifax to Bedford, 15 April 1749; Beaumont, *Colonial America,* 41–68.
148. The paradigm of "salutary neglect" is, however, far from dead. For discussions of the deeper roots of the century's imperial conflicts, see, for example, Beneke, "Critical Turn"; Clayton, "Duke of Newcastle"; Greene, "An Uneasy Connection"; Mason, "Britain and the Administration."

4. The Seven Years' War and the Patriot Alternative to Professionalization

1. National Library of Scotland (hereafter NLS) MS 11014, f. 31. Charles Townshend to Sir Gilbert Elliot, [24 June 1756].
2. See, for example, the variety of anonymous letters sent to William Pitt as Secretary of State: TNA PRO 30/8/78, f. 4. [Anonymous] to William Pitt, 21 February 1757; TNA PRO 30/8/78, f. 24. [Anonymous] to Pitt, 7 February 1757.
3. TNA SP 36/135, f. 192. E. F. to Robert Darcy, Earl of Holdernesse, 21 August 1756.
4. WCL George Grenville Papers, Box 1, Folder 15. Thomas Potter to George Grenville, 11 September 1756. The ballad referenced is *The Block and Yard Arm: A New Ballad. On the Loss of Minorca, and the Danger of Our American Rights and Possession* ([London], [1756]).

5. Articles of War, 1749, in Markus Eder, *Crime and Punishment in the Royal Navy of the Seven Years' War, 1755–1763* (Aldershot, UK: Ashgate, 2004), 158–173.
6. M. John Cardwell, *Arts and Arms: Literature, Politics and Patriotism during the Seven Years' War* (Manchester: Manchester University Press, 2004), 4–5, 10–11, 68, 74; Nicholas Rogers, *Crowds, Culture, and Politics in Georgian Britain* (Oxford: Clarendon Press, 1998), 58–64; Spector, *English Literary Periodicals.* Historians have explained the virulence of the response to the Byng affair in several ways. Some have suggested that the popular response was essentially irrational: people blamed both Byng and the administration equally without really thinking things through. Another explanation is that the reactions to the loss of Minorca were politically motivated: the establishment whigs vilified Byng and exaggerated his deficiencies as a way to exonerate themselves. Meanwhile, the opposition, both patriots and tories, used Minorca as an excuse to embarrass the administration, in a purely strategic move unmotivated by other beliefs or principles. A more nuanced third explanation has been that hostilities against Byng and against the administration were linked because Byng was emblematic of other perceived failings in aristocratic government. For an attribution of both Byng's and Newcastle's disgraces to blind popular anger, see Marie Peters, *Pitt and Popularity: The Patriot Minister and London Opinion during the Seven Years' War* (Oxford: Clarendon Press, 1980), 52, 70. For an explanation of the Minorca controversy as political opportunism, see N. A. M. Rodger, *The Command of the Ocean: A Naval History of Britain, 1649–1815* (New York: Norton, 2004); Nicholas Rogers, *Whigs and Cities: Popular Politics in the Age of Walpole and Pitt* (Oxford: Clarendon Press, 1989); Robert Donald Spector, *English Literary Periodicals and the Climate of Opinion during the Seven Years' War* (The Hague: Mouton, 1966). For an analysis of the perceived connection between Byng and aristocratic government, see Kathleen Wilson, *The Sense of the People: Politics, Culture, and Imperialism in England, 1715–1785* (Cambridge: Cambridge University Press, 1995), 183–189.
7. For a recent example of the continuing emphasis on the periphery, see P. J. Marshall, *The Making and Unmaking of Empires: Britain, India, and America c. 1750–1783* (Oxford: Oxford University Press, 2005); Matt Schumann and Karl Schweizer, *The Seven Years' War: A Transatlantic History* (London: Routledge, 2008). For an emphasis on continental entanglements, see Brendan Simms, *Three Victories and a Defeat: The Rise and Fall of the First British Empire, 1714–1783* (London: Allen Lane, 2007).
8. Daniel Baugh, *The Global Seven Years War, 1754–1763: Britain and France in a Great Power Contest* (Harlow, UK: Pearson, 2011), 35; Wilson, *Sense of the People,* 193.
9. BL Add. MSS 32860, f. 65v. Newcastle to William, Count Bentinck, 16 October 1755.

10. *Some remarks on the Royal Navy. To which are annexed some Short but Interesting Reflections on a Future Peace* (London, 1760), 38–40.
11. As has been well documented: see, among many others, David A. Fleming, "Patriots and politics in Navan, 1753–5," *Irish Historical Studies* 36 (2009): 502–521; Christine Gerrard, *The Patriot Opposition to Walpole: Politics, Poetry, and National Myth, 1725–1742* (Oxford: Clarendon Press, 1994); Harris, *Patriot Press;* Bob Harris, "The Patriot Clubs of the 1750s," in *Clubs and Societies in Eighteenth-Century Ireland,* ed. James Kelly and Martyn J. Powell (Dublin: Four Courts Press, 2010), 224–243; Jacqueline Hill, "'Allegories, Fictions and Feigned Representations': Decoding the Money Bill Dispute, 1752–6," *Eighteenth-Century Ireland* 21 (2006): 66–88; Declan O'Donovan, "The Money Bill Dispute of 1753," in *Penal Era and Golden Age,* ed. Thomas Bartlett and D. W. Hayton (Belfast: Ulster Historical Foundation, 1979), 55–87; Martyn J. Powell, "The Society of Free Citizens and Other Popular Political Clubs, 1749–89," in Kelly and Powell, *Clubs and Societies,* 243–263; Rogers, *Whigs and Cities;* Rogers, *Crowds, Culture, and Politics;* Wilson, *Sense of the People.*
12. Rogers, *Whigs and Cities,* 141.
13. See, for example, Public Record Office of Northern Ireland (hereafter PRONI) T2915 / 3 / 22, copy of WA HMC 8, vol. XXXV, p. 50. Bedford to Pitt, 12 November 1757; PRONI T3228 / 2 / 5. John Ryder, Archbishop of Tuam, to Nathaniel Ryder, 16 December 1760; PRONI T2915 / 10 / 72, copy of WA HMC 8, vol. XLII, p. 294. Lords Justices of Ireland to Bedford, 27 December 1760; see also Martyn Powell, *Britain and Ireland in the Eighteenth-Century Crisis of Empire* (New York: Palgrave Macmillan, 2003), 48–65.
14. PRONI T2915 / 7 / 43, copy of WA HMC 8, vol. XXXIX, p. 180. Bedford to George Armagh, 22 May 1759.
15. PRONI T2915 / 3 / 22, copy of WA HMC 8, vol. XXXV, p. 50. Bedford to Pitt, 12 November 1757; PRONI T2915 / 3 / 28, copy of WA HMC 8, vol. XXXV, p. 62. Same to same, 17 November 1757; PRONI T2915 / 3 / 36, copy of WA HMC 8, vol. XXXV, p. 81. Pitt to Bedford, 26 November 1757; see also Eoin Magennis, *The Irish Political System, 1740–1765* (Dublin: Four Courts Press, 2000), 117–20.
16. Bedford was somewhat sympathetic to Irish Catholics. He expressed his support for a plan to remove some of the restrictions on Catholic priests in Ireland and reconcile them to the regime, which he hoped would "make the Papists of Ireland good Subjects to the King." PRONI T2915 / 2 / 32, copy of WA HMC 8, vol. XXXIV, p. 113. Earl of Clanbrassill to Bedford, 17 July 1757; PRONI T2915 / 2 / 38, copy of WA HMC 8, vol. XXXIV, p. 137. Bedford to Clanbrassill, 4 August 1757.
17. WA HMC 8, vol. XL, p. 242. Bedford to Pitt, 25 December 1759; PRONI T2915 / 9 / 1, copy of WA HMC 8, vol. XLI, p. 2. Pitt to Bedford, 5 January 1760; Magennis, *Irish Political System,* 132–140; Sean Murphy, "The

Dublin Anti-Union Riot of 3 December 1759," in *Parliament, Politics, and People: Essays in Eighteenth-Century Irish history,* ed. Gerard O'Brien (Blackrock: Irish Academic Press, 1989), 49–68. For other accounts of the riots, see PRONI T3228 / 2 / 4. Archbishop of Tuam to Ryder, 7 December 1759; PRONI T3019 / 6458 / 572. Rigby to Robert Wilmot, 26 November 1759; PRONI T3019 / 6458 / 577. Thomas Waite to Wilmot, 18 December 1759.

18. PRONI T3019 / 6458 / 575. Rigby to Wilmot, 10 December [1759]; PRONI T3019 / 6458 / 579. Same to same, 23 December 1759; PRONI T3019 / 6458 / 580. Same to same, 26 December 1759.
19. Debate in the Commons on the Number of Seamen for the year 1750, 27 November 1749. *Cobbett's Parliamentary History of England,* 36 vols. (London, 1806–1820), 14:618.
20. *A Modest Address to the Commons of Great Britain, and in Particular the Free Citizens of London; Occasioned by the Ill Success of Our Present Naval War with France, and the Want of a Militia Bill* (London, 1756), 6.
21. TNA SP 94 / 148, f. 196. Memorial sent to Emmanuel-Félicité de Durfort de Duras, French ambassador to Spain, and forwarded by Benjamin Keene, British ambassador to Spain, to Sir Thomas Robinson, Secretary of State, [1755]. "se sabe que hay muchas personas del primero rango en Inglaterra, que embarrazandose muy poco del sucesso de la ultima guerra en Europa, hubieran querido que su nación hubiesse empleado todas sus fuerzas, contra la America Española y Francesa, y por esta consideración, han objetado á los que travasaron al Tratado de Aix la Chapelle."
22. TNA SP 78 / 251, f. 76. Hans Stanley, British ambassador to France, to Pitt, 3 June 1761.
23. BL Add. MSS 32866, ff. 44v–45. Newcastle to Bentinck, 6 July 1756.
24. BL Add. MSS 32866, f. 230. Joseph Yorke, British ambassador to the Dutch Republic, to Newcastle, 20 July 1756.
25. BL Add. MSS 32860, f. 36v. Newcastle to George William Hervey, Earl of Bristol, 13 October 1755.
26. BL Add. MSS 32860, f. 1v. Newcastle to Philip Yorke, Earl of Hardwicke, 11 October 1755; NLS MS 11001, ff. 14–15. Gilbert Elliot [son] to Sir Gilbert Elliot [father], 15 November 1755; Debate in the Commons on the Address of Thanks, 14 November 1755. *Cobbett's Parliamentary History,* 15:333–372.
27. BL Add. MSS 32868, f. 118. George Lyttelton to Newcastle, 7 October 1756. Lyttelton had been closely associated with Pitt in the 1730s and 1740s, though relations had cooled between them in the 1750s.
28. Peter Warren to Stephen Corbett, 6 February 1742 / 3, in *The Royal Navy and North America: The Warren Papers, 1736–1752,* ed. Julian Gwyn (London: Navy Records Society, 1973), 35–39; Newcastle to John Russell, Duke of Bedford, and others, 28 March 1746, in *Correspondence of John, fourth Duke of Bedford: Selected from the originals at Woburn Abbey,* 3 vols. (London, 1842–1846), 1:64; Bedford to Andrew Stone, 10 November 1746, in ibid., 1:182–185.

29. *London Evening Post,* 4 June 1754.
30. BL Add. MSS 32868, f. 114. Lyttelton to Newcastle, 7 October 1756.
31. BL Add. MSS 41346, ff. 133–134. Samuel Martin [father] to Samuel Martin [son], 20 May 1755; BL Add. MSS 41347, f. 124. Same to same, 15 February 1762.
32. TNA SP 42 / 38, f. 45. M. Alexis to [unknown], 10 August 1755. "Nous savons qu'il n'y a pas de guerre en France, mais elle est furieuse en ce pais ci."
33. France began what the British ambassador to Spain, Benjamin Keene, called a "paper war" in an attempt to persuade the Spanish to enter the fray. For the pamphlet mentioned above, see TNA SP 94 / 148, f. 196. Memorial to Duras, [1755]. "Aunque es quimerico, el proyecto de la monarquía universal, el de una influencia general, por medio de las riquezas, vendría á ser realidad, si algún estado, llegara á hacerse dueño absoluto, de todo el comercio de la America." For Keene's observations on French pamphleteering in Spain, see TNA SP 94 / 149, f. 321. Keene to Henry Fox, 28 December 1755.
34. The French ambassador warned the Spanish court that if the French West Indies were lost, Spanish Mexico would be next. See, for example, TNA SP 94 / 148, f. 175. Keene to Robinson, 7 April 1755; TNA SP 94 / 149, f. 135. Keene to Holdernesse, 27 August 1755.
35. TNA SP 94 / 148, f. 189. [Antoine-Louis] Rouillé, [comte de Jouy,] to [François de Baschi,] Comte de Baschi [Saint Esteve], 25 March 1755. "l'Europe ne pourra certainement voir, que avec une extreme surprise. . . . Que les Anglois pour satisfaire des vues ambitieuses, et de conquete, entreprennent de detruire dans le Nouveau Monde l'Equilibre de Puissance, qu'il n'est pas moins important d'y maintenir qu'en Europe, et auquel toutes les nations commerciantes sont essentiellement interessées."
36. *Considerations on the Approaching Peace* (London, 1762), 30.
37. BL Add. MSS 32924, f. 172. Intelligence from Versailles to Newcastle, 19 June 1761; Beinecke Manuscript and Rare Book Library OSB MSS File 7847. James Hutton to Mr. Phelps, 3 December 1762.
38. Spector, *English Literary Periodicals,* 112–114, 124–125.
39. By the middle of 1757, the war appeared to be very much on a downward spiral; Grenville suggested that within a few months, "the good people of England & Scotland may be furnished with a better reason for hanging themselves than they have hitherto been able to assign." NLS MS 11014, ff. 69–70. Grenville to Sir Gilbert Elliot, 14 September 1757; see Baugh, *Global Seven Years War,* 169–270.
40. David Mallet, for example, offered and was hired to write a pamphlet attacking Byng. BL Add. MSS 32866, f. 115. Mallet to Newcastle, 10 June 1756; A Plain Man [David Mallet], *Observations on the Twelfth Article of War: Wherein the Nature of Negligence, Cowardice, and Disaffection, Is Discussed* (London, 1757). See also BL Add. MSS 35594, ffs. 103, 236–237, 254 (for

correspondence between Mallet and Hardwicke regarding his pamphleteering activities).

41. Or at least that was the establishment whigs' hope. See, for example: BL Add. MSS 32866, ff. 211–214. Newcastle to Hardwicke, 19 July 1756; BL Add. MSS 32866, f. 280. Thomas Knox to Robert Nugent, 26 July 1756; BL Add. MSS 32866, f. 456v. Nugent to Newcastle, 15 August 1756.
42. BL Add. MSS 32866, f. 113. Newcastle to Hardwicke, 19 July 1756.
43. *An Appeal to Reason and Common Sense: or, a Free and Candid Disquisition of the Conduct of A__ B__* (London, 1756), 21.
44. *A Poetical Epistle from Admiral Byng, in the Infernal Shades to His Friend L__d A__, an Inhabitant on Earth* (London, 1757).
45. See for example: Staff. RO D1798/HMDrakeford/22. Samuel Faulkner to Richard Drakeford, 31 July 1756. Daniel Baugh argues that in fact the majority of sea officers agreed that Byng was in the wrong, though that did not necessarily mean they thought he should be executed: Daniel Baugh, "'Too Much Mixed in This Affair': The Impact of Ministerial Politics in the Eighteenth-Century Royal Navy," in *New Interpretations in Naval History: Selected Papers from the Fourteenth Naval History Symposium*, ed. Randy Carol Balano and Craig L. Symonds (Annapolis, MD: Naval Institute Press, 2001), 36; Baugh, *Global Seven Years War*, 234.
46. Barnet (Byng's estate), Bewdley, Birmingham, Bristol, Cleveland, Darlington, Devizes, Dublin, Dudley, Exeter, Falmouth, Gateshead, Gravesend, Harborough, Hertford, Higham Ferrars, Leeds, London (several times), Market Worcester, Newcastle, Richmond, Salisbury, South Shields, North Shields, Southampton, Sunderland, Tynemouth, York, and the Isle of Wight, among others. Cardwell, *Art and Arms*, 65.
47. BL Add. MSS 32860, f. 273. Newcastle to Lyttleton, 1 November 1755.
48. BL Add. MSS 32866, f. 328. Newcastle to Henry Campion, 31 July 1756.
49. BL Add. MSS 32866, f. 62. Joseph Watkins to Newcastle, 7 July 1756.
50. BL Add. MSS 32866, ff. 210–214. Newcastle to Hardwicke, 19 July 1756.
51. NMM KEP/11. "Resolutions of the Court, with the Sentence & a Representation to the Lords of the Admiralty," 27 January 1757. A pamphlet supporting this view explained, "I little thought to see the day, when omniscience should be expected as a necessary qualification in a sea-officer" and condemned the policy of "murdering for mistake." An Old Sea Officer, *A Candid Examination of the Resolutions and Sentence of the Court-Martial on the Trial of Admiral Byng* (London, 1757), 3; Proceedings of the Commons on the Bill to release Admiral Byng's Court Martial from the Oath of Secrecy, 25 February 1757. *Cobbett's Parliamentary History*, 15:804–807; Proceedings of the Lords on the Bill to release Admiral Byng's Court Martial from the Oath of Secrecy, 1 March 1757. *Cobbett's Parliamentary History*, 15:807–821.
52. *A letter from the C__t M__l upon Admiral Byng, to the L__ds of the A__dm__lty* ([London?], [1757?]).

53. Baugh, *Global Seven Years War,* 182–194.

54. Charles Townshend, for example, bemoaned the support the establishment whig administration continued to receive from George II and suggested that the country would have benefitted had George II died four years previously, allowing George III—whose views were suspected to be more sympathetic to colonial causes—to come to the throne: "how different a rank would this reign have held in the history of this island, if the four last years of this had made a part of the next reign." Bedford likewise expressed his unhappiness at the "fatal consequences, that have followed the measures that have been hitherto taken" and warned of "the destructive tendency of any others, that may be hereafter proposed, upon the same unsteady, and inconsistent principles, which have hitherto prevailed." BL Add. MSS 63079, ff. 93–95. Charles Townshend to Etheldreda Townshend, Viscountess Townshend, 13 July 1757; BL Add. MSS 51385, ff. 5–6. Bedford to Fox, 14 October 1756.

55. BL Add. MSS 51385, ff. 5–6, Bedford to Fox, 14 October 1756. Some have cited Bedford's response to Byng's sister as evidence that he was in fact disposed to mercy. Bedford's words in that instance were that "in case his Majesty shall be pleased to refer the sentence of the court martial to the Cabinet Council," he would "be very happy if, upon a short examination into the proceedings of the court martial, I shall find myself at liberty to adopt those sentiments of mercy which that court has so strongly recommended to his Majesty." Bedford did not promise to intervene, nor did he say that he currently supported mercy, nor did he promise to support mercy in the future. It is a sentence full of conditional statements (*if* the king refers the matter to the cabinet, Bedford *would* be happy *if* Byng appears to deserve mercy), written to an immediate relative of the condemned—an instance in which a firm reiteration of the legitimacy of a death sentence might be an act of cruelty. Bedford to Mrs. Osborne, 2 February 1757, in *Correspondence of John, fourth Duke of Bedford,* 2:233.

56. BL Add. MSS 32870, f. 260. Hardwicke to Newcastle, 11 March 1757.

57. BL Add. MSS 32870, ff. 218–219. [Anonymous] to Newcastle, [February 1757].

58. See, for example: *The Voice of Liberty. An Occasional Essay. On the Behaviour and Conduct of the English Nation, In Opposition to Min_st___l Oppression* (London, 1756); *All Is Out—or, Admiral Byng to the Tune of Tantararara* ([London?], [1756?]).

59. This was Byng's version of the story, expressed in his pamphlet *An Appeal to the People.* Byng argued that his force was so weak, he showed poorer judgment in seeking out the enemy at all than he did in retreating to Gibraltar, which he thought he could save. One establishment whig responded, "From whence I suppose we are to infer, that this gentleman was sent out with a respectable squadron of line of battle ships for a pleasant summer's trip as it were, not by any means to fight, but only to

be a tame spectator of Mr. Blakeney's distress." [John Byng], *An Appeal to the People: Containing, The Genuine and Entire Letter of Admiral Byng to the Secr. of the Ad__y, Observations on Those Parts Which Were Omitted by the Writers of the* Gazette: *and What Might be the Reasons for Such Omissions* (London, 1756), 46; BL Add. MSS 32868, f. 157. James Burrow to Newcastle, 9 October 1756.

60. Spector, *English Literary Periodicals,* 31.
61. *A Letter to a Member of Parliament in the Country, from His Friend in London, Relative to the Case of Admiral Byng* (London, 1756), 1, 46.
62. Vernon also admitted, though, that if he had been in Byng's situation, "however unequal my force had been I think, I should have pushed the [fleet?] to its utmost period, and left to others to have accounted for the insufficiency of the force." NMM VER / 1 / 5 / G. Edward Vernon to Francis Vernon, 6 June 1756.
63. Cardwell, *Art and Arms,* 83.
64. *London Evening Post,* 11 January 1757.
65. TNA SP 36 / 135, f. 206. 14 August 1756.
66. NMM VER / 1 / 5 / F. Edward Vernon to Francis Vernon, 2 January 1755.
67. BL Add. MSS 32861, f. 145. Newcastle to Hardwicke, 30 November 1755.
68. BL Add. MSS 32866, ff. 206–206v. Hardwicke to Newcastle, 18 July 1756.
69. TNA SP 78 / 250, f. 150. Rouillé to [Gaston Pierre de Lévis,] Duc de Mirepoix, 31 March 1755. "Nous sommes, dit ce Ministre, persuadés des intentions pacifiques de la Cour de Londres."
70. BL Add. MSS 32868, f. 42. Intelligence from Versailles to Newcastle, 3 October 1756.
71. Rogers, *Whigs and Cities,* 101–102. Rogers lists thirty-six constituencies; however, Wigton also petitioned, for a total of thirty-seven.
72. TNA SP 36 / 135, f. 192. E. F. to Holdernesse, 21 August 1756.
73. BL Add. MSS 32868, f. 390. West to Newcastle, 23 October 1756.
74. An Old Sea Officer, *A Candid Examination,* 1–2.
75. Augustus Hervey, *Augustus Hervey's Journal: The Adventures Afloat and Ashore of a Naval Casanova,* ed. David Erskine (London: Chatham, 2002), 80–81.
76. BL Add. MSS 32860, f. 89. Newcastle to Hardwicke, 18 October 1755; BL Add. MSS 32860, f. 471. West to Newcastle, 13 November 1755; NLS MS 11001 ff. 14–15. Gilbert Elliot [son] to Sir Gilbert Elliot [father], 15 November 1755; BL Stowe 263, f. 2. Henry Digby to Charles Hanbury Williams, 23 December 1755.
77. Proceedings of the Commons on the Bill to release Admiral Byng's Court Martial from the Oath of Secrecy, 26 February 1757. *Cobbett's Parliamentary History,* 15:804; Debate in the Commons on the Number of Seamen for the Year 1751, 25 January 1751. *Cobbett's Parliamentary History,* 14:849–851; BL Add. MSS 32889, ff. 400–401. "List of Persons present at the Militia Meeting April 7th 1759"; BL Add. MSS 32870, f. 194. Hardwicke to Newcastle, 29 February 1757.

78. Suff. RO 941 / 50 / 5, p. 111. Augustus Hervey, draft for a pamphlet printed 18 February 1749.
79. Hervey, *Journal*, 234.
80. Ibid., 236–237.
81. NMM VER / 1 / 5 / G. Edward Vernon to Francis Vernon, 2 March 1756; NMM VER / 1 / 5 / J. Edward Vernon to Pitt, [1757].
82. David J. Starkey, "The Origins and Regulation of Eighteenth-Century British Privateering," in *Bandits at Sea: A Pirates Reader*, ed. C. R. Pennell (New York: New York University Press, 2001), 79.
83. Rogers, *Whigs and Cities*, 111–112.
84. An Officer of a Privateer during the Late War, *Useful Remarks on Privateering. Addressed to the Laudable Association of Anti-Gallicans* (London, 1756), 1.
85. *Monitor*, 30 October 1756.
86. Rogers, *Crowds, Culture, and Politics*, 101; Western, *English Militia*, 144.
87. For more on the difficulties the state encountered in trying to regulate privateers, see Guy Chet, *The Ocean Is a Wilderness: Atlantic Piracy and the Limits of State Authority, 1688–1856* (Amherst: University of Massachusetts Press, 2014).
88. BL Eg. MSS 3438, f. 281. Customs Commissioners to Treasury, 18 July 1758.
89. Starkey, "Eighteenth-Century Privateering," 74; *Monitor*, 7 April 1759.
90. Staff. RO D615 / P(S) / 1 / 2 / 23. Elizabeth Anson to George Anson, 1 September 1758.
91. 32 George II c 25; Starkey, "Eighteenth-Century Privateering," 74.
92. The Admiralty expressed concern over competing with privateers for sailors. TNA ADM 7 / 341, ff. 76–77. Admiralty Board to George II, 20 March 1759.
93. J. R. Western, *The English Militia in the Eighteenth Century: The Story of a Political Issue, 1660–1802* (London: Routledge and Kegan Paul, 1965), 116.
94. Philip Stanhope, Earl of Stanhope, Debate in the Lords on the Militia Bill, 24 May 1756. *Cobbett's Parliamentary History*, 15:708–709.
95. Horatio Walpole to Hardwicke, 4 April 1756. *Cobbett's Parliamentary History*, 15:705–706.
96. Proceedings of the Commons on the Bill to release Admiral Byng's Court Martial from the Oath of Secrecy, 26 February 1757. *Cobbett's Parliamentary History*, 15:804; Debate in the Commons on the Number of Seamen for the Year 1751, 25 January 1751. *Cobbett's Parliamentary History*, 14:849–851; BL Add. MSS 32889, ff. 400–401. "List of Persons Present at the Militia Meeting April 7th 1759"; BL Add. MSS 32870, f. 194. Hardwicke to Newcastle, 29 February 1757.
97. NMM VER / 1 / 5 / G. Edward Vernon to Francis Vernon, 2 March 1756; NMM VER / 1 / 5 / J. Edward Vernon to Pitt, [1757].
98. *London Chronicle*, 8 January 1757.
99. NLS MS 11001 ff. 50–51. Gilbert Elliot [son] to Sir Gilbert Elliot [father], [March 1760]; NLS MS 11001 ff. 52–54. Same to same, 15 March 1760; NLS MS 11001 f. 74. Same to same, 7 March 1762.
100. *A Modest Address to the Commons*, 27–28.

101. *London Evening Post,* 11 January 1757.
102. NMM VER / 1 / 5 / J. Edward Vernon to Pitt, [1757].
103. Cardwell, *Art and Arms,* 112.
104. BL Add. MSS 41346, f. 167. Samuel Martin [father] to Samuel Martin [son], 15 June 1756.
105. Richard Grenville-Temple, Earl Temple, Debate in the Lords on the Militia Bill, 24 May 1756. *Cobbett's Parliamentary History,* 15: 767; *London Evening Post,* 25 January 1757.
106. BL Add. MSS 41346, ff. 125–128. Samuel Martin [father] to Samuel Martin [son], 20 December 1754.
107. Western, *English Militia,* 125, 437.
108. Gentlewoman, *A Poem. Occasioned by the Militia Bill, Now Depending. Addressed to the Ladies of Great Britain* (London, 1757), 4–8.
109. Western, *English Militia,* 119.
110. WCL George Townshend Papers, Letterbook vol. 1, pp. 160–166. George Townshend to John Perceval, Second Earl of Egmont, 5 September 1768.
111. Ibid., 221–229. Townshend to Attorney General De Grey, 21 October 1768.
112. BL Add. MSS 15916, ff. 50–51. Bedford, draft of a speech to be given on the Militia Bill, [April 1757].
113. This may have stemmed from the authoritarian whig perception that the Irish population was rather less than trustworthy. Neal Garnham, *The Militia in Eighteenth-Century Ireland: In Defence of the Protestant Interest* (Woodbridge, UK: Boydell, 2012), 64; Magennis, *Irish Political System,* 142.
114. PRONI T2915 / 9 / 30, copy of WA HMC 8, vol. XLI, p. 118. Francis Russell, Marquess of Tavistock, to Bedford, 30 March 1760; WA HMC 8, vol. XLI, p. 194. Same to same, 5 May 1760.
115. NMM SAN / F / 41 / 8. John Montagu, earl of Sandwich, to [William Augustus, duke of Cumberland], 27 May 1757.
116. Baron Samuel Sandys, Debate in the Lords on the Militia Bill, 24 May 1756. *Cobbett's Parliamentary History,* 15:757.
117. Hardwicke, Debate in the Lords on the Militia Bill, 24 May 1756. *Cobbett's Parliamentary History,* 15:731–732.
118. UNott Ne C 258. Michael Lee Dicker to Henry Pelham, 27 January 1746.
119. Ian Gilmour, *Riot, Risings and Revolution: Governance and Violence in Eighteenth-Century England* (London: Pimlico, 1993), 295–296.
120. *Lloyd's Evening Post,* 5 September 1757.
121. TNA SP 36 / 138, ff. 1–2. Bedford to Pitt, 1 September 1757; see also WA HMC 8, vol. XLI, p. 60. Tavistock to Bedford, 10 February 1760.
122. BL Eg. MSS 3436, f. 137. Henry Willoughby to Conyers D'Arcy, 15 September 1757; TNA SP 36 / 138, f. 115. Thomas Powell to Gabriel Hangers, [October or November] 1757; TNA SP 36 / 138, f. 117. Hangers to [Pitt?], 6 November 1757; *Lloyd's Evening Post,* 5 September 1757; *London Chronicle,* 6 October 1757.

123. BL Eg. MSS 3436, f. 138. Henry Ingram, viscount of Irwin [Irvine], published declaration, 15 September 1757.
124. TNA PRO 30 / 8 / 64, ff. 151–152. George Townshend to Pitt, 28 February 1758.
125. BL Eg. MSS 3436, ff. 141–142. Holdernesse to [George Fox Lane,] Lord Mayor of York, 17 September 1757.
126. BL Eg. MSS 3436, ff. 152–153. Irwin to Holdernesse, 28 September 1757. Bedford, true to form, thought the administration should make "proper examples of some of the ringleaders of the late riots" which would "prevent . . . the like enormities being committed for the future." WA HMC 8, vol. XXXIV, p. 189. Bedford to Richard Astell, 3 September 1757.
127. *London Chronicle,* 6 October 1757.
128. TNA SP 36 / 138, f. 43. Lane to Pitt, 1 October 1757.
129. BL Add. MSS 32874, ff. 161–162. Anonymous to Samuel Dashwood and James Bateman, [September 1757].
130. TNA PRO 30 / 8 / 53, ff. 115–116. John Poulett, earl Poulett, to Pitt, qtd. in Western, *English Militia,* 151–152.
131. TNA SP 36 / 135, f. 176. Lord Mayor, Aldermen and Commons of the City of London in Common Council Assembled to George II, 17 August 1756.
132. TNA SP 36 / 136, f. 184. Tavistock to George II, 1756; ibid., f. 195. Wigtownshire to George II, 1756; ibid., f. 198. Southwark to George II, 1756; BL Add. MSS 32866, f. 449v. West to Newcastle, 14 August 1756; Rogers, *Whigs and Cities,* 100.
133. NMM ELL / 400, no. 22. Jack Elliot to George Elliot, 11 January 1758.
134. TNA ADM 1 / 384. Edward Boscawen to John Clevland, secretary of the Admiralty, 20 August 1759.
135. TNA ADM 1 / 161, f. 346. George Pocock to Clevland, 12 October 1759. Pocock became a supporter of George Grenville's administration in the 1760s.
136. BL Add. MSS. 45580, f. 21. "Neptune's Resignation," 1759.
137. Brian Lavery, *The Ship of the Line,* 2 vols. (Annapolis, MD: Naval Institute Press, 1983), 1:9, 127.
138. Similarly, Spain's late entry into the war did give Britain time to face down France without the support of its Bourbon ally. This however cannot explain the shift toward more aggressive naval warfare demonstrated in that war and continued in subsequent conflicts. For accounts of the diplomatic currents of the Seven Years War, see, for example, Matt Schumann and Karl Schweizer, *Seven Years War: A Transatlantic History* (London: Routledge, 2008), 157–226; Karl Schweizer, *Frederick the Great, William Pitt, and Lord Bute: The Anglo-Prussian Alliance, 1756–1763* (New York: Garland, 1991); Brendan Simms, *Three Victories and a Defeat: The Rise and Fall of the First British Empire, 1714–1783* (London: Allen Lane, 2007), 387–500.
139. BL IOR H / 95, f. 191. Pocock to Pitt, 22 July 1758.
140. TNA ADM 1 / 384. Henry Osborn to Clevland, 12 March 1758.

141. Clive Wilkinson, *The British Navy and the State in the Eighteenth Century* (Woodbridge, UK: Boydell, 2004), 99.
142. J. R. Jones, "Limitations of British Sea Power in the French Wars, 1689–1815," in *The British Navy and the Use of Naval Power in the Eighteenth Century*, ed. Jeremy Black and Philip Woodfine (Leicester: Leicester University Press, 1988), 47.
143. N. A. M. Rodger, *The Wooden World: An Anatomy of the Georgian Navy* (New York; London: Norton, 1986), 345.
144. Rodger, *Command of the Ocean*, 288.
145. Lavery, *Ship of the Line*, 1:99, 102.
146. Edward Loveden, Debate in the Commons respecting Promotions of Flag Officers, 29 April 1788. *Cobbett's Parliamentary History*, 27:376.
147. See, among others, Charles Alfred Ashburton, *A New and Complete History of England* (London, 1791–1794), 814–815; Edward Barnard, *The New, Impartial and Complete History of England; from the Very Earliest Period of Authentic Information* (London, [1790?]), 615–617; Robert Beatson, *Naval and Military Memoirs of Great Britain, from the Year 1727, to the Present Time*, 3 vols. (London, 1790), 2:45–93; William Belsham, *History of Great Britain, from the Revolution to the Session of Parliament Ending A.D. 1793*, 4 vols. (London, 1798), 3:415–420.

5. The Authoritarian Navy and the Crisis of Empire

1. *New England Weekly Journal*, 10 April 1732.
2. Letters written to the Board of Admiralty by Alexander Colvill, Lord Colville, as naval commander in chief of the North American station are rife with descriptions of colonial hostility to the navy, sea officers, and those who collaborated with them. These reports were confirmed by colonial newspapers—for example, the *Providence Gazette*, along with several other New England newspapers, printed a story in June 1772 about a colonial pilot who had served on a naval ship being forcibly sheared. For accounts of colonists attempting to prevent peers from collaborating with the navy, see TNA ADM 1 / 482, ff. 370–372. Colville to Philip Stephens, Secretary of the Admiralty, 26 July 1764; TNA ADM 1 / 482, ff. 404–405. Colville to Stephens, 9 November 1764; *Providence Gazette*, 13 June 1772; Steven Harley Park, "The Burning of HMS *Gaspee* and the Limits of Eighteenth-Century British Imperial Power" (PhD diss., University of Connecticut, 2005), 75. For accounts of sea officers being threatened with arrest or violence or being actually assaulted, see TNA ADM 1 / 482, ff. 341–342. John Brown to Colville, 12 December 176; TNA ADM 1 / 482, ff. 370–372. Colville to Stephens, 26 July 1764; TNA ADM 1 / 482, ff. 437–438. Colville to Stephens, 16 February 1765; TNA ADM 1 / 482, ff. 486–488. Charles Leslie to Francis Ward, 1–5 September 1765; Park, "Burning of HMS *Gaspee*," 77.

3. Historical Society of Pennsylvania (hereafter HSP) Box 1 Folder 7, Bradford Family Papers (Collection 1676). John Lathrop to Thomas Bradford, 6 September 1775.
4. For an explanation that focuses on the role of the American Revolution, see, for example, C. A. Bayly, *Imperial Meridian: The British Empire and the World 1780–1830* (London: Longman, 1989), 8–9; Henry P. Ippel, "British Sermons and the American Revolution," *Journal of Religious History* 12 (1982): 197. For explanations that focus on the role of the French Revolution, see Michael Duffy, "World-Wide War and British Expansion, 1793–1815," in *The Oxford History of the British Empire*, ed. P. J. Marshall, vol. 2, *The Eighteenth Century* (Oxford: Oxford University Press, 1998), 184–207; E. P. Thompson, *The Making of the English Working Class* (New York: Pantheon Books, 1963), 102–186; Linda Colley, "The Apotheosis of George III: Loyalty, Royalty and the British Nation 1760–1820," *Past & Present* 102 (1984): 99–111.
5. For example, Paul Langford argues that the Americans' affiliation with radicals in Britain, such as the Wilkites, swayed the propertied classes toward supporting the principle of parliamentary sovereignty. Paul Langford, "Old Whigs, Old Tories and the American Revolution," *Journal of Imperial and Commonwealth History* 8 (1980): 121–127.
6. One potential problem was that the territorial acquisitions of the war, which included large nonwhite, non-Protestant populations, necessitated a different form of government than that which had been used with the settler colonies previously. A second problem was that the war left a vast war debt that had to be paid by someone; James Vaughn argues that Britain's ruling class believed collecting the taxes necessary to fund this debt at home would exacerbate radical claims for political reform, and chose instead to turn the colonies into arenas for revenue extraction. For the importance of new subject populations, see P. J. Marshall, *The Making and Unmaking of Empires: Britain, India, and America c. 1750–1783* (Oxford: Oxford University Press, 2005), 7, 183–206; Robert Travers, *Ideology and Empire in Eighteenth-Century India: The British in Bengal* (Cambridge: Cambridge University Press, 2007), 49–50. For the importance of the war debt, see James Vaughn, "The Politics of Empire: Metropolitan Socio-Political Development and the Imperial Transformation of the British East India Company, 1675–1775" (PhD diss., University of Chicago, 2009), 444–450, 507–540, 516–522.
7. The experience of the war convinced many in Britain that the American colonies were not doing enough to uphold their end of the colonial bargain—they had been too slow to contribute to the war effort against France and were trying to evade the rules that governed imperial trade. Even for authors who acknowledge the desire for imperial reform as early as the 1740s, the Seven Years' War remains an important turning point as it convinced the majority of the political classes in Britain of the necessity of

that reform. For the Seven Years' War highlighting a problem of authority in the colonies and creating a consensus around a preexisting reform project, see Marshall, *Making and Unmaking of Empires,* 102–113; Jack P. Greene, "An Uneasy Connection: An Analysis of the Preconditions of the American Revolution," in *Essays on the American Revolution,* ed. Stephen G. Kurtz and James H. Hutson (Chapel Hill: University of North Carolina Press, 1973), 73–75; Keith Mason, "Britain and the Administration of the American Colonies," in *Britain and the American Revolution,* ed. H. T. Dickinson (London: Longman, 1998), 36–40.

8. James Bradley and J. A. W. Gunn both argue for a resurgence of high-church toryism under George III, which emphasized episcopacy but also respect for the Crown and the political judgments of social superiors. Gunn highlights the post-1760s resurrection of paternalist political theory based on the writings of Charles Leslie and Robert Filmer, both noted theorists of divine-right monarchy. In her study of Oxfordshire clergy, Diana McClatchey argues that criminals were more aggressively prosecuted under George III, as clerical justices of the peace—who previously had been proscribed for their tory leanings—once again became involved in judicial proceedings. James Bradley, *Religion, Revolution, and English Radicalism: Nonconformity in Eighteenth-Century Politics and Society* (Cambridge: Cambridge University Press, 1990), 23–25; J. A. W. Gunn, *Beyond Liberty and Property: The Progress of Self-Recognition in Eighteenth-Century Political Thought* (Kingston, ON: McGill–Queen's University Press, 1983), 164–179; Diana McClatchey, *Oxfordshire Clergy, 1777–1869: A Study of the Established Church and the Role of the Clergy in Local Society* (Oxford: Clarendon Press, 1960), 178–201.

9. For how each side tried to use taxation and fiscal policy to achieve their larger ends, see Justin du Rivage, *Revolution against Empire: Taxes, Politics, and the Origins of American Independence* (New Haven, CT: Yale University Press, 2017).

10. The *London Evening Post,* for example, which Bob Harris cites as an example of the patriot press in the early 1750s, supported John Wilkes in the 1760s and 1770s on the basis of many of the same issues. Additionally, James Bradley has discussed extensively the links between Dissent and political radicalism throughout the eighteenth century. See John Brewer, "English Radicalism in the Age of George III," in *Three British Revolutions: 1641, 1688, 1776,* ed. J. G. A. Pocock (Princeton, NJ: Princeton University Press, 1980), 338; Bradley, *Religion, Revolution, and English Radicalism;* Bob Harris, "The *London Evening Post* and Mid-Eighteenth-Century British Politics," *English Historical Review* 110 (1995): 1134, 1151–1153; H. T. Dickinson, "Introduction," in Dickinson, *Britain and the American Revolution,* 1–20, esp. 10–12.

11. Bradley, *Religion, Revolution and English Radicalism,* 9, 133–147; John Brewer, *Party Ideology and Popular Politics at the Accession of George III* (Cam-

bridge: Cambridge University Press, 1976); Neil McKendrick, John Brewer, and J. H. Plumb, *The Birth of a Consumer Society: The Commercialization of Eighteenth-Century England* (Bloomington: Indiana University Press, 1982); Nicholas Rogers, *Whigs and Cities: Popular Politics in the Age of Walpole and Pitt* (Oxford: Clarendon Press, 1989), 46–129; Lorna Weatherill, *Consumer Behaviour and Material Culture in Britain, 1660–1760* (London: Routledge, 1988).

12. Brewer, "English Radicalism," 361–362.
13. Ibid., 351; Bradley, *Religion, Revolution, and English Radicalism,* 9.
14. Bradley, *Religion, Revolution, and English Radicalism,* 134–139, 174–184; John Brewer, "The Wilkites and the Law, 1763–4: A Study of Radical Notions of Governance," in *An Ungovernable People: The English and Their Law in the Seventeenth and Eighteenth Centuries,* ed. John Brewer and John Styles (New Brunswick, NJ: Rutgers University Press, 1980), 137; Brewer, "English Radicalism," 338–351.
15. Bradley, *Religion, Revolution, and English Radicalism,* 142–153; Brewer, *Party Ideology and Popular Politics,* 201–216; John Sainsbury, *Disaffected Patriots: London Supporters of Revolutionary America, 1769–1782* (Kingston, ON: McGill–Queen's University Press, 1987).
16. The American colonists were not unified in their resistance to the British government. This chapter fully acknowledges the degree of ideological division among the colonists; nevertheless, it focuses on the beliefs of the patriot radicals because they were the ones for whom the professional navy was most problematic and who were most in conflict with the British imperial administration. For discussions of the commonwealth tradition in the mainland American colonies, see Bernard Bailyn, "The Central Themes of the American Revolution: An Interpretation," in *Essays on the American Revolution,* ed. Stephen G. Kurtz and James H. Hutson (Chapel Hill: University of North Carolina Press, 1973), 27; Bernard Bailyn, *Ideological Origins of the American Revolution* (Cambridge, MA: Belknap Press of Harvard University Press, 1967), 23–48, 56–59.
17. The followers of Chatham and Temple opposed restructuring the economic relationships of the empire because they believed that if that American markets were retained, commerce could expand infinitely to counterbalance the taxes not charged. If taxation generated resistance, then it was not worth the threat of alienating American affections in case they began to buy another country's manufactures or to make their own. Chatham, however, wavered on exactly the relationship between the colonies and Britain and was not willing to give up all claims to authority over America. The establishment whigs, now led by the Marquess of Rockingham, believed in parliamentary supremacy over the American colonies, but opposed much of official British policy in the 1760s and 1770s from a fear that imperial restructuring would place too much concentrated power in the hands of the Crown and the Crown's ministers, independent from Parlia-

ment. This should not be taken as sympathy for the patriot or radical cause; Edmund Burke, a close associate of Rockingham, described the establishment whigs as an "aristocratic party." In an influential pamphlet, he criticized a system in which it could be "avowed, as a constitutional maxim, that the King might appoint one of his footmen, or one of your footmen, for Minister." W. M. Elofson, *The Rockingham Connection and the Second Founding of the Whig Party, 1768–1773* (Montreal: McGill–Queen's University Press, 1996), 3; [Edmund Burke], *Thoughts on the Cause of the Present Discontents* (London, 1770), 9.

18. James Kelly, "'Era of Liberty': The Politics of Civil and Political Rights in Eighteenth-Century Ireland," in *Exclusionary Empire: English Liberty Overseas, 1600–1900,* ed. Jack P. Greene (Cambridge: Cambridge University Press, 2010), 98.
19. Thomas Bartlett, "Ireland, Empire, and Union, 1690–1801," in *Ireland and the British Empire,* ed. Kevin Kenny (Oxford: Oxford University Press, 2004), 74.
20. In the 1760s and 1770s, authoritarian whig positions on imperial, constitutional, and financial affairs also received sustained support from bishops in the House of Lords. See William C. Lowe, "Bishops and Scottish Representative Peers in the House of Lords, 1760–1775," *Journal of British Studies* 18, no. 1 (1978): 86–106, esp. 91–95; James E. Bradley, *Popular Politics and the American Revolution in England: Petitions, the Crown, and Public Opinion* (Macon, GA: Mercer University Press, 1986), 14, 136–137, 201.
21. For a discussion of Grenville's split from Pitt and how authoritarian whiggism manifested itself in the context of imperial rule in India, see Vaughn, "Politics of Empire," 524–527. See also, for example, BL Add. MSS 57815, ff. 39–40. James Fife, Earl of Fife, to Grenville, 3 September 1766.
22. In 1766 political negotiations with William Pitt, Earl of Chatham, every person Bedford put forward for office (whose voting record is known) had opposed the repeal of the Stamp Act. WA HMC 8, vol. LIII, p. 16. Bedford, "Thoughts on the proper manner of proceeding in the house, on the papers laid before the House, by H Majesty's command, in relation to the tumults &c in No. America, laid before the Lords at Ld Halifax's on Friday Jan. 24th 1766," 24 January 1766; WA HMC 8, vol. LIV, p. 132. Bedford, "Précis of the conversation between Ld Chatham and me," 1 December 1766.
23. Bedford had a taste of mob disorder as early as 1747, when he was horsewhipped by a man associated with a disaffected crowd at the Litchfield races. BL Add. MSS 34712, f. 56. John Russell, Duke of Bedford, to George Montagu-Dunk, Earl of Halifax, 19 May 1765; BL Add. MSS 34712, f. 83. Bedford to Richard Rigby, 20 May 1765; BL Add. MSS 34712, f. 51. John Montagu, Earl of Sandwich, and Halifax to Justices of the Tower Division and Finsbury Division, Sheriffs of London, and Robert Pell, 17 May 1765; BL Add. MSS 34712, f. 93. Sandwich and Halifax to Welbore

Ellis, 20 May 1765; Eveline Cruickshanks, *Political Untouchables: The Tories and the '45* (London: Duckworth, 1979), 107; Paul Monod, *Jacobitism and the English People, 1688–1788* (Cambridge: Cambridge University Press, 1989), 199.

24. WA HMC 8, vol. LVIII, p. 126. Rigby to Bedford, 4 August 1769; WA HMC 8, vol. LVII, p. 40. Rigby to Bedford, 20 April 1767.
25. William Knox, "Considerations on the Great Question, What Is Fit to Be Done with America," WCL Germain Papers, vol. 17, in Leland J. Bellot, ed., "William Knox Asks What Is Fit to Be Done with America?," in *Sources of American Independence: Selected Manuscripts from the Collections of the William L. Clements Library,* ed. Howard H. Peckham, 2 vols. (Chicago: University of Chicago Press, 1978), 1:140–187, quotations 166, 171, 176. Bellot argues that Knox's policy recommendations were broadly approved within the North administration.
26. A Wilkite crowd burned Sandwich and Halifax in effigy during the 1768–1769 disorder over the Middlesex elections. A different Wilkite crowd in Exeter "laid violent hands on" Bedford in the belief that he opposed their attempts to "secure their ancient and unalienable liberties." For a discussion of the domestic manifestations of authoritarian whiggery's concern with order and hierarchy, see Bradley, *Religion, Revolution, and English Radicalism,* 23–25; Brewer, *Party Ideology,* 184; Gunn, *Beyond Liberty and Property,* 164–179; McClatchey, *Oxfordshire Clergy,* 178–201; Alison Gilbert Olson, "Parliament, Empire, and Parliamentary Law, 1776," in Pocock, *Three British Revolutions,* 291–311; P. J. Marshall, "Empire and Authority in the Later Eighteenth Century," *Journal of Imperial and Commonwealth History* 15, no. 2 (1987): 105–122; Vaughn, "Politics of Empire," 516–522. For harassment of authoritarian whigs by crowds, see WA HMC 64, f. 112. Untitled newspaper clipping, 19 July 1769; Brewer *Party Ideology and Popular Politics,* 184.
27. North, Debate in the Commons on the Address of Thanks, 9 January 1770. *Cobbett's Parliamentary History of England,* 36 vols. (London, 1806–1820), 16:718.
28. For the authoritarian whigs' insistence on maintaining their American policy, see Bedford, extracts from journal, 11 July 1767, in *Correspondence of John, Fourth Duke of Bedford: Selected from the Originals at Woburn Abbey,* 3 vols. (London, 1842–1846), 3:365–366; George Grenville to Rigby, 16 July 1767, ibid., 3:369–371.
29. For examples of the whig account, see Charles M. Andrews, *The Colonial Background of the American Revolution: Four Essays in Colonial American History* (New Haven, CT: Yale University Press, 1924); Bailyn, *Ideological Origins of the American Revolution;* Jack P. Greene, *Peripheries and Center: Constitutional Development in the Extended Polities of the British Empire and the United States 1607–1788* (Athens: University of Georgia Press, 1986); John Pocock, "1776: The Revolution against Parliament," in *Virtue, Commerce, and*

History: Essays on Political Thought and History, Chiefly in the Eighteenth Century (Cambridge: Cambridge University Press, 1985), 73–88; Gordon Wood, *The Radicalism of the American Revolution* (New York: Alfred A. Knopf, 1991). For naval historians describing the Navy's constitutional position as essentially unassailable, see Jeremy Black, "Introduction," in *The British Navy and the Use of Naval Power in the Eighteenth Century*, ed. Jeremy Black and Philip Woodfine (Leicester: Leicester University Press, 1988), 1–31, esp. 3; John Brewer, *The Sinews of Power: War, Money, and the English State, 1688–1783* (Cambridge, MA: Harvard University Press, 1989), 33; Jeremy Black, *The British Seaborne Empire* (New Haven, CT: Yale University Press, 2004), 8, 110; N. A. M. Rodger, *The Command of the Ocean: A Naval History of Britain, 1649–1815* (New York: Norton, 2004), 178, 577; N. A. M. Rodger, "Queen Elizabeth and the Myth of Sea-Power in English History," *Transactions of the Royal Historical Society* 14 (2004): 153–174.

30. For examples of the progressive account, see, for example, Woody Holton, *Forced Founders: Indians, Debtors, Slaves & the Making of the American Revolution in Virginia* (Chapel Hill: University of North Carolina Press, 1999); John Franklin Jameson, *The American Revolution Considered as a Social Movement* (Princeton, NJ: Princeton University Press, 1923); Merrill Jensen, *The American Revolution within America* (New York: New York University Press, 1974); Gary Nash, *The Urban Crucible: The Northern Seaports and the Origins of the American Revolution*, abridged ed. (Cambridge, MA: Harvard University Press, 1986). Neil R. Stout repeatedly emphasizes that "most objections [to new revenue measures] were on commercial, rather than political, grounds," that the new imperial policy was about debt and imperial defense, that "taxation was the main point of conflict between Britain and her American colonies," and that colonists cared whether taxes were enforced, not whether they were legislated. See Stout, *The Royal Navy in America, 1760–1775: A Study of Enforcement of British Colonial Policy in the Era of the American Revolution* (Annapolis, MD: Naval Institute Press, 1973), 25–26, 40, 165–170; James M. Volo, *Blue Water Patriots: The American Revolution Afloat* (Westport, CT: Praeger, 2007), 35.

31. On the military generally, see Fred Anderson, *Crucible of War: The Seven Years' War and the Fate of Empire in British North America, 1754–1766* (New York: Vintage Books, 2001); John Resch and Walter Sargent, eds., *War and Society in the American Revolution: Mobilization and Home Fronts* (DeKalb: Northern Illinois University Press, 2007). Anderson links the new military settlement in the colonies following the Seven Years' War to the nascent imperial conflict, arguing persuasively that acts such as the Quartering Act and the Mutiny Act were part of a longer imperial story and must be understood as much in the context of the Seven Years' War as in that of the Revolution. Resch and Sargent's edited volume contains a number of essays discussing colonial conceptions of military service. On the emotional impact of the military, see T. H. Breen, *American Insurgents,*

American Patriots: The Revolution of the People (New York: Hill and Wang, 2010), which argues that the Revolution emerged as an emotionally fueled insurgency of ordinary Americans against a cruel and oppressive British regime embodied by the military. On cities, see Richard Buel Jr., *In Irons: Britain's Naval Supremacy and the American Revolutionary Economy* (New Haven, CT: Yale University Press, 1998); Benjamin L. Carp, *Rebels Rising: Cities and the American Revolution* (Oxford: Oxford University Press, 2007); Paul A. Gilje, *Liberty on the Waterfront: American Maritime Culture in the Age of Revolution* (Philadelphia: University of Philadelphia Press, 2004); Peter Linebaugh and Marcus Rediker, *The Many-Headed Hydra: Sailors, Slaves, Commoners, and the Hidden History of the Revolutionary Atlantic* (Boston: Beacon Press, 2000). Carp's work emphasizes the importance of port cities in disseminating revolutionary sentiment, while Gilje, Linebaugh, and Rediker stress the important role played by waterfront workers in revolutionary action. Buel makes a compelling case for the Royal Navy's efficacy in disrupting the American economy during the Revolution by preventing waterborne trade and by capturing port cities, thereby disrupting the regional economies of which they were the hubs.

32. The navy, though present in Anderson's account of the Seven Years' War, largely disappears from his story following the end of open warfare against a foreign enemy. Breen identifies the army alone as being the source of cruelty that spurred Americans to resist the imperial regime. Resch and Sargent's volume does not include discussion of any naval element within the context of motivation, mobilization, or the impact of warfare.
33. For example, Captain Charles Knowles sparked a riot in Boston in 1747 following his impressment of forty men; New Yorkers complained of the same in 1746 and Virginians in 1748; more impressment riots took place in the 1760s. TNA ADM 1/234, ff. 74–77. Charles Knowles to [Thomas Corbett, Secretary to the Admiralty], 18 January 1747/8; Sir Peter Warren to George Clinton, Governor of New York, 24 June 1746, in *The Royal Navy and North America: The Warren Papers, 1736–1752*. ed. Julian Gwyn (London: Navy Records Society, 1973), 279–280 (hereafter *Warren Papers*); TNA ADM 3/60. Admiralty Board minutes, 28 January 1748/9; TNA SP 42/26, f. 284. Admiralty Board to Lords Justices, 26 September 1743. See also Denver Alexander Brunsman, "The Knowles Atlantic Impressment Riots of the 1740s," *Early American Studies: An Interdisciplinary Journal* 5, no. 2 (2007): 324–366; John Lax and William Pencak, "The Knowles Riot and the Crisis of the 1740s in Massachusetts," *Perspectives in American History* 10 (1976): 153–214; Pauline Maier, "Popular Uprisings and Civil Authority in Eighteenth-Century America," *William and Mary Quarterly* 27, no. 1 (1970): 8–9, 22.
34. Stephen Conway, "Another Look at the Navigation Acts and the Coming of the American Revolution," in *The Royal Navy and the British Atlantic World, c. 1750–1820*, ed. Christer Petley and John McAleer (London: Palgrave Macmillan, 2016), 77–96.

35. Allyn B. Forbes, "Greenwich Hospital Money," *New England Quarterly* 3, no. 3 (1930): 519–526; TNA ADM 80 / 131, p. 13. Henry Hulton to Commissioners [for managing the Revenue of Customs in America], 1 December 1769.
36. TNA ADM 80 / 131, f. 1. Hulton to Commissioners for managing the Revenue of Customs in America, 11 September 1768; TNA ADM 80 / 131, ff. 42–43. Hulton to Commissioners for managing the Revenue of Customs in America, 31 January 1772; TNA ADM 80 / 131, f. 66. Alexander Thompson to Hulton, 31 August 1774.
37. TNA ADM 80 / 131, f. 13. Hulton to Commissioners [for managing the Revenue of Customs in America], 1 December 1769; TNA ADM 80 / 131, f. 14. Hulton to Thomas Hicks, 2 December 1769.
38. Houghton Library, Harvard University, MS Can 16, vol. 1, pp. 42–43. Hulton to [unknown], 21 April 1772.
39. The monopoly extended to all white pines which were not growing inside the limits of a township or had not been privately owned before October 7, 1690. Olson "Parliament, Empire, and Parliamentary Law," 302–303; Thomas L. Purvis, *Colonial America to 1763* (New York: Facts on File, 1999), 86.
40. Joseph J. Malone, *Pine Trees and Politics: The Naval Stores and Forest Policy in Colonial New England, 1691–1775* (New York: Arno Press, 1979), 124–136; Maier, "Popular Uprisings and Civil Authority," 8–12; *Pennsylvania Gazette,* 3 July 1729 and 17 July 1729.
41. John Trenchard, *An argument, Shewing That a Standing Army Is Inconsistent with a Free Government and Absolutely Destructive to the Constitution of the English Monarchy* (London, 1697), 7, 20; Bailyn *Ideological Origins,* 35–36, 84; Heather E. Barry, *A "Dress Rehearsal" for Revolution: John Trenchard and Thomas Gordon's Works in Eighteenth-Century British America* (Lanham, MD: University Press of America, 2007), 27–50.
42. The Levellers were a political movement during the English Civil War who wanted to "level" all distinctions between men, or in other words, to make all citizens equal. Peter Warren to Thomas Pelham-Holles, Duke of Newcastle, 18 June 1745, in *Warren Papers,* 125–126.
43. *Newport Mercury,* 10 June 1765; *Oxford English Dictionary,* 3rd ed., June 2003, online version June 2011, http://www.oed.com/view/Entry/124572.
44. Brewer, "English Radicalism," 347.
45. For the act, see *A Collection of all the Statutes Now in Force, Relating to the Duties of Excise in England* (London, 1764), 566–570. The statutory reference is 3 Geo. 3, c. 22. In theory, the Treasury had been able to deputize sea officers as customs officials since the seventeenth century, but it had rarely done so. Grenville's act codified naval participation in customs enforcement, and the Treasury and Admiralty in conjunction immediately began deputizing sea officers. Though Grenville had been a commissioner of the Admiralty Board from 1744 to 1747, he was not strongly associated with

Bedford's reforms—he was not responsible for creating the professional navy, but once his views shifted toward authoritarianism in the 1760s, it fit well into his model of imperial administration. See Stout, *Royal Navy,* 27–28; Daniel A. Baugh, "Maritime Strength and Atlantic Commerce: The Uses of 'a Grand Marine Empire,'" in *An Imperial State at War: Britain from 1689 to 1815,* ed. Lawrence Stone (London: Routledge, 1994), 206–207.

46. The "consternation" reference is John Tyler's: John W. Tyler, *Smugglers and Patriots: Boston Merchants and the Advent of the American Revolution* (Boston: Northeastern University Press, 1986), 68. For the quote from the *Boston Gazette,* see *Boston Gazette,* November 28, 1763; also qtd. in Stout, *Royal Navy,* 40.
47. Volo, *Blue Water Patriots,* 3.
48. The date 25 October 1763 represents the first time in his correspondence with the Admiralty that Colville mentions taking an active part in regulating and suppressing smuggling. Naval commanders previously assisted customs officials in apprehending and preventing smuggling in the British Isles and reported illegal trade in the colonies, but had not, with a few occasional exceptions, tried to prevent it. Colville's letter to the Secretary of the Admiralty informed him that "I have made some alteration in the stations of several of the ships. . . . I am in hopes from the disposition I have made that smuggling will receive a severe check this winter. . . . I have thoughts of sending another ship to Newport in Rhode Island: this and New London . . . have been long noted for nests of smugglers." From that point on, the efforts of Colville and his squadron to suppress illicit colonial trade came to comprise a massive proportion of the correspondence between Colville and the Admiralty. TNA ADM 1 / 482, ff. 304–306. Colville to Stephens, 25 October 1763; TNA ADM 1 / 482, ff. 308–309. Colville to the captains of the North American squadron, 15 October 1763.
49. Tyler, *Smugglers and Patriots,* 90–91.
50. *Boston Evening-Post,* 20 June 1768; see also *Boston Chronicle,* 13–20 June 1768; *Boston Post-Boy & Advertiser,* 20 June 1768.
51. *Massachusetts Spy,* 5 March 1772.
52. *New-London Gazette,* 21 May 1773; *Boston-Gazette, and Country Journal,* 24 May 1773; *Massachusetts Spy,* 27 May 1773; Stout, *Royal Navy,* 43.
53. For objections to the use of general warrants in customs cases in England, see Brewer, "English Radicalism," 339. For the use of general warrants in the American colonies, see Carl Ubbelohde, *The Vice-Admiralty Courts and the American Revolution* (Chapel Hill: University of North Carolina Press, 1960), 12–21.
54. This leaves aside the entire issue of impressment, which radicals argued was also unconstitutional.
55. [Arthur Lee], *A Speech, Intended to Have Been Delivered in the House of Commons, in Support of the Petition from the General Congress at Philadelphia* (London, 1775), 5.
56. Ibid., 3–5, 45.

57. Although the *Gaspee* was often referred to as a revenue schooner, its commander, William Dudingston, was a lieutenant of the Royal Navy and under the command of Admiral John Montagu. The ship was a royal schooner that had been purchased by Colville for coast guard duty. J. J. Colledge and Ben Warlow, *Ships of the Royal Navy: The Complete Record of All Fighting Ships of the Royal Navy from the 15th Century to the Present* (London: Chatham, 2006), 138; David Syrett, *The Commissioned Sea Officers of the Royal Navy, 1660–1815*, 2 vols. (London: Navy Records Society, 1994), 1:272; Stout, *Royal Navy*, 141–143. According to a statement given by one of the participants when he was near his deathbed in 1839, the assailants included John Brown, John Hopkins, Benjamin Dunn, John Mawney, Benjamin Page, Joseph Bucklin, and Turpin Smith. William R. Staples, *The Documentary History of the Destruction of the* Gaspee (Providence: Rhode Island Publications Society, 1990), 12–14.
58. *Providence Gazette*, 9 January 1773.
59. Dudingston previously seized a ship belonging to the Greene family, a merchant family that included Nathaniel Greene, who would later serve as a high-ranking officer under George Washington. Charles Dudley, a tax collector for Newport, wrote that "the attack upon the *Gaspée* was not the effect of sudden passion and resentment, but of cool deliberation and forethought . . . it had been long determined she should be destroyed . . . tho it was notorious that the armed vessel in question sailed under British colors, and belonged to his Britannic Majesty." TNA T 1 / 494, ff. 144–145. Charles Dudley to [unknown], 23 July 1772; Park, "Burning of HMS *Gaspee*," 24–26, 111.
60. For discussion of the commission's composition and Pownall's imperial involvements, see *Boston Weekly News-Letter*, 17 December 1772; Park, "Burning of HMS *Gaspee*," 54–66; Franklin B. Wickwire, "John Pownall and British Colonial Policy," *William and Mary Quarterly*, 3rd ser., 20, no. 4 (1963): 543–554, esp. 549–553. Stout notes that Montagu's "ideas of conciliation seemed to run mostly to cannon and Marines," unlike James Gambier, the previous commander. Stout, *Royal Navy*, 154–155.
61. *Massachusetts Spy*, 17 December 1772.
62. *Providence Gazette*, 26 December 1772. Adams was writing under the pseudonym "Americanus." Park, "Burning of the *Gaspee*," 89n5.
63. *Newport Mercury*, 21 June 1773.
64. In two years, this pamphlet went through seven editions published in four cities. [John Allen], *An Oration, Upon the Beauties of Liberty, Or the Essential Rights of the Americans* (Boston, 1773), xii, ix; John M. Bumsted and Charles E. Clark, "New England's Tom Paine: John Allen and the Spirit of Liberty," *William and Mary Quarterly*, 3rd ser., 21, no. 4 (1964): 561.
65. Paul Leicester Ford, *The Works of Thomas Jefferson*, 12 vols. (New York: G. P. Putnam's Sons, 1904), 1:9–10; Pauline Maier, *From Resistance to Revolution: Colonial Radicals and the Development of American Opposition to Britain, 1765–1776*

(New York: Knopf, 1972), xiii; L. H. Butterfield, *The Adams Papers: Diary and Autobiography of John Adams,* 4 vols. (Cambridge MA: Belknap Press of Harvard University Press, 1961), 2:76; all cited in Park, "Burning of the *Gaspee,*" 69–70, 93.

66. Radicals repeatedly claimed that violence on the part of colonists was deliberately stirred up by royal or naval officers in order to create the illusion that colonists were disloyal and to have an excuse to garrison them. In June 1768 customs seized one of John Hancock's vessels in Boston and towed it away from the wharf to be protected by the *Romney.* The Bostonians rioted, and later excused themselves by saying they had been insulted at the implication that they would rescue a seized ship (despite the fact that every ship seized in the preceding several months had been rescued by colonists). The Massachusetts Governor's Council twice officially claimed this reaction had been deliberately provoked by the use of armed force, and that the vessel had been seized purely "in order to excite a riot, and furnish a plausible pretence for requesting troops." These arguments were repeated at the time of the *Gaspée,* arguing after the attack that the ministry exaggerated their ongoing fears for Lt. Dudingston's life in order to "bring a further odium upon Lord Hillsborough's *loyal colony* of Rhode Island." It was also reiterated regarding the actions of a man of war in New York in July 1773 and following the Boston Tea Party in December 1773. The "proceedings of Council on the 27th and 29th of July" in the *Boston Evening-Post,* 10 October 1768; an address from the "subscribers, members of his Majesty's Council of the province of Massachusetts Bay" to General Gage in the *Boston Evening-Post,* 31 October 1768; *Boston Gazette,* 31 October 1768; *Boston Post-Boy & Advertiser,* 31 October 1768; *Massachusetts Spy,* 20 August 1772; *New-York Journal,* 8 July 1773; Benjamin L. Carp, *Defiance of the Patriots: The Boston Tea Party & the Making of America* (New Haven, CT: Yale University Press, 2010), 182; Ubbelohde, *Vice-Admiralty Courts,* 93, 122.

67. Ezra Stiles to Elihu Spencer, 16 February 1773, in *The Literary Diary of Ezra Stiles,* ed. Franklin Bowditch Dexter, 3 vols. (New York: Charles Scribner's Sons, 1901), 1:349; cited in Park, "Burning of the *Gaspee,*" 51n166.

68. Peter Oliver, *Peter Oliver's Origin & Progress of the American Rebellion: A Tory Perspective,* ed. Douglass Adair and John A. Schutz (San Marino, CA: Huntington Library, 1961), 99; cited in Park, "Burning of the *Gaspee,*" 126.

69. *Essex Gazette,* 21 December–28 December 1773.

70. In 1765, for example, a Providence mob threatened to board a king's sloop in order to release a man onboard; the plans involved taking over the fort in Providence and firing on the ship. This was not as far-fetched as it might seem, as the mob had already taken over Fort George in Narragansett Bay and fired on the *St. John,* another naval ship engaged in supporting the revenue laws, the year before. TNA ADM 1/482, ff. 486–488. Captain Leslie to Francis Ward, 1–5 September 1765; TNA ADM 1/482, ff. 370–372. Colville to Stephens, 26 July 1764.

71. *Newport Mercury,* 3 May 1773.
72. NMM COO / 1, p. 88. William Owen, "Narrative—Voyages, Travels, &c, Volume 2d," 23 August 1767.
73. CO 5 / 1278, f. 144. Frederick Smyth to William Legge, Earl of Dartmouth, 8 February 1773; CO 5 / 1104, ff. 113–118v. Daniel Horsmanden to Dartmouth; both cited in Park, "Burning of HMS *Gaspee,*" 111–112.
74. See, for example, UNott Ne C 243. Michael Lee Dicker to Henry Pelham, 24 November 1744.
75. During the War of the Austrian Succession, the American and Caribbean colonies fitted out around a thousand privateers over the course of ten years, roughly as many as Britain itself. See Michael J. Jarvis, *In the Eye of All Trade: Bermuda, Bermudians, and the Maritime Atlantic World, 1680–1783* (Chapel Hill: Published for the Omohundro Institute of Early American History and Culture, Williamsburg, Virginia, by the University of North Carolina Press, 2010), 243.
76. Volo, *Blue Water Patriots,* 2.
77. See No. 520, 5 October 1763, in *Acts of the Privy Council of England: Colonial Series,* ed. W. L. Grant, James Munro, and Almeric W. FitzRoy, 6 vols. (London: Printed for His Majesty's Stationery Office, 1911), 4:569–572.
78. Radicals' arguments against a professional military applied equally to land and sea forces; radicals did not in theory fear a navy more. However, the professional navy was far more of a presence in the lives of many mercantile colonists than the army; it therefore embodied stronger imperial governance in a very real and very physical way. See Stout, *Royal Navy,* 61–89, 130, 217–220.
79. TNA T 1 / 502, f. 145. Merchants of the town of Dartmouth trading to Newfoundland to the Lords of the Treasury, [1773].
80. The Collector of the Customs at Falmouth refused to assist Allen in prosecuting these seizures. TNA ADM 1 / 482, ff. 432–433. Colville to Stephens, 12 January 1765.
81. See, for example, TNA ADM 1 / 3866. Edward Stanley, Secretary to the Commissioners of the Customs, to Stephens, 15 August 1771; TNA T 1 / 501, f. 366. Commissioners of Customs in America to the Lords of the Treasury, 19 November 1773.
82. TNA ADM 80 / 131, f. 1. Hulton to Commissioners for managing the Revenue of Customs in America, 11 September 1768.
83. BL Add. MSS 57835, f. 108. Anonymous account of social unrest in Boston, September [1768]; Francis Bernard to Hillsborough, 9 July 1768, in *Letters to the Ministry from Governor Bernard, General Gage, and Commodore Hood . . .* (Boston, 1768), 38–41; Peter D. G. Thomas, *The Townshend Duties Crisis: The Second Phase of the American Revolution, 1767–1773* (Oxford: Clarendon Press, 1987), 192–193.
84. In this comment, Allen referred as well to the sailors he believed were imprisoned on the ship through impressment. [Allen], *An Oration,* xii.

85. *New-York Gazette,* 24 October 1768.
86. *Boston Evening-Post,* 20 June 1768.
87. *Connecticut Courant,* 5–12 January 1773; see also *Massachusetts Spy,* 14 January 1773.
88. *Boston Evening-Post,* 3 May 1773.
89. Stout, *Royal Navy in America,* 155, qtd. in Volo, *Blue Water Patriots.*
90. WCL Charles Townshend Papers, Box 8/34/57. "Advantages resulting from keeping up Armed Vessells on the Lakes" [1760s?]; *New-York Journal,* 29 October 1772; Berthold Fernow, *The Ohio Valley in Colonial Days* (Albany, NY, 1890), 278.
91. This account is contained in a letter from Colville to the Secretary of the Admiralty. TNA ADM 1/482, ff. 502–503. Colville to Stephens, 10 February 1766.
92. The customs officer backed down and reopened the port of Brunswick, but Captain Jacob Lobb of the *Viper* seized three ships for sailing without stamped clearances, turning them over to the customhouse. Before the vessels could be tried in a vice admiralty court, a mob of nearly one thousand people surrounded the customs officers of the town and forced them to give up the ships. Ubbelohde, *Vice-Admiralty Courts,* 83–87.
93. Halifax, 11 March 1766, in *Proceedings and Debates of the British Parliaments Respecting North America, 1754–1783,* ed. R. C. Simmons and P. D. G. Thomas, 7 vols. to date (Millwood, NY: Kraus Reprint, 1982–), 2:339.
94. TNA CO 5/658, ff. 116–117. James Wright to Henry Seymour Conway, 7 February 1766; TNA CO 5/658, ff. 127–128. Wright to Conway, 10 March 1766; TNA ADM 1/482, ff. 490–491. Colville to Stephens, 7 November 1765; TNA ADM 1/482, ff. 483–484. Colville to Stephens, 21 September 1765; *Gazetteer and New Daily Advertiser,* 3 March 1766; Stout, *Royal Navy,* 108.
95. TNA ADM 1/482, ff. 304–306. Colville to Stephens, 25 October 1763.
96. Under standard practice, customs auctioned off goods seized from vessels condemned for smuggling. The informant or customs officer who brought the smuggling case to court received one-third of the profits, the judge of the vice admiralty court one-third, and the colonial governor one-third. Under the law making sea officers into customs officers, one-half was given to the navy (a fourth of that to go to the commander in chief and the remaining three-quarters to be divided between officers and crew) and one-half went to the king, leaving customs officers and colonial governors out of the profits. Ubbelohde, *Vice-Admiralty Courts,* 40–44. For resistance to sea officers from other officials ostensibly serving the central government, see TNA ADM 1/482, f. 344. John Temple, Surveyor General of the Customs in North America, to Capt. John Brown, 19 December 1763; TNA ADM 1/482, f. 342. Capt. Thomas Bishop to Colville, 22 December 1763; TNA ADM 1/482, f. 334. Colville to Stephens, 22 January 1764; TNA ADM 1/482, ff. 393–394. Colville to Stephens, 22 September 1764.

97. TNA ADM 1/2012. Admiralty to Capt. Archibald Kennedy, 14 December 1765, qtd. in Stout, *Royal Navy,* 100; Articles of War, 1749, in Markus Eder, *Crime and Punishment in the Royal Navy of the Seven Years' War, 1755–1763* (Aldershot, UK: Ashgate, 2004), 158–173. See also Neil Stout, "Captain Kennedy and the Stamp Act," *New York History* 45, no. 1 (1964): 44–58.
98. For a discussion of the comparative rapacity of different categories of customs enforcers, see Stout, *Royal Navy,* 98–103, 129. For a discussion of the background and general milieu of colonial customs officers, see Thomas C. Barrow, *Trade and Empire: The British Customs Service in Colonial America, 1660–1775* (Cambridge, MA: Harvard University Press, 1967), 86–87; Ubbelohde, *Vice-Admiralty Courts,* 11, 24–30, 58–59.
99. He made the comment with regards to the difficulty of manning in the American colonies, but the same truth clearly applied to the difficulties of preventing smuggling and tax evasion. TNA ADM 1/482, f. 445. Colville to Stephens, 12 March 1765.
100. For example, in 1726 the Lieutenant Governor and Council of Massachusetts complained to George I about Captain James Cornwall's extreme sloth in convoying merchant ships and refusal to seek out a pirate who had been plaguing the nearby coast. Stationed at Boston close to two years, he sat in port the entire time, excepting one three-month trip to Barbados when he "sequestered and engrossed a great quantity of salt to his own use, to the great damage and discouragement of the trade." In the 1760s, the Admiralty admitted these previous failings: when Captain Walter Stirling was ordered to North America, his orders noted that "commanders of His Majesty's ships formerly stationed in North America took an unwarrantable liberty of loitering in port, instead of guarding the coast, and trade, to the dishonor of his Majesty's service." In contrast, Stirling was ordered to be constantly at sea and to send reports to the Admiralty as often as possible, along with a full log of his activities at least once every six months. These orders reiterate the importance to authoritarian whig governance of dedication to duty, under the onus of central surveillance. TNA SP 44/221. [William Dummer,] Lieutenant Governor, and Council of Massachusetts to George I, 8 July 1726; TNA ADM 2/90. Admiralty to Walter Stirling, 23 June 1763, qtd. in Stout, *Royal Navy,* 30.
101. TNA ADM 1/482, ff. 370–372. Colville to Stephens, 26 July 1764; TNA ADM 1/482, ff. 437–438. Colville to Stephens, 16 February 1765; TNA ADM 1/482, ff. 486–488. Leslie to Ward, 1–5 September 1765.
102. TNA ADM 1/482, ff. 437–438. Colville to Stephens, 16 February 1765; see Stephens's minutes on reverse.
103. John Perceval, Earl of Egmont. Debate in the Commons on a Plan for Speedily Manning the Navy, 14 April 1749. *Cobbett's Parliamentary History,* 14:5425–5450; Suff. RO, 941/50/5, p. 115. Augustus Hervey, draft of a pamphlet, 18 February 1749.

104. BL Add. MSS 57809, ff. 85–87. Charles Jenkinson to Grenville, 20 April 1763.
105. *The Late Occurrences in North America, and Policy of Great Britain, Considered* (London, 1766), 32.
106. Resistance to naval enforcement of imperial law did spread throughout the thirteen colonies, but it was strongest in New England and the mid-Atlantic, in part because earlier acts such as the Sugar Act affected the northern colonies more than the southern, which did not import much molasses. (When later acts such as the Stamp Act were enforced across the mainland colonies, southern colonies demonstrated a similar response to northern ones.) An additional reason for greater resistance among New Englanders lay in their different religious traditions and socioeconomic backgrounds, which created a more fertile ground for radicalism.
107. Lawrence D. Cress, *Citizens in Arms: The Army and the Militia in American Society to the War of 1812* (Chapel Hill: University of North Carolina Press, 1982), 1–50.
108. Michael McDonnell, "Popular Mobilization and Political Culture in Revolutionary Virginia: The Failure of the Minutemen and the Revolution from Below," *Journal of American History* 85, no. 3 (1998): 948–949.
109. Craig L. Symonds, *Navalists and Antinavalists: The Naval Policy Debate in the United States, 1785–1827* (Newark: University of Delaware Press, 1980), 13, 24.
110. Jeffery M. Dorwart and Jean K. Wolf, *The Philadelphia Navy Yard: From the Birth of the U.S. Navy to the Nuclear Age* (Philadelphia: University of Pennsylvania Press, 2001), 34–42.
111. Stout, *Royal Navy,* 129.
112. Q. E. D. [Benjamin Franklin], "Rules by which a Great Empire May Be Reduced to a Small One," *Public Advertiser,* 11 September 1773.
113. BL Add. MSS 18020, f. 13. Thomas Thynne, Viscount Weymouth, to [George Colebrooke] Chairman and [Peregrine Cust] Deputy Chairman of the EIC, 13 March 1769; BL Add. MSS 18020, ff. 14–15. Henry Crabb Boulton and Colebrooke to Weymouth, 17 March 1769.
114. BL Add. MSS 18020, f. 13. Weymouth to [Colebrooke and Cust], 13 March 1769; BL IOR / H / 100, pp. 359–361. Colebrooke and Cust to Robert Wood, 1 August 1769.
115. BL IOR H / 100, pp. 443–448. Weymouth to Colebrooke and Cust, 10 August 1769; BL Add. MSS 18020, ff. 10v–11v. George III to John Lindsay, 7 September 1769; BL Add. MSS 18020, ff. 2v–4. EIC Directors to Lindsay, 8 September 1769; BL IOR H / 101, pp. 175–188. Minutes of the General Court of the EIC, 30 August–13 September 1769.
116. BL Add. MSS 18020, ff. 72v–75v. EIC Council at Fort St. George to Lindsay, 3 August 1770.
117. BL IOR H / 103, pp. 189–196. EIC Council at Fort St. George to Lindsay, 16 August 1770.

118. BL IOR H/104, pp. 489–490. EIC Council at Fort St. George to Lindsay, 15 July 1771.
119. H. V. Bowen, *Revenue and Reform: The Indian Problem in British Politics, 1757–1773* (Cambridge: Cambridge University Press, 1991), 76–82; H. W. Richmond, *The Navy in India, 1763–1783* (Aldershot, UK: Gregg Revivals, 1993), 40–42; see also Philip Lawson, *The East India Company: A History* (London: Longman, 1993). Not coincidentally, Weymouth had also been active in suppressing Wilkite unrest surrounding the contested Middlesex election in 1768–1769.
120. Among his points of complaint were that the EIC had requested naval support because of self-proclaimed financial weakness, but had done so immediately after paying a dividend to its stockholders; had said they would use a stronger marine force to combat an enemy on the Malabar coast they had previously claimed to have destroyed; and both claimed to fear French encroachments in India while also swearing they had no idea what those plans might look like. BL Add. MSS 18020, f. 13. Weymouth to [Colebrooke and Cust], 13 March 1769; BL Add. MSS 18020, ff. 19v–23v. Weymouth to [Colebrooke and Cust], 12 June 1769.
121. BL Add. MSS 18020, ff. 10v–11v. George III to Lindsay, 7 September 1769; BL IOR/H/101, pp. 101–131. Weymouth to Lindsay, 13 September 1769.
122. BL IOR H/103, pp. 137, 150, 153. Lindsay to Weymouth, 13 October 1770.
123. This program entailed the expansion of the active fleet (from 16,000 to 25,000 men, though he was forced to compromise at 20,000), the repair of ships not in active service, the rebuilding of stockpiles of naval stores, the resumption of visits to the dockyards, and a general return to the principles of rationalization and reform which had characterized the authoritarian whig Admiralty of the 1740s. Sandwich supported the innovation of copper plating for ships' hulls, instituted good storage techniques for timber, introduced carronades (smaller guns, but heavier cannonballs), put guardships into a better state of readiness for real service, and used them for training cruises. TNA SP 42/48, f. 25a. Admiralty Board to William Henry van Nassau van Zuylestein, Earl of Rochford, 1 March 1771; TNA SP 42/48, f. 25c. Admiralty Board, "Plan for the disposition of his Majesty's Ships to Be Employed in time of peace," 1 March 1771; Nicholas Tracy, *Navies, Deterrence, and American Independence: Britain and Seapower in the 1760s and 1770s* (Vancouver: University of British Columbia Press, 1988), 35–38.
124. Michael R. Snyder, "A Victim of Circumstance: The Timber Bill of 1772 and the East India Company," *Past Imperfect* 1 (1992): 27–47.
125. W. M. Elofson, "The Rockingham Whigs in Transition: The East India Company Issue, 1772–1773," *English Historical Review* 104 (1989): 948–949, 952; *Bingley's Journal*, 7–14 March 1772; *The History, Debates, and Proceedings of Both Houses of Parliament of Great Britain, from the year 1743 to the year 1774*, 7 vols. (London, 1792), 6:250; Sheffield Archives WWM/R/1/1419. William Dowdeswell to Charles Watson-Wentworth, 2nd Marquess of

Rockingham, 20 December 1772; BL Add. MSS 43771, ff. 88–89. John Calcraft to William Pitt, Earl of Chatham, 14 December 1770; Debate in the Commons on the Number of Seamen, 29 January 1772. *Cobbett's Parliamentary History,* 17:239–243; Debate in the Commons on the Navy Estimates, 1 November 1775. *Cobbett's Parliamentary History,* 18:841.

126. For an analysis of the larger history of Caribbean slave rebellions, see Michael Craton, *Testing the Chains: Resistance to Slavery in the British West Indies* (Ithaca, NY: Cornell University Press, 1982); see also Andrew Jackson O'Shaughnessy, *An Empire Divided: The American Revolution and the British Caribbean* (Philadelphia: University of Pennsylvania Press, 2000), 34–57.
127. If such a request was made, there is no record of it in the main registers of correspondence between these respective colonies and the Board of Trade, Secretaries of State, or Admiralty.
128. TNA CO 137 / 20, f. 157. William Nedham, Speaker of the Council of Jamaica, to Admiral Chaloner Ogle, 6 July 1733; TNA ADM 1 / 231, Part 1, ff. 53–56. Admiral Charles Stewart to Josiah Burchett, Secretary of the Admiralty, 16 March 1729 / 30; TNA ADM 1 / 231, Part 2, ff. 321–323. Same to same, 14 January 1731 / 32; TNA ADM 1 / 231, Part 2, ff. 359–360. Same to same, 4 April 1732; TNA CO 137 / 20, ff. 144–145. Robert Hunter, Governor of Jamaica, to the Board of Trade, 7 July 1733; TNA CO 137 / 20, f. 191. Ogle to Burchett, 12 September 1733.
129. TNA ADM 1 / 236, ff. 41–42. Admiral Charles Holmes to John Clevland, Secretary of the Admiralty, 11 June 1760; TNA ADM 51 / 717, Part 8. Captain's log of the *HMS Antonio,* 1 May 1760.
130. TNA ADM 1 / 309, f. 190. Admiral William Parry to Stephens, 2 August 1772; TNA ADM 1 / 309, ff. 194–198. Same to same, 19 September 1772; TNA ADM 1 / 309, ff. 221–222. Same to same, 19 November 1772; TNA ADM 1 / 309, f. 225v. Captain William Garnier to Parry, 20 November 1772.
131. Sam Willis, *The Struggle for Sea Power: A Naval History of the American Revolution* (New York: Norton, 2016).
132. TNA ADM 1 / 309, f. 75. Robert Stewart, President of the Island of Tobago, to Admiral Robert Man, 25 November 1770.
133. TNA ADM 1 / 239. Richard Hoare, chairman of the British settlement at St. George's Kay to George Brydges Rodney, 18 June 1773; TNA ADM 1 / 239. Captain Thomas Davey to Rodney, 21 June 1773; TNA ADM 1 / 239. Rodney to Stephens, 10 September 1773.
134. TNA CO 40 / 10. Minutes of the Bermuda Council in Assembly, 10 March 1762; TNA CO 37 / 19, f. 58. William Popple, Governor of Bermuda, to Charles Wyndham, Earl of Egremont, 31 March 1762; TNA CO 37 / 19, f. 60. Address of the Council & General Assembly of Bermuda to Popple, 24 March 1762.
135. TNA ADM 1 / 309, ff. 7–8. Man to Stephens, 24 August 1769; TNA ADM 1 / 309, f. 14. Henry Sharpe to Man, 31 August 1769.

136. TNA ADM 1 / 236, ff. 41–42. Holmes to Clevland, 11 June 1760; TNA ADM 51 / 717, Part 8. Captain's log of the HMS *Antonio,* 1 May 1760.
137. TNA ADM 1 / 236, ff. 191–198. Holmes to Clevland, 18 March 1761.
138. This is leaving aside, of course, the role played by the Royal Navy in protecting the slave trade on the African coast and the view taken by many sea officers that the slave trade was an important part of Britain's naval strength. See Joshua D. Newton, "Slavery, Sea Power and the State: The Royal Navy and the British West African Settlements, 1748–1756," *Journal of Imperial and Commonwealth History* 41, no. 2 (2013): 171–193; Christer Petley, "The Royal Navy, the British Atlantic Empire and the Abolition of the Slave Trade," in Petley and McAleer, *Royal Navy and the British Atlantic World,* 97–121.
139. Thomas Bartlett, "Viscount Townshend and the Irish Revenue Board, 1767–73," *Proceedings of the Royal Irish Academy. Section C: Archaeology, Celtic Studies, History, Linguistics, Literature* 79 (1979): 153–175.
140. Thomas Bartlett, "The Townshend viceroyalty," in *Penal Era and Golden Age: Essays in Irish History, 1690–1800,* ed. Thomas Bartlett and D. W. Hayton (Belfast: Ulster Historical Foundation, 1979), 88–112; Eoin Magennis, *The Irish Political System, 1740–1765* (Dublin: Four Courts Press, 2000), 124, 193; Martyn Powell, "Reassessing Townshend's Irish Viceroyalty, 1767–72: The Caldwell–Shelburne Correspondence in the John Rylands Library, Manchester," *Bulletin of the John Rylands University Library of Manchester* 89, no. 2 (2012): 155–176.
141. WCL George Townshend Papers, Letterbook vol. 2, pp. 122–129. George Townshend to Weymouth, 7 March 1770, 5 April 1770; ibid., pp. 225–269. Same to same, 16 October [1770]; National Archives of Ireland M 730 / 48. Thomas Allen to Townshend, 17 December 1770; National Archives of Ireland M 730 / 92. Same to same, 12 April 1772; National Archives of Ireland M 730 / 94. Same to same, 16 April 1772; Martyn Powell, *Britain and Ireland in the Eighteenth-Century Crisis of Empire* (New York: Palgrave Macmillan, 2003), 95–126.
142. WCL George Townshend Papers, Letterbook vol. 1, pp. 393–399. Townshend to [Thomas?] Astle, 15 February 1769; ibid., pp. 400–403. Townshend to Lady Greenwich, 20 February 1769; National Archives of Ireland M 5040, pp. 14–17. Townshend to Luke Gardiner, 3 June. 1779. On the other hand, he supported a militia both in England and in Ireland, proving that individuals sometimes charted their own ideological paths.
143. Patrick Walsh, "Ireland and the Royal Navy in the Eighteenth Century," in Petley and McAleer, *Royal Navy and the British Atlantic World,* 62–63.
144. WCL William Knox Papers, Box 11, Folder 55. William Knox, "Reasons in support of the Bill for encouraging the Trade of Ireland," 1778.
145. Marshall, *Making and Unmaking of Empires,* 7, 183–206.
146. L. B. Namier, *The Structure of Politics at the Accession of George III* (London: Macmillan, 1957).

147. In the cabinet meeting regarding the repeal of the duties, the five members who voted for retaining the duty on tea were all associated with the authoritarian whigs (Lord North, Hillsborough, Gower, Weymouth, and Rochford); the four who voted against retaining the duty were followers of Chatham or Rockingham (Grafton, Camden, Granby, and Conway). Moreover, William Strahan, a printer associated with the North administration, believed that the lack of full repeal "is not owing to Lord North, our present premier, but to the influence of the Duke of Bedford, and his friends, who cannot be brought to consent to it." HSP AM.162, p. 20. William Strahan to David Hall, 19 March 1770; Thomas, *Townshend Duties*, 138.
148. Langford, "Old Whigs, Old Tories," 126; National Library of Ireland, 52 / K / 2b. Lord Midleton to Thomas Townshend, 16 August 1775, qtd. in Powell, *Britain and Ireland*, 141; Marshall, "Empire and Authority," 116.
149. Josiah Quincy Jr., *Observations on the act of Parliament Commonly Called the Boston Port-Bill; with Thoughts on Civil Society and Standing Armies* (Boston, 1774), 6–7; A Farmer, *Free Thoughts on the Proceedings of the Continental Congress, held at Philadelphia, Sept. 5, 1774: Wherein Their Errors Are Exhibited* (New York, 1775), 37.
150. TNA T 1 / 483. Capt. Philip Durell to Customs Board, 14 August 1766, qtd. in Stout, *Royal Navy*, 64.
151. John Ruskin, "Lectures on Art," in *The Works of John Ruskin*, 39 vols., ed. E. T. Cook and Alexander Wedderburn (London: G. Allen, 1905), 20:42; see Denver Brunsman, *The Evil Necessity: British Naval Impressment in the Eighteenth-Century Atlantic World* (Charlottesville: University of Virginia Press, 2013), 6.

Conclusion

1. John Derry, *English Politics and the American Revolution* (New York: St. Martin's Press, 1976), 182.
2. Andrew Jackson O'Shaughnessy, *The Men Who Lost America: British Leadership, the American Revolution, and the Fate of the Empire* (New Haven, CT: Yale University Press, 2013), 11–12.
3. Peter Whiteley, *Lord North: The Prime Minister Who Lost America* (London: Hambledon Press, 1996), 162–163.
4. David Syrett, *The Royal Navy in European Waters during the American Revolutionary War* (Columbia: University of South Carolina Press, 1998), ix. See also Derry, *English Politics*, 178–179; David Syrett, *The Royal Navy in American Waters, 1775–1783* (Aldershot, UK: Scolar Press, 1989).
5. Silas Deane, "Estimate for Fitting Out Warships for a Three Months Cruise 30 October 1775," in *Naval Documents of the American Revolution*, ed. William Bell Clark et al., 12 vols. (Washington, DC: Naval History Division, 1964–2014), 2:647–652. For American fears about the navy, see James M. Volo,

Blue Water Patriots: The American Revolution Afloat (Westport, CT: Praeger, 2007), 252.

6. William M. Fowler Jr., *Rebels under Sail: The American Navy during the Revolution* (New York: Charles Scribner's Sons, 1976), 43.
7. Ibid., 64, 171, 246–252; Volo, *Blue Water Patriots,* 8.
8. Stephen Conway, "British Governments and the Conduct of the American War," in *Britain and the American Revolution,* ed. H. T. Dickinson (London: Longman, 1998), 183.
9. Houghton Library, Harvard University, MS Can 16, vol. 1, pp. 146–153. Henry Hulton to [unknown], 7 May 1775.
10. On this point, see especially Richard Buel Jr., who estimates that trade in and out of Rhode Island in 1776, for example, was only about 36 percent of the annual trade between 1768 and 1772. He notes, "During 1776, only one foreign vessel is recorded as entering and only two as clearing in Rhode Island's naval records." Richard Buel Jr., *In Irons: Britain's Naval Supremacy and the American Revolutionary Economy* (New Haven, CT: Yale University Press, 1998), 41, 43. See also David Syrett, *Admiral Lord Howe* (Staplehurst, UK: Spellmount, 2006), 63; Volo, *Blue Water Patriots,* 8.
11. Buel, *In Irons,* 107–113.
12. Jeremy Black, "Naval Power, Strategy and Foreign Policy, 1775–1791," in *Parameters of British Naval Power, 1650–1850,* ed. Michael Duffy (Exeter: University of Exeter Press, 1992), 102.
13. Conway, "British Governments," 159, 183; N. A. M. Rodger, *The Insatiable Earl: A Life of John Montagu, Fourth Earl of Sandwich, 1718–1792* (London: HarperCollins, 1991), 213–232.
14. Daniel Baugh, "The Atlantic of the Rival Navies, 1714–1783," in *English Atlantics Revisited: Essays Honouring Professor Ian K. Steele,* ed. Nancy Rhoden (Montreal: McGill–Queen's University Press, 2007), 224; Buel, *In Irons,* 217–226.
15. Syrett, *Royal Navy in European Waters,* 13, 15, 21–22; TNA ADM 8/52, 1 December 1776; *The Private Papers of John, Earl of Sandwich, First Lord of the Admiralty, 1771–1782,* ed. G. R. Barnes and J. H. Owen, 4 vols. (London: Navy Records Society, 1932–1938), 1:163, 2:235–238.
16. Edmund Burke, Debate in the Commons on the Navy Estimates, 26 November 1777. *Cobbett's Parliamentary History of England,* 36 vols. (London, 1806–1820), 19:458–459.
17. Qtd. in Daniel A. Baugh, "Why Did Britain Lose Command of the Sea during the War for America?," in *The British Navy and the Use of Naval Power in the Eighteenth Century,* ed. Jeremy Black and Philip Woodfine (Leicester: Leicester University Press, 1988), 149.
18. O'Shaughnessy, *Men Who Lost America,* 14.
19. Syrett, *Royal Navy in European Waters,* 21–22; N. A. M. Rodger, *Command of the Ocean: A Naval History of Britain, 1649–1815* (New York: Norton, 2004), 342.

20. James E. Bradley, *Popular Politics and the American Revolution in England: Petitions, the Crown, and Public Opinion* (Mason, GA: Mercer University Press, 1986).
21. Fox, Debate on the Navy Estimates—Sir Hugh Palliser's Defence, 4 December 1780. *Cobbett's Parliamentary History,* 21:916.
22. Temple Luttrell, Debate in the Commons on the Navy Estimates, 8 November 1778. *Cobbett's Parliamentary History,* 18:1449, 1453–1454.
23. Luttrell, Debate in the Commons on the Navy Estimates, 26 November 1777. *Cobbett's Parliamentary History,* 19:448, 451.
24. Debate in the Lords on the Duke of Bolton's Motion respecting the State of the Navy, 2 March 1778. *Cobbett's Parliamentary History,* 19:818–834; Debate in the Commons on the State of the Navy, 11 March 1778. *Cobbett's Parliamentary History,* 19:874–893; Debate on the Earl of Effingham's Motion relative to the State of the Navy, 31 March 1778. *Cobbett's Parliamentary History,* 19:980–996.
25. For the version attacking Palliser, see *General Advertiser and Morning Intelligencer,* 15 October 1778; for the version attacking Keppel, see *London Evening Post, London Chronicle, London Morning Post, The Morning Intelligencer,* and *The Gazetteer,* all 5 November 1778.
26. For more on the Keppel-Palliser controversy, see Nicholas Rogers, "The Dynamic of News in Britain during the American War: The Case of Admiral Keppel," *Parliamentary History* 25, no. 1 (2006): 49–67; Syrett, *Royal Navy in European Waters,* 17–60; Daniel Baugh, "'Too Much Mixed in This Affair': The Impact of Ministerial Politics in the Eighteenth-Century Royal Navy," in *New Interpretations in Naval History: Selected Papers from the Fourteenth Naval History Symposium,* ed. Randy Carol Balano and Craig L. Symonds (Annapolis, MD: Naval Institute Press, 2001), 21–43.
27. Debate on Mr. Dunning's Motion respecting the Power of the Board of Admiralty to Grant or Refuse Courts Martial, 15 March 1779. *Cobbett's Parliamentary History,* 20:304–305.
28. Debate on Mr. Fox's Motion for the Removal of the Earl of Sandwich, 19 April 1779. *Cobbett's Parliamentary History,* 20:399. See also Barré's comments in the same debate, 400–401. See also *An Address to the Lords of the Admiralty on their Conduct towards Admiral Keppel* (London, 1778), 30; A Freeholder [Thomas Erskine], *To the Independent Freeholders of the County of Surry* [1780], 12–13.
29. Debate on Mr. Fox's Motion of Censure on the Conduct of the Admiralty, in sending out Admiral Keppel with too small a Force, 3 March 1779. *Cobbett's Parliamentary History,* 20:174–203; Debate on Mr. Fox's Motion for the Removal of the Earl of Sandwich, 19 April 1779. *Cobbett's Parliamentary History,* 20:372, 377.
30. Debate on the Earl of Bristol's Motion for the Removal of the Earl of Sandwich, First Lord of the Admiralty, 23 April 1779. *Cobbett's Parliamentary History,* 20:426–469.

31. Debate on the Duke of Richmond's Motion respecting the intended Court Martial upon Sir Hugh Palliser, 31 March 1779. *Cobbett's Parliamentary History,* 20:406–426; Debate on the Navy Estimates—Sir Hugh Palliser's Defence, 4 December 1780. *Cobbett's Parliamentary History,* 21:908–949; Debate on Mr. Fox's Motion relative to the Appointment of Sir Hugh Palliser to the Government of Greenwich Hospital, 1 February 1781. *Cobbett's Parliamentary History,* 21:1106–1161.
32. Debate on Mr. Fox's Motion for the Removal of the Earl of Sandwich, 19 April 1779. *Cobbett's Parliamentary History,* 20:382.
33. Debate on Mr. Fox's Motion respecting the State of the Navy upon the breaking out of the War with France, 8 March 1779. *Cobbett's Parliamentary History,* 20:216.
34. Sandwich, Debate on the Earl of Bristol's Motion for the Removal of the Earl of Sandwich, First Lord of the Admiralty, 23 April 1779. *Cobbett's Parliamentary History,* 20:447.
35. Duke of Richmond, Debate on the Duke of Richmond's Motion respecting the intended Court Martial upon Sir Hugh Palliser, 31 March 1779. *Cobbett's Parliamentary History,* 20:408, 414.
36. Rogers, "Dynamic of News," 55, 64.
37. Debate on Mr. Fox's Motion of Censure on the Conduct of the Admiralty, in sending out Admiral Keppel with too small a Force, 3 March 1779. *Cobbett's Parliamentary History,* 20:174.
38. Rogers, "Dynamic of News," 55–56.
39. Tessa Murdoch and Michael Snodin, "Admiral Keppel's 'Freedom Box' from the City of London," *Burlington Magazine* 35 (1993): 403–410.
40. Qtd. in Syrett, *Royal Navy in European Waters,* 59.
41. NMM SAN/V/13, pp. 204–210. Sandwich to Rodney, 8 March 1780.
42. Debate on Mr. Fox's Motion for the Sentence of the Court Martial on Sir Hugh Palliser, 13 May 1779. *Cobbett's Parliamentary History,* 20:627–628.
43. Debate on Mr. Fox's Motion for the Removal of the Earl of Sandwich, 19 April 1779. *Cobbett's Parliamentary History,* 20:397.
44. Derry, *English Politics,* 181.
45. Debate in the Committee of the House of Commons on the Causes of the Want of Success of the British Navy, 7 February 1782. *Cobbett's Parliamentary History,* 22:931.
46. Edmund Burke, Debate on Mr. Fox's Motion for the Sentence of the Court Martial on Sir Hugh Palliser, 13 May 1779. *Cobbett's Parliamentary History,* 20:626, 629; Hugh Pigot, Debate in the Committee of the House of Commons on the Causes of the Want of Success of the British Navy, 7 February 1782. *Cobbett's Parliamentary History,* 22:932.
47. Debate on Mr. Fox's Motion for the Removal of the Earl of Sandwich, 19 April 1779. *Cobbett's Parliamentary History,* 20:386–387.
48. Rodger, *Command of the Ocean,* 354.

49. NMM SAN / T / 6, folder 1. Sandwich, notes for parliamentary speech, 1781; Baugh, "Why Did Britain Lose Command of the Sea?," 153–154. See also R. J. B. Knight, "The Royal Navy's Recovery after the Early Phase of the American Revolutionary War," in *The Aftermath of Defeat: Societies, Armed Forces, and the Challenge of Recovery*, ed. George J. Andreopoulos and Herold E. Selesky (New Haven, CT: Yale University Press, 1994), 10–25.
50. Rodger, *Insatiable Earl*, 173–183.
51. R. J. B. Knight, "Sandwich, Middleton and Dockyard Appointments," *Mariner's Mirror* 57, no. 2 (1971): 175–192; Rodger, *Insatiable Earl*, 191.
52. A. B. McLeod, *British Naval Captains of the Seven Years' War: The View from the Quarterdeck* (Woodbridge, UK: Boydell, 2012), 21–23, 229; Daniel K. Benjamin and Anca Tifrea, "Learning by Dying: Combat Performance in the Age of Sail," *Journal of Economic History* 67, no. 4 (2007): 991; N. A. M. Rodger, *The Wooden World: An Anatomy of the Georgian Navy* (New York: Norton, 1996), 273–303.
53. TNA PRO 30 / 20 / 26 / 3, pp. 161–163. Will[iam] Knox to Rodney, 28 July 1789; Rodney to Philip Stephens, 28 October 1780. *Letter-Books and Order-Book of George, Lord Rodney, Admiral of the White Squadron, 1780–1782*, 2 vols. (New York: New York Historical Society, 1932), 1:192–193; Macintyre, *Admiral Rodney*, 128; Ruddock Mackay and Michael Duffy, *Hawke, Nelson and British Naval Leadership, 1747–1805* (Woodbridge, UK: Boydell, 2009), 132.
54. Rodney to Sir Peter Parker, 5 March 1782. *Letter-Books*, 1:264–265; NMM MID / 1 / 93 / 1 / 6. Hood to Charles Middleton, 13 December 1781; NMM MID / 1 / 93 / 1 / 12. Same to same, 13 April 1782; NMM MID / 1 / 93 / 1 / 14. Same to same, 30 April 1782; NMM MID / 1 / 93 / 66. Hood to Rear Admiral Robert Digby, 13 November 1782.
55. Debate on Mr. Fox's Motion relative to the Appointment of Sir Hugh Palliser to the Government of Greenwich Hospital, 1 February 1781. *Cobbett's Parliamentary History*, 21:1133–1134.
56. Mackay and Duffy, *Hawke, Nelson and British Naval Leadership*, 127; see also Michael A. Palmer, *Command at Sea: Naval Command and Control since the Sixteenth Century* (Cambridge, MA: Harvard University Press, 2005), 123–162.
57. Richard Kempenfelt to Middleton, 18 January 1780, in Charles Middleton, *Letters and Papers of Charles, Lord Barham, Admiral of the Red Squadron, 1758–1813*, ed. Sir John Knox Laughton, 3 vols. (London: Navy Records Society, 1907–1911), 1:309–313 (hereafter *Barham Papers*).
58. Mackay and Duffy, *Hawke, Nelson and British Naval Leadership*, 147; see also Macintyre, *Admiral Rodney*, 256.
59. Kempenfelt to Middleton, 28 December [1779?], *Barham Papers*, 1:304–305.
60. Candidus, *Public Advertiser*, 27 March 1786.
61. Thomas Fitzherbert, Debate in the Commons on Mr. Fox's Motion for an Enquiry into the Causes of the Want of Success of the British Navy, 24 January 1782. *Cobbett's Parliamentary History*, 22:902.

62. Lord Samuel Hood, Debate on Mr. Pitt's Motion for fortifying the Dock Yards, 27 February 1786. *Cobbett's Parliamentary History,* 25:1117.
63. An Officer, *An Address to the Right Honourable The First Lord Commissioner of the Admiralty* (London, 1786), 8–9.
64. See, for example, the discussion of the Duc de Choiseul's post–Seven Years' War building program: H. M. Scott, "The Importance of Bourbon Naval Reconstruction to the Strategy of Choiseul after the Seven Years' War," *International History Review* 1, no. 1 (1979): 17–35; M. C. Morison, "The Duc de Choiseul and the Invasion of England, 1768–1770," *Transactions of the Royal Historical Society* 4 (1910): 83–115.
65. Fox, Debate in the Commons on Mr. Fox's Motion for an Enquiry into the Causes of the Want of Success of the British Navy, 24 January 1782. *Cobbett's Parliamentary History,* 22:887–889.
66. James Luttrell, Debate on Sir W. Meredith's Motion respecting the Equipment and Sailing of the French Fleet from Toulon—and on the State of the British Navy, 25 May 1778. *Cobbett's Parliamentary History,* 19:1169–1170.
67. Debate on Mr. Fox's Motion for the Sentence of the Court Martial on Sir Hugh Palliser, 13 May 1779. *Cobbett's Parliamentary History,* 20:629, 632.
68. Debate on Mr. Pitt's Motion for fortifying the Dock Yards, 27 February 1786. *Cobbett's Parliamentary History,* 25:1096–1157.
69. Pitt, ibid., 1098, 1110.
70. George Berkeley, ibid., 1121.
71. Despite William Pitt's concern with economy and financial retrenchment, his administration spent freely on the navy during the 1780s, building eight new ships of the line, repairing forty-eight others, and accumulating new stockpiles of resources. See Syrett, *Admiral Lord Howe,* 110; P. C. Webb, "The Rebuilding and Repair of the Fleet, 1783–1793," *Bulletin of the Institute of Historical Research* 50 (1977): 194–209.
72. John Burgoyne, Debate on Mr. Pitt's Motion for fortifying the Dock Yards, 27 February 1786. *Cobbett's Parliamentary History,* 25:1116.
73. John Courtenay, ibid., 1136–1138.
74. Sir William Lemon, ibid., 1115.
75. See, for example, the Debate on the Bill for disabling persons in the Office of Ordnance, Navy, &c from voting at Elections, 30 March 1786. *Cobbett's Parliamentary History,* 25:1323–1338; the new debate over whether sea officers should be allowed to make commercial seizures discussed in the *Public Advertiser,* 9 May 1786; Debate in the Commons on the Clause in the Mutiny Bill, subjecting Brevet Officers to Martial Law, 28 February 1787. *Cobbett's Parliamentary History,* 26:639–645; Debate on the Clause of the Mutiny Bill for incorporating the New Corps of Military Artificers, 12 March 1788. *Cobbett's Parliamentary History,* 27:163–168.
76. Debate in the Commons on the Navy Estimates, 11 December 1782. *Cobbett's Parliamentary History,* 23:297.

77. Sam Willis, *The Struggle for Sea Power: A Naval History of the American Revolution* (New York: Norton, 2016), 442–460.
78. Baugh, "Why Did Britain Lose Command of the Sea?," 152; see also Volo, *Blue Water Patriots*, 243; Willis, *Struggle for Sea Power*, 460.
79. Debate on the Earl of Bristol's Motion for the Removal of the Earl of Sandwich, First Lord of the Admiralty, 23 April 1779. *Cobbett's Parliamentary History*, 20:461.
80. Derry, *English Politics*, 187.
81. Baugh, "Why Did Britain Lose Command of the Sea?," 153.
82. *Morning Chronicle*, 5 May 1786.
83. Linda Colley, "The Apotheosis of George III: Loyalty, Royalty and the British Nation 1760–1820," *Past & Present* 102 (1984): 94–129.

Epilogue

1. According to his biographer, Jervis "could not endure to hear of the word 'trouble': there ought, he said, to be no such word in the naval dictionary. When any one said they could not do a thing they were desired to do, he used to tell them to 'rub out "can't" and put in "try."'" Edward Pelham Brenton, *Life and Correspondence of John, Earl of St. Vincent*, 2 vols. (London, 1837), 1:339.
2. A. B. McLeod, *British Naval Captains of the Seven Years' War: The View from the Quarterdeck* (Woodbridge, UK: Boydell, 2012), 21–23, 229; Daniel K. Benjamin and Anca Tifrea, "Learning by Dying: Combat Performance in the Age of Sail," *Journal of Economic History* 67, no. 4 (2007): 991; N. A. M. Rodger, *The Wooden World: An Anatomy of the Georgian Navy* (New York: Norton, 1996), 273–303.
3. Earlier in the century, letters of recommendation tended to reference the author's connections while later letters referenced connections but also "merit." By the 1780s, it was common to do as Admiral Augustus Keppel did when he wrote a letter of recommendation on behalf of a young relative in which he explained that "young Keppel is good but requires a strict hand over him, his preferment, need not take place of Lumley's. Indeed it cannot be better than his waiting till you think his behaviour thoroughly merited your favour." Catherine Macartney wrote a similar letter, requesting that the recipient take "my nephew William Greville under your protection[.] Those better acquainted with his professional merit than I can pretend to be, assure me that he will not disgrace my recommendation nor render himself unworthy of any favour you will be pleased to grant him." TNA PRO 30/20/26/3, p. 95. Keppel to George Rodney, 5 June 1780; TNA PRO 30/20/26/3, pp. 181–182. Cath[erine] Macartney to Rodney, 4 October 1782.

4. Jan Glete, *Navies and Nations: Warships, Navies and State Building in Europe and America, 1500–1860,* 2 vols. (Stockholm: Almqvist & Wiksell International, 1993), 1:291.
5. Benjamin Rush to Richard Henry Lee, 21 December 1776, in *Naval Documents of the American Revolution,* ed. William Bell Clark et al., 12 vols. (Washington, DC: Naval History Division, 1964–2014), 7:543.
6. Robert H. Patton, *Patriot Pirate: The Privateer War for Freedom and Fortune in the American Revolution* (New York: Pantheon Books, 2008), 107; William M. Fowler Jr., *Rebels under Sail: The American Navy during the Revolution* (New York: Charles Scribner's Sons, 1976), 268; Richard B. Morris, *Government and Labor in Early America* (New York: Columbia University Press, 1946), 272, qtd. in Fowler, *Rebels under Sail,* 274.
7. Scholars who have tended to see the navy primarily through a coercive lens include Scott Claver, *Under the Lash: A History of Corporal Punishment in the British Armed Forces* (London: Torchstream, 1954); Niklas Frykman, "Seamen on Late Eighteenth-Century Warships," *International Review of Social History* 54 (2009): 67–93; Jonathan Neale, *The Cutlass and the Lash* (London: Pluto, 1985); and Marcus Rediker, *Between the Devil and the Deep Blue Sea* (New York: Cambridge University Press, 1987). Those who have tended to see it more through a cooperative lens include John D. Byrn, *Crime and Punishment in the Royal Navy* (Aldershot, UK: Scolar Press, 1989); Markus Eder, *Crime and Punishment in the Royal Navy of the Seven Years War, 1755–1763* (Aldershot, UK: Ashgate, 2004); A. G. Jameson, "Tyranny of the Lash? Punishment in the Royal Navy during the American War," *Northern Mariner* 9, no. 1 (1999): 53–66; and Rodger, *Wooden World.*

ACKNOWLEDGMENTS

So many people were so helpful while this book was being researched, written, and rewritten that I am absolutely petrified I'll leave someone really important off the list. If I have, I promise it's me, not you.

Most of the research and writing of this book took place under the patronage of Yale University. I cannot imagine a more supportive environment for scholarship, and I will forever be grateful for my time there. I also cannot imagine a more supportive (and provocatively challenging) advisor than Steve Pincus. He consistently pushed me to think deeper, to do the hard work I wanted to be too lazy to do, and he taught me not to be afraid to fight my corner. I can never thank him enough for his good advice, high standards, and kind heart. Paul Kennedy likewise has always been a stalwart source of wisdom and warmth; I am deeply grateful to him for his insights and his unfailing generosity with his time. Keith Wrightson and Julian Hoppit are compelling historians and genuine human beings; their comments on earlier stages of this project have unquestionably improved the final product. I would also like to express my appreciation to the wider Yale community of scholars interested in the early modern world, among them Julia Adams, John Demos, Alejandra Dubcovsky, Joanne Freeman, Stuart Schwartz, Vivek Sharma, and Francesca Trivellato. Each of them has been a role model—when I grow up, I hope to be like them. Eleanor Hughes has been a friend, a mentor, and an inspiration. Julia Marciari-Alexander and Amy Meyers welcomed me into the Yale Center for British Art family, while Maggie Powell and Nicole Bouché did the same at the Lewis Walpole Library. The Department of History is lucky to have Marcy Kaufman. The best part of the work that went into this book was the hours (and hours) spent around seminar tables, at the Skinners Arms, and occasionally on Hampstead Heath debating the nuances of historiography with Amanda Behm, Justin Brooks, Christian Burset, Megan Lindsay Cherry, Justin du Rivage, Richard Huzzey, Rachel Herrmann, Lucy Kaufman, Matthew Lockwood, Leslie Theibert, Courtney Thomas, Jennifer Wellington, Nicholas Wilson, and Alice Wolfram. Thank you.

I had the opportunity to present parts of this research in a variety of forums. At Yale, this included the British Historical Studies Colloquium, the Center for Historical Enquiry and the Social Sciences, the Early Modern Empires Workshop, the Early Modern Studies Colloquium, and the International Security Studies Brady-Johnson Colloquium in Grand Strategy and International History; at the University of Sydney, the History on Monday Seminar Series; at Cambridge University, the Maritime and Oceanic History Workshop; at the Institute for Historical Research in London, the British Maritime History Seminar (cosponsored by the National Maritime Museum) and the British History in the Long Eighteenth Century Seminar, as well as at the Britain and the World Conference, New Maritime Researchers Conference, North American Conference on British Studies, Northeast American Society for Eighteenth-Century Studies Conference, and Society for Court Studies Conference. To the organizers and participants, thank you for the opportunity and for your insightful comments and questions.

I received generous financial support for my research from the Beinecke Rare Book and Manuscript Library, the John F. Enders Fellowship, the Georg W. Leitner Program in International and Comparative Political Economy, and the MacMillan Center, all of Yale University, as well as from the Smith Richardson Foundation and the Yale Club of Philadelphia. A Mrs. Giles Whiting Fellowship in the Humanities supported the writing, as did a postdoctoral position courtesy of the European Studies Council of Yale University and the American Society for Eighteenth-Century Studies. The final research was completed with the help of support from the Department of History and the John C. Baker Fund of Ohio University.

Chapter 3 reprints, with minor edits, the text of "Disorder, Discipline, and Naval Reform in Mid-Eighteenth-Century Britain," *The English Historical Review* 128 (2013): 1451–1482. Portions of Chapter 5 were first published in "The King's Pirates? Naval Enforcement of Imperial Authority, 1740–76," *William and Mary Quarterly* 71 (2014): 3–34. I thank Oxford University Press and the Omohundro Institute of Early American History and Culture, respectively, for permission to reprint. Chapter 4 builds on ideas first discussed in "Saving Admiral Byng: Imperial Debates, Military Governance, and Popular Politics at the Outbreak of the Seven Years' War," *Journal for Maritime Research* 13, no. 1 (2011): 3–19. I am furthermore sincerely grateful to the Duke of Bedford for his permission to use the archives at Woburn Abbey; all material cited from there appears by kind permission of the Duke of Bedford and the Trustees of the Bedford Estate.

Many other individuals made this project possible in a variety of ways. Bob Wofford and Phyllis Wright were, no joke, the *most* amazing high school English teachers: thank you for teaching me how to read and write. Gabrielle Jungels-Winkler made it possible for me to become a Scripps woman; I strive to live up to the confident, courageous, and hopeful ideals that education embodies. I owe a substantial debt to Andre Wakefield: thank you for your mentorship and for embodying the teacher-scholar. Martin Cooles, Peter James, Gilly and

Simon King, Nicholas Wrightson, and Nicoletta Vogg-Wrightson all provided hospitality on various research trips, and I must particularly thank Suzanne Ashman and Euan Blair for the Sarah R. Kinkel Memorial Bedroom. You're the best. I have felt extremely fortunate in my choice of colleagues at Ohio University, but would like to single out Robert Ingram, Katherine Jellison, and Brian Schoen for helping me hit the ground running. Thank you for your friendship. Michael Gerber and Michael Mangan, undergraduate research fellows with the George Washington Forum at Ohio University, provided important research and logistical support in the final stages of this project. I'm very grateful to Andrew Kinney at Harvard University Press for his guidance and editorial acumen, as well as to the rest of the HUP team and the manuscript's anonymous readers. You too were helpful and provocatively challenging, and I appreciate that.

A massive, massive thank you to my family, who have provided love and support from Byron Bay, Australia, to Bowling Green, Kentucky, and everywhere in between. To Bailey, Hannah, Adam, and Brandy for letting me go on historical rants and sometimes acting like they were interesting. To Mom and Dad, for everything—truly.

To Jamie, for always letting me know when I wasn't taking something seriously enough, or too seriously, and for always believing that I'm a better person than I am, and for making me laugh.

INDEX